GENERAL RECORDKEEPING

NINTH EDITION

HARRY HUFFMAN, Ed.D.

Formerly Professor of Business Education
Ohio State University and
    Colorado State University
Currently Business Education Consultant

JEFFREY R. STEWART, Jr., Ed.D.

Professor of Business Education
Virginia Polytechnic Institute and State University
Blacksburg, Virginia

DAISY L. STEWART, Ph.D.

Associate Professor of Vocational and Technical
    Education
Virginia Polytechnic Institute and State University
Blacksburg, Virginia

GREGG DIVISION • McGRAW-HILL BOOK COMPANY

NEW YORK ATLANTA DALLAS ST. LOUIS
SAN FRANCISCO AUCKLAND BOGOTÁ GUATEMALA
HAMBURG LISBON LONDON MADRID MEXICO MILAN
MONTREAL NEW DELHI PANAMA PARIS SAN JUAN
SÃO PAULO SINGAPORE SYDNEY TOKYO TORONTO

Sponsoring Editor: Leo Gafney
Editing Supervisor: Vivian Koenig/Arthur Pomponio
Design and Art Supervisor: Caryl Valerie Spinka
Production Supervisor: S. Steven Canaris
Photo Editor: Rosemarie Rossi

Interior Design: Keithley and Associates
Cover Design: Renée Kilbride Edelman
Cover Art: Jon Weiman

Technical Studio: Burmar Technical Corp.

Credits for the photographs shown in this book are provided on page 566.

Library of Congress Cataloging-in-Publication Data

Huffman, Harry.
    General recordkeeping.

    Includes index.
    1. Bookkeeping. I. Stewart, Jeffrey Robert,
date. II. Stewart, Daisy L. III. Title.
HF5635.H8834 1987   657'.2   87-2982
ISBN 0-07-031054-8

General Recordkeeping, Ninth Edition

1 2 3 4 5 6 7 8 9 0 VNHVNH 8 9 4 3 2 1 0 9 8 7

ISBN 0-07-031054-8

CONTENTS

Keeping records is a part of everyone's personal and business lives. As individuals, we maintain personal records for taxes, budgets, credit, and banking. As employees, we prepare and use records of many kinds: sales, purchases, payroll, inventory, and accounting. Office workers especially need basic recordkeeping knowledge and skill. *General Recordkeeping,* Ninth Edition, provides the information and activities necessary to develop competency in both personal and business recordkeeping.

The ninth edition has been revised both to update features of the previous editions and to add entirely new topics and chapters. Expanded emphasis is given to cashier's activities, business banking, inventory control, and payroll records. To provide additional recordkeeping practice, the number of exercises and application problems has been increased. Throughout the text, important computer recordkeeping applications are introduced. The critical component of basic skills development has been enhanced in this edition with the inclusion of reading, math, and vocabulary practice.

PROGRAM COMPONENTS

Textbook. The textbook is divided into four parts: personal recordkeeping, basic business records, applied business records, and basic accounting records. Each part contains several chapters which are further divided into topics. Topics are complete lessons and include goals, key terms, instructional content and illustrations, questions to check reading, and exercises. At the end of every chapter there are both vocabulary practice on the terms introduced and application problems that cover the entire chapter's content. Most chapters also include related math practice in the end-of-chapter activities. The last chapter in each part concludes with a computer application which describes how computers are used in recordkeeping. The 20 textbook chapters are supplemented by separate projects which appear at the end of each of the four parts.

Part One, Personal Recordkeeping, provides instruction on the use of forms, personal banking, budgeting, and credit records. It offers important information that all consumers need and introduces fundamental recordkeeping procedures.

Part Two, Basic Business Records, explains recordkeeping for cash receipts, petty cash, travel accounts, and business banking. Many jobs require a knowledge of these basic business records and the skill to maintain them.

Part Three, Applied Business Records, deals with the major business record systems: sales and accounts receivable, inventory control, purchases and accounts payable, payroll preparation, and payroll taxes. Experience in working with these record systems provides realistic and valuable exposure to the business activities of many employees as well as of entrepreneurs.

Part Four, Basic Accounting Records, introduces double-entry accounting procedures and provides practice in keeping a general ledger system. Content includes accounts, journals, general and subsidiary ledgers, trial balances, and financial statements. This part provides both entry-level employment skills and a foundation for further study of accounting.

Activity Guides. Accompanying the textbook are two student activity guides that contain the working papers necessary to complete all of the text exercises and the other activities, including the four projects. The first activity guide is used with Parts One and Two of the textbook; the second with Parts Three and Four. The activity guides follow the textbook format and are divided into topics, end-of-chapter activities, and projects. There are also supplementary problems that reinforce textbook content and build basic skills.

Software. A software package that accompanies the *General Recordkeeping* program is available, and it provides experience in several recordkeeping applications. For example, practice is given in verifying computer information, data entry, database management, and spreadsheet use.

Instructor's Editions of Activity Guides. Instructor's editions of the activity guides contain answers to all the exercises, which are printed in a second color for ease in checking student work.

Resource Manual and Tests. The instructor's resource manual contains teaching suggestions, several options for scheduling instruction, and transparency masters of commonly used forms. A completely revised and expanded testing program also appears in the manual. Both an objective test and a performance test are included for each of the 20 chapters, and test keys with item point values are provided.

HIGHLIGHTS

Special features of the ninth edition of *General Recordkeeping* include the following:

Goals and Key Terms. Each topic begins with clear statements of what the student should achieve through the completion of topic activities. Also in each topic opening is a list of definitions for the most important terms introduced in the topic. These key terms are supplemented with marginal notes throughout the topics that support the strong emphasis on vocabulary development in the *General Recordkeeping* program.

Basic Skills Development. Reading comprehension is assessed and reinforced by the "Check Your Reading" feature at the end of each topic. Further attention is given to verbal skills through the "Vocabulary Skillbuilder" quizzes that end each chapter. Mathematics instruction, drill, application, and reinforcement are provided throughout the textbook. Topic exercises and end-of-chapter application problems contain many math operations. The "Math Skillbuilder" at the end of most chapters gives special reinforcement to skills related to chapter content.

Computer Applications. The ninth edition of *General Recordkeeping* focuses on the fact that much personal and business recordkeeping is done with computers. Spreadsheet, graphics, and database examples are included in the relevant topics as well as in the "Computer Applications" sections at the end of each of the four parts.

Color and Graphics. The use of full color in this edition enhances the appearance and motivational impact of the textbook. Full-color illustrations and improved graphic presentations include attractive photographs, charts, and recordkeeping forms.

Projects. Each of the four textbook parts concludes with a complete recordkeeping project, which is one more than in the previous edition. The first project deals with personal recordkeeping, the second with cash receipts and payments for a business, the third with purchases and sales records, and the fourth with double-entry accounting procedures.

ACKNOWLEDGMENTS

Appreciation is expressed to the many recordkeeping instructors and businesspersons who have provided comments and suggestions related to the content and presentation of *General Recordkeeping*, Ninth Edition. Special thanks are also extended to the Gregg/McGraw-Hill staff for its valuable support and assistance throughout the preparation of this new edition.

Harry Huffman
Jeffrey R. Stewart, Jr.
Daisy L. Stewart

CONSULTANTS AND REVIEWERS

The following experienced reviewers and consultants read and commented on the materials for *General Recordkeeping,* Ninth Edition. They worked out the exercises and made numerous suggestions for improving the text and supporting materials. We are grateful for their assistance in making this text clear and instructionally correct.

Edith Baldree
Bradley High School
Cleveland, Tennessee

Paul Bertrand
Marinette High School
Marinette, Wisconsin

William Dodge
Santa Cruz High School
Santa Cruz, California

Mildred M. Lester
State Department of Education
Jackson, Mississippi

Daniel Marrone
College of St. Elizabeth
Convent Station, New Jersey

Celestine Mongo
Detroit Public Schools
Detroit, Michigan

Wanda R. Smith
Butler High School
Huntsville, Alabama

Barbara Trent-Langdon
Franklin Heights High School
Columbus, Ohio

Richard H. Wirth
Cleveland Heights High School
Cleveland Heights, Ohio

PART
ONE

PERSONAL
RECORDKEEPING

CHAPTER 1

WORKING WITH RECORDS

All during your life you will work with records. For example, you will fill in job applications and tax forms. You will receive records such as report cards, receipts, and licenses and you will have to decide where to put them. Sometimes you will have to find a record quickly.

You should check the records you receive or fill in. You may find later that it takes more time to correct an error if you do not catch it right on the spot. In this chapter you will learn about handling many of the records you will use in your personal and business life.

TOPIC 1 ▲ FORMS

GOALS

1. To describe and complete descriptive forms.
2. To describe and complete financial forms.
3. To describe and complete combination forms.

KEY TERMS

Forms are records that have spaces and lines to show where you are to enter information.

Descriptive forms usually answer questions such as: Who? What? When? Where? and Why?

Financial forms usually answer questions such as: How much? and How many?

Combination forms usually answer both descriptive and financial questions.

In your personal and business life, there will be many reasons for you to fill out forms. Here are some.

To get a job
To put money in the bank
To get money out of the bank
To place an order by mail
To get a Social Security number
To get a driver's license
To apply to college
To enter a hospital

To file an income tax return
To apply for insurance

A *form* is made to help you give complete information. Printed guide words tell you what to write, such as your name and address, and where to write it. As you will see, forms have spaces or lines for writing the information.

DESCRIPTIVE FORMS

A *descriptive* form is one that asks: Who? What? When? Where? and Why? When completed, the form answers these questions and gives a description of something.

One simple descriptive form is the address list shown here.

Name	Street Address	City, State, ZIP	Telephone No.
Gravel, Gary	231 View Point	Wichita, KS 67213	(316) 555-6410
Sorto, Mark	8731 Hickory Street	Memphis, TN 38112	(901) 555-0132
Bank, Jon	4870 Quail Road	Columbus, MS 39701	(601) 555-3102

This form provides one line each for writing a person's (1) name, (2) street address, (3) city, state, and ZIP code, and (4) phone number. When completed, the information is arranged in columns such as one column for names and one for street addresses.

Note the advantages of using a form such as the telephone message shown here. The person taking the message knows that all the important information will be there. The person receiving the message knows exactly where to find everything. Businesses save a great deal of time and money just because of this simple form.

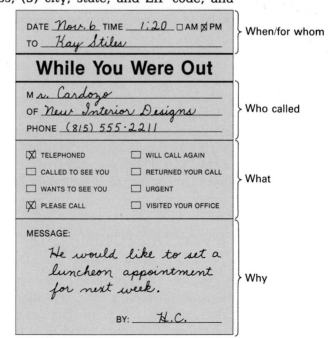

DATE Nov. 6 TIME 1:20 ☐ AM ☒ PM
TO Kay Stiles
} When/for whom

While You Were Out

M r. Cardozo
OF New Interior Designs
PHONE (815) 555-2211
} Who called

☒ TELEPHONED   ☐ WILL CALL AGAIN
☐ CALLED TO SEE YOU   ☐ RETURNED YOUR CALL
☐ WANTS TO SEE YOU   ☐ URGENT
☒ PLEASE CALL   ☐ VISITED YOUR OFFICE
} What

MESSAGE:
He would like to set a luncheon appointment for next week.

BY: H.C.
} Why

Business forms are useful tools. Many employers believe they can learn something about people by studying their job application forms. Is the form neat? Is the writing clear and legible? Is the information written in the right place? Employers look at these things when they are deciding whether to hire someone.

APPLICATION FOR EMPLOYMENT

FEDERAL AND STATE LAW REQUIRES THAT ALL APPLICATIONS BE CONSIDERED WITHOUT REGARD TO RACE, RELIGION, COLOR, SEX, AGE OR NATIONAL ORIGIN. WE BELIEVE IN AND FULLY SUPPORT THE PRINCIPLE OF EQUAL EMPLOYMENT OPPORTUNITY AND WILL FULFILL OUR OBLIGATION TO THE FULLEST.

PLEASE TYPE OR PRINT

LAST NAME	FIRST NAME	M.I.
TRILLING	JOHN	W.

SOCIAL SECURITY NO.	ADDRESS		
101-37-5316	31 W. 86TH ST.		

CITY	STATE	ZIP	POSITION APPLIED FOR
NEW YORK	NY	10024	SALESPERSON

DATE YOU CAN START	WAGE EXPECTED	HOW DID YOU HEAR OF OPENING?
10/1/--	PER HR. $ 8.50	FRIEND

FULL TIME?	IF PART TIME, HRS. YOU CAN WORK	
YES	MON.–FRI.:	SAT.–SUN.:

PREVIOUS EMPLOYER (NAME AND ADDRESS)

HOUSE OF LIGHTS, 300 E. 40TH ST., NY, NY 10016

When completing descriptive forms, therefore, be sure to follow the directions given on the form. For example, some descriptive forms should be typed. Others should be carefully completed in ink. The directions may ask you to print. If the form has no directions, enter the information as neatly as possible.

FINANCIAL FORMS

A *financial* form deals with money. The order blank below is a financial form that includes catalog numbers, quantities, unit prices, and totals. Note that the form asks for answers to the questions: How much? and How many?

ORDER BLANK

Davis Supply Company
1672 Military Trail
Boca Raton, Florida 33434

Lauren Madison
87 Market Street
Philadelphia, PA 19103

Catalog Number	Quantity	Size	Color	Description	Price of Items	
					Each	Total
8 9 0 3	1	Med.	Yellow	Sweater	18.95	18 95
4 7 1 2	2	10	Red	Knit top	10.95	21 90
6 8 5 4	3	—	White	Socks	4.95	14 85
				Total Price of Items	55	70

In addition to the suggestions given earlier for descriptive forms, be sure to follow these rules when filling out financial forms:

1. Write numbers so that each figure is sharp and clear, like the numbers shown in the margin. Be especially careful about the difference between 1s and 7s, 2s and 3s, and 4s and 9s. Also, write all numbers about the same size.

2. If the form has a vertical rule to separate dollars and cents, line up the dollars and cents properly in columns, as shown to the left.

3. If the form has *unit rules*—that is, one box for the cents amount and an individual box for each figure in the dollar amount—use only about half the vertical space for each number, as shown to the right for $134.60, $8,000, and $586.27.

4. Omit dollar signs and decimals on financial forms such as those illustrated.

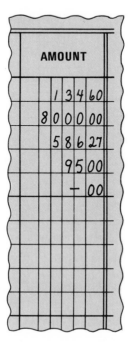

AMOUNT		
1 3 4	60	
8 0 0 0	00	
5 8 6	27	
9 5	00	
—	00	

COMBINATION FORMS

A *combination* form has space for descriptive and financial information. This restaurant receipt asks for descriptive information:

The number of customers
The server's initials
The check number

The table number
The food ordered
The date

BEEF BARON Restaurant

Guests 2	Server FS	Check No. 5793	Table No. 14		
Order			Price		
Shrimp Platter				15	15
T-Bone				17	65
2 Coffee				1	50
			Subtotal	34	30
			Tax	2	06
			Total	36	36
Date 10/1					

At the same time, it also asks for financial information:

The cost of each item
The amount of tax

The subtotal
The total cost

Note the way the form is set up:

Column heading: A title describing data that follows.

Vertical: From top to bottom.

Horizontal: From side to side.

1. Headings (Guests, Server) identify the purpose of each space.
2. One vertical rule separates dollars and cents.
3. A second vertical rule separates the financial information from the rest of the form.
4. Horizontal rules are lines on which to write entries.

1. Forms that answer questions such as Who? What? When? Where? and Why? are called ___?___ forms.

2. Forms that answer questions such as How much? and How many? are called ___?___ forms.

3. Forms that answer a mixture of questions are called ___?___ forms.

4. Rules from top to bottom are called ___?___ rules.

5. Rules from left to right are called ___?___ rules.

6. Rules that create boxes for individual figures are called ___?___ rules.

7. What are three reasons for you to fill out forms in your personal or business life?

Exercises for Topic I

1. Use a telephone message form to record the following telephone message accurately: "On October 6 at 9:15 a.m., Lisa Chambers called from Northeast Services Corp. to speak with Joan Gaskins. Ms. Chambers wants to make an appointment. Please have Joan call Ms. Chambers. The telephone number is 614-555-8137."

2. On December 6, at 3 o'clock in the afternoon, you answered Eunice Zuko's telephone while she was out of the office. The caller, Ms. Janice Trathem, wanted to make an appointment with Eunice on Thursday, December 18, at 10 a.m. Ms. Zuko's number is (516) 555-2300. Complete a message form for Eunice.

3. Organize this information to create an address list.

   Joe Knoff, (214) 555-4301, 1521 Pine Street, Dallas, Texas (TX) 75228

   Marie Santana, 507 N. 17th Street, Boston, Massachusetts (MA) 02215, (617) 555-5089

   Harvey Vectora, (501) 555-1488, 2314 Camellie Highway, Conway, Arkansas (AR) 72032

4. Rewrite the following words clearly and neatly.

ninety	cooperate
seventeen dollars	forty
January	February
calculator	computer

5. Copy the following numbers. Write neatly and then ask someone to tell you if all your numbers are legible.

9 8 7 6 5 4 3 2 1 0   1 2 3 4 5 6 7 8 9 0

1,2 3 4   5, 6 7 8   9, 0 9 8   7, 6 5 4   3, 2 1 0

6. Write the following amounts on separate lines. Do not write the dollar sign or decimal point.

$1,256.70	$3,957.60	$28.84	$481.25
$828.24	$3.09	$229.78	$4,984.00
$359.75	$2,777.77	$2.74	$37.37

7. Complete an employment application form using your own personal, employment, and educational data. Before you begin, review the following instructions:

▲ Assume that the position applied for is a part-time sales job (on Saturdays and Sundays from 10 a.m. to 6 p.m.) with Benson's, a local department store. For starting rate of pay, enter the minimum wage.

▲ Write that you heard about this sales position from a friend, Ted Godwin, who is an employee at Benson's.

▲ Write "NA" (for "not applicable") whenever appropriate.

▲ For personal references, write the names of friends, business people, and former teachers who know you well.

▲ Remember to enter information neatly and correctly.

8. Complete the Active Sports order form provided in the Activity Guide using all the fitting details (sizes, lengths) that are right for you. You are ordering two items:

▲ One pair of wool pants. The item number (as listed in the Active Sports catalog) is 2298. Color choices: white, blue, tan. Price: $39.

▲ One wool shirt, Item 2282. Color choices: white, blue, tan. Price: $32.

If you must add any special fitting instructions, use the "Will It Fit?" box at the bottom of the form.

TOPIC 2 ▲ VERIFYING RECORDS

GOALS

1. To verify lists of words, names, and numbers.
2. To identify the parts of a computer and their functions.
3. To verify computer information.

KEY TERMS

Verifying is the process of checking information for completeness and accuracy.

A *source document* is a form that is known to be correct and that gives information for a record or report.

Recording information does not guarantee accuracy. *Verifying* information does. Think about entering catalog numbers and prices in a computer. If the computer printout shows all the wrong numbers and prices, then time has been wasted. Worse, people using the printout may order the wrong things or use the wrong prices.

Whenever you record information of any kind, you must check the accuracy of your entries. Whether the final copy is handwritten, typed, or computer-printed, it is always your responsibility to verify that your work is correct. Your careful work will not go unnoticed: Employers value workers who are accurate.

CHECKING FOR ACCURACY

When completing a form, you will often need to copy information from other sources. Most errors result from carelessness in copying information. To check that a completed form is correct, use the original source that you know is correct.

Now let's review three steps to verify or check for accuracy.

Step 1 Examine the completed form to make sure that the information entered is clear, accurate, and complete.

Step 2 Compare the items on the completed form with source documents:

a. Match the information you recorded number by number and letter by letter against the original document. For example, note the differences below.

Source Document	Completed Form
F137Ab/182	E137Ab/182
Catherine Jeffries	Katherine Jeffries
reserved	reversed

b. Watch especially for transpositions. Note the following:

Source Document	Completed Form	Error
185643	186543	The numbers "5" and "6" are transposed.
dairy	diary	The letters "a" and "i" are transposed.

c. Check for omissions. Note the following:

Source Document	Completed Form	Error
Prepare two copies of the form.	Prepare copies of the form.	The word "two" was omitted.

Step 3 Check the accuracy of all computations—that is, double-check addition, subtraction, multiplication, and division.

USING COMPUTERS FOR RECORDKEEPING

Computers help make business and office work efficient and profitable. Computer forms are used to simplify and standardize recordkeeping. Information entered into a computer must also be verified, just as information handwritten onto a form must be verified.

Let's take a closer look at a typical computer setup:

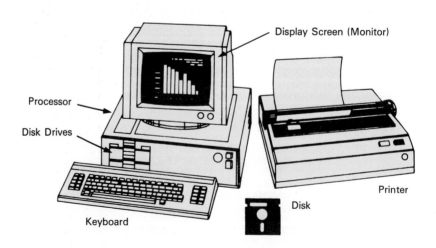

As you see, the computer setup includes several parts, each of which is discussed below.

Keyboard The computer *keyboard* (a typewriter keyboard with some additional keys) is used to enter data.

Display Screen Also called a monitor, the *display screen* shows information as it is entered into the computer. It also displays computations that the computer performs.

Processor The brains of the computer, the *processor,* controls all computer activities and is the most important part of the computer. Many modern devices now have processors, including automated bank tellers, calculators, cash registers, and dishwashers.

Disks A *disk* is a flat piece of plastic that stores information in the same way that audiotapes store sound.

Depending on the kind of information it stores, a disk is called a *program disk* or a *work disk* (also called a *data disk*).

▲ A program disk tells the computer what to do and how to do it. It gives instructions.
▲ A work disk stores information or records. For example, a work disk may contain the names and addresses of a store's customers.

Disk Drive Each *disk drive* has a slot into which the disk is inserted. Then the disk drive ''reads'' the information stored on the disk (similar to the way a tape player ''reads'' the information stored on an audiotape).

Most computers have one or two disk drives. The drives may be hooked up separately or may be part of the computer.

Printer The *printer,* as its name tells, prints the information from the computer onto paper. It does its job by following the instructions on the program disk.

Check Your Reading

1. An error that results from switching two consecutive letters or numbers is called a(n) ___?___ .

2. The process of checking the accuracy of an entry by comparing it to an original document is known as ___?___ .

3. The keyboard of a computer is similar to that of a(n) ___?___ .

4. The computer part that allows you to see the information that you are entering is the ___?___ .

5. The brains of the computer is its ___?___ .

6. The two kinds of computer disks are the ___?___ disk and the ___?___ disk.

7. The computer part that "reads" disk information is the ___?___ .

Exercises for Topic 2

1. Comparing Words. Compare the words in the two columns below to verify that each pair matches. On a separate sheet, indicate each pair that does not match by writing the letter of the pair. (Hint: Place a ruler under each pair as you match them.) Ten pairs do not match.

a.	progressive	progressive
b.	autumn	autumn
c.	morality	mortality
d.	debate	rebate
e.	Earl's	Earl's
f.	cordially	Cordially
g.	Wingate Haus	Wingate House
h.	programmer	programmer
i.	Mississippi	Missisippi
j.	advise	advise
k.	Your truly	Yours Truly
l.	affect	effect
m.	recommend	reccommend
n.	Mr.	Ms.
o.	morning	mourning
p.	clerical	clerical

2. Comparing Numbers and Symbols. Follow the directions in Exercise 1. Ten pairs do not match.

a.	8.0%	0.8%
b.	$796,240	$769,240
c.	33-3333	33-33333
d.	6:50 p.m.	6:50 p.m.
e.	96	96
f.	4011.26	4011.26
g.	4 cm	4 cc

h.	9 ml	9 ml
i.	#8350	8350#
j.	$3,220.96	$3,22069
k.	464-04-3511	464-04-3511
l.	63-52-38	63-52-83
m.	628-6953	628-6593
n.	$8\frac{1}{2}'' \times 11''$	$8\frac{1}{3}'' \times 11''$
o.	24210	24201

3. Comparing Names. Follow the directions in Exercise 1. Twelve pairs do not match.

a.	David Rigney	David Rigney
b.	Max Elkin	Max Elkind
c.	Sondra Johnson	Sandra Johnson
d.	Bill Olson	Will Olson
e.	M. C. Evans	M. O. Evans
f.	Lee Hanson	Lee Hanson
g.	R. B. Lefkowitz	R. P. Lefkowitz
h.	Saul Phyfer	Saul Phyfer
i.	Gregory Lafon	Gregory Lafon
j.	Susan Owens	Susan Owens
k.	C. F. Davis	C. E. Davis
l.	Lew Lilly	Lou Lilly
m.	Julie Petersen	Julie Peterson
n.	William H. Thomason	William H. Thomason
o.	A. L. Tayler	A. L. Tyler
p.	Kurt von Helzing	Kurt von Helzing
q.	Anthony Franconia	Anthony Franconia
r.	Phyllis T. Emenhiser	Phyllis Emenhiser
s.	Maria Cervantes	Marie Cervantes
t.	Joan Ramos	Juan Ramos

4. Comparing Number Combinations. Follow the directions in Exercise 1. Twelve pairs do not match.

a.	8:00–3:57	8:00–3:56
b.	9:15–3:30	9:15–3:30
c.	26.53876 grams	26.53786 grams
d.	196 degrees F	169 degrees F
e.	77 degrees C	77 degrees C
f.	4.52 hl	4.52 hl
g.	#46555686	#46555686
h.	October 16 19—	October 16, 19—
i.	#12232321	#12223231
j.	9:03–5:00	9:30–5:00
k.	1,786,980k	1,786,980k
l.	250-404-743	250-404-734

m.	60GK872	60GK872
n.	4844489	4848489
o.	7:15–3:30	7:15–3:30
p.	10E782610	10F782610
q.	38′ 6$\frac{3}{8}$″	38′ 6$\frac{5}{8}$″
r.	10100100	10100010
s.	3C298765	30298765
t.	3 ha	3 ha

5. Comparing Words and Numbers. Follow the directions in Exercise 1. Fourteen pairs are different.

a.	822,296	822.296
b.	487-66618	478-666-18
c.	headstart	headstart
d.	indifferent	in different
e.	L. F. Strong	L. F. Strong
f.	7:45 a.m.	7:45 A.M.
g.	11/10/86	10/11/86
h.	Lansing	Lanssin
i.	$744,613.58	744,613.58
j.	Cincinnati	Cincinnati
k.	latter	later
l.	George Morales	George Morales
m.	#2982765	2982765#
n.	632-65-1840	632-56-1840
o.	42-28-83	42-28-38
p.	982.017	9820.17
q.	deferred	defered
r.	Febuary	February

6. Assume that you wrote the following messages and then entered them into a computer. Verify the copy on the computer screens below. In your Activity Guide or on separate paper correct any errors that appear on the screens. Assume that the hand-written copy is correct. On separate paper, list any errors that appear on the screens.

a. *Meet Sally Burnot in her office at 6:00 p.m. Bring notes of the supervisors' meeting and related reports.*

Meet Sally Burnot in her
office at 6:00. Bring
notes of the supervisors'
meeting and related

b. *Send the current report by Express Mail. Be sure to include your proposal and the survey results.*

Send the current by
Express mail. Be sure to
include your proposal and
the survey results.

c. *Remember Dan's birthday party to be held immediately after work. No gift should cost more than $10.*

Remember Dan's birthday
party to held immediately
after work. No should
more than $10.

7. Assume that you wrote the following addresses and then entered them into a computer. Verify the copy on the computer screens below. On separate paper list any errors that appear on the screen.

a. *D'Almore, Carol*
1003 Jackson Blvd.
Lakeland, FL 33802
(813) 555-9023

D'Almore, Carol
1003 Jackson St.
Lakeland, LA 33802
(813) 555-9032

b. *Gonzales, Carol*
2930 Lincoln Highway
Forrest, CA 92655
(714) 555 - 0723

Gonzales, Carlos
2390 Lincoln Highway
Forrest, CA 92655
(714) 555-0723

GOALS

1. To arrange names of persons in indexing order.
2. To arrange names of persons or businesses in alphabetic order.

KEY TERMS

Filing is the process of classifying, sorting, and storing information for quick and easy reference.

Alphabetic filing is the process of arranging records in order by name.

Indexing order is the special order in which a name is arranged for filing.

Many business records are filed in alphabetic order. These records include customers' records, creditors' records, payroll records, sales records, and purchases records. *Alphabetic filing* is arranging records like these in alphabetic order by the letters of the name of the person or business to whom they refer.

File workers use standard rules for the alphabetic filing of names of people and of businesses. Three basic rules for alphabetic filing that apply to most business records are listed below.

Rule 1: *Names of people are filed by last names.* Names are arranged in a special order for filing called *indexing order*. To write a name in indexing order, you must first transpose the name. *Transposing* a name means changing the order of the parts of a name to last name, first name, and middle name.

If two or more people have the same last name, then the first name determines the alphabetic order. If the first and last names are the same, then the middle name or initial determines the alphabetic order. If the names are exactly alike, then the name of a person's town or state may determine the order. For example:

Transposing is the process of arranging names of persons in indexing order or field order by changing the parts to last name, first name, then middle name.

Meadows, Ralph

Meadows, Ralph J.

Meadows, Ralph James (New York)

Meadows, Ralph James (Tennessee)

The following names are in alphabetic order and have been transposed into indexing order:

Name	Indexing Order
William E. Bankston	Bankston, William E.
John L. Crafton	Crafton, John L.
Dewayne McDowell	McDowell, Dewayne
Calvin Rymer	Rymer, Calvin
H. J. Trout	Trout, H. J.

Rule 2: *Nothing comes before something.* A last name alone comes before the same last name with a first name or a first initial. A last name with a first initial comes before the same last name with a complete first name beginning with the same letter as the initial. Here are some examples of this rule:

Crandall	comes before	*M.* Crandall
M. Crandall	comes before	*Martin* Crandall
Martin Crandall	comes before	Martin *D.* Crandall
Martin *D.* Crandall	comes before	Martin *Dean* Crandall

Here are the above names written in indexing order:

Name	Indexing Order
Crandall	Crandall
M. Crandall	Crandall, M.
Martin Crandall	Crandall, Martin
Martin D. Crandall	Crandall, Martin D.
Martin Dean Crandall	Crandall, Martin Dean

Rule 3: *Names of businesses and institutions are generally filed as written.* In almost all cases the names of businesses and institutions are filed exactly as written. The only exception is when the word "the" is the first part of the name. In this case, "the" is moved to the end of the name. The following examples show the names of businesses arranged in alphabetic order:

Taylor *Autos*	comes before	Taylor *Supply*
Taylor Supply	comes before	*Temple* Lumber
Temple Lumber	comes before	*Thompson* Contractors
Thompson Contractors	comes before	Thompson *Landscaping*
Thompson Landscaping	comes before	The *University* Clinic
The *University* Clinic	comes before	Ursula Haywood Landscaping

Here are the above names written in indexing order:

Name	Indexing Order
Taylor Autos	Taylor Autos
Taylor Supply	Taylor Supply
Temple Lumber	Temple Lumber
Thompson Contractors	Thompson Contractors
Thompson Landscaping	Thompson Landscaping
The University Clinic	University Clinic The
Ursula Haywood Landscaping	Ursula Haywood Landscaping*

*Note that the name "Ursula Haywood" is not transposed. This is because it is part of the business name.

1. The process of classifying, sorting, and storing information is known as ___?___ .

2. Records arranged in order by name are in ___?___ order.

3. The process of changing names to indexing order is called ___?___ .

Exercises for Topic 3

1. Durand Gift Shop has 12 employees. Julia Durand, the owner, must set up a filing system for her employees. Julia wants each employee's earnings record to be filed in a separate file folder. The names of the employees are listed below.

   a. Write each name in indexing order.
   b. List the names in alphabetic order.

   Kelly R. Hilbert   Paul R. Cabretti
   Steven M. Eliason   Kelly A. Hilbert
   Elaine Lupone   Francine Milgram
   Joy L. Arkwright   Joe Lupone
   Frances Milgram   Kenneth Hilbert
   Louis J. McCabe   Daniel Elias

2. At the Boylan Company the suppliers' folders are filed in alphabetic order by the suppliers' names. List the following suppliers' names in alphabetic order:

   Buy and Save Grocery
   The Houseman Electric Supply
   Continental Products Inc.
   Miguel Carillo Plumbing Company
   Mike Houseman Trucking Company
   Mary Millian Construction
   Carillo Family Clothing Store
   The Buyer's Market
   The Taylor Laundering Company
   Carillo and Carillo Inc.
   Houseman and Milan Inc.
   The Martha McMillian Company
   The Tanenbaum Company
   Conti Service Company

3. Granger's Greenhouse has several new customers. The customers' folders are filed in alphabetic order according to the

customers' names. List the following new customers' names in alphabetic order:

Paul's Plants
Main Street Florists
Florence's Flowers
The Plants and Pots Place
Fowler's Flower Shop

The Flower Pot
Sandford's Flower Shop
Flowers ''N'' Such
Sara's Flowers
The Flower Box

4. Using the sales slips below, prepare a report summarizing the information in alphabetic order by customers' last names. Keep related information on the same line.

Running Sports
No. 1001
Date: Nov. 16, 19-
Sold to: Jerri Burnstone
Amount Due: $59.63

Running Sports
No. 1002
Date: Nov. 18, 19-
Sold to: Dan W. Rasch
Amount Due: $78.50

Running Sports
No. 1003
Date: Nov. 20, 19-
Sold to: Gladys C. Andreas
Amount Due: $78.50

Running Sports
No. 1004
Date: Dec. 4, 19-
Sold to: Julio D. Manchego
Amount Due: $26.87

Running Sports
No. 1005
Date: Dec. 5, 19-
Sold to: Lucy A. Gibbs
Amount Due: $52.45

Running Sports
No. 1006
Date: Dec. 10, 19-
Sold to: Cheryl M. Laurin
Amount Due: $19.43

TOPIC 4 ▲ YOUR PERSONAL PAPERS

GOALS

1. To describe ways to care for and protect important records.
2. To decide where to store records for safekeeping.

KEY TERMS

A *record book* has pages for listing important information.

An *expandable file* is a heavy paper folder containing pockets.

A *fireproof box* is a container that will protect valuables from heat damage caused by fire.

A *safe-deposit box* is a locked container within a bank vault.

All of us have important personal papers: birth certificates, canceled checks, receipts, insurance policies, car-ownership papers, and special licenses. All of these records should be carefully protected.

PROTECTING VALUABLE RECORDS

If you are careful, you will keep copies of records such as certificates, diplomas, checks, bank records, licenses, and agreements. There are various ways to protect records and other valuable items.

Expandable File An *expandable file* is a heavy paper folder with pockets that provide places for storing papers. The pockets usually have tabs for alphabetic filing or for filing by dates. An expandable file is ideal for storing the following papers:

Warranties and guarantees
Rental leases
Earnings records
Savings account passbooks
Installment contracts
Receipts
Canceled checks
School records
Written agreements

Record Book A *record book* has pages for listing information. Here are some examples of the kinds of information that are best kept in a record book:

List of insurance companies, policy numbers, and amounts
Due dates for rent or mortgage payments, installments, and insurance payments
List of banks and savings and checking account numbers
Income tax information, including donations, medical expenses, and business expenses
Employment facts, including names and addresses of companies worked for, dates of employment, and beginning and ending salaries
Dates for warranties and guarantees on major appliances, tires, and automobiles
Social Security number
Credit card account numbers
List of locations of important documents

Safe-Deposit Box For a yearly fee banks rent locked *safe-deposit boxes* within bank vaults. Only depositors whose signatures are on file may enter the vault area. Two keys are needed to open each safe-deposit box. The bank has one key and the depositor has the other key to the box.

Safe-deposit boxes provide a very high degree of protection against loss from theft and fire. They are very popular for valuables such as these:

Savings certificates

Bonds

Expensive jewelry

Mortgage papers

Stock certificates

Deeds

Copies of wills

Fireproof Box A good *fireproof box* will protect its contents from damage in fires up to 1800 degrees Fahrenheit. In addition, it can be locked.

People often use fireproof boxes to store the following:

Insurance policies
Marriage certificate
Naturalization papers
Passports
Credit cards not carried in wallet or purse
Written agreements and contracts
Title certificates to cars, motorcycles, boats
Birth certificates
Adoption certificates
Tax records
Spare cash
Photographs of household furnishings (in case of fire)
Jewelry
Receipts for expensive items (cameras, computers)

Check Your Reading

1. A heavy paper folder with pockets for storing papers is called a(n) ___?___ .

2. A locked container that resists heat is a(n) ___?___ .

3. A locked container within a bank vault is a(n) ___?___ .

4. Rental leases should be stored in a(n) ___?___ .

5. Birth certificates should be stored in a(n) ___?___ .

1. Select the item in column 2 that is best suited for protecting each record in column 1.

Column I	Column 2
1. Bond	a. Expandable file
2. Stock certificate	b. Fireproof box
3. Installment contract	c. Safe-deposit box
4. High school diploma	d. Record book
5. Last year's tax records	
6. Savings account passbook	
7. TV set guarantee form	
8. List of medical expenses	
9. Earnings record	
10. List of insurance policies	
11. Birth certificate	
12. Photographs of furnishings	
13. Apartment lease agreement	
14. Marriage certificate	
15. Date for expiration of TV guarantee	

2. Why is it unwise to store important records in a cardboard file or a plain metal box?

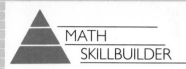

Skill: Basic addition.

Sample Problem: Find the sum of 52, 17, and 26.

Solution:

1. Set the problem up in standard addition form. Be sure that the numbers on the right side are in a column.

$$
\begin{array}{r}
52 \\
17 \\
\underline{26}
\end{array}
$$

2. Starting at the right, add all the numbers in that column. Record the 5 under the right column, and carry the 1 to the left column.

$$
\begin{array}{r}
1 \\
52 \\
17 \\
\underline{26} \\
5
\end{array}
$$

3. Add the left column (including the number you carried). Record the 9 under the left column to complete your answer.

$$
\begin{array}{r}
1 \\
52 \\
17 \\
\underline{26} \\
95
\end{array}
$$

4. Answer: 95

Practice: Find the sum of the following:

1. 6, 7, and 5
2. 27 and 42
3. 86 and 49
4. 52, 36, and 74
5. 36, 59, and 72
6. 89, 96, and 78
7. 372, 634, and 125
8. 123, 536, and 263
9. 809, 576, and 427
10. 969, 936, and 768

Skill: Adding dollars and cents.

Sample Problem: Find the sum of $9.30, $17, 50¢, and $4.09.

Solution:

1. Set up the problem for addition. Be sure all decimal points are in a vertical column. Then add. Notice that $17 is written as 17.00 and 50¢ is written as .50.

$$
\begin{array}{r}
\$\ 9.30 \\
17.00 \\
.50 \\
\underline{4.09} \\
\$30.89
\end{array}
$$

2. Answer: $30.89

Practice: Find the sum for each of the following:

1. $6.80 and $4.46
2. $29.65 and $15.38
3. $493.57 and $521.93
4. $1.38, $3.23, and $8.60
5. $21.47, $49.62, and $13.18
6. $893.64, $696.79, and $874.78
7. $14.06, $5.43, $12.93, and $4.28
8. $14.97, $18, $52.41, and $3
9. $42.60, 66¢, 48¢, $4.95, and $6.50
10. $248.51, $24, $150, 36¢, and $1.46

Skill: Basic subtraction.

Sample Problem: Find the difference between 52 and 38.

Solution:

1. Set up the problem in standard subtraction form. Be sure the larger number is above the smaller number.

$$
\begin{array}{r}
52 \\
\underline{-38}
\end{array}
$$

2. Subtract the right column. You cannot subtract 8 from 2. Therefore, you must borrow 10 from the left column, or tens column, and add it to the right column $(10 + 2 = 12)$. Now subtract and record your answer (4) under the right column $(12 - 8 = 4)$.

$$\begin{array}{r} 52 \\ -38 \\ \hline 4 \end{array}$$

3. Subtract the left column. Remember that you are now subtracting 3 from 4 since you borrowed before $(4 - 3 = 1)$.

4. Record the 1 to complete the problem.

$$\begin{array}{r} 52 \\ -38 \\ \hline 14 \end{array}$$

5. Answer: 14

Practice: Find the difference for the following:

1. 15 and 9
2. 78 and 61
3. 82 and 76
4. 32 and 15
5. 93 and 76
6. 158 and 37
7. 451 and 296
8. 956 and 464
9. 672 and 487
10. 783 and 586

Skill: Subtracting dollars and cents.

Sample Problem: Find the difference between $173.50 and $8.30.

Solution:
1. Set the problem up for subtraction. Be sure the decimal points are in a vertical column. Subtract.

$$\begin{array}{r} \$173.50 \\ -8.30 \\ \hline \$165.20 \end{array}$$

2. Answer: $165.20

Practice: Find the difference for the following:

1. $67.50 and $1.25
2. $168 and $71
3. $83.60 and $19.60
4. $858.90 and $264.50
5. $756.10 and $103.95
6. $682.49 and $457.51
7. $300 and $29.27
8. $605.48 and $40.30
9. $82.06 and $1.29
10. $3,253.90 and $515.40

Skill: Writing numbers on forms.

Sample Problem: Write the following amounts on a unit-ruled form: $32.70, $145.68, $3,479.25, and $403.05.

Solution: Some forms provide a separate space for each digit on an amount. They are called unit-ruled forms. When you write numbers on these forms, omit the dollar sign and decimal point. Write small, neat figures that are the same size. Use the lower half of each box as shown below. Do this because if you have to correct an error, you will need the space above the error to write in the correction.

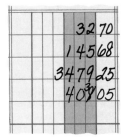

Practice: Write the following amounts in the spaces of a unit-ruled form. If necessary, make corrections by drawing a single line through the error and writing the correction above it.

1. $92.27
2. $29.64, $632.66, $8.78
3. $950.80, $83.83, $4,388, $11.32

4. $7,903.37, $45.80, $600, $33.50
5. $700, $582.67, $421.66, $3.86
6. $711.52, $167.17, $2,735.98, $55.33
7. $4,006.55, $910.21, $2,650.40, $30.50

8. $342.91, $666.45, $3,971, $6.80
9. $478.12, $31,243, $832,160.10, $99.12
10. $933,246.18, $688,432.51, $822,364.47, $789,564.81

VOCABULARY SKILLBUILDER

Read each of the following statements. From the words below each statement, choose the term that best matches the statement.

1. A rule going up and down.

    horizontal   column   vertical

2. Rule that goes left to right.

    entry   horizontal   vertical

3. Checking data to see if it is accurate and complete.

    reporting   transposing   verifying

4. A sheet of paper with lines, or rules, and columns.

    entry   form   report

5. A disk that gives instructions to the computer.

    data   work   program

6. A personal computer stores information on.

    form   disk   paper

7. A safe deposit box is found in.

    bank   store   home

8. Part of a computer used to enter data.

    keyboard   processor

9. Numbers or letters in the wrong order.

    matching   transposition   verifying

APPLICATION PROBLEMS

1. Assume that you are applying for a part-time job. Complete the job application form provided in the Activity Guide. Fill out the form neatly, using your name, address, Social Security number, and dates of previous employment. Do not leave any blanks; write "NA" (for "not applicable") if necessary. As you complete the form, remember to be neat and careful.

2. Draw up a form asking for the following:

Line 1, current date, date of birth; line 2, last name, first name, middle initial; line 3, street address, city, state, ZIP Code.

3. Draw up a form to record your personal financial information:

    a. Title the form "Personal Finances."

    b. Create column headings for date, item, amount paid, and amount received.

c. Make the following entries:
Total the amount paid and amount received columns

July 6   Received salary of $89.20 from part-time job.

7   Bought a gift for $12.50 for Cindy.

8   Jud Brown paid a debt of $15.

8   Paid $3.50 for the movies.

8   Bought a paperback for $4.95.

8   Paid $5 club dues.

9   Sold guitar for $60.

9   Paid $15 at amusement park.

d. Review the completed form to make sure that it is legible. Verify each entry. If any entry is missing or if the form has errors, develop a new form and record the entries again.

4. Mark Slovitz is applying for admission to a community college. Complete the form in the Activity Guide for him. Use the following information:

Social Security number: 892-01-1650
Present mailing address: 755 Elm Avenue, Englewood, NJ 07631
Permanent mailing address: 8076 Kennedy Boulevard, Elizabeth, NJ 07201
Birth date: January 22, 1972
Home telephone: (201) 555-1920
Business telephone: None

CHAPTER 2

PERSONAL BANKING

Banking is an important activity in your life. Banking services help you keep track of your money and keep it safe. A bank is a *service business,* so you can expect a friendly welcome there. To find out more about banking, visit a local bank to pick up information about its services. After you've reviewed the materials, visit the bank again, this time to see a customer service representative. Ask how the bank might help you with your finances.

In this chapter, you will learn how to open a personal checking account and write checks. You will also learn how to keep your account balance and confirm that your balance and the bank's record of your balance agree. This chapter, therefore, will help you control an important part of your personal finances.

TOPIC 1 ▲ BANKING SERVICES AND CHECKING ACCOUNTS

GOALS

1. To identify banking services.
2. To complete a signature card.
3. To endorse checks properly.
4. To complete deposit slips.

KEY TERMS

A *check* is an order to a bank to pay someone money.

A *checking account* is a service provided by a bank that lets a person deposit money and write checks.

A *signature card* shows the official signature of each person opening the account.

A *deposit slip* is a form that shows the amount of money to be deposited, the date, the name of the bank, the account number, and the name of the account holder.

BANKING SERVICES

Banks are businesses. They make a profit by charging fees for services and by collecting interest on loans. Because banks offer safety, they are good places to keep money. But banks do more than just hold money. Banks also offer a variety of general services:

Checking Accounts A checking account is set up to make day-to-day payments without the risk of using cash. Banks pay interest on some checking accounts.

Savings Accounts A savings account is set up to keep money and build up the balance. Not only does the bank store the savings safely, but it also pays interest.

Interest is a fee paid for the use of money.

Safe-Deposit Boxes Small boxes within bank vaults provide a very safe place to store valuables such as jewelry and important papers. The bank charges a rental fee for each safe-deposit box.

Traveler's Checks Banks issue traveler's checks to their customers so they can obtain cash when on a trip.

Bank Credit Cards Some banks issue credit cards that make buying on credit convenient. The card holder pays interest on outstanding balances and may pay an annual fee for the card.

Loans Banks lend money for various purposes and charge interest for the loan. Some reasons for borrowing money are to buy a home or a car, to pay for school, and to buy business equipment.

Automated Teller Machines As a convenience to their customers, many banks have *automated teller machines* (ATMs). An ATM can be used both to withdraw money from an account and to deposit money in an account. An ATM is often open 24 hours a day. ATMs are located in shopping centers and other convenient places.

    To use the machine, a customer must have a special card that comes from the bank. The bank will also provide a brochure explaining how to use the ATM and listing the locations of its ATMs.

Automated teller machine

SELECTING A BANK

How do you choose the bank that is best for you? First, consider which banking services you might need in the future. For example, you may not need a safe-deposit box now, but you may need one soon. Think also about ease of banking. You should not pick a bank solely because it is close to your home or your office, but you should consider distance. In addition, you should ask these questions: Are the tellers friendly? Do they wait on you promptly? Will the bank pay interest on your money? What are the fees for checks? Does the bank require a minimum balance for a checking account? Before you open an account, try to find out as much as possible about the bank's people.

The rest of this chapter is concerned with two important banking services—checking accounts and savings accounts.

THE CHECKING ACCOUNT

Whichever bank you select, you will benefit from having a personal checking account. First of all, nearly all businesses now accept personal checks as payments for purchases. With a checking account, you do not need to carry large amounts of cash with you when you shop, and you do not need to keep too much cash at home. In addition, checks provide the only easy way to pay bills by mail.

Opening an Account Once a bank has been chosen, opening a checking account is a matter of filling out a form and depositing money to start the account. For example, let's see how Stacey C. Walters opened her first checking account.

The Signature Card When Stacey met with a customer service representative at the First Savings & Loan, she was first asked for personal identification. Then she completed both sides of this signature card:

	INDIVIDUAL
Walters, Stacey C.	703-6446-7

AUTHORIZED SIGNATURES, CHECKING ACCOUNT WITH

First Savings & Loan
El Toro, CA 92658

SIGNATURE _Stacey C. Walters_
SIGNATURE _____
ADDRESS _1262 Main St._
El Toro, CA 92658
TELEPHONE NO. _555-7600_
TYPE OF ACCOUNT _Checking_
INITIAL DEPOSIT _$100_
DATE _Oct 20,19—_ OPENED BY _Stacey C. Walters_

Signature Card

Stacey Walters will sign her name on her checks just like she signs her name on this signature card. Signature cards are used for both checking and savings accounts.

The card asks for basic information—her address and phone number, and the type of account she wishes to open. The blanks are small, so Stacey was careful to write neatly within the space provided.

The card also shows Stacey's official signature. The bank will use this signature to verify that checks presented for payment were indeed signed by Stacey C. Walters. Remember: The bank has authority only to pay checks signed by Stacey. Therefore, this signature card is very important. It shows how Stacey will sign all her checks.

Of course, Stacey also deposited money into her new account. Later, you will see how to complete a deposit slip. Having completed the signature card and deposited money into the account, Stacey was given temporary checks to use until she gets her printed checks. Then, within two weeks or so, Stacey will receive printed checks like this one:

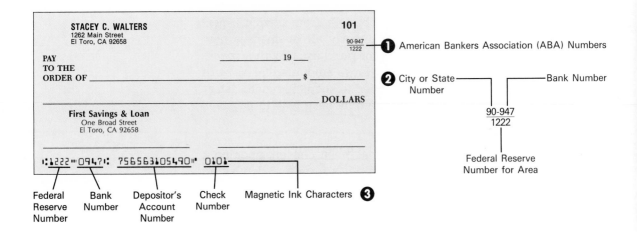

Stacey now has her own personal checking account, also known as an *individual* checking account. This means that only one person can write checks. When two persons can write checks—such as a married couple—both persons complete the signature card. Then the bank has both official signatures on file. For this reason, the signature card shown on page 29 has a space for a second signature.

Later you will learn how to write a check. On Stacey's printed check shown above, note these three numbers:

1. In the upper-right corner, the number of the check appears: *101*. Stacey's check numbers are printed in order, so that she does not have to number checks as she writes them.
2. Below the check number is the American Bankers Association (ABA) number:

$$\frac{50\text{-}947}{219}$$

   The ABA number identifies the location of a bank (50), the bank number (947), and the Federal Reserve Number (219) used in sorting checks for payment.
3. At the bottom of the check is a computer-readable number printed in magnetic ink.

Endorsing Checks Both cash and checks may be deposited in a checking account. Banks provide easy-to-complete deposit tickets, as you will see later.

When checks are deposited, the bank will collect the amount of each check and credit it to the account. But before a check can be deposited, it should be properly endorsed. To understand what endorsement means, let's see how Stacey Walters handles her paychecks.

When Stacey receives her paycheck, she has two options. She can sign the check and cash it; the bank will give her the full amount of the check. Or if she wishes, she can deposit the check in her checking account. In both cases, she should sign the check, and her signature is the endorsement.

Blank Endorsement To cash the check, Stacey must sign it on the left end of the back, as shown here.

By signing only her name, Stacey wrote a *blank endorsement* One thing to remember about a blank endorsement is that if the check is lost or stolen, it can be cashed by someone else. Stacey uses the blank endorsement only when she is at the bank.

To endorse a check, turn it over and sign it at the left end.

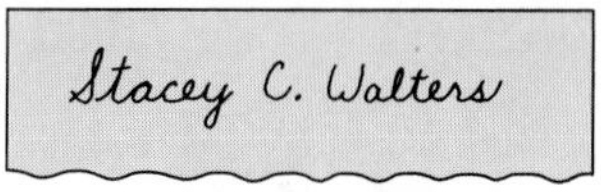

Stacey C. Walters

For-Deposit-Only Endorsement A second endorsement, called a *for-deposit-only endorsement,* is safer to use. As its name clearly tells, a for-deposit-only endorsement is used when a check is to be deposited, not cashed. By signing the following check and then writing the words "For Deposit Only," Stacey orders the bank to deposit the full amount of the check in her account.

Because this check cannot be cashed, the for-deposit-only endorsement provides a safe way to mail deposits to the bank.

For-deposit-only endorsement

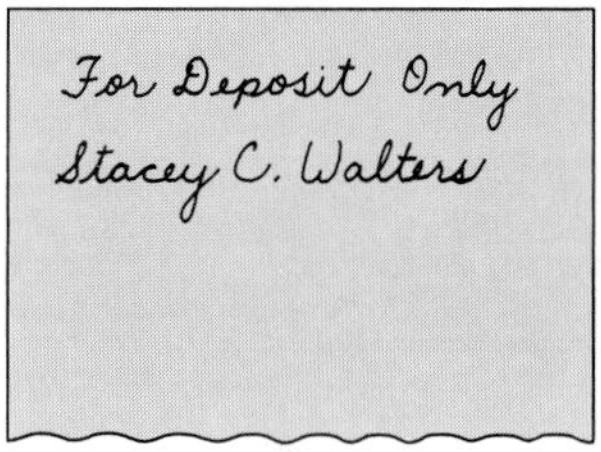

For Deposit Only
Stacey C. Walters

Third-Party Endorsement Sometimes Stacey uses another kind of endorsement, called a *third-party endorsement.* For instance, Stacey gave her friend Bruce Bernstein a check made out to her. The back of the check is shown to the right.

Because she endorsed the check to Bruce, he can deposit or cash the check. Three persons are involved: the person who wrote the check, Stacey, and Bruce. You can see why this is called a third-party endorsement.

Third-party endorsement

Pay to the Order of
Bruce Bernstein
Stacey C. Walters

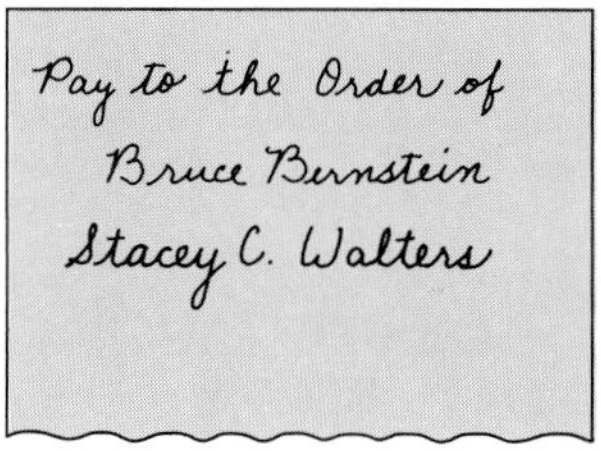

Making Deposits To prepare checks for deposit, as you read above, Stacey should properly endorse them. Stacey often writes her account number on each check under her endorsement—just in case the check and the deposit slip should be separated.

Next, Stacey completes a *deposit slip.* Her bank, like most others, gives Stacey deposit slips with her name, address, and account number printed on them.

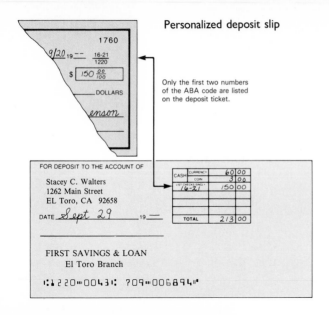

Personalized deposit slip

Only the first two numbers of the ABA code are listed on the deposit ticket.

Stacey simply fills in the amount of cash deposited and lists each check separately, as shown here. Stacey lists $60 in bills and $3 in coins. For each check, Stacey writes the top part of the ABA number and the amount of the check, as shown.

The printed form is easy for Stacey to use. The *magnetic-ink character recognition* (MICR) numbers at the bottom of the form can be read by computer, so the bank can identify the account. The ABA number, which appears in the upper right corner of a check, identifies the bank's location, it's number, and the Federal Reserve number.

Check Your Reading

1. Name three services provided by banks.

2. An order to a bank to pay money is called a(n) ___?___ .

3. The form listing the checks and money to be deposited to an account is called a(n) ___?___ .

4. The form with an account holder's official signature is called a(n) ___?___ card.

5. Before a check can be deposited, it should be ___?___ .

6. A simple signature on the back of check is called a(n) ___?___ endorsement.

7. To show that a check is to be deposited, not cashed, a depositor uses a(n) ___?___ endorsement.

Exercises for Topic 1

1. You are opening a checking account at the First State Bank. Complete the signature card provided in the Activity Guide. Use the following information:

   For the past 14 months, you have been employed by Shopper's Galaxy, located at 360 East Van Buren, Phoenix, Arizona 85044. Use this company as your financial reference. Its telephone number is (602) 555-2174. Your driver's license number is P3221867NJ.

2. A friend, Judy C. Lockmer, filled in the following signature card to open a new account at Central Bank. On a separate sheet, list any errors or omissions Judy made in completing the card.

Central Bank   Signature Card

NAME *Judy C. Lockmer*
ADDRESS *897 Central Avenue*
Houston
TELEPHONE NUMBER *(713) 555-2046*
PERSONAL REFERENCE: NAME *A. C. Richards*
               ADDRESS
               TELEPHONE NUMBER *(713) 555-7692*
FINANCIAL REFERENCE: NAME *SuperMart*
               ADDRESS *1490 Tidwell Road*
               Houston
               TELEPHONE NUMBER *(713) 555-4200*
TYPE OF ACCOUNT
INITIAL DEPOSIT *$100*
SIGNATURE

3. Endorse the following paychecks in the space provided in your Activity Guide. Terri usually signs her name *Terri Blakmer.* Kevin signs *Kevin Butler.* Use a blank endorsement.

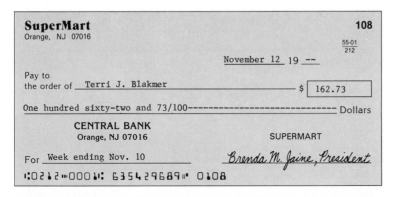

SuperMart		**108**
Orange, NJ 07016		$\frac{55\text{-}01}{212}$
	November 12 19 --	
Pay to the order of Terri J. Blakmer		$ 162.73
One hundred sixty-two and 73/100------------------------------- Dollars		
CENTRAL BANK Orange, NJ 07016	SUPERMART	
For Week ending Nov. 10	*Brenda M. Jaine, President*	
⑈0212⑈000⑈: 635429689⑈ 0108		

SuperMart		**1008**
Orange, NJ 07016		$\frac{55\text{-}01}{212}$
	December 7 19 --	
Pay to the order of Kevin Andrew Butler		$ 155.35
One hundred fifty-five and 35/100-------------------------- Dollars		
CENTRAL BANK Orange, NJ 07016	SUPERMART	
For Week ending December 4, 19--	*Brenda M. Jaine, President*	
⑈0212⑈000⑈: 635429689⑈ 1008⑈		

Use "for-deposit-only" endorsements for exercises 4. and 5.

4. Now show how you would endorse your paycheck, shown below. Then prepare a deposit slip for the paycheck.

SuperMart   **1005**
Orange, NJ 07016
                                                                       $\frac{55\text{-}01}{212}$

                                               October 28 19 __

Pay to
the order of ____ (Your Full Name) _____ $ | 178.29

One hundred seventy-eight and 29/100----------------------- Dollars

    CENTRAL BANK
    Orange, NJ 07016   SUPERMART

For Week ending October 25, 19--   Brenda M. Jaine, President

⑈0212⑈0001⑈ 635429689⑈ 1005⑈

5. Show how you would endorse these two checks. Both are made payable to you. Then prepare two deposit slips. Date the one for the first check October 15 of this year. For the second check, date the deposit slip November 6 of this year.

      GORDON C. WALCO   **114**
         1261 Larch St.
         Orange, NJ 07016   October 5 19 __   55-175/212

PAY TO THE
ORDER OF (Your full name) _____ $ 68 $\frac{00}{100}$

Sixty - eight $\frac{00}{100}$ _____ Dollars

    Garden State Bank
    4328 Moulton Parkway
    Orange, NJ 07016

Memo ____ Typing ____   Gordon C. Walco

⑈0212⑈0175⑈ 015800297300⑈ 0114

      GORDON C. WALCO   **118**
         1261 Larch St.
         Orange, NJ 07016   November 2 19 __   55-175/212

PAY TO THE
ORDER OF (Your full name) ____ $ 34 $\frac{50}{100}$

Thirty - four $\frac{50}{100}$ _____ Dollars

    Garden State Bank
    4328 Moulton Parkway
    Orange, NJ 07016

Memo Proofreading ____   Gordon C. Walco

⑈0212⑈0175⑈ 015800297300⑈ 0118

6. Prepare three deposit slips for the following dates. For each check, be sure to include the ABA number, which is listed before the amount of each check. Use your own name and address. Your account number is 608-53355.

August 1:
Bills: $87. Coins: $34.57. Checks: 22-41, $18.30; 22-59, $7.18; 22-980, $128.70; 22-460, $2.98.

August 15:
Bills: $34. Coins: $10.47. Checks: 69-118, $9.87; 68-609, $7.54; 68-629, $24.98; 68-704, $280; 68-806, $39.78.

August 30:
Bills: two $20 bills, one $5 bill, seven $1 bills. Coins: one half-dollar, three quarters, twenty dimes, five nickels, seventeen pennies. Checks: 80-118, $22.18.

7. Deposit six checks for the following amounts in your account (number 608-53355).

Amount of Check	ABA Number
$225.00	70-21
$96.00	00-28
$25.50	71-00
$43.25	04-08
$53.00	01-34
$60.00	02-6001

TOPIC 2 ▲ WRITING CHECKS

GOALS

1. To write checks.
2. To review a written check for accuracy and completeness.
3. To enter checks in a check register.

KEY TERMS

The *drawer* is the person who writes a check.

The *payee* is the person who receives the check.

The *check register* is the customer's record of all deposits made and checks written.

USING THE CHECK REGISTER

The *check register* is a book of forms that provide space for writing in the dates, amounts, and payees for all checks. The *payee* is the person who receives the check. As this page from Stacey Walters' check register shows, a register also provides space for deposits:

		19— PLEASE BE SURE TO **DEDUCT** CHARGES THAT AFFECT YOUR ACCOUNT						BALANCE FORWARD		
NO.	DATE	ISSUED TO OR DESCRIPTION OF DEPOSIT	AMOUNT OF PAYMENT	✓	OTHER DEDUCT	AMOUNT OF DEPOSIT		*147* *63*	— ❶
501	9/26	TO *Edison Gas & Electric* FOR *9/22 Invoice*	35 29					*35 29* *112 34*	— ❷ — ❸
	9/27	TO *Deposit* FOR *Paycheck*				237 61		*237 61* *349 95*	— ❹ — ❺
		TO FOR							
		TO FOR							

Check register

In the No. column, Stacey enters the number of each check she writes. In the Date column, she enters the date for each check and for each deposit.

The next column provides both a To and a For line for each check. Stacey writes the payee's name on the To line and the reason for the payment on the For line. Then, in the Amount of Payment column, she writes the check amount. For each deposit, she writes Deposit on the To line and a brief explanation on the For line. Then, in the Amount of Deposit column, she writes the deposit total.

Let's see how Stacey uses the Balance Forward column:

1. Before she wrote Check 501, Stacey had a balance of $147.63 in her account. She copied this balance from the previous page of her check register.
2. Then, on September 26, she wrote Check 501, in the amount of $35.29, to Edison Gas and Electric Company for electric service.
3. After writing Check 501, Stacey deducted the amount, $35.29, from the old balance, $147.63, to get a new balance, $112.34.
4. On September 27, Stacey deposited her paycheck, $237.61.
5. Having made the deposit, Stacey added the deposit amount, $237.61, to the old balance, $112.34, to get a new balance, $349.95.

As you can see, Stacey computes a new balance by (1) *deducting* from the old balance each check written or (2) *adding* to the old balance each deposit made. In this way, Stacey uses the check register to keep her checkbook balance up to date.

WRITING CHECKS

The best way to write checks and keep the check register is to follow a step-by-step procedure. First of all, always complete the check register before writing the check. Fill in the date, amount, and other information.

After you have entered the data in the check register, calculate a new balance to see whether you have enough money to cover the check you are about to write. If you do, then you are ready to write the check, as follows:

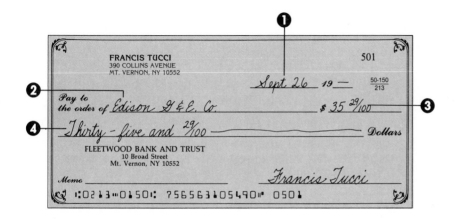

1. Using a pen, fill in the date—month, day, and year.
2. Clearly write or print the name of the payee on the line following the words "Pay to the Order of."
3. Enter in figures the exact amount of the check close to the dollar symbol. Note the illustration.
4. On the line below "Pay to the Order of," write the dollar amount of the check in words.
   a. If the amount is a whole-dollar amount, also write "and 00/100" to indicate "and no cents."
   b. If the amount does include part of a dollar, use figures to write the cents amount—for example, 39/100 for 39 cents. See the above illustration.
   If the amount in figures and the amount in words are different, the bank will use the amount in words.
5. Review the check to make sure that the date, the payee, the amount in figures, and the amount in words are written correctly, then sign the check.

Spelling Numbers:
twenty   sixty
thirty   seventy
forty   eighty
fifty   ninety

Spelling Numbers:
eleven   sixteen
twelve   seventeen
thirteen   eighteen
fourteen   nineteen
fifteen

Spelling Hyphenated Numbers:
twenty-one   fifty-six
thirty-two   sixty-eight
forty-four

Use the Least Number of Words:
seventeen hundred (for $1,700)
thirty-eight hundred (for $3,800)

Check Your Reading

1. The person who writes a check is called the ___?___ .

2. The person to whom a check is written is called the ___?___ .

3. The booklet of forms used to record written checks and account balances is called the ___?___ .

Exercises for Topic 2

1. Write the following numbers in words as they should appear on a check. Write the cents as a fraction of 100. The word "dollars" does not need to be written. (Use the fewest words possible.)

$105.00	$42.76	$19.50
$1,275.00	$14.45	$1,700.00
$5,620.00	$96.98	$18.25
$13.20	$1,482.00	$11.50

2. Verify the following check endorsements by matching them against the signature cards on file at the bank. In your Activity Guide, make any necessary corrections and note whether any signature card is missing.

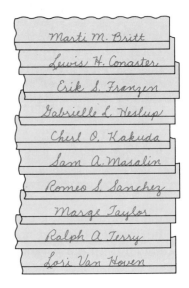

How the Check Was Signed

Twenty-eight ⁴³/₁₀₀ DOLLARS
Erik S. Franzen
Cherl O. Kakuda
Ralph Terry
Lew Conaster
Marge Taylor
Lori Van Hoven
Marti M. Britt
Gabrielle L. Heslup
Samuel A. Masalin
Romeo S. Sanchez
Linda Barclay

What the Signature Card Shows
(Alphabetized)

Marti M. Britt
Lewis H. Conaster
Erik S. Franzen
Gabrielle L. Heslup
Cherl O. Kakuda
Sam A. Masalin
Romeo S. Sanchez
Marge Taylor
Ralph A. Terry
Lori Van Hoven

3. In your Activity Guide, correct any errors or omissions in the following checks.

```
Marti M. Britt                                    NO. _____
2340 Main Street
Chicago, IL 60620                                        2-310
                                                          710
PAY                                 2/6      19 __
TO THE
ORDER OF  Outdoor Sports Shop ————— $ 31 42/100

Thirty-one 00/100 ——————————————— DOLLARS

Shore National Bank
   Chicago, Illinois
                                  Marti Britt

⑈0310⑈0710⑈ 706000733⑈
```

```
Marti M. Britt                                    NO. 102
2340 Main Street
Chicago, IL 60620                                        2-310
                                                          710
PAY                                 2/6      19 __
TO THE
ORDER OF _____ $ 28 50/100

Twenty-eight 50/100 ——————————————— DOLLARS

Shore National Bank
   Chicago, Illinois
                                  Marti

⑈0310⑈0710⑈ 706000733⑈
```

4. In the Activity Guide, write the checks indicated below and complete the check register. Your completed check register should include all the necessary information for each check and deposit as well as the new balance.

Dec. 1 Deposited $525 from your savings account. Make an entry in the check register.

1 Issued Check 101 for $19.50 to Lee's Book Store for two books.

3 Issued Check 102 for $60.50 to Ace Garage for car inspection and repair.

4 Deposited $153.73, pay from Woody's Restaurant.

9 Issued Check 103 for $67 to Lynne's Shoes Inc. for new boots.

11 Issued Check 104 for $35.98 to Mountain Gifts for a gift.

13 Issued Check 105 for $50 to Dr. Jane Kilgore for office visit.

16 Deposited $148, pay from Woody's.

16	Issued Check 106 for $36.80 to the SuperMart for groceries.
17	Issued Check 107 for $25.90 to Metro Cycle Shop for bicycle repairs.
19	Issued Check 108 for $185 to Neighborhood Finance Company for car payment.
23	Issued Check 109 to Sal's Music Place for $8.98 for a record.
28	Deposited $79, pay from Woody's.
31	Issued Check 110 for $90 to Stonebrooke National Bank for loan payment.

TOPIC 3 ▲ MAINTAINING YOUR CHECKBOOK

GOALS

1. To keep the check register up to date.
2. To write checks for cash.
3. To identify the problems related to an overdrawn account.
4. To identify advantages of electronic banking.

KEY TERMS

An *overdrawn account,* or *overdraft,* results from writing a check for an amount that is greater than the balance in the account. *NSF* means "not sufficient funds."

A *voided* check is one that is written in error and not used.

CHECKS FOR CASH

At times, you may write a check not to make a payment but to take out money for your own use. To do this, you write "Cash" on the "Pay to the Order of" line. Fill in the rest of the check in the usual way. Remember that anyone can cash such checks. To be on the safe side, write checks made out to "Cash" only when you are in the bank.

OVERDRAWN ACCOUNT

As you have seen, the purpose of your check register is to provide you with accurate records and to tell you the balance in your account at all times. By carefully recording all checks and deposits and by calculating a new balance after each entry, you will always know how much you have in your account.

But what happens when you make a mistake? What happens if you have only $50 in your account and you write a check for $100?

When the bank receives the check for $100, it cannot honor the payment. It stamps the check *NSF*, for not sufficient funds, and returns the check unpaid. Perhaps you have heard this referred to as a bounced check.

For protection against overdrafts, many banks offer *automatic loan protection*. This is an agreement with the bank to deposit money in your account as a loan in the event of an overdraft. You must pay interest on the loan.

VOIDING CHECKS

Sometimes you will write a check and then find you have made a mistake. In this case you can tear up the check and throw it away, noting in your check register that you did not use it for payment. A better procedure that is followed by most businesses is to write "VOID" across the check and keep it. A voided check is shown below.

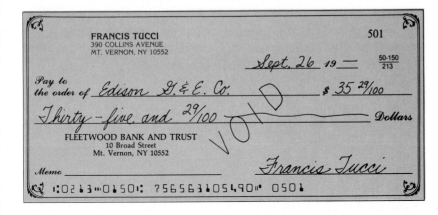

Voided check

STOP PAYMENTS

Occasionally, after you have written a check, you may need to *stop payment*. Suppose, for instance, you mailed a check to MasterCard on September 26. Then, on October 15, MasterCard sends you a late-notice reminder. When you phone the MasterCard office, you are told that your check did not arrive. What do you do?

You must assume that the check has been lost in the mail. In this case, you inform the bank not to pay Check 504 to Master-

A *stop payment* is an order not to pay a specific check.

Card, dated September 26, for $145.50. For this stop payment, the bank will charge you a fee, but you will no longer worry about the lost check. Then write another check to pay your MasterCard bill.

ELECTRONIC BANKING

As you learned earlier, some banks place automated teller machines (ATMs) in shopping centers or other convenient areas. Customers can then withdraw or deposit money without going into a bank. ATMs are an example of *electronic banking*

In addition to ATMs, depositors may use their home telephones to link their home computers to a computer at the bank and do their banking electronically. Certain codes must be entered, including personal codes that prevent unauthorized money transfers. Electronic banking allows you to:

Have your pay automatically deposited to your account each payday.

Have money transferred automatically from your savings account to your checking account (or vice versa).

Use a phone to transfer money from one account to another.

Use a phone to pay bills or to make loan payments.

Use a phone to find your account balance.

Use an ATM to withdraw or deposit money.

Electronic banking allows customers to transfer money at all hours of the day. This is a great advantage to many depositors who can't get to the bank during normal business hours.

Check Your Reading

1. When a check is written incorrectly, the check should be ___?___ .

2. When a check amount is greater than the account balance, the check is called a(n) ___?___ check.

3. NSF means ___?___ .

4. To protect customers from overdrafts, many banks offer ___?___ protection.

1. Compute the balance after each check and each deposit in the following check register on separate paper.

NO.	DATE	ISSUED TO OR DESCRIPTION OF DEPOSIT	AMOUNT OF PAYMENT	✓	OTHER DEDUCT	AMOUNT OF DEPOSIT	BALANCE FORWARD − 00
		19— PLEASE BE SURE TO **DEDUCT** CHARGES THAT AFFECT YOUR ACCOUNT					
	3/23	TO *Deposit*					230 27
		FOR *Paycheck*				230 27	230 27
201	3/24	TO *Tracy J. Wells*					23 00
		FOR *Dues*	23 00				
202	3/25	TO *Dr. James O. Apler*					56 25
		FOR *Dental work*	56 25				
203	3/28	TO *Lous B. Downs*					35 60
		FOR *Car repair*	35 60				
	3/30	TO *Deposit*					256 40
		FOR *Paycheck*				256 40	
204	3/31	TO *GM Rental Agency*					240 00
		FOR *April rent*	240 00				
	4/11	TO *Service charges*					3 25
		FOR *Bank statement*	3 25				
205	4/12	TO *The Telephone Co.*					10 35
		FOR *April bill*	10 35				
		TO					
		FOR					
		TO					

2. In your Activity Guide, write checks as instructed below. Be sure to enter check information in the register before writing each check. Also, to prevent overdrafts, be sure to figure a new balance after each check and each deposit.

Oct. 1 Deposited paycheck for $185.25. Made an entry in the register.

3 Wrote Check 501 to College Book Store for supplies for $12.65.

5 Wrote Check 502 to MusicHeaven for two records for $17.96.

9 Deposited $65 from the sale of ski boots.

12 Wrote Check 503 to the Mall Shop for clothes for $18.45; then voided it.

12 Wrote new Check 504 to Mall Shop for $18.95.

17	Wrote Check 505 to Running Shoes for sport shoes for $27.32.
24	Wrote Check 506 to College Club for dues for $5.
25	Wrote Check 507 to Cash for personal use for $25.
26	Stopped payment on Check 505 for $27.32 because the wrong shoes were delivered. Add $27.32 to register balance. Deduct stop payment fee of $5.

TOPIC 4 ▲ BANK RECONCILIATION

GOALS

1. To reconcile the bank statement and the check register.
2. To update the check register.

KEY TERMS

A *bank statement* is a monthly record of checks, deposits, and service charges for one account.

Reconciling is the process of making the check register balance and the bank statement balance agree.

An *outstanding check* is a check that has been written but does not appear on the bank statement.

A *deposit in transit* is a deposit that has been made but does not appear on the bank statement.

BANK STATEMENTS

Each check you write is given or sent to the payee of the check. The payee then cashes or deposits the check. The check is returned to your bank, and the amount is subtracted from your checking account balance. Then the check is canceled by a machine that stamps it ''Paid.'' A paid check is also called a canceled check.

The bank keeps a record of each customer's checking account. This record shows the amounts of all checks written as well as charges subtracted from the account and deposits and interest added to the account. A copy of the bank's record is sent to the depositor each month. Many banks also return the canceled checks to the customer.

The record of checks, bank charges, and deposits that the bank sends to the depositor each month is called a *bank statement* Look at the bank statement shown on page 45.

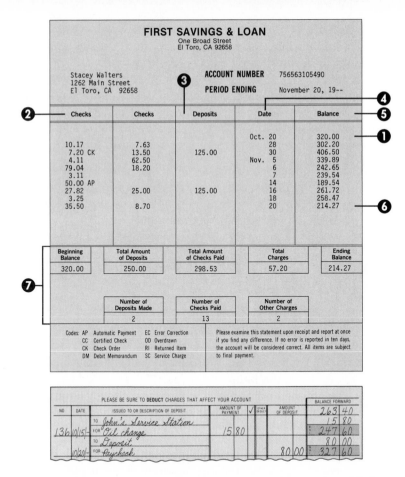

FIRST SAVINGS & LOAN
One Broad Street
El Toro, CA 92658

Stacey Walters
1262 Main Street
El Toro, CA 92658

ACCOUNT NUMBER 756563105490

PERIOD ENDING November 20, 19--

Checks	Checks	Deposits	Date	Balance
			Oct. 20	320.00
10.17	7.63		28	302.20
7.20 CK	13.50	125.00	30	406.50
4.11	62.50		Nov. 5	339.89
79.04	18.20		6	242.65
3.11			7	239.54
50.00 AP			14	189.54
27.82	25.00	125.00	16	261.72
3.25			18	258.47
35.50	8.70		20	214.27

Beginning Balance	Total Amount of Deposits	Total Amount of Checks Paid	Total Charges	Ending Balance
320.00	250.00	298.53	57.20	214.27

	Number of Deposits Made	Number of Checks Paid	Number of Other Charges	
	2	13	2	

Codes: AP Automatic Payment EC Error Correction
CC Certified Check OD Overdrawn
CK Check Order RI Returned Item
DM Debit Memorandum SC Service Charge

Please examine this statement upon receipt and report at once if you find any difference. If no error is reported in ten days, the account will be considered correct. All items are subject to final payment.

PLEASE BE SURE TO **DEDUCT** CHARGES THAT AFFECT YOUR ACCOUNT

NO	DATE	ISSUED TO OR DESCRIPTION OF DEPOSIT	AMOUNT OF PAYMENT	✓	OTHER DEDUCT	AMOUNT OF DEPOSIT	BALANCE FORWARD
							263 40
		TO John's Service Station					15 80
136	10/15	FOR Oil change	15 80				247 60
		TO Deposit					80 00
	10/20	FOR Paycheck				80 00	327 60

Stacey Walters received this statement on November 25. It covers the period from October 20 to November 20, 19—.

1. The bank listed the balance of the account at the beginning of the period. Stacey's balance on October 20 is $320.

2. In the Checks column, the bank listed each check that it paid from Stacey's account during the period. The bank also uses this section to show any charges against the account, such as service charges. The bank listed two charges against Stacey's account. The $7.20 charge is for printing checks. The $50 charge is for an automatic payment from Stacey's checking account into her savings account. The letters *CK* and *AP* identify the reason for the charges. (Note the Codes at the bottom of the statement.) All the checks and charges were deducted from her account.

3. In the Deposits column, the bank listed each deposit that it received from Stacey. All the deposits were added to her account.

4. In the Date column, the bank listed the dates on which it paid the checks and received the deposits.

5. In the Balance column, the bank listed the updated balances of the account during the period. Every time a check or charge was paid or a deposit was received, the bank computed the new balance.
6. The bank listed the balance of the account at the end of the month. Stacey's balance on November 20 is $214.27.
7. The bank listed the totals of the checks and charges paid and the totals of the deposits to Stacey's account.

After Stacey read her bank statement, she compared it with the information in her check register. Her check register showed a balance of $327.60. This amount did not agree with the ending balance of $214.27 on the bank statement.

RECONCILING THE BANK STATEMENT AND THE CHECK REGISTER

The ending balance on the bank statement usually does not agree with the balance in the check register on the same date.

If there is a difference between the ending balance on the bank statement and the balance shown in the check register, the depositor must find out what is causing the difference. Then the depositor must try to make the balances agree. This is called *reconciling* the bank statement and the check register. Stacey Walters followed these steps to reconcile her bank statement and her check register.

1. Compare the listing of paid checks with the check register. Place a check mark beside the amount of each check in the check register for which there is a paid check. Make sure that the amount of each check agrees with the amount listed in the check register. If there are any mistakes, make a note of them. Then look at the amounts to see which ones have no check marks in the register. These amounts are for *outstanding checks,* or checks that have not yet been received or paid by the bank. Make a note of the check numbers and the amounts. Stacey Walters found that the following checks had not yet been paid by the bank: Check 135 for $8.07 and Check 136 for $15.80.
2. Compare the deposits shown on the bank statement with the deposits shown in the check register. If any deposits are not listed, make a note of the amount and the date. Stacey noticed that a deposit on November 20 for $80 was not listed on the bank statement. An amount that has been deposited but does not appear on the bank statement is called a *deposit in transit.*

Next Stacey prepares a *bank reconciliation statement.* This record helps Stacey find the reasons for the difference between the bank statement balance and the check register balance.

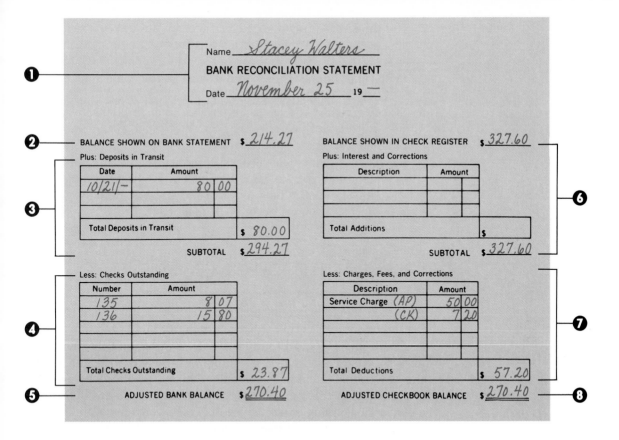

①

Name *Stacey Walters*

BANK RECONCILIATION STATEMENT

Date *November 25* 19 —

② BALANCE SHOWN ON BANK STATEMENT $ *214.27*

③ Plus: Deposits in Transit

Date	Amount
10/21/—	*80 00*
Total Deposits in Transit	$ *80.00*

SUBTOTAL $ *294.27*

④ Less: Checks Outstanding

Number	Amount
135	*8 07*
136	*15 80*
Total Checks Outstanding	$ *23.87*

⑤ ADJUSTED BANK BALANCE $ *270.40*

BALANCE SHOWN IN CHECK REGISTER $ *327.60*

⑥ Plus: Interest and Corrections

Description	Amount
Total Additions	$

SUBTOTAL $ *327.60*

⑦ Less: Charges, Fees, and Corrections

Description	Amount
Service Charge *(AP)*	*50 00*
(CK)	*7 20*
Total Deductions	$ *57.20*

⑧ ADJUSTED CHECKBOOK BALANCE $ *270.40*

Many banks provide a form on which the depositor may prepare the reconciliation. This form is often printed on the back of the bank statement. Stacey used such a form when she reconciled her bank statement on November 25. The form she completed is shown above. Stacey followed these steps in reconciling her statement.

1. She filled in her name and the date.
2. She filled in the balance shown on the bank statement ($214.27).
3. She recorded the deposit in transit ($80). Then, Stacey added the two figures to get a subtotal ($214.27 + $80 = $294.27).
4. Stacey listed the check numbers and amounts of each outstanding check. She added to find the total of all the outstanding checks ($8.07 + $15.80 = $23.87).
5. Next, Stacey subtracted the total of the outstanding checks from the subtotal to obtain the adjusted balance of the bank statement ($294.27 − $23.87 = $270.40).
6. Stacey filled in the balance shown in her check register ($327.60). Since she had already recorded all deposits in her check register, she wrote the subtotal of $327.60.

Bank Reconciliation Statement:
Helps the depositor find the reasons for a difference between the bank statement balance and the check register balance.

7. She then listed the charges she had not already written in her check register. These charges are for the automatic payment (AP $50) and the bank charge for printing checks (CK $7.20). Then she added these items and listed the total ($50 + $7.20 = $57.20).
8. Stacey finished the check register side of the bank reconciliation statement by subtracting the total of the charges from the balance shown in her check register ($327.60 − $57.20 = $270.40). Stacey was pleased to notice that both sides of the reconciliation had the same balance, $270.40. That means that the check register balance and the bank statement balance now agree. Stacey's account is reconciled.

UPDATING THE CHECK REGISTER

After the bank statement and the check register are reconciled, the depositor must bring the check register up to date. The depositor does this by entering in the check register any charges, fees, interest, or corrections. The amounts of these items are listed on the bank reconciliation statement. For example, Stacey Walter's reconciliation statement shows an automatic payment of $50 and a charge for having checks printed of $7.20. Stacey entered these items in her check register as shown and checked them off, since they have already been deducted from her account by the bank as shown on the bank statement.

Suppose Stacey had made an error in recording the amount of a check in her check register. That is, suppose she had written a check for one amount, but recorded a different amount in the check register. If she had recorded an amount that was more than the actual check, she would *add* the difference to her balance. If she had recorded an amount that was less than the actual check, she would *subtract* the difference from her balance.

After all changes have been made on the check register, the balance of the check register must agree with the adjusted balances on the bank reconciliation statement.

NO.	DATE	ISSUED TO OR DESCRIPTION OF DEPOSIT	AMOUNT OF PAYMENT	✓	OTHER DEDUCT	AMOUNT OF DEPOSIT	BALANCE FORWARD 263 40
		PLEASE BE SURE TO **DEDUCT** CHARGES THAT AFFECT YOUR ACCOUNT					
		TO John's Service Station					15 80
136	10/15/-	FOR Oil change	15 80				247 60
		TO Deposit					80 00
	10/20/-	FOR Paycheck				80 00	327 60
		TO Charge for printing checks					7 20
	10/20/-	FOR	7 20	✓			320 40
		TO Automatic payment					50 00
	10/20/-	FOR to savings account	50 00	✓			270 40

Updating the check register

COMPUTERIZED CHECK REGISTER

In this day of personal computers, many depositors keep their check registers up to date electronically. With a special software program—that is, a disk specifically designed for the job—you can enter the information that you usually write in your register. The computer can also perform the calculations to balance the checkbook.

When entering check information, you leave the Deposit column blank. When entering deposit information, you leave the Check Number and the Amount of Check columns blank. The Explanation column can be used both for check entries and deposit entries.

As soon as a deposit amount or a check amount is entered, the computer instantly figures a new balance. The following illustration shows how the computer balances the register.

Check No.	Date	Payee	Explanation	Deposit	Amt. Check	Balance	
	Jun 01		Bal. on hand			500.00	❶
	Jun 02		Paycheck	170.00		670.00	❷
830	Jun 03	Electric Co.	May bill		45.00	625.00	❸

Look at the three balances on the screen.

1. The first balance is the beginning balance, $500.
2. When the June 2 deposit is entered in the Deposit column, the computer immediately shows the new balance that results from this deposit, $670.00.
3. On June 3, when $45 is entered in the Amount of Check column, the computer again shows a new balance—$625.00—by deducting the check amount from the previous balance.

Check Your Reading

1. The monthly record listing the checks, deposits, and charges for an account is the ___?___ .

2. The form that helps a customer find the reasons for differences between the bank's balance and the customer's register balance is the ___?___ .

3. A deposit that the bank has not recorded on the customer's monthly statement is a(n) ___?___ .

4. Making the bank statement balance and the check register balance agree is ___?___ .

5. Checks that the customer has written but the bank has not yet recorded are ___?___ checks.

6. Checks that the bank has paid and deducted from the customer's account are ___?___ checks.

7. Do you have to figure your checking account balance if you are using a computerized check register?

Exercises for Topic 4

1. Using the following information, figure the adjusted bank statement balance.

   Bank statement balance: $486.08
   Deposit in transit: $203.80
   Outstanding checks: 308 $23.00
                       310   $14.75

2. Using the following information, figure the adjusted check register balance.

   On December 31, the check register balance was $524.50. A check for $22.35 was written but not deducted from the register.
   The December service charge was $4.35.

3. Prepare a bank reconciliation using Emily's December bank statement and her check register, both of which are shown below. Be sure to follow the same steps Stacey Walters followed on pages 47 and 48. Update Emily's check register in the Activity Guide.

FIRST NATIONAL BANK
One Main Street
Kettering, OH 45429

Emily McFarland
372 Pine Street
Kettering, OH 45429

ACCOUNT NUMBER   701-6111-0

PERIOD ENDING   December 31, 19--

CHECKING ACCOUNT ACTIVITY

TYPE	DATE	AMOUNT	TYPE	DATE	AMOUNT
Deposit	1203	341.00			
Service Charge	1226	5.00			
103	1201	34.23			
104	1216	350.00			
105	1218	18.50			

SUMMARY OF ACTIVITY

Beginning Balance	Total Amount of Deposits	Total Amount of Checks Paid	Total Charges	Ending Balance
492.85	341.00	402.73	5.00	426.12

	Number of Deposits Made	Number of Checks Paid	Number of Other Charges	
	1	3	1	

Codes: AP   Automatic Payment   EC   Error Correction
        CC   Certified Check   OD   Overdrawn
        CK   Check Order   RI   Returned Item
        DM   Debit Memorandum   SC   Service Charge

Please examine this statement upon receipt and report at once if you find any difference. If no error is reported in ten days, the account will be considered correct. All items are subject to final payment.

NO	DATE	ISSUED TO OR DESCRIPTION OF DEPOSIT	AMOUNT OF PAYMENT	✓	OTHER DEDUCT	AMOUNT OF DEPOSIT	BALANCE FORWARD
		19— PLEASE BE SURE TO DEDUCT CHARGES THAT AFFECT YOUR ACCOUNT					458 62
	12/3	TO Deposit					341 00
		FOR Monthly paycheck				341 00	799 62
							350 00
104	12/14	TO The Rental Co.					
		FOR Monthly bill	350 00				449 62
							18 50
105	12/15	TO The Telephone Co.					
		FOR Monthly bill	18 50				431 12
							213 00
106	12/19	TO Mall Department Store					
		FOR Sofa	213 00				218 12
							150 00
	12/23	TO Deposit					
		FOR Bonus				150 00	368 12
		TO					
		FOR					

4. You received the bank statement below. Reconcile it with the check register provided. Use the reconciliation form in your Activity Guide.

NO	DATE	ISSUED TO OR DESCRIPTION OF DEPOSIT	AMOUNT OF PAYMENT	✓	OTHER DEDUCT	AMOUNT OF DEPOSIT	BALANCE FORWARD 0
	7/13	TO *Deposit* / FOR *Monthly check*				478 75	478 75 / 478 75
601	7/14	TO *Sally B. Chekor* / FOR *Dues*	10 00				10 00 / 468 75
602	7/16	TO *Dr. James O. Apler* / FOR *Eye checkup*	40 00				40 00 / 428 75
603	7/18	TO *The Repair Shop* / FOR *Motorcycle*	38 14				38 14 / 390 61
	7/18	TO *Deposit* / FOR *Paycheck*				197 50	197 50 / 588 11
604	7/20	TO *Ace Rental Agency* / FOR *April rent*	190 00				190 00 / 398 11
	7/28	TO *Deposit* / FOR *Commission*				200 00	200 00 / 598 11
		TO / FOR					
		TO / FOR					
		TO / FOR					
		TO / FOR					
		TO / FOR					

PLEASE BE SURE TO **DEDUCT** CHARGES THAT AFFECT YOUR ACCOUNT

19—

CHECKING ACCOUNT ACTIVITY

TYPE	DATE	AMOUNT	TYPE	DATE	AMOUNT
Deposit	0713	478.75	601	0715	10.00
Deposit	0718	197.50	602	0718	40.00
Automatic Payment	0714	25.00	604	0731	190.00
Check Order	0713	6.25			
Service Charge	0720	3.00			

SUMMARY OF ACTIVITY

Beginning Balance	Total Amount of Deposits	Total Amount of Checks Paid	Total Charges	Ending Balance
0	676.25	240.00	34.25	402.00

	Number of Deposits Made	Number of Checks Paid	Number of Other Charges	
	2	3	3	

Codes: AP Automatic Payment   EC Error Correction
CC Certified Check   OD Overdrawn
CK Check Order   RI Returned Item
DM Debit Memorandum   SC Service Charge

Please examine this statement upon receipt and report at once if you find any difference. If no error is reported in ten days, the account will be considered correct. All items are subject to final payment.

5. You have received the bank statement below. Reconcile it with the check register provided. Use the reconciliation form in your Activity Guide.

NO.	DATE	ISSUED TO OR DESCRIPTION OF DEPOSIT	AMOUNT OF PAYMENT	✓	OTHER DEDUCT	AMOUNT OF DEPOSIT	BALANCE FORWARD 325 00
		19— PLEASE BE SURE TO **DEDUCT** CHARGES THAT AFFECT YOUR ACCOUNT					
	10/1	TO *Deposit* FOR *Monthly check*				445 00	445 00 / 770 00
605	10/5	TO *Dr. Harold Greengold* FOR *Ankle cast*	52 00				52 00 / 718 00
606	10/7	TO *Business Club* FOR *Monthly dues*	5 00				5 00 / 713 00
607	10/9	TO *Jack's Motors* FOR *Car Repair*	123 45				123 45 / 589 55
	10/12	TO *Deposit* FOR *Commission*				200 00	200 00 / 789 55
608	10/20	TO *Travel Agent* FOR *Air ticket*	45 00				45 00 / 744 55
	10/25	TO *Deposit* FOR *Commission*				225 00	225 00 / 969 55
609	10/30	TO *Talhausers* FOR *Air ticket*	228 76				228 76 / 740 79
610	10/30	TO *Houghs Market* FOR *Supplies*	13 87				13 87 / 726 92
		TO FOR					
		TO FOR					
		TO FOR					
		TO FOR					

CHECKING ACCOUNT ACTIVITY

TYPE	DATE	AMOUNT	TYPE	DATE	AMOUNT
Deposit	1001	445.00			
Deposit	1012	200.00			
Automatic Payment	1013	25.00			
Service Charge	1002	3.00			
605	1005	52.00			
606	1007	5.00			
607	1009	123.45			
610	1030	13.87			

SUMMARY OF ACTIVITY

Beginning Balance	Total Amount of Deposits	Total Amount of Checks Paid	Total Charges	Ending Balance
325.00	645.00	194.32	28.00	747.68

	Number of Deposits Made	Number of Checks Paid	Number of Other Charges	
	2	4	2	

Codes: AP Automatic Payment   EC Error Correction
CC Certified Check   OD Overdrawn
CK Check Order   RI Returned Item
DM Debit Memorandum   SC Service Charge

Please examine this statement upon receipt and report at once if you find any difference. If no error is reported in ten days, the account will be considered correct. All items are subject to final payment.

6. Prepare a bank reconciliation statement for Arlene Edwards using the following information:

   a. Arlene's bank statement shows an ending balance of $478.20 on October 30.
   b. Her check register balance is $372.85.
   c. There are three outstanding checks:
      Check 182, $23.90
      Check 184, $86.25
      Check 189, $15.20
   d. The bank statement shows an automatic teller machine payment of $20, which is not recorded in the register.

7. Prepare a bank reconciliation statement for Anita Helms using the following information:

   a. On June 1, Anita receives a bank statement from Peninsula Federal Bank. It shows an ending balance of $678.33.
   b. Her check register balance is $711.05.
   c. On May 30, Anita deposited $100, which is not listed on the bank statement.
   d. The outstanding checks are:
      Check 728, $37.00
      Check 729, $6.86
      Check 732, $20.00
      Check 734, $5.50
   e. The bank added $3.72 to her account for interest.
   f. The bank deducted a $5.80 service charge for printed checks.

TOPIC 5 ▲ SAVINGS ACCOUNTS

GOALS

1. To explain why people use savings accounts.
2. To identify types of savings accounts.
3. To prepare savings deposit slips and withdrawal slips.

KEY TERMS

Interest is money that banks pay for the use of depositors' money.

A *regular savings account* is a bank account that earns interest at a set rate.

A *certificate of deposit* pays higher interest than a regular savings account but requires a minimum deposit. Further, the money in the certificate cannot be withdrawn for a certain length of time.

A *money market account* pays higher interest than a regular account and permits withdrawals and deposits, but it requires a minimum balance at all times.

WHAT IS A SAVINGS ACCOUNT?

Banks make money in different ways—mostly from interest received on loans. To lend money, of course, banks need money, and their major source of money is customers' deposits.

Savings accounts have several advantages. First of all, savings accounts earn interest for depositors. Second, savings accounts are safe. Third, depositing money into or withdrawing money from savings accounts is very convenient.

A *depositor* is a person who has a bank account.

Interest Banks pay depositors interest for the use of their money. Think of interest as money that the bank pays you for depositing your money.

Interest is always expressed in percents such as 5 percent, 6 percent, $6\frac{1}{2}$ percent. The interest rate is always for a full year's period. Interest rates vary from one bank to another. In addition, interest rates may vary from day to day at the same bank.

Suppose you have deposited $1,000 in a savings account. If the bank pays 6 percent interest, then at the end of one full year your account will be credited for $60 in interest:

$$\$1,000 \times 0.06 = \$60$$

You now have $1,060 in your account. If you deposit no more money in your account and the interest rate stays the same, how much interest will you receive at the end of the second year?

$$\$1,060 \times 0.06 = \$63.60$$

Thus you will have $1,123.60 at the end of the second full year.

In this way, savings accounts make depositors' money grow. The longer the money is in the bank, the more interest it accumulates.

Safety An important consideration for savings is safety. Money kept in a savings account is safe because banks have special vaults, electronic equipment, and guards to keep money safe.

Banks have something else to protect depositors' money: *insurance.* The federal government offers banks special insurance to protect depositors if the bank goes out of business for any reason. Perhaps you have seen *FDIC* or *FSLIC* before. Each means that the U.S. government insures accounts. (In addition, some states have their own insurance against bank failures.)

FDIC, which stands for Federal Deposit Insurance Corporation, insures depositors' accounts up to $100,000.

FSLIC, which stands for Federal Savings & Loan Insurance Corporation, is similar to FDIC and also insures depositors' accounts.

Convenience Opening a savings account is easy to do. And depositing money into or withdrawing money from a savings account is easy. Thus savings accounts are convenient.

TYPES OF ACCOUNTS

Savings accounts are available in various types according to the savings needs of the depositor.

Regular Savings Accounts A *regular savings account* offers a fixed rate of interest. This means that as other interest rates rise and fall, the savings account will continue to pay the same interest rate.

In addition, usually only $5 is required to open a regular account. Other accounts may require $500 or $1,000.

Certificate of Deposit Accounts Another account is known as the *certificate of deposit (CD)*. Unlike the regular savings account, a minimum deposit of $500 must be made to obtain a CD. See, for example, the following notice for a CD:

Great Lakes Bank

SAVINGS PLAN

- Certificate of Deposit.

- Time: One Year.

- Minimum: $500.

- Compounded Daily at 8.4%.

- Yield: 8.76%, if interest remains in the account for one year.

- $500 grows to $543.81.

Notice that you must leave the full amount in the bank for a certain period of time. This means that you cannot withdraw the money until the end of the time period, nor can you add to the amount of money in the CD.

Money Market Accounts A *money market account* also requires a minimum deposit. But the money market account allows the depositor to add money to or withdraw money from the account as long as the account keeps a minimum balance.

Assume, for example, that you open a money market account with a minimum deposit of $2,500. You may add money to the account whenever you wish. Whenever you have more than the $2,500 minimum, you may withdraw money—again, always leaving the minimum.

OPENING A REGULAR SAVINGS ACCOUNT

You already learned how to open a checking account. Opening a regular savings account is similar.

As before, you must complete and sign a signature card. Of course, you must also deposit some money. Before you open your account, visit several banks to find out the various rules about savings accounts.

DEPOSITING AND WITHDRAWING MONEY

As with checking account deposits, savings account deposits are entered on deposit slips. A *deposit slip* is a form on which you enter your name, the date, the amount of the deposit, and your account number. See the sample deposit slip shown below.

A *deposit slip* is a form on which you enter your name, the date, the amount of the deposit, and your account number.

	Dollars	Cents
Cash		
Checks	200	00
Total	200	00

Deposited with
Pacific Savings Bank
Date *November 1*   19 —
For account of
Janet Kaye

Savings Account No.
1 0 3 - 1 9 3 7 6 5

List each check separately
Endorse all checks

Deposit slip for savings account

When you make a deposit, the teller gives you a summary slip. A *summary slip* is a record of a bank deposit or withdrawal. It shows the date, the account number, the amount of the deposit or the withdrawal, and the current balance in the account. In addition, the summary slip shows any interest credited to the account.

Summary Slip			
Pacific Savings Bank		Account No. 103–193765	
Date	Withdrawal	Deposit	Balance
Oct. 10		100.00	250.00

Summary slip for savings account

A summary slip is a record showing the amount of a bank deposit or withdrawal and the current account balance.

Because summary slips are important bank records, they should be stored for possible future use, perhaps in one pocket of an expandable file.

To take money out of a savings account, you complete a withdrawal slip. A *withdrawal slip* is a form on which you enter your name, the date, the amount of the withdrawal, and your account number. See the sample withdrawal slip below.

Savings Account Withdrawal

Received from **Pacific Savings Bank**   Date *December 15, 19—*

The sum of *Fifty and 00/100* _____ Dollars

Signature *Janet Kaye*

☒ Cash
☐ Check

Savings Account Number									
1	0	3	–	1	9	3	7	6	5

Dollars	Cents
50	00

Withdrawal slip for savings account

When a customer makes a withdrawal, the teller gives the customer a summary slip.

Savings account deposits and withdrawals can also be made using an automated teller machine. The machine gives you a summary slip for each transaction.

STATEMENTS

By keeping summary slips, you can maintain accurate records. You will always know the correct balance in your account. In addition, most banks send regular statements showing deposits, withdrawals, interest earned, and the new balance. If you receive account statements, you must use the summary slips to check the statement. Follow these steps:

1. Arrange the slips in order by date.
2. On the statement, check off each deposit and each withdrawal indicated by your summary slips.
3. a. If all deposits and withdrawals are listed on the statement, the balance on the statement and the balance on your last summary slip should agree.
   b. If you deposited or withdrew money after the closing date on the statement, save the summary slips to use for checking the next statement.

Check Your Reading

1. A person who has a savings account is called a(n) ___?___ .

2. For the use of depositors' funds, banks pay ___?___ .

3. In addition to vaults, electronic equipment, and guards, banks protect depositors' money with government ___?___ , such as FDIC and FSLIC.

4. FDIC insures an account up to $ ___?___ .

5. A savings account that offers a fixed rate of interest is called a(n) ___?___ savings account.

6. An account that requires a minimum deposit for a certain period of time is called a(n) ___?___ .

7. An account that requires a minimum balance yet allows the depositor to deposit more money or to withdraw funds is called a(n) ___?___ account.

Exercises for Topic 5

1. Answer the following questions about the form shown on the bottom of page 57.
   a. What is the form used for?
   b. Who is the customer?
   c. To whom is the form given?
   d. What record of the deposit and the new balance does the customer receive?
   e. Where is the money deposited?

2. The following questions refer to the form shown on the top of page 58.
   a. What type of form is it?
   b. What is the form used for?
   c. To whom is the form given?

3. Prepare deposit slips for the following deposits made by Victor Strong. His address is 228 Spring Drive, Casper, WY 82601. His savings account number is 565-798460.
   a. September 1: cash, $85; check, $125.
   b. October 1: cash, $95; check, $35.70.

4. Prepare withdrawal slips for the following withdrawals made by Peggy Curcio. Her savings account number is 999-908736.
   a. January 15: $140   b. June 12: $395.80

5. In November Sharon Bouco received the following information on her summary slips. She also received a savings account statement shown below.

SUMMARY SLIP INFORMATION			
Date	**Withdrawal**	**Deposit**	**Balance**
Oct. 20	100.00		345.00
Nov. 5		120.00	465.00
Nov. 10	40.00		425.00
Nov. 20		25.00	450.00
Nov. 25	14.00		436.00
Nov. 29		21.00	457.00
Nov. 30	12.50		444.50

Great Lakes Bank

Savings Account Statement

Sharon Bouco
7691 Main Street
Chicago, IL 60601

Account No. 12340001

Oct. 22   Beginning balance   345.00

DEPOSITS
Nov. 5   120.00
      20   25.00
      29   21.00
Total deposits   166.00

WITHDRAWALS
Nov. 10   40.00
     25   14.00
     30   12.50
Total withdrawals   66.50
Nov. 30   Ending balance   444.50

   a. Compare the summary slip information with the savings account statement.
   b. Compute the ending balance by adding the beginning balance to the total deposits; then subtracting the withdrawals.
   c. The ending balance on the last summary slip should equal the ending balance on the account statement.

MATH
SKILLBUILDER

Skill: Adding different bills and coins.

Sample Problem: Find the total amount of cash in the following.

Bills and Coins	Number
$5	3
$1	9
25¢	10

Solution:

1. Multiply the unit of bill or coin by the number of bills or coins, and record the amount of money for each unit of bill or coin.

$$\$5 \times 3 = \$15.00$$
$$\$1 \times 9 = \$9.00$$
$$\$0.25 \times 10 = \$2.50$$

2. Add the totals of each denomination to find the total amount of cash.

$$\$15.00 + \$9.00 + \$2.50 = \$26.50$$

3. Answer: $26.50

Practice: Find the total amount of cash in each of the following.

	$50	$20	$10	$5	$1	25¢	10¢	5¢	1¢
1.			3	2	5	4	5	2	5
2.			1	5	15	8	14	12	15
3.			4	2	12	15	10	11	18
4.			8	6	11	6	18	14	16
5.			3	2	14	12	15	10	28
6.		2	9	3	10	13	16	8	13
7.	1	4	2	4	15	12	13	6	32
8.	2	3	6	8	6	11	15	12	19
9.	3	5	2	3	12	14	12	13	37
10.	1	10	8	5	13	10	13	5	40

Skill: Writing money amounts in words.

Sample Problem: Write $283.50 in words as it would be written on a check.

Solution:

1. Each number to the left of the decimal point (the dollar amount) is written in words as it would be read.

$283: Two hundred eighty-three

2. The word "and" replaces the decimal:

Two hundred eighty-three and

3. Cents are expressed as a fraction of 100:

$$\frac{50}{100}$$

4. Answer: Two hundred eighty-three and $\frac{50}{100}$

Practice: Write the following amounts in words as they would be written on a check. (Items 6 and 7 should be written in as few words as possible because of the limited amount of space on a check.)

1. $35
2. $67
3. $149
4. $594.25
5. $889
6. $1,284
7. $3,567
8. $403
9. $1,015
10. $3,008.43

Read each of the following statements. From the words below each statement, choose the term that best matches the statement.

1. A check that has been written but does not appear on the bank statement.

   canceled check   outstanding check

2. An account with too little money in it to pay a check that the depositor has written.

   overdrawn account   regular account

3. A record of checks, service charges, and deposits that the bank sends to depositors each month.

   bank statement   check register

4. A form that helps the depositor find the reasons for the difference between the bank statement balance and the checkbook balance.

   deposit slip   reconciliation statement

5. Depositor's written order to the bank to pay out a certain amount from the depositor's checking account.

   check   endorsement   receipt

6. A banking service that allows a person to store money safely and conveniently and also to get interest on the money.

   safe-deposit box   savings account

7. A form listing the amount of money that a depositor is putting into a bank account.

   deposit slip   outstanding check

8. Depositor's record of checks written and deposits made.

   bank statement   check register

9. The payee's signature on the back of a check.

   certification   endorsement

10. Check that a bank has paid and returned to the depositor.

    canceled check   promissory note

11. The person or business who writes a check.

    drawer   payee

12. The person or business to whom a check is made out.

    drawer   maker   payee

APPLICATION PROBLEMS

1. Abigail Kassin receives a paycheck of $1,240 on the first of each month.

   a. Prepare a deposit slip for her February paycheck.

   b. Issue the following checks for bills that Abigail must pay by the 10th of the month. Use February 1, 19—, as the date of the checks. Be sure to fill in the check register before you prepare each check. Begin with Check 2378. Her balance is $525.10.

   ### Bills to Be Paid

   $250 to Central Realty Inc. for rent for apartment.

   $27.95 to Metropolitan Telephone for telephone bill.

   $23.17 to MasterCard for charge sales. (Payee is the Regional Bank.)

   $95 to All-County Insurance Company for car insurance.

   $42.50 to Northwest National Bank for a payment on a personal loan.

   $25 to Fashion Beauty Shop for permanent.

   $35 to Brookville Medical Center for an office visit last month.

2. Ernie Fowler has a checking account at Gold Coast State Savings. His check register for August is shown on page 64. The bank statement he received on August 31 and a list of his canceled checks is shown on page 65. Notice that Ernie did not fill in the new balance in his check register as he wrote checks during the month. He believes that it saves time if he does not compute the balance each time he writes a check or makes a de-

posit. He computes his balance when he reconciles his checking account at the end of the month.

   a. Did Ernie know the balance of his account when he wrote each check in August?

   b. Complete Ernie's check register for August by filling in the Balance Forward column. Use your Activity Guide.

   c. Why should Ernie compute the new balance each time he writes a check?

   d. Compare Ernie's August check register with the numbers and amounts of the canceled checks. Make a list of the checks that are outstanding as of September 1. Notice that Ernie made a mistake on Check 2610. The actual amount of the check was $73.58, but he recorded it as $73.18 in the check register. (Do not try to correct this mistake now. The checkbook balance will be updated after the account is reconciled.)

   e. Prepare a bank reconciliation statement as of September 1, 19—.

   f. Update the check register. Bring the balance forward to the new page in the check register. Then record the correction for the mistake on Check 2610. Label this transaction "Error, Check 2610." Also record the bank service charge. Then enter the new balance. The new balance must agree with the balance computed on the bank reconciliation statement.

NO	DATE	ISSUED TO OR DESCRIPTION OF DEPOSIT	AMOUNT OF PAYMENT	✓	OTHER DEDUCT	AMOUNT OF DEPOSIT	BALANCE FORWARD 810 12
		PLEASE BE SURE TO **DEDUCT** CHARGES THAT AFFECT YOUR ACCOUNT					
2600	8/3/-	TO Bayview Realty FOR Rent	200 00				BAL
2601	8/3/-	TO Gulf Telephone Co. FOR Telephone bill	21 17				BAL
2602	8/4/-	TO Southern Electric Co. FOR Electric bill	43 10				BAL
2603	8/6/-	TO Quality Foods, Inc. FOR Food	61 10				BAL
2604	8/10/-	TO Gold Coast State Savings Bank FOR Car payment	90 00				BAL
2605	8/12/-	TO Regional Bank FOR Master Card credit charges	25 16				BAL
2606	8/15/-	TO Atlas Company Credit Union FOR Savings	100 00				BAL
	8/15/-	TO Deposit FOR Paycheck				375 00	BAL
2607	8/20/-	TO Cash FOR Spending money	62 00				BAL
2608	8/23/-	TO Marshall's Department Store FOR Clothes	38 17				BAL
2609	8/25/-	TO Motor Vehicles Department FOR Car license	15 00				BAL
2610	8/25/-	TO Quality Foods, Inc FOR Food	73 18				BAL
	8/30/-	TO Deposit FOR Paycheck				375 00	BAL

GOLD COAST STATE SAVINGS BANK
Shreveport, LA 71106

Ernie Fowler
706 Bayou Road
Shreveport, LA 71102
589-8877

ACCOUNT NUMBER   788-3220-8

PERIOD ENDING   August 31, 19--

CHECKING ACCOUNT ACTIVITY

TYPE	DATE	AMOUNT	TYPE	DATE	AMOUNT
Deposit	0818	375.00			
Service Charge	0829	2.50			
2600	0805	200.00			
2601	0805	21.17			
2602	0812	43.10			
2603	0818	61.10			
2604	0818	90.00			
2606	0820	100.00			
2608	0828	38.17			
2610	0829	73.58			

SUMMARY OF ACTIVITY

Beginning Balance	Total Amount of Deposits	Total Amount of Checks Paid	Total Charges	Ending Balance
810.12	375.00	627.12	2.50	555.50

Number of Deposits Made	Number of Checks Paid	Number of Other Charges
1	8	1

Codes:
AP	Automatic Payment	EC	Error Correction
CC	Certified Check	OD	Overdrawn
CK	Check Order	RI	Returned Item
DM	Debit Memorandum	SC	Service Charge

Please examine this statement upon receipt and report at once if you find any difference. If no error is reported in ten days, the account will be considered correct. All items are subject to final payment.

CHAPTER 3

PERSONAL BUDGETING

Do you feel that you never have enough money? This is a feeling that many people have. Most of us would be happier if we managed our money better.

Good money management will help you avoid too much borrowing. Careful money management will let you save money for the things you want and the things you need.

Effective money management will help you get the most for your money. But good money management is not accidental. It is planned. It results from careful budgeting. This chapter will help you learn to manage and budget your money and keep personal financial records.

TOPIC I ▲ PLANNING PERSONAL FINANCES

GOALS

1. To identify personal values and goals.
2. To determine personal needs and wants.
3. To prepare weekly and monthly budgets.

KEY TERMS

A *budget* is a plan showing how money is to be received and spent.
Income is money earned or received.
An *expense* is money spent.

VALUES AND GOALS; NEEDS AND WANTS

Susan Yates and Larry O'Donnell were in the same graduating class at Richmond High School two years ago. Susan now works for the Barron Advertising Agency, and Larry works for the Richmond Bank. They earn about the same salary. Susan has her own apartment. Larry shares an apartment with a roommate. Each owns a car and goes to college at night. They have many things in common, but Susan's budget and Larry's budget are different. Why? Let's take a closer look.

Values are things that are important to a person.

Values and Goals *Values* are things that we rate very highly, things that are important to us. Honesty, freedom, education, family, religion, health, wealth—these are examples of common values. We learn values from our parents, teachers, friends, and from our own experience. Many values learned during childhood are strengthened as we grow older. Other values develop later in life.

For Susan Yates, health and education are two very important values. She teaches at a health club and wants to learn more about nutrition and exercising. After she graduates, she plans to take courses that interest her. Susan values education very highly.

Larry's interest in education is different. He knows that he will need a degree to become an executive. Larry values education as a tool for getting ahead in business. Outside of work Larry's greatest interests are his sailboat and his sports car.

Values affect a person's goals. *Goals* are the things we want to accomplish. They are objectives.

Goals are the things we want to accomplish.

Susan and Larry both share this common goal: to get a college degree. Larry's professional goal is to become an executive. Because Susan has such a strong interest in exercise and nutrition, her professional goal is to own and manage her own business, a health and exercise club.

The time it takes you to reach a goal will vary, depending on the specific goal. A *long-term goal* may take a year or more to reach. A *short-term goal* takes less time to achieve. Sometimes a long-term goal is accomplished through several short-term goals.

Needs and Wants All of us have needs and wants. *Needs* are the things that we must have. Food, shelter, and clothing are examples of the most basic physical needs.

Needs are the things you must *have.*

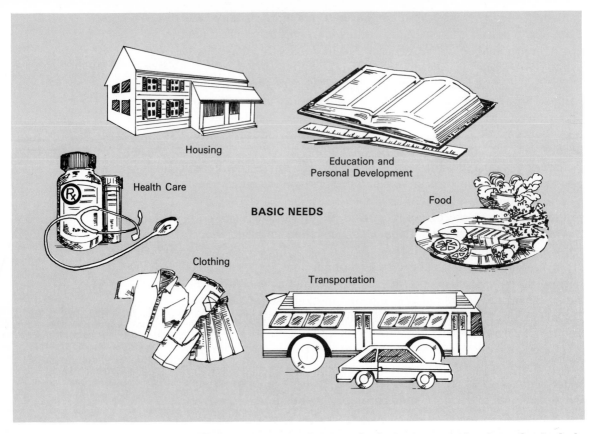

Housing

Education and
Personal Development

Health Care

BASIC NEEDS

Food

Clothing

Transportation

There are many other needs that are not as basic as food, shelter, and clothing but are still important. For instance, transportation, safety, and education are also needs. You can satisfy your need for transportation, for example, by walking or by using a bike, motorcycle, car, bus, or train.

Wants are things you would *like* to have.

Wants, on the other hand, are things that we would like to have or to do. Tickets to a rock concert, a new camera, a sports car, a leather jacket—these are examples of wants. A bicycle, for example, may adequately satisfy your need for transportation to and from school. However, you may want a motorcycle or a sports car.

As you will see, knowing the difference between needs and wants is useful in planning your personal budget. Knowing your goals is also important. For example, to help her budget properly, Susan Yates develops a list of goals each month:

GOALS FOR APRIL

1. Save money each payday for health and exercise club (savings).
2. Set aside money for new tennis racket, tickets to a play, and club dinner on April 20 (personal development).
3. Buy a dress, a blouse, a gym suit, and a pair of shoes (clothing).

4. Set aside money for next semester's tuition (education).
5. Set aside money for new tires and a tune-up (transportation).
6. Save money for finding and moving to a new apartment (housing).

By listing her goals, Susan can plan her budget better. Susan's planning helps her manage her money. If she does not have enough money in April for all the goals listed, she may then decide to put off buying clothing until May. But because she made this list, Susan will be able to control her expenses.

Susan set her goals based on her values. She uses her goals to help her prepare a budget.

The need for transportation can be met in a number of ways.

PREPARING A PERSONAL BUDGET

A *budget* is a plan for using your income to meet your needs and wants and to reach your goals. This plan will not solve all your problems, but it will help you make sensible decisions about money.

A budget may cover only a week or it may be for one month or more. Susan Yates receives a weekly paycheck from the Barron Advertising Agency. In addition, she teaches exercise classes at the Midtown Physical Fitness Club. She is also paid weekly by Midtown. Therefore, Susan prepares weekly budgets.

Susan's budget for the week of April 1 is shown on page 70. Let's follow the steps Susan takes to complete her budget each week.

```
                        Susan Yates
              Budget for Weeks of April 1-April 7

Income
    Barron. . . . . . . . . . . . . . .$342
    Midtown Club. . . . . . . . . . .  52
        Total income                               $394


Estimated Expenses
Fixed expenses:
    Rent. . . . . . . . . . . . . . .$ 75
    Car insurance . . . . . . . . . .  10
        Total fixed expenses                       $ 85
Variable Expenses
    Clothing. . . . . . . . . . . . .$ 75
    Groceries . . . . . . . . . . . .  25
    Lunch and dinner. . . . . . . . .  35
    Electricity . . . . . . . . . . .  12
    Gas and oil . . . . . . . . . . .  15
    Gifts . . . . . . . . . . . . . .  10
    Recreation. . . . . . . . . . . .  15
    Savings . . . . . . . . . . . . .  62
    Books, magazines. . . . . . . . .  10
    Miscellaneous (tennis racquet). . . 50
        Total variable expenses                    $309
Total estimated expenses                           $394
```

1. Susan writes her name and enters the date.
2. Susan's take-home pay at Barron is $342 a week. Her take-home pay at Midtown is $52 a week. Susan adds these numbers to get her total weekly income, $394.
3. From her experience in preparing budgets in the past few years, Susan knows the categories of expenses that she needs in her weekly budgets. She lists these in the left column. Then she enters the estimated expense on each line.

Note that Susan separates expenses into *fixed* and *variable* expenses:

A *fixed expense* is one that does not change from one budget period to the next.

▲ Fixed expenses do not change from one week to the next. Susan's rent, for instance, is $300 a month. She sets aside $75 every week for her rent. Her car insurance is $520 a year. She sets aside $10 every week for her car insurance.

A *variable expense* is one that changes from one budget period to the next.

▲ Variable expenses may change from one week to the next. For the week of April 1, Susan estimates that she will spend $75 for clothing. Her weekly budget for April 8 may allow no money for clothing. Clothing is a variable expense.

On Susan's budgets, estimated expenses and total income are always equal. Of course, she does not spend more than she makes. And if she changes her budget and has extra money, she either puts it in her savings account or spends it. Thus estimated expenses and total income are always equal.

Larry O'Donnell receives a monthly paycheck from the Richmond Bank. As a result, Larry does a monthly budget. His budget for the month of April is shown below.

```
                     Larry O'Donnell
                     Budget for April

Income
Richmond Bank. . . . . . . . . . .              $1482

Estimated Expenses
Fixed expenses:
    Rent. . . . . . . . . . . . . . . .$385
    Car insurance . . . . . . . . . . 100
    Boat insurance. . . . . . . . . .  15
    Car loan. . . . . . . . . . . . . 117
        Total fixed expenses                   $ 617
Variable expenses:
    Clothing. . . . . . . . . . . . .  60
    Groceries . . . . . . . . . . . . 120
    Lunch and dinner. . . . . . . . . 130
    Electricity . . . . . . . . . . .  50
    Gas and oil . . . . . . . . . . .  80
    Car maintenance . . . . . . . . .  50
    Recreation. . . . . . . . . . . .  60
    General savings . . . . . . . . .  90
    Tuition savings . . . . . . . . .  85
    Books and magazines . . . . . . .  40
    Miscellaneous . . . . . . . . . . 100
        Total variable expenses                $ 865
Total estimated expenses                       $1482
```

In addition to being prepared monthly, Larry's budget is different from Susan's in other ways:

1. Larry has only one source of income.
2. Larry shares an apartment with a roommate. His rent expense each month is less than Susan's.
3. Larry has monthly car payments.
4. Larry's insurance expenses are greater than Susan's because he insures both his sports car and his boat.

Your budget will be different from both Susan's and Larry's. Even if your take-home pay were the same, your budget would reflect your values, needs, wants, and goals. To make your budget decisions, you must identify your needs and think of possible ways to meet each need. Then, as shown in the chart below, you can choose from among the ways you have suggested.

Deciding How Much to Put in the Budget		
Need	**Possible Ways to Meet Need**	**Choice**
Food	Prepare own meals, eat at a pizza place, a fast-food place, or a fancy restaurant.	Make own meals, eat out occasionally.
Clothing	Make alterations, buy mix and match, go to a budget shop, or go to a high-fashion shop.	Go to a budget shop.
Housing	Live with parents, share an apartment, or rent an apartment by yourself.	Share an apartment.

For example, you need housing. You identify three possible ways to meet your need for housing:

You may continue to live with your parents.
You may share an apartment.
You may get your own apartment.

You may want your own apartment, but if you cannot afford it, you must make another choice. You may decide that the best choice is to share an apartment.

As you can see, budgeting forces you to make realistic decisions—decisions that will help you manage your money well.

Check Your Reading

1. Things that are important to a person are ___?___ .

2. Things that a person wants to accomplish are ___?___ .

3. Things that a person must have are ___?___ .

4. Things that a person would like to have are ___?___ .

5. Which basic need is met when

    a. You live at home with your parents?
    b. You participate in on-the-job training?
    c. Your employer provides medical insurance?
    d. You eat in a fast-food restaurant?
    e. You alter your own clothing?
    f. You participate in team sports?
    g. You use your bicycle to go to work?
    h. You have your hair styled?

6. The plan that shows how money is to be spent is a(n) _____?_____ .

7. Money that is received is _____?_____ .

8. Money that is spent is a(n) _____?_____ .

9. An expense that does not change from one budget period to the next is a(n) _____?_____ expense.

10. An expense that does change from one budget period to the next is a(n) _____?_____ expense.

Exercises for Topic I

1. List each value on a sheet of paper. Match each value to a goal by writing the letter of the goal beside the value.

Values	Goals
1. Greater responsibility	a. Buy a new stereo.
2. Education	b. Earn a promotion at work.
3. Family	c. Enroll in a community college.
4. Health	d. Exercise twice a week.
5. Music	e. Spend time with grandparents.

2. Think about your personal goals. List three long-term goals that you hope to achieve. Write a short-term goal you are working toward which will help you reach that long-term goal.

3. **a.** Make a list of your financial goals for the next 12 months. See how Susan Yates made her list that appears on pages 68–69.
    b. Check your goals with the list of basic needs to be certain you have not left out anything.
    c. Rearrange your list in order of importance to you.

4. Shakeep Rashad would like to plan a weekly budget to help him save money. His weekly take-home pay from his part-time job is $85. He estimates that he will have the following expenses: clothes, $20; lunches, $12; miscellaneous, $12.50; recreation, $17.50; school supplies, $4.50; and subway fare, $7.50.

a. Prepare a budget for Shakeep. Subtract the expenses listed above from his income, and put the difference in his budget as the amount of his weekly savings. Shakeep will use this money to begin a new savings account.

b. After following the budget for 15 weeks, Shakeep wants to buy a camera that costs $183. Does he have enough in his savings to pay for the camera? If your answer is yes, how much will he have left in his savings after buying it? If he does not have enough, how many more weeks must he save before he has enough money to buy the camera?

5. Janice Link, a high school senior, has decided to prepare a weekly budget. She would like to begin a savings account and save $520 to make a down payment on a used motorcycle.

Janice works as a cashier at the Thrifty Discount Store in the evenings and on weekends. Her take-home pay is $80 each week. Janice's weekly expenses are bus fare, $6.50; lunches, $11; miscellaneous, $12; personal care, $5.50; recreation, $15; and school supplies, $4.

a. Prepare a weekly budget for Janice. Any income that is not used for the expenses should go into savings.

b. How many weeks will Janice have to follow this budget to save $520?

c. After buying the motorcycle, Janice decides that she now needs a monthly budget. Prepare the budget for her using the following information:

Janice got a pay raise at work, and her take-home pay is now $372 a month. Her new budget should have a separate listing for fixed expenses.

Her new fixed expenses are $31 a month for insurance on her motorcycle and $87 a month for the payment on her motorcycle loan.

Janice's variable expenses will no longer include bus fare, because she will ride her motorcycle to school and work. She estimates that it will cost her $15 a month for gas, oil, and maintenance expense.

To figure Janice's other variable expenses, multiply the weekly expense amounts by 4 to get her new monthly estimate. Any income that is not used for her expenses should go into savings.

6. Fernando Munilla attends Central Community College and works as a taxi driver. He shares an apartment with two roommates who are also students. He needs a monthly budget to help him manage his money better. Fernando receives an educational grant of $100 a month to help with his college expenses. His other income is $750 a month in take-home pay from Taylor Cabs. He has the following monthly expenses:

Fixed expenses: college expenses (tuition, books), $125; payments on TV and stereo, $65; rent, $174; and telephone, $13.
Variable expenses: bus fare, $45; clothes, $70; food, $185; miscellaneous, $25; personal care, $30; recreation, $80.

a. Prepare a budget for Fernando. Any income that is not used for the expenses listed above should go to savings.
b. Fernando's current debt on his TV and stereo is $325 including interest. How many months will it take him to pay off this debt?
c. After Fernando makes all the payments on his TV and stereo, he will be able to increase his monthly savings by the amount of that payment. What will be the amount of his new monthly savings?

8. Prepare a budget for Josie Washburn. Josie is 18 and is a part-time teller at the Federal National Bank. She is enrolled in college classes.
a. Her job pays $380 a month. Her grandmother offered to give her $40 a month as long as she continues her education.
b. Her variable expenses include the following: bus fare, $60; clothing, $64; lunches and snacks, $62; miscellaneous (magazines, books, and donations), $48; personal care (permanents, cosmetics), $38; savings, $50; educational supplies, $36; educational expenses (tuition and fees), $42; and recreation, $30.
c. If her expected expenses are less than her expected income, put the difference in savings.
d. If her expected expenses are greater than the budget she prepared, deduct half the difference from her savings and the other half from recreation.

GOALS

1. To prepare a cash record.
2. To prepare a classified cash record.
3. To prove a classified cash record.

KEY TERMS

A *cash record* is a form that lists a beginning balance, income, expenses, and a balance of money left to spend.

A *classified cash record* is a form similar to a cash record, but it includes columns for expense items.

A *beginning balance* is the amount of money you have at the beginning of a time period.

An *ending balance* is the amount you have at the close of a time period.

CASH RECORDS

A *cash record* is a form that lists cash received and cash spent. As the following example shows, a cash record is a simple form. Let's look at the entries column by column.

Earnings and Expenses for the Week of November 1

		❶	❷	❸	❹	❺
	Date	Explanation	Received	Paid Out	Balance
Nov.	1	Balance on hand			240.00
	2	Paycheck	71.20		311.20
	3	Lunch ticket		10.00	301.20
	4	School Supplies		4.70	296.50
	5	Class dues		10.00	286.50
	6	VCR tapes rental		5.20	281.30
	6	Bus tickets		6.00	275.30
	6	Field trip expense		30.00	245.30

Column 1 shows the date that cash is received or spent.

Column 2 gives a brief explanation of each entry. The explanation helps identify the source of cash received and the reason for cash paid out.

Column 3 is used only to enter amounts of cash received.

Column 4 is used only to enter amounts of cash paid out.

Column 5 is used to compute the balance. The balance is the amount remaining after cash has been received or spent.

The cash record provides an easy way of recording cash received and cash paid out. It also is an easy way to find the balance.

CLASSIFIED CASH RECORDS

A *classified cash record* is a form that has columns for certain kinds of monthly expenses. Study the classified cash record on pages 78 and 79.

Jack Cordello prepared this classified cash record of his expenses for the month of October. Note the column numbers across the form and the line numbers from top to bottom. Note, too, the headings of the columns.

In addition to columns for expenses, the completed form also has a column (column 4) for listing income. Jack finds this monthly form very helpful in tracking his expenses and managing his money.

Completing the Classified Cash Record Now follow Jack as he completes his classified cash record for October.

1. Jack enters his beginning balance by writing the date, "Oct. 1," in columns 1 and 2, "Balance on hand" in column 3, and "$220" in the Balance column, column 16.
2. When Jack receives his monthly paycheck on October 2, he enters the date and writes "Pay from Mall" in the Explanation column. Then he enters $355 in the Income column and computes the new balance by adding the old balance, $220, to the amount of the paycheck, $355:

$$\$220 + \$355 = \$575$$

3. On October 3, Jack pays $9 cash for lunch and $3 cash for a notebook. On line 8 he enters the date. Then he enters $9 in the Meals column, $3 in the School Supplies column and $12 in the Paid Out column. He then subtracts the $12 and enters the new balance.

	1	2	3	4	5	6	7	
						CLASSIFICATION		
					Car	Club	Payment	
5	Date		Explanation	Income	Ins.	Dues	Car Loan	
6	Oct.	1	Balance on hand					
7		2	Pay from Mall Dis. Cen.	355 00				
8		3	Lunch ticket/notebook					
9		5	Payment on car loan				35 00	
10		8	Gas, movies, dues			8 00		
11		12	Sweater, supplies					
12		14	Donation to Wild Life Fd.					
13		17	Savings, car insurance		50 00			
14		20	Restaurant, VCR tapes					
15		24	Dance date, car repair					
16		26	Gas, meal tickets					
17		26	Cassette, clothes					
18		27	Charity donation					
19		29	Camping trip					
20			Totals	355 00	50 00	8 00	35 00	
21	Nov.	1	Balance on hand					
22								
23								

Jack Cordello
Classified Cash Record

4. From October 5 through October 29, Jack enters the total of each day's expenses in the Paid Out column and each individual expense in the appropriate expense columns. After each entry, he computes a new balance.

After the last expense entry, Jack is ready to total the expenses and double-check the figures to make sure they are correct.

Pencil-footing is the process of adding columns of numbers and penciling the total in small numbers at the bottom of each column.

Pencil-Footing and Proving the Classified Cash Record When he adds the numbers in each column, Jack writes the total in pencil at the bottom, or the foot, of each column. This process is called *pencil-footing*

In the classified cash record above, Jack writes the totals in small numbers just below line 19. Before he enters the numbers in ink, he must first verify the totals. He must make sure that all the numbers are correct. This process of checking the accuracy of

8	9	10	11	12	13	14	15	16	
									1
									2
OF PAYMENTS (EXPENSES)									3
	Transpor-				Personal	School	Paid		4
Clothing	tation	Meals	Misc.	Savings	Development	Supplies	Out	Balance	5
								220 00	6
								575 00	7
		9 00				3 00	12 00	563 00	8
							35 00	528 00	9
	13 50		4 00				25 50	502 50	10
24 00						13 50	37 50	465 00	11
			5 00				5 00	460 00	12
				20 00			70 00	390 00	13
		5 25	6 30				11 55	378 45	14
	75 00				12 00		87 00	291 45	15
	12 00	18 00					30 00	261 45	16
19 00			5 10				24 10	237 35	17
			3 00				3 00	234 35	18
					30 00		30 00	204 35	19
43 00	100 50	32 25	23 40	20 00	42 00	16 50	370 65	204 35	20
								204 35	21
									22
									23

the numbers is called *proving*. It provides proof that the numbers are correct.

Proving is the process of checking the accuracy of numbers.

With the pencil-footed numbers, Jack can begin proving the totals. He prepares a proof in three parts.

1. **The Heading.** Jack writes his name, the purpose of the form (Proof of Classified Cash Record), and the date.
2. **Classification of Payments.** Jack writes the names of columns 5 through 14 and their pencil-footed totals and adds them to get $370.65. He verifies that $370.65 is correct by checking it against the total of the Paid Out column, which is also $370.65. See the illustration on page 80. The two amounts are the same, proving the accuracy of the totals. On the proof, Jack draws two lines under $370.65 to show that the Classification of Payments section is complete.

Jack Cordello
Proof of Classified Cash Record
October 31, 19—

Classification of Payments:

Car insurance	$ 50.00
Club dues	8.00
Payment on car loan	35.00
Clothing	43.00
Transportation	100.50
Meals	32.25
Miscellaneous	23.40
Personal development	42.00
Savings	20.00
School supplies	16.50
Total payments	$370.65

Cash balance on October 1	$220.00
Income for October	355.00
Total cash available for October	$575.00
Less: Payments for October	370.65
Cash balance on November 1	$204.35

3. The Balance Section. In the Balance section, Jack lists the beginning balance for October, $220, and adds to it the total in the Income column, $355, to get $575. Then he subtracts the total expenses, $370.65, from $575 to get the ending balance, $204.35.

Jack compares this ending balance with the last amount shown in the Balance column of the classified cash record and finds that they are the same. The ending balance for October on the classified cash record is $204.35, and the beginning balance for November on the proof is $204.35.

When the totals match, Jack draws two lines under the total to show that the classified cash record has been proved.

If the totals do not match, Jack adds the numbers again. If he finds no errors, he checks whether he transferred the right column totals from the classified cash record.

After the classified cash record is proved, it must be made ready for the next month. First

6	78
4	93
5	46
7	34
3	22
27	73

the classified cash record is totaled and ruled. Then the balance for the beginning of the new month is entered. Use the following procedures.

4					Car	School	Paid			4
5 Date		Explanation	Income	Ins.	Supplies	Out	Balance			5
6 Oct.	1	Balance on hand						220 00		6
19		29 Camping trip					30 00	204 35		19
20		Total	355 00	50 00		16 50	370 65	204 35		20
21 Nov.	1	Balance on hand						204 35		21

③   ①   ②

1. Use a ruler to draw a single line across all the money columns except the Balance column. This line should be just above the pencil footings. Enter the word "Totals" in the Explanation column. Then write the totals in regular-sized figures under the pencil footings.
2. Use a ruler to draw two lines below the Date column and all the money columns, including the Balance column.
3. Enter the beginning balance for the new month. Jack wrote "Nov. 1" in the Date column and "Balance on hand" in the Explanation column. Then he recorded $204.35 in the Balance column. Note that the beginning balance for the new month is the same as the ending balance for the old month.

Check Your Reading

1. A record that lists a beginning balance, income, expenses, and a running balance of money available to spend is called a(n) ___?___ record.

2. A record that has columns for expenses is called a(n) ___?___ record.

3. The process of adding columns of numbers and writing the total in small numbers at the bottom of each column is called ___?___ .

4. The process of checking the accuracy of the classified cash record is called ___?___ .

5. To show that a total is completed and proved, draw ___?___ under the number.

1. Fernando Rivera had the following cash transactions during the first ten days of November. Prepare a cash record for him similar to the one on page 76.

   Nov. 1 Balance $157.50.
   2 Paid $25.75 for books.
   3 Paid $45.90 for car repair.
   5 Received paycheck of $129.60.
   6 Paid $12.40 for dinner out.
   7 Paid $9.90 for birthday gift.
   9 Paid $3.50 for movie ticket.
   10 Paid $29.20 for tennis shoes.

2. Geraldine Murray wants to set up a cash record for the first week of December. Do it for her using the following information.

   Dec. 1 Balance $100.43.
   2 Paid $14.37 for tapes.
   3 Received paycheck for $157.69.
   4 Paid phone bill of $21.74.
   5 Paid back loan of $20.00.
   6 Bought gift for $13.20.

3. Julie Young is in a high school co-op program. She works part time at a local department store, and Julie's take-home pay is $250 a month.
   a. Prepare a budget for Julie. Her estimated monthly expenses are as follows:
      Fixed expenses: club dues, $5; payment on loan, $20. Variable expenses: clothing, $40; lunches and snacks, $50; miscellaneous, $25; personal development, $20; savings, $30; school supplies, $20; transportation, $40.
   b. Julie is planning to use a classified cash record. This record will help her keep track of her income and expenses. Set up Julie's classified cash record. Enter the necessary headings. In the Classification of Payments section, Julie will need a column for each of the expenses shown on her budget.

4. Julie's income and expenses for September are listed below. First enter a balance of $44 on September 1. Then, enter the following in her classified cash record.

   Sept. 1 Received pay of $250 from East Plaza Department Store.
   1 Paid $10 for bus tickets.
   1 Paid $25.98 for a blouse.
   2 Paid $14.50 to buy a gift (miscellaneous).

5	Paid $4.50 to buy notebooks and pens (school supplies).
5	Paid $12 to buy a lunch ticket for the school cafeteria.
6	Paid $5 dues for the school business club
6	Paid $5.50 to buy a concert ticket (miscellaneous).
8	Paid $8.98 to buy a record album (miscellaneous).
8	Paid $20 to buy a softball glove (personal development).
9	Paid $12 to buy a lunch ticket for the school cafeteria.
10	Paid $30 to deposit savings in the bank.
10	Paid $10 for bus tickets.
12	Paid $4 to buy a movie ticket (miscellaneous).
14	Paid $12.50 to buy a pair of earrings (miscellaneous).
15	Paid $5 as a donation (miscellaneous).
16	Paid $12 for a lunch ticket for the school cafeteria.
16	Paid $3.15 to buy typing paper (school supplies).
18	Paid $10 for bus tickets.
19	Paid $5 to buy a softball cap (personal development).
23	Paid $2.75 for a snack.
24	Paid $12 for a lunch ticket for the school cafeteria.
25	Paid $3 to buy notebook paper (school supplies).
26	Paid $10 for bus tickets.
28	Paid $20 on loan.

5. Julie wants to make sure that all the entries in her classified cash record are correct.

   a. Pencil-foot the money columns on the classified cash record.

   b. Prepare a proof of the classified cash record.

   c. Total and rule the classified cash record. Enter the balance for October 1.

   d. Compare Julie's estimated expenses and her actual expenses. The estimated expenses are listed on the budget you prepared in Exercise 1. The actual expenses are shown by the totals in the Classification of Payments section of the classified cash record. Are any of the actual expenses larger than the estimated expenses? Which amounts are larger and by how much?

1. To prepare a statement of income and expenses.
2. To prepare a budget analysis.

A *statement of income and expenses* is a record that summarizes information about all the money received and spent during a period of time.

A *budget analysis* is a record that compares estimated income and expenses with actual income and expenses.

At the end of the month, how do you know how well you are doing financially? What was your income during the month? Were your expenses within your budget? How much money do you have now?

The best way to answer such questions is to prepare a statement of income and expenses and a budget analysis.

PREPARING A STATEMENT OF INCOME AND EXPENSES

A *statement of income and expenses* summarizes information about all the money received and spent during a time period, usually a month. It may also be prepared every three months or every six months.

You already saw the classified cash record that Jack Cordello prepared during the month of October (pages 78–79). Now, look at the statement of income and expenses Jack prepared for October.

Let's see how Jack completes this statement. The numbers are keyed to Jack's statement of income and expenses.

1. Jack enters the heading information which includes his name, the title of the record, and the time period.
2. Next to October 1, he enters the beginning balance, $220. This is the amount shown on the classified cash record for October.
3. Jack writes Income and $355. He also identifies how he earned the income: Earnings from Mall Discount Center. The $355 income was listed under the Income column on the classified cash record.

```
                        Jack Cordello
 ❶          Statement of Income and Expenses
                 October 1, 19— to October 31, 19—

 ❷   Cash balance on October 1                    $220.00
 ❸   Income:
          Earnings from Mall Discount Center      355.00
               Total cash available for October   $575.00
 ❹   Expenses:
          Car insurance                    $  50.00
          Club dues                            8.00
          Car loan                            35.00
          Clothing                            43.00
          Transportation                     100.50
          Meals                               32.25
          Miscellaneous                       23.40
          Personal development                42.00
          Savings                             20.00
          School supplies                     16.50
               Total expenses.                    $ 370.65


 ❺   Cash balance on October 31                   $ 204.35
```

Jack adds the beginning balance, $220, and the income, $355, to get the total cash available for the month:

$$\$220 + \$355 = \$575$$

The total cash available is the actual amount of money that Jack had on hand for the month of October.

4. Jack writes "Expenses" and lists his expenses for the month. He finds this information in the classified cash record that he prepared.

   When he listed all the expenses for October, Jack totals the column to get $370.65. This figure matches the total of the Paid Out column in the classified cash record.

5. Jack computes the ending balance. He subtracts the total expenses from the total cash available:

$$\$575.00 - \$370.65 = \$204.35$$

His ending balance is $204.35. He draws a double rule under the ending balance to show that the statement is completed.

Jack's statement of income and expenses helps him summarize his finances at the end of October. Now he can compare his actual income and expenses with his estimated income and expenses.

PREPARING A BUDGET ANALYSIS

Jack's statement of income and expenses shows his actual income and expenses for the month of October. He now wants to compare these actual figures with the figures he had estimated for income and expenses. He does this by preparing a *budget analysis* such as the one shown below.

Jack Cordello
Budget Analysis
October 1 to October 31, 19—

	Budgeted	Actual	Difference
Income:			
Earnings from the Mall Discount Center	$355.00	$355.00	$00.00
Expenses:			
Car insurance	$ 50.00	$ 50.00	$ 00.00
Club dues	8.00	8.00	00.00
Car loan	35.00	35.00	00.00
Clothing	40.00	43.00	(3.00)
Transportation	80.00	100.50	(20.50)
Meals	35.00	32.25	2.75
Miscellaneous	10.00	23.40	(13.40)
Personal development	55.00	42.00	13.00
Savings for new car	10.00	10.00	00.00
Savings for starting own business	10.00	10.00	00.00
School supplies	22.00	16.50	5.50
Total:	$355.00	$370.65	($15.65)

Let's follow Jack as he prepares his budget analysis. Jack begins by entering the heading information, which includes his name, the title of the record, and the time period.

Jack completes the rest of the analysis by columns.

1. In the first column Jack writes "Income" and the source of his income. Then he writes "Expenses" and lists each type of expense. He finds this information in his budget.

2. In the Budgeted column, Jack lists the estimated amounts for income and expenses. These are the amounts he had estimated in his budget. He draws two lines under his total income and under his total expenses.

3. In the Actual column, Jack lists the income he actually received in October. Then he lists the actual expenses. These amounts are found in his classified cash record as well as in his statement of income and expenses.

4. Now Jack must compute the figures to enter in the Difference column. In other words, he must compare the budgeted amount with the actual amount to see whether they are the same.

   a. When the budget amount and the actual amount are the same, Jack enters "00.00" to show that there is no difference. Note that Jack enters "00.00" in the Income row and in the first three expense rows listed.

   b. When the budgeted amount is greater than the actual amount, Jack has spent less than he estimated. For example, Jack budgeted $35 for meals but actually spent only $32.25. He computes the difference:

$$\$35.00 - \$32.25 = \$2.75$$

   He enters $2.75 in the Difference column.

   c. When the actual amount is greater than the budget amount, Jack has spent more than he estimated. For example, Jack budgeted $40 for clothing but actually spent $43. He spent $3 more than he had planned to spend. He computes the difference by subtracting the smaller number from the larger number:

$$\$43 - \$40 = \$3$$

   Now, however, Jack cannot simply write $3 in the Difference column. He needs a way to indicate that some differences are in his favor and some differences are not. Remember: A difference is in Jack's favor whenever he spends less than he budgets.

   Jack uses parentheses whenever a difference is not in his favor—that is, whenever an actual expense is greater than the budgeted expense. Thus for clothing he writes ($3.00) in the Difference column.

5. Now Jack totals the numbers in the Difference column.
    a. He adds all the numbers in parentheses, the overspent amounts:

    $$\$3.00 + \$20.50 + \$13.40 = \$36.90$$

    b. Then he adds all the other numbers:

    $$\$2.75 + \$13.00 + \$5.50 = \$21.25$$

    c. Again, he subtracts the smaller number from the larger. Remember that the larger number, $36.90, represents overspent amounts.

    $$\$36.90 - \$21.25 = \$15.65$$

6. Jack's total expenses for October were $15.65 more than his budgeted expenses. He spent $15.65 more than he had planned to, so he writes the amount in parentheses. To check this amount, Jack subtracts his budgeted expenses, $355, from his actual expenses, $370.65:

    $$\$370.65 - \$355.00 = \$15.65$$

Now Jack does the analysis. The budget analysis will be helpful to Jack only if he uses what he learns.

The completed budget analysis tells Jack which items were overspent. If the same item is often overspent, Jack should do something about it. For example, during the month of October he spent $100.50 on transportation. Because he had budgeted only $80, he overspent $20.50 in this one category. For the month of November, Jack may decide to increase his budget for transportation to $100. Only by completing and studying the budget analysis will Jack improve his money management.

Check Your Reading

1. The record that summarizes information about all the money received and spent during a period of time is called a(n) ___?___ .

2. The record that compares estimated income and expenses with actual income and expenses is called a(n) ___?___ .

3. At the top of every record, the name, title, and date are entered. This information is called the ___?___ .

4. How often is the statement of income and expenses usually prepared?

1. Ellen Hahn attends a community college, and she also works part time at the Craft Cellar. Her cash balance on September 1 was $60. The amount of her income during September was $495. Her expenses for the month are listed below.

Auto insurance	$ 55.00
Tuition for college	100.00
Books and supplies	29.00
Clothing	55.00
Gas, oil, and repairs	105.00
Lunches	56.00
Miscellaneous	42.00
Personal development	42.00
Savings	20.00

a. Prepare a statement of income and expenses for Ellen. The period covered by this statement is September 1 to September 30, 19—.

b. The total of the estimated expenses on Ellen's budget was $495. Did she stay within this amount during September? What is the difference between Ellen's estimated expenses and the total expenses shown on the statement of income and expenses?

c. Is Ellen's cash balance on September 30 more or less than her cash balance on September 1? What is the difference between the two balances?

2. Dean Jenkins is a high school senior. He has a part-time job at Burger City. He wants to buy a motorcycle but is having trouble saving. He often runs out of money before the end of the month. To manage his finances better, Dean started using a classified cash record. He also plans to prepare a statement of income and expenses every month so that he can see exactly where his money is going.

On November 1, Dean had a cash balance of $152. His classified cash record shows that his income was $287 during November. It also shows the following expenses:

Club dues	$ 9.00
Payment on stereo	15.00
Bus fare	45.00
Clothing	45.00
Lunches	46.40
Miscellaneous	56.25
Personal development	48.50
Savings	20.00
School supplies	37.30

a. Prepare a statement of income and expenses for Dean. The period covered by this statement is November 1 to November 30, 19—.

b. Did Dean spend more money than he earned? What is the difference between his expenses and his income?

c. Was Dean's cash balance on November 30 more or less than his cash balance on November 1? What is the difference between the two balances?

3. Dean has decided that he also needs to prepare a budget analysis. He would like to know how his actual expenses differed from his budgeted expenses. He feels that this information will help him spend his money more wisely next month. Dean's monthly budget shows an estimated income of $287. The estimated expenses are listed below.

Club dues	$ 9.00
Payment on stereo	15.00
Bus fare	40.00
Clothing	38.00
Lunches	40.00
Miscellaneous	45.00
Personal development	40.00
Savings	20.00
School supplies	40.00

a. Prepare a budget analysis for Dean. The period covered by this analysis is November 1 to November 30, 19—. Use the budgeted amounts given above. The actual amounts are shown on the statement of income and expenses that you prepared in Exercise 2.

b. Which of Dean's actual expenses are larger than his budgeted expenses?

c. Did Dean save more or less money than he had planned to save in his budget? How much more or less?

d. Dean deposits his savings in the bank during the last week of each month. Since he is usually short of money at that time, he often saves less than he has planned. One of his friends suggests that Dean put his savings in the bank right after he is paid at the beginning of the month. If he does this, his friend believes that Dean can save the full amount each month. Do you agree with Dean's friend? Why or why not?

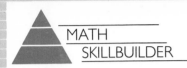

MATH SKILLBUILDER

1. Copy the following problems on separate paper in columns and add.

					Total
a.	204.50	317.25	50.00	135.75	?
b.	56.00	265.00	35.70	208.00	?
c.	76.25	40.00	98.00	45.30	?
d.	46.00	35.80	254.50	23.50	?

2. Add the following rows of numbers without copying the numbers, if you can.

				Total
a.	308.20	321.40	=	?
b.	289.00	78.10	=	?
c.	95.00	125.00	=	?
d.	427.00	153.00	=	?

3. Add the following rows of numbers without copying the numbers, if you can.

					Total
a.	45.00	23.50	12.00	=	?
b.	73.00	45.50	18.50	=	?
c.	48.00	124.20	51.00	=	?
d.	360.00	22.00	361.00	=	?

VOCABULARY SKILLBUILDER

Read each of the following statements. Then, from the words below each statement, choose the term that best matches the statement.

1. A plan showing how money is to be received and spent.

budget   goals

2. Money earned or received.

payments   income

3. Money spent.

invoices   expenses

4. A form that lists a beginning balance, income, expenses, and a balance of money available to spend.

balance form   cash record

5. A form that lists a beginning balance and income and has columns for expenses.

classified cash record   balance form

6. The amount of money you have at the start of a time period.

net income   beginning balance

7. A record that summarizes information about all the money received and spent during a period of time.

statement of income and expenses
income summary

8. A record that compares estimated income and expenses with actual income and expenses.

budget analysis   estimate form

APPLICATION
PROBLEMS

1. Debbie Campbell has been entering her income and expenses in a notebook. She has decided to begin using a classified cash record that will give her more complete information.

a. Set up Debbie's classified cash record. In the Classification of Payments section, arrange the following headings alphabetically: housing, savings, transportation, personal care, personal development, school supplies, miscellaneous, and clothing.

b. On September 1, Debbie had a balance of $142. Enter this balance on her classified cash record. Then enter the following income and expenses:

Sept. 2 Received monthly pay of $268 from East Supermarket.

3 Paid $50 to parents for household expenses (housing).

4 Paid $50 to deposit in the savings bank.

4 Paid $5 to deposit money in the Holiday Club bank account (savings).

5 Paid $15 for bus tickets.

6 Paid $3.98 for shampoo (personal care).

8 Paid $3.90 for notebooks and pencils (school supplies).

9 Paid $12 to buy a lunch ticket for the school cafeteria.

10 Paid $1.50 for a magazine (miscellaneous).

10 Paid $19.07 for a skirt.

11 Paid $5 for a ticket to a concert (miscellaneous).

12 Paid $4.20 for a pocket dictionary (school supplies).

15 Paid $8.14 for a gift (miscellaneous).

15 Paid $16.98 for a blouse.

17 Paid $5 as a donation to the Red Cross (miscellaneous).

20 Paid $4.25 for a movie ticket (miscellaneous).

22 Paid $15 for bus tickets.

23 Paid $5.75 for cosmetics (personal care).

24 Paid $12 for school lunch ticket.

25 Paid $12 for haircut (personal care).

26 Paid $4.75 for a belt.

29 Paid $10 dues for community bowling team (personal development).

30 Paid $5.25 for a record album (miscellaneous).

c. Pencil-foot the money columns on the classified cash record.

d. Prepare a proof of the classified cash record.

e. Total and rule the classified cash record. Enter the balance for October 1.

2. Debbie would like to compare her actual income and expenses with her budgeted income and expenses.

a. Prepare a budget analysis for Debbie for the period September 1 to September

30, 19——. Look at Debbie's budget below to find the budgeted amounts. The classified cash record that you prepared in Problem 1 shows the actual amounts.

b. Are Debbie's total expenses for September within her budget? What is the difference between the total of her actual expenses and the total of her budgeted expenses?

3. Debbie will go to a local community college after she graduates from high school. She is planning her expenses for her first year.

a. The college that Debbie will attend has four quarterly terms. The tuition is $100 a term. In addition, books and supplies will cost about $120 a term. Debbie would like to attend four terms during her first year. How much will she need for these expenses for one year?

b. Debbie saved $142 during her junior year in high school. She is planning to save $50 a month for 9 months in her senior year. What will be the total of Debbie's savings? Is this enough to pay for her tuition and books and supplies during the first year? If not, how much more money will Debbie have to save when she works full time during the summer?

```
                    Debbie Campbell
                    Monthly Budget


Estimated income
Take-home pay (from part-time job).......................... $248.00


Estimated expenses
Fixed expenses:
   Holiday Club in bank.........................$ 5.00
   Payment to parents (to help with household expenses.. 50.00
      Total fixed expenses.................................. $ 55.00
Variable expenses:
   Bus fare....................................$30.00
   Clothing.................................... 40.00
   Lunches..................................... 25.00
   Miscellaneous (magazines, books, donations).......... 15.00
   Personal care (shampoo, cosmetics)................  8.00
   Recreation (movies, rock concerts)................ 20.00
   Savings..................................... 50.00
   School supplies.............................  5.00
      Total variable expenses...........................  193.00
   Total estimated expenses............................. $248.00
```

CHAPTER 4

CREDIT RECORDS

If you are like most people, you often want to buy something before you have saved enough money. For example, if you are interested in a compact disc player and find one on sale, you may decide to buy it on credit. Buying on credit means that you purchase something now and pay for it later. Buying a compact disc player on credit is an example of short-term credit. Short-term credit means that you pay for the item purchased over a short period of time—a month to a year or two.

You may also want to make an expensive purchase such as a car and make monthly payments for it over several years. This is an example of long-term credit because the purchase is paid for over two years or more.

In this chapter, you will learn about using credit wisely. You will also study procedures for obtaining and using both short-term and long-term credit and what it costs you to use credit.

TOPIC 1 ▲ HANDLING CREDIT WISELY

GOALS

1. To identify reasons for using credit.
2. To describe types of credit.
3. To list things that will help you qualify and apply for credit.
4. To identify procedures for keeping a good credit rating.

KEY TERMS

Credit is the right to buy something now and pay for it later.

Short-term credit means that you pay for an item in a short period of time.

Long-term credit means that you pay for an expensive item over a period of several years.

A *finance charge* or *interest* is a fee paid for the use of credit.

A *credit application* is a form on which you report information a bank or store will use to decide if you should receive credit.

A *credit rating* is a record of how dependable you have been in making credit payments.

USES OF CREDIT

Consumers buy goods and services on credit for several reasons:

▲ Safe Shopping. The shopper who uses credit does not need to get and carry a large amount of cash.

▲ Convenient Payments. A credit buyer receives a bill for all purchases made during the month and pays for all the purchases with only one check.

▲ Small Payments for Expensive Items. Credit makes it easier to fit expensive items, such as cars and major appliances, into your budget. Few people can afford to pay $10,000 in cash for a car. But many people can make a payment of $250 a month for a car.

▲ Invest in Your Future. Borrowing money to go to business school or college, for example, is often a good investment in your future because of the likelihood of increased earnings.

As you can see, credit is very valuable. There are several types that are available for you to use.

Monthly bill for a charge account

YOUR ACCOUNT NUMBER	BILL OPENING DATE	BILL CLOSING DATE	30 Day Account means accounts beginning with the number 1 or 2 or 3. PBA means accounts beginning with the number 4 or 5 or 6. CPA means accounts beginning with the number 7.			J. DELWAY & CO.
250-06-319	04|17 --	05|15 --				

REFERENCE NUMBER FOR INQUIRIES	PURCHASES AND OTHER CHARGES	PAYMENTS AND CREDITS	STORE CODE DEPARTMENT NAME OR TRANSACTION DESCRIPTION AND DEPT NO ✷ SEE OTHER SIDE FOR DETAILED DESCRIPTION	TRANSACTION DATE	YOUR RECEIPT NUMBER
9043078	37.26		COOKWARE	04/28	C28240
6056047	5.65		DELICACIES	04/28	D28316
2118078	3.78		GREETING CARDS/GIFT WRAP	04/28	W28247
4148065	37.80		GIFTS	04/28	G28575
2148068	16.40		GIFTS	04/28	G28576
		163.73	✷ PAYMENT -- THANK YOU ✷	05/10	
5003229	30.24		UMBRELLAS OR RAINWEAR	05/12	R12109
7226223	21.08		GLASS DEPARTMENT	05/12	H12254
4159771		37.80	CREDIT -- GIFTS	05/12	G12576
9159803		37.26	CREDIT -- COOKWARE	05/14	C14240

PREVIOUS BALANCE	TOTAL ADDED	TOTAL SUBTRACTED	NO. DAYS IN BILL PERIOD	BALANCE SUBJECT TO FINANCE CHARGE	FINANCE CHARGE	NEW BALANCE	AMOUNT NOW DUE
163.73	152.21	238.79	29	0.00	0.00	77.15	77.15

You need not pay any part of your New Balance which you have questioned in writing pending our compliance with Regulation Z, Section 226.14.
30 Day Account—Full payment of the New Balance must be received within 27 days of the Bill Closing Date shown above.
PBA and CPA—To avoid a **FINANCE CHARGE** on your next statement, payment of all but **$4.99** of the New Balance must be received within 27 days of the Bill Closing Date shown above; you may pay your total balance at any time; if **FINANCE CHARGE** exceeds **50¢**, its **ANNUAL PERCENTAGE RATE** is 18% on the first **$500** of the Balance Subject to **FINANCE CHARGE** and 12% on any remaining part of the Balance Subject to **FINANCE CHARGE**. For CPA only, if the full amount of any purchase is paid within 90 days of the date of purchase, the **FINANCE CHARGE** on that purchase will be credited if requested by you within 30 days of payment. NOTICE: See reverse side for important information.

CR means Credit Balance ▲

INCLUDES PAST DUE PAYMENTS. IF ANY

TYPES OF CREDIT

As you learned in the introduction, the two major kinds of credit are short term and long term. Types of short-term credit include charge accounts at stores, bank credit cards, gasoline credit cards, and installment buying. Long-term credit includes loans for expensive items such as cars and homes. You will learn more about these types of credit in Topics 2 and 3.

Most types of credit require that you pay back the cost of the goods or services plus a fee called a *finance charge* or *interest*.

APPLYING FOR CREDIT

Before a store or bank will grant you credit, you will be required to fill in an application. The purpose of the application is to provide proof that you have enough income and can be trusted to make your payments. Therefore, it is important that you fill in credit application forms carefully and accurately.

Review the sections of the application form shown here. The form asks for information such as in the table below.

Section	Description
1	Name, address, and phone number
2	Employment and monthly salary
3	Co-applicant information
4	Bank account
5	List of credit references

The bank or store takes a financial risk by giving you credit. The information on the application can help determine how much of a risk the bank or store is taking. Here are three things that you can do to improve your chances of having your credit application approved:

1. Remember that the bank or store will consider your salary as your major means of paying for purchases. Enter accurate salary information. The bank or store will check your statements.
2. Open a savings account if you do not already have one. Try to deposit money regularly, even if the amounts are small.
3. Open a checking account if you do not already have one. If your application is approved, you will pay your monthly bills by check.

KEENEY'S CLOTHING STORE CHARGE APPLICATION

❶ ACCOUNT TO BE IN THE NAME OF:

MR. MRS. MISS MS. (TITLE OPTIONAL)

NAME FIRST **Norma** INITIAL **E.** LAST **Simpkin**

STREET ADDRESS **1806 Driftwood Lane** HOW LONG? **4** YRS. **X** OWN RENT BOARD LIVE WITH PARENTS OTHER

PREVIOUS ADDRESS IF LESS THAN 2 YRS. AT PRESENT ADDRESS

CITY **Wichita**

STATE **Kansas** ZIP **67217** HOW LONG? YRS.

HOME PHONE AREA CODE **316** NUMBER **653-4354** AGE **26**

❷ ACCOUNT HOLDER'S EMPLOYER **Emerson Supply Company** HOW LONG? **5** YRS.

EMPLOYER'S ADDRESS **2218 Park, Wichita** DEPT. NO. BUSINESS PHONE **462-4161**

OCCUPATION **Office Manager** SALARY $ **1,500** WEEKLY **X** MONTHLY YEARLY

PREVIOUS EMPLOYER IF LESS THAN 1 YR WITH PRESENT EMPLOYER HOW LONG? YRS.

COMPLETE FOR CO-APPLICANT (IF AUTHORIZED TO USE ACCOUNT)

FIRST NAME **Frank** INITIAL **J.** LAST **Simpkin** AGE **24**

❸ EMPLOYER **Morris Realtors** HOW LONG? **3** YRS.

EMPLOYER'S ADDRESS **3720 Oak, Wichita** DEPT. NO.

BUSINESS PHONE **527-8132** SALARY $ **315** WEEKLY **X** MONTHLY YEARLY

❹ OTHER INCOME $ **None** WEEKLY MONTHLY YEARLY SOURCES

BANK NAME **First Security Bank** BANK ADDRESS **1800 Glenview, Wichita, KS 67217** **X** SAVINGS **X** CHECKING LOAN

CREDIT REFERENCES: BANK CARDS, NAT'L CREDIT CARDS, STORES, FINANCE COMPANIES, ETC.

NAME **Bellville's Dept. Store** ACCT. NO. **73-046-2A** ADDRESS **1310 Western Drive Wichita, KS 67210**

❺ NAME **Dorland Finance** ACCT. NO. **9812347** ADDRESS **417 Rogers Avenue Wichita, KS 67226**

NEAREST RELATIVE NOT AT YOUR PRESENT ADDRESS

NAME **Ronald Simpkin** ADDRESS **7228 Valley Drive, Wichita KS 67226**

APPLICANT SIGN HERE *Norma E. Simpkin* SOCIAL SECURITY NUMBER **441-36-6470** DATE **1/12/—**

CO-APPLICANT SIGN HERE *Frank Simpkin* SOCIAL SECURITY NUMBER **079-26-1253** DATE **1/12/—**

☐ I HEREBY REQUEST A KEENEY'S CHARGE PLATE.

CREDIT LIMITS

Each bank or store that grants you credit will set a limit for your account. The limit will vary from one store or bank to another. Your credit limit will be based on your credit record, your income, and other important factors. One store may set your credit limit at $500 and another at $750.

A *credit limit* is the maximum balance a customer can have on an account.

KEEPING A GOOD CREDIT RATING

Your *credit rating* is a record of how dependable you have been in making your credit payments.

To keep a good credit rating, you must pay your bills on time. Late payments will hurt your credit rating and reduce your chances of getting other applications for credit approved. Those who pay the full amount of their bills on time have the best credit ratings.

Think before you buy. Will you be able to pay next month for all the purchases you want to make today? Some people buy things they don't really need because credit makes buying so easy.

Keep copies of all receipts, and use them to check your monthly bills. Only by checking your bills can you be sure they are correct. When you receive a monthly bill, compare the items on the bill with the receipts you have saved.

Check Your Reading

1. What is the word that means the right to buy something and pay later?

2. Name three reasons why credit may be useful.

3. Is a home loan an example of short-term credit?

4. Is a charge account at a store an example of short-term credit?

5. Name three examples of information that you would list on a credit application.

6. What are two things you should do to keep a good credit rating?

Exercises for Topic 1

1. Jayne Bryant wants to buy a $439 videocassette recorder (VCR). She works full-time at the Center Mall Plaza Shop, where she earns $235 a week. She attends college classes but finds it difficult to schedule study time and still participate in social and sports activities.

   Each week, Jayne spends more than her budget allows, forcing her to borrow about $100 a month from her parents. She has a $50 furniture payment each month, and she often buys on impulse during a lunch hour walk.

   The salesperson at P&J's Electronics is urging Jayne to take advantage of the sale price of $439 for the VCR by signing a purchase agreement for "just $99 down and $35 a month."

   Assume that you are Jayne's best friend. Help her answer these questions:

   a. Do you think the VCR should be Jayne's most important goal at this time? Why or why not?

b. Are Jayne's finances in good shape? Explain your answer.

c. What should Jayne say to the P&J salesperson?

2. Check the monthly bill for Albert M. Jalsly.

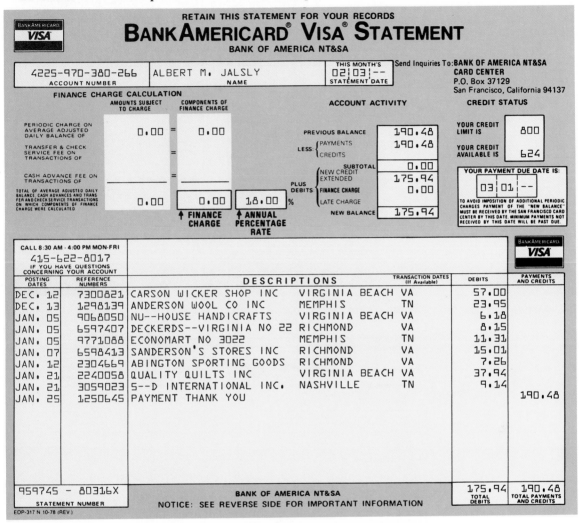

Albert kept his purchase slips and his canceled check for last month's payment.

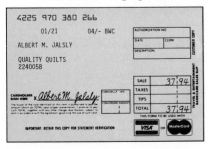
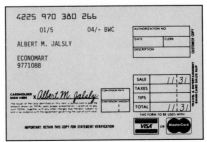

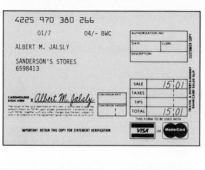

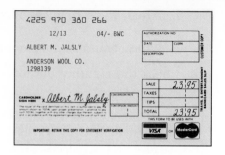

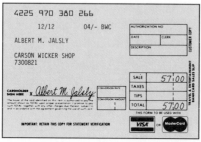

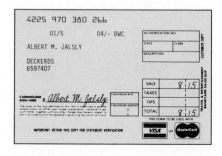

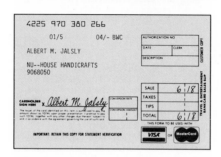

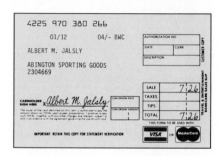

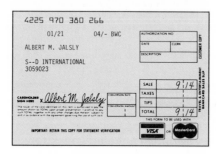

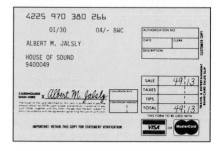

Albert M. Jalsly	235
	20-532 / 712

PAY TO THE ORDER OF ___VISA___ Jan. 23 19— $110 48/100

One hundred ten and 48/100 ——————— DOLLARS

Bank of Indiana
Indianapolis, IN 46200

Albert M. Jalsly

⑆0712⑈0947⑉ 68741⑈2

a. Check that each purchase slip appears on the monthly bill.

b. Check that the amount on each slip agrees with the amount on the bill. List any differences. If there are none, write "none."

c. Make a list of purchase slips that do not appear on the monthly bill. These purchases were made after the closing date of the bill. Albert will use these slips to check next month's statement.

d. Has Albert's canceled check, dated 1/23/19—, been deducted from the monthly bill?

e. Does the amount of the check agree with the amount of the payment shown on the monthly bill?

f. If Albert pays the bill on time, how much should he pay?

3. Check the Delway charge account bill for M. O. Wilson on page 95.

   Ms. Wilson kept her purchase and return slips and her canceled check for her payment to Delway last month. These records are shown below:

J. Delway & Co.	J. Delway & Co.	J. Delway & Co.	J. Delway & Co.
Purchase Slip	Purchase Slip	Purchase Slip	Purchase Slip
Date: 4/28/—	Date: 4/28/—	Date: 4/28/—	Date: 4/28/—
Item: 2148068	Item: 9043078	Item: 4148065	Item: 2118078
Price: 16.40	Price: 37.26	Price: 37.80	Price: 3.78

J. Delway & Co.	J. Delway & Co.	J. Delway & Co.	J. Delway & Co.
Purchase Slip	Purchase Slip	Purchase Slip	Credit Slip
Date: 4/28/—	Date: 5/12/—	Date: 5/12/—	Date: 5/12/—
Item: 6056047	Item: 7226223	Item: 5003229	Item: 4159771
Price: 5.65	Price: 21.80	Price: 30.24	Price: 37.80

J. Delway & Co.	J. Delway & Co.	J. Delway & Co.	J. Delway & Co.
Credit Slip	Purchase Slip	Purchase Slip	Credit Slip
Date: 5/14/—	Date: 5/17/87	Date: 5/20/—	Date: 5/25/—
Item: 9159803	Item: 9836402	Item: 6723407	Item: 8883592
Price: 37.26	Price: 45.60	Price: 9.04	Price: 9.04

Martha O. Wilson   159

May 8 19 --   60-214 / 313

Pay to the order of   J. Delway & Co. $ 163 73/100

One hundred sixty-three 73/100 ————————— Dollars

Central State Bank
Harrisburg, PA 17001

Memo _____   M. O. Wilson

⑈:0313⑈0214⑈: 792410

a. Check that each purchase slip appears on the monthly bill.

b. Check that the amounts on the purchase slips agree with the amounts on the bill. List any differences. If there are none, write "none."

c. Make a list of purchase slips that do not appear on the monthly bill. These purchases were made after the closing date of the bill. She will use these slips to check next month's statement.

d. Check that return slips appear on the monthly bill. Note any missing return slips. If there are none, write "no missing return slips."

e. Check that the amount on each slip agrees with the amount on the bill. List any differences. If there are none, write "none."

f. Has Ms. Wilson's canceled check, dated 5/8/19—, been deducted from the monthly bill?

g. Does the amount of the check agree with the amount of the payment shown on the monthly bill?

h. If Ms. Wilson pays the bill on time, how much should she pay?

GOALS

1. To identify two types of store charge accounts.
2. To describe procedures for using bank and other credit cards.
3. To determine when installment credit should be used.
4. To calculate costs of short-term credit.

KEY TERMS

A *charge account* is an agreement with a store that allows a customer to buy merchandise and pay for it later.

A *bank credit card* allows a customer to make credit purchases at many different stores and businesses.

An *installment contract* is an agreement to pay a store an amount plus interest each month for a purchase such as an appliance or furniture.

A *down payment* is the part of an installment purchase that is paid immediately rather than in installments.

TYPES OF CHARGE ACCOUNTS

A store charge account is one kind of short-term credit. Most stores that offer charge accounts give each of their charge customers a card to be used when buying on credit. Stores offer different kinds of charge accounts, which give customers different methods for paying their monthly charges. Let's look at two of the more popular types.

Regular Charge Account Under the terms of a *regular charge account,* the customer pays the total of each monthly bill within 30 days. The store charges the customer no finance charge and no extra fee for this type of account. The customer pays only for the goods purchased plus any sales tax.

Revolving Charge Account A *revolving charge account* allows a customer to pay the total bill over several months. The customer may pay only part of the total bill each month.

For example, Ken Griffin charged the purchase of a $300 compact disc player. Under the terms of his revolving charge account, he paid $30 a month for 10 months plus a finance charge of $1\frac{1}{2}$ percent (0.015) a month. The finance charge is applied to the total amount owed. His first payment, therefore, was $30 plus $1\frac{1}{2}$ percent of $300, the amount owed for the first month.

$$
\begin{array}{lr}
& \$30.00 \\
0.015 \times \$300 \quad = & \underline{4.50} \\
\text{Monthly payment} & \$34.50
\end{array}
$$

One benefit of the revolving charge account is that it permits the buyer to make payments over a period of time. One drawback is that the buyer must pay a finance charge.

A credit card issued by a store is used only to charge purchases made from the store. For example, a department store where you live may issue a credit card which can be used for purchases only from that store and its branches. The monthly bill shown on page 95 lists purchases made from one store.

BANK CREDIT CARDS

Banks also issue credit cards, often called *bank credit cards.* This is another type of short-term credit. Examples of bank credit cards are MasterCard and VISA. The cards can be used in many different stores and other businesses. The monthly bill for a bank credit card shown on page 99, for example, lists purchases in four different cities.

Banks collect interest on credit purchases. They may also charge an annual fee, usually between $25 and $50. You can avoid paying interest charges on bank credit card purchases by paying the full amount owed each month.

Bank credit cards can be used to pay for such different purchases as food, clothing, gasoline, hotel services, and airline tickets. Some bank credit cards can also be used to borrow cash. Used with care, bank credit cards are a convenience.

A *cash advance* is a small loan made on a bank credit card.

Cash Advances Using a bank credit card, you can obtain small amounts of cash quickly, just by presenting the card to a bank. The process is like using a credit card to buy something. In this case, however, the merchandise is cash.

There are rules concerning the use of bank cards for cash. For example, there may be a minimum, or smallest, amount that you must borrow. There is also a maximum, or largest, amount.

$800 Credit limit
−450 Already charged
$350 Available for cash advance

Suppose that your credit limit is $800 and you have already charged $450 on your account. The maximum cash advance that you can get is $350.

A finance charge will be added to what you owe on a cash advance.

Other Credit Cards Large companies such as American Express and Diners Club issue credit cards that serve the same purposes as bank cards. Card holders must pay annual fees for membership. These cards can be used for a variety of purchases throughout the world.

INSTALLMENT PURCHASES

Installment purchases are another kind of short-term credit. *Installments* are partial payments on items such as appliances, computers, stereo equipment, and furniture. When an installment sale is made, the customer is usually asked to sign a legal paper. This legal paper is called an installment contract.

COURTESY TITLES ARE OPTIONAL		PLEASE PRINT	

☐ MR. ☐ MRS. ☐ MISS ☐ MS. _____

First Name / Initial / Last Name

Street Address / City / State / Zip Code

Phone No: Home _____ Phone No: Business _____ Soc. Sec. No. _____ Age _____ Number of Dependents _____ (Excluding Applicant)

Are you a United States citizen? ☐ Yes ☐ No   If NO, explain immigration status: _____

How Long at Present Address _____ Own ☐ Rent-Furnished ☐ Rent-Unfurnished ☐ Board ☐ Monthly Rent or Mortgage Payments $_____

Name of Landlord _____ Street Address _____ City and State _____

Former Address (if less than 2 years at present address) _____ How long _____

Employer _____ Street Address _____ City and State _____

How long _____ Occupation _____ Net Income $_____ Monthly ☐ Weekly ☐

Former Employer (if less than 1 year with present employer) _____ How long _____

ALIMONY, CHILD SUPPORT, OR SEPARATE MAINTENANCE INCOME NEED NOT BE REVEALED IF YOU DO NOT WISH TO HAVE IT CONSIDERED AS A BASIS FOR PAYING THIS OBLIGATION.

Alimony, child support, separate maintenance received under:
☐ Court order ☐ Written agreement ☐ Oral understanding Amount $_____

Other Income, if any: Amount $_____ Source _____

Name and Address of Bank _____ Savings ☐ Acc't No. _____ Checking ☐ Acc't No. _____ Loan ☐ Acc't No. _____

Previous Sears Account ☐ Yes ☐ No At What Sears Store _____ Account No. _____ Is Account ☐ Yes ☐ No Date Final Payment Made _____ Paid in Full

Relative or Personal Reference Other than Spouse _____
(Name) / (Street Address) / (City and State) / (Relationship)

CREDIT REFERENCES Attach additional sheet if necessary List all references (Open or closed within past two years)

Charge Accounts Loan References Store/Company Address	Date Opened	Name Account Carried In	Account Number	Balance	Monthly Payments

Authorized buyer _____ First Name / Initial / Last Name / Relationship to applicant

Authorized buyer _____ First Name / Initial / Last Name / Relationship to applicant

This contract will be filled in by the seller when a customer buys on the installment plan. The customer must sign the contract in order to complete the sale. Before signing an installment contract, a customer should read it carefully. If any of the terms are unclear, the customer should ask the seller to explain them. People should never sign legal papers that they do not understand or that are not filled out completely.

The *installment contract* lists the details of the purchase and the terms of the sale. It lists the following information:

The price of the merchandise
The amount of the down payment
The amount of interest
The amount of each monthly payment
The total number of payments

When you sign an installment contract, you must pay a certain amount of money. This amount is called a *down payment* and is your first payment toward the total amount. Each month you pay an installment.

Each installment payment includes money paid toward the total amount of the purchase plus money paid as a finance charge or interest. The amount of the finance charge for an installment purchase will vary from store to store and from one item to another.

Before you sign an installment contract, ask yourself the following:

1. Can I afford to pay the installments?
2. What happens if I miss a payment? Can the merchandise be repossessed—that is, taken away from me?
3. Does the contract have small, easy payments in the beginning and a large "balloon" payment at the end?
4. Has the salesperson made any promises that are not in writing?
5. How can I cancel the contract if I change my mind? What fee or penalty is there if I decide to cancel?
6. Is this a spur-of-the-moment decision? Will I regret this purchase later?
7. Have I compared prices elsewhere? Am I sure that the quality, the price, and the contract terms are satisfactory?

COSTS OF SHORT-TERM CREDIT

Some short-term credit is free. That is, you do not always have to pay interest or finance charges to use credit. For example, if you pay the full amount owed each month on your store charge account or bank credit card, you do not have to pay interest.

If you do not pay the full amount owed each month or if you have an installment contract, you will pay interest. Interest rates from 9 to 22 percent a year are charged on bank credit cards and store charge accounts. Let's see how these rates translate into dollars you must pay.

Suppose you buy an $800 computer and charge the whole amount on your bank credit card:

1. The balance at the end of the first month is $800, and you pay $100.
2. The balance on your next monthly bill will be $700 plus a finance charge. At $1\frac{1}{2}$ percent per month, this charge will be

$$\$700 \times 0.015 = \$10.50$$

making a total of $710.50.

3. You pay $110.50 leaving a balance of $600. Your next monthly balance will be $609.

$$\$600 \times 0.015 = \$9 + \$600 = \$609$$

4. You then pay the entire balance of $609. How much did the computer cost you?

The actual cost of the computer was $819.50. For the use of the bank's money for three months, you paid $19.50. If you had waited three months and then purchased the computer for $800, you would have saved $19.50 but would not have had the use of the computer for three months.

If you are charged a monthly rate of interest, such as $1\frac{1}{2}$ percent, you can compute the annual rate by multiplying the monthly rate by 12.

The *annual percentage rate* you are paying in this case is 18 percent. No matter how they choose to advertise their finance charges or interest rates, all stores and banks must inform you of their APR. The APR, then, is a good figure to use when you are shopping for credit.

If one store has an APR of 18 percent and another charges 21 percent, you may decide to open a charge account at the one that charges 18 percent.

1.5% Monthly rate
×12 Months in a year
18% Annual percentage
     rate (APR)

Annual percentage rate (APR) is the monthly cost of credit converted to a yearly cost.

Check Your Reading

1. A(n) ___?___ charge account allows the customer to pay the total bill over several months.

2. The total balance of a(n) ___?___ charge account must be paid within 30 days.

3. A credit card that can be used to charge purchases at many different stores and businesses is a(n) ___?___ credit card.

4. A small loan made on a bank credit card is a cash ___?___.

5. A payment made when you sign an installment contract is a(n) ___?___ payment.

6. The three-letter abbreviation for yearly interest rate is ___?___.

Exercises for Topic 2

1. Maria and Tony Martino have charge accounts in several stores. They keep a list of all their charge purchases. Here is their list for the last seven weeks. Items that have already been paid for are crossed out.

Charge Account Purchases

~~Oct. 1 Coffee maker, $29.95 - Marshall's Housewares~~ Paid, Oct. 16, 19-

~~Oct. 15 Towels, $12.90 - Tracey's Sportswear~~ Paid, Oct. 24, 19-

Oct. 29 Dishes, $89.98 - Marshall's Housewares

Nov. 1 Shoes, $22.95 - Tracey's Sportswear

Nov. 5 Slacks, $29.98 - Tracey's Sportswear

Nov. 8 Curtains, $9.98 - Marshall's Housewares

Nov. 15 Sweater, $12.95 - Tracey's Sportswear

    a. What is the total amount that Maria and Tony owe for all their charge account purchases as of November 15?

    b. Maria and Tony budget $60 a month for clothing. What is the total amount of their charge purchases for clothing from November 1 through November 15? Should they buy any more clothing in November?

    c. Maria and Tony have a revolving charge account at Marshall's Housewares with a $300 credit limit. How much do they owe Marshall's Housewares as of November 1? Can they charge a chair for $250?

2. Lynette Marsh has a $1,200 credit limit on her VISA card. She has already charged $142.37. What is the upper limit of the amount she can borrow on her VISA card?

3. Joe Russo has a MasterCard with a $700 credit limit. He has made the following purchases and payments. Find the balance he owes and the credit he still has available after each purchase.

    Aug. 1 Purchased gasoline, $12.50.
             2 Paid for lunch at restaurant, $5.35.
             5 Bought clothes, $35.97.
             7 Bought furniture, $198.35.
          15 Made payment on MasterCard account, $35.82.
          19 Paid for dinner at restaurant, $10.72.
          28 Had car tuned up, $56.28.

4. Pat and Cliff Mooney work full-time. Pat's monthly take-home pay is $670 and Cliff's is $606. Last year they bought a car, some furniture, and a color TV set on the installment plan. Their monthly payments on these items are as follows:

car, $140; furniture, $60; TV set, $55. The Mooneys are now thinking of buying a microwave oven and a stereo on the installment plan. Their monthly payments would be $35 for the oven and $52 for the stereo.

a. What is the total amount that Pat and Cliff pay each month for the car, furniture, and TV set? If they buy the oven and the stereo, what will their new total monthly payment be?

b. Suppose that Cliff loses his job. He collects $282 a month in unemployment insurance. What is the difference between the total monthly income that the Mooneys had before Cliff lost his job and their present monthly income?

c. Suppose that Pat and Cliff stop making payments on their oven and stereo. What might happen to these items?

5. In March you bought clothes that cost $185 and charged the total amount to your new VISA account. When you received the April bill, you paid $50 of the $185 balance. The monthly finance charge is $1\frac{1}{2}$ percent.

a. If you do not make any other VISA purchases, what will be the balance of your May VISA bill?

b. If you pay $50 in May and make no other VISA purchases, what will be the balance of your June VISA bill?

c. If you pay the entire balance of your VISA bill in June, what is the total amount, including interest, that you paid for the clothes you bought in March?

d. What is the APR charged on your VISA account?

e. You receive in the mail an offer to apply for a VISA card issued by another bank. The APR offered is 15 percent. Is this a better rate than the one charged on the VISA account you now have?

TOPIC 3 ▲ LONG-TERM CREDIT

GOALS

1. To identify purposes of loans.
2. To identify the parts of a promissory note.
3. To compute monthly loan payments using a table.
4. To list types of car expenses and records.

KEY TERMS

A *note* is a written promise to repay a loan. It may also be called a *promissory note*.

The *principal* of a note is the amount of money borrowed.

The *maturity date* of a note is when the loan must be repaid.

Long-term credit is used to buy an expensive item such as a home or a car and pay for it over several years. Long-term credit is usually obtained at a bank, savings and loan, finance company, or credit union. When you borrow from one of these institutions, you obtain a loan by signing a note. A *note* is a written promise to repay a loan.

PURPOSES OF LOANS

Loans are made to people who need money now and are able to pay it back over several years. They may need the money for such things as:

A car. Most people cannot afford to buy a car for cash, so they get a *car loan.*

A home. Nearly everyone who buys a home obtains a loan, called a *mortgage loan.*

An education. To pay for tuition and other educational expenses, a person may get a *student loan.*

NOTES

A *note* or *promissory note* is a written promise to repay a loan. Most notes include a promise to repay with interest. Some notes must be repaid in monthly payments. Others are repaid in full on a certain date. Notes state the rate of interest to be paid and what will happen if the loan plus interest is not repaid.

Review the promissory note on page 111. The parts of the note are described below.

1. The *principal* is $1,050. The principal of a note is the amount of money borrowed. The principal is written in both figures (1A) and words (1B).
2. The *date* of the note is November 1, 19—. This is the date when the note is signed.
3. The *time* is 90 days. The time of a note is the number of days, months, or years from the date the note is written to the date that payment is due.
4. The *lender* is Cooper Savings Bank. The lender is the person, bank, or business to which the money must be repaid. The name of the lender follows the words "promise to pay to the order of."
5. The lender's address is the location where the note is to be repaid.

$ 1,050.00 _____ November 1 , 19 --

Ninety days ------- after date, without grace, _____ I _____ , promise to

pay to the order of Cooper's Savings Bank _____

at Laguna Hills, CA 92653 _____

One thousand fifty and 00/100 _____ DOLLARS

in lawful money of the United States of America, with interest thereon, in like lawful money, at the rate

of ____ 10 ____ per cent per ____ year ____ from November 1, 19 -- _____ until

paid for value received. Interest to be paid on due date _____ and if not
so paid, the whole sum of both Principal and Interest to become immediately due and payable, at the option of the holder of this note. And in case suit or action is instituted to collect this note or any portion

thereof _____ I _____ promise and agree to pay, in addition to the costs and disbursements provided
by statute, such additional sum, in like lawful money, as the Court may adjudge reasonable, for Attorney's
fees to be allowed in said suit or action.

Dwight M. Petersen

Due January 30, , 19 —   76 Pine St.
No. 57   Laguna Hills, CA 92653

NOTE—ATTORNEY'S FEES—WOLCOTTS FORM 1459

Promissory note

6. The *interest rate* is 10 percent. The borrower promises to pay the principal ($1,050) plus interest at 10 percent per year.
7. The *terms* of the note state that failure on the part of Dwight to pay on time gives the bank the right to sue to recover the principal and interest, as well as any court and legal costs.
8. The *maturity date* is January 30, 19—. The maturity date, or due date, is the date when the money must be paid back.
9. The *borrower* is Dwight M. Petersen. The borrower is the person or business that signs a note and promises to repay the money.

The *maturity date* is the date that the loan is to be repaid.

A *note payable* is a loan that you must repay on a certain date.

A *note receivable* is a loan that will be repaid to you on a certain date.

To Dwight, the signer of the note, this is a *note payable* because he must repay it. To the bank, this is a *note receivable* because it expects to receive the principal plus the interest when the note is due.

CAR LOANS AND RECORDS

A common reason for borrowing money is to buy a car. Owning a car also involves other expenses and records.

Car Loans Money to buy a car can be borrowed from banks, savings and loans, finance companies, credit unions, and car manufacturers. Many auto dealers have agreements with banks to simplify getting loans for the dealers' customers.

Auto loans are available with monthly payment plans, usually for 24, 36, or 48 equal installments. The rate of interest varies from one lender to another, so you should check two or three lenders to find the best rate.

Computing Monthly Payments Lenders may provide you with a chart showing the monthly payments at different interest rates and for different lengths of time, as shown in the table below. Using this table you can calculate payments on a loan.

INTEREST RATES AND TIME PERIODS FOR AUTOMOBILE LOANS
(Figures are payments per $100 borrowed)

%	\multicolumn{5}{c}{MONTHS}
	12	24	36	48	60
6	$8.61	$4.44	$3.05	$2.35	$1.94
7	8.66	4.48	3.09	2.40	1.99
8	8.70	4.53	3.14	2.45	2.03
9	8.75	4.57	3.18	2.49	2.08
10	8.80	4.62	3.23	2.54	2.13
11	8.84	4.67	3.28	2.59	2.18
12	8.89	4.71	3.33	2.64	2.23
13	8.94	4.76	3.37	2.69	2.28
14	8.98	4.81	3.42	2.74	2.33
15	9.03	4.85	3.47	2.79	2.38
16	9.08	4.90	3.52	2.84	2.44
17	9.13	4.95	3.57	2.89	2.49
18	9.17	5.00	3.62	2.94	2.54

Look at the table carefully to be sure that you know how to use it. Note the column headings at the top. The first column, labeled %, lists interest rates from 6 to 18 percent. The other five columns, labeled 12 through 60, represent the number of monthly payments.

If the current rate for car loans is 9 percent, find 9 in the % column, and then read from left to right.

%	12	24	36	48	60
9	8.75	4.57	3.18	2.49	2.08

Read the above line as follows: "At a rate of 9 percent, the monthly payment for every 100 dollars borrowed will be $8.75 for a 12-month loan, $4.57 for 24-month loan, $3.18 for a 36-month loan," and so on.

With this table you can figure how much the monthly payment will be for a 9 percent loan for any length of time. If you need to borrow $5,000 for a car, figure the monthly payment at 9 percent as follows:

1. Figure how many hundreds there are in $5,000.

$$\frac{5,000}{100} = 50$$

There are 50 hundreds in 5,000.

2. Multiply the number in each column by 50:

%	12	24	36	48	60
9	8.75	4.57	3.18	2.49	2.08
	×50	×50	×50	×50	×50
	437.50	228.50	159.00	124.50	104.00

You know that you can afford no more than $165 a month for car payments, and you want to pay off the loan as soon as possible. Which loan would you choose? Answer: The 36-month loan, because it is the shortest loan period that has monthly payments less than $165.

Reviewing Loan Needs As with any loan, you should first consider whether you really should borrow money to buy a car. If you decide that you should, then be sure to ask yourself these questions:

Where can you get the best rate—from a bank? credit union? the dealer?
What is the minimum down payment?
Can you afford the minimum down payment?
Can you afford to put down more than the minimum?
How many monthly payments are best for you?
Can you afford the monthly payments?

Taking on monthly car payments is a serious matter. It is also an expensive matter. Figure out how much it will cost, for example, to finance a $5,000 loan for 36 months at a rate of 9 percent. The monthly payments are $159 a month.

$$\$159 \times 36 = \$5,724$$

The cost of borrowing $5,000 for three years is $724. That's about $241 a year for interest. You need to decide if you want to spend that much each year for interest on your car loan. If not, you may want to save money before you buy the car.

Costs of Car Use When you borrow money for a car, one of your car expenses is the interest you pay for the car loan. As a car owner, it is important for you to keep track of interest as well as all your other car expenses.

Louis Jeffers is a student who works part-time as a salesperson for Clemmons Drapery Shop. He uses his own car to visit homes, take measurements, and hang draperies. Knowing and recording his car expenses helps Louis budget expenses. Louis keeps records of five kinds of car expenses:

Car loan
Insurance
License and registration
Gasoline and oil
Repairs and tires

Let's see how Louis computes and records each of these expenses.

Car Loan Most people buy a car by making a down payment and taking out a car loan for three or four years. After the loan is paid, it is no longer an expense. Often the down payment money comes from the sale or trade of another car.

Louis Jeffers is paying on a four-year loan. His payments are $140 per month.

To find his yearly expenses for the loan he multiplies by 12.

$$\$140 \times 12 = \$1,680$$

CAR EXPENSES FOR 19—	
Car loan	$1,680

Quarterly means four times a year. Each quarter is three months long:

First quarter: January, February, and March
Second quarter: April, May, and June
Third quarter: July, August, and September
Fourth quarter: October, November, and December

Insurance Louis pays his insurance quarterly. Each payment is $150; the total is $600 for the year.

Louis includes this expense on his list:

Insurance	$600

License and Registration Other costs are for a driver's license and license plates. There are also local fees in some areas. Louis paid $50 to the state motor vehicle department for his license plates, and he paid $20 for his driver's license—a total of $70 for license and registration.

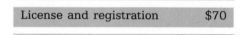

License and registration	$70

Gas and Oil Louis keeps careful records of gas expenses—a major cost of operating a car. In addition, Louis records all the expenses for oil changes and lubrication. His gas and oil costs for the year are $850, and he adds this expense to his list:

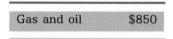

Gas and oil	$850

Repairs and Tires During the year, Louis had his car repaired twice. He also bought new tires. He totaled his repair and tire expenses.

Repairs, Feb. 4	$ 420
Repairs, Aug. 7	480
Tires, Sept. 19	300
	$1,200

He then added this expense to his list:

CAR EXPENSES FOR 19—	
Car loan	$1,680
Insurance	600
License and registration	70
Gas and oil	850
Repairs and tires	1,200
Total	$4,400

Figuring Mileage Costs With his completed list of car expenses, Louis now knows the total yearly cost of using his car is $4,400.

In addition to listing his expenses, Louis also keeps a record of the number of miles he drives. He does this by recording the car's odometer mileage at the beginning of the year and subtracting it from the mileage at the end of the year:

Odometer mileage, Dec. 31	74,627
Odometer mileage, Jan. 1	52,414
Total miles for 19—	22,213

To figure the average cost per mile of using his car, Louis divides his total cost, $4,400, by the number of miles driven, 22,213.

$$\frac{\$4,400}{22,213} = \$0.20$$

His average cost per mile is 20 cents.

After buying a car, you should begin keeping the important car records that you will need.

Other Car Records In addition to keeping records of mileage and expenses, Louis Jeffers must keep records of other car information.

▲ He is responsible for renewing driver's license and license plates on a regular basis.
▲ He must pay his car insurance when it is due.
▲ He must have his car inspected on a regular basis.

To make sure that he does not forget, Louis keeps a list in a record book, shown below. He also makes notes in his calendar to remind himself.

Car Records		
Record	Renewal Date	
License plates	March 31	
City sticker	March 31	
Driver's license	4 years, June 15, 19—	
Insurance bills	January 1, April 1 July 1, October 1	
Inspection sticker	August 1	

He also makes notes in his calendar to remind himself.

MARCH 19—		MARCH 19—
15 Monday		**18 Thursday**
Car licenses and sticker due March 31.		
16 Tuesday		**19 Friday**
H. A. Burns 5:00 p.m. 1208 Martin St.		*Ms. Valke 6:00 p.m. 3352 High St.*
17 Wednesday		**20 Saturday/21 Sunday**

Check Your Reading

1. Name three things you might borrow money for.

2. A(n) ___?___ is a written promise to repay a loan.

3. The amount of money borrowed is the ___?___ of a note.

4. The due date of a note is also called the ___?___ date.

5. If you borrow money and sign a note, is it a note payable for you?

6. Name five kinds of car expenses.

7. To figure your average car cost per mile, divide the total expenses by the total ___?___ .

Exercises for Topic 3

1. On a slip of paper, George Curton wrote the following and gave the paper to his friend Patty Allstair:

   "January 24, I make a promise to repay a loan of $20 to Patty Allstair on February 1."
   (signed) George Curton

    a. Does this paper state who is to receive the money? Why is this statement important?

    b. Does the paper give the date payment is due? Why is this date important?

    c. What is the advantage of George's paying Patty by check? What is the advantage of having Patty mark the paper paid and then giving it back to George?

2. Answer the following questions about the promissory note shown below:

$ _2,000.00_   _January 15_   , 19 _—_

Sixty days ————————— after date, without grace, _____, promise to

pay to the order of _____ _Celia A. Woodsen_

at _____ _174 Main St. Minneapolis MN_

___ _Two thousand and 00/100_ ———————————————— DOLLARS

in lawful money of the United States of America, with interest thereon, in like lawful money, at the rate

of ____ _11_ ____ per cent per ____ _year_ ____ from ____ _January 15, 19—_ ____ until

paid for value received. Interest to be paid ____ _on the due date_ ____ and if not

so paid, the whole sum of both Principal and Interest to become immediately due and payable, at the op-

tion of the holder of this note. And in case suit or action is instituted to collect this note or any portion

thereof _____ promise and agree to pay, in addition to the costs and disbursements provided

by statute, such additional sum, in like lawful money, as the Court may adjudge reasonable, for Attorney's

fees to be allowed in said suit or action.

                                   Paul J. Andosky

Due ____ _March 16_ ____, 19 _—_   _6600 France Ave._

No. ____ _23_   _Edina, MN 55421_

NOTE—ATTORNEY'S FEES—WOLCOTTS FORM 1459

---

    a. What is the interest rate?

    b. Who is the borrower?

    c. Who is the lender?

    d. What is the date of the note?

    e. What is the maturity date?

    f. Where is the note to be paid?

    g. For whom is it a note payable?

    h. For whom is it a note receivable?

3. Mitsy and Ted Tabor need an additional $600 to furnish their apartment. They decide to take out a loan and repay the entire amount at the end of one year. The Tabors compared interest rates at a commercial bank, a finance company, and their credit union. They wrote down the amounts from the three financial institutions. Here are the rates they were quoted for a $600 loan for one year:

First National Bank: 18% APR
Budget Finance Company: 28% APR
Credit Union: 16% APR

    a. What amount of interest would the Tabors pay for the bank loan? the finance company loan? the credit union loan?

    b. Which place is offering the best terms?

4. Write promissory notes using the following information:

    a. Date: December 10, 19—
        Time: 45 days
        Interest: 10%
        Maturity date: January 24, 19—
        Lender: Fidelity National Bank
        Address: 12 West Thompson Avenue
                   Lake Forest, IL 60045
        Number: 18
        Borrower: Annette Pirelli
        Principal: $400

    b. Date: May 23, 19—
        Time: 120 days
        Interest: 15%
        Maturity date: September 20, 19—
        Lender: Pam Mahoney
        Address: 605A Westcott Boulevard
                   Worcester, MA 01609
        Number: 42
        Borrower: Jay Weaver
        Principal: $250

5. Compute the monthly payments for the following auto loans. Use the table on page 112.

	Principal	Interest Rate	Number of Monthly Payments
a.	$3,000	10%	12
b.	$6,000	12%	24
c.	$8,000	11%	36
d.	$4,000	14%	48
e.	$9,000	9%	60
f.	$4,500	8%	24

6. Dan Furtado, a student, works as a salesperson for the Kustom Shutter Company. The company refers Dan to prospective customers. He drives to their homes to show samples, take measurements, and quote prices. Dan uses his own car.

   Dan's records and bills for the past year are shown below. Use them to find his average cost per mile.

   a. The odometer readings on Dan's car are as follows: beginning reading, 20,536; ending reading 50,836.
   b. Dan paid quarterly insurance premiums of $150 each.
   c. Dan paid $20 for his driver's license and $40 for his license plates.
   d. During the past year, Dan paid $375 for a new transmission and $425 for a partial overhaul. Also, he bought two new tires for $50 each.
   e. Dan's notebook shows that he spent $840 on oil and gasoline. He also has four lubrication bills: $42, $28, $10, and $20.

Skill: Finding the percentage—multiplying dollars by decimals.

Sample Problem: What is 75% of $3,250?

Solution:
1. Change 75% to 0.75 by dropping the percentage sign and moving the decimal point two places to the left.

2. Multiply 0.75 × $3,250 as if the decimal point were not there.

$$
\begin{array}{r}
3250 \\
\times 0.75 \\
\hline
16250 \\
22750 \\
\hline
\$243750
\end{array}
$$

3. Count the total number of digits to the right of the decimal point in the two numbers you multiplied.

4. Starting from the right of the answer, count that number of digits (in this case, two) to determine the correct placement of the decimal point.

$$\$2{,}437.50$$

5. Answer: $2,437.50

Practice: Find the percentage in each of the following:

1. 70% of $50
2. 80% of $745
3. 65% of $3,000
4. 55% of $696
5. 70% of $1,307
6. 41% of $3,032
7. 24% of $8,240
8. 96% of $55,794
9. 59% of $528,320
10. 87% of $5,653,688

Skill: Basic division.

Sample Problem: Divide 525 by 25.

Solution:
1. Set up the problem in standard division form with the number to be divided under the division sign.

$$25\overline{)525}$$

2. Estimate how many times the divisor (25) will go into the first two digits of the number to be divided (525). In this case, 25 will go into 52 a total of 2 times.

$$
\begin{array}{r}
2 \\
25\overline{)525}
\end{array}
$$

3. Multiply 2 times 25, and record the answer under the first two digits to be divided.

$$
\begin{array}{r}
2 \\
25\overline{)525} \\
50
\end{array}
$$

4. Subtract 50 from 52.

$$
\begin{array}{r}
2 \\
25\overline{)525} \\
50 \\
\hline
2
\end{array}
$$

5. Bring down the next digit in the number to be divided (5) and place it beside the 2.

$$
\begin{array}{r}
2 \\
25\overline{)525} \\
50 \\
\hline
25
\end{array}
$$

6. The divisor 25 goes into 25 once. Place the 1 in the answer, and multiply as you did in step 3.

$$
\begin{array}{r}
21 \\
25\overline{)525} \\
50 \\
\hline
25 \\
25 \\
\hline
\end{array}
$$

7. Answer: 21

Practice: Divide the following:

1. 32 by 8
2. 72 by 4
3. 954 by 9
4. 272 by 16

5. 414 by 23
6. 7,644 by 91
7. 4,738 by 103
8. 34,036 by 508
9. 48,766 by 659
10. 267,208 by 526

VOCABULARY SKILLBUILDER

Read each of the following statements. From the words below each statement, choose the term that best matches the statement.

1. An agreement with a store that allows a customer to pay for purchases at a later date.

   charge account   down payment

2. A fee paid for the use of money.

   finance charge   installment plan

3. A payment made at the time of signing an installment contract.

   credit payment   down payment

4. A loan obtained with a bank card.

   cash advance   personal loan

5. The maximum balance a customer can have on an account.

   credit limit   total charges

6. The figure used to compare interest rates.

   annual percentage rate (APR)
   compounded rate

7. A written promise to repay a certain amount of money.

   installment loan   promissory note

8. The amount of money borrowed.

   limit   principal

9. The person who receives money as a result of a loan.

   borrower   lender

10. The person who lends money.

    borrower   lender

11. Payments made every three months.

    quarterly payments
    semiannual payments

APPLICATION PROBLEMS

Charles Gilbert needs a loan of $3,500 to help pay for his new car.

1. Charles first went to a local bank to ask about financing. He was offered a $3,500 loan with three different time periods, each at 12%. Charles can afford a maximum pay-

ment of about $170 a month and wants to pay off his loan as quickly as possible. Which time period should he choose, 12, 24, or 36 months? Why? (Use the table on page 112.)

2. Charles then went to the credit union where he works. There, he was also offered a $3,500 loan with three different time periods. Keeping in mind that Charles can afford to pay a maximum monthly payment of about $170, which time period from the three choices listed below should he choose? Why?

a. Time period, 12 months; monthly payment, $309.01; finance charge, $208.12; APR, 10.97%.

b. Time period, 24 months; monthly payment, $162.81; finance charge, $407.44; APR, 11.18%.

c. Time period, 36 months; monthly payment, $114.25; finance charge, $613.36; APR, 11.3%.

3. Should Charles choose the bank loan or the credit union loan? Why?

COMPUTER
APPLICATION

Exploring Computers in Recordkeeping—Part I

Computers have changed the way we live and the way we work. They play an important role in personal recordkeeping, in the office, and in other work places where records are kept.

Computers have changed the way we process information. For hundreds of years information has been written out or printed on paper and then filed by hand. Now the same type of information, or data, can be organized, moved around, filed, and stored—all with a computer. Much less work is involved and much less space is used.

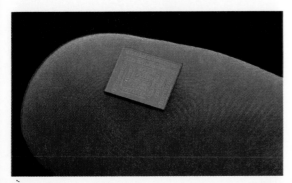

Silicon chip

In recent years small computers, called microcomputers, have become very popular. As you learned in Chapter 1, the basic parts of a microcomputer are a processor, a keyboard, a disk drive, a display screen, and a printer. These parts are called hardware. How does a computer work? The tiny silicon chips located in the body of the computer can store, process, and organize enormous amounts of information quickly in a very tiny amount of space.

Programs tell the computer what to do. They are written on a program disk. When you put it into the disk drive and turn the computer on, the computer is ready to follow the program.

Computer programs, often called software, are written by programmers. These people are trained to write instructions in special computer languages. Programs are prepared for the computer by keyboarding the instructions at the computer and then saving them on a disk. The disk is copied so that others can buy and use the program. When you are at the computer you usually do not see the instructions; you only see how the computer works.

Below is an example of a series of instructions written in BASIC, one of the most commonly used computer languages. As you can see it really does look like a different language.

This is a very short program—only three lines long. If a person named Joe ran this program and entered his name, the screen would look like this:

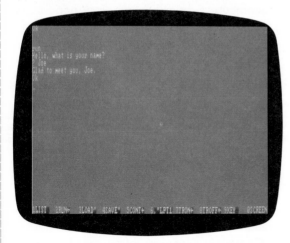

Some programs for business and personal recordkeeping are thousands of lines long. When you use a computer, you don't have to think about the programs, but remember that someone did have to tell the computer to do each thing that it does.

Many types of programs have been designed to help people perform recordkeeping tasks. Special programs are used to do budgets, keep banking records, predict sales figures, keep inventory records, and work with written mate-

rial. Programs that tell a computer how to work with written material are called word processing programs. They are very helpful to people who type and write at home and on the job. They are valuable because they enable these people to correct, change, organize, and print written materials such as letters and reports with very little effort.

For example, if you were sending the same letter to five different companies and you were using a typewriter, you would have to type it five times. With a word processing program in your computer you would keyboard the letter once, print it out, change only the address on the letter still in the computer, and then print out the new version. In the letter below the highlighted words would be different from one letter to another. They would not appear in color.

A word processing program also makes your work easier if you make a mistake or want to make a last minute change. If you were using a typewriter you might have to retype the entire letter. With word processing you simply correct the error and print out a new copy in seconds. Imagine how much time this saves. Even if you are an excellent typist and make very few mistakes, you will need to make changes in the things you write.

Another advantage of word processing is that copies of letters can be stored on disks. Whenever you need to send a type of letter, such as a request for payment past due, you can get the disk from your file and change only the part of the letter that is different. In this way a letter can be completed in much less time than it would take to keyboard it from scratch.

Check Your Reading

1. Name five parts of a microcomputer.

2. What is another name for computer programs?

3. Computer programs are written by people who are called ___?___.

4. One of the most commonly used computer languages is ___?___.

5. A program that works with written material is a(n) ___?___ program.

George and Sally Walters are a young couple. Sally is attending a community college. She expects to graduate in six months. Meanwhile, she is working part-time. George has been working full-time for several years. The Walters are saving as much money as possible for a down payment on a house. Buying a house is their major goal at this time.

George and Sally use a number of different records to help manage their finances. Their monthly recordkeeping activities include preparing deposit slips for their checking and savings accounts, making entries in their household income and expense record, preparing a budget analysis, reconciling the bank statement, and filing receipts and canceled checks.

In this project, you will do the Walters' recordkeeping for the month of January. Follow all the instructions given below and on the following pages.

Preparing Deposit Slips, Checks, and the Household Income and Expense Record

Sally and George Walters deposit all their income in their checking account each month. They write checks during the month to pay for expenses and to get spending money. When they want spending money, they write a check payable to "Cash." The Walters also have a savings account in the credit union at the company where George works. They make a deposit in the credit union once a month.

After the Walters receive income or pay an expense, they enter the information in their household income and expense record. This record shows all their income and expenses, including expenses paid by check and expenses paid in cash.

Exercise 1. Prepare deposit slips and issue checks for the following transactions. Be sure that you first enter each transaction in the check register. When you fill in the check register, be certain to include what the payment was for. A balance of $415.50 has been already entered in the check register. Do not sign the checks.

Deposits and Payments by Check

Jan. 2 Deposited George's monthly salary check of $1,915.50 in the checking account.

2 Wrote Check 201 to Cash for $75 for spending money.

2 Wrote Check 202 to Midwest Employee's Credit Union for $200 to deposit money in the savings account.

3 Wrote Check 203 to Midwest Fuel Company for $154.38 to pay heating fuel bill (utilities).

4 Wrote Check 204 to Twain Furniture Company for $138 to make monthly furniture payment (rent and furniture).

5 Wrote Check 205 to Kansas Insurance Company for $36.25 to make monthly hospital insurance payment.

5 Wrote Check 206 to Central Investment Company for $425 to make monthly rent payment (rent and furniture).

6 Wrote Check 207 to College Short Course for $60 to pay short course fee (personal development).

8 Wrote Check 208 to Cash for $100 for spending money.

8 Wrote Check 209 to KC Finance Company for $200 to make monthly car payment.

8 Wrote Check 210 to Family Fashions for $73.15 to buy clothing.

10 Wrote Check 211 to Mid-Continent Telephone Company for $17.80 to pay monthly telephone bill (utilities).

12   Wrote Check 212 to River Power Company for $35.50 to pay electric bill (utilities).

16   Deposited Sally's part-time wages of $381.25 in the checking account.

16   Wrote Check 213 to Cash for $150 for spending money.

16   Wrote Check 214 to Jimmy's Motors for $73.28 to pay for car repairs.

23   Wrote Check 215 to Rockwell Insurance Company for $48 to pay monthly premium on life insurance policy.

26   Wrote Check 216 to Centerville Medical Center for $45 for treatment of sprained wrist.

26   Wrote Check 217 to Circuit Center for $250 to pay for a tape player (miscellaneous).

26   Wrote Check 218 to Rossi's Drugstore for $8.50 to pay for prescriptions.

26   Wrote Check 219 to Cash for $175 for spending money.

30   Wrote Check 220 to College Book Store for $23.50 to pay for textbooks (personal development).

31   Wrote Check 221 to Boston Insurance Company for $80 to pay premium on car insurance.

Exercise 2. Prepare the household income and expense record for January. The information you need is shown in the list of deposits and checks above and in the list of cash payments shown on page 128. Enter all items in order by date. Do not include any of the checks written for cash. The money from these checks is recorded in the list of cash payments. If there is more than one payment on a date, find the total of the payments. Put the total amount paid for that date in Paid Out column; then classify the individual payments.

When you finish making entries in the household income and expense record, pencil-foot the money columns. Prove the expenses. Then total and rule the record.

Cash Payments

Jan.   2   Spent $4.25 for lunch (food).

2   Spent $48.25 for groceries (food).

3   Spent $15 for gasoline (repairs, gas, and oil).

6   Spent $35 for special dinner and movie (miscellaneous).

6   Spent $8.40 for scarf (clothing).

10   Spent $11 for stamps (miscellaneous).

11   Spent $45.20 for groceries (food).

12   Spent $17.10 for gasoline (repairs, gas, and oil).

12   Spent $7.50 on bowling (miscellaneous).

14   Spent $20 for a contribution to the hospital fund (contributions and gifts).

15   Spent $37.95 for a gift (contributions and gifts).

15   Spent $8.95 for a cake (food).

17   Spent $4.25 for lunch (food).

17   Spent $28 for repairs on TV set (miscellaneous).

18   Spent $50.25 for groceries (food).

18   Spent $15.95 for textbook (personal development).

23   Spent $20 for a contribution to Helping Hands Charity (contributions and gifts).

25   Spent $15.88 for gasoline (repairs, gas, and oil).

25   Spent $44.77 groceries (food).

27   Spent $11 for movie tickets and snacks (miscellaneous).

27   Spent $41.40 for groceries (food).

29   Spent $5.60 for gasoline (repairs, gas, and oil).

31   Spent $2.50 for parking (miscellaneous).

Preparing the Budget Analysis

At the end of each month the Walters compare their actual income and expenses with the amounts on their monthly budget in order to see how they are doing.

```
                        George and Sally Walters
                             Monthly Budget

        Estimated Income
          George's salary (take-home pay from full-time job)........... $1,915.50
          Sally's earnings (take-home pay form part-time job)..........    381.75
                   Total estimated income............................. $2,297.25

        Estimated Expenses
          Fixed expenses:
            Car loan....................................... $200.00
            Insurance......................................  164.25
            Rent/Furniture payments........................  563.00
            Savings........................................  300.00
                   Total fixed expenses.............................. $1,227.25
          Variable expenses:
            Clothing....................................... $ 60.00
            Contributions..................................   60.00
            Food...........................................  250.00
            Repairs, gas, and oil..........................  120.00
            Medical........................................   30.00
            Miscellaneous..................................  200.00
            Personal development...........................  120.00
            Utilities......................................  230.00
                   Total variable expenses...........................  1,070.00
                   Total estimated expenses.......................... $2,297.25
```

Exercise 3. Prepare a budget analysis for January. The budgeted amounts are shown above. The actual amounts will be shown in the household income and expense record you complete.

Exercise 4. On which items did the Walters spend more than they had budgeted? Write a possible reason for each one.

Exercise 5. On which items did the Walters spend less than they had budgeted? Write a possible reason for each one.

Exercise 6. Do you think the Walters did a good job of managing their money in January. Why or why not?

Preparing the Bank Reconciliation Statement

The Walters receive a bank statement once a month. As soon as the bank statement arrives, they reconcile it with their checkbook. The bank statement on page 129 covers the period of January 1 to January 31, 19—. The checks received and cashed by the bank are listed on the statement.

Exercise 7. Prepare the bank reconciliation statement for January 31, 19—.

Exercise 8. Do the Walters have more or less money in their checking account on January 31 than they did on January 1. (Compare their adjusted balance at the end of the month with their beginning balance of $415.50.)

Exercise 9. Suppose that the Walters find a house they like and need $10,000 for the down payment. Can they make this down payment now if they take all the money from their savings account in the Employee's Credit Union (which now has $2,500)? They also plan to borrow $6,000 from George's parents and take out $500 from their checking account. (Be sure to examine the checking account to determine the amount of the adjusted balance.)

Exercise 10. Sally and George have been discussing whether or not it would be wise to use all their savings for a down payment on a house. George can see nothing wrong with this. Sally feels they should always keep some money in the savings account for

LINCOLN NATIONAL BANK
Kansas City, Kansas

George and Sally Walters

1492 Elmwood Ave.
Kansas City, KS 66101
555-7500

ACCOUNT NUMBER 888-74303

PERIOD ENDING January 31, 19--

CHECKING ACCOUNT ACTIVITY

TYPE	DATE	AMOUNT	TYPE	DATE	AMOUNT
Deposit	0102	1,915.50	210	0120	73.15
Deposit	0116	381.25	212	0120	35.50
Service Charge	0129	3.00	213	0120	150.00
201	0105	75.00	214	0120	73.28
202	0107	200.00	216	0127	45.00
203	0110	154.38	219	0127	175.00
204	0114	138.00			
205	0114	36.25			
206	0115	425.00			
207	0116	60.00			
208	0117	100.00			

SUMMARY OF ACTIVITY

Beginning Balance	Total Amount of Deposits	Total Amount of Checks Paid	Total Charges	Ending Balance
415.50	2,296.75	1,740.56	3.00	968.69

Number of Deposits Made	Number of Checks Paid	Number of Other Charges
2	14	1

Codes: AP Automatic Payment   EC Error Correction
CC Certified Check   OD Overdrawn
CK Check Order   RI Returned Item
DM Debit Memorandum   SC Service Charge

Please examine this statement upon receipt and report at once if you find any difference. If no error is reported in ten days, the account will be considered correct. All items are subject to final payment.

---

emergencies. Do you agree with Sally or George? Why?

Filing Canceled Checks, Receipts, and Other Records

The Walters use an expandable file to store some of their records. The file is divided into the 15 sections listed below. By having different sections, Sally and George can arrange their records by subject. For example, they can put all the canceled checks for insurance in one section and canceled checks for utilities in another.

A. Automobile
B. Bank statements
C. Clothing
D. Contributions and gifts
E. Earnings and deductions
F. Furniture and household equipment
G. Guarantees and warranties
H. Insurance
I. Medical
J. Miscellaneous
K. Personal development
L. Rent
M. Savings account
N. Taxes
O. Utilities

Exercise 11. The records the Walters must store during January are listed below. Show where these records should be stored. For each record, write a capital letter identifying the correct section of the file. Use the miscellaneous category for any records that do not belong in any of the other sections.

Checks to Be Stored

Assume that you have the following canceled checks as shown on the bank statement for January 31.

a. Check 201 to Cash.
b. Check 202 to Midwest Employee's Credit Union.
c. Check 203 to Midwest Fuel Company.
d. Check 204 to Twain Furniture Co.
e. Check 205 to Kansas Insurance Co.
f. Check 206 to Central Investment Co.
g. Check 207 to College Short Course.
h. Check 208 to Cash.
i. Check 210 to Family Fashions.
j. Check 212 to River Power Co.
k. Check 213 to Cash.
l. Check 214 to Jimmy's Motors.
m. Check 216 to Centerville Medical Center.
n. Check 219 to Cash.

Receipts

o. Receipt for money given to hospital fund.

p. Receipt for money spent on a new tape player.
q. Receipt for money given to Helping Hands Charity.

Other Items

r. Statement of monthly earnings and deductions that George received with his pay.
s. Guarantee on new tape player.
t. Bank statement.
u. Statement of monthly earnings and deductions that Sally received with her pay.

Exercise 12. The Walters think that it is important for them to keep their canceled checks and the bank statement. Their friend Denise Parker throws away her canceled checks and bank statement after she reconciles her bank statement. Do you agree with the Walters or with Denise? Why?

PART
TWO

BASIC BUSINESS
RECORDS

CHAPTER 5

RECEIVING CASH

Businesses must keep accurate, up-to-date records of the cash they receive and pay out. Owners and managers would find it difficult to make wise business decisions without these records. Cash that businesses receive, or take in, is called cash receipts.

In this chapter, you will learn how to prepare sales slips and sales receipts, compute sales taxes, make change, handle cash refunds, and receive cash by mail. Understanding basic cash receipts procedures will help you in almost any job you may find in business.

TOPIC | ■ SALES SLIPS AND SALES RECEIPTS

GOALS

1. To prepare sales slips.
2. To prepare sales receipts.
3. To identify procedures for bank credit card sales.
4. To compute total cash.

KEY TERMS

Cash receipts are the payments received by a business for goods and services.

A *sales slip* is a form that lists information about a sale, usually of goods.

A *sales receipt* is a form that lists information about a sale, usually of services.

CASH RECEIPTS

The term *cash receipts* is used to refer to all the payments a business receives for goods or services, not just bills and coins. Depending on the business, the payments may be bills and coins, checks, or both. Payments may also be in the form of money orders and traveler's checks. Credit card sales slips are also considered cash receipts.

Cash receipts for a newsstand and a bakery may be only bills and coins. The cash receipts for your local electric company will be only checks. Cash receipts for supermarkets and drugstores will include bills and coins as well as checks. For some businesses, payments are made in person; for others, payments are made by mail.

One of the common forms that businesses use to record cash receipts is the sales slip.

SALES SLIPS

In many stores, the customer is given a sales slip after making a purchase. A *sales slip* is a form that lists information about a sale—the date, the item purchased, and the amount of the purchase. The sales slip is important because it provides both the customer and the business with a record of the purchase.

At Denton's Department Store, salespersons issue sales slips such as the one shown below.

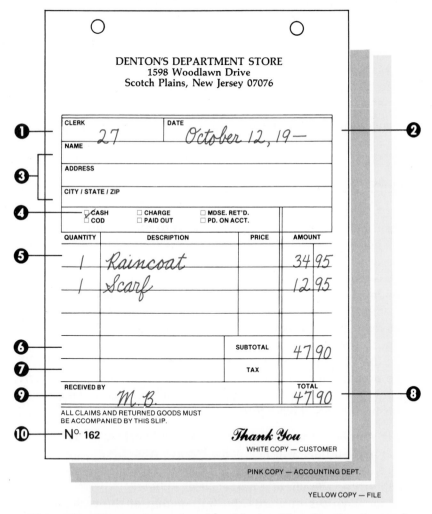

This sales slip was completed by Marion Blanchard, who works in the clothing department. Look at the information Marion listed on this sales slip.

1. Marion enters her employee number. Under "Clerk," she writes "27."
2. She writes the date of the sale.
3. Marion omits the customer's name and address whenever the customer pays cash for the purchase. She fills this information in when a customer charges merchandise.
4. Marion checks the Cash box to show how the customer paid.
5. To enter the first item purchased, she writes "1" in the Quantity column, "Raincoat" in the Description column, and "$34.95" in the Amount column. Marion enters each of the other items the same way.
6. Marion adds the amounts to get the subtotal: $47.90.
7. Because New Jersey does not tax clothing, Marion leaves the tax line blank.
8. She writes "$47.90" under the Total column.
9. Marion initials the slip "M.B.," again identifying the person who made the sale.
10. Marion uses the slip number, 162, to arrange her sales slips in numeric order each day. Sales slips are printed with consecutive numbers to simplify recordkeeping.

Marion then gives the customer a copy of the sales slip.

SALES RECEIPTS

As you have seen, sales slips are used to record the details of a sale, usually of goods. *Sales receipts* are used to record many sales of services and for some other cash receipts. The sales receipt is similar to a sales slip except that it is usually prepared to provide the person who pays with proof of payment.

George Weaver, a legal secretary for Atkins and Pierce, often receives cash payments from clients for services. For each payment, George writes a sales receipt for the client. The sales receipt that George prepared for Hal Rogers is shown on page 135.

To prepare two copies of this receipt, an original and one copy, George places a sheet of carbon paper between two blank forms. Then he follows these steps:

1. He numbers the form "125." George keeps sales receipts in numeric order. The last sales receipt was 124.
2. He dates the receipt.
3. He writes the client's name: "Hal Rogers."
4. George writes in words the full amount of the payment.
5. He identifies the purpose of the payment, "Legal consultation fee," and the date of the service, "April 25, 19—."

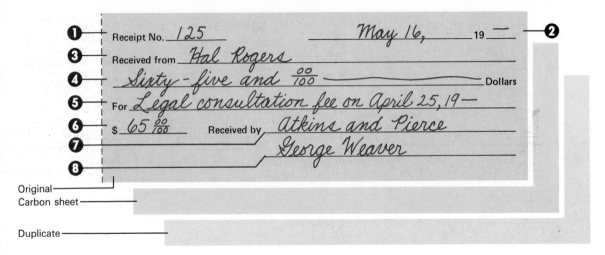

① Receipt No. _125_   _May 16,_   19 ___ ②

③ Received from _Hal Rogers_

④ _Sixty-five and 00/100_ ——————— Dollars

⑤ For _Legal consultation fee on April 25, 19—_

⑥ $ _65 00/100_   Received by _Atkins and Pierce_

⑦ _George Weaver_

⑧

Original ———
Carbon sheet ———

Duplicate ———

6. He writes in figures the amount of the payment.
7. George fills in the name of the firm, "Atkins and Pierce."
8. Finally, George signs his name to the sales receipt.

Because he used carbon paper, George now has two completed sales receipts. He gives the original to Hal Rogers. He files the copy. He places the cash in the firm's cash box.

BANK CREDIT CARD SALES SLIPS

Shopping with bank credit cards such as VISA or MasterCard is very common. Stores welcome customers using such cards. The store can convert credit card slips to cash quickly by depositing them in the bank. The bank then collects from the customer. For the service it provides, the bank charges the store a fee, usually 2 percent of the sale.

Marion and the other salespersons at Denton's use a special *imprinting machine* to record information on credit sales slips. The imprinting machine is shown at the right. These machines are found in almost all stores and restaurants.

When a customer uses a VISA card, for example, Marion places the card in the imprinting machine. Then she positions a blank sales slip over the card. As she pushes the handle from one end of the machine to the other, the information on the customer's VISA card is imprinted onto the sales slip form. At the same time, the machine imprints the store's name, address, and VISA account number. The store information is permanently in the machine. See the bank credit card sales slip on page 136.

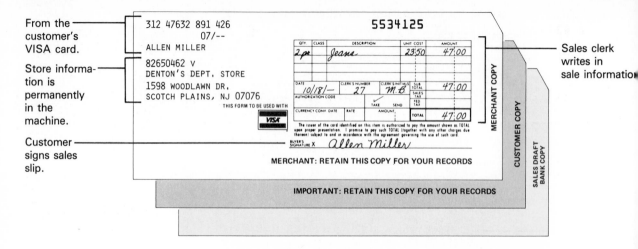

312 47632 891 426
07/--
ALLEN MILLER

82650462 v
DENTON'S DEPT. STORE
1598 WOODLAWN DR.
SCOTCH PLAINS, NJ 07076
THIS FORM TO BE USED WITH
VISA

5534125

QTY.	CLASS	DESCRIPTION	UNIT COST	AMOUNT
2 pr		Jeans	23.50	47.00

DATE 10/18/--	CLERK'S NUMBER 27	CLERK'S INITIALS M.B.	SUB TOTAL	47.00
AUTHORIZATION CODE		TAKE ✓ SEND	SALES TAX	
CURRENCY CONV DATE	RATE	AMOUNT	FED TAX	
			TOTAL	47.00

The issuer of the card identified on this item is authorized to pay the amount shown as TOTAL upon proper presentation. I promise to pay such TOTAL (together with any other charges due thereon) subject to and in accordance with the agreement governing the use of such card.

BUYER'S SIGNATURE X *Allen Miller*

MERCHANT: RETAIN THIS COPY FOR YOUR RECORDS

IMPORTANT: RETAIN THIS COPY FOR YOUR RECORDS

MERCHANT COPY

CUSTOMER COPY

SALES DRAFT BANK COPY

By using pressure, an imprinting machine records on a blank sales slip (1) the store's name, address, and account number and (2) the customer's name and account number.

Marion must now add the sale information—the date, the item purchased, and the price. She writes this information in the blanks provided on the form. After she completes and checks this information, she has the customer sign the slip.

Credit card sales slips are prepared in triplicate. One copy is for the customer, one is for the bank, and the third is for the store.

TOTAL CASH

You have learned that cash receipts include all the payments a business collects. Cash, checks, money orders, traveler's checks, and credit card sales slips are all part of cash receipts. As soon as possible, usually on the same day the payments are received, these receipts will be deposited in the bank. Even before cash receipts are deposited, they are considered part of the business's total cash.

To compute total cash, therefore, you must add the money in the bank to all cash receipts not deposited.

Cash in bank account + Cash receipts not deposited = Total cash

Check Your Reading

1. Cash, checks, and other forms of payment that a business receives are called ___?___ .

2. A form that lists sales information, usually about a sale of goods or merchandise, is a(n) ___?___ .

3. A form that lists sales information, usually about a sale of services, is a(n) ___?___ .

4. Would a store consider a completed and signed bank credit card slip as cash?

5. A machine that uses pressure to record information about the store and a credit card customer is called a(n) ___?___ machine.

Exercises for Topic I

1. Christine Schultz is a salesperson at the Skyway Sports Center. Prepare a sales slip for each of the following six cash sales that Christine made today. Her clerk number is 12. Find the subtotal of each sales slip. Save your work. You will add tax and total the slips in the next topic.

Sale	Quantity	Description	Price
a.	1 pr.	Ice skates	$ 59.95
	1 pr.	Thermal socks	7.25
b.	1	Fishing rod	23.88
	1	Spinning reel	27.39
c.	1	Camping tent	149.95
	1	Sleeping bag	29.66

2. Check the computations on the following sales slips. Make any corrections necessary, and find the correct subtotal for each slip. Save your work for use in the next topic.

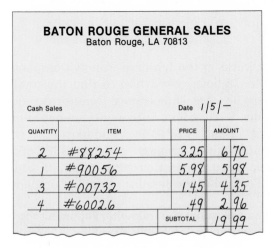

BATON ROUGE GENERAL SALES
Baton Rouge, LA 70813

Cash Sales   Date 1/5/—

QUANTITY	ITEM	PRICE	AMOUNT
2	#88254	3.25	6 70
1	#90056	5.98	5 98
3	#00732	1.45	4 35
4	#60026	.49	2 96
		SUBTOTAL	19 99

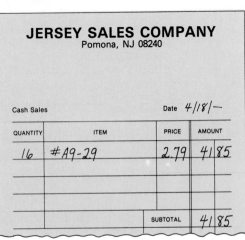

JERSEY SALES COMPANY
Pomona, NJ 08240

Cash Sales   Date 4/18/—

QUANTITY	ITEM	PRICE	AMOUNT
16	#A9-29	2.79	41 85
		SUBTOTAL	41 85

3. You are the receptionist for Dr. Kim Ortiz. Today four patients made payments by check for past medical services. Prepare sales receipts for these patients. The last receipt that you wrote was Receipt 318.

	Customer	Amount of Check Written	Date of Medical Service
a.	Johnny Gonzales	$75.00	June 19, 19—
b.	Stella Clarkson	46.50	May 6, 19—
c.	Terry Hoffman	38.00	July 27, 19—
d.	Donna Ventura	64.00	August 8, 19—

4. L. S. Manning, the new receptionist at the law firm of Cuka and Baro, wrote the following receipts. Because the telephone rang constantly and several clients were waiting to pay their bills, the receptionist made a few errors. Make a list of corrections needed on the following receipts.

a.
Receipt No. 519   Feb. 5   19 —
Received from Carol M. Werken
One hundred and 00/100 ———— Dollars
For Legal fees
$ 175 00   Received by Cuka and Baro, Attorneys
          L. S. Manning

b.
Receipt No. 520   Feb. 5   19 —
Received from John Burnstone
One hundred and 00/100 ———— Dollars
For Consultation
$ 100 00   Received by Cuka and Baro, Attorneys
          L. S. Manning

c.
Receipt No. ____   Feb. 5   19 —
Received from Inez Santos
Fifty and 00/100 ———— Dollars
For Legal services
$ ____   Received by Cuka and Baro, Attorneys
          L. S. Manning

d.
Receipt No. 522   19 ___
Received from Ivan Bensky
Two hundred fifty and 00/100 ——— Dollars
For Fees
$ 250 00   Received by Cuka and Baro, Attorneys

5. Dennis McCoy works at the Jennings Supply Company. The bookkeeper, Mr. Dubois, asked him to find the total cash that the business has. Mr. Dubois gave Dennis the following information: bills, $424; coins, $68; money on deposit at the First National Bank, $7,129; undeposited checks, $1,672.80; undeposited money orders, $322.65; undeposited bank credit card sales slips, $925.76. Find the total amount of cash that the Jennings Supply Company has.

6. Assume that you are given the following report by the office manager of Greeting and Holiday Supplies. Compute the total cash the business has on hand and in the bank. Be sure

to take into account only cash items. Do not include paid out slips.

SUMMARY SHEET

Total coins on hand	$ 87.42
Total bills on hand	982.00
Total checks received	1,506.72
Total store coupons received	35.70
Total bank credit card slips	492.41
Total money orders	75.00
Balance in Buehler National Bank	3,905.73
Total of paid out slips	12.35

TOPIC 2 ■ SALES TAXES

GOALS

1. To compute sales taxes.
2. To use sales tax tables to find the amount of tax for a sale.
3. To add the sales tax to the subtotal on a sales slip.

KEY TERMS

A *sales tax* is a government fee added to the cost of a purchase.

A *sales tax table* is a chart on which you can find the amount of tax for a sale.

State and local governments must raise money to pay their expenses. They must pay teachers, police officers, and firefighters. They must build and repair highways and provide many other government services. Money for these services comes from taxes.

An important kind of tax that is collected by state and local governments is the sales tax. A *sales tax* is a government fee added to the cost of a purchase.

Many different items are subject to sales taxes. Cars, jewelry, radios, clothing, books—these are some of the items we purchase that may be taxed. Types of items that are taxed vary from one place to another; for example, some states tax food and some do not. The amount of the tax also varies. The sales tax may be 6 percent in one state and 8 percent in another.

COMPUTING SALES TAXES

Sales taxes are always stated in *percentages* such as 1 percent, 3 percent, or $7\frac{1}{2}$ percent. This means that the amount of tax is a percentage of the price of the item purchased.

To compute the total cost of a $210 stereo with a 6 percent sales tax, follow these steps:

1. Convert the percentage to a decimal:

$$6 \text{ percent} = 0.06$$

2. Multiply the price of the item by the sales tax:

$$\begin{array}{r} \$210 \\ \times 0.06 \\ \hline \$12.60 \end{array}$$

3. Add the tax to the price of the item to find the total cost:

$$\begin{array}{r} \$210.00 \\ + \ 12.60 \\ \hline \$222.60 \end{array}$$

Now compute the total cost of a $29.99 videotape with a 5.5 percent sales tax:

1. Convert the percentage to a decimal:

$$5.5 \text{ percent} = 0.055$$

2. Multiply the price of the item by the sales tax percentage:

$$\$29.99 \times 0.055 = \$1.64945$$

Note: Round off the tax to the nearest cent whenever necessary: $1.64945 = $1.65.

3. Add the tax to the price of the item to find the total cost.

$$\begin{array}{ll} \$29.99 & \text{Price} \\ +1.65 & \text{Sales tax} \\ \hline \$31.64 & \text{Total cost} \end{array}$$

In the sales slip shown to the left, note how an 8 percent tax is computed on the subtotal of $46.35. Then the tax is added to the subtotal to get the total cost.

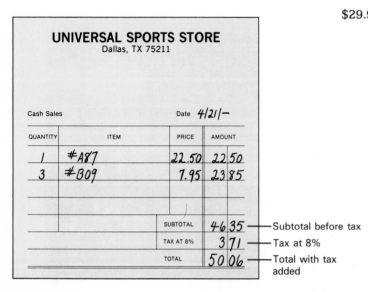

UNIVERSAL SPORTS STORE
Dallas, TX 75211

Cash Sales · Date 4/21/—

QUANTITY	ITEM	PRICE	AMOUNT
1	#A87	22.50	22 50
3	#B09	7.95	23 85
		SUBTOTAL	46 35
		TAX AT 8%	3 71
		TOTAL	50 06

— Subtotal before tax
— Tax at 8%
— Total with tax added

SALES TAX TABLES

Most stores use printed sales tax tables to help employees find sales taxes quickly without computation. The tax table shown below lists the sales tax at a rate of 6 percent for all sales from 1 cent to $10.

SALES TAX COLLECTION CHART FOR A RATE OF 6 PERCENT

Amount of Sale	Tax to Be Collected	Amount of Sale	Tax to Be Collected
$0.01 to $0.08	None	$5.09 to $5.24	$.31
.09 to .24	$.01	5.25 to 5.41	.32
.25 to .41	.02	5.42 to 5.58	.33
.42 to .58	.03	5.59 to 5.74	.34
.59 to .74	.04	5.75 to 5.91	.35
.75 to .91	.05	5.92 to 6.08	.36
.92 to 1.08	.06	6.09 to 6.24	.37
1.09 to 1.24	.07	6.25 to 6.41	.38
1.25 to 1.41	.08	6.42 to 6.58	.39
1.42 to 1.58	.09	6.59 to 6.74	.40
1.59 to 1.74	.10	6.75 to 6.91	.41
1.75 to 1.91	.11	6.92 to 7.08	.42
1.92 to 2.08	.12	7.09 to 7.24	.43
2.09 to 2.24	.13	7.25 to 7.41	.44
2.25 to 2.41	.14	7.42 to 7.58	.45
2.42 to 2.58	15	7.59 to 7.74	.46
2.59 to 2.74	.16	7.75 to 7.91	.47
2.75 to 2.91	.17	7.92 to 8.08	.48
2.92 to 3.08	.18	8.09 to 8.24	.49
3.09 to 3.24	.19	8.25 to 8.41	.50
3.25 to 3.41	.20	8.42 to 8.58	.51
3.42 to 3.58	.21	8.59 to 8.74	.52
3.59 to 3.74	.22	8.75 to 8.91	.53
3.75 to 3.91	.23	8.92 to 9.08	.54
3.92 to 4.08	.24	9.09 to 9.24	.55
4.09 to 4.24	.25	9.25 to 9.41	.56
4.25 to 4.41	.26	9.42 to 9.58	.57
4.42 to 4.58	.27	9.59 to 9.74	.58
4.59 to 4.74	.28	9.75 to 9.91	.59
4.75 to 4.91	.29	9.92 to 10.00	.60
4.92 to 5.08	.30		

The salesperson looks at the chart to find the sales tax. Other tables are available for use in places where the sales tax is different from 6 percent.

In Chapter 6 you will see that many cash registers compute the sales tax automatically.

1. A government fee added to the price of a purchase is called ___?___.

2. Sales taxes are always stated in ___?___.

3. In decimals, a sales tax of $6\frac{1}{2}$ percent would be stated ___?___.

4. On a sales slip, the sales tax is added to the ___?___ of the prices of goods purchased.

5. A printed chart that lists sales taxes is called a(n) ___?___.

Exercises for Topic 2

1. Refer to Exercises 1 and 2 on page 137. Complete each sales slip you saved by computing the sales tax and the total due. The sales tax is 6 percent.

2. You are a salesperson at the Camera Center. Prepare a sales slip for each of the following cash sales. Your clerk number is 62. The sales tax is 5 percent.

Sale	Quantity	Description	Unit Price
a.	1	Automatic camera	$139.50
b.	1	#67 electronic flash	49.25
c.	3	#110 film	2.35
d.	2	#36 film	3.25

3. You are a cashier at the Center Mall Hobby Shop. Find the sales tax at 6 percent for the following sales. Use the tax table on page 141.

   a. $9.42   e. $2.89   i. $2.62
   b. $4.95   f. $6.77   j. $6.99
   c. $8.75   g. $5.10
   d. $7.10   h. $8.20

4. As manager of the Shoe and Boot Shop, you must compute the sales tax at 7 percent on the following sales:

   a. $57.95   e. $ 2.89   i. $110.00
   b. $62.20   f. $19.98   j. $ 48.50
   c. $39.95   g. $41.75
   d. $28.75   h. $86.50

5. Find the sales tax and total cost on the following sales. Note that the tax rate is different for each item.

Sale	Sales Amount	Tax Rate
a.	$ 46.20	5%
b.	$ 19.75	8%
c.	$ 26.00	$8\frac{1}{2}$%
d.	$ 52.00	$6\frac{1}{2}$%
e.	$125.00	7%
f.	$ 20.00	$6\frac{1}{4}$%

6. Check the math on the six sales slips shown in your Activity Guide.

    a. Is the quantity multiplied by the price correctly?
    b. Is the subtotal of each sales slip correct?
    c. Is the 6 percent sales tax computed correctly? Use the tax table on page 141, or calculate the tax yourself.
    d. Is the total of each slip correct? Make any necessary corrections.

TOPIC 3 ■ MAKING CHANGE AND ACCEPTING CHECKS

GOALS

1. To compute the correct change, given specific sales information.
2. To list the coins and bills given as change.
3. To determine whether a check is acceptable as payment.

KEY TERMS

A *change fund* is the amount of money in a cash drawer at the beginning of the day.
To *tender* means to offer money in payment.

MAKING CHANGE

At the start of each business day, a certain amount of money is placed in the cash drawer. Because this money is used to make change for customers, it is called the *change fund*

At Glenda's Flower Shop, Cathy D'Amato begins the day with a change fund of $150. Cathy is responsible for this money, so she counts it to check that there is $150 in the drawer.

Because her cash register does not automatically figure the amount of change, Cathy follows certain procedures to make sure that she always makes change correctly. Cathy knows that customers sometimes pay without really noticing the bills they hand to the cashier. For each sale, Cathy always states the amount the customer gives her. This is called the *amount tendered.* She says aloud "Five dollars" or "Ten dollars" to remind the customer exactly what was given to her. Then she leaves the bill on (not in) the cash drawer until she finishes making change. Then she places the bill in the drawer. When Cathy follows this procedure, customers always know exactly what bill they gave her.

Cathy uses the smallest number of coins or bills to make change. This saves time and avoids error. She follows the same procedure every time she makes change. For example, if she has a sale of $3.64 and the customer tenders a ten-dollar bill, Cathy says, "That's ten dollars," places the bill on the drawer, and makes change as follows:

1. Cathy says "$3.64" and begins counting from this amount as she makes change.
2. From her drawer she takes 1 cent and says "$3.65."
3. She takes a dime and says "$3.75."
4. She takes a quarter and says "$4."
5. Cathy takes a $1 bill and says "$5."
6. She takes a $5 and says "$10."

Then Cathy counts the change aloud as she hands the coins and bills to the customer. By saying each step aloud, Cathy reduces the chances of making an error. By giving the customer a quarter instead of two dimes and a nickel and by giving 1 five-dollar bill instead of 5 one-dollar bills, she again reduces the chances of making an error.

ACCEPTING CHECKS

Cathy accepts almost as many payments by check as she receives by bills and coins. She also knows that accepting checks requires just as much care. Even the most honest people can make mistakes in writing checks. An alert cashier can help avoid many errors by following standard procedures for accepting checks.

Cathy reviews all checks before she accepts them. For example, when a customer gives Cathy the check shown on page 145, she reviews it as follows:

1. She checks the legibility of the writing. She makes sure that the check is written in ink and that there are no changes on the check.

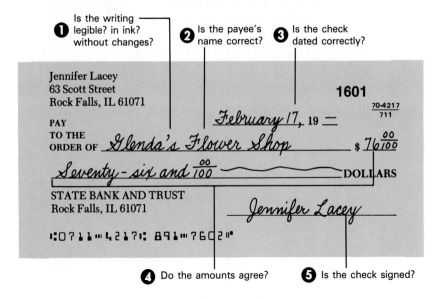

① Is the writing legible? in ink? without changes?
② Is the payee's name correct?
③ Is the check dated correctly?

Jennifer Lacey
63 Scott Street
Rock Falls, IL 61071

1601

70-4217
711

February 17, 19 —

PAY TO THE ORDER OF *Glenda's Flower Shop* $ 76 00/100

Seventy-six and 00/100 ——————— DOLLARS

STATE BANK AND TRUST
Rock Falls, IL 61071

Jennifer Lacey

⑈0711⑈4217⑈ 891⑈7602⑈

④ Do the amounts agree?
⑤ Is the check signed?

2. Cathy makes sure that the payee's name is correct: "Glenda's Flower Shop."

3. She checks that it has today's date. A postdated check, one that is dated in the future, cannot be deposited or cashed until that future date.

A postdated check is one that is dated for the future.

4. She checks that both the written words and the figures agree and that they are for the correct amount.

5. Cathy reviews the signature of the check writer. She makes sure it agrees with the name printed at the top of the check.

6. On the back of the check, Cathy writes information, such as the customer's phone number and driver's license number, to identify the check writer.

7. Cathy knows some customers well. For checks from customers she does not know, Cathy must get her supervisor's approval. Her supervisor writes "OK" and her initials on the back of the check.

8. Cathy rubber-stamps the check. The rubber stamp says "For Deposit Only" and identifies the store, its bank, and its account number. Now no one can use this check except Glenda's Flower Shop.

Check Your Reading

1. The amount of money in a cash drawer at the beginning of the day is the ____?____.

2. To ____?____ means to offer money in payment.

3. Salespersons should use the ____?____ number of coins and bills to make change.

4. Checks should be written in ___?___ .

5. A check that is dated in the future is call a(n) ___?___ check.

6. Before checks are accepted, they must be ___?___ for errors.

1. Using the form in your Activity Guide, write the number of coins and bills you would use to make change for each of the following sales. Note that the amount of each sale and the amount tendered by the customer are both listed.

Amount of Sale	Amount Tendered		Amount of Sale	Amount Tendered
a. $ 2.51	$ 3.00	i.	$ 8.60	$10.00
b. 5.07	10.00	j.	9.16	20.00
c. 14.63	20.00	k.	46.26	50.01
d. 16.14	20.04	l.	5.60	10.00
e. 23.78	30.00	m.	18.37	20.00
f. 17.61	20.01	n.	15.06	40.00
g. 22.91	30.01	o.	19.08	50.00
h. 28.68	50.00			

2. Are the following checks acceptable? Review each check carefully; then answer the following questions:

   a. Is the writing legible?
   b. Has information on the check been changed in any way?
   c. Is the check dated correctly? Today's date is April 25.
   d. Does the signature match the name printed at the top of the check?
   e. Do the amounts written in figures and in words agree?
   f. Is the check writer's address included on the check?

Bob or June Keenan
930 Twin City Drive
Kansas City, KS 66100

189

PAY
TO THE
ORDER OF _Cash_

April 25 19 —

18-230
1010

$ _123 50/100_

One hundred twenty three and 50/100 _____ DOLLARS

**Lincoln National Bank
Kansas City, KS 66100**

June Keenan

⑆1010⑈0230⑆ 888⑈74303⑆

Check 190

Bob or June Keenan
930 Twin City Drive
Kansas City, KS 66100

190

PAY
TO THE
ORDER OF _Toy Barn_

April 25 19 __

18-230
1010

$ _25 00/100_

Seventy five and 00/100 ———————————— DOLLARS

Lincoln National Bank
Kansas City, KS 66100

Bob Keenan

⑆1010⑈0230⑆ 888⑈74303⑉

Check 191

Bob or June Keenan
930 Twin City Drive
Kansas City, KS 66100

191

PAY
TO THE
ORDER OF _Runners World_

April ___ 19 __

18-230
1010

$ _42 59/100_

Forty two and 0%/100 ———————————— DOLLARS

Lincoln National Bank
Kansas City, KS 66100

⑆1010⑈0230⑆ 888⑈74303⑉

TOPIC 4 ■ MAKING CASH REFUNDS

GOALS

1. To prepare a cash refund slip.
2. To determine the amount of sales tax for a cash refund.

KEY TERMS

A *cash refund* is a return of cash for a returned purchase.

A *proof of purchase* such as a sales slip is a form that shows where an item was bought and how much was paid.

A *refund slip* is a form that lists the customer's name and address, the item returned, and the purchase price.

REFUNDS

Customers return merchandise for many reasons. A lamp may be damaged, a shirt may be soiled, or a dress may be torn. Such things are often exchanged. A damaged item may be exchanged for one in good condition.

Customers sometimes decide that they do not want to keep or exchange the merchandise. They may not like the color or the style. They may need a different size or want a different model. Instead of exchanging the merchandise, they want their money back.

A *cash refund* is a return of the purchase price of merchandise to the customer. Before a store will refund money, the salesperson asks to see the sales slip the customer received. The sales slip serves as a *proof of purchase*. It lists the price of the merchandise, the sales tax, if any, and the date of purchase. If the merchandise is accompanied by a sales slip, a store will usually grant a refund.

Different stores have different refund policies. Most stores post their policies so that customers will know of any restrictions. For example:

"Refunds will be allowed within 30 days of purchase."

"Refunds must be accompanied by sales slips."

"Refunds not allowed on sales merchandise."

COMPLETING THE REFUND SLIP

Whenever a store does grant a refund, the salesperson must complete a refund slip. It is often similar to the form used for sales slips. Note that the refund slip always requires the customer's signature. See the refund slip shown on page 149.

Marion Blanchard, who works in the clothing department at Denton's, completes this refund slip when a customer, Luis Garcia, returns an umbrella. Note how Marion completes this refund slip:

1. She fills in her clerk number, "27."
2. She fills in the date: "November 9, 19—."
3. She fills in the customer's name and address.
4. Marion checks the Paid Out box and the Merchandise Returned box.
5. In the Quantity column she writes "1." In the Description column she writes "Cash refund for umbrella." In the Amount column she writes the cost.
6. Next to Subtotal, Marion again writes the cost. Then she adds the tax, if any, and totals the refund.
7. Marion asks Mr. Garcia to sign the refund slip. Then she gives him a copy of the refund slip along with the money refunded. This completes the transaction.

```
                    DENTON'S DEPARTMENT STORE
                         1598 Woodlawn Drive
                    Scotch Plains, New Jersey 07076
```

CLERK	DATE
27	*November 9, 19—*

NAME *Luis Garcia*

ADDRESS *481 Oak St.*

CITY / STATE / ZIP *Jersey City, N. J. 07304*

☐ CASH	☐ CHARGE	☑ MDSE. RET'D.
☐ COD	☑ PAID OUT	☐ PD. ON ACCT.

QUANTITY	DESCRIPTION	PRICE	AMOUNT
1	*Cash refund for umbrella*	15 99	
		SUBTOTAL	15 99
		TAX	

RECEIVED BY *Luis Garcia* **TOTAL** 15 99

ALL CLAIMS AND RETURNED GOODS MUST
BE ACCOMPANIED BY THIS SLIP.

N°· 448

Thank You

WHITE COPY — CUSTOMER

❶ ❷ ❸ ❹ ❺ ❻ ❼

Check Your Reading

1. A return of cash for returned merchandise is called a(n) ___?___ .

2. A form that proves where merchandise was bought and what price was paid is called a(n) ___?___ .

3. A form used by customers to return merchandise for refunds is the ___?___ that the customer originally received with the purchase.

4. A form that lists the customer's name and address, the merchandise returned, and the purchase price, along with the customer's signature, is called a(n) ___?___ .

1. Bill Kim, a salesperson at Berry's Drugstore, has to prepare a cash refund slip for a Sharp Cut electric razor (Model #6321). The razor was returned today by Steve Douglas of 2229 Birch Drive, Oklahoma City, OK 73106. The razor cost $44.95 plus 6 percent sales tax. Bill's clerk number is 6. Prepare the cash refund slip for Bill. Sign Steve's name on the refund slip.

2. Curt Sloan, a salesperson at Sharp Lens Camera Store, receives a camera for refund from Karen Bell of 844 Alpine Drive, Los Angeles, CA 90026. Her sales slip shows that the camera cost $43.50 plus 6 percent sales tax. Curt's clerk number is 45. Prepare the cash refund slip for Curt. Sign Karen Bell's name to the refund slip.

3. Compute the amount of the cash refund for each of the following returns. The sales tax rate is 7 percent. In all cases a sales slip accompanied the returns.

   a. Cosmetics, $21.50.
   b. Jeans, $29.
   c. Shirt, $14.95.
   d. Sweater, $48.
   e. Shirt and skirt combination, $79.95.
   f. 1 facial cream at $4.95 and 2 lipsticks at $2.95 each.
   g. 4 slips at $10.95 each.
   h. 5 small bottles of cologne at $6.95 each.

4. Compute the amount of the cash refund for each of the following returns. If a sales slip is not present with the return, indicate *no refund.* If the store manager rejects the refund because the package had been opened and used, indicate *no refund.* The sales tax rate is 5 percent.

	Quantity	Items Returned	Unit Price	Accompanied by Sales Slip?	Approved by Manager?
a.	2	Tapes	7.95	Yes	Yes
b.	3	Records	8.95	No	No
c.	1	Record	6.50	Yes	Yes
d.	1	Tape	9.95	Yes	No
e.	2	Tape holders	29.95	Yes	No
f.	1	Record	6.95		
	1	Record	8.98	Yes	Yes
g.	3	Tapes	5.50	Yes	Yes

GOALS

1. To compare checks received by mail with bill stubs.
2. To prove the total of checks received against the total of bill stubs received.
3. To complete payment slips.

KEY TERMS

A *bill stub* is that part of a bill that is torn off and returned with the payment.

A *payment slip* is a receipt that a company gives or sends to a customer.

BILL STUBS

Many businesses receive payments by mail for their goods and services. A large company may receive thousands of checks and money orders each day. The company must identify the purpose of the payment, the customer's account number, and the amount of the payment.

To keep track of mail payments, businesses provide their customers with two-part bills. One part is for the customer to keep; the other part, the stub, is for the customer to return with the payment. The stub that Dale Olson sent with his check to pay his electricity bill is shown here.

By returning the stub with his payment, Dale helps the Marysville Power Company credit the payment to the right account. At Marysville Power, cashiers such as Tammy Grace open hundreds of envelopes each day. When a check or money order is accompanied by a stub, Tammy compares the amount of the check or money order with the amount shown on the stub. For example, when she receives Dale's payment, she notes that Dale's check is for $48.72 and that the amount due at the bottom of his stub is $48.72. When the stub amount and the check amount agree, she makes a check mark on the stub and places all checkmarked stubs in a certain pile.

When the stub amount and the check amount do not agree, on the stub she circles the Amount Due box and writes the actual amount of the check that was received. She separates all circled stubs by placing them in another pile.

When an envelope includes a check or money order but no stub, she creates a stub. Tammy takes a blank stub and writes in the customer's name, account number, and the amount paid. Again, she sorts the stubs into piles.

Tammy also takes all the checks and reviews them carefully. She makes sure that each check and money order is ready to be deposited.

Tammy uses a calculator to total the checks and money orders received each day. She totals the day's stubs to prove that the total of the checks and the total of the stubs agree.

PAYMENT SLIPS

Some companies do not provide bill stubs. Cycle World, for example, sends its charge customers monthly bills, but the bills do not have stubs attached.

Kate Gleason, who works in the business office at Cycle World, completes a payment slip each time she receives a check or money order from a customer. When she receives a check from Ellen Steinberg, a Cycle World charge customer, Kate reviews the check as usual. Then she writes a payment slip.

1. Kate numbers the payment slip. She checks the last slip number (324) and numbers the new slip "325."
2. She writes in the customer's name.
3. From the customer's check, she copies the amount paid ($63.47), the check number (479), and the check date (April 7, 19—).
4. She explains the purpose of the payment.
5. Kate dates and initials the payment slip.

Kate uses the payment slips to record the payment amount in each customer's account file. At the end of the day, Kate arranges all the payment slips in numeric order and totals the amounts on the slips. Then she totals the amounts of the checks and money orders to make sure that both totals agree.

Ellen Steinberg
1328 East 52nd
Sterling, IL 61081

479

70-2672
711

PAY
TO THE
ORDER OF _Cycle World_ _____ $ 63 47/100

Sixty-three and 47/100 _____ **DOLLARS**

First Commercial Bank
Sterling, IL 61081

Ellen Steinberg

⑆0711⑈2672⑆ 617⑈9396⑈

Customer's Payment Slip	NO. 325 ──❶

❷── NAME _Ellen Steinberg_

❸── | AMOUNT $ 63 47/100 | CHECK NO. 479 | CHECK DATE April 7, 19— |

❹── EXPLANATION _Payment on account_

❺── | DATE April 10, 19— | RECEIVED BY K. G. |

1. The part of a bill that is torn off and sent along with the customer's payment is the ___?___ .

2. Most payments made by mail are in the form of ___?___ and ___?___ .

3. The form that companies send to notify customers of payments received is the ___?___ .

1. As a cashier for Marysville Power Company, Rick Beskian received bill stubs and checks as shown on pages 154—155.

   a. Check the amount of each stub with the amount of the corresponding check. Note any differences.
   b. Examine each check to see whether it is made out correctly and whether the amount in numbers is the same as the amount in writing. Note any differences.
   c. Total the amounts of the stubs.
   d. Total the amounts of the checks.
   e. Compare the two totals. If the totals are not equal, explain why.

a.

Billing Code	Billing Date	Amount
A5	MAY 10	65.20
		Amount 65.20

Felipe Bautisti
165 Cypress
Jacksonville, FL 32212

161

63-851 / 630

PAY TO THE ORDER OF _Marysville Power Company_ $ 65 20/100

Sixty-five and 20/100 ———————— DOLLARS

Sunshine State Bank
Jacksonville, Florida 32203

Felipe Bautisti

⑆0630⑉0851⑆ 75192⑈9

b.

Billing Code	Billing Date	Amount
EL1	MAY 10	107.33
		Amount 107.33

Daisy Fortier
44 Sea Pine Ln.
Jacksonville, FL 32207

234

63-851 / 630

PAY TO THE ORDER OF _Marysville Power Company_ $ 107 33/100

One hundred seven and 33/100 ———————— DOLLARS

Sunshine State Bank
Jacksonville, Florida 32203

Daisy Fortier

⑆0630⑉0851⑆ 14267⑈9

c.

Billing Code	Billing Date	Amount
EL1	MAY 10	87.65
		Amount 87.65

James Albens
1243 Beck Ave.
Jacksonville, FL 32206

26

63-851 / 630

PAY TO THE ORDER OF _Marysville Power Company_ $ 87 60/100

Eighty-seven and 60/100 ———————— DOLLARS

Sunshine State Bank
Jacksonville, Florida 32203

James Albens

⑆0630⑉0851⑆ 27659⑈0

d.

Billing Code	Billing Date	Amount
EL1	MAY 10	48.75
		Amount 48.75

Luis J. Luna
3124 Knott Ave.
Jacksonville, FL 33205

423

63-851 / 630

PAY TO THE ORDER OF _Marysville Power Company_ $ 48 75/100

Forty-eight and 75/100 ———————— DOLLARS

Sunshine State Bank
Jacksonville, Florida 32203

Luis J. Luna

⑆0630⑉0851⑆ 39814⑈6

e.

Billing Code	Billing Date	Amount
EL1	MAY 10	98.45
		Amount 98.45

Mr. & Mrs. Henry Jennings
2644 E. Sycamore
Jacksonville, FL 32214

181

63-851 / 630

June 10, 19 —

PAY TO THE ORDER OF *Marysville Power Company* $ *90 45/100*

Ninety and 45/100 —————————————— DOLLARS

Sunshine State Bank
Jacksonville, Florida 32203

Henry Jennings

⑈0630⑈0851⑈ 29471⑈1

---

f.

Billing Code	Billing Date	Amount
EL1	MAY 10	115.61
		Amount 115.61

H. Hassan
403 BrookHurst St.
Jacksonville, FL 32201

206

63-851 / 630

June 1, 19 —

PAY TO THE ORDER OF *Marysville Power Company* $ *115 61/100*

One hundred fifteen and 61/100 —————— DOLLARS

Sunshine State Bank
Jacksonville, Florida 32203

H. Hasson

⑈0630⑈0851⑈ 11842⑈6

---

g.

Billing Code	Billing Date	Amount
EL1	MAY 10	86.43
		Amount 86.43

Rick Macias
5010 6th Avenue
Jacksonville, FL 32215

29

63-851 / 630

June 13, 19 —

PAY TO THE ORDER OF *Marysville Power Company* $ *86 43/100*

Eighty - six and 43/100 —————————— DOLLARS

Sunshine State Bank
Jacksonville, Florida 32203

Rick Macias

⑈0630⑈0851⑈ 20300⑈9

---

h.

Billing Code	Billing Date	Amount
EL1	MAY 10	120.41
		Amount 120.41

Robert Foy
67 Rosewood Ln.
Jacksonville, FL 32210

47

63-851 / 630

June 10 19 —

PAY TO THE ORDER OF *Marysville Power Company* $ *120 41/100*

One hundred twenty and 41/100 —————— DOLLARS

Sunshine State Bank
Jacksonville, Florida 32203

Robert Foy

⑈0630⑈0851⑈ 91874⑈2

2. Prepare a payment slip for the checks below. Number the slips from 682. Explanation: payment on account. Date: August 1, 19—. Initial each slip.

a.

J.M. Hoot 604A Hacienda Ave. Mission City, CA 92656	**215** ₉₀₋₃₁₆₅ 1222

PAY
TO THE
ORDER OF *Harrison Hardware* $ *22 3¹/100*

June 22 19 —

Twenty – two and ³¹/100 ———— DOLLARS

Pacific Coast Bank
Laguna Beach, California 92652

J. M. Hoot

⑈1222⑈3165⑈ 29148⑈6

b.

M.J. Froelich 10 Blue Jay Ln. Laguna Beach, CA 92677	**29** ₉₀₋₃₁₆₅ 1222

PAY
TO THE
ORDER OF *Harrison Hardware* $ *45 ⁶⁰/100*

June 30 19 —

Forty – five and ⁶⁰/100 ———— DOLLARS

Pacific Coast Bank
Laguna Beach, California 92652

M. J. Froelich

⑈1222⑈3165⑈ 28654⑈0

c.

W.C. Bordoni	**87** ₉₀₋₃₁₆₅ 1222

PAY
TO THE
ORDER OF *Harrison Hardware* $ *19 ⁸⁶/100*

July 15 19 —

Nineteen and ⁸⁶/100 ———— DOLLARS

Pacific Coast Bank
Laguna Beach, California 92652

W. C. Bordoni

⑈1222⑈3165⑈ 28742⑈0

d.

D.P. Dezotell 544 Woodland St. Laguna Beach, CA 92651	**305** ₉₀₋₃₁₆₅ 1222

PAY
TO THE
ORDER OF *Harrison Hardware* $ *56 ⁰⁵/100*

August 1, 19 —

Fifty – six and ⁰⁵/100 ———— DOLLARS

Pacific Coast Bank
Laguna Beach, California 92652

D. P. Dezotell

⑈1222⑈3165⑈ 74159⑈9

3. As a cashier for the Ohio Electric Power Company, you receive the stubs and checks shown below.

Account No.: A5049	Date: 3/1/–
Amount Due	38.45

G. T. Swanson
4782 W. Highway
Columbus, OH 43214

Act. No. A5049

8002

25-366 / 412

PAY TO THE ORDER OF *Ohio Electric Power Company* $ 68 45/100

3/21 19 —

Sixty-eight and 45/100 ———————— DOLLARS

Columbus Bank & Trust
Columbus, OH 43210

G. T. Swanson

⑆0412⑈0366⑆ 67821⑈0

Account No.: B0037	Date: 3/1/–
Amount Due	35.90

Joy and Will Ashton
8065 Worth Rd.
Columbus, OH 43217

Act. No. B0037

225

25-366 / 412

PAY TO THE ORDER OF *Ohio Electric Power Company* $ 35 90/100

3/8 19 —

Thirty-five and 90/100 ———————— DOLLARS

Columbus Bank & Trust
Columbus, OH 43210

Joy Ashton

⑆0412⑈0366⑆ 54919⑈8

Account No.: C0062	Date: 3/1/–
Amount Due	78.45

S. M. Scorri
462 Birch St.
Columbus, OH 43211

Act. No. C0062

3009

25-366 / 412

PAY TO THE ORDER OF *Ohio Electric Power Company* $ 75 45/100

3/14 19 —

Seventy-five and 45/100 ———————— DOLLARS

Columbus Bank & Trust
Columbus, OH 43210

S. M. Scorri

⑆0412⑈0366⑆ 46729⑈8

Account No.: B2286	Date: 3/1/–
Amount Due	39.52

Maria and Jose Sanches
287 Birch St.
Columbus, OH 43211

3585

25-366 / 412

PAY TO THE ORDER OF *Ohio Electric Power Company* $ 39 52/100

3/19 19 – –

Thirty-nine and 52/100 ———————— DOLLARS

Columbus Bank & Trust
Columbus, OH 43210

Maria Sanches

⑆0412⑈0366⑆ 98402⑈0

a. Match each stub to its proper check. In your Activity Guide, write "OK" on each stub you match and make a note on the stub when you find an error. If the check amount differs from the stub amount, on the stub write the check number and the check amount. Do not write on the stubs in your textbook.

   NOTE: The company often reminds customers to write their account numbers on their checks, but customers sometimes forget to do so. Use account numbers, when provided, and check amounts to guide you in matching stubs and checks.

   b. Total all the stubs. Use the actual amounts of the checks received, the amounts that you wrote on the stubs.

   c. Total all the checks using the amount in words.

   d. Make sure that the total of the checks and the total of the stubs agree. If they do not, recheck your work.

   e. Make a list of the checks that do not have account numbers. On the list indicate (1) the check number, (2) the check amount, (3) the name of the customer, and (4) the account number that should have been written on the check.

MATH SKILLBUILDER

Skill: Using percentages.

Sample Problem: Convert the following percentages to decimal numbers:

a. 4%
b. $4\frac{1}{2}$%
c. $4\frac{3}{4}$%

Solution:

1. Place a decimal after the whole number in the percentage.

   a. 4 percent = 4.0 percent

2. If the percentage includes a fraction, express the fraction as a decimal.

   b. $4\frac{1}{2}$ percent = 4.5 percent

   c. $4\frac{3}{4}$ percent = 4.75 percent

3. Move the decimal two places to the left:

   a. 4.0 percent = 0.04

   b. 4.5 percent = 0.045

   c. 4.75 percent = 0.0475

Practice: Convert the following percentages to decimals:

1. 3 percent
2. $3\frac{1}{2}$ percent
3. $4\frac{3}{4}$ percent
4. 5 percent
5. $5\frac{1}{4}$ percent
6. $6\frac{1}{4}$ percent
7. $6\frac{3}{4}$ percent
8. 10 percent
9. $10\frac{1}{2}$ percent
10. $11\frac{1}{2}$ percent

Skill: Rounding amounts to the nearest cent.

Sample Problem: Round $6.1274 and $78.4837 to the nearest cent.

Solution:

1. When working with dollars and cents, the digit to be rounded is always the second digit to the right of the decimal point.

   $6.1274 $78.4837
      ↑   ↑
   Digit to be rounded   Digit to be
                             rounded

2. See if the next digit to the right is 5 or more or if it is less than 5.

   $6.127 $78.483
      ↑   ↑
   5 or more   Less than 5

3. Because the 7 in $6.127 is 5 or more, add 1 to the 2 and drop the 7: $6.13. Because the 3 in $78.483 is less than 5, simply drop the 3: $78.48.

4. Answers: $6.13, $78.48

Practice: Round the following amounts to the nearest cent.

1. $7.383
2. $18.432
3. $24.377
4. $74.383
5. $104.293
6. $281.435
7. $779.288
8. $1,041.345
9. $1,237.495
10. $1,383.699

VOCABULARY SKILLBUILDER

Read each of the following statements. From the words below each statement, choose the term that best matches the statement.

1. Payments received by a business for goods and services.
   cash receipts   cash on hand

2. A form that lists information about a sale of goods.
   credit card   sales slip

3. A form that lists information about a sale of services.

sales receipt   sales tax

4. A machine that uses pressure to record information on blank sales slips.

imprinting machine   credit card machine

5. A government fee added to the cost of a purchase.

tolls   sales tax

6. Amount of money in a cash drawer at the beginning of the day.

change fund   coins and currency

7. To offer money in payment.

tender   deposit

8. A check dated for some future time.

postdated   undated

9. A return of cash for a returned purchase.

canceled check   cash refund

10. Anything that confirms where merchandise was bought and how much was paid.

proof of purchase   stamped receipt

11. A form that lists the customer's name and address, the merchandise returned, and the full purchase price.

exchange form   refund slip

12. The part of a bill that the customer returns with payment.

stub   payment part

13. A form that is completed and sent to a customer when payment is received.

payment slip   check receipt

APPLICATION PROBLEMS

1. Use the following report to compute the total cash that Speciality and Gourmet Foods has on hand and in the bank.

SUMMARY SHEET

Balance in Capitol	
National Bank	$4,490.33
Coins on hand	83.90
Bills on hand	1,640.00
Checks received	3,448.20
Store coupons received	55.90
Bank credit card sales slips	2,400.12
Money orders	127.00

2. Check the computations on the following sales slip. Make any corrections necessary and find the correct total.

PRINT AND PHOTOCOPY SHOP
Detroit, MI

Cash Sales   Date 2/17/—

QUANTITY	ITEM	PRICE	AMOUNT	
55	#88254	.10	5	50
4	#83003	5.25	21	00
3	#AB898	43.20	86	40
12	#66635	5.95	71	40
		SUBTOTAL	184	30
		TAX AT 8%	14	74
		TOTAL	199	04

3. Compute the sales tax and total cost for each sale below.

Sale	Sales Amount	Tax Rate
a.	$75.00	6%
b.	$39.33	$7\frac{1}{2}$%
c.	$46.50	$8\frac{1}{2}$%
d.	$19.00	$6\frac{1}{2}$%
e.	$235.00	8%
f.	$80.00	$6\frac{1}{4}$%

4. Using the form in your Activity Guide, indicate the number of coins and bills you would use to make change for each of the following sales.

	Amount of Sale	Amount Tendered
a.	$ 2.27	$ 3.00
b.	6.19	10.00
c.	13.73	20.00
d.	9.14	20.04
e.	21.68	30.00
f.	16.51	20.01
g.	27.81	30.01
h.	34.66	50.00
i.	9.60	10.00
j.	8.14	20.00
k.	36.16	50.01
l.	7.80	10.00
m.	17.91	20.00
n.	36.55	40.00
o.	21.80	50.00

5. Compute the cash refund for each of the following returns. The sales tax rate is 6 percent. In all cases a sales slip accompanied the returns.

a. Jeans, $23.59

b. Shirt, $19.95

c. Shirt, $16.95

d. Jacket, $68

e. Tailored suit, $229.95

6. You are a receptionist for Dr. Warren Barr. These patients made payments for dental work. Use today's date.

Patient	Amount of Check Received
Inez Ortega	$45
Wanda Benares	36
William Cortez	58
Donna Mitchell	64

You prepared the following sales receipts:

To Donna Mitchell, 672, $64
To Inez Ortega, 673, $55
To Wanda Benares, 674, $36
To William Cortez, 675, $58

a. Add the amounts on the sales receipts.

b. Add the amounts on the checks.

c. Compare the total of the sales receipts with the total of the checks. **Note:** If the totals are not equal, explain why.

7. As a cashier for Eastern Utility Company, Chuck Wilasky received the bill stubs and checks shown on page 162.

a. Check the amount of each stub with the amount of the corresponding check. Note any differences.

b. Examine each check to see whether it is made out correctly and whether the amount in numbers is the same as the amount in writing. Note any differences on the stub.

c. Total the amounts on the stubs.

d. Total the amounts on the checks using the amounts in words.

e. Compare the two totals. If the totals are not equal, explain why.

Account No.: 10288	Date: 3/1/-
Amount Due	120.50

M.J. Colbury   *Account No. 10288*   **943**

25-366 / 412

April 1 19 —

PAY
TO THE
ORDER OF *Eastern Utility Company* $ 120 5%/100

One hundred forty and 5%/100 ———— DOLLARS

Eastern National Bank
Harrisburg, PA

M. J. Colbury

⑆0412⑈0366⑆ 305⑈613?

Account No.: 10083	Date: 3/1/-
Amount Due	48.49

P.D. Levitz   *Account No. 10083*   **412**

25-366 / 412

March 28 19 —

PAY
TO THE
ORDER OF *Eastern Utility Company* $ 48 49/100

Forty-eight and 49/100 ———— DOLLARS

Eastern National Bank
Harrisburg, PA

P. D. Levitz

⑆0412⑈0366⑆ 721⑈6244

Account No.: 10201	Date: 3/1/-
Amount Due	52.82

Celia Strassen   *Account No. 10201*   **698**

25-366 / 412

March 15, 19 —

PAY
TO THE
ORDER OF *Eastern Utility Company* $ 52 82/100

Fifty-two and 82/100 ———— DOLLARS

Eastern National Bank
Harrisburg, PA

Celia Strassen

⑆0412⑈0366⑆ 402⑈7210

Account No.: 10406	Date: 3/1/-
Amount Due	37.20

Jason Brukner   *Account No. 10406*   **715**

25-366 / 412

March 20 19 —

PAY
TO THE
ORDER OF *Eastern Utility Company* $ 37 7%/100

Thirty-seven and 7%/100 ———— DOLLARS

Eastern National Bank
Harrisburg, PA

Jason Brukner

⑆0412⑈0366⑆ 399⑈7645

CHAPTER 6

CASHIERS' ACTIVITIES

"I'm applying for a part-time job at Hugh's Market as a checkout cashier," said Tom Benton. "It looks like fun to operate a cash register. They can do all kinds of things, like figure the change and then print out reports. You meet a lot of nice people as a cashier and can learn how the business operates."

"I'll be operating a cash register too," said Sue Harko. "But I'm going to be at the service desk of Robertson's Department Store. I'll be taking in cash and checking out the credit of customers who want to pay by credit card. I found out that at the end of the day, you can get reports from cash registers on the amounts of cash and credit sales without using a calculator."

The cash register is one of the most popular and useful business machines. In this chapter you will learn how it operates. You will also learn to prepare some of the reports that a cashier is responsible for.

TOPIC I ■ USING ELECTRONIC CASH REGISTERS

GOALS

1. To identify the common features of electronic cash registers.
2. To select the correct cash register keys for routine sales.
3. To arrange coins, bills, and checks in cash-drawer compartments.

KEY TERMS

An *electronic cash register* is a machine that uses a computerlike processor to compute and record sales information.

A *keyboard* is that part of a cash register that contains the number keys and other keys needed to enter sales information.

A *cash drawer* is a place within the cash register with compartments for storing coins, bills, and checks.

A *cash register tape* provides customers with a printout of the items purchased and the costs.

WHAT IS AN ELECTRONIC CASH REGISTER?

A *cash register* is a machine that records the cost of a sale for both the customer and the business. Older models of cash registers simply provide a tape that shows the cost of each item, the tax (if

any), and the total. The tape also shows the date of the purchase. This tape is the customer's receipt. Each entry is also recorded in the machine. At the end of each day, the cashier can read and record the total of all sales that were registered that day. Then the cashier resets the machine to zero for the start of the next day.

Newer cash registers, such as the one shown in the margin, are *electronic.* They include the same electronic devices used to operate computers and calculators. Electronic cash registers do many different kinds of math calculations with ease.

Look at this tape from an electronic cash register.

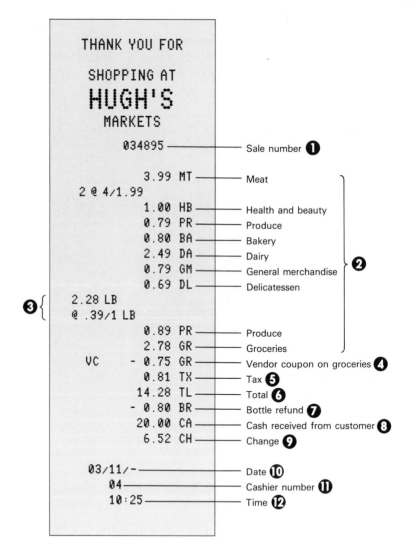

As you can see, this supermarket tape gives the customer more information than the cost and the date of the purchase:

1. It identifies the sale number: 034895.

2. It identifies each purchase by department such as meat or health and beauty.
3. It computes the cost of 2.28 pounds of produce at a rate of 39 cents a pound. The cashier merely enters the weight and the cost per pound. The register does the rest.
4. It deducts the value of any coupons the customer submits.
5. It computes the tax on taxable items only.
6. It prints the total of the sale.
7. It subtracts the bottle refund.
8. It tells how much money the customer tendered.
9. It computes the amount of change to be given to the customer.
10. It gives the date of purchase.
11. It identifies the cashier who handled the sale.
12. It gives the time of the sale.

Electronic cash registers have several advantages. They assist the cashier by making computations. They provide the customer with specific, clearly labeled information about each sale. Within electronic cash registers are duplicate tapes that provide the business with the same kind of information. These duplicate tapes, which are known as *detailed audit tapes*, will be discussed in Topic 4. As you can see, then, electronic cash registers are very useful to a business.

THE CASH REGISTER KEYBOARD

The keyboard of the electronic cash register is used to enter information about sales at the touch of a key. Tom Benton obtained the job he wanted as a checkout cashier at Hugh's Market. One thing he had to learn was the keyboard of his cash register.

Tom found the keyboard easy to learn when he divided it into five blocks, as shown on page 166.

Block 1 The 11 keys in the lower middle section are used for entering amounts of sales. These number keys are the first ones to be touched when entering the items a customer has purchased. The 00 key is used when Tom wants to enter an even dollar amount such as $1. He touches 1 and 00. This is faster than touching the 1 and then the 0 key twice.

Block 2 The keys on the left are for various functions. They are most often used after all the dollar amounts are entered. Can you find the abbreviation *Tend?* This means tendered, or given in

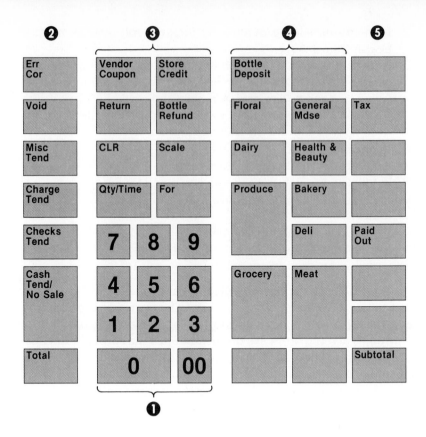

payment. Study the keys in the left column from the top down.

Err Cor is for the correction of errors.
Void is used to void, or cancel, an item that has been entered.
Tend keys are for entering the amount of various kinds of payments given by customers.
Total is used to find the total.

Block 3 Tom found that these eight keys are helpful for the following purposes:

Vendor Coupon is for a clipped coupon for price reduction.
Store Credit is used for a price discount on an item.
Return is used when a customer returns an item.
Bottle Refund is used when a customer brings in returnable bottles for credit.
CLR is used when the cashier wishes to correct an amount before the department key is touched. (CLR means clear.)
Scale is used when Tom has to weigh produce to compute the price.
Qty/Time is used when more than one item is sold or with the *for* key as described below.

For is used when a customer purchases one of something that is quoted at two, or three, for a certain price, as in the example "2 @ 4/1.99" on the tape shown on page 164.

Block 4 Bottle Deposit is used when a customer purchases beverages in returnable bottles. The nine department keys are used as the last step in recording an item sold. When Tom touches one of these keys, the register prints the transaction on the cash register slip. Two of the departments are grocery and meat. Can you find the other seven departments? The blank keys may be assigned new functions when needed.

Block 5 Tax is used when the cashier wants the tax computed. The cashier uses Paid Out when giving a customer cash on a returned item. Subtotal is touched when the cashier or the customer wishes to see the total so far.

EXAMPLES OF TRANSACTIONS

Here are some examples of transactions that Tom had to record.

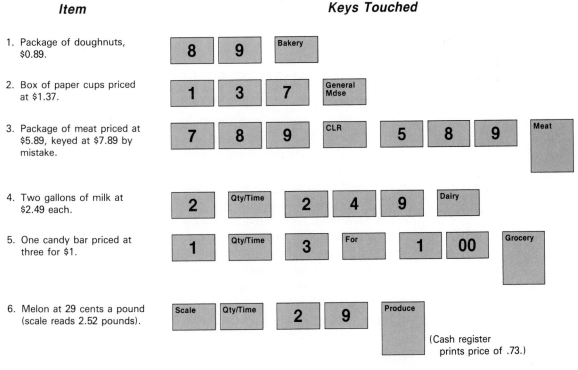

Item	Keys Touched

1. Package of doughnuts, $0.89.
2. Box of paper cups priced at $1.37.
3. Package of meat priced at $5.89, keyed at $7.89 by mistake.
4. Two gallons of milk at $2.49 each.
5. One candy bar priced at three for $1.
6. Melon at 29 cents a pound (scale reads 2.52 pounds). (Cash register prints price of .73.)

Item	**Keys Touched**

7. Bottle of cola for $1.19.

1	1	9	Grocery

8. Bottle deposit of 10 cents.

1	0	Bottle Deposit

9. Coupon for 25-cent discount on cola.

2	5	Vendor Coupon	Grocery

10. Customer decides to return paper cups at $1.37.

1	3	7	Return	General Mdse

11. Find the tax. (The cash register is set for 6 percent sales tax.)

Tax

(Cash register prints .83.)

12. Find the total.

Total

(Cash register prints 14.69.)

13. Customer offers $20.

2	0	00	Cash Tend/ No Sale

(Cash register prints 5.31 change due.)

OTHER CASH REGISTER FEATURES

The display window allows the customer to see the price of each item as the checkout cashier enters it on the keys.

The cash drawer has compartments for storing coins, bills, and checks. The compartments for coins are arranged from left to right: half-dollars, quarters, dimes, nickels, and pennies. The compartments for bills are arranged from left to right: rolls of coins, twenties, tens, fives, and ones. Checks and coupons may be placed in the large back compartment. In some parts of the country half-dollars are not often used. The half-dollar compartment may then be used for rolls of coins.

Universal Product Code (UPC): Coded lines and numbers printed on products which identify the manufacturer and specific item.

Some electronic cash registers have an attached scanner that can read the *Universal Product Code (UPC)* which is printed on grocery packages. The UPC has lines and numbers which identify the manufacturer and the specific product. The scanner is usually built into the counter.

Guard bars to assure readability
of UPC symbols.

21275 13500

Manufacturer's 5 digit
number coded into
symbols.

Product identification
(size, flavor, color).

The checkout cashier passes each item over the face of the scanner, with the UPC facing down, until a tone sounds on the register. The tone means that the scanner has read the UPC, looked up the price in the computer, and recorded the sale in the register.

Scanner: Reads the UPC on items passed over it and sends the information to a computer to find the price.

Check Your Reading

1. What part of the cash register is used to make entries?

2. In what part of the cash register do you keep the money received from customers?

3. What is the name of the device that reads the Universal Product Code?

4. List from left to right the compartments in the cash drawer for coins.

5. List from left to right the compartments in the cash drawer for bills and rolled coins.

Exercises for Topic 1

1. Write in order what keys you would touch for the following: (Refer to the cash register keyboard on page 166.)

   a. One head of lettuce at 79 cents.
   b. Two loaves of bread at $1.19 each.
   c. One can of peaches at $1.07.
   d. Two quarts of milk at 69 cents each.
   e. Two bottles of ginger ale at 99 cents each.

f. Two bottles, deposit of 10 cents each.
g. One vendor coupon for bread at 10 cents.
h. A $10 bill offered in payment.
i. Three bottles returned at 10 cents each.
j. Customer wants one can of tomatoes at 97 cents taken off the amount already entered in the cash register.

2. Write in order what keys you would touch for the following: (Refer to the cash register keyboard on page 166.)

a. One tube of toothpaste at 98 cents.
b. One box of breakfast cereal at $1.45.
c. Package of meat for $5.76.
d. One bunch of radishes at 39 cents.
e. Three packages of noodles at 77 cents each.
f. One can of corn, priced at 2 for 97 cents.
g. One roll of paper towels at 99 cents.
h. Potatoes at 49 cents a pound.
i. A can of beans keyed at 89 cents, instead of 79 cents, by mistake (department not entered).
j. A $20 check offered in payment.

TOPIC 2 ■ USING SPECIALIZED CASH REGISTERS

GOALS

1. To describe the features of a fast-food restaurant cash register.
2. To identify the parts of a retail service center cash register.
3. To identify in order the steps for entering a sale on a specialized cash register.

KEY TERMS

A *service center* is a counter where sales and returns are processed in a retail store.

A *keyboard-display* contains all the number keys and function keys that are needed to ring up sales and a display window that shows the cashier each entry.

FAST-FOOD RESTAURANT CASH REGISTERS

To fill orders very quickly, fast-food restaurants look for ways to save time. One way they save time is by using specialized cash registers—cash registers with keyboards that are tailored to the needs of each restaurant.

The removable panels for this electronic cash register are changed for breakfast, lunch, and dinner menus.

When Tom Benton visited Wally's Place, a fast-food restaurant in his city, he talked with his friend Mark Alvarez, the assistant manager at Wally's. Mark showed Tom the special electronic cash register shown above.

Each key on this cash register is for an item that Wally's sells. To record the sale of a double burger, the cashier touches only one key: the DOUBLE BURGER key. Because the register stores prices in its computer memory, it records the correct amount. The cash register flashes the item name and price on a display screen for the customer to see. In addition, the register prints "DOUBLE BURGER" on the customer's tape to help identify the item.

Mark explained how the keyboard can easily be changed for a different menu. Each cash register has a different panel for breakfast, lunch, and dinner. At the beginning of the day, Mark prepares each machine by placing the breakfast keyboard panel on the cash register. Before lunch, he removes the breakfast panel and places the lunch menu panel on the register. Each time Mark changes a menu panel, he also changes the setting of the cash register to match the new panel. Sample panels are shown on page 172.

With the breakfast menu panels in place, the cashiers are ready to begin. To record an order of apple pancakes, Mark touches the APPLE PANCAKE key on the top row. The register automatically en-

First Keyboard

Orange Juice	Grapefruit Juice	Tomato Juice	Melon	Coffee	Tea	Milk	Hot Choc.	Choc. Milk
Straw-berries	Orange Slices	Cold Cereal	Hot Cereal	Toast	Bagel	Plain Muffin	Raisin Muffin	Danish
One Egg	Two Eggs	Cheese Omelet	Western Omelet	Eggs Ben.	S. Dol. Pancs.	Straw. Panc.	Pecan Panc.	French Toast
Bacon	Sausage	Canadian Bacon	Ham	C. Beef Hash	Home Fries	French Fries	Donut	Choc. Donut
		Quantity	Clear Error	Delete Last Item	Cancel Exit	Void Item	Void Tran.	
		Special Promo	Aux. Sales	Screen	No Sale Data Entry	Price Look-Up	Paid Out	Tran. Code
		Open Disc.	7	8	9	Server #	Check #	Previous Balance
			4	5	6	Eat In	Carry Out	
		Coupon Food	1	2	3	Add Checks	Total	
		Coupon Bev.	0			Amount Tend.		

Second Keyboard

Ham Sand.	Am. Ch. Sand.	Sw. Ch. Sand.	Combo	Tuna Sand.	Chk. Salad Sand.	Turkey Sand.	R. Beef Sand.	P.&J. Sand.
Tuna Salad	Potato Salad	Coleslaw	Chk. Salad	Fruit Salad	Shrimp Salad	Veg. Salad	Pasta Salad	Egg Salad
Soup	Hot Turkey	Hot R. Beef	Veg.	Apple	Banana	Fruit Cup	Melon	Green Salad
Cake	Pie	Ice Cream	Jello	Fruit Juice	Cider	Milk	Coffee	Tea
		Quantity	Clear Error	Delete Last Item	Cancel Exit	Void Item	Void Tran.	
		Special Promo	Aux. Sales	Screen	No Sale Data Entry	Price Look-Up	Paid Out	Tran. Code
		Open Disc.	7	8	9	Server #	Check #	Previous Balance
			4	5	6	Eat In	Carry Out	
		Coupon Food	1	2	3	Add Checks	Total	
		Coupon Bev.	0			Cash Tend.		

ters the correct price, $2.49, and prints it on the customer's tape, as shown below.

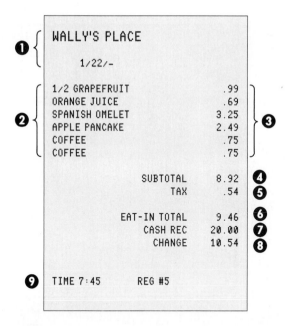

The tape shows the customer:

1. The name of the restaurant and the date.
2. The items ordered.
3. The price of each item.
4. The subtotal, which is the cost of all items purchased before tax is included.
5. The amount of the sales tax. Note, however, that the keyboard has no TAX key. The tax is computed automatically when the cashier touches one of the TOTAL keys.
6. The total. The tape identifies each total as either an Eat-In Total or a Carry-Out Total.
7. The cash received from the customer.
8. The customer's change.
9. The time of the sale and the register number.

The internal record for a fast-food cash register is very helpful. It can list the total sales for each category, such as burgers or fries. Therefore, it gives the restaurant both an inventory report and a sales report.

Inventory is the total number of items of each kind that a store or business has.

SERVICE CENTER CASH REGISTERS

In retail stores, a *service center* is a counter where sales and returns are processed. A service center handles all sales—cash, check, and credit card sales. To meet their special needs, retail stores use *service center cash registers*

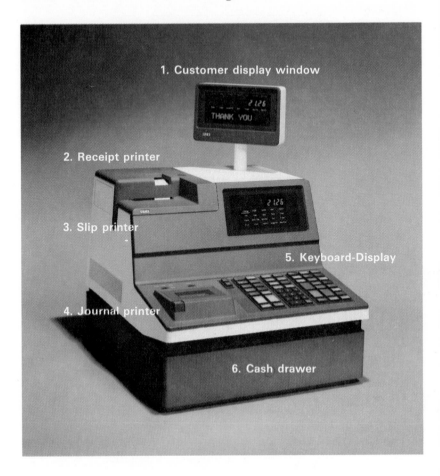

1. Customer display window
2. Receipt printer
3. Slip printer
5. Keyboard-Display
4. Journal printer
6. Cash drawer

Let's look at the parts of this cash register:

To *validate* means to approve a refund slip or credit memo and enter it into the cash register system.

A *slip printer* endorses checks and validates forms.

The *journal printer* provides the store with a printed record (or journal) of all transactions.

The *receipt printer* prints the customer's sales receipt.

The *customer's display window* shows each cash register entry.

1. **The Keyboard-Display.** The keyboard has all the keys needed to enter sales prices and tax for items purchased. As you will see later, it also has keys to identify the department for each item purchased. Just above the keyboard is the *display*, the window that shows each entry.
2. **The Slip Printer.** The slip printer endorses checks and validates forms such as credit memos and refund slips.
3. **The Journal Printer.** The journal printer creates the detailed audit tape, which is the tape the store keeps as a record (or journal) of all transactions.
4. **The Receipt Printer.** The customer's tape or receipt is printed by the receipt printer.
5. **The Customer's Display Window.** The display window shows each cash register entry. The window can be turned so that it faces the customer.

6. The Cash Drawer. The cash drawer has a removable tray that can be locked, allowing the cashier to take the tray with all its cash to the safe.

Take a close look at the special keyboard for a service center cash register.

Cash	Check	Bank Card	Gift Cert	1 Auto-motive	2 Sports
Sale	Refund	Lay Away	Lay Away PMT	3 House-wares	4 Health Beauty
QTY X	Clear	Void	Coupon	5 Shoes	6 Child's Clothing
Subtotal	**7**	**8**	**9**	7 Men's Clothing	8 Women's Clothing
Tax	**4**	**5**	**6**		
Total	**1**	**2**	**3**		
	0 0		**0**	9 Jewelry	10 Cameras

As the keyboard above shows, the register has number keys like the ones on other electronic registers. It also has function keys that instruct the register (CLEAR, VOID, SUBTOTAL) and that identify departments (AUTOMOTIVE, SPORTS).

Sue Harko, an experienced cashier at Robertson's Department Store, finds this cash register easy to use. For example, when a customer brings Sue four purchase items and one return item, Sue uses the price tags on the four items and the refund slip to record the transaction. The price tags and the refund slip are shown below.

Sue follows these steps:

1. She looks at the tag on the first item, a woman's blouse, and enters "$34.99," by touching 3 4 9 9.

2. Sue finds the department code number on the tag, 8, and touches key 8, WOMEN'S CLOTHING, on her register.
3. Sue records the sale of two pillows at $13.90 each by (a) entering 2, (b) touching the QTY X key, (c) entering $13.90, and, finally, (d) touching the key for department 3, HOUSEWARES.
4. Because she knows that the next item, an oil filter, is on sale for $12.70, she enters this amount, touches the SALE key, and then touches the key for department 1, AUTOMOTIVE. The cash register prints "SALE" next to this item so that it can be returned only at the sale price, not the regular price.
5. Sue takes the return item, a boy's shirt that is the wrong size, and enters $16.95. She puts a refund form in the slip printer and then touches the REFUND key and the key for department 6, CHILDREN'S CLOTHING. Sue attaches one copy of the validated refund form to the receipt she gives to the customer. She puts the other copy in her cash drawer.
6. Sue touches the SUBTOTAL key; the register shows a subtotal of $58.54.
7. She touches the TAX key; the register calculates the tax at 6 percent and prints the tax amount, $3.51.
8. Sue touches the TOTAL key; the register prints "$62.05."
9. The customer tenders a check for the full amount, $62.05. Sue places the check in the slip printer to have it endorsed; then she enters $62.05 and touches the CHECK key. The register prints the amount of the check on the tape and calculates a zero balance for the transaction.
10. Sue puts the check and one copy of the refund form in the cash drawer. She gives the customer's receipt and the other copy of the refund form to the customer. The customer's receipt is shown at the left.

```
        ROBERTSON'S

          7/23/-

           1:37


          34.99    DEPT 8
     2@ 13.90
          27.80    DEPT 3
     SALE 12.70    DEPT 1
     RETURN-16.95  DEPT 6

    SUBTOTAL 58.54

        TAX  3.51

      TOTAL 62.05

      CHECK 62.05

    BALANCE  0.00


      THANK YOU
```

Check Your Reading

1. To change the keys on a fast-food restaurant's cash register, cashiers use different ___?___ .

2. The keyboard for a service center cash register also includes a(n) ___?___ , which shows the cashier each item entered.

3. The part of the cash register that endorses checks and validates forms is the ___?___ .

4. The part of the cash register that prints the customer's tape is ___?___ .

5. The part of the cash register that maintains all the store's cash register records is the ___?___ .

6. The part of the cash register that shows customers each entry is the ___?___ .

7. The part of the cash register that contains a removable tray that can be locked is the ___?___ .

1. Refer to the breakfast menu of the fast-foods cash register on page 172. Find the space to touch for the following items by indicating the row number and the column number. For example, the answer to the first item is row 1, column 9.

Food Item
a. Orange juice
b. Cheese omelet
c. Coffee
d. Tomato juice
e. Silver dollar pancakes
f. Hot chocolate
g. Corned beef hash
h. Melon
i. Cold cereal
j. Chocolate milk

2. You are a cashier at Wally's Place. Use the breakfast menu on page 172 to list in order the keys you would touch to record each of the following orders:

   a. Pecan pancakes, bacon, milk, carry out, $10 tendered.
   b. Eggs benedict, grapefruit juice, hot tea, eat in, $20 tendered.
   c. One egg scrambled, home fries, coffee, carry out, $5 tendered.
   d. Raisin muffins, chocolate milk, eat in, $3 tendered.

3. Refer to the service center cash register keyboard on page 175 to write how you would enter the sales represented by the tags on the following page. List in order the keys you would touch, including the full names of the departments.

Also indicate when a refund form or check would be placed in the slip printer. Amount tendered is at the right.

a.

ROBERTSON'S	ROBERTSON'S	ROBERTSON'S	ROBERTSON'S
DEPT.2	DEPT.10	DEPT.4	DEPT.9
$19.89	$ 5.75	$ 3.97	$24.99

Cash: $60.00

b.

ROBERTSON'S	ROBERTSON'S	ROBERTSON'S	ROBERTSON'S	ROBERTSON'S
DEPT.7	DEPT.8	DEPT.3	DEPT.3	DEPT.5
$ 9.78	$33.89	$ 4.76	$ 4.76	$49.59

Check: $102.78

c.

ROBERTSON'S	ROBERTSON'S	ROBERTSON'S	ROBERTSON'S
DEPT.1	DEPT.6	DEPT.10	DEPT.8
$32.57	$13.89	$15.35	$54.99 (crossed out) SALE $39.95

Cash: $110.00

d.

ROBERTSON'S	ROBERTSON'S	ROBERTSON'S	ROBERTSON'S	ROBERTSON'S
DEPT.5	DEPT.7	DEPT.7	DEPT.7	DEPT.2
$37.79	$29.99	$29.99	$29.99	$17.45

Check: $145.21

e.

ROBERTSON'S	ROBERTSON'S	ROBERTSON'S	ROBERTSON'S	ROBERTSON'S
DEPT.4	DEPT.4	DEPT.6	DEPT.9	DEPT.3
$ 5.79	$ 5.79	$17.99 (crossed out) SALE $14.79	$35.75	$ 8.98 REFUND

Cash: $60.00

GOALS

1. To total currency and cash correctly.
2. To total checks and paid-out slips correctly.
3. To compute total cash receipts.

KEY TERMS

A *paid-out slip* is a cash register tape that records cash refunds and small cash expenses.

A *cashier's voucher* is a written form that records cash refunds and small cash expenses.

A *cash drawer count form* is a record of all the cash in the register.

PAID-OUT SLIPS

As you have seen, the cash register records all sales. The *detailed audit tape,* which is a record of all of the customers' tapes, provides the business with a record of all cash received.

But what about cash that is paid out? The cashier may refund money to a customer who returns an item. The cashier must account for that money. In addition, the cashier may be asked to pay for certain deliveries. Whenever the cashier pays out cash, that cash must be recorded on a paid-out slip.

A *paid-out slip* is a form that cashiers use to record refunds and expenses paid. If the cash register has a PAID-OUT key, the cashier simply uses this key to record the amount paid out. The cash register shown on page 166 has a PAID-OUT key. The cashier rings up the amount paid out and asks the customer to sign the tape. The cashier places the signed tape in the cash drawer and then gives the customer the refund.

```
           051451

            2.73
            0.08 TX
            2.81  TL
            2.81

      2 21   --
             02
      12: 40
```

Paid-out slips

CASHIER'S VOUCHERS

If the cash register does not have a key to record paid-out amounts, then the cashier must use a form such as the cashier's voucher on the next page.

The *cashier's voucher* also serves as a paid-out slip. It, too, records the amount of money that the cashier removed from the cash drawer. Again, note that the customer must sign the voucher.

CASHIER'S VOUCHER

NO. 42

CASHIER: *M. H.*   *February 21,* 19 —

PAY *Tom's Bakery Supplies* $ *197 78/100*

Nineteen and 78/100 ——————— DOLLARS

CHARGE ——————— ACCOUNT   NO. ———

DESCRIPTION *Bakery supplies purchased*

APPROVED FOR PAYMENT	RECEIVED PAYMENT
J. T.	*Marion Fletcher*

CASH DRAWER COUNT FORM

At the end of each day, the cashier must complete a cash drawer count form. On October 3, for example, Tom Benton completed this cash drawer count form.

CASH DRAWER COUNT

Date: *October 3,* 19 —

Number	Type of Cash	Amount
42	Pennies	42
38	Nickels	1 90
41	Dimes	4 10
52	Quarters	13 00
	Half-dollars	
21	$1 bills	21 00
16	$5 bills	80 00
46	$10 bills	460 00
19	$20 bills	380 00
	Checks	1,732 40
Total cash in drawer		2,692 82

Prepared by *T. B.*

As you can see, the form provides an easy way to record the contents of the cash drawer item by item. To complete the form, Tom enters the date. Then he lists the number of each coin and each bill in the drawer, as well as the number of checks in the drawer. He multiplies the number by the value. For example, Tom computed the total value of 52 quarters as follows:

$$52 \times \$0.25 = \$13$$

Tom entered "$13.00" in the Amount column.

Tom totaled all 22 checks and entered that figure in the Amount column. Finally, Tom added all the coins, bills, and checks and entered that amount on the "Total cash in drawer" line.

TOTAL CASH SALES

The total cash in the drawer at the end of the day is not all sales money. Remember: At the beginning of the day, the cashier begins with a change fund.

The money in the change fund is what the cashier had before the first sale. Therefore, to compute the total cash sales for the day, Tom Benton subtracts the amount of the change fund he had at the beginning of the day from the total cash in his register at the end of the day. His cash drawer count form (see page 180) shows $2,692.82 at the end of the day. His change fund was $200. With these figures, Tom computes the total cash sales for the day:

$2,692.82 Cash in drawer at end of day
−200.00 Change fund
$2,492.82 Cash sales for the day

The total cash sales for Tom's register was $2,492.82.

Check Your Reading

1. A cash register tape that records cash refunds and small cash expenses is a(n) ___?___ .

2. A written form that records cash refunds and small cash expenses is a(n) ___?___ .

3. The coins, bills, and checks in the register at the end of the day are recorded on a(n) ___?___ .

4. The cash in the drawer at the beginning of the day is the ___?___ .

5. To compute total cash sales, the cashier must subtract the ___?___ from the total cash in the drawer at the end of the day.

Compute the total of the coins and bills for both exercises below.

1.

Denomination	Number of Items
Penny	73
Nickel	51
Dime	23
Quarter	36
$1 bill	102
$5 bill	70
$10 bill	45
$20 bill	68

2.

Denomination	Number of Items
Penny	108
Nickel	82
Dime	45
Quarter	53
$1 bill	126
$5 bill	92
$10 bill	55
$20 bill	86

3. a. Prepare a cash drawer count for the following items. Use today's date and your initials.

Coins	Bills	Checks
38 pennies	27 $1 bills	$16.35
41 nickels	15 $5 bills	26.93
16 dimes	35 $10 bills	40.78
38 quarters	22 $20 bills	58.16

b. If your change fund was $150, what were the total cash sales?

4. a. Marie Gonzales is a cashier, and at the end of the day on March 4, she had the following money in her cash register. Complete a cash drawer count form for Marie.

Coins	Bills	Checks
29 pennies	36 $1 bills	$16.32
32 nickels	22 $5 bills	28.07
87 dimes	41 $10 bills	15.96
39 quarters	62 $20 bills	42.35

b. Marie began the day with a change fund of $200. Prepare a report of total cash sales.

TOPIC 4 ■ PROVING CASH

GOALS

1. To prepare a proof of cash report.
2. To determine whether actual cash received agrees with the detailed audit tape.

KEY TERMS

A *proof of cash* report is a form used to compare the actual amount of cash received with the amount of cash sales recorded by the cash register.

A *detailed audit tape* is the store's record of a cash register's transactions.

THE PROOF OF CASH REPORT

The *detailed audit tape* is a record that shows all the transactions made on a cash register. If Tom Benton begins the day with $200 in his change fund and his audit tape reads $2,000 in cash sales, then Tom should have $2,200 at the end of the day.

The process of checking that the register does have the right amount of cash at the end of the day is called proving the cash. To simplify the process, cashiers complete a *proof of cash* form. The one shown below was completed by Tom Benton on October 3.

Cash is not necessarily all in coins and bills. Tom usually has checks, coupons (which the store will convert to cash), and paid-out slips in addition to cash.

PROOF OF CASH

Date: *Oct. 3, 19—*

	Amount	
Total cash in drawer	2692 82	❶
Plus: coupons and paid out slips	27 58	❷
Total cash handled	2720 40	❸
Less: change fund	200 00	❹
Cash received, cashier's count	2520 40	❺
Cash received, detailed audit strip	2520 40	❻
Amount short or over	0 00	❼

Cash proved ☑
Cash short ☐
Cash over ☐

Prepared by *T.B.*

Let's see how Tom completes this form:

1. Tom records the total cash in his drawer, $2,692.82. He gets this figure simply by copying it from the cash drawer count form that he completed on October 3. See page 180.
2. Tom then adds his coupons and paid-out slips, which total $27.58, and enters this amount on the second line.
3. Tom adds the first two lines to get the total cash handled: $2,720.40.
4. Tom subtracts the change fund. On October 3, he started the day with $200.
5. After he subtracts the change fund, Tom sees that he should have received $2,520.40 during the day.
6. Tom checks the detailed audit tape and notes that the total cash received according to this tape is $2,520.40.
7. Because the amounts on lines 5 and 6 are the same, Tom writes 0.00 on line 7. Then he checks the Cash Proved box, to show that he has proved cash.

CASH SHORT AND CASH OVER

Sometimes, the total for Tom's actual cash and the total on the audit tape do not agree. A mistake in making change could have been the reason. Or perhaps the wrong keys were pressed for a transaction.

For example, if the amount of cash in the register is $2 less than the amount on the audit tape—it is short of the amount on the tape. Tom checks the Cash Short box.

When the actual amount of cash is less than the cash register total, cash is short.

Less: change fund	150	00
Cash received, cashier's count	1,521	85
Cash received, detailed audit strip	1,523	85
Amount short or over	2	00

Cash proved ☐
Cash short ☑
Cash over ☐

When the amount of actual cash is more than the audit tape amount, cash is over, and Tom checks the Cash Over box.

When the actual amount of cash is more than the cash register total, cash is over.

Less: change fund	150	00
Cash received, cashier's count	1,524	85
Cash received, detailed audit strip	1,523	85
Amount short or over	1	00

Cash proved ☐
Cash short ☐
Cash over ☑

Check Your Reading

1. The store's record of all cash register transactions is the ___?___ .

2. The process of checking to see that the register has the right amount of cash at the end of the day is called ___?___ .

3. The form that helps cashiers check the register amount against the actual amount of cash at the end of the day is the ___?___ form.

4. In addition to coins and bills, "cash" also includes these three items: (a) ___?___ , (b) ___?___ , and (c) ___?___ .

5. When the actual amount of cash in the register is more than the amount shown on the audit tape, cash is ___?___ .

6. When the actual amount of cash in the register is less than the amount shown on the audit tape, cash is ___?___ .

1. On March 16 you started the day with a $100 change fund. At the end of the day, your cash drawer contains the following items:

Coins	Bills	Checks	Other
61 pennies	78 $1 bills	$28.46	Coupons: $2.34
28 nickels	39 $5 bills	43.96	Paid-out slips: 5.15
45 dimes	51 $10 bills	21.17	
21 quarters	23 $20 bills	37.43	

The total cash sales amount on the detailed audit tape is $1,293.27. Prepare a proof of cash report. Use your initials.

2. On September 3 you started the day with $200 in your change fund. At the end of the day, your cash drawer contains the following items:

Coins	Bills	Checks	Other
39 pennies	49 $1 bills	$28.43	Coupons: $10.14
51 nickels	58 $5 bills	50.00	Paid-out slips: 8.23
61 dimes	35 $10 bills	39.62	
46 quarters	29 $20 bills	41.86	

The total cash sales amount on the detailed audit tape is $1,269.32. Prepare a proof of cash report. Use your initials.

3. On December 12 Mark Delgado started the day with a change fund of $150. When his department manager unlocked the cash register and looked at the detailed audit strip, she said, "Mark, see if your cash proves to $1,947.23." Here is what Mark has in his register:

Coins	Bills	Checks	Other
65 pennies	41 $1 bills	$28.70	Coupons: $16.35
28 nickels	62 $5 bills	40.00	Paid-out slips: 7.65
39 dimes	39 $10 bills	25.73	
18 quarters	57 $20 bills	51.96	
		36.47	

Prepare a proof of cash report for Mark.

4. One of Rochelle Hobson's duties at The Pet Palace is to prove cash at the end of the day. On July 6 the bills and coins in her cash drawer at the end of the business day are as follows:

Type of Bill	Number in Drawer	Type of Coin	Number in Drawer
$ 1	83	1¢	45
5	11	5	50
10	17	10	75
20	16	25	40

There are also checks for $10.49, $16.08, and $47.68 in the drawer. Rochelle started the day with a change fund of $100, and she made one cash refund for $6.25. The amount on the detailed audit strip is $628.95.

Prepare a cash drawer count form and a proof of cash report for Rochelle.

TOPIC 5 ■ DEPARTMENT SUMMARY REPORTS

GOALS

1. To prepare a daily register report.
2. To prepare a department summary report of cash sales.

KEY TERMS

A *daily register report* lists cash sales by department for a cash register.

A *checkout counter* is a work station where a cashier records customers' purchases.

A *department summary report* lists cash sales by department for all cash registers.

DAILY REGISTER REPORTS

As you learned in Topic 4, at the end of the day the cashier counts all the money in the register and prepares a proof of cash report. This report helps the store keep track of total cash sales for each day.

But knowing total cash sales is not enough for the store's manager. The manager also needs to know the amount of cash sales by department. To help provide this information, cashiers prepare daily register reports.

8:00 A.M. — 9:00 P.M.		
	Register No. 1	
Grocery		400.00
Produce		340.00
Meat		300.00
Dairy		120.00
Miscellaneous		210.00
Register Total		1,370.00

A *daily register report* lists the total sales recorded at one cash register, and it breaks down cash sales by department. At the Hugh's Market, where Tom Benton works, each cashier completes a register report at the end of the day. At the left is the daily register report that Tom completed on November 5.

Tom's report gives the total cash sales for the day, $1,370.00, collected at Register 1. But the report also lists cash sales for each of these five departments: grocery, produce, meat, dairy, and miscellaneous.

DEPARTMENT SUMMARY REPORT

Hugh's Market has six checkout counters. A *checkout counter* is a work station where a cashier records customers' purchases. Each checkout counter has a cash register.

At the end of the day, Tom and the other Hugh's Market cashiers give their daily register reports to the head cashier, Gloria Fuentes. Gloria takes these six register reports and prepares a *department summary report*

Cash Receipts Summary of 6 Cash Registers							
8:00 a.m. — 9:00 p.m.					Date:	1105 —	
			Cash Register Summary				Department
	Register 1	Register 2	Register 3	Register 4	Register 5	Register 6	Total
Grocery	400.00	520.00	930.00	510.00	750.00	200.00	3,310.00
Produce	340.00	600.00	710.00	430.00	510.00	90.00	2,680.00
Meat	300.00	410.00	480.00	310.00	420.00	80.00	2,000.00
Dairy	120.00	200.00	310.00	150.00	320.00	60.00	1,160.00
Miscellaneous	210.00	2,320.00	350.00	160.00	310.00	70.00	3,420.00
Register Total	1,370.00	4,050.00	2,780.00	1,560.00	2,310.00	500.00	12,570.00

To complete this form, Gloria copies the information from the six daily register reports. She labels the first column

"Register 1." Then she enters the total for "Grocery," "Produce," "Meat," "Dairy," and "Miscellaneous." Gloria repeats this process with the other daily register reports.

After Gloria enters the totals, she does the following:

1. She adds the numbers in each column and enters the column totals on the Register Total line. Beginning with the Register 1 column, she adds the numbers and checks her total, $1,370, against the total on Tom's daily register report. The totals agree. In the Register 1 column, she writes "$1,370." By doing this for each column, Gloria can be sure that she entered the numbers correctly.

2. Now Gloria adds the department amounts from left to right and writes the totals in the Department Total column. She begins with the Grocery line. Gloria finds the sum of these six numbers, $3,310. Then, in the Department Total column, she enters "$3,310" on the Grocery line. She does the same for the other departments.

3. a. After Gloria has entered all five department totals, she adds this column too:

$$
\begin{array}{r}
3,310 \\
2,680 \\
2,000 \\
1,160 \\
\underline{3,420} \\
12,570
\end{array}
$$

b. To double-check that $12,570 is correct, she adds all the numbers to the left of this total. That is, she adds the six register totals from left to right:

$$1,370 + 4,050 + 2,780 + 1,560 + 2,310 + 500 = 12,570$$

Gloria has proved in two ways that $12,570 is correct.

Check Your Reading

1. A work station where a cashier records customers' purchases is a(n) ___?___ .

2. A report that lists cash sales by department for one particular cash register is a(n) ___?___ report.

3. A report that lists cash sales by department for all cash registers is a(n) ___?___ report.

1. Check the totals of the following six daily register reports. Correct any errors on the reports in your Activity Guide.

8:00 A.M. — 9:00 P.M.	
	Register No. 1
Grocery	610.00
Produce	420.00
Meat	380.00
Dairy	250.00
Miscellaneous	210.00
Register Total	1,870.00

8:00 A.M. — 9:00 P.M.	
	Register No. 2
Grocery	940.00
Produce	560.00
Meat	410.00
Dairy	315.00
Miscellaneous	305.00
Register Total	2,530.00

8:00 A.M. — 9:00 P.M.	
	Register No. 3
Grocery	560.00
Produce	380.00
Meat	320.00
Dairy	280.00
Miscellaneous	165.00
Register Total	1,605.00

8:00 A.M. — 9:00 P.M.	
	Register No. 4
Grocery	410.00
Produce	290.00
Meat	307.00
Dairy	280.00
Miscellaneous	140.00
Register Total	1,427.00

8:00 A.M. — 9:00 P.M.	
	Register No. 5
Grocery	830.00
Produce	450.00
Meat	430.00
Dairy	380.00
Miscellaneous	210.00
Register Total	2,400.00

8:00 A.M. — 9:00 P.M.	
	Register No. 6
Grocery	740.00
Produce	410.00
Meat	390.00
Dairy	370.00
Miscellaneous	225.00
Register Total	2,135.00

2. Use the daily register reports you just checked to prepare a department summary report.

3. Prepare a department summary report using the following information:

   Cash Register 1: Grocery, $550; Produce, $430; Meat, $260; Dairy, $160; Miscellaneous, $380.
   Cash Register 2: Grocery, $630; Produce, $520; Meat, $340; Dairy, $210; Miscellaneous, $420.
   Cash Register 3: Grocery, $330; Produce, $420; Meat, $230; Dairy, $170; Miscellaneous, $240.
   Cash Register 4: Grocery, $720; Produce, $530; Meat, $310; Dairy, $230; Miscellaneous, $280.
   Cash Register 5: Grocery, $640; Produce, $425; Meat, $345; Dairy, $250; Miscellaneous, $320.

4. The cashier for Register 1 omitted the amount for miscellaneous. If the register total is correct, what is the amount for miscellaneous?

8:00 A.M. — 9:00 P.M.	
	Register 1
Grocery	525.00
Produce	321.50
Meat	234.70
Dairy	141.20
Miscellaneous	
Register Total	1,428.60

MATH
SKILLBUILDER

Skill: Totaling coins and bills.

Sample Problem: Total the following coins and bills:

72 pennies	12 one-dollar bills
35 nickels	9 five-dollar bills
22 dimes	11 ten-dollar bills
17 quarters	3 twenty-dollar bills

Solution:

1. Write the value of the coin or bill in decimals:

$$\text{Penny} = 0.01$$
$$\text{Nickel} = 0.05$$

2. Multiply the number of each coin or bill by its value, and write the totals in a column.

$$72 \times 0.01 = 0.72$$
$$35 \times 0.05 = 1.75$$

3. Add the column.

$$
\begin{array}{rcl}
72 \times 0.01 & = & 0.72 \\
35 \times 0.05 & = & 1.75 \\
22 \times 0.10 & = & 2.20 \\
17 \times 0.25 & = & 4.25 \\
12 \times 1.00 & = & 12.00 \\
9 \times 5.00 & = & 45.00 \\
11 \times 10.00 & = & 110.00 \\
3 \times 20.00 & = & \underline{60.00} \\
& & 235.92 \\
\end{array}
$$

Practice: Total the following coins and bills:

1. 22 pennies
   24 nickels
   31 dimes
   19 quarters
   21 one-dollar bills
   11 five-dollar bills
   21 ten-dollar bills
   9 twenty-dollar bills

2. 43 pennies
   53 nickels
   41 dimes
   21 quarters
   49 one-dollar bills
   19 five-dollar bills
   9 ten-dollar bills
   8 twenty-dollar bills

3. 19 pennies
   38 nickels
   45 dimes
   32 quarters
   27 one-dollar bills
   18 five-dollar bills
   21 ten-dollar bills
   13 twenty-dollar bills

VOCABULARY
SKILLBUILDER

Read each of the following statements. From the words below each statement, choose the term that best matches the statement.

1. A machine that uses a computerlike processor to compute and record sales data.

   electronic cash register
   imprinting machine

2. The part of a cash register that contains all the keys needed to enter sales information.

   scanner   keyboard

3. Part of a cash register that has compartments for storing coins, bills, and checks.

   slots   cash drawer

4. A printout that identifies for customers the items purchased and costs.

   cash register tape   refund slip

5. The part of the cash register that shows the customer the price of each item.

   keyboard   display window

6. The meaning of UPC.

   Universal Product Code
   Uniform Price Code

7. The device that reads the UPC.

   reader   scanner

8. A cash register tape that records cash refunds and small cash expenses.

   paid-out slip   expense slip

9. A written form that records cash refunds and small cash expenses.

   summary form   cashier's voucher

10. A record of all the cash in the register.

    cash-drawer count form   paid-out slip

11. Form used to compare actual amount of cash received with the amount of cash recorded by the cash register.

    proof of cash report   cashier's report

12. More actual cash received than is recorded by the cash register.

    cash over   cash short

13. The store's record of a cash register's transactions.

    deposit slip   detailed audit tape

14. A form that lists cash sales by department for all the cash registers in a store.

    daily register report
    department summary report

APPLICATION PROBLEMS

1. Write in order the keys you would touch for the following. Use the grocery store cash register keyboard on page 166.

   One dozen eggs, $1.07
   Oranges, 39 cents a pound
   Two cans of green beans, 3 for $1.19
   Vendor coupon for 25-cent discount on green beans
   Sliced luncheon meat from the delicatessen, 99 cents a pound
   Two boxes of tissues, 93 cents each
   One package of breakfast rolls, $1.59
   Two bottles returned, 15 cents each
   Customer returns shampoo, $1.29
   Customer tenders $25

2. Use the breakfast menu of the fast-food cash register on page 172 to list in order the keys you would touch for each of these orders.

   a. Two eggs over medium, link sausage, tomato juice, coffee, carry out, $10 tendered.

   b. Strawberry pancakes, ham, milk, eat in, $20 tendered.

   c. French toast, melon, hot chocolate, carry out, $5 tendered.

d. Corned beef hash and eggs, orange slices, hot tea, eat in, $20 tendered.

e. Canadian bacon, bagel, strawberries, coffee, eat in, $20 tendered.

3. Using the keyboard on page 175, write in order the keys you would touch, including department keys, to enter the sales shown below. Also indicate in order when a refund slip or a check is placed in the slip printer.

4. Burt Moskovitz was asked to compute the total coins, bills, and checks in the cash drawer. Complete a cash drawer count form for Burt using the form at the right.

Denomination	Number of Items	Checks
Penny	82	$45.00
Nickel	45	34.90
Dime	35	90.00
Quarter	23	17.35
$1 bill	115	
$5 bill	72	
$10 bill	55	
$20 bill	47	

a.

```
ROBERTSON'S        ROBERTSON'S        ROBERTSON'S

DEPT.3             DEPT.1             DEPT.1

$ 8.79            $12.45            $12.45
```
Check: $33.69

b.

```
ROBERTSON'S        ROBERTSON'S        ROBERTSON'S

DEPT.7             DEPT.9             DEPT.6

$48.79            $35.99            $ 8.44

                                     REFUND
```
Cash: $100

c.

```
ROBERTSON'S        ROBERTSON'S        ROBERTSON'S

DEPT.10            DEPT.10            DEPT.10

$ 5.49            $ 5.49            $ 5.49
```
Check: $16.47

Coins	Bills	Checks	Paid-Out Slips	Coupons	
35 pennies	45 $1 bills	$26.32	$3.79	40¢	25¢
40 nickels	36 $5 bills	29.07	8.43	25	30
65 dimes	72 $10 bills	35.96	2.28	60	50
44 quarters	36 $20 bills	40.00			

5. a. On March 4 Ramon Martinez, a cashier for Oak Street Auto Supplies, had the following in his cash register at the end of the day. Complete a cash drawer count form for Ramon.

b. Ramon began the day with a change fund of $200. The detailed audit tape shows cash receipts of $1,633. Prepare a proof of cash report.

6. One of Sabrina Jabar's duties at the Stop and Go Store is to prove the cash at the end of each day. On June 6, the bills and coins in her cash register are as follows:

Bills	Number in Drawer	Coins	Number in Drawer
$1	45	1¢	84
$5	22	5¢	46
$10	38	10¢	87
$20	51	25¢	68

The drawer also contains checks for $40, $25, and $38.56; coupons for $14.50; and paid-out slips for $21.25. Sabrina started the day with a $300 change fund. The detailed audit strip lists cash sales at $1,562.46.

a. Prepare a cash-drawer count.

b. Prepare a proof of cash report.

7. Janie Wautet, head cashier for the Farmers' Market, was asked to prepare a department summary using the following information.

Cash Register 1: Grocery, $820; Produce, $530; Meat, $390; Dairy, $220; Miscellaneous, $350.

Cash Register 2: Grocery, $620; Produce, $540; Meat, $460; Dairy, $320; Miscellaneous, $472.

Cash Register 3: Grocery, $430; Produce, $650; Meat, $610; Dairy, $270; Miscellaneous, $263.

Cash Register 4: Grocery, $820; Produce, $630; Meat, $510; Dairy, $415; Miscellaneous, $470.

Cash Register 5: Grocery, $670; Produce, $430; Meat, $320; Dairy, $365; Miscellaneous, $325.

Prepare the department summary report for Janie. Be sure to prove your total.

CHAPTER 7

RECORDS FOR SMALL BUSINESSES

Many of the new jobs in our country are in small businesses. The records kept by small businesses are similar to those you have already studied for individuals and families. But businesses usually need a more complete recordkeeping system. In this chapter you will study some of the records used by small businesses.

TOPIC 1 ■ CLASSIFIED CASH BOOK

GOALS

1. To record receipts and payments in a classified cash book.
2. To prove and close the classified cash book.

KEY TERMS

A *classified cash book* is a record that groups similar cash receipts and similar cash payments together.

Proving means checking to see that the sum of the subtotals equals the total and that the classified cash book balance equals the checkbook balance.

Closing means computing the ending and beginning balances of the classified cash book.

Ready-made system: Blank forms available from office supply stores.

It can take a lot of time and effort to establish a special recordkeeping system for a business. Therefore, many small businesses, such as restaurants, hairstyling salons, service stations, and doctors' offices use ready-made systems.

An example of a ready-made recordkeeping system is the classified cash book. The *classified cash book* is a record of all cash transactions, both cash receipts and cash payments, for each business day. Classifying information means arranging it in different categories. This is the purpose of the classified cash record. All similar cash receipts and cash payments are classified; that is, grouped together. In Chapter 3, you saw how a classified cash book can be used for personal recordkeeping.

Classified cash books are made to meet the special needs of different kinds of businesses. The classified cash book is divided into columns. These columns have headings that show what type of cash payment or cash receipt should be entered in each column. The types of headings depend on the business which uses the record. A business can purchase the type of classified cash book that fits the number of receipt (income) and payment (expense) categories the business uses.

CLASSIFIED CASH BOOK ENTRIES

Laura Cinalli owns a small business named Video World. Her business has video equipment (cassette recorders and cameras) and videocassette tapes which are rented by customers. Video World's electronic cash register classifies and labels each income transaction as equipment rental or tape rental and totals each type of receipt. Laura uses a ready-made classified cash book that has columns for two types of income.

Video World's payments for expenses are classified in six categories: Advertising, Miscellaneous, Repairs, Salaries, Supplies, and Utilities. Laura's classified cash book has six columns for expenses so she can put each type of expense in a separate column. Data for these columns is taken from the checkbook stubs.

Here are the steps Laura follows in making entries in the classified cash book. As you read the steps, look at Video World's classified cash book for June, which is shown on pages 198–199.

1. Laura writes the business name, the month, the page number, and the income and expense accounts at the top of the form.
2. The first entry of the month is the cash balance. The amount of the beginning cash balance is taken from the last check stub in the checkbook. She enters the date, June 1, 19—, in the Date column and the word ''Balance'' and the cash balance of $9,547.66 in the Explanation column.
3. The amount of the cash receipts is entered at the end of each business day. This information is taken from the detailed audit strip of the electronic cash register. On June 1, Laura entered ''Daily receipts'' in the Explanation column and the total receipts of $781.50 in the Cash Receipts column. She then wrote the subtotals of $293.75 and $487.75 in the Equipment and Tapes columns to show the amount of income in each category.
4. Laura records payments from the information on Video World's checkbook stubs on the day she issues each check. On June 1, she entered a payment to A-1 Office Supply for station-

Video World				CLASSIFIED CASH	
DATE	EXPLANATION	CASH RECEIPTS	Income Accounts		
			Equipment	Tapes	
June 19—	1 Balance $9,547.66				
	1 Daily receipts	781 50	293 75	487 75	
	1 A-1 Office Supply				
	2 Daily receipts	828 65	304 61	524 04	
	2 Station KDGB				
	2 Midland Phone Co.				
	3 Daily receipts	842 41	322 76	519 65	
	3 U.S. Postal Service				
	4 Daily receipts	703 27	271 08	432 19	
	4 Carpet City				
	4 Reagal Sign Co.				
	5 Daily receipts	715 68	265 51	450 17	
	5 Exeter Cable TV				
	5 Dayton Electronics				
	6 Daily receipts	776 96	280 80	496 16	
	6 Kraft Supply Co				
	7 Daily receipts	847 23	313 11	534 12	
	7 Apex Payroll Service				
June	8 Balance $10,917.18	5495 70	2051 62	3444 08	

ery. She wrote "A-1 Office Supply" in the Explanation column and "619" in the Check Number column. The amount of the payment, $78.40, was recorded in two places: the Cash Payments column and the expense column for Supplies.

5. She recorded the remaining entries for the week of June 1 through 7. On June 7 she wrote a check to Apex Payroll Service for salaries. Apex keeps payroll records for Video World and prepares individual salary checks.

PROVING AND CLOSING THE CLASSIFIED CASH BOOK

Laura proves and closes the classified cash book every week. On June 7, she proved and closed the book for the week of June 1 through 7. Here are the steps she followed:

1. She drew a rule under all the columns except the Explanation

BOOK FOR _____June_____, 19 – –   Page ___1___

CHECK NO.	CASH PAYMENTS	Expense Accounts						
		Advertising	Miscellaneous	Repairs	Salaries	Supplies	Utilities	
								1
								2
619	78 40					78 40		3
								4
620	326 50	326 50						5
621	218 15						218 15	6
								7
622	180 00		180 00					8
								9
623	119 00			119 00				10
624	111 71	111 71						11
								12
625	63 50						63 50	13
626	426 00			426 00				14
								15
627	124 47					124 47		16
								17
628	2478 45				2478 45			18
	4126 18	438 21	180 00	545 00	2478 45	202 87	281 65	19
								20
								21

and Check Number columns. She added and pencil-footed each amount column of the cash book.

2. Laura proved the total of the Cash Receipts column by adding the totals of the Equipment and Tapes columns ($2,051.62 + $3,444.08 = $5,495.70).

3. She proved the total of the Cash Payments column by adding the totals of all the expense columns ($438.21 + $180.00 + $545.00 + $2,478.45 + $202.87 + $281.65 = $4,126.18).

4. Laura found the ending cash balance using the following procedure:

   a. She added the beginning cash balance ($9,547.66) to the Cash Receipts total ($5,495.70) to find the total cash available for the week ($9,547.66 + $5,495.70 = $15,043.36).

   b. She subtracted the Cash Payments total ($4,126.18) from the total cash available for the week ($15,043.36) to find the ending cash balance ($15,043.36 − $4,126.18 = $10,917.18).

5. She proved the ending cash balance of $10,917.18 by comparing this amount with the checkbook balance. These two totals

Pencil-footing means adding the numbers in the column and writing the sum in small numbers as a check on the final total.

Chapter Seven: RECORDS FOR SMALL BUSINESSES ■ **199**

should be the same. Video World's checkbook stub showed a balance of $10,917.18 at the close of business on June 7, which is the same as the ending cash balance from the classified cash book. Laura's cash book was proved for the week.

6. To close the cash book, Laura entered the totals of all the columns in ink. Then she drew a double rule under all the columns except the Explanation and Check Number columns.

7. To complete the closing process, Laura prepared the cash book for the next week's entries. First she entered the date, June 8, in the Date column and the beginning cash balance for the new week, $10,917.18, in the Explanation column. The beginning cash balance for the new week is the ending cash balance from the last week.

Check Your Reading

1. What is a classified cash book?

2. What does "proving" mean?

3. What is the term that means computing ending and beginning balances?

4. The two most important kinds of entries in a classified cash book are cash ___?___ and cash ___?___ .

Exercises for Topic I

1. Set up page 2 of Video World's classified cash book for June by listing the business name, month, page number, column headings, and beginning balance. The checkbook stub and previous cash book show a balance of $8,693.80 at the beginning of the day on June 15.

   a. Record the transactions for June 15 through June 21. Number the checks in order beginning with Check 638.
   b. Prove and close the classified cash book, and enter the cash balance as of June 22.

   June 15 Recorded daily receipts of $287 for equipment and $492.16 for tapes.
       15 Paid $48 to Shoppers' Weekly for advertising.
       16 Recorded daily receipts of $314.65 for equipment and $518.70 for tapes.
       16 Paid $83.75 to City Water Department for water bill (Utilities).

17   Recorded daily receipts of $335.80 for equipment and $478.78 for tapes.

17   Paid $487.50 to Dayton Electronics for repairs.

18   Recorded daily receipts of $263.75 for equipment and $457.20 for tapes.

18   Paid $92.72 to Kraft Supply Company for computer paper.

19   Recorded daily receipts of $270.95 for equipment and $530.45 for tapes.

19   Paid $365.50 to *News Leader* for advertising.

20   Recorded daily receipts of $315.60 for equipment and $488.19 for tapes.

20   Paid $216.75 to Video Cameras, Inc., for camera repairs.

21   Recorded daily receipts of $323.90 for equipment and $510.25 for tapes.

21   Paid $2,506.45 to Apex Payroll Service for salaries.

(Hint: Video World's check stub balance at the end of the day on June 21 is $10,305.51.)

c. Record the transactions for June 22 through June 28.
d. Prove and close the classified cash book, and enter the balance as of June 29.

June 22   Recorded daily receipts of $268.75 for equipment and $460.18 for tapes.

22   Paid $317 to Ace Manufacturing for repairs.

23   Recorded daily receipts of $294.60 for equipment and $495.76 for tapes.

23   Paid $116.90 to A-1 Office Supply for office supplies.

24   Recorded daily receipts of $240.65 for equipment and $435.85 for tapes.

25   Recorded daily receipts of $285.40 for equipment and $435.85 for tapes.

25   Paid $345.60 to United Electric for electric bill (Utilities).

25   Paid $120 to U.S. Postal Service for postage (Miscellaneous).

26   Recorded daily receipts of $306.45 for equipment and $507.60 for tapes.

26   Paid $298 to Station KDGB for radio commercials (Advertising).

27   Recorded daily receipts of $275.35 for equipment and $465.44 for tapes.

28 Recorded daily receipts of $311.55 for equipment and $517.80 for tapes.

28 Paid $58.75 to Kraft Supply Company for computer paper (Supplies).

28 Paid $2,465.90 to Apex Payroll Service for salaries.

2. Alan Chu owns a food service business named Oriental Specialties. The business offers catering services and also has a small restaurant. Alan keeps a classified cash book that has columns for two types of income: Catering and Restaurant. The cash payments for expenses are classified in six categories: Advertising, Food Purchases, Miscellaneous, Salaries, Supplies, and Utilities. Alan proves and closes the cash book twice a month. The cash balance at the opening of business on July 1 is $5,376.90.

a. Set up a classified cash book for Oriental Specialties for July by listing the business name, date, page number, column headings, and beginning balance.

b. Record the following transactions for the period from July 1 through July 15. Number the checks in order beginning with Check 384.

c. Prove and close the classified cash book, and enter the balance as of July 16.

July 1 Recorded daily receipts of $145.50 for catering and $792.56 for restaurant.

1 Paid $1,368.90 to Union Power Company for electric bill (Utilities).

2 Recorded daily receipts of $817.90 for restaurant.

2 Paid $62.50 to *Daily News* for advertising.

3 Recorded daily receipts of $225.00 for catering and $748.77 for restaurant.

4 Recorded daily receipts of $890.38 for restaurant.

4 Paid $2,235.90 to Central Payroll Service for salaries.

5 Recorded daily receipts of $902.40 for restaurant.

5 Paid $178.39 to Adams Office Supply for supplies.

5 Paid $975.63 to Atlantic Seafood Company for food purchases.

6 Recorded daily receipts of $317.80 for catering and $768.14 for restaurant.

6 Paid $225 to Al's Cleaning Service for carpet cleaning (Miscellaneous).

7 Recorded daily receipts of $837.85 for restaurant.

7 Paid $663.40 to Miller's Produce for food purchases.

8 Recorded daily receipts of $910.22 for restaurant.

8 Paid $438.95 to Oven Fresh Bakery for food purchases.

9 Recorded daily receipts of $185 for catering and $863.75 for restaurant.

10 Recorded daily receipts of $95.75 for catering and $724.36 for restaurant.

10 Paid $118.75 to City Water Service for water bill (Utilities).

11 Recorded daily receipts of $876.19 for restaurant.

11 Paid $2,268.35 to Central Payroll Service for salaries.

12 Recorded daily receipts of $798.66 for restaurant.

12 Paid $285.75 to Station WLIR for radio commercials (Advertising).

13 Recorded daily receipts of $940.87 for restaurant.

14 Recorded daily receipts of $274.50 for catering and $765.95 for restaurant.

14 Paid $419.88 to Kitchen Supply, Inc., for paper products (Supplies).

14 Paid $337.16 to Gourmet Foods for food purchases.

15 Recorded daily receipts of $165 for catering and $837.86 for restaurant.

15 Paid $2,618.58 to Wholesale Grocery Company for food purchases.

15 Paid $50 to United Charities as a contribution (Miscellaneous).

d. Set up page 2 of Oriental Specialties' classified cash book for July.

e. Record the transactions below for the last half of July.

f. Prove and close the classified cash book and enter the cash balance as of August 1.

July 16 Recorded daily receipts of $216.80 for catering and $736.76 for restaurant.

16 Paid $379.18 to Lee's Catering Supply for supplies.

17 Recorded daily receipts of $877.90 for restaurant.

17 Paid $3,963.88 to Sam's Meat Market for food purchases.

18 Recorded daily receipts of $428 for catering and $837.16 for restaurant.

18   Paid $203.85 to Midland Phone Company for telephone bill (Utilities).

18   Paid $2,305.18 to Central Payroll Service for salaries.

19   Recorded daily receipts of $797.43 for restaurant.

20   Recorded daily receipts of $813.65 for restaurant.

20   Paid $56.50 to *Shoppers' News* for advertising.

21   Recorded daily receipts of $195.50 for catering and $778.41 for restaurant.

21   Paid $736.45 to Miller's Produce for food purchases.

22   Recorded daily receipts of $845.37 for restaurant.

22   Paid $210 to Al's Cleaning Service for window washing (Miscellaneous).

22   Paid $267.79 to Kitchen Supply, Inc., for supplies.

23   Recorded daily receipts of $903.68 for restaurant.

24   Recorded daily receipts of $312.80 for catering and $866.92 for restaurant.

24   Paid $503.65 to Oven Fresh Bakery for food purchases.

25   Recorded daily receipts of $136 for catering and $783.62 for restaurant.

25   Paid $2,216.95 to Central Payroll Service for salaries.

26   Recorded daily receipts of $945.16 for restaurant.

27   Recorded daily receipts of $823.73 for restaurant.

27   Paid $678.38 to National Gas Company for gas bill (Utilities).

28   Recorded daily receipts of $784.17 for restaurant.

29   Recorded daily receipts of $245 for catering and $873.95 for restaurant.

29   Paid $933.49 to Sunlight Dairy for food purchases.

30   Recorded daily receipts of $866.38 for restaurant.

30   Paid $315.50 to Station WLIR for radio commercials (Advertising).

31   Recorded daily receipts of $903.19 for restaurant.

31   Paid $46.90 to Speedy Delivery for package delivery (Miscellaneous).

1. To use classified cash book totals to calculate estimated receipts and payments for a later budget period.
2. To total and prove a small business budget spreadsheet.
3. To prepare a budget analysis for a small business.

A *budget* is a financial plan which includes estimated receipts and payments.

Cash flow refers to the increases and decreases in the amount of cash on hand as a result of receipts and payments within a time period.

An *estimate* is a calculation based on opinion or previous data.

A *spreadsheet* is a form that has columns and rows for entering data.

A *budget analysis* is a comparison of estimated and actual receipts and payments.

PREPARING A BUDGET SPREADSHEET

Like individuals and families, small businesses use budgets to help them manage their finances. A *budget* is a written plan of the amounts of money the business expects to receive and pay out during a future period of time, such as a month or a year. Using a budget can help a business study its cash flow to be sure that there are always enough receipts to make the payments. A budget can also give the business owner information to use in making business decisions.

Because a budget is a plan for a future period of time, the amounts in the budget can only be the owner's best guess of what the receipts and payments will be. To make the budget as accurate as possible, the owner's estimate of these amounts is usually based on the actual receipts and payments from a previous time period. For example, the owner might estimate that the utilities payments would be $50 more than the previous month or that the sales receipts would be 10 percent higher than the same month last year.

A form which includes columns for actual and estimated receipts and payments could be called a *budget spreadsheet*. A *spreadsheet* is a form that has columns and rows for entering data.

Don Volhein owns a food service business named Country Kitchen. Don proves and closes his classified cash book at the end of each month instead of twice a month as was done by Oriental

Specialties. Don prepared a budget spreadsheet for Country Kitchen for the first quarter of next year: January, February, and March. As a basis for his estimates, Don used the totals from his classified cash book for the first three months of last year. Because Don's business had been growing steadily, he estimated that the receipts and payments for next year would be 10 percent higher than they were for last year.

❶ *Country Kitchen*
Budget Spreadsheet
1st Quarter, 19—   **❷**

DESCRIPTION	January LAST YEAR ACTUAL	January NEXT YEAR ESTIMATE	February LAST YEAR ACTUAL	February NEXT YEAR ESTIMATE	March LAST YEAR ACTUAL	March NEXT YEAR ESTIMATE	1st Quarter TOTAL ESTIMATE	
Receipts								
Catering	$ 5,672	$ 6,239	$ 4,836	$ 5,320	$ 5,937	$ 6,531	$ 18,090	**❻**
Restaurant	18,387	20,226	16,498	18,148	21,314	23,445	61,819	
Total Receipts	$ 24,059	$ 26,465	$ 21,334	$ 23,468	$ 27,251	$ 29,976	$ 79,909	
Payments								
Advertising	$ 553	$ 608	$ 418	$ 460	$ 635	$ 699	$ 1,767	
Food Purchases	9,074	9,981	7,687	8,456	9,368	10,305	28,742	
Miscellaneous	375	413	342	376	416	458	1,247	
Salaries	7,216	7,938	6,735	7,409	7,488	8,237	23,584	**❼**
Supplies	783	861	523	575	843	927	2,363	
Utilities	1,668	1,835	1,389	1,528	1,731	1,904	5,267	
Total Payments	$ 19,669	$ 21,636	$ 17,094	$ 18,804	$ 20,481	$ 22,530	$ 62,970	
Balance	$ 4,390	$ 4,829	$ 4,240	$ 4,664	$ 6,770	$ 7,446	$ 16,939	**❽**

❸ (left margin marker)   **❹** **❺** (bottom markers)

Look at the Country Kitchen budget spreadsheet above as you read the steps Don followed in developing it.

1. Don wrote the name of the business (Country Kitchen) and the name of the form (Budget Spreadsheet) in the heading. He also listed the time period for which the budget was made (1st Quarter, 19—).
2. He wrote the words "January," "February," "March," and "1st Quarter" as column headings. There are two money columns for each month, one for the actual figure from last year and one for the estimate for the next year. The last money column lists the total estimate for the first quarter.

3. In the Description column Don wrote the two major classifications (Receipts and Payments) and the names of the individual income and expense accounts under each. He also labeled a row for total receipts, one for total payments, and one for balance.

4. Don listed the classified cash book totals for January, February, and March of last year as the amounts for the Last Year Actual columns. When he entered the figures on the budget spreadsheet, Don rounded the numbers and listed them as whole-dollar amounts. For example, $5,672.13 was listed as $5,672 and $18,386.96 was listed as 18,387.

To round an amount to the nearest whole dollar:

1. Look at the digit immediately to the right of the decimal point.
2. If the digit is 4 or less, simply drop the decimal point and the digits after it.
3. If the digit is 5 or more, increase the digit to the left of the decimal point by 1. Then drop the decimal point and the numbers after it.

The Math Skills Builder section at the end of this chapter will help you in rounding amounts to the nearest dollar.

---

5. He calculated the estimates for January, February, and March of next year. Because he had estimated that the receipts and payments would increase by 10 percent, Don multiplied each actual amount by 1.1 to get the estimated amount (100% + 10% = 110%, or 1.1). For example, $5,672 × 1.1 = $6,239.20. Don then rounded the amount to the nearest whole dollar, so $6,239.20 was listed as $6,239. For each month, he added the estimates for the individual income and expense accounts to get the total receipts and the total payments.

6. For each of the two types of receipts, catering and restaurant, Don added the estimates for January, February, and March of next year. He listed the totals in the 1st Quarter Total Estimate column. He then added these two totals: $18,090 + $61,819 = $79,909. He checked his work by adding the estimated total receipts for January, February, and March: $26,465 + $23,468 + $29,976 = $79,909. The two totals were the same, so Don drew a single line under the money columns in the Receipts section.

7. For each type of payment, Don added the January, February, and March estimates and listed the total in the 1st Quarter Total Estimate column. He added the totals for each type of payment to get the total estimated payments for the first quar-

ter. Don checked his work by adding the estimated total payments for January, February, and March. Then he drew a single line under the money columns in the Payments section.

8. Don found the balance for each month and for the quarter by subtracting the amount of total payments from the amount of total receipts. For all three months, the actual and estimated receipts were more than the payments, so the business had a *positive cash flow*. If the payments had been more than the receipts, the balance would have been a negative number. A negative balance may be listed with a minus sign or in parentheses to indicate a *negative cash flow*. Don added the estimated balances for January, February, and March to check the balance of the 1st Quarter Total Estimate column. The total balances were the same, so he drew a double line under the balance amounts to indicate that the budget spreadsheet was complete.

Positive cash flow: The amount of receipts is larger than the amount of payments.

Negative cash flow: The amount of payments is larger than the amount of receipts.

PREPARING A BUDGET ANALYSIS

At the end of the first quarter of the next year, Don wanted to compare his budget estimates with his actual receipts and payments. To do this, he prepared a budget analysis. Look at the budget analysis shown below as you read the steps Don followed to prepare it.

Country Kitchen
Budget Analysis
1st Quarter, 19—

DESCRIPTION	ESTIMATED	ACTUAL	DIFFERENCE
Receipts			
Catering	$18,090	$19,367	$1,277
Restaurant	61,819	60,983	(836)
Total Receipts	$79,909	$80,350	$441
Payments			
Advertising	$1,767	$1,990	$223
Food Purchases	28,742	27,239	(1,503)
Miscellaneous	1,247	1,631	384
Salaries	23,584	24,389	805
Supplies	2,363	2,296	(67)
Utilities	5,267	5,718	451
Total Payments	$62,970	$63,263	$293

1. In the heading, Don wrote the name of the business, the name of the record (Budget Analysis), and the time period covered.
2. In the description column, he listed the classifications of receipts and payments from his budget spreadsheet. He also listed total receipts and total payments.
3. Don listed the amounts from the 1st Quarter Total Estimate column of the budget spreadsheet in the Estimated column of the budget analysis.
4. He used his classified cash book totals, rounded to the nearest whole dollar, to compute the amounts in the Actual column. For example, he added the totals of the Catering columns for January, February, and March to get the actual catering receipts for the first quarter.
5. Don computed and listed the differences between the amounts in the Estimated and Actual columns. For each line, he subtracted the smaller amount from the larger amount. If the actual amount was larger, he listed the difference as a positive number. He did better than his estimate. If the estimated amount was larger, he listed the difference in parentheses to indicate that it was a negative number. He did worse than his estimate. For example, the actual receipts for catering were more than the estimate, so the difference is positive. The actual receipts for the restaurant were less than the estimate, so the difference is negative.
6. Don computed the difference for the total receipts. If both of the differences had been positive or both had been negative, he would have added the two amounts. Because the catering difference was positive and the restaurant difference was negative, he subtracted the smaller number, $836, from the larger, $1,277. The larger amount is positive, so the difference for the total receipts, $441, is positive. Don checked his calculation by subtracting the total receipts estimate from the actual total receipts, which also gave a positive difference of $441. He then drew a double line under the Receipts section.
7. Don calculated the difference for the total payments. He added all the positive amounts in the Difference column: $223 + $384 + $805 + $451 = $1,863. Then he added the negative amounts: $1,503 + $67 = $1,570. Finally, he subtracted the smaller total from the larger total: $1,863 − $1,570 = $293. The larger total was a positive amount, so the difference is also positive. Don checked the difference by subtracting the total of his estimated payments from the total of his actual payments, which also gave a positive difference of $293. He then drew a double line under the Payments section.

The budget analysis gives Don information about how accurate his budget was. This can help him in making business decisions for later periods of time. For example, the catering part of his business did better than he estimated, but his restaurant did worse. He may want to revise his future budgets to show more receipts for catering. He might also decide to advertise his restaurant more, in order to increase the restaurant receipts.

Check Your Reading

1. ___?___ refers to increases and decreases in the amount of cash on hand as a result of receipts and payments within a time period.

2. ___?___ cash flow means that the amount of cash received is larger than the amount of payments.

3. In a budget, an amount based on opinion or calculated from previous data is a(n) ___?___ .

4. What is a spreadsheet?

5. A comparison of estimated and actual receipts and payments is a(n) ___?___ .

Exercises for Topic 2

1. Kevin's Clean Center is a small business that offers dry cleaning and laundry services. Prepare a budget spreadsheet for Kevin's Clean Center for the first quarter of next year. Use last year's actual amounts, which are listed below, as a basis for your estimates. Kevin expects his receipts and payments to be 10 percent more this year than last year. After computing the estimates, round the numbers to whole-dollar amounts.

	January	February	March
Receipts			
Dry Cleaning	$ 8,438	$ 7,163	$ 8,779
Laundry	4,516	3,847	4,686
Total Receipts	$12,954	$11,010	$13,465
Payments			
Advertising	$ 385	$ 370	$ 415
Cleaning Supplies	1,344	1,273	1,427
Miscellaneous	38	115	146
Packaging Supplies	1,526	1,397	1,638
Salaries	3,546	3,148	3,358
Utilities	1,793	1,562	1,984
Total Payments	$ 8,632	$ 7,865	$ 8,968

2. Prepare a budget analysis for Kevin's Clean Center for the first quarter. Use the first quarter total estimates from Exercise 1 and the actual amounts listed below. Remember that negative differences should be listed in parentheses.

	Actual First Quarter Amounts
Receipts	
Dry Cleaning	$23,675
Laundry	16,537
Total Receipts	$40,212
Payments	
Advertising	$ 1,390
Cleaning Supplies	4,203
Miscellaneous	385
Packaging Supplies	4,867
Salaries	10,613
Utilities	5,913
Total Payments	$27,371

3. Custom Video rents videotapes and equipment to its customers. Prepare a budget spreadsheet for Custom Video for the fourth quarter of next year. Use last year's actual amounts, which are listed below. Alicia Brownfield, the owner of Custom Video, estimates that her receipts and payments will increase by 20 percent, so you will multiply last year's amounts by 1.2 to calculate the estimates for next year. Round amounts to the nearest whole dollar.

	October	November	December
Receipts			
Equipment	$ 4,523	$ 4,475	$ 4,718
Tapes	8,479	8,936	9,443
Total Receipts	$13,002	$13,411	$14,161
Payments			
Advertising	$ 637	$ 598	$ 685
Miscellaneous	389	470	523
Repairs	1,076	1,130	1,292
Salaries	5,920	5,990	6,339
Supplies	996	1,087	1,142
Utilities	1,378	1,297	1,438
Total Payments	$10,396	$10,572	$11,419

4. Prepare a budget analysis for Custom Video for the fourth quarter. Use the fourth quarter total estimates from Exercise 3 and the actual amounts listed below. List negative differences in parentheses.

	Actual Fourth Quarter Amounts
Receipts	
Equipment	$15,959
Taxes	33,985
Total Receipts	$49,944
Payments	
Advertising	$ 2,210
Miscellaneous	1,738
Repairs	3,866
Salaries	21,480
Supplies	3,734
Utilities	5,198
Total Payments	$38,226

TOPIC 3 ■ COMPUTERIZED BUDGET RECORDS

GOALS

1. To identify advantages of using an electronic spreadsheet for budget records.
2. To indicate ways of using computer graphics to illustrate budget data.
3. To interpret information from computerized budget records and graphs.

KEY TERMS

An *electronic spreadsheet* is a computer program that makes calculations using data entered in columns and rows.

A *column* is a vertical section of a spreadsheet.

A *row* is a horizontal section of a spreadsheet.

A *cell* is the point where a column and a row meet.

Personal computer: A small computing system used by an individual or a small business. Also called a *microcomputer.*

As you will remember from Topic 2, Don Volhein owns a small catering and restaurant business named Country Kitchen. He bought a personal computer to keep the records for his business. Don also bought an integrated software package that included an electronic spreadsheet and a graphics program. Don used both of these programs in computerizing his budget records.

ELECTRONIC SPREADSHEET

In the last topic you learned that a spreadsheet is a form that has rows and columns for entering data. An *electronic spreadsheet* is a computer program that lets users set up their own forms and enter information in columns and rows. An electronic spreadsheet is often simply called a *spreadsheet.*

The *columns* on a spreadsheet are the vertical (up and down) sections. Each column is identified by a letter of the alphabet. In the example shown below, column A contains the descriptions and column B contains last year's actual amounts for January.

Integrated software package: A combination of computer programs that can be used together. A typical example would include word processing, database, spreadsheet, and graphics programs.

	A	B	C	D	E	F	G	H
1				COUNTRY KITCHEN				
2				BUDGET SPREADSHEET				
3				1ST QUARTER, 19--				
4								
5		JANUARY		FEBRUARY		MARCH		1ST QTR
6	DESCRIPTION	LAST YR	NEXT YR	LAST YR	NEXT YR	LAST YR	NEXT YR	TOTAL
7		ACTUAL	ESTIMATE	ACTUAL	ESTIMATE	ACTUAL	ESTIAMTE	ESTIMATE
8								
9	RECEIPTS							
10	CATERING	5,672	6,239	4,836	5,320	5,937	6,531	18,090
11	RESTAURANT	18,387	20,226	16,498	18,148	21,314	23,445	61,819
12	TOTAL RECEIPTS	24,059	26,465	21,334	23,468	27,251	29,976	79,909
13								
14	PAYMENTS							
15	ADVERTISING	553	608	418	460	635	699	1,767
16	FOOD PURCHASES	9,074	9,981	7,687	8,456	9,368	10,305	28,742
17	MISCELLANEOUS	375	413	342	376	416	458	1,247
18	SALARIES	7,216	7,938	6,735	7,409	7,488	8,237	23,584
19	SUPPLIES	783	861	523	575	843	927	2,363
20	UTILITIES	1,668	1,835	1,389	1,528	1,731	1,904	5,267
21	TOTAL PAYMENTS	19,669	21,636	17,094	18,804	20,481	22,530	62,970
22								
23	BALANCE	4,390	4,829	4,240	4,664	6,770	7,446	16,939
24								

The *rows* on a spreadsheet are the horizontal (side to side) sections. Each row is identified by a number. In the example, row 1 contains the name of the business (Country Kitchen) and row 10 contains the amounts received from catering.

The point where a column and a row meet is called a *cell.* Cells are identified by stating the letter of the column, then the number of the row. This is called the cell's *address,* or *coordinates.* In the Country Kitchen spreadsheet, cell B10 contains the amount of last January's catering receipts: 5,672.

Labels are words that are listed on a spreadsheet to tell what the numbers mean by giving titles to columns and rows. The column headings in rows 5, 6, and 7 and the row descriptions in column A are examples of labels on the Country Kitchen spreadsheet.

Values are numbers that are entered into the cells of a spreadsheet and used for making calculations. Don entered the value 5,672 in cell B10 and the value 18,387 in cell B11.

Formulas are mathematical statements that give directions for calculating numbers. Formulas are entered into cells of a spread-

sheet and stored in the computer's memory or on a disk. When you look at the spreadsheet on the monitor or on a printed report, however, only the value that was calculated using the formula appears in the cell.

Let's see how spreadsheet formulas work. Don wanted the computer to calculate the total receipts for last January and enter the results in cell B12. If he had told the computer to calculate 5,672 + 18,387, it would have gotten the correct answer of 24,059. Later, however, he might have found that one of the figures had changed. Then he would have had to change both the value and the formula. Instead, for cell B12 Don entered a formula: +B10+B11. This told the computer to add the value in cell B10 to the value in cell B11.

Don also entered a formula in cell C10. Because he estimated that the next year's receipts would be 10 percent more than last year's, he used the formula 1.1 * B10. This told the computer to multiply 1.1 times the value in cell B10.

In cell B21, Don wanted to calculate the total of the payments for last January. He entered the formula: @SUM(B15.B20). The computer then summed (added) the values in cells B15 through B20.

An important advantage of using an electronic spreadsheet instead of a handwritten spreadsheet is the speed of making calculations. If the value in one cell is changed, all values which were based on that cell will automatically be recalculated.

This feature of automatic recalculation gives a small business owner an easy way to answer "what if" questions. For example, Don might want to know what if his catering receipts had been $1,000 more for each of the three months. After he changes the three monthly values, the computer will recalculate all the totals, estimates, and balances. This "what if" feature makes it possible to see the results of changes very quickly and without making many time-consuming calculations.

Multiplication symbol: On a spreadsheet, the symbol * (asterisk) means to multiply.

GRAPHICS PROGRAM

Another part of Don's integrated software package is a graphics program. A *graphics program* can be used to illustrate numerical data visually by using line, bar, and circle graphs.

Don used the *line graph* below to show the changes in his total receipts, total payments, and balance for the first three months of last year. The line graph makes it easy to see that Country Kitchen's volume of business was lower in February, then increased greatly in March.

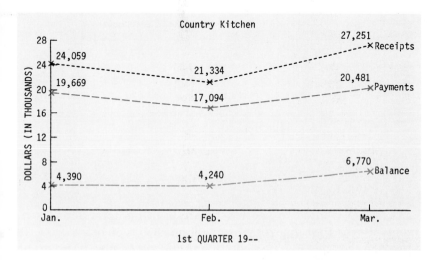

Don put his budget analysis for the first quarter on his electronic spreadsheet program. The computer printout of the budget analysis is shown below.

	A	B	C	D
1		COUNTRY KITCHEN		
2		BUDGET ANALYSIS		
3		1ST QUARTER, 19--		
4				
5	DESCRIPTION	ESTIMATED	ACTUAL	DIFFERENCE
6				
7	---			
8	RECEIPTS			
9	CATERING	18,090	19,367	1,277
10	RESTAURANT	61,819	60,983	-836
11	TOTAL RECEIPTS	79,909	80,350	441
12				
13	PAYMENTS			
14	ADVERTISING	1,767	1,990	223
15	FOOD PURCHASES	28,742	27,239	-1,503
16	MISCELLANEOUS	1,247	1,631	384
17	SALARIES	23,584	24,389	805
18	SUPPLIES	2,363	2,296	-67
19	UTILITIES	5,267	5,718	451
20	TOTAL PAYMENTS	62,970	63,263	293

He used the *bar graph* below to compare visually the estimated and actual payments for the quarter. The graph shows clearly that the estimated and actual figures for some expenses were very close, while the estimates for others, such as food purchases and salaries, were less accurate.

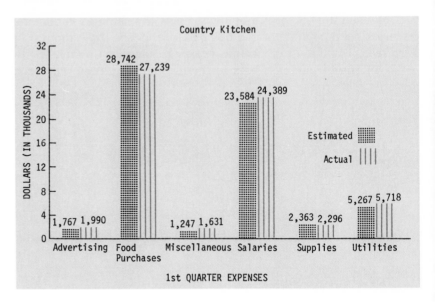

Don also wanted to see what portion of his total actual payments for the first quarter was spent on each type of expense. To illustrate this visually, he used the *circle graph* below. The graph makes it clear that most of Country Kitchen's payments go for food purchases, with salaries as the next largest category.

Country Kitchen–First Quarter Actual Expenses

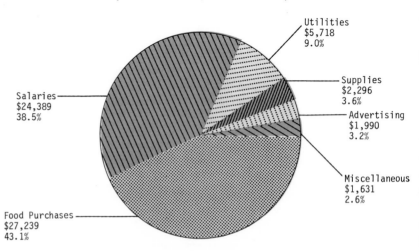

Using a computer graphics program gives a small business owner a very quick way to make visual comparisons of financial data. Line, bar, and circle graphs can be used to present information in a way that is often easier to understand than just looking at the numbers. Programs for circle graphs also give percentages.

1. A computer program that makes calculations using data entered in columns and rows is a(n) ___?___ .

2. What is the difference between a column and a row on a spreadsheet?

3. What is a spreadsheet cell?

4. The letter and number that identify a cell make up its ___?___ .

5. What is the difference between labels and values on a spreadsheet?

6. A mathematical statement that gives directions for calculation is a(n) ___?___ .

7. Name one advantage of using an electronic spreadsheet.

8. What does a graphics program do?

Exercises for Topic 3

1. Look at the electronic spreadsheet of Country Kitchen's budget analysis on page 215 to answer these questions.

   a. Give three examples of labels from the budget analysis spreadsheet.
   b. Give three examples of values.
   c. What is the address of the cell that contains the word "Advertising"?
   d. What is the address of the cell that contains the actual restaurant receipts for the quarter?
   e. The formula for the estimated total receipts, cell B11, is +B9+B10. What would be the formula for cell C11, the actual total receipts?
   f. The formula for the difference between the actual and estimated catering receipts, cell D9, is +C9−B9. What would be the formula for cell D14, the difference between the actual and estimated advertising payments?
   g. The formula for the total estimated payments, cell B20, is @SUM(B14.B19). What would be the formula for cell C20, the total actual payments?

2. Look at the computer bar graph below to answer the following questions.

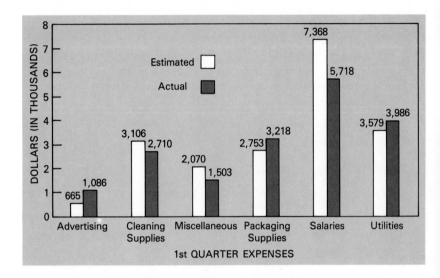

a. Which expense accounts had actual amounts higher than the estimated amounts?

b. Which expense accounts had actual amounts lower than the estimated amounts?

c. What is the name of the expense account that had the lowest actual amount for the quarter?

d. What is the name of the expense account that had the highest estimated amount for the quarter.

e. Which expense account had the largest difference between estimated and actual accounts?

f. Which expense account had an estimated amount of about $2,000?

g. Which expense account had an actual amount of about $4,000?

MATH
SKILLBUILDER

Skill: Given an amount of money, round it to the nearest dollar.

Solution: To round an amount to the nearest dollar, look at the digit immediately to the right of the decimal point.

1. If the digit is 4 or less, simply drop the decimal point and the digits after it. For example, round $4,968.26 to the nearest dollar. The digit to the right of the decimal point is 2, so drop the decimal point and numbers after it.

$4,968.26 rounds to $4,968

2. If the digit is 5 or more, increase the digit to the left of the decimal point by 1, then drop the decimal point and the digits after it. For example, round $11,673.85 to the nearest dollar. The digit to the right of the decimal

point is 8, so add 1 to the digit to the left of the decimal point and drop the .85.

$11,673.85 rounds to $11,674

Practice: Round each amount to the nearest dollar.

1. $478.18	11. $8,990.83
2. $5,231.92	12. $12,409.65
3. $3,979.76	13. $307.12
4. $280.42	14. $4,385.55
5. $14,372.01	15. $75.49
6. $942.41	16. $16,411.36
7. $519.00	17. $25.92
8. $8,737.75	18. $1,086.27
9. $8.19	19. $270.88
10. $46,053.64	20. $364.53

VOCABULARY
SKILLBUILDER

Read each of the following statements. From the words below each statement, choose the term that best matches the statement.

1. A record that groups together similar cash receipts and similar cash payments.

   budget   classified cash book   formula

2. Checking to see that the sum of the subtotals equals the total.

   closing   estimating   proving

3. A financial plan that includes estimated receipts and payments.

   budget   classified cash book   coordinate

4. When the amount of receipts is larger than the amount of payments.

   negative cash flow   positive cash flow
   proof of cash

5. A form that compares estimated and actual receipts and payments.

   budget analysis   classified cash book
   graphics program

6. A computer program that makes calculations using data entered in columns and rows.

   electronic spreadsheet   graphics program
   integrated package

7. A horizontal section of a spreadsheet.

   cell   column   row

8. The letter and number that identify a cell.

   address   labels   values

9. A mathematical statement that gives directions for calculating numbers.

formula   label   value

10. This is used to illustrate data visually.

budget   electronic   graphics
analysis   spreadsheet   program

APPLICATION PROBLEMS

1. Quality Cleaners is a small business that offers dry cleaning and laundry services. Lisa Stein, the owner of Quality Cleaners, keeps a classified cash book which she proves and closes at the end of each month. She deposits cash in the bank each day but records the receipts in the classified cash book only at the end of each week. Lisa records payments as each check is written. The classified cash book for Quality Cleaners has two income accounts (Dry Cleaning and Laundry) and six expense accounts (Advertising, Cleaning Supplies, Miscellaneous, Packaging Supplies, Salaries, and Utilities).

a. Set up a classified cash book for Quality Cleaners for March. The beginning cash balance at the opening of business on March 1 is $7,346.80.

b. Record the following transactions for the month of March. Number the checks in order, beginning with Check 687.

c. Prove and close the classified cash book and enter the balance as of April 1. Save your work for use in Problem 2.

Mar. 1   Paid $237.68 to Midland Phone Company for telephone bill (Utilities).

      2   Paid $362.90 to Laundry Supply Company for hangers (Packaging Supplies).

      3   Paid $25 to United Charities for contribution (Miscellaneous).

      5   Recorded weekly receipts of $2,437.16 for dry cleaning and $1,878.34 for laundry.

      5   Paid $278.56 to Smith Chemical Company for cleaning supplies.

      6   Paid $1,376.55 to Carter Payroll Service for salaries.

      8   Paid $315 to Station WKEO for radio commercials (Advertising).

      8   Paid $406.35 to Ace Paper Products for packaging supplies.

    10   Paid $697.93 to Allstate Gas Service for gas bill (Utilities).

    11   Paid $413.52 to Cleaning Products, Inc., for cleaning supplies.

    12   Recorded weekly receipts of $2,642.57 for dry cleaning and $1,951.17 for laundry.

    13   Paid $1,423.30 to Carter Payroll Service for salaries.

    13   Paid $120 to U.S. Postal Service for postage (Miscellaneous).

    13   Paid $316.83 to Smith Chemical Company for cleaning supplies.

    15   Paid $187.50 to News Leader for advertising.

    16   Paid $1,183.76 to Union Electric for electric bill (Utilities).

    17   Paid $348.37 to Laundry Supply Company for plastic bags (Packaging Supplies).

    18   Paid $36.75 to Speedy Delivery for delivery service (Miscellaneous).

    19   Recorded weekly receipts of $2,578.32 for dry cleaning and $2,044.39 for laundry.

    20   Paid $1,390.85 to Carter Payroll Service for salaries.

22 Paid $388.14 to A-1 Cleaning Supply for cleaning supplies.

22 Paid $50 to 4-H Clubs for contribution (Miscellaneous).

23 Paid $298.30 to Lee's Laundry service for packaging supplies.

24 Paid $265.30 to Station WKEO for radio commercials (Advertising).

25 Paid $592.80 to City Water Department for water bill (Utilities).

26 Recorded weekly receipts of $2,581.58 for dry cleaning and $1,722.37 for laundry.

27 Paid $1,435.75 to Carter Payroll Service for salaries.

29 Paid $342.50 to Joe's Appliance Repair for repairs (Miscellaneous).

31 Paid $379.65 to A-1 Cleaning Supply for cleaning supplies.

2. Prepare a budget spreadsheet for Quality Cleaners for the first quarter of next year. As a basis for the estimates, use last year's actual amounts for January and February, which are listed below. For March, use the totals of the classified cash book you prepared for Problem 1. Round each amount to the nearest whole dollar. Lisa Stein estimates that the business's receipts and payments will be 10 percent more next year than last year. Save your work for use in Problem 3.

	January	February
Receipts		
Dry Cleaning	$10,892	$ 9,381
Laundry	7,868	6,954
Total Receipts	$18,760	$16,335
Payments		
Advertising	$ 813	$ 675
Cleaning Supplies	1,733	1,483
Miscellaneous	603	492
Packaging Supplies	1,854	1,667
Salaries	6,214	5,031
Utilities	3,027	2,248
Total Payments	$14,244	$11,596

3. Prepare a budget analysis for Quality Cleaners for the first quarter. Use the first quarter total estimates from Problem 2 and the actual amounts listed below. Remember that negative differences should be listed in parentheses.

	Actual 1st Quarter Amounts
Receipts	
Dry Cleaning	$37,199
Laundry	23,442
Total Receipts	$60,641
Payments	
Advertising	$ 2,750
Cleaning Supplies	4,247
Miscellaneous	2,366
Packaging Supplies	5,764
Salaries	20,604
Utilities	8,578
Total Payments	$44,309

CHAPTER 8

PETTY CASH AND TRAVEL RECORDS

In Chapter 7 you learned how small businesses keep records of cash receipts and payments. In this chapter you will learn to keep records for two kinds of payments that need special attention: (1) payments of small amounts of cash (petty cash) for business expenses and (2) payments to employees and others for business travel. Both kinds of payments require the use of special records that must be prepared before the payments are actually made. Petty cash and travel records are kept not only by small businesses but also by large firms and government agencies.

TOPIC 1 ■ PETTY CASH RECORDS

GOALS

1. To identify which of several cash payments should be paid from the petty cash fund and which should be paid by check.
2. To prepare petty cash vouchers.
3. To prepare a petty cash summary.
4. To make entries in a petty cash book.
5. To prove and close a petty cash book.

KEY TERMS

A *petty cash fund* is an amount of cash set aside to pay for small business expenses.

A *petty cash voucher* is a form used to record information about a petty cash expense.

A *petty cash summary* is a report that lists the total petty cash payments for each type of expense.

A *petty cash book* is a record in which petty cash transactions are recorded.

Many businesses have a petty cash fund for small expenses. The word "petty" means small; thus the name *petty cash*. The petty cash fund saves the owners from having to write many checks for small amounts of money. Such small expenses as taxi and bus fares for employees on business errands, dinner for employees who work late, small amounts of office supplies, and cleaning supplies may be paid from a petty cash fund. The petty cash fund is usually kept in a locked cash box.

PREPARING PETTY CASH VOUCHERS

Before money is paid from the petty cash fund, a petty cash voucher must be prepared. A *petty cash voucher* is a form used to record information about a petty cash expense. The voucher must be approved and signed by the manager or department head. The voucher must also be signed by the person who receives the money. A signed petty cash voucher serves as proof that money has been paid out of the petty cash fund.

The employee in charge of the petty cash fund is often called the *petty cash clerk*. When an employee needs money from the petty cash fund, the employee presents an approved petty cash voucher to the petty cash clerk. If the employee has already spent personal funds and has a receipt, the receipt is attached to the voucher. The clerk gives the employee the amount of money shown on the voucher. Then the employee receiving the money signs the voucher.

Petty cash clerk: Employee in charge of the petty cash fund.

Darla McGuire works for the Kwik-Lok Corporation. She spent $4 for taxi fare to make a delivery. She fills in a petty cash voucher, attaches the $4 taxi receipt, and gives it to her manager for approval. The manager then gives it to Curtis Knox, the petty cash clerk. Curtis gives Darla the amount that she spent for taxi fare.

Note the following about the petty cash voucher that Darla McGuire prepared, which is shown here.

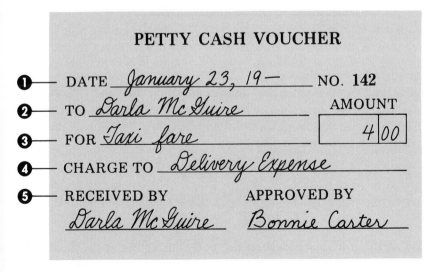

1. The date is entered on the first line. (Vouchers are prenumbered in numeric order.)
2. The name of the person who will receive the cash is entered on the second line.

3. The reason for the payment and the amount are entered on the third line. In this case, $4 is to be paid out for taxi fare.
4. The classification of the payment is entered on the fourth line. The classification of this payment is "Delivery Expense." This information is used later when the payments from the petty cash fund are recorded.
5. The person who receives the money signs the petty cash voucher. In this case, Darla McGuire signed the voucher. The person who approves the petty cash payment also signs the voucher. Bonnie Carter, Darla's manager, signed the voucher.

Four common petty cash expenses:

1. Advertising
2. Delivery
3. Office
4. Miscellaneous

There are many different types of petty cash expenses. However, the four most common petty cash expenses are advertising expense, delivery expense, office expense, and miscellaneous expenses. Examples of advertising expenses are newspaper ads and posters. Examples of delivery expenses are messenger service, transportation for employees on business errands, and payments for COD packages. Examples of office expenses are small amounts of postage, stationery, carbon paper, pencils, erasers, and file folders. Miscellaneous expenses include small expenses that do not occur often. Examples are window washing, minor repairs, cleaning, and donations.

PROVING THE PETTY CASH FUND

Proving petty cash: Making sure that the cash plus the vouchers equal the amount at which the fund was set up.

When a business establishes a petty cash fund, it sets aside a certain amount to be used for petty cash payments. For example, the amount set can be $50, $300, or $750, depending on the needs of the business. The cash in the petty cash box plus the vouchers should equal the amount at which the fund was set up. Each day the petty cash clerk proves petty cash by adding the cash and the vouchers to see whether they equal the amount at which the fund was set up.

PREPARING A PETTY CASH SUMMARY

When the amount of cash in the petty cash fund at the Kwik-Lok Corporation gets low, Curtis Knox, the petty cash clerk, proves the fund and prepares a petty cash summary. A *petty cash summary* is a report that lists the total petty cash payments for each type of expense. It also shows the amount of cash currently in the box. Curtis prepared the petty cash summary that is shown on the following page.

```
          Kwik-Lok Corporation
           Petty Cash Summary
            January 30, 19--

Advertising Expense ..................$221.00
Delivery Expense ..................... 115.00
Office Expense  ...................... 219.70
Miscellaneous Expenses ............... 116.30
   Total petty cash vouchers ..........$672.00
   Plus cash in box ..................... 78.00
   Total petty cash fund ..............$750.00
```

REPLENISHING THE PETTY CASH FUND

To bring the amount of cash in the petty cash fund back up to the amount originally set aside, Curtis must replenish the fund. *Replenishing the petty cash fund* means that an amount of cash is placed in the fund to bring it back up to its original amount. To do this, Curtis gives the petty cash vouchers and the petty cash summary to the cashier at the Kwik-Lok Corporation. The vouchers and summary are given to the person responsible for issuing checks for a business. In some companies, this may be the treasurer or the owner. This person writes a check for the total of the petty cash vouchers.

Curtis replenished the petty cash fund at the Kwik-Lok Corporation on January 30. A check for $672 was issued. The check was cashed, and the cash was placed with the cash on hand in the petty cash box. In this way, the petty cash fund was brought back up to its original amount ($672 + $78 = $750).

Replenishing the petty cash fund: Putting an amount of cash in the fund to bring it back up to its original amount.

USING A PETTY CASH BOOK

The petty cash clerk may keep a *petty cash book*. This book helps the clerk prove the petty cash fund and organize a record of all transactions. Note the following about the page from the petty cash book shown on the following page.

- The totals of the columns from the previous page are entered on the first line of this page. "Brought forward" is written in the Explanation column. The last line on the preceding page

PETTY CASH BOOK   Page 5

| PETTY CASH FUND | | DATE | EXPLANATION | VOUCHER NO. | DISTRIBUTION OF PAYMENTS | | | |
RECEIVED	PAID OUT				ADVERTISING EXPENSE	DELIVERY EXPENSE	MISC. EXPENSES	OFFICE EXPENSE
750 00	588 50	19— Jan. 23	Brought forward		191 00	111 00	76 30	210 20
	4 00	23	Taxi fare	142		4 00		
	30 00	25	Newspaper ad	143	30 00			
	15 00	26	Contribution	144			15 00	
	9 50	26	File folders	145				9 50
	25 00	27	Floor cleaning	146			25 00	
750 00	672 00		Totals		221 00	115 00	116 30	219 70
	78 00	30	Cash on hand					
750 00	750 00							
78 00		30	Cash on hand					
672 00		30	Replenish fund, Ck.4360					

would be the same except that the explanation would say "Carried forward."

■ The information on the second line of this page is found on the petty cash voucher shown on page 223. Curtis Knox records the date (January 23, 19—), the explanation (Taxi fare), and the voucher number (142). Then he enters the amount ($4) in two places: the Paid Out column and the Delivery Expense column. He does not record the name of the person who received the money. If he needs the person's name, he can look at the petty cash voucher.

■ When the fund is replenished, Curtis uses the following procedure to prove and close the petty cash book:

1. He pencil-foots all the money columns. Then he checks that the totals of all the Distribution of Payments columns equal the total of the Paid Out column ($221 + $115 + $116.30 + $219.70 = $672). Since they are equal, he enters the totals.

2. He draws a double rule below all the Distributions of Payments columns.

3. He computes the difference between the Received column and the Paid Out column ($750 − $672 = $78). This is the cash on hand. He enters this amount in the Paid Out column. The amount of cash on hand must be checked. Curtis does this by counting the money left in the petty cash box.

4. He totals the Received and Paid Out columns. He draws a double rule below them and the Date column.

5. He transfers the current cash on hand ($78) to the Received column. This is the amount left in the petty cash fund.

6. He records the date, explanation, and number of the check used to replenish the fund. Then he enters the amount put into the petty cash fund in the Received column.

1. What form is used to record information about a petty cash expense?

2. What summary report lists the total petty cash payments for each type of expense?

3. Name three common categories of petty cash expenses.

4. Putting an amount of cash in the petty cash fund to bring it back up to its original amount is called ___?___ the petty cash fund.

5. What is the meaning of the word "petty"?

6. If you add the cash in any petty cash box to the totals of the vouchers, the answer should be what amount?

1. Betsy Lewis is a cashier at the Globe Travel Agency. The Globe Travel Agency has a petty cash fund of $100. Use the following procedure to show whether Betsy should pay for each item listed below by check or with money from the company's petty cash fund. On a separate sheet of paper, write the letters "a" through "m" in a column. Next to each letter, write "check" if Betsy should pay by check or "petty cash" if she should use money from the petty cash fund.

    a. $145 for an electricity bill.
    b. $1 for bus fare.
    c. $250 for a weekly salary.
    d. $975 for a new typewriter.
    e. $15 for an advertising sign.
    f. $8.75 for taxi fare.
    g. $5.75 for a parking lot fee.
    h. $7.50 for postage.
    i. $6 for file folders.
    j. $86 for a telephone bill.
    k. $19.50 for window repair.
    l. $21.50 for office cleaning.
    m. $25 for a donation.

2. Kathy Smith is a cashier for The Bicycle Center. She prepares petty cash vouchers for the employees. The petty cash transactions for February follow.

Feb. 10 Gave $1.50 to Ron Martin for bus fare (Delivery Expense).

12 Gave $15 to Sue Wang for stamps (Office Expense).

15 Gave $4.75 to David Morrow for stationery (Office Expense).

18 Gave $5.73 to Sue Wang for light bulbs (Miscellaneous Expenses).

22 Gave $7.30 to David Morrow for note pads (Office Expense).

24 Gave $16.50 to Bill Gerrity for repair work (Miscellaneous Expenses).

a. Prepare a petty cash voucher for each of the transactions. Sign the names of the employees who received the money. Sign the name of the manager, Wanda Baker, who must approve each voucher.

b. Prepare a petty cash summary dated February 28, 19—. The petty cash fund was established at $65. How much money is needed to replenish the fund?

3. As co-owner of the Eastside Insurance Agency, Mary Houston must prepare the second page of a petty cash book. The petty cash fund began with $175. The totals of the columns from the first page are as follows: Received, $175; Paid Out, $57; Advertising Expense, $18; Delivery Expense, $12.25; Miscellaneous Expenses, $9.50; Office Expense, $17.25.

Start with July 28, and enter the totals brought forward on the first line. Then enter the following transactions. Number the vouchers beginning with 31.

July 28 Paid $5.75 for postage (Office Expense).

31 Paid $20 for advertising brochures (Advertising Expense).

Aug. 2 Made a $15 donation to the Red Cross (Miscellaneous Expenses).

4 Paid $3 for taxi fare (Delivery Expense).

4 Paid 30 cents postage due on mail received (Office Expense).

6 Spent $14 on flowers for office (Miscellaneous Expenses).

7 Purchased party decorations for $12.75 (Miscellaneous Expenses).

7 Purchased printer ribbons for $12.50 (Office Expense).

    9   Paid $17.50 for window-washing service (Miscel-
        laneous Expenses).
   12   Replenished fund with Check 93.

TOPIC 2 ■ TRAVEL RECORDS

GOALS

1. To prepare travel expense authorizations.
2. To prepare travel expense vouchers.

KEY TERMS

A *travel expense authorization* is a form on
which the estimated expenses for a trip
are approved.

A *travel expense voucher* is a report of an
employee's actual expenses on a business
trip.

Most businesses pay their employees for the cost of travel while
on company business. Two main types of records used for these
expenses are travel expense authorizations and travel expense
vouchers.

PREPARING TRAVEL EXPENSE
AUTHORIZATIONS

Kathy Marino works in the accounting department of Midway
Manufacturing Company. One of her responsibilities is to prepare
travel expense authorizations for employees who will be making
trips on company business. A *travel expense authorization* is a
form which provides information about the trip and the estimated

Authorization: Permission or
approval.

expenses. It must be approved by the employee's supervisor before the trip is taken.

Frank Fleschner, an employee in the sales department, gave Kathy information about a business trip he was planning. Look at the travel expense authorization below as you read the steps Kathy followed in completing the form.

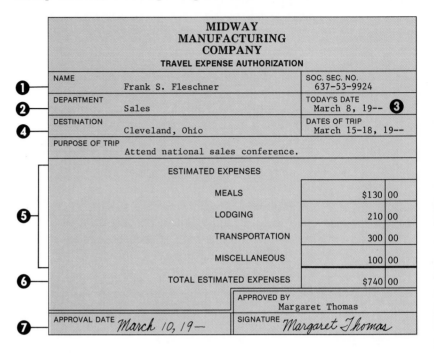

MIDWAY
MANUFACTURING
COMPANY
TRAVEL EXPENSE AUTHORIZATION

❶ NAME Frank S. Fleschner | SOC. SEC. NO. 637-53-9924
❷ DEPARTMENT Sales | TODAY'S DATE March 8, 19-- ❸
❹ DESTINATION Cleveland, Ohio | DATES OF TRIP March 15-18, 19--
PURPOSE OF TRIP Attend national sales conference.

ESTIMATED EXPENSES

❺
MEALS $130 00
LODGING 210 00
TRANSPORTATION 300 00
MISCELLANEOUS 100 00
❻ TOTAL ESTIMATED EXPENSES $740 00

APPROVED BY Margaret Thomas
❼ APPROVAL DATE *March 10, 19—* | SIGNATURE *Margaret Thomas*

1. Kathy listed Frank's full name and his Social Security number on the first line of the form.
2. She wrote the name of the department where he is employed.
3. She listed the date the form was completed.
4. Kathy used the information Frank had given her to fill in his destination, the dates he would be gone, and the purpose of his trip.
5. In the Estimated Expenses section, Kathy listed Frank's estimates of how much the trip would cost. The expenses were divided into four categories: Meals, Lodging (hotel or motel), Transportation, and Miscellaneous. Miscellaneous expenses included things such as telephone charges, hotel tips, and conference registration fees.
6. Kathy added the amounts for the four types of expenses and listed the sum as the Total Estimated Expenses.
7. She entered the name of Frank's supervisor, Margaret Thomas, in the space labeled "Approved By." Margaret signed and dated the form to show that she approved the trip and the estimated expenses.

Destination: Where you are going.

PREPARING TRAVEL EXPENSE VOUCHERS

After Frank Fleschner returned from his trip, he gave Kathy Marino a list of his actual expenses. She then prepared the *travel expense voucher* on page 232, which was used to reimburse Frank for the money he had spent. Some of the information on the voucher was copied from the travel expense authorization which had already been approved. Look at the voucher as you read the steps in completing the form.

Reimburse: Pay back.

1. Kathy used the information on the travel expense authorization to enter Frank's name, Social Security number, department, and the destination and purpose of his trip.

2. She used the expense list Frank had given her to complete the remainder of the voucher. Note that beside the word "Date" is "(MM/DD)." This means that the date should be entered in the format which has the number of the month in two digits (MM) and the number of the day in two digits (DD). Frank left on Monday, March 15, so Kathy wrote 03/15 above the abbreviation for Monday in the Date section. He returned on Thursday, March 18, so she entered 03/16, 03/17, and 03/18 above Tuesday, Wednesday, and Thursday, respectively.

3. Beginning with lunch on Monday, Kathy wrote the costs of Frank's meals in the spaces under each day. The last meal he had on the trip was lunch on Thursday. The meal costs on Frank's list included tips.

4. Kathy wrote the amounts of Frank's hotel bills for Monday, Tuesday, and Wednesday nights on the line labeled "Lodging."

5. She followed these steps in completing the Transportation section.

   a. On Monday and Thursday, Frank drove his personal car 30 miles to and from the airport. Kathy multiplied 30 miles by the rate of $0.25 per mile and entered $7.50 on the Mileage line in the columns for Monday and Thursday.

   b. On Thursday, he paid $24 for parking at the airport, and Kathy listed this amount on the Parking line.

   c. The cost of Frank's airplane ticket to Cleveland was $118.45 each way. Kathy wrote this amount on the Fares line under both Monday and Thursday.

   d. He paid $8 for taxi rides between the airport and his hotel, and these amounts were listed on the Taxi line.

6. Kathy listed the following miscellaneous expenses from the information Frank had given her: conference registration of $75 on Monday, a telephone charge of $2.75 on Wednesday, and hotel tips of $5 on Thursday.

MIDWAY
MANUFACTURING
COMPANY

TRAVEL EXPENSE VOUCHER

NAME	SOC. SEC. NO.
Frank S. Fleschner	637-53-9924

DEPARTMENT	DESTINATION
Sales	Cleveland, Ohio

PURPOSE OF TRIP

Attend national sales conference.

DATE (MM/DD)

ITEMS	SUN.	03/15 MON.	03/16 TUES.	03/17 WED.	03/18 THURS.	FRI.	SAT.	ITEM TOTALS
MEALS, INCLUDING TIPS								
BREAKFAST			4 80	3 95	5 35			14 10
LUNCH		6 75	5 65	7 20	5 80			25 40
DINNER		17 87	19 25	16 82				53 94
LODGING		70 65	70 65	70 65				211 95
TRANSPORTATION								
MILEAGE @ $0.25/MILE		7 50			7 50			15 00
TOLLS								
PARKING					24 00			24 00
FARES (AIR, TRAIN, BUS)		118 45			118 45			236 90
TAXI		8 00			8 00			16 00
CAR RENTAL								
MISCELLANEOUS (LIST)								
conference registration		75 00						75 00
telephone				2 75				2 75
hotel tips					5 00			5 00
DAILY TOTALS		304 22	100 35	101 37	174 10			680 04

EMPLOYEE'S SIGNATURE	APPROVED BY
Frank Fleschner	Margaret Thomas
DATE 03/18/-	SIGNATURE *Margaret Thomas* DATE 03/19/-

7. Kathy added the amounts on each line and entered the sums in the Item Totals column on the right side of the form. Then she added the amounts in each column and listed the sums in the Daily Totals row at the bottom of the form. She checked to be sure that the sum of the item totals was the same as the sum of the daily totals.

8. Kathy entered the name of Margaret Thomas, supervisor, in the Approved By space. She then gave the form to Frank for his signature and to Margaret to sign and date.

After the form was completed, Kathy gave it to the cashier who wrote Frank a check to reimburse him for the total amount of his expenses. She then filed the travel expense authorization and travel expense voucher.

Check Your Reading

1. Look at the travel expense authorization on page 230 to answer the following questions.

   a. Where is Frank Fleschner going on this business trip?
   b. How much does he estimate his hotel bill will be?
   c. What is the name of the person who authorized this travel expense?

2. Refer to the travel expense voucher on page 232 to answer these questions.

   a. How much was Frank paid for each mile he drove his personal car?
   b. What type of expense is a conference registration fee?
   c. What is the total amount of travel expenses for which Frank will be reimbursed for this trip?

3. What is the difference between a travel expense authorization and a travel expense voucher?

Exercises for Topic 2

1. Prepare a travel expense authorization for Melody Raines, 937-42-6836, an employee in the marketing department of Top Line Furniture. Use July 11 as the date the authorization is prepared and July 20 to 22 as the dates of the trip. Melody is traveling to Atlanta, Georgia, to attend a meeting of the National Furniture Council. Her estimated expenses are as follows: meals, $75; lodging, $126; transportation, $350; miscellaneous, $150. Total the estimated expenses; then

complete the Approval section with the date July 13 and your name and signature. Save your work for use in Exercise 2.

2. After Melody returned from her meeting, she gave you the following list of her actual expenses. Use this data and the information on the travel expense authorization you prepared in Exercise 1 to prepare a travel expense voucher. Total all the rows and columns, and be sure the sum of the Item Totals column equals the sum of the Daily Totals row. Leave the signature and Approval section of the form blank.

   Tuesday, July 20: mileage, 40 miles; tolls, $0.50; airline ticket, $149.80; taxi, $7.50; lunch, $5.40; meeting registration, $110; dinner, $16.95; lodging, $61.58.

   Wednesday, July 21: breakfast, $3.98; telephone, $2.85; lunch, $6.25; dinner, $15.42; lodging, $61.58.

   Thursday, July 22: breakfast, $4.25; hotel tips, $6; lunch, $5.95; taxi, $8; airline ticket, $149.80; parking, $18; tolls, $0.50; mileage, 40 miles.

3. Prepare a travel expense authorization for Kim Sims, 463-90-8015, an employee in the engineering department of Eagle Products Company. Use November 1 as the date the authorization is prepared and November 8 to 11 as the dates of the trip. Kim is traveling to Dallas, Texas, to meet with the engineering staff at the corporate headquarters. Her estimated expenses are as follows: meals, $95; lodging, $215; transportation, $400; miscellaneous, $50. Total the estimated expenses; then complete the Approval section with the date November 3 and your name and signature. Save your work for use in Exercise 4.

4. After Kim returned from Dallas, she gave you the following list of her actual expenses. Use it and the travel expense authorization from Exercise 3 to prepare a travel expense voucher. Total all the rows and columns and cross-check to be sure your totals are correct. Leave the signature and Approval section blank.

   Wednesday, November 8: taxi, $11.50; airline fare, $105; dinner, $18.45; lodging, $72.40; hotel tips, $5.

   Thursday, November 9: breakfast, $3.70; lunch, $6.95; dinner, $16.35; lodging, $72.40; telephone, $3.60.

   Friday, November 10: breakfast, $5.25; lunch, $5.80; dinner, $17.60; lodging, $72.40.

   Saturday, November 11: breakfast, $4.84; lunch, $7.10; hotel tips, $10; car rental, $178.50; airline fare, $105; taxi, $10.75.

MATH
SKILLBUILDER

Problem: Compute mileage charges using the rate per mile and the number of miles driven. The employee drove 75 miles at $0.25 per mile.

Solution: Multiply the number of miles driven (75) by the rate ($0.25) to find the amount of mileage charges. Be sure to include two decimal places in your answer.

$$75 \times \$0.25 = \$18.75$$

Practice: Find the mileage charges for each of the following distances and rates.

1. 125 miles at $0.30 per mile
2. 371 miles at $0.23 per mile
3. 278 miles at $0.27 per mile
4. 542 miles at $0.29 per mile
5. 733 miles at $0.31 per mile
6. 651 miles at $0.24 per mile

7. 78 miles at $0.28 per mile
8. 1,236 miles at $0.25 per mile
9. 837 miles at $0.33 per mile
10. 481 miles at $0.27 per mile
11. 1,143 miles at $0.23 per mile
12. 286 miles at $0.31 per mile
13. 793 miles at $0.27 per mile
14. 288 miles at $0.26 per mile
15. 432 miles at $0.29 per mile
16. 987 miles at $0.25 per mile
17. 316 miles at $0.22 per mile
18. 408 miles at $0.32 per mile
19. 576 miles at $0.30 per mile
20. 849 miles at $0.25 per mile

VOCABULARY
SKILLBUILDER

Read each of the following statements. From the words below each statement, choose the term that best matches the statement.

1. Cash paid out, or spent.

   cash payments   cash receipts

2. An amount of cash set aside to pay for small business expenses.

   checking account   petty cash fund

3. A record that gives information about a petty cash expense.

   petty cash fund   petty cash voucher

4. A common petty cash expense.

   deliveries   rent   utilities

5. A report that lists the total petty cash payments for each type of expense.

   petty cash summary   petty cash voucher

6. The term commonly used for permission or approval.

   authorization   information

7. The place where you are going.

   travel   destination

8. To pay back for expenses.

   reimburse   return

APPLICATION
PROBLEMS

1. Steve Cardin is a cashier at the Gomez Flower Shop. He prepares petty cash vouchers for the employees. The petty cash transactions for August follow.

Aug. 1 Gave $4.50 to John Ballard for taxi fare (Delivery Expense).
3 Gave $10.25 to Paul Odonsky for stationery (Office Expense).
5 Gave $18.75 to Rob Coleman for cleaning (Miscellaneous Expenses).
9 Gave $2 to Diane LaCosta for bus fare (Delivery Expense).
12 Gave $5 to George Gibson for COD package (Delivery Expense).
14 Gave $10 to Jay Burns for donation to the Heart Fund (Miscellaneous Expenses).

a. Prepare a petty cash voucher for each of the transactions listed above. Sign your name as the person who approves each payment. Sign each voucher with the name of the person who receives the cash.

b. Prepare a petty cash summary dated August 15. If the petty cash fund was established at $70, how much money is needed to replenish the fund?

2. Sharon Hinds is a student who works at the Village Flower Shop. Prepare the second page of the shop's petty cash book for Sharon. The petty cash fund began with $200. The totals of the columns from the first page are as follows: Received, $200; Paid Out, $111; Advertising Expense, $25; Delivery Expense, $17.50; Miscellaneous Expenses, $31.80; Office Expense, $36.70. Start with May 14, and enter the totals brought forward on the first line. Then enter

the following transactions. Number the vouchers, beginning with 28.

May 16 Paid a parking fee of $1.75 (Delivery Expense).
18 Paid $5 for washing the van (Delivery Expense).
18 Paid $6.50 for wrapping cord (Office Expense).
21 Paid $9 for stamps (Office Expense).
22 Paid $12.50 for newspaper ad (Advertising Expense).
25 Paid $10 for stationery (Office Expense).
29 Paid $8.60 for wrapping paper (Office Expense).
31 Replenished fund with Check 113.

3. Prepare a travel expense authorization for Ramon Martinez, 357-88-4391, an employee in the sales department of Ace Equipment Company. Use April 28 as the date the authorization is prepared and May 5 to 9 as the dates of the trip. Ramon is traveling to Los Angeles, California, to meet with regional sales agents. His estimated expenses are as follows: meals, $150; lodging, $290; transportation, $550; miscellaneous, $50. Total the estimated expenses; then complete the Approval section with the date May 1 and your name and signature. Save your work for use in Problem 4.

4. After Ramon returned from his trip, he gave you the following list of his actual expenses. Use this data and the travel expense authorization you completed in Problem 3 to prepare a travel expense voucher. Total all the rows and columns, and be sure the sum of the Item Totals column equals the sum of the Daily Totals row. Leave the signature and Approval section of the form blank.

Monday, May 5: mileage, 40 miles; airline ticket, $138.75; lunch, $6.80; dinner, $17.85; telephone, $1.90; lodging, $71.90.

Tuesday, May 6: breakfast, $5.25; telephone, $3.25; lunch, $6.70; tolls, $0.50; parking, $6; dinner, $16.50; lodging, $71.90.

Wednesday, May 7: breakfast, $4.18; lunch, $5.90; parking, $8; telephone, $2.85; dinner, $19.20; lodging, $71.90.

Thursday, May 8: breakfast, $4.90; lunch, $6.35; tolls, $1; parking, $6; telephone, $4.60; dinner, $17.93; lodging, $71.90.

Friday, May 9: breakfast, $5.20; lunch, $6.38; hotel tips, $10; rental car, $210.50; airline ticket, $138.75; parking, $24; mileage, 40 miles.

CHAPTER 9

BUSINESS BANKING RECORDS

In Chapter 2 you learned how to keep a personal checking account. In this chapter you will learn how businesses keep their checking accounts. You will prepare bank deposits, write checks, and prepare bank reconciliations for businesses. Keeping business banking records is like keeping personal banking records except that the amounts of money and the number of deposits and checks are usually larger.

TOPIC I ■ PREPARING BILLS AND COINS FOR DEPOSIT

GOALS

1. To count and wrap bills and coins.
2. To prepare a cash tally sheet for bills and coins.
3. To prepare a bank deposit slip for bills and coins.

KEY TERMS

A *cash tally sheet* is a form used to figure the total value of bills and coins.

A *deposit slip* is a form used to record information about a bank deposit.

A *check stub* is a record of deposits and checks written.

COUNTING AND WRAPPING BILLS AND COINS

In Chapter 6 you learned how to count and record the amount of bills and coins in a cash drawer. Next the money must be prepared for deposit in a bank. The first step in preparing money for deposit is to put the bills and coins in separate piles by denomination. A *denomination* is a bill or coin of one value, such as a ten-dollar bill or a quarter.

The *denomination* of a bill or a coin is its face value.

After the bills and coins have been placed in piles by denomination, the next step is to wrap the items in each pile.

Counting and Wrapping Bills After bills are sorted by denomination, they are counted and then wrapped by placing a paper strap around a certain number of bills. Before bills are wrapped, they are all placed face up, with the top of each bill facing in the same direction. For example, 100 one-dollar bills would be wrapped with a strap marked "100," as shown here.

Many businesses place 100 bills in each wrapper. The value of a full wrapper (that is, 100 bills) of one-, five-, ten-, or twenty-dollar denomination is shown here.

Denomination of Bill		Number of Bills in Full Wrapper		Value of Bills in Full Wrapper
$20	×	100	=	$2,000
10	×	100	=	1,000
5	×	100	=	500
1	×	100	=	100

Fewer than 100 bills are still wrapped, with the amount clearly written on the wrapper. For example, the wrapper for 73 one-dollar bills would be labeled as follows.

Bills that do not make up a full wrapper are called *loose items* They are counted separately on the cash tally sheet.

Counting and Wrapping Coins Coins are counted and then wrapped in a paper coin wrapper or *roll*. A roll of quarters is shown here.

Loose items are bills or coins that do not make up a full wrapper or roll.

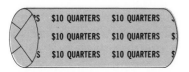

A standard number of coins of each denomination is placed in each roll, as shown here.

Coin		Number of Coins in Full Roll		Value of Coins in Full Roll
$0.50	×	20	=	$10.00
0.25	×	40	=	10.00
0.10	×	50	=	5.00
0.05	×	40	=	2.00
0.01	×	50	=	0.50

Just as with bills, fewer coins are wrapped and clearly labeled with the amount. For example, the wrapper for 36 quarters would be labeled as follows.

$10 QUARTERS $10 QUARTERS
$9 ONLY
$10 QUARTERS $10 QUARTERS
$10 QUARTERS $10 QUARTERS

PREPARING A CASH TALLY SHEET

The next step in preparing bills and coins for deposit is to fill in a *cash tally sheet*. Assume, for example, that you wrapped the bills and coins shown on page 241 and then completed the cash tally sheet illustrated below the bills and coins.

Let's trace the steps to fill in the cash tally sheet:

1. Under the Loose Items section, record the number of loose $20 bills. Enter "14" under the Number column on the $20 line.
2. Multiply the denomination of the bill by the number of loose bills: $20 × 14 = $280.
3. Under the Loose Items section, record the number and the value of the loose $10, $5, and $1 bills in the same way as for loose $20 bills.
4. Under Full Wrappers or Rolls section, record the number of full wrappers of $1 bills. Enter "1" under the Number column on the $1 line.
5. Multiply the number of full wrappers by the value shown on the form for one wrapper: 1 × $100 = $100. Enter "$100" under the Full Wrappers or Rolls section.
6. For each denomination, add across the amounts under the Loose Items and the Full Wrappers or Rolls sections. Enter answers in the Total Value column. For example, on the $1

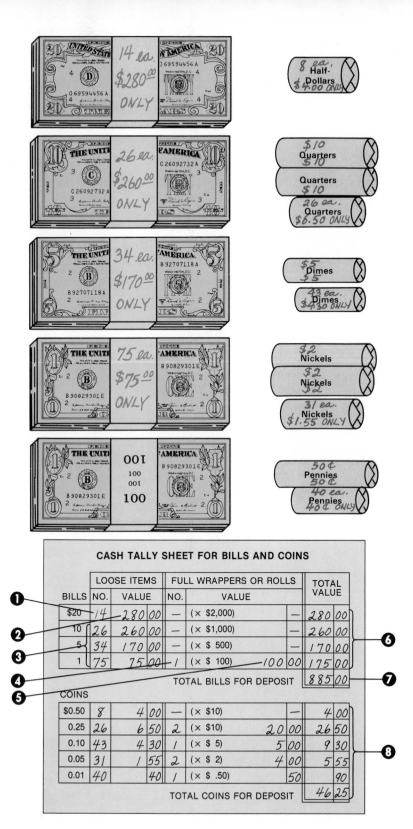

CASH TALLY SHEET FOR BILLS AND COINS

BILLS	LOOSE ITEMS NO.	VALUE	FULL WRAPPERS OR ROLLS NO.	VALUE		TOTAL VALUE	
$20	14	280 00	—	(× $2,000)	—	280 00	
10	26	260 00	—	(× $1,000)	—	260 00	
5	34	170 00	—	(× $ 500)	—	170 00	
1	75	75 00	1	(× $ 100)	100 00	175 00	
				TOTAL BILLS FOR DEPOSIT		885 00	

COINS							
$0.50	8	4 00	—	(× $10)	—	4 00	
0.25	26	6 50	2	(× $10)	20 00	26 50	
0.10	43	4 30	1	(× $ 5)	5 00	9 30	
0.05	31	1 55	2	(× $ 2)	4 00	5 55	
0.01	40	40	1	(× $ .50)	50	90	
				TOTAL COINS FOR DEPOSIT		46 25	

line, add $75 + $100 = $175. Enter "$175" on the $1 line under the Total Value column.

7. Add the amounts in the Total Value column for bills. Enter "$885" beside the Total Bills for Deposit line.

8. Follow steps 1 through 7 to complete the Coins section of the cash tally sheet.

PREPARING A BANK DEPOSIT SLIP FOR BILLS AND COINS

After you have completed the cash tally sheet for bills and coins, follow these steps in preparing a *deposit slip:*

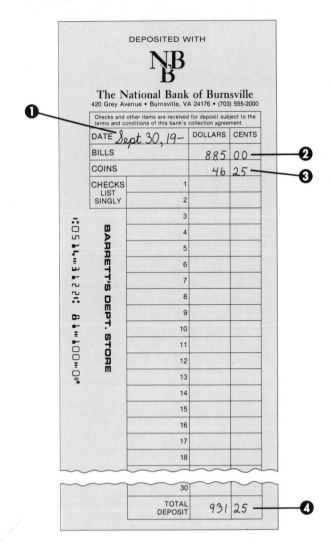

1. Fill in the date. Note that the name of the business and the checking account number are already printed on the slip.
2. On the cash tally sheet for bills and coins, find the Total Bills for Deposit line. Write this amount, $885, on the deposit slip beside the Bills line.
3. On the cash tally sheet for bills and coins, find the Total Coins for Deposit line. Write this amount, $46.25, on the deposit slip beside the Coins line.
4. Add the amounts for bills and coins, and write the total, $931.25, beside the Total Deposit line.

You must also be sure to keep a copy of the deposit slip and to enter the total amount of the deposit on the checkbook stub, shown at the right.

Then, to deliver the cash to the bank, place all bills and coins to be deposited, as well as the deposit slip, in a bank deposit bag, such as this one.

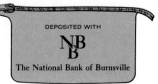

A *bank deposit bag* is a container for items to be taken to the bank.

NO.	$_____
DATE _____	
TO _____	
_____	
FOR _____	

	DOLLARS	CENTS
BALANCE	4,261	13
AMT. DEPOSITED *September 30, 19—*	931	25
TOTAL		
AMT. THIS CHECK		
BALANCE		

DEPOSITED WITH
NB
B
The National Bank of Burnsville

1. What is the first step in preparing bills and coins for deposit?

2. Name an example of a denomination of a bill and a denomination of a coin.

3. How should the bills be arranged before they are wrapped?

4. What are bills or coins called that do not make up a full wrapper or a full roll?

5. What is a bank deposit bag used for?

Exercises for Topic 1

1. How many full wrappers and how many loose bills do you have in each of the following cases. How much money do you have in each case? Refer to the table on page 239.

   a. 372 $1 bills
   b. 210 $10 bills
   c. 195 $5 bills
   d. 275 $20 bills
   e. 127 $1 bills
   f. 32 $20 bills
   g. 927 $5 bills
   h. 476 $10 bills
   i. 661 $1 bills
   j. 338 $10 bills

2. How many rolls of coins and how many loose coins do you have in each of the following cases? How much money do you have in each case? Refer to the table on page 240.

a. 45 nickels   **f.** 1,246 pennies

b. 146 pennies   **g.** 273 quarters

c. 227 dimes   **h.** 487 dimes

d. 12 half-dollars   **i.** 193 nickels

e. 378 quarters   **j.** 625 pennies

3. a. Prepare a cash tally sheet for the following items. Before you begin, figure out how many full wrappers or rolls and how many loose items you have for each denomination. Refer to the tables on pages 239 and 240.

Number of Items	Denomination
12	$20 bill
22	$10 bill
37	$5 bill
148	$1 bill
6	Half-dollar
65	Quarter
87	Dime
56	Nickel
93	Penny

b. Check your work. The total bills for deposit should be $793; the total coins for deposit should be $31.68.

c. Prepare a bank deposit slip for the bills and coins. Use today's date.

4. a. Prepare a cash tally sheet for the following items.

Number of Items	Denomination
67	$20 bill
110	$10 bill
81	$5 bill
234	$1 bill
4	Half-dollar
51	Quarter
120	Dime
64	Nickel
82	Penny

b. Check your work. The total bills for deposit and total coins for deposit should be $3,109.77.

c. Prepare a bank deposit slip for the bills and coins. Use today's date.

5. a. Prepare a cash tally sheet for the following items.

Number of Items	Denomination
134	$20 bill
263	$10 bill
111	$5 bill
376	$1 bill
12	Half-dollar
178	Quarter
110	Dime
89	Nickel
78	Penny

b. Check your work. What is the amount of total bills for deposit and total coins for deposit?

c. Prepare a bank deposit slip for the bills and coins. Use today's date.

TOPIC 2 ■ PREPARING CHECKS AND CREDIT CARD SALES SLIPS FOR DEPOSIT

GOALS

1. To prepare checks for deposit.
2. To prepare credit card sales slips for deposit.
3. To prepare deposit slips for checks and credit card sales slips.

KEY TERMS

To *endorse* a check is to sign or stamp the back of the check so that it can be cashed or deposited.

A *merchant sales slip summary* records information about the credit card sales slips being sent to the bank for deposit.

An *ABA number* is the American Bankers Association number on checks that are used to identify the bank. An example is $\frac{96-974}{1232}$. The number "96" refers to the city or state, which in this case is Oregon. The number "974" is the bank number. The number "1232" is the Federal Reserve number for the area.

PREPARING CHECKS FOR DEPOSIT

Besides bills and coins, you will also deposit checks in the bank. Before they can be deposited, however, checks must be endorsed.

To *endorse* a check is to sign it or stamp it so that the check can be cashed or deposited. Some businesses use a handwritten endorsement, others use rubber stamps to endorse checks, and some firms have electronic cash registers that automatically endorse the customer's check as the customer's receipt is printed. For example, note the rubber stamp endorsement at the left, which is used by Capital Appliance Repair.

The words "For deposit only" on the endorsement mean that the check cannot be cashed. It can only be deposited in Capital Appliance Repair's bank account.

Some businesses accept checks that are made payable to others. For example, Myra Husak, a customer at Barrett's Department Store, paid her Barrett's bill with her payroll check. Before Barrett's accepted Myra's payroll check, she had to endorse it by signing the check. (Businesses often require such endorsements to include the payee's address and telephone number.)

Having accepted such a check, Barrett's must also endorse the check in order to deposit it in Barrett's account. With both endorsements—Myra's and Barrett's—the back of the check will look like this.

It is a good business practice to endorse checks and money orders "For deposit only" as soon as they have been accepted to protect them against theft or loss.

For deposit only
Capital Appliance Repair

Myra Husak

For deposit to the
account of
Barrett's Dept. Store

Mary Gee verifies the customer records and payments at Barrett's Department Store.

PREPARING CREDIT CARD SALES
SLIPS FOR DEPOSIT

Millions of times each day, customers use bank credit cards, such as VISA or MasterCard, to buy goods and services. At the time of each sale, three copies of a *credit card sales slip* are prepared. The customer receives one copy, and the business keeps one copy. The business sends the third copy to the bank for deposit in the business's checking account. Likewise, if the business makes a refund for a credit card sale, three copies of a *refund slip* are prepared.

A *merchant sales slip summary,* shown below, is used to record and summarize information about all the credit card sales slips sent to the bank for deposit on one particular day.

A *credit card sales slip* is a form used to make a record of a bank credit card sale.

A *refund slip* is a form used to make a record of a bank credit card refund.

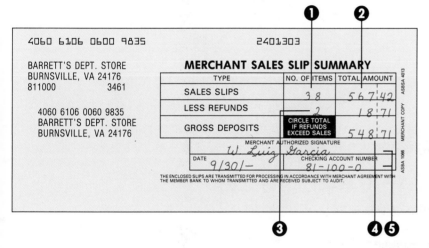

To complete the merchant sales slip summary at the close of each business day, cashiers do the following:

1. Enter the total number of credit card sales slips for the day.
2. Enter the total dollar amount of credit card sales slips for the day.
3. Enter the number of refunds (if any) and their total amount on the Less Refunds line.
4. In the Total Amount column, subtract the refunds total from the sales slips total and enter the answer on the Gross Deposits line. *Gross deposits* is the amount to be deposited in the business's account before bank card service fees are charged to the account.
5. Sign, date, and enter the checking account number on the form.

Three copies of the merchant sales slip summary are prepared. The business keeps one copy along with its copies of the credit

A *merchant deposit envelope* is used for sales slips, refund slips, and the merchant sales slip summary before they are taken to the bank.

card sales slips. The other two copies, along with all the sales slips and refund slips, are placed in a merchant deposit envelope. These two copies are placed in the envelope so that information on the top copy shows through the windows on the envelope. The envelope is sealed and given to the office worker who will prepare the bank deposit.

PREPARING DEPOSIT SLIPS FOR CHECKS AND CREDIT CARD SALES SLIPS

To complete a deposit slip for checks and credit card slips, follow these steps:

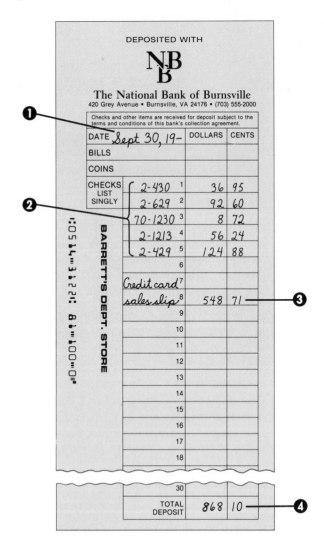

1. Fill in the date.
2. Review each check for a correct endorsement. Enter the top part of the ABA number and the amount of each check on a separate line on the deposit slip.
3. Enter the gross deposits amount from the merchant sales slip summary. Next to this amount, write ``Credit card sales slips'' to explain the entry.
4. Add the checks and the credit card sales slips, and enter the total beside the Total Deposit line.

As you did when depositing cash, be sure to enter the amount of the deposit on the business's checkbook stub. Keep a copy of the deposit slip. Then place all items to be deposited and the deposit slip in a bank deposit bag.

Check Your Reading

1. What must a business do to a check before depositing it?

2. Name three ways that a business can write an endorsement on a check.

3. Why might a check have two endorsements?

4. How many copies of a credit card sales slip are prepared at the time of sale? Who receives each copy?

5. What is placed in the merchant deposit envelope along with two copies of the merchant sales slip summary?

6. What information about a check is entered on the deposit slip?

Exercises for Topic 2

1. Write an endorsement for a check for deposit in the account of Scottie's TV Repair.

2. A check payable to Andre Perez was accepted by Gold-Way Grocery. Write an endorsement for the check for deposit in the business's account.

3. Prepare a merchant sales slip summary for Barrett's Department Store for the credit card sales slips listed below. There are no refunds. Use today's date and sign your name. Barrett's checking account number is 81-100-0.

   Credit card sales slip amounts: $17.95, $25.70, $44.63, $121.49, $80.40, $24.89.

4. Prepare a merchant sales slip summary for Barrett's Department Store for the credit card sales and refund slips listed below. Use today's date and sign your name. Barrett's checking account number is 81-100-0.

   Credit card sales slip amounts: $212.70, $89.46, $33.45, $14.32, $10.07, $9.84; $84.63, $127.43, $50.56, $12.23, $119.50, $32.20.

   Refund slip amounts: $42.77, $11.64, $8.48.

5. Prepare a bank deposit slip for the Unix Cycle Shop. The following have been prepared for deposit.

   Checks: 94-32, $37.50; 94-06, $50.71; 94-62, $82.21; 94-10, $239.80; 94-49, $121.75; 94-73, $99.82.

   Credit card sales slips (gross deposits): $724.38.

   Use today's date.

6. Prepare a bank deposit slip for the Cho Chang Motel. The following have been prepared for deposit:

   Checks: 29-3, $42.76; 28-13, $89.55; 23-7, $134.42; 29-6, $39.90; 28-21, $94.40; 29-7, $47.25; 28-2, $76.62; 29-2, $147.02.

   Credit card sales slips (gross deposits): $2,327.84.

   Use today's date.

7. Prepare a cash tally sheet for bills and coins, a merchant sales slip summary, and a bank deposit slip for Youngs Auto Repair. The following are to be deposited.

   Bills and coins:

Number of Items	Denomination
8	$20 bill
12	$10 bill
7	$5 bill
24	$1 bill
40	Quarter
43	Dime
27	Nickel
50	Penny

   Checks: 32-121, $112.50; 32-101, $94.70; 31-212, $274.75; 33-40, $412.76.

   Credit card sales slips total (7 items): $682.73.

   Refund slip total (1 item): $40.00.

   Use today's date. Sign your name on the merchant sales slip summary. Youngs' checking account number is 42-021-3.

8. Prepare a cash tally sheet for bills and coins, a merchant sales slip summary, and a bank deposit slip for Sarro Lumber Company. The following are to be deposited:

Bills and coins:

Number of Items	Denomination
142	$20 bill
118	$10 bill
78	$5 bill
242	$1 bill
3	Half-dollar
121	Quarter
88	Dime
47	Nickel
72	Penny

Checks: 41-1312, $1,207.76; 40-1201, $48; 41-772, $818.40; 40-2120, $174.44; 43-121, $604.35; 40-201, $6,724.37; 43-212, $717.42; 44-121, $175.50.

Credit card sales slip total (41 items): $5,320.20.

Refund slips total (2 items): $257.92.

Use today's date. Sign your name on the merchant sales slip summary. Sarro's checking account number is 37-112-1.

TOPIC 3 ■ KEEPING A BUSINESS CHECKING ACCOUNT

GOALS

1. To identify the different kinds of business checks.
2. To maintain a business checkbook.

KEY TERMS

A *check stub* is a record of each individual check that remains in the checkbook after the check has been torn out.

A *check register* is a separate booklet of check records.

A *voucher check* is a check with an attached form explaining the purpose of the check.

IDENTIFYING BUSINESS CHECKS

A business must keep records of every check that it writes. Without records, how would a business know if it paid a bill—and if so, when and how much? In addition, a business would have no way of keeping track of the amount left in its checking account. How businesses choose to keep checking account records varies, as you will see.

Checks With Stubs Some businesses use checks with stubs. A *stub* is a short, perforated form attached to the check. Before a check is written, the stub is completed. Because the stub remains when the check is torn out of the book, the stub provides a permanent record. For an example of a check with a stub, see the illustration below.

NO. 5630 $ 216.00
DATE Aug. 19, 19—
TO Garland Wholesale Supplies
FOR Paper towels and floor wax

	DOLLARS	CENTS
BALANCE	6,930	50
AMT. DEPOSITED		
. .		
TOTAL	6,930	50
AMT. THIS CHECK	216	00
BALANCE	6,714	50

Wells Cosmetic Company
7609 Wellington
Chicago, IL 60633
NO. 5630
55-713/212
August 19, 19 --
PAY TO THE ORDER OF Garland Wholesale Supplies $ 216.00
Two hundred sixteen and 00/100 ---------------- DOLLARS
Central National Bank
2520 Parker Avenue
Chicago, IL 60633
Sue Fordham
⑆0212⑈0713⑆ 0815⑈02249⑈

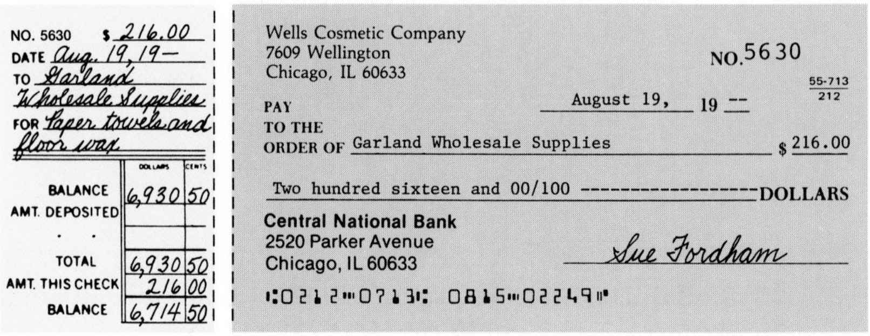

Check Register A separate booklet called a *register* also provides a record of checks written. The register is a book of blank forms in which dates, names, deposits, and information about checks can easily be entered. You learned how to keep a personal check register in Chapter 2. See the register for a business illustrated below.

PLEASE BE SURE TO **DEDUCT** CHARGES THAT AFFECT YOUR ACCOUNT

NO	DATE	ISSUED TO OR DESCRIPTION OF DEPOSIT	AMOUNT OF PAYMENT		✓	OTHER DEDUCT	AMOUNT OF DEPOSIT		BALANCE FORWARD	
									6,930	50
5630	8/19/-	TO Garland Wholesale Supplies FOR Paper towels and floor wax	216	00					216	00
									6,714	50
		TO FOR								
		TO FOR								
		TO								

Wells Cosmetic Company
7609 Wellington
Chicago, IL 60633
NO. 5630
55-713/212
August 19, 19 --
PAY TO THE ORDER OF Garland Wholesale Supplies $ 216.00
THE SUM 216 DOLS 00 CTS DOLLARS
Central National Bank
2520 Parker Avenue
Chicago, IL 60633
Sue Fordham
AUTHORIZED SIGNATURE
⑆0212⑈0713⑆ 0815⑈02249⑈

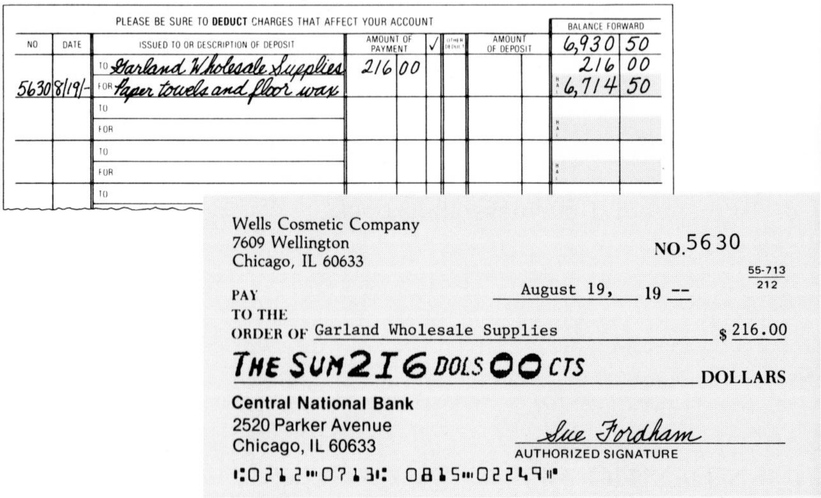

Voucher Check Voucher checks provide a third method for keeping records of checks. A *voucher check* has three parts. It has a check, of course, but it also has an attached form that tells the

payee the purpose of the check. In this way, even after the payee deposits the check, the voucher provides the payee with an important record. The company that sent the check has a copy of the entire voucher.

The *payee* is the person or business to whom a check is made out.

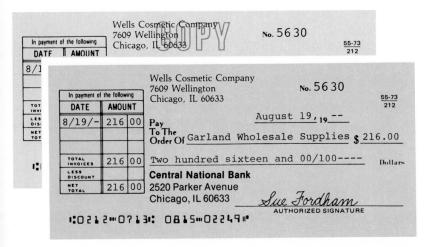

Note that the voucher check illustrated above shows a three-part form. Another voucher check is illustrated below. This voucher records information on the face of the check. The check is given to a vendor or supplier. The business keeps a copy of the entire check.

Check-writing machine: A machine that prints the amount of the check so that the amount cannot be changed.

Whichever system a business may use, business checks are generally typed or are printed by computer. In fact, some businesses use *check-writing machines,* special equipment that prints the amount of the check so that the amount cannot be changed.

To control possible misuse of company money, businesses limit the number of people who have the authority to sign checks. Some businesses, in fact, require two signatures on each check.

MAINTAINING A BUSINESS CHECKBOOK

Whichever checkbook system a business uses, the purpose is to keep accurate records. For the rest of this discussion and for the exercises that follow, you will use checks with stubs.

Let's see, then, how a business records check information step by step:

1. Look at the stub for Check 100:

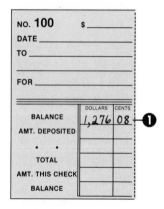

The balance, $1,276.08, was recorded after the last check was written.

2. On September 30, $578.10 was deposited in the account. This deposit must be recorded on the Amount Deposited line.

The balance and the deposit are not totaled until another check is written. Reason: There may be another deposit—and therefore another number to add—before the next check is written.

3. When you are ready to write a check, you add the balance and the deposit, and you write the sum, $1,854.18, on the Total line.

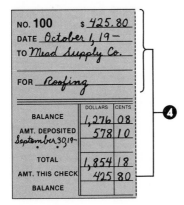

4. To write a check, write the stub information first.
   a. Enter the check amount, $425.80, at the top right, next to the dollar sign, and fill in the date.

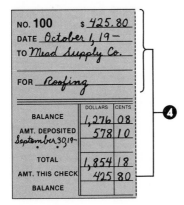

   b. Write the payee's name on the To line and the purpose of the check on the For line.
   c. Again write the amount of the check, $425.80, on the Amount This Check line.
5. Fill in the check only after you have completed the stub information so that you do not forget to complete the stub.

Filling in the check follows the same procedure you learned earlier (see page 37).

6. Subtract the amount of the check from the Total line to get the new balance. Enter this new balance, $1,428.38, on two stubs: at the bottom of the stub for the check that was just written (Check Stub 100) and on the Balance line of the next stub (Check Stub 101).

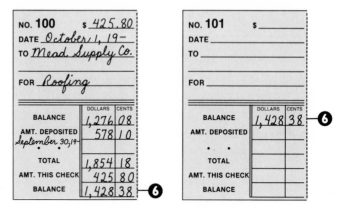

Repeat steps 1 through 6 when writing each check.

Check Your Reading

1. How does a business keep a record of voucher checks that are written?

2. What type of machine is used to print the amount of a business check? What is the purpose of using this machine?

3. When should you add the beginning balance and a deposit on the checkbook stub?

4. When should the check stub information be filled in? Why?

Exercises for Topic 3

1. As an office worker for Central Appliance, one of your jobs is to maintain the business's checkbook. The beginning balance on the stub for Check 1300 is $2,740.75. Record deposits and issue checks as follows.

Apr. 7 Record deposit, $250.
     8 Issue Check 1300 to Magi-Clean Ovens for oven parts, $321.71. (Remember to fill in the information on the stub first. Then write the check and bring the new balance forward to the stub for Check 1301.)

      9 Record deposit, $400.

    11 Issue Check 1301 to Master Toast Inc. for toasters, $728.84.

    14 Issue Check 1302 to Delta Supply Co. for display case, $607.72.

2. Record deposits and issue checks for Mobile Data Services as follows. The beginning balance on the stub for Check 525 is $4,482.98.

May 14 Record deposit, $720.

    15 Issue Check 525 to Southern Power Co. for electric service, $184.40.

    18 Issue Check 526 to Micro Sales Co. for computer printer, $426.76.

    21 Record deposit, $100.

    22 Record deposit, $1,270.

    25 Issue Check 527 to Sohio for gasoline, $174.82.

3. Record deposits and issue checks for the Kite Shack as follows. The beginning balance on the stub for Check 140 is $1,474.82.

Nov. 20 Issue Check 140 to Chung Silk Co. for kite material, $240.

    22 Record deposit, $718.21.

    23 Record deposit, $624.42.

    25 Issue Check 141 to Gar Management Co. for rent, $1,000.

    27 Record deposit, $618.25.

    29 Issue Check 142 to Mary Tollison for legal services, $200.

4. Verify these four consecutive check stubs. List any necessary corrections on a separate sheet of paper. If no deposits are listed, assume that none was made.

NO. 117	$ 23 00/100	NO. 118	$ 14 95/100	NO. 119	$ 12 11/100	NO. 120	$ 32 85/100
DATE July 8, 19–		DATE July 8, 19–		DATE July 10, 19–		DATE July 11, 19–	
TO U. S. Postmaster		TO Wood Co.		TO Karl Jones		TO Kay Todd	
FOR Stamps		FOR Supplies		FOR Refund		FOR Cleaning	

	DOLLARS	CENTS		DOLLARS	CENTS		DOLLARS	CENTS		DOLLARS	CENTS
BALANCE	532	20	BALANCE	509	20	BALANCE	495	25	BALANCE	578	64
AMT. DEPOSITED			AMT. DEPOSITED			AMT. DEPOSITED	95	50	AMT. DEPOSITED		
• •			• •			• •			• •		
TOTAL			TOTAL			TOTAL	590	75	TOTAL		
AMT. THIS CHECK	23	00	AMT. THIS CHECK	14	95	AMT. THIS CHECK	12	11	AMT. THIS CHECK	32	85
BALANCE	509	20	BALANCE	495	25	BALANCE	578	64	BALANCE	546	06

TOPIC 4 ■ RECONCILING BANK STATEMENTS FOR A BUSINESS

GOAL

1. To reconcile business bank statements that have outstanding checks, deposits in transit, and service charges.

KEY TERMS

To *reconcile* means to bring the bank balance and the checkbook balance into agreement.

A *bank statement* is a form sent by the bank to the customer, usually monthly. The statement lists checks paid, deposits received, service charges, and the account balance.

An *outstanding check* is a check that has been issued by the customer but has not yet been recorded by the bank on the customer's statement.

Just as holders of personal checking accounts receive monthly bank statements, business checking accounts also receive monthly statements. To see how a business uses its monthly statement to prepare reconciliations, you will follow Doris Wyrick, an employee of Stalling Millwork, Inc., as she reviews, then reconciles, Stalling's latest statement.

REVIEWING THE BANK STATEMENT

On March 31, Doris Wyrick received Stalling's monthly statement from the Security Bank and Trust. Follow her as she reviews the statement, which is illustrated on page 259.

Doris looks over the entire statement, but she is especially interested in the sections numbered 1 through 4 in the illustration:

1. The date, check number, and amount of each check paid by the bank for the Stalling account
2. The date and amount of each deposit
3. The bank service charge
4. The ending balance

Doris will use these four sections of the statement to reconcile the statement for Stalling Millwork.

```
SECURITY BANK AND TRUST
                          1171 Shirley Boulevard
                          Atlanta, GA 30310

                                  ACCOUNT NO.  03 14104270
  Stalling Millwork Inc.    DATE THIS STATEMENT  03/28/--
  14 North Star Drive       DATE LAST STATEMENT  02/27/--
  Atlanta, Ga 30310               PAGE NUMBER              1
```

SERVICES SUMMARY	SERVICE	ACCOUNT	BEGINNING BALANCE 02/27/--	ENDING BALANCE 03/28/--	
	CHECKING	03 14104270	9,361.27	8,320.19	❹

CHECKS PAID	CHECK NO.	DATE POSTED	AMOUNT	CHECK NO.	DATE POSTED	AMOUNT	
	1126	03/03	632.19	1138	03/18	63.70	
	* 1131	02/28	328.07	1139	03/18	824.73	
	1132	02/28	2,141.10	1140	03/20	192.00	❶
	1133	03/03	400.00	* 1142	03/21	1,120.06	
	1134	03/10	1,921.68	1143	03/21	127.73	
	1135	03/11	82.51	1144	03/27	92.16	
	1136	03/11	631.11	1145	03/27	215.78	
	1137	03/18	141.48	* 1149	03/27	183.86	

* GAP IN CHECK SEQUENCE

OTHER DEBITS	SERVICE CHARGE	DATE POSTED 03/27	AMOUNT 10.00	❸

CREDITS		DATE POSTED	AMOUNT	
	DEPOSIT-DELWOOD OFFICE	03/10	2,783.24	
	DEPOSIT-DELWOOD OFFICE	03/18	1,863.65	❷
	DEPOSIT-BLAIR OFFICE	03/21	3,420.19	

CHECKING BALANCE BY DATE	DATE	BALANCE	DATE	BALANCE	
	02/28	6,892.10	03/18	6,841.59	
	03/03	5,859.91	03/20	6,649.59	
	03/10	6,721.47	03/21	8,821.99	
	03/11	6,007.85	03/27	8,320.19	❹

RECONCILING THE STATEMENT

Reconciling is the process of bringing the bank balance and the checkbook balance into agreement. The monthly statement shows the ending balance that the bank has on record. But what about checks that were written but not received by the bank? Doris must account for such checks.

She does so by completing the bank reconciliation statement shown on page 260. As you see, Doris's goal is to figure out an adjusted checkbook balance, as shown at the end of the reconciliation.

Let's follow Doris step by step as she fills in the bank reconciliation statement.

1. Doris writes the name of the company and the date at the top of the form.

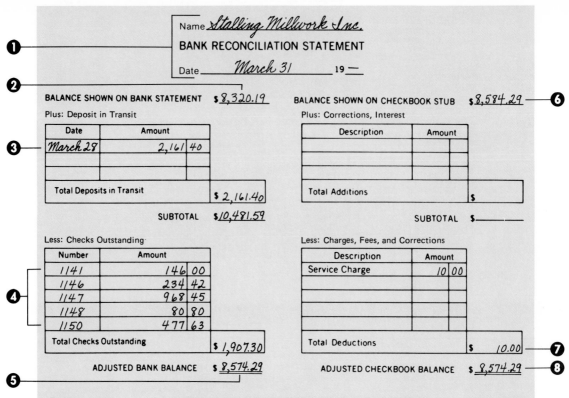

①

②

Name *Stalling Millwork Inc.*

BANK RECONCILIATION STATEMENT

Date _____ *March 31* _____ 19 —

BALANCE SHOWN ON BANK STATEMENT	$8,320.19			BALANCE SHOWN ON CHECKBOOK STUB	$8,584.29	**⑥**

Plus: Deposit in Transit

③

Date	Amount
March 28	2,161 40
Total Deposits in Transit	$ 2,161.40

Plus: Corrections, Interest

Description	Amount
Total Additions	$

SUBTOTAL $10,481.59

SUBTOTAL $_____

Less: Checks Outstanding

④

Number	Amount
1141	146 00
1146	234 42
1147	968 45
1148	80 80
1150	477 63
Total Checks Outstanding	$ 1,907.30

Less: Charges, Fees, and Corrections

Description	Amount
Service Charge	10 00
Total Deductions	$ 10.00	**⑦**

⑤

ADJUSTED BANK BALANCE $ 8,574.29

ADJUSTED CHECKBOOK BALANCE $ 8,574.29 **⑧**

These totals represent the correct amount of money you have in the bank and should agree. Differences, if any, should be reported to the bank within ten days after the receipt of your statement.

A *deposit in transit* is a deposit that has been sent to the bank but is not recorded on the customer's bank statement.

2. She enters the ending balance that appears on the bank statement, $8,320.19.

3. She looks at the check stubs to see if any deposits have not been listed on the statement. A March 28 deposit of $2,161.40 is not included in the statement, so Doris lists that amount under the Deposits in Transit section.

4. She looks at the check stubs to see which checks have been written that are not listed on the statement. She finds that five checks are outstanding, so she lists the number and amount of each under the Checks Outstanding section.

5. Doris totals the five outstanding checks and enters the amount on the Total Checks Outstanding line. Then she figures the adjusted bank balance by adding deposits in transit to the balance shown on the bank statement. From this subtotal she subtracts the amount of checks outstanding. The difference, $8,574.29, is written on the Adjusted Bank Balance line.

A *service charge* is money deducted by the bank from the customer's account as payment for keeping the account.

6. She enters the balance shown on the last check stub, $8,584.29.

7. Doris enters the amount of the bank service charge, $10, on the Service Charge line and again on the Total Deductions line.

8. She figures the adjusted checkbook balance by subtracting total deductions, $10, from the balance shown on the check stub, $8,584.29. Doris has reconciled the bank account because both adjusted balances are the same: $8,574.29.

Now that Doris has completed the bank reconciliation statement, she subtracts the $10 service charge from the balance on the last check stub in order to bring her checkbook balance up to date. Her last check stub then looks like this.

NO. **1151**	$_____	
DATE		
TO		
FOR		
	DOLLARS	CENTS
BALANCE	8,584	29
AMT. DEPOSITED		
Service charge TOTAL	-10	00
	8,574	29
AMT. THIS CHECK		
BALANCE		

Check Your Reading

1. What are three reasons why a bank statement balance and a checkbook stub balance might be different?

2. How do you tell whether there are any deposits in transit?

3. On a bank reconciliation statement, should deposits in transit be added to, or subtracted from, the bank statement balance?

4. How do you tell which checks are outstanding?

5. On a bank reconciliation statement, should outstanding checks be added to, or subtracted from, the bank statement balance?

Exercises for Topic 4

1. On July 31 Miller Lumber Company received a monthly bank statement dated July 26 showing the following:

Checks paid: 171, $624.80; 172, $178.27; 173, $430.80; 174, $992.67; 176, $522.89; 177, $46.44.

Deposits: July 20, $2,186.40; July 22, $914.80.

Service charge: $8.

Ending balance: $6,962.25.

The check stubs show a balance of $8,726.11. They also show that the following checks have been written and deposits made:

Checks written: 171, $624.80; 172, $178.27; 173, $430.80; 174, $992.67; 175, $1,182.20; 176, $522.89; 177, $46.44; 178, $178.40.

Deposits: July 20, $2,186.40; July 22, $914.80; July 27, $3,116.46.

Prepare a bank reconciliation statement for Miller Lumber Company dated July 31.

2. On March 31 Cupino's Jewelry received a monthly bank statement dated March 26 showing the following:

Checks paid: 430, $624; 431, $181.18; 432, $46.84; 433, $933.12; 435, $626.77; 436, $2,121.80; 438, $500; 439, $772.93.

Deposits: March 8, $823.18; March 13, $797.66.

Service charge: $10.

Ending balance: $5,161.18.

The check stubs show a balance of $6,070.82. They also show that the following checks have been written and deposits made:

Checks written: 430, $624; 431, $181.18; 432, $46.84; 433, $933.12; 434, $95.03; 435, $626.77; 436, $2,121.80; 437, $164.25; 438, $500; 439, $772.93; 440, $420.20; 441, $117.21.

Deposits: March 8, $823.18; March 13, $797.66; March 28, $1,011.81; March 30, $684.52.

Prepare a bank reconciliation statement for Cupino's Jewelry dated March 31.

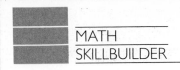

Example: What is the total value of these bills?

Number of Bills	Denomination
16	$20
23	10
18	5
34	1

Solution:

1. Multiply: 16 × 20 = 320
   23 × 10 = 230
   18 × 5 = 90
   34 × 1 = 34

2. Add: 674

3. Record the answer: $674

Practice:

1. What is the total value of these bills?

Number of Bills	Denomination
24	$20
31	10
22	5
64	1

2. What is the total value of these bills?

Number of Bills	Denomination
236	$20
174	10
108	5
370	1

Example: What is the total value of these coins?

Number of Coins	Denomination
7	50¢
18	25¢
23	10¢
16	5¢
31	1¢

Solution:

1. Multiply: 7 × 0.50 = 3.50
   18 × 0.25 = 4.50
   23 × 0.10 = 2.30
   16 × 0.05 = 0.80
   31 × 0.01 = 0.31

2. Add: 11.41

3. Record the answer: $11.41

Practice:

1. What is the total value of these coins?

Number of Coins	Denomination
4	50¢
36	25¢
41	10¢
22	5¢
58	1¢

2. What is the total value of these coins?

Number of Coins	Denomination
9	50¢
126	25¢
94	10¢
88	5¢
121	1¢

Example: What are (1) the total of sales slips, (2) the total refunds, and (3) the gross deposits for these credit card sales slip and refund slip amounts?

Credit card sales slip amounts: $43.25, $18.63, $31.02, $68.85, $101.38.

Refund slip amounts: $9.50, $34.77.

Solution:

1. Add credit card sales slips: $ 43.25
                                   18.63
                                   31.02
                                   68.85
                                  101.38
   Record total sales slips: $263.13

2. Add refund slips: $ 9.50
                                   34.77
   Record total refunds: $ 44.27

3. Subtract total refund slips from total credit card sales slips:
                                 $263.13
                                 − 44.27

4. Record gross deposits $218.86

Practice:

1. What are (a) the total of the credit card sales slips, (b) the total refunds, and (c) the gross deposits for the following?

   Credit card sales slip amounts: $83.27, $10.99, $64.02, $4.73, $112.40, $26.30, $48.

   Refund slip amounts: $16.88, $72.81.

2. What are (a) the total of the credit card sales slips, (b) the total refunds, and (c) the gross deposits for the following?

   Credit card sales slip amounts: $218.41, $170.06, $92.42, $15, $309.69, $420.20, $90, $144.46, $197.24, $88.43.

   Refund slip amounts: $163.72, $11.55.

VOCABULARY SKILLBUILDER

Read each of the following statements. From the words below each statement, choose the term that best matches the statement.

1. A form used to figure the value of bills and coins.

   cash tally sheet   currency sheet

2. A form used to record information about a bank deposit.

   account balance form   deposit slip

3. A record of deposits and checks written.

   balance record   checkbook stub

4. The face value of a bill or a coin.

   denomination   total worth

5. To sign or stamp the back of a check so that it can be cashed or deposited.

   approve   endorse

6. The bank-identifying number that appears on checks.

   ABA number   account number

7. A form used to make a record of a bank credit card sale.

   bank voucher slip   credit card sales slip

8. A booklet for recording checks written and deposits made.

check register   checking form booklet

9. A check that has been issued by the customer but has not yet been recorded by the bank on the customer's statement.

blank check   outstanding check

10. Money deducted by the bank from the customer's account as payment for keeping the account.

monthly fees   service charge

APPLICATION
PROBLEMS

1. As an employee of the Western Wear Shop, you must maintain the business's checking account (number 44-606-9). You are to prepare deposits, issue checks, and prepare the monthly bank reconciliation statement as follows. The beginning balance on Check Stub 701 is $2,127.64.

June 23 Prepare a cash tally sheet for bills and coins, a merchant sales slip summary, and a bank deposit slip for the following.

Bills and coins:

Number of Items	Denomination
41	$20 bill
55	$10 bill
38	$5 bill
121	$1 bill
2	Half-dollar
96	Quarter
70	Dime
43	Nickel
79	Penny

Checks: 21-171, $89.72; 22-170, $145; 21-170, $74.57; 22-171, $34.63

Credit card sales slip amounts: $68.85, $247.65, $128.77, $33.27, $74.51, $99.22.

Refund slips: none.

Record the total deposit on the stub for Check 701.

24 Issue Check 701 to Rambler Fashions for merchandise, $854.75. (Remember to fill in the information on the check stub first. Then write the check and bring the balance forward to the stub for Check 702.)

25 Issue Check 702 to Carlos Sanchez for rent, $900.

26 Prepare a cash tally sheet for bills and coins, a merchant sales slip summary, and a bank deposit slip for the following:

Bills and coins:

Number of Items	Denomination
32	$20 bill
49	$10 bill
30	$5 bill
117	$1 bill
4	Half-dollar
107	Quarter
58	Dime
39	Nickel
66	Penny

Checks: 22-170, $50; 21-170, $84.36; 20-171, $18.35; 22-171, $319.44; 21-171, $111.63; 23-172, $80.70.

Credit card sales slip amounts: $121.40, $11.55, $63.27, $65.59, $232.67.

Refund slip amounts: $68.85, $8.44.

Record the total deposit on the stub for Check 703.

27 Issue Check 703 to Boots and Saddles Inc. for merchandise, $1,450.

30 You received a monthly bank statement dated June 25 showing the following:

Checks paid: 696, $324.42; 697, $85; 698, $166.75; 699, $427.77; 700, $188.20; 701, $854.75.

Deposits: June 12, $643.27; June 20, $2,712.13.

Service charge: $8.

Ending balance: $3,977.02

The check stubs show that the following checks have been written and deposits made:

Checks written: 696, $324.42; 697, $85; 698, $166.75; 699, $427.77; 700, $188.20; 701, $854.75; 702, $900; 703, $1,450.

Deposits: June 12, $643.27; June 20, $2,712.13; June 27, $2,515.83.

Prepare a bank reconciliation statement dated June 30. Then deduct the $8 service charge from the stub for Check 704.

2. As an office worker for Star Pharmacy, you have been given the job of maintaining the business's checking account (number 38-008-9). You are to prepare deposits, issue checks, and prepare the monthly bank reconciliation statement as follows. The beginning balance on the stub for Check 2100 is $4,643.40.

Feb. 21 Prepare a cash tally sheet for bills and coins, a merchant sales slip summary, and a bank deposit slip for the following.

Bills and coins:

Number of Items	Denomination
183	$20 bill
148	$10 bill
106	$5 bill
371	$1 bill
12	Half-dollar
247	Quarter
164	Dime
88	Nickel
170	Penny

Checks: 12-81, $12.75; 14-82, $26.67; 13-82, $49.80; 12-82, $35; 16-21, $9.43; 14-82, $21.83.

Credit card sales slip amounts: $43.72; $18.41; $112.70; $78.38; $7.40; $89.63; $32.41; $6.88; $93.27.

Refund slip amount: $18.47.

Record the total deposit on the stub for Check 2100.

22 Issue Check 2100 to Woody Laboratory for cough medicines, $327.62. (Remember to fill in the information on the stub first. Then write the check and bring the balance forward to the stub for Check 2101.)

23 Issue Check 2101 to Bay Area Phone Co. for telephone service, $172.42.

24 Prepare a cash tally sheet for bills and coins, a merchant sales slip summary, and a bank deposit slip for the following.

Bills and coins:

Number of Items	Denomination
164	$20 bill
131	$10 bill
92	$5 bill
322	$1 bill
6	Half-dollar
218	Quarter
151	Dime
75	Nickel
121	Penny

Checks: 13-82, $17.41; 16-21, $88.80; 14-82, $10.17; 13-81, $68.47.

Credit card sales slip amounts: $18.55, $93.27; $121.30, $24.70, $9.18, $14.60, $34.54.

Refund slip amounts: $7.40, $26.33.

Record the total deposit on the stub for Check 2102.

25 Issue Check 2102 to City National Bank for note payment, $4,500.

28 You received a monthly bank statement dated February 23 showing the following:

Checks paid: 2091, $43.18; 2092, $357.90; 2093, $181.21; 2094, $878.16; 2095, $743.22; 2096, $95.45; 2097, $873.11; 2099, $1,100.

Deposits: Feb. 9, $2,326.85; Feb. 16, $6,751.06.

Service charge: $10.

Ending balance: $11,527.77.

The check stubs show that the following checks have been written and deposits made:

Checks written: 2091, $43.18; 2092, $357.90; 2093, $181.21; 2094, $878.16; 2095, $743.22; 2096, $95.45; 2097, $873.11; 2098, $143.21; 2099, $1,100; 2100, $327.62; 2101, $172.42; 2102, $4,500.

Deposits: Feb. 9, $2,326.85; Feb. 16, $6,751.06; Feb. 24, $5,916.72.

Prepare a bank reconciliation statement dated February 28. Then deduct the $10 service charge from the stub for Check 2103.

COMPUTER
APPLICATION

Exploring Computers in Recordkeeping —Part 2

At the end of Part 1 you learned how word processing programs are used with computers to save time and work in preparing written materials. Other types of computer programs that are popular in recordkeeping are spreadsheet, graphics, and database programs. You learned about spreadsheet and graphics programs in Chapter 7 when you worked with computerized budget records.

Computers can store very large amounts of information in a small amount of space. *Databases* are programs that tell the computer how to store, organize, and manage data.

The information in a database is collected in *records*. An individual student record, for example, might contain the student's name, address, phone number, ID number, and class. A customer record might contain the customer's name, address, credit history, occupation, and additional information that would help a

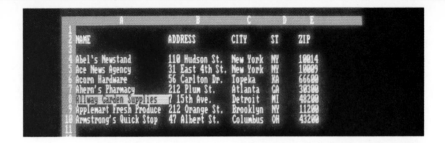

	A	B	C	D	E
1					
2	NAME	ADDRESS	CITY	ST	ZIP
3					
4	Abel's Newstand	110 Hudson St.	New York	NY	10014
5	Ace News Agency	31 East 4th St.	New York	NY	10009
6	Acorn Hardware	56 Carlton Dr.	Topeka	KA	66600
7	Ahern's Pharmacy	212 Plum St.	Atlanta	GA	30300
8	Allway Garden Supplies	7 15th Ave.	Detroit	MI	48200
9	Applemart Fresh Produce	212 Orange St.	Brooklyn	NY	11200
10	Armstrong's Quick Stop	47 Albert St.	Columbus	OH	43200
11					

salesperson pinpoint the customer's buying needs. A collection of related records is called a *file*.

A database is made of one or more files. Above is a section of a file listing customer names and addresses. The entire file contains hundreds of names. The database not only stores these names but can also organize them in various ways. In the example above the list is organized alphabetically by name.

Imagine that you want to organize the list in some other way such as by ZIP Code or telephone area code. You may want to distribute customer lists to regional salespeople. You would simply tell the database to organize, or *sort*, records numerically by using the ZIP Code. The computer would display the file in numeric order according to ZIP Codes, as shown below.

A database can also be used to select certain items from a file. You might want a list of all the pharmacies from your file of customers. Using the FIND command of the database, you would tell the computer to make a list of pharmacies. The computer would go through the file and print only the names and addresses of pharmacies.

A database can be connected with a word processing program. You might write a sales letter and have it printed over and over again. The database provides the names and addresses and the word processing program provides the letter. With this system many letters can be printed and individually addressed in a very short time and with no errors.

Check Your Reading

1. Name four types of computer programs that are popular in recordkeeping.

2. Programs that tell the computer how to store, organize, and manage data are called ____?____ programs.

3. A collection of related database records is called a(n) ____?____.

4. A database program can organize, or ____?____, the records in a file alphabetically or numerically.

5. A database can be connected with a(n) ____?____ program to prepare individually addressed letters.

	A	B	C	D	E
1					
2	NAME	ADDRESS	CITY	ST	ZIP
3					
4	Union Grocery	41 Court St.	New York	NY	10002
5	Penelton Shoe Store	220 Water St.	New York	NY	10004
6	Hall Street News	205 Henry St.	New York	NY	10005
7	Topper's Delicatessen	415 Morris St.	New York	NY	10006
8	Lindell's Pharmacy	4 Abbot St.	New York	NY	10007
9	Ace News Agency	31 East 4th St.	New York	NY	10009
10	Chelsea Pharmacy	200 West 23rd St.	New York	NY	10011
11					

Belinda Johnson and Kareem Rasvan own a retail store named Super Sounds. They sell compact discs, records, and tapes on a cash basis. This means that customers pay by cash or check or use a bank credit card when they buy merchandise. Operating on a cash basis also means that Belinda and Kareem pay for recordings as they are billed. They pay by check, which is a form of cash.

In this project you are going to work with the cash records of Super Sounds for the month of February. The cash records are kept in a classified cash record. The word "classified" means that some of the items on the record are listed by type.

The classified cash record for Super Sounds is shown on pages 270–271. Note that the receipts, deposits, and expenses have been classified into types. The record has been filled in for the first week of February. Let's see where the information comes from for the items in the classified cash record.

Date. The shop is open seven days a week. There is at least one entry for each day.

Cash Receipts. The total receipts for each day are entered in this section. Each classification of receipts has its own heading.

- Compact Discs. The total daily receipts for the sale of compact discs are entered here. On February 1, the total is $109.20, not including sales tax.
- Records. The total daily receipts for record sales are entered in this column. The total for February 1 is $148.75, not including sales tax.
- Tapes. This column shows the total daily receipts for the sale of tapes. On February 1, the total is $252.60, not including sales tax.
- Tax. The total daily receipts for the 6 percent sales tax are entered in this

column. The total amount of sales tax on February 1 is $30.63.
- Total Receipts. The total daily receipts for the sale of compact discs, records, and tapes and for the tax on those sales are entered here. On February 1, the total is $541.18.

The information for the above types of receipts comes from a printed tape that is made by the electronic cash register at the end of each day. After Super Sounds has closed, Kareem or Belinda totals the cash register and it prints the tape. The tape for February 1 is shown below. When each sale is made, a classification key on the cash register is touched. The cash register at Super Sounds has classification keys labeled CD for compact discs, R for records, T for tapes, and TAX for sales tax. When the cash register is totaled, the tape shows the total receipts for each type of sale, the total taxes, and the total of all cash received.

```
     SUPER SOUNDS

        *109.20 CD
        *148.75 R
        *252.60 T
        * 30.63 TAX
FEB. 1  *541.18 TOTAL
```

Deposits. Daily receipts are always deposited in the bank on the same day they are received. The night depository is used if the bank is closed. After the cash register has been totaled, the bills, coins, checks, and bank credit card slips are removed from the cash drawer. They are totaled and then prepared for deposit.

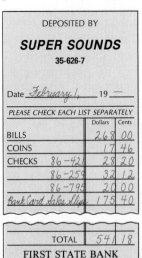

DEPOSITED BY		
SUPER SOUNDS		
35-626-7		
Date February 1, 19 —		
PLEASE CHECK EACH LIST SEPARATELY	Dollars	Cents
BILLS	268	00
COINS	17	46
CHECKS 86–421	28	20
86–259	32	12
86–795	20	00
Bank Card Sales Slips	175	40
TOTAL	541	18
FIRST STATE BANK		

Date	Cash Receipts					Deposits			
	Compact Discs	Records	Tapes	Tax	Total Receipts	Currency and Coins	Checks	Bank Card	Total Deposits
Feb. 19-- 1									
1	109 20	148 75	252 60	30 63	541 18	285 46	80 32	175 40	541 18
2	108 59	172 90	272 17	33 22	586 88	298 58	110 38	177 92	586 88
3	78 94	98 74	191 94	22 18	391 80	202 22	70 14	119 44	391 80
3									
4	112 47	165 20	276 02	33 22	586 91	300 19	98 56	188 16	586 91
5	70 28	124 37	184 77	22 77	402 19	199 60	79 98	122 61	402 19
6	99 25	138 90	240 84	28 74	507 73	261 61	95 47	150 65	507 73
7	96 52	157 45	255 23	30 55	539 75	273 32	104 50	161 93	539 75

The deposit slip is the source of information for the entries in the Deposits section of the classified cash record. The deposit slip for February is shown on page 269.

The total amount of currency and coins is entered in the classified cash record in the Bills and Coins column. Note that the total for February 1 is $285.46.

The total amount of checks received from customers is entered in the Checks column. For February 1, the total of this column is $80.32.

The total amount received from bank credit card sales slips is entered in the Bank Card column. The total of the bank credit card sales slips for February 1 is $175.40.

The total amount of the bank deposit ($285.46 + $80.32 + $175.40 = $541.18) is entered in the Total Deposit column. The amount in the Total Deposit column should always be the same as the amount in the Total Receipts column.

Cash Payments. It costs money to operate a business. The largest payments made by Belinda Johnson and Kareem Rasvan for their store, Super Sounds, are for the purchase of recordings. Other payments must be made for salaries, utilities, and miscella-neous expenses such as advertising and supplies. Note the following columns in the Cash Payments section of the Classified Cash Record.

- Check Number. Because payments are made by check, the number of each check is entered in the Check Number column. Check 2161 was written on February 1. A separate line is used for each check.
- Explanation. The Explanation column is used to explain the first balance amount each month. This column is also used to explain the purpose of each payment. The payment on February 1 was for rent.
- Amount. The amount of each check is entered in the Amount column. The amount of check 2161 was $780.

Expense Accounts. The Expense Account section has four columns. These columns are used to classify each payment into one of the four main types of expenses that Super Sounds has. The amount of the check from the Amount column is listed in the correct Expense Account column.

- Miscellaneous. Miscellaneous ex-

Sounds Cash Record								Page 6	
	Cash Payments			Expense Accounts				Balance	
Check Number	Explanation	Amount	Miscellaneous	Recordings	Salaries	Utilities			
	Balance for January							5,826.07	1
2161	Rent	780.00	780.00					5,587.25	2
								6,174.13	3
2162	Electricity	117.18				117.18		6,448.75	4
2163	Gas	48.60				48.60		6,400.15	5
2164	Recordings	1,615.91		1,615.91				5,371.15	6
2165	Display Equipment	39.78	39.78					5,733.56	7
								6,241.29	8
2166	Salaries	1,080.20			1,080.20			5,700.84	9

penses include those that do not occur often. Examples are payments for rent and display equipment.

- Recordings. Payments to suppliers for compact discs, records, and tapes are listed in the Recordings column.
- Salaries. Each week, Super Sounds makes a payment to a payroll service for the total amount of the salaries the employees have earned that week. The payroll service then pays the individual employees.
- Utilities. Super Sounds has utility expenses each month which include electricity, gas, water, and telephone.

Balance. Belinda and Kareem must know how much money they have on hand each day. They need this information to be sure that they have enough money in their checking account to pay their bills. Each day they add the total receipts to the previous balance and then subtract the payments to find the new balance.

For example, on February 7 they added the total receipts ($539.75) to the balance on February 6 ($6,241.29) and subtracted the payment for salaries ($1,080.20) to find the new balance for the day ($5,700.84). Note that the total deposit for the day was not added because it is the same as the total receipts.

Week of February 1

The cash receipts, deposits, cash payments, expense accounts, and balance have been entered in the classified cash record for the week of February 1 shown above. Make the same entries for the week of February 1 in a classified cash record using the information that follows. After each date, the receipt tape for that day is shown, followed by that day's deposits and payments. When you are finished, check your work against the classified cash record above.

February 1   Balance for January is $5,826.07.
   See page 269 for the February 1 receipt tape.
   See page 269 for the February 1 deposit slip. Be sure to total bills and coins before recording the amount in the Bills and Coins column. Also, total the checks before recording the amount in the Checks column.

Payments: Check 2161 for rent (Miscellaneous)—$780.

In recording these transactions, be sure to follow the dates down each column.

```
      SUPER SOUNDS

        *108.59 CD
        *172.90 R
        *272.17 T
        * 33.22 TAX
  FEB. 2 *586.88 TOTAL
```

Deposit: Bills and coins — $298.58; checks — $110.38; bank credit cards — $177.92.

```
      SUPER SOUNDS

        * 70.28 CD
        *124.37 R
        *184.77 T
        * 22.77 TAX
  FEB. 5 *402.19 TOTAL
```

Deposit: Bills and coins — $199.60; checks — $79.98; bank credit cards — $122.61.

Payment: Check 2165 for display equipment (Miscellaneous) — $39.78.

```
      SUPER SOUNDS

        * 78.94 CD
        * 98.74 R
        *191.94 T
        * 22.18 TAX
  FEB. 3 *391.80 TOTAL
```

Deposit: Bills and coins — $202.22; checks — $70.14; bank credit cards — $119.44.

Payments: Check 2162 for electricity (Utility) — $117.18; Check 2163 for gas (Utility) — $48.60.

```
      SUPER SOUNDS

        * 99.25 CD
        *138.90 R
        *240.84 T
        * 28.74 TAX
  FEB. 6 *507.73 TOTAL
```

Deposit: Bills and coins — $261.61; checks — $95.47; bank credit cards — $150.65.

```
      SUPER SOUNDS

        *112.47 CD
        *165.20 R
        *276.02 T
        * 33.22 TAX
  FEB. 4 *586.91 TOTAL
```

Deposit: Bills and coins — $300.19; checks — $98.56; bank credit cards — $188.16.

Payment: Check 2164 for recordings — $1,615.91.

```
      SUPER SOUNDS

        * 96.52 CD
        *157.45 R
        *255.23 T
        * 30.55 TAX
  FEB. 7 *539.75 TOTAL
```

Deposit: Bills and coins — $273.32; checks — $104.50; bank credit cards — $161.93.

Payment: Check 2166 for salaries — $1,080.20.

Week of February 8

Now make the entries in the classified cash record for the week of February 8. The transactions for the week follow.

```
       SUPER SOUNDS

         *133.39 CD
         *168.17 R
         *301.23 T
         * 36.17 TAX
FEB. 8  *638.96 TOTAL
```

Deposit: Bills and coins — $327.73; checks — $122.45; bank credit cards — $188.78.

```
       SUPER SOUNDS

         *102.24 CD
         *169.85 R
         *274.16 T
         * 32.78 TAX
FEB. 9  *579.03 TOTAL
```

Deposit: Bills and coins — $285.43; checks — $115.39; bank credit cards — $178.21.

```
       SUPER SOUNDS

         *110.17 CD
         *157.48 R
         *269.41 T
         * 32.22 TAX
FEB. 10 *569.28 TOTAL
```

Deposit: Bills and coins — $290.74; checks — $109.39; bank credit cards — $169.15.

Payment: Check 2167 for telephone (Utility) — $78.26.

```
       SUPER SOUNDS

         * 78.19 CD
         * 98.39 R
         *178.75 T
         * 21.32 TAX
FEB. 11 *376.65 TOTAL
```

Deposit: Bills and coins — $189.39; checks — $72.85; bank credit cards — $114.41.

Payment: Check 2168 for recordings — $874.73.

```
       SUPER SOUNDS

         *107.23 CD
         *174.13 R
         *276.32 T
         * 33.46 TAX
FEB. 12 *591.14 TOTAL
```

Deposit: Bills and coins — $311.24; checks — $105.90; bank credit cards — $174.

```
       SUPER SOUNDS

         *100.99 CD
         *148.99 R
         *250.37 T
         * 30.02 TAX
FEB. 13 *530.37 TOTAL
```

Deposit: Bills and coins — $264.80; checks — $106.22; bank credit cards — $159.35.

```
         SUPER SOUNDS

         *  77.49 CD
         *123.17 R
         *200.82 T
         * 24.09 TAX
 FEB. 14 *425.57 TOTAL
```

Deposit: Bills and coins — $212.55; checks
           — $83.98; bank credit cards —
           $129.04.

Payment: Check 2169 for salaries —
         $1,132.13.

```
         SUPER SOUNDS

         *100.23 CD
         *141.18 R
         *251.45 T
         * 29.57 TAX
 FEB. 17 *522.43 TOTAL
```

Deposit: Bills and coins — $261.03; checks
           — $104.56; bank credit cards —
           $156.84.

Payment: Check 2171 for advertising
         (Miscellaneous) — $55.81.

Week of February 15

Now make the entries in the classified cash record for the week of February 15. The transactions for the week follow.

```
         SUPER SOUNDS

         *182.91 CD
         *257.91 R
         *442.26 T
         * 52.98 TAX
 FEB. 15 *936.06 TOTAL
```

Deposit: Bills and coins — $468.95; checks
           — $184.80; bank credit cards —
           $282.31.

Payment: Check 2170 for sales tax
         (Miscellaneous) — $742.29.

```
         SUPER SOUNDS

         * 93.64 CD
         *148.95 R
         *253.08 T
         * 29.74 TAX
 FEB. 18 *525.41 TOTAL
```

Deposit: Bills and coins — $266.66; checks
         — $110.90; bank credit cards —
         $147.85.

```
         SUPER SOUNDS

         *148.83 CD
         *192.38 R
         *342.93 T
         * 41.05 TAX
 FEB. 16 *725.19 TOTAL
```

Deposit: Bills and coins — $362.81; checks
         — $142.39; bank credit cards —
         $219.99.

```
         SUPER SOUNDS

         * 74.45 CD
         *106.50 R
         *181.58 T
         * 21.75 TAX
 FEB. 19 *384.28 TOTAL
```

Deposit: Bills and coins — $193.46; checks
           — $72.95; bank credit cards —
           $117.87.

Payment: Check 2172 for recordings —
         $2,013.81.

```
        SUPER SOUNDS

          *105.94 CD
          *163.38 R
          *266.14 T
          * 32.13 TAX
  FEB. 20 *567.59 TOTAL
```

Deposit: Bills and coins — $282.17; checks
— $93.55; bank credit cards —
$191.87.

Payment: Check 2173 for water (Utility) —
$27.90.

```
        SUPER SOUNDS

          *125.62 CD
          *168.18 R
          *291.41 T
          * 35.11 TAX
  FEB. 23 *620.32 TOTAL
```

Deposit: Bills and coins — $310.28; checks
— $118.97; bank credit cards —
$191.07.

Payment: Check 2175 for recordings —
$1,198.56.

```
        SUPER SOUNDS

          *104.97 CD
          *138.70 R
          *243.59 T
          * 29.24 TAX
  FEB. 21 *516.50 TOTAL
```

Deposit: Bills and coins — $263.32; checks
— $97.63; bank credit cards —
$155.55.

Payment: Check 2174 for salaries —
$1,075.37.

```
        SUPER SOUNDS

          * 97.53 CD
          *137.95 R
          *256.60 T
          * 29.52 TAX
  FEB. 24 *521.60 TOTAL
```

Deposit: Bills and coins — $266.54; checks
— $105.35; bank credit cards —
$149.71.

Payment: Check 2176 for supplies
(Miscellaneous) — $15.54.

Week of February 22

Now make the entries in the classified cash record for the week of February 22. The transactions for the week follow.

```
        SUPER SOUNDS

          *158.30 CD
          *231.14 R
          *378.69 T
          * 46.09 TAX
  FEB. 22 *814.22 TOTAL
```

Deposit: Bills and coins — $407.77; checks
— $159.86; bank credit cards —
$246.59.

```
        SUPER SOUNDS

          * 96.52 CD
          *135.42 R
          *232.50 T
          * 27.87 TAX
  FEB. 25 *492.31 TOTAL
```

Deposit: Bills and coins — $249.98; checks
— $94.37; bank credit cards —
$147.96.

SUPER SOUNDS

```
        * 75.26 CD
        *117.80 R
        *302.83 T
        * 29.75 TAX
FEB. 26 *525.64 TOTAL
```

Deposit: Bills and coins — $248.41; checks — $108.18; bank credit cards — $169.05.

SUPER SOUNDS

```
        * 83.98 CD
        *122.88 R
        *206.09 T
        * 24.78 TAX
FEB. 27 *437.73 TOTAL
```

Deposit: Bills and coins — $218.; checks — $87.89; bank credit cards — $131.84.

Payment: Check 2177 for recordings — $526.52.

SUPER SOUNDS

```
        *111.53 CD
        *152.25 R
        *261.16 T
        * 31.50 TAX
FEB. 28 *556.44 TOTAL
```

Deposit: Bills and coins — $313.19; checks — $96.87; bank credit cards — $146.38.

Payment: Check 2178 for salaries — $1,114.44.

Proving and Closing the Classified Cash Record

At the end of each month, Belinda Johnson and Kareem Rasvan prove and close the classified cash record. Your job is to prove and close the record that you kept for the month of February. Follow these steps.

1. Draw a single rule under all the money columns. Pencil-foot each money column by writing the totals just below the rule in small pencil figures.

2. To check the accuracy of your classified cash record before you record final totals, do the following work:

a. Add the totals for the Compact Discs, Records, Tapes, and Tax columns. The result should be equal to the total of the Total Receipts column.

b. Add the total of the Bills and Coins, Checks, and Bank Card columns. The result should be the same as the total of the Total Deposit column.

c. Compare the total of the Total Receipts column with the total of the Total Deposit column. They should be the same.

d. Add the total of the four expense account columns (Miscellaneous, Recordings, Salaries, and Utilities). The result should be the same as the total of the Amount column in the Cash Payments section.

e. Add the balance for January in the February 1 entry to the total deposits. From this, subtract the total of the Amount column in the Cash Payments section. The result should be the same as the ending balance for February.

f. Compare the ending cash balance with the balance in the checkbook. The two amounts should be the same. The checkbook balance is $8,702.20.

3. Enter the totals. Write the date (28) in the Date column. Write the word "Totals" in the Explanation column. Draw a double rule under all the columns except the Explanation column.

4. On the first line after the double rules, enter the date (Mar. 1, 19—). Enter the words "Balance for February" in the Explanation column. Enter the balance from February 28 in the balance column.

APPLIED
BUSINESS
RECORDS

CHAPTER 10

SALES RECORDS AND REPORTS

In Chapter 4, you learned about credit from the consumer's point of view. In this chapter, you will learn about credit from the point of view of a business. You've seen how to complete a credit application. In this chapter, you will see what a business looks for when credit applications are reviewed. You already know about the costs of credit for a consumer. In this chapter, you will discover that credit also has costs for a business.

A *charge sale* means that the customer does not pay cash for the items at the time of purchase but pays for them at a later date. In Chapter 4, you found out how important it is for consumers to keep accurate records of their charge sales. Businesses, too, must keep accurate records. You will learn how that is done in this chapter. Finally, you will see how businesses use records to examine their sales by department and territory.

TOPIC 1 ● RECORDING RETAIL CHARGE SALES

GOALS

1. To review charge account applications.
2. To prepare charge sales slips.
3. To prepare credit memos.

KEY TERMS

On a sales slip, the *extension* is the unit price of an item multiplied by the quantity of that item.

A *credit memorandum*, also called a *credit memo,* is a form used to record the return of goods bought on a charge account by a customer.

REVIEWING CHARGE ACCOUNT APPLICATIONS

A *retail business* is a business that sells goods or services directly to the public.

As you learned in Chapter 4, to open a charge account in a retail store, a customer first must complete a credit application. Vicki Turner completed the application shown on page 279 to apply for a charge account at Nina's Fashion Boutique.

Nina's
Fashion Boutique

CREDIT APPLICATION

FOR OFFICE USE ONLY ACCOUNT NUMBER	DATE OPENED
☐ - ☐☐☐ - ☐☐☐ - ☐	

# OF CARDS	LIMIT	APPROVED—BY	EMP NO.

1 TELL US ABOUT YOURSELF

First Name	Middle Name (Account will be carried in this name)	Last Name	Age	Spouse's First Name
Vicki	Rose	Turner	23	—

Present Address Residence:	City/State	Zip Code	Own / ☒ Rent / ☐ Live w/parents	How Long (Yrs.) Mos.	Mortgage/Rent Payments	Telephone
1481 Royal Lane,	Dallas, TX	75230		3	$ 340 /Mo.	(214) 555-7946

Previous Address (If less than two years of present address)	City/State	Zip Code		How Long Yrs. Mos.	Social Security Number

Present Employer	Address	Position	Phone No.	Salary		How Long (Yrs.) Mos.
Blakely Corp.	5942 Greenville Ave. Dallas, TX	Secretary	(214)555-8971	$1,850	Wk. (Mo.) Yr.	3

Previous Employer (If less than two years at present employment)	Address	Position		How Long Yrs. Mos.

Nearest relative not living with you (Other than spouse)	Relationship	Address	City/State	Phone No.
Helen Turner	Mother	2619 Alameda Ave.	El Paso, TX	(915) 555-8916

Alimony, child support, or separate maintenance income need not be revealed if you do not wish to have it considered as a basis for repaying this obligation.	Other Source(s) of income	Amount	Wk. Mo. Yr.

MARITAL STATUS	☐ MARRIED	☐ SEPARATED	☒ UNMARRIED	(INCLUDING SINGLE DIVORCED AND WIDOWED)

2 AND YOUR CO-APPLICANT

First Name	Middle Name	Last Name	Age

Present Employer	Address	Phone No.	Salary Wk. Mo. Yr.	How Long Yrs. Mos.

Previous Employer (If less than two years at present employment)	Address		How Long Yrs. Mos.	Social Security Number

3 AND YOUR CREDIT REFERENCES

PREVIOUS NINA'S ACCOUNT	☐ YES	☒ NO	(PLEASE INDICATE NAME IN WHICH ACCOUNT WAS ESTABLISHED AND ACCOUNT NUMBER IF KNOWN)

BANK REFERENCES	CK	SV	LN	CREDIT REFERENCES
Bank: Dallas Central Savings		X		Store: Greer's Dept. Store
Account No. 046-842936				Account No. 892-437-50
Bank: Park Cities Trust	X			Store: Junior Dimension
Account No. 079-239461				Account No. 462378

4 YOUR SIGNATURE

I hereby apply for a Nina's Charge Account.

A copy of our Charge Account Agreement, also Truth-in-Lending Disclosures will be provided upon approval of this application.

APPLICANT'S SIGNATURE _Vicki R. Turner_ CO-APP SIGNATURE _—_ DATE _5/1/—_

A *charge account application* is a form requesting that a charge account be opened.

Legible means easy to read.

Credit references are the names of banks and stores where a charge account applicant has an account.

A *charge card* is a plastic card issued so that a customer can buy goods and services on credit.

An *imprinting machine* is a device that uses pressure to "print" information from a charge card onto a sales slip or a credit memorandum.

In the office at Nina's Fashion Boutique, the charge account application is then reviewed to be sure that:

1. Each item is easy to read. If any item is not legible, the customer will be asked to correct it.
2. No information is missing. The customer will be asked to supply any missing information.
3. The application is signed and dated. If it is not, the customer will be asked to sign and date the form.

Some stores will also compare specific information on the completed form with the customer's driver's license or other identification.

After the application has been reviewed, the store manager or the credit manager checks the applicant's credit references. If the manager finds that the person pays bills promptly and has a steady income, the application will be approved. A charge account will then be opened, and the customer will receive a charge card. The card can be used to charge items that are purchased.

PREPARING CHARGE SALES SLIPS

To record a charge sale, a salesperson needs the customer's charge card, a sales slip, and an imprinting machine. You saw what an imprinting machine looks like in Chapter 5.

To complete the sales slip, the salesperson places the customer's charge card in the imprinting machine. The salesperson places a blank sales slip in position over the card and pulls the handle quickly from left to right. Pulling the handle presses the card firmly against the sales slip and imprints the information from the card onto the slip.

Now the salesperson removes the printed slip and writes in the sales information:

1. The date, the department number, the clerk number, and the salesperson's initials. The salesperson also checks off either the Send or Take line, depending on whether the customer takes the merchandise or not.
2. The quantity; class, or number used by the store to classify the item; a description of the item, or article; the unit price (that is, the price of *one* item); and the extension, which is the unit price times the quantity.
3. The subtotal (the total before sales tax is added).
4. The sales tax.
5. The total, which is the subtotal plus the sales tax.

When the customer signs the sales slip, the salesperson compares the signature with the one on the back of the charge card. The salesperson gives the charge card and one copy of the sales slip to the customer along with the items that were purchased.

As you learned in Chapter 5, electronic cash registers automatically print sales information on the sales slip. A charge sales slip that has been filled out by an electronic cash register is shown here.

The *unit price* is the price of one item.

The *subtotal* is the total cost of a sale before the sales tax is added.

A *sales slip* is a form used to record specific sales information.

PREPARING CREDIT MEMOS

When charge customers return goods, they receive *credit* for the returned items (including the sales tax). The salesperson makes a record of the return by preparing a *credit memorandum,* or a *credit memo,* such as the one shown below.

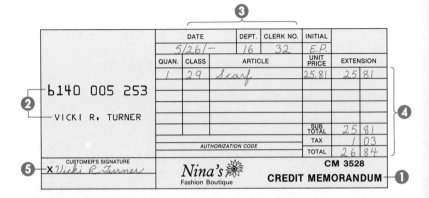

Note the following:

1. The words ''Credit'' or ''Credit Memorandum'' are printed on the face of the form.
2. The customer's name and account number are imprinted with the customer's charge card, just as they were for a charge sale.
3. The date, department number, clerk number, and clerk's initials are written on the top line, just as they were for a sale.
4. Information about the item being returned is written on the sales slip—again, just as for a sale.
5. The customer signs the credit memo.

One copy of the credit memo is given to the customer. The other copy is kept by the business to credit the customer's charge account.

Check Your Reading

1. What is the first thing a customer must do to open a charge account in a retail store?

2. What three items does the salesperson use to record a charge sale?

3. On a sales slip, what term is used for the result when you multiply the unit price by the quantity?

4. When customers return items, do they receive credit for the sales tax they were charged?

1. Review the charge account application shown below. Then answer the questions that follow.

LOWELL'S CHARGE ACCOUNT APPLICATION (Please print or type)

OFFICE USE ONLY	STATUS	DATE RATED	LC	PLATES	SOURCE					
	CR RPT	EMP	OTHER ACCOUNT		DESG	STORE	EMPLOYEE NO.	RATER	DATE	

TITLE (Optional) APPLICANT'S NAME: Leave one blank between first name, middle initial and last name.

`R A N D O L P H   R   M O O R E`

CHECK ONE:
☒ Option Account
☐ Revolving Contract Account
☐ Table Top Account

Telephone No. (205) 377-1658
Business Telephone No. (205) 294-1672

STREET ADDRESS

`6 7 2   G A R D E N   S P R I N G   D R`

Social Security Number | No. of Dependents 3

CHECK ONE:
☒ Individual Account
☐ Spouse User Account

CITY `H U N T S V I L L E` STATE `A L` ZIP CODE `3 5 8 0 3`

Length of Time at Present Address YEARS 14 MONTHS 6

☒ Own ☐ Rent
☐ Live with Relative
Monthly Mtge./Rent $ 890.00

If at above home address for less than 3 years, please furnish former address information below.

Former Address Street City State Zip Code | Length of Time YEARS | MONTHS

Name of Employer (or Business if Self-Employed): FLIGHT TEST ENGINEERING INC. | Occupation: ENGINEER | Business Address: 1700 FREEWAY, HUNTSVILLE, AL 35807 | Salary Amount ☐ Week $ ☒ Month $5,600.00 | Length of Time YEARS 14 MONTHS 6

Former Employer (or Business if Self-Employed): U.S. ARMY | Occupation: TECHNICIAN | Business Address: FORT BENNING, GA 31905 | Salary Amount ☐ Week $ ☒ Month $850.00 | Length of Time YEARS 3 MONTHS 0

Source and amount of other income (Income from alimony, child support, or maintenance payments need not be disclosed unless you rely on it in applying for credit). | Source | | Amount ☐ Week $ — ☐ Month $

Bank: ALABAMA BANK & TRUST | Branch: MONTE SANO | ☒ Checking ☒ Savings ☒ Loan

Nearest Relative (not living with you): PAUL R. MOORE | Relationship: BROTHER | Street Address: 316 EAST DR. | City: DENVER | State: CO | Zip Code: 80218 | Phone: (303) 622-8217

Complete only if you checked Spouse User Account or if you rely on your spouse's income in making this application.

SPOUSE'S NAME Leave One Blank Between First Name, Middle Initial and Last Name | Address (if different from yours) City State Zip | Soc. Security No.

Spouse's Employer (or Business if Self-Employed) | Occupation | Business Address | Salary Amount Week $ Month $ | Length of Time YEARS MONTHS

CREDIT REFERENCES: If you completed shaded area above, also include accounts carried in your spouse's name.

Reference	City	Account No.	Reference	City	Account No.
SEARS	HUNTSVILLE, AL	7-17025-11682-9			
TEXACO	HOUSTON, TX	33-247-10419-1127			

NOTICE: ANY HOLDER OF THIS CONSUMER CREDIT CONTRACT IS SUBJECT TO ALL CLAIMS AND DEFENSES WHICH THE DEBTOR COULD ASSERT AGAINST THE SELLER OF GOODS OR SERVICES OBTAINED PURSUANT HERETO OR WITH THE PROCEEDS HEREOF. RECOVERY HEREUNDER BY THE DEBTOR SHALL NOT EXCEED AMOUNTS PAID BY THE DEBTOR HEREUNDER.

_____ Date _____ 19 ___
Applicant's Signature

a. Are all entries legible? If not, list the heading of each entry that is not legible.

b. Is any information missing? If so, list the heading of each entry that is missing.

c. Has the form been signed? dated?

d. Does the information on the application agree with this information from the customer's driver's license?

Name: Randolph E. Moore
Address: 672 Garden Spring Dr.
Huntsville, AL 35807
S.S. No.: 219-84-6768

If not, list the items that are different.

2. As a salesperson for Nina's Fashion Boutique, you are to prepare charge sales slips for the following sales. For all sales slips, use today's date, department number 16, clerk number 32, and your own initials. All customers will take their purchases with them. The sales tax rate is 4 percent. Do not sign the sales slips.

a. You sold one class 23 winter coat, priced at $159.95, to Vicki R. Turner, account number 6140 005 253. (Multiply $159.95 by 0.04 to figure the tax.) Your completed sales slip should match the one shown on page 280.

b. You sold two class 21 blouses, priced at $40 each, to Angela Garcia, account number 6162 080 171.

c. You sold one class 24 skirt, priced at $39.95, and one class 21 blouse, priced at $28.50, to Kim Wong, account number 6203 061 177.

d. You sold one class 23 raincoat, priced at $89.95; two class 21 blouses, priced at $34.50 each; and three class 29 scarves, priced at $9.50 each to Janet E. Williams, account number 6177 070 194.

3. As a salesperson for Nina's Fashion Boutique, you are to prepare credit memos for the following returns. For both credit memos, use today's date, department number 16, clerk number 32, and your own initials. The sales tax rate is 4 percent. Do not sign the credit memos.

a. Mona L. Freeman, account number 6308 073 149, returned one class 23 ski jacket, priced at $124.95.

b. Nicole R. Perez, account number 6269 019 193, returned two class 21 blouses, priced at $43.75 each.

TOPIC 2 ● MAINTAINING ACCOUNTS RECEIVABLE

GOALS

1. To prepare charge sales slips for posting.
2. To post charge sales to a customer's account.
3. To post sales returns to a customer's account.
4. To prepare a customer's statement of account.
5. To post cash receipts to a customer's account.

KEY TERMS

Accounts receivable are amounts that will be received by a business at a later date in payment of charge sales.

A *customer's account* is a record of charges, returns, and payments for a charge customer.

To *post* means to transfer information from one source to another. Information from sales slips, credit memos, and other source documents is posted to a customer's account.

The *debit* column of a customer's account is used to record amounts charged to the account. A debit increases the amount that a customer owes.

The *credit* column of a customer's account is used to record the amounts of returns and payments. A credit decreases the amount that a customer owes.

PREPARING CHARGE SALES SLIPS FOR POSTING

At the end of each business day, sales slips from charge sales are collected. They are sent to the office where the store's accounts receivable records are kept. *Accounts receivable* are amounts that will be received by a business at a later date in payment of charge sales.

Danielle Benjamin, an employee in the accounts receivable department, first prepares the charge sales slips for posting. You will learn about posting later in this topic. To prepare charge sales slips for posting:

1. She audits each sales slip. She checks the extensions, subtotal, sales tax, and total for accuracy. She makes corrections if she finds errors.
2. She adds the totals of all charge sales slips to figure total charge sales for the day. She gives the calculator tape showing

this total to the accounting assistant who keeps records on charge sales.

3. She sorts the charge sales slips according to customer name.

POSTING CHARGE SALES TO CUSTOMERS' ACCOUNTS

When a customer opens a charge account at Nina's Fashion Boutique, John Wrenn, the bookkeeper, prepares a form such as this.

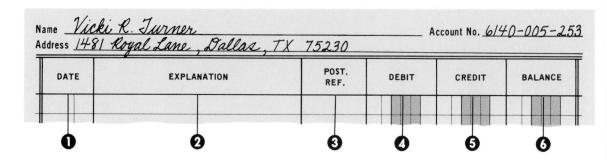

To prepare the form, John fills in the customer's name, address, and account number. Then, as the customer charges purchases, John can post charge sales to this form. Recording in customers' accounts information that is on charge sales slips is called posting charge sales.

Let's see how the six columns of this form identify the information that will be entered:

The *explanation* column on a customer's account is used to show that a balance has been brought forward from another page of the account.

The *Posting Reference* (Post. Ref.) column on the customer's account is used to record the source of the information that was posted.

The *Balance* column on a customer's account is used to record the current amount owed by the customer.

The *previous balance* is the amount that was recorded in the Balance column of a customer's account before the current charge or payment is posted.

1. The Date column is for the date of each transaction in the account.
2. The Explanation column is used to show that a balance has been brought forward from another page of the account. Because this is the first page of Vicki Turner's account, the Explanation column will not be used.
3. The Posting Reference (Post. Ref.) column is used to record the number of the charge sales slip.
4. The Debit column on a customer's account is for amounts charged to the account. A debit increases the balance of a customer's account.
5. The Credit column on a customer's account is for the amounts of returns or payments made by the customer. A credit decreases the balance of a customer's account.
6. The Balance column shows what the customer owes after each purchase and each payment. The balance is figured by adding a debit to or subtracting a credit from the previous balance.

When John received the charge sales slip, he used it to post the charge to Vicki's account form.

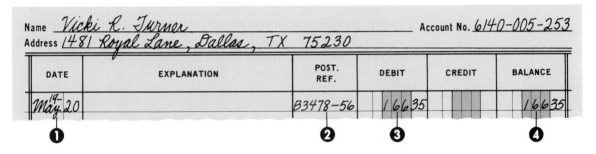

DATE	EXPLANATION	POST. REF.	DEBIT	CREDIT	BALANCE
May 20		B3478-56	166 35		166 35

Name *Vicki R. Turner* Account No. *6140-005-253*
Address *1481 Royal Lane, Dallas, TX 75230*

Follow John's steps as he posts the charge to Vicki's account:

1. John writes the date of the sales slip in the Date column.
2. He writes the sales slip number in the Post. Ref. column.
3. He writes the total amount of the sales slip in the Debit column.
4. Because there is no previous balance, John also writes the amount of the debit in the Balance column.
5. He makes a check mark beside the total on the charge sales slip to show that the amount has been posted.

DATE		DEPT.	CLERK NO.	INITIAL	SEND	
5/20/—		16	32	F.P.	TAKE	✓

QUAN.	CLASS	ARTICLE	UNIT PRICE	EXTENSION
1	23	Winter coat	159.95	159 95
			SUB TOTAL	159 95
			TAX	6 40
			TOTAL	166 35 ✓

6140 005 253

VICKI R. TURNER

SALE CONFIRMED AND DRAFT ACCEPTED
X *Vicki R. Turner*

AUTHORIZATION CODE

B3478-56

Nina's ❀
Fashion Boutique

On May 24 John posted a second charge sales slip, number B3479-32 in the amount of $26.84, to Vicki Turner's account. After he posted the sales slip, the account looked like this.

Name *Vicki R. Turner* Account No. *6140-005-253*
Address *1481 Royal Lane, Dallas, TX 75230*

DATE	EXPLANATION	POST. REF.	DEBIT	CREDIT	BALANCE
May 20		B3478-56	166 35		166 35
24		B3479-32	26 84		193 19

Note that the debit amount, $26.84, was added to the previous balance, $166.35, to get the new balance, $193.19:

$$\$26.84 + \$166.35 = \$193.19$$

POSTING CREDIT MEMOS TO CUSTOMERS' ACCOUNTS

On May 26 Vicki Turner returned an item she had purchased and received the credit memo below. When the bookkeeper, John Wrenn, receives his copy of the credit memo, he posts the credit to Vicki's account, as follows:

Name	Vicki R. Turner		Account No. 6140-005-253			
Address	1481 Royal Lane, Dallas, TX 75230					
DATE	EXPLANATION	POST. REF.	DEBIT	CREDIT	BALANCE	
May 20		B3478-56	166 35		166 35	
24		B3479-32	26 84		193 19	
26		CM3528		26 84	166 35	

❶   ❷   ❸   ❹

1. John writes in the date of the credit memo.
2. He writes the number of the credit memo in the Post. Ref. column.
3. He writes the amount of the credit memo in the Credit column.
4. He subtracts the amount of the credit from the previous balance and writes the difference in the Balance column. Remember: A credit decreases the balance of a customer's account.
5. John makes a check mark beside the total on the credit memo to show that the amount has been posted.

	DATE	DEPT.	CLERK NO.	INITIAL	
	5/26/—	16	32	E.P.	
	QUAN.	CLASS	ARTICLE	UNIT PRICE	EXTENSION
6140 005 253	1	29	Scarf	25.81	25 81
VICKI R. TURNER					
				SUB TOTAL	25 81
		AUTHORIZATION CODE		TAX	1 03
				TOTAL	26 84 ✓ ❺
CUSTOMER'S SIGNATURE				CM 3528	
X Vicki R. Turner	Nina's Fashion Boutique			CREDIT MEMORANDUM	

PREPARING THE STATEMENT OF ACCOUNT

A *statement of account* is a bill that is sent to a customer, usually monthly, listing amounts charged to the account, returns, and payments on the account.

Near the end of each month, the accounts receivable department of Nina's Fashion Boutique prepares a *statement of account* for each charge customer who owes money. The statement of account, or bill, tells the customer how much to pay and when the payment is due. Vicki Turner's statement of account for May 28 is shown here.

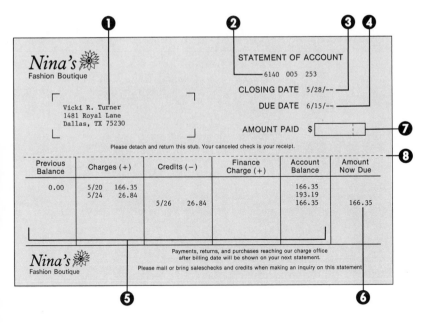

Note the following on the statement of account:

1. The customer's name and address are in the address block.
2. The customer's account number is at the top right of the statement.
3. The *closing date* is the date the statement was prepared and mailed.
4. The *due date* is the date the payment is due.
5. The previous balance and all charges, credits, and account balances from the customer's account are listed on the form.
6. The Amount Now Due column shows the amount to be paid, which is the amount of the last balance listed.
7. The Amount Paid box is for the customer to fill in. When Vicki writes her check, she then fills in the amount paid in this box.
8. There is a broken line across the middle of the statement. Vicki tears the statement across this broken line and returns the top part, the stub, with her check. She keeps the bottom part for her records.

The *closing date* is the date on which the statement of account is prepared and mailed.

The *due date* is the date the customer's payment is due. The Amount Now Due total shown on the statement of account is expected no *later* than this date.

The *statement stub* is the part of the statement of account that the customer tears off and sends along with the payment check.

POSTING CASH RECEIPTS TO CUSTOMERS' ACCOUNTS

Payments received from charge customers must be posted to the customers' accounts.

Vicki Turner's statement stub and her check are shown here. Also shown is Vicki Turner's account form.

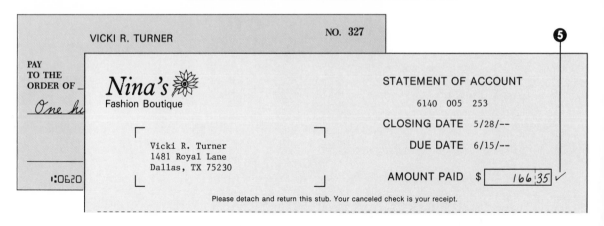

Yolanda Guerro, who works in the accounts receivable department, follows these steps in posting this cash receipt to Vicki Turner's account:

1. Yolanda writes the date the payment was received.
2. In the Posting Reference column she enters "Ck 327," for Check 327, Vicki Turner's check number.
3. Yolanda writes the amount of the check in the Credit column.
4. She subtracts the amount in the Credit column from the previous balance and writes the difference in the Balance column. When the balance is zero, she writes the figures "—00" in the Balance column.
5. Yolanda makes a check mark beside the Amount Paid box on the statement stub to show that the amount has been posted.

Check Your Reading

1. Which four amounts should be checked for accuracy when a charge sales slip is reviewed?

2. What happens to a customer's account balance for each of the following? Answer either increase or decrease for each item.

    a. The customer returns an item for credit.
    b. The customer buys an item on account.
    c. The customer makes a payment on account.

3. What does a bookkeeper do to a charge sales slip to show that it has been posted to the customer's account?

4. What does a bookkeeper do to a credit memo to show that it has been posted to the customer's account?

5. What term describes the date on which the statement of account is prepared and mailed?

6. Which two items does a customer send to make a payment on account?

7. What does a bookkeeper do to a statement stub to show that a customer's payment has been posted to the customer's account?

Exercises for Topic 2

1. Shown below and on the next page are parts of six charge sales slips. Review the extensions, subtotal, tax (at 4 percent), and total for each sales slip. On a separate sheet list any errors you find and the corrected amounts. Then figure the total amount of all six sales slips.

a.

QUAN.	CLASS	ARTICLE	UNIT PRICE	EXTENSION	
2	17	Tapes	8.95	17	80
			SUB TOTAL	17	80
		AUTHORIZATION CODE	TAX		71
			TOTAL	18	51

b.

QUAN.	CLASS	ARTICLE	UNIT PRICE	EXTENSION	
1	17	Headphones	27.50	27	50
2	17	Battery pak	9.95	19	90
			SUB TOTAL	46	90
		AUTHORIZATION CODE	TAX	1	88
			TOTAL	48	78

c.

QUAN.	CLASS	ARTICLE	UNIT PRICE	EXTENSION	
1	14	Printer cable	26.00	26	00
1	14	mouse	34.50	34	50
1	14	Language card	44.95	44	95
1	14	Head cleaner	9.50	9	50
			SUB TOTAL	114	95
		AUTHORIZATION CODE	TAX	4	60
			TOTAL	119	55

d.

QUAN.	CLASS	ARTICLE	UNIT PRICE	EXTENSION	
2 pr	23	Earrings	42.20	84	40
2	23	Necklace	63.90	127	80
			SUB TOTAL	212	20
		AUTHORIZATION CODE	TAX	8	48
			TOTAL	220	68

e.

QUAN.	CLASS	ARTICLE	UNIT PRICE	EXTENSION	
4 pr	40	Men's socks	3.95	15	80
			SUB TOTAL	15	80
AUTHORIZATION CODE			TAX		63
			TOTAL	16	33

f.

QUAN.	CLASS	ARTICLE	UNIT PRICE	EXTENSION	
2	12	Cheese tray	26.95	53	90
1	12	Cheese knife	18.50	18	50
2	12	Candle holder	31.00	62	00
3	12	Sewing dish	14.45	43	35
			SUB TOTAL	177	75
AUTHORIZATION CODE			TAX	7	11
			TOTAL	184	86

2. In your Activity Guide are three completed charge sales slips. Review the slips, making any necessary corrections. Figure the total amount of all three sales slips.

3. As an employee in the accounts receivable department of Nina's Fashion Boutique, your duties include setting up new customer accounts, posting charge sales slips and credit memos, preparing statements of account, and posting cash receipts to customer's accounts.

a. Set up a new account for the following customers by entering each name, address, and account number at the top of a customer account form.

(1) Pauline Bowers
6184 Ninth Avenue
Dallas, TX 75239
Acct. No. 5036 812 288

(2) Carol Ford
4126 South Woodson
Dallas, TX 75224
Acct. No. 3842 065 982

(3) Betsy Jamison
928 Belmont Drive
Dallas, TX 75212
Acct. No. 4416 840 318

(4) Marie Rossi
1229 Princeton
Dallas, TX 75218
Acct. No. 2102 428 261

b. Post each of the following charge sales slips or credit memos to the correct account.

Charge Sales Slip No. B2463-29; Betsy Jamison; March 13, 19—; total, $142.57.

Charge Sales Slip No. B2463-33; Pauline Bowers; March 13, 19—; total, $48.63.

Charge Sales Slip No. B2463-40; Carol Ford; March 16, 19—; total, $28.76.

Charge Sales Slip No. B2463-48; Betsy Jamison; March 16, 19—; total, $17.50.

Credit Memo No. 3529; Betsy Jamison; March 17, 19—; total, $17.50.

Charge Sales Slip No. B2463-55; Carol Ford; March 17, 19—; total, $218.33.

Charge Sales Slip No. B2463-59; Marie Rossi; March 18, 19—; total, $89.95.

Charge Sales Slip No. B2463-62; Pauline Bowers; March 18, 19—; total, $143.22.

Charge Sales Slip No. B2463-68; Carol Ford; March 20, 19—; total, $82.20.

Credit Memo No. 3530; Pauline Bowers; March 21, 19—; total, $48.63.

Charge Sales Slip No. B2463-74; Betsy Jamison; March 23, 19—; total, $84.47.

Credit Memo No. 3531; Carol Ford; March 26, 19—; total, $82.20.

Charge Sales Slip No. B2463-81; Marie Rossi; March 26, 19—; total, $101.67.

c. Prepare a statement of account for each of the four customers. The closing date is March 26, 19—, and the due date is April 15, 19—.

d. The following list represents checks and statement stubs received from customers on the dates shown at the left. Post each payment to the correct account.

April 7, Check 1170; Carol Ford; $247.09.
April 12, Check 418; Marie Rossi; $191.62.
April 14, Check 336; Betsy Jamison; $100.
April 15, Check 4120; Pauline Bowers; $143.22.

TOPIC 3 ● EXAMINING SALES REPORTS

GOALS

1. To examine departmental sales report data.
2. To examine territorial sales report data.

KEY TERMS

Net income is the money left over after business expenses are paid.

A *departmental sales report* is a listing of the dollar amount of sales by the company unit, or department, in which the sales were made.

A *territorial sales report* is a listing of the dollar amount of sales by the state, city, or other area or territory in which the sales were made.

In order to stay in business, a retailer or wholesaler must sell enough goods or services to earn a profit, or net income. *Net income* is the money left over after expenses are paid. Sales managers must closely review their company's sales records because the success of a business depends on knowing what items are selling. A sales manager may ask questions like these:

- How much is each department selling?
- How much is each territory selling?
- How much is each salesperson selling?
- How much of each product or service is selling?

Sales and advertising managers use the answers to these questions to help improve sales. Information from cash sales and charge sales records is organized into *sales reports*. The type of business will determine the types of sales reports prepared. Two commonly used sales reports are the departmental sales report and the territorial sales report.

DEPARTMENTAL SALES REPORT

A *departmental sales report* sums up sales information for each department of a store or other organization. The report shown below, for example, gives the departmental sales for Toys Galore for the week of May 15.

TOYS GALORE

DEPARTMENTAL SALES REPORT

WEEK ENDING *May 15,* 19 —

DAY	Dolls	Games	Electronics	Miscellaneous	TOTAL
Monday	729 60	456 40	591 75	946 20	2,723 95
Tuesday	858 25	321 30	686 20	765 35	2,631 10
Wednesday	687 40	541 85	432 95	843 75	2,505 95
Thursday	798 35	428 35	803 50	671 40	2,701 60
Friday	926 80	621 10	562 50	1,003 25	3,113 65
Saturday	1,225 95	832 05	981 60	1,121 45	4,161 05
Totals	5,226 35	3,201 05	4,058 50	5,351 40	17,837 30

Note that this sales report shows (1) the daily sales for each department of the store, (2) the total sales for the store for each day, (3) the total sales for each department for the week, and (4) the total store sales for the entire week.

By comparing the sales report for May 15 with sales reports for other weeks, the managers of Toys Galore can run the store better. For example, the reports can help show trends in sales and where and when more salespersons may be needed. In this way, departmental sales reports are very helpful.

TERRITORIAL SALES REPORTS

A *territorial sales report* sums up the sales information for each salesperson's assigned area. A computer screen of a territorial sales report is shown below.

Humming Electronic Control Company			May 31, 19--	
Territorial Sales Report ($)				
	May Sales		Year to date Sales	
Territory	This Year	Last Year	This Year	Last Year
Sacramento, CA	$ 21,845	$ 23,284	$ 65,180	$ 62,520
Bartow, FL	$ 56,600	$ 51,080	$ 180,516	$ 170,913
Atlanta, GA	$ 12,497	$ 10,234	$ 38,578	$ 29,190
Peoria, IL	$ 41,912	$ 38,586	$ 133,004	$ 139,450
Monroe, LA	$ 35,267	$ 31,908	$ 103,654	$ 95,369
Totals	$ 168,121	$ 155,092	$ 520,932	$ 497,442

The sales manager notes that in Bartow, Humming sold $56,600 worth of goods during May of this year. For May of last year, Humming sold $51,080 worth of goods. Therefore, Humming's sales for May in the Bartow territory have gone up by $5,520 ($56,600 − $51,080 = $5,520). In the Bartow territory, Humming has sold $180,516 worth of goods so far this year. In the same time period last year, $170,913 worth of goods were sold. Therefore, Humming's year-to-date sales for the Bartow territory have gone up by $9,603 ($180,516 − $170,913 = $9,603).

This sales report does more than show increases and decreases. It helps the sales manager see the problem sales areas. It helps the manager report accurate information to company executives. Thus, the manager can see sales patterns and plan for the future.

Planning Suppose the manager wants to plan the quota for next May. This requires taking the sales for this May and calculating a percentage of increase. For example, to plan a 9 percent increase for the month of May, follow three steps:

1. Change the percentage to a decimal:

$$9\% = 0.09$$

2. Multiply the decimal by this May's sales:

$$
\begin{array}{r}
\$\ 56{,}600 \\
\times 0.09 \\
\hline
\$5{,}094.00
\end{array}
$$

3. Add the increase to this May's sales:

$$
\begin{array}{l}
\$56{,}600 \\
+5{,}094 \\
\hline
\$61{,}694 \text{ Quota for next May}
\end{array}
$$

Check Your Reading

1. Why are sales important to a business?

2. What term means the same as "profit"?

3. What is the difference between a departmental sales report and a territorial sales report?

4. What information does the departmental sales report provide?

5. What information does the territorial sales report provide?

1. Use the departmental sales report for Toys Galore on page 294 to answer the following:
   a. Which department had the highest sales on each of the following days: Monday, Tuesday, Wednesday, Thursday, Friday, and Saturday?
   b. Which department had the highest sales that week?
   c. Which department had the lowest sales that week?
   d. Which day had the highest sales?
   e. Which day had the lowest sales?
   f. What was the total amount of sales for the week?

2. Use the Humming territorial sales report on page 295 to answer these questions:
   a. Compare the monthly sales for this year and for last year. In which territories have sales gone up? In which territories have sales gone down?
   b. Compare the year-to-date sales for this year and for last year. In which territories have sales gone up? In which territories have sales gone down?
   c. Each month Humming awards two sales prizes. Which territory will win the prize for the highest sales for the month? the highest sales for the year?

3. Vulcan Metals Inc. is planning to increase its total dollar sales. Each department will be given a sales quota for next year that is a percentage increase over this year's sales.
   Figure the new quota for each department. First, convert the percentage increase to a decimal (for example, 4 percent = 0.04), and round the answer to the nearest dollar. Multiply the decimal increase by this year's sales and round the answer to the nearest dollar. Then add the answer, which is the amount of sales increase, to this year's sales. The sum is the new department quota for next year.

Department	Percentage Increase	This Year's Sales
Alloys	4	$174,210
Aluminum	5	214,993
Brass	2	93,208
Chrome plating	1	118,454
Iron casting	4	378,226
Steel milling	5	401,756
Welding	6	124,153
Zinc products	12	63,289

Skill: Figuring the extension, subtotal, tax, and total for a sale.

Sample Problem: Figure the following sales information:

3 items at $18.00	___?___
2 items at $6.50	___?___
Subtotal	___?___
Tax at 4%	___?___
Total	___?___

Solution:

1. Multiply quantity times unit price to figure the extensions:

$$3 \times \$18.00 = \$54.00$$
$$2 \times \$6.50 = \$13.00$$

2. Add the extensions to find the subtotal:

$$\frac{\$54.00}{\underline{+13.00}} \\ \$67.00$$

3. Multiply the subtotal by 0.04 to figure the tax:

$$\frac{\$\ 67.00}{\underline{\times 0.04}} \\ \$2.6800 = \$2.68$$

4. Add the tax to the subtotal to find the total:

$$\frac{\$67.00}{\underline{+\ 2.68}} \\ \$69.68$$

Practice: Figure extensions, subtotal, tax at $4 percent, and total for sales 1 through 8.

1. 4 items at $2.75
1 item at $6.21
6 items at $4.70

2. 2 items at $13.72
3 items at $18.95
6 items at $21.98

3. 1 item at $126.50
2 items at $45.00
12 items at $11.75
6 items at $4.35

4. 4 items at $142.75
1 item at $518.13
2 items at $26.75
3 items at $42.00

5. 4 items at $454.70
2 items at $1,102.27
6 items at $673.41

6. 2 items at $1,627.45
1 item at $800.10
2 items at $2,107.62

7. 75 items at $0.75
43 items at $0.82
96 items at $1.07

8. 126 items at $79.95
300 items at $42.50
418 items at $112.75

Skill: Finding the customer's balance, given the beginning or the previous account balance and a debit or credit amount.

Sample Problem: Find the customer's balance, given the following information:

Beginning balance	$300.00
Debit amount	50.00
Credit amount	100.00

Solution:

1. Sales to customers on account (debits) are added to the previous balance.

$$\$300 \text{ (balance)} + \$50 \text{ (debit)} = \$350$$

2. Customer's payments on account (credits) are subtracted from the previous balance.

$$\$350 - \$100 = \$250$$

Practice: Find the balance after each debit or credit.

	Debit	Credit	Balance
	—	—	$400.00
1.	$100.00	—	
2.	—	$ 50.00	
3.	55.00	—	
4.	—	25.50	
5.	—	10.75	
6.	75.20	—	
7.	17.50	—	
8.	—	56.25	
9.	48.95	—	
10.	—	212.00	

VOCABULARY SKILLBUILDER

Read each of the following statements. From the words below each statement, choose the term that best matches the statement.

1. Money that is owed to a business as a result of charge sales.

   accounts receivable   net income

2. On a sales slip, the unit price of an item multiplied by the quantity of that item.

   extension   total

3. A form used to record returned merchandise.

   credit memo   debit form

4. A sale for which the customer does not pay cash at the time of purchase but pays at a later date.

   charge sale   delayed sale

5. A business that sells goods or services directly to the public.

   retail business   wholesale business

6. A device that uses pressure to "print" information from a charge card onto a sales slip.

   card printer   imprinting machine

7. The price of *one* item.

   individual price   unit price

8. The cost of a sale before the sales tax is added.

   nontaxed sale   subtotal

9. A record of charges, returns, and payments for a charge customer.

   customer's account   customer's stub

10. To transfer information from one source to another.

    copy   post

11. An increase in the balance of a customer's account.

    debit   payment

12. A decrease in the balance of a customer's account.

    credit   explanation

13. The current total amount owed in a customer's account.

    balance   payment due

14. A bill sent to a customer, usually monthly, listing amounts charged to the account, returns, and payments on the account.

    credit memo   statement of account

15. The date on which a statement of account is prepared and mailed.

    closing date   preparation date

16. The date by which the customer's payment should be paid.

    due date   payment date

17. The part of a statement of account that the customer tears off and sends along with the payment check.

    customer copy   statement stub

18. The money left over after business expenses are paid.

    excess cash   net income

19. A report listing the dollar sales by company unit or division.

    departmental sales report
    territorial sales report

20. A report listing dollar sales by state, city, or other area.

departmental sales report
territorial sales report

APPLICATION PROBLEMS

As a trainee employed by Benn's Department Store, you are assigned to several jobs that concern charge sales and accounts receivable.

1. Review the charge account application. Then answer the following questions:

    a. Are all entries legible? If not, list the heading of each entry that is not legible.

    b. Is any information missing? If so, list the heading of each entry that is missing.

    c. Has the form been signed? dated?

    d. Does the information on the application agree with this information from the customer's driver's license?

Name: Doris R. Hofheimer
Address: 2008 Orchard Hill Road
          Roanoke, VA 24018
S.S. No.: 231-16-4127

If not, list the items that are different.

2. Your next job is to work as a salesperson in the women's clothing department, which is department 135. Your employee number is 30.

    a. Prepare sales slips for your charge sales for April:

Apr. 2 Tonya Watson: 1 dress at $94 and 2 blouses at $40 each.

      6 Jill Jensen: 1 handbag at $56 and 2 skirts at $49.95 each.

      8 Frieda Younos: 1 coat at $219.95 and 1 pair of boots at $79.50.

   10 Willette Price: 2 jackets at $84.75 each and 2 blouses at $34.95 each.

INDIVIDUAL CREDIT ACCOUNT APPLICATION

APPLICATION TO BE COMPLETED IN NAME OF PERSON IN WHICH THE ACCOUNT IS TO BE CARRIED.

COURTESY TITLES ARE OPTIONAL   PLEASE PRINT

☐ MR. ☐ MRS. ☐ MISS ☒ MS.   DORIS   R   HOFHEIMER

                 First Name   Initial   Last Name

Mailing Address If Different than Residence Address

2008 ORCHARD HILL RD. ROANOKE   24018

Residence Address   Street Address   Apt. #   City   State   Zip Code

Phone No: Phone No: Soc. Sec.   Number of
Home (703)711-4110 Business (703)724-1000 No. 231-16-4127 Age 23 Dependents 0
                                          (Excluding Applicant)

Are you a United ☒ Yes   If No, explain
States Citizen? ☐ No   immigration status: _____

How Long at   Own ☐ Rent-Furnished ☐ Rent-Unfurnished ☐ Board ☐ Live With Parents ☒ Monthly Rent or
Present Address 23 Yrs. 2 Mos.   Mortgage Payments $ ____

Name of Landlord or Mortgage Holder   Street Address   City and State
Former Address (If less than 2   How
years at present address) _____   long

HOLIDAY MOTORS   127 ELM ST.   ROANOKE VA 24018
Employer   Street Address   City and State
How   Net   Monthly ☒
long 4 Yrs. 6 Mos. Occupation: MECHANIC   Income $ ____ Weekly ☐
Former Employer   (Take Home Pay)
(If less than 1 year with present employer) _____ How long ____ Yrs. ____ Mos.

ALIMONY, CHILD SUPPORT, OR SEPARATE MAINTENANCE INCOME NEED NOT BE REVEALED IF YOU
DO NOT WISH TO HAVE IT CONSIDERED AS A BASIS FOR PAYING THIS OBLIGATION.
Alimony, child support, separate maintenance received under: Monthly ☐
    ☐ Court order ☐ Written agreement ☐ Oral understanding ☐ Amount $ ____ Weekly ☐

                Monthly ☐
Other income, if any: Amount $ ____ Weekly ☐ Source ____

DOMINION BANK   Savings ☐ Checking ☒ 84-173-8
Name and Address of Bank or Credit Union   Acc't No.

                      Savings ☐ Checking ☐ ____
Name and Address of Bank or Credit Union   Acc't No.

Previous
Credit ☐ Yes   Is Account ☐ Yes Date Final
Account ☒ No VALLEY VIEW   Paid in Full ☐ No Payment Made ____
       At What Branch do you usually shop? Account No.

       X Doris R. Hofheimer
         (Signature of person on whose income or   Date
          assets applicant is relying.)
Finance charges not in excess of those permitted by law will be charged
on the outstanding balances from month to month.

15 Jill Jensen: 1 suit at $249.50 and 2 scarves at $15 each.

20 Tonya Watson: 1 belt at $15 and 2 handkerchiefs at $5 each.

23 Willette Price: 2 pairs of jeans at $49.95 each and 2 shirts at $40 each.

25 Frieda Younos: 2 pairs of shoes at $42.98 each.

All sales are class 88, and the sales tax rate is 4 percent. Number the sales slips in order from C5634-75 to C5634-82. The customers will take the items with them. Sign each customer's name on the sales slips. The customers' names and account numbers follow.

Jill N. Jensen
1000 Cutler Ave.
Dayton, OH 45414
Acct. No. 37-424-71

Tonya R. Watson
P.O. Box 4272
Dayton, OH 45419
Acct. No. 36-422-17

Willette D. Price
144 Wintergreen
Fairborn, OH 45324
Acct. No. 40-307-91

Frieda G. Younos
37 Glade Street
Dayton, OH 45426
Acct. No. 37-719-22

b. Prepare a credit memo for each of the following returns:

Apr. 26 Frieda Younos returned one pair of shoes that were purchased on April 26.

27 Willette Price returned two shirts that were purchased on April 23.

Use the sales slips for information about the items returned. Use credit memo numbers CM2860 and CM2861.

3. You have now been assigned to the accounts receivable department. Use the charge sales slips and credit memos that you have already prepared as you complete the following work.

a. Review each sales slip and credit memo. Make any necessary corrections. After you review the slips, initial each in the lower-right corner.

b. Figure the following amounts for the accounting department:
1. The total of the eight charge sales slips not including the sales tax.
2. The total sales tax on the eight charge sales slips.
3. The total amount of the eight charge sales slips including the sales tax.
4. The total of the two credit memos not including the sales tax.
5. The total sales tax on the two credit memos.
6. The total amount of the two credit memos including the sales tax.

c. Set up an account for each of the four customers listed at the left by entering each name, address, and account number at the top of a customer account form.

d. Post each charge sales slip and credit memo to the correct account. Make a check mark beside the total of each sales slip or credit memo after you have posted the item.

e. Prepare a statement of account for each of the four customers. The closing date is April 30, 19—, and the due date is May 25, 19—.

f. You received the following statement stubs and checks from the four customers. Post each cash receipt to the correct account.

May 10 Check 177 for $352.88 was received from Willette Price.

15 Check 477 for $356.13 was received from Frieda Younos.

21 Check 1209 for $452.82 was received from Jill Jensen.

24 Check 385 for $206.96 was received from Tonya Watson.

4. Your final training assignment is in the office of the assistant manager of Benn's Department Store. The assistant manager is in charge of the following departments: appliances, carpeting, draperies, and furniture. Sales reports for the week ending May 25 have been sent to the assistant manager from each of the four departments. The sales, rounded to the nearest dollar, were as follows:

Monday: appliances, $2,178; carpeting, $1,626; draperies, $863; furniture, $3,442.

Tuesday: appliances, $2,302; carpeting, $1,489; draperies, $904; furniture, $4,170.

Wednesday: appliances, $2,874; carpeting, $2,092; draperies, $1,127; furniture, $2,961.

Thursday: appliances, $2,445; carpeting, $945; draperies, $951; furniture, $3,212.

Friday: appliances, $3,178; carpeting, $1,620; draperies, $1,055; furniture, $4,227.

Saturday: appliances, $4,625; carpeting, $1,845; draperies, $1,286; furniture, $5,679.

a. Prepare a departmental sales report for the week ending May 25.

b. Which department had the highest sales that week?

c. Which department had the lowest sales that week?

d. Which day had the highest sales?

e. Which day had the lowest sales?

f. What was the total amount of sales for the week?

CHAPTER 11

INVENTORY RECORDS

The stock of goods that a business has for sale is called its *inventory*. For example, the clothes for sale in a clothing store are the store's inventory, or merchandise.

Inventory changes every business day. When sales are made, inventory decreases. When the business buys more items, inventory increases. It is important for a business to keep accurate inventory records, so the owner or manager will know what new merchandise to order, when to order it, and how much to order. If there is too little inventory in a store, sales will be lost. If there is too much inventory, the cost of storing and paying for it will be too high. A good business manager knows just how much inventory should be on hand to make the most sales possible at the lowest cost to the business.

In this chapter you will learn how to keep some important inventory records: the low-stock report, the stock card, the receiving report, and the inventory sheet. These records can be kept manually, as you will do in the textbook exercises, or by computer, as is done in many businesses.

TOPIC 1 ● LOW-STOCK REPORT

GOALS

1. To determine which items on an inventory listing need to be reordered.
2. To prepare a low-stock report.

KEY TERMS

Inventory is the stock of goods and merchandise that a business has for sale.

On-hand inventory refers to goods in the stockroom or in the store.

A *low-stock report* is a form that lists inventory items that need to be reordered.

REORDERING INVENTORY ITEMS

Once each week, Jefferson Scale Company uses its computer to print out an inventory list. As an employee in the stockroom of Jefferson Scale Company, you must decide which items to reorder. First, take the inventory listing to the stockroom, where the inventory is stored. Count the number of each item on hand, and write the number in the On Hand column of the inventory listing.

An *inventory listing* is a list or a printout of all the items a business has for sale.

After you have counted and recorded items on hand, your inventory listing looks like this.

Jefferson Scale Company

Inventory Listing

Item	Stock No.	Unit	Maximum	On Hand	Min. Order
Dial scale	S-100	EA	30	20	12
Digital scale	S-140	EA	40	14	20
Hopper scale	S-200	EA	50	11	25
Platform scale	S-240	EA	2	0	1

Next, you must determine which items to reorder. Follow these steps for the first item on the inventory list, dial scale:

The *maximum* is the largest number of an item that the manager wants to have on hand at one time.

1. Subtract the number in the On Hand column from the number in the Maximum column. The *maximum* is the largest number of an item that the manager wants to have on hand at one time.

$$30 \text{ (maximum)} - 20 \text{ (on hand)} = 10$$

The *minimum order* is the smallest quantity that the business orders for an inventory item.

2. The answer means that you need 10 more dial scales to bring the number of that inventory item up to the maximum of 30. Now look at the Minimum Order column. The number 12 is the smallest order that the manager will place for that item. Reason: There is a discount for orders of 12 or more.

To *reorder* means to purchase more inventory because stock is low.

3. You decide not to reorder dial scales because 10 is less than the minimum order.

Follow the same steps for the second item on the inventory list, digital scale:

1. Subtract the on hand number from the maximum number:

$$40 \text{ (maximum)} - 14 \text{ (on hand)} = 26$$

2. You need 26 digital scales to bring the number up to maximum. The minimum order is 20.
3. You decide to reorder digital scales, because 26 is more than the minimum order; you order 26.

Follow the same steps for the third item on the list, hopper scale:

1. Step 1 is figured as follows:

$$50 \text{ (maximum)} - 11 \text{ (on hand)} = 39$$

2. You need 39 hopper scales to bring the number up to maximum. The minimum order is 25.

3. You decide to reorder hopper scales; you order 39.

For the fourth item on the list, platform scale:

1. Step 1 is as follows:

$$2 \text{ (maximum)} - 0 \text{ (on hand)} = 2$$

2. You need 2 platform scales. The minimum order is 1.

3. You decide to reorder platform scales.

PREPARING A LOW-STOCK REPORT

You decide to reorder the last three items on the inventory listing. The stock for those three items is low. The manager wants a complete picture of low stock before placing an order for expensive scales, so your next job is to prepare a low-stock report for the three items to be reordered. A low-stock report is shown here.

Note how you fill in the low-stock report using the information on the inventory listing:

LOW STOCK REPORT

Date _August 20_, 19 _ _

Item	Stock No.	Unit	Maximum	On Hand	Order
Digital scale	S-140	E A	40	14	26
Hopper scale	S-200	E A	50	11	39
Platform scale	S-240	E A	2	0	2

1. In the Item column, write the name of the item to be reordered.

2. In the Stock Number column, write the stock number of the item to be reordered.

3. In the Unit column, write the abbreviation "EA" for "each," for items that are sold one by one. For items sold by the box, write "BOX" in the Unit column; by the dozen, write "DOZ."; and by the pair, write "PR." Each is one unit.

4. In the Maximum column, copy the maximum number from the inventory listing.

5. Write the number on hand in the next column.

6. In the Order column, write the number of items to be ordered. To get this number, subtract the number in the On Hand column from the number in the Maximum column.

A *unit* is the number of pieces that a customer must buy for a particular inventory item. If the unit is *each,* the item may be sold one at a time. If the unit is *pair,* as with stereo speakers, then the customer must buy two. If the unit is *dozen,* as with eggs, then the customer must buy the item by the dozen.

1. What causes inventory to decrease? to increase?

2. Why is it important for a business to keep accurate inventory records?

3. What is the purpose of the low-stock report?

4. What would you write in the Unit column of a low-stock report if the name of the item was skis?

5. What would you write in the Unit column of a low-stock report if the name of the item was clock?

Exercises for Topic 1

1. As an employee of Le Chef Kitchen Specialties, you have been given the following inventory listing:

Le Chef Kitchen Specialities

Inventory Listing

Item	Stock No.	Unit	Maximum	On Hand	Min. Order
Beverage mixer	3124	EA	60	42	20
Blender	3125	EA	72	8	36
Broiler	3200	EA	60	14	30
Citrus juicer	3220	EA	48	24	24
Coffee grinder	1855	EA	24	0	12
Coffee maker	1875	EA	144	25	72
Electric can opener	6440	EA	72	11	36
Electric kettle	2120	EA	36	19	12
Electric mixer	3255	EA	96	46	60
Electric skillet	2150	EA	48	4	24
Electric wok	2170	EA	36	9	12
Ice cream machine	9140	EA	24	14	6
Ice crusher	7124	EA	36	30	12
Meat slicer	1970	EA	48	13	24
Microwave oven	8185	EA	12	2	6
Microwave stand	8195	EA	12	4	6
Pasta machine	3377	EA	6	6	1
Toaster	1440	EA	144	27	72
Toaster-broiler	1480	EA	72	4	36
Waffler	1774	EA	96	22	40

a. Which items on the inventory listing need to be reordered?

b. Prepare a low-stock report for those items. Use today's date.

2. As an employee of Vibes Unlimited Sound Shack, you have been given the following inventory listing:

Vibes Unlimited Sound Shack

Inventory Listing

Item	Stock No.	Unit	Maximum	On Hand	Min. Order
AM/FM recorder	B-400	EA	18	2	6
Automatic turntable	A-701	EA	6	6	1
Danzig stereo	C-212	EA	24	7	12
Digital disc player	D-101	EA	18	0	6
Double cassette deck	B-420	EA	36	12	12
Dual cassette system	B-427	EA	12	1	6
Exeter video system	B-409	EA	4	2	1
Four-way stereo	C-218	EA	18	14	6
Harp portable stereo	C-200	EA	36	8	12
M-VOX portable stereo	C-225	EA	36	9	12
Marx stereo system	C-235	EA	2	1	1
Miniature LCD TV	H-190	EA	12	3	6
Music composer	K-400	EA	2	0	1
Cassette player	C-242	EA	60	43	24
Stereo headphones	C-243	EA	144	26	48
Stereo receiver	C-240	EA	12	6	6
Super Walkman	L-310	EA	72	20	24
Suzanna speakers	A-740	PR	18	4	6
Walkman II	L-320	EA	50	39	12
Watchman TV	H-198	EA	12	5	6

a. Which items on the inventory listing need to be reordered?

b. Prepare a low-stock report for those items.

GOALS

1. To keep a perpetual inventory using stock cards.
2. To answer inquiries about stock card data.

KEY TERMS

A *perpetual inventory* method keeps records of the items on hand on a daily basis.

A *stock card* is an inventory record for one item. It shows the number of items received and sold, and it shows the balance on hand.

The *minimum* is the smallest number of an inventory item in stock before more items are ordered.

KEEPING A PERPETUAL INVENTORY USING STOCK CARDS

Instead of using the low-stock reports that you studied in Topic 1, many retail stores and other businesses keep a daily record of each item in inventory. When inventory records are kept up to date daily, the store is keeping a *perpetual inventory*. Perpetual means constant or continuous.

Most perpetual inventory records are kept on a computer. When items of merchandise are received, the computer operator keys the number of items received into the files for each item. The computer then adds the number of items received to the balance on hand for each item. As items of merchandise are sold, the salesperson keys the item number into an electronic cash register, which is connected to the computer. The items sold are automatically subtracted from the balance on hand to give the new balance.

If a business is small and does not have a large number of items in inventory, the owner may keep a perpetual inventory on *stock cards*, rather than on a computer. Items received are added to inventory by hand, and items sold are subtracted from inventory by hand. A stock card used by Diane's Camera Corner is shown on the following page.

Note that to use the stock card, you:

1. Write the name of the product, Luxar 35-mm camera, in the Item block. A separate stock card is kept for each inventory item.
2. Write the stock number, 2-1720, in the Stock Number block.

STOCK CARD

ITEM			STOCK NO.	
❶ *Luxar 35 mm camera*			2-1720 ❷	

MINIMUM		MAXIMUM	
❸ 4		8 ❹	

❺ DATE ❻		NUMBER RECEIVED	NUMBER SOLD ❼	BALANCE ❽
19- May	3	6		6
	7		1	5
	10		2	3
	15	5		8
	19		1	7
	21		1	6
	23	3		9
	25		3	6
	31		1	5

3. Write in the Minimum block the smallest number of this item that is to be in stock before more items are ordered.
4. Write in the Maximum block the largest number of this item that should be in stock at any time.
5. Record the date that items are received or sold in the Date column.
6. Enter the number of items received in the Number Received column.
7. Enter the number of items sold in the Number Sold column.
8. Figure the balance by (a) adding the number received to, or (b) subtracting the number sold from, the previous balance.

STOCK CARD DATA

Perpetual inventory records, whether kept on stock cards or on computers, are used to help business managers make good decisions. These decisions will make the business more efficient and

profitable. For example, using the stock card shown on page 309, you can answer the following questions:

1. Q: Did the balance ever fall below the minimum?
   A: Yes, on May 10 the balance was 3 and the minimum is 4. When the balance falls below the minimum, it is likely that a decision will be made to reorder Luxar 35-mm cameras.

2. Q: How many cameras needed to be reordered on May 10?
   A: The balance on May 10 was 3, and the maximum is 8. Therefore, five cameras needed to be reordered ($8 - 3 = 5$).

3. Q: Did the balance ever go above the maximum?
   A: Yes, on May 23 the balance was 9 and the maximum is 8. When the balance goes above the maximum, this item might be put on sale at a special reduced price.

4. Q: How many of these cameras were received in May? How many were sold? Is the stock card correct?
   A: The total of the Number Received column is 14. The total of the Number Sold column is 9. The ending balance, the difference between the total number received and the total number sold, should be 5 ($14 - 9 = 5$). If not, then an error has been made in adding or subtracting on the card, and the balances will have to be figured again. There should be five Luxar 35-mm cameras in the store. The manager can check the number of those cameras on hand against the number shown on the card to be sure that none is missing.

Check Your Reading

1. What term describes keeping inventory records on a daily basis?

2. What does a receipt of new merchandise do to the balance of an item in inventory?

3. What does a sale of merchandise do to the balance of an item in inventory?

4. Describe how a computer might be used to keep perpetual inventory records.

5. Under what conditions might a business owner decide to use stock cards instead of a computer to keep perpetual inventory records?

6. How many stock cards would be needed to keep perpetual inventory records for 75 different inventory items?

1. As an employee of Diane's Camera Corner, you are to prepare stock cards for four new inventory items. Fill in the following information on four stock cards:

   Avanti talking camera; Stock No. 2-1840; minimum, 6; maximum, 12.
   Lens brush; Stock No. 4-1700; minimum, 12; maximum, 24.
   Mixton camera case; Stock No. 3-1826; minimum, 2; maximum, 6.
   Pulsar telephoto lens; Stock No. 1-1440; minimum, 2; maximum, 5.

2. Record the following receipts and sales on the stock cards you prepared in Exercise 1:

   June 2 Received 12 Avanti talking cameras, 18 lens brushes, 6 Mixton camera cases, and 4 Pulsar telephoto lenses.

   3 Sold 3 Avanti talking cameras and 1 Mixton camera case.

   4 Sold 2 lens brushes and 1 Pulsar telephoto lens.

   5 Sold 1 Avanti talking camera, 3 lens brushes, 2 Mixton camera cases, and 1 Pulsar telephoto lens.

   7 Sold 2 Mixton camera cases.

   9 Sold 2 lens brushes.

   10 Sold 1 Avanti talking camera and 1 Pulsar telephoto lens.

   14 Received 13 lens brushes, 5 Mixton camera cases, and 4 Pulsar telephoto lenses.

   18 Sold 2 Avanti talking cameras and 1 Mixton camera case.

   21 Sold 4 lens brushes.

   22 Received 7 Avanti talking cameras.

   23 Sold 2 Pulsar telephoto lenses.

   25 Sold 2 Mixton camera cases.

   26 Sold 4 Avanti talking cameras, 3 lens brushes, and 3 Pulsar telephoto lenses.

   27 Sold 1 lens brush and 1 Mixton camera case; received 5 Pulsar telephoto lenses.

   28 Sold 3 Avanti talking cameras, 2 lens brushes, and 1 Mixton camera case.

   29 Sold 1 Avanti talking camera, 1 lens brush, and 1 Pulsar telephoto lens.

   30 Sold 1 Pulsar telephoto lens; received 7 Avanti talking cameras and 5 Mixton camera cases.

3. Use the stock cards you prepared in Exercises 1 and 2 to answer the following questions:
   a. For which items did the balance fall below the minimum? Identify both the items and the dates.
   b. For each item in **a** above, list the reorder quantity.
   c. Did the balance go above the maximum for any item? If so, which item(s)?
   d. How many of each item were received and sold? Total the Number Received and Number Sold columns of each stock card. Then check your work by subtracting the total number sold from the total number received for each card. The answer should be the ending balance. If it is not, check each addition and subtraction and make the correction on the stock card.

4. One of your duties at Fashion Phone Center is to keep perpetual inventory records. Your first job is to prepare four stock cards for the following new items at the store:

   ADX Answerphone; Stock No. 14-233; minimum, 10; maximum, 40.

   ADX cordless phone; Stock No. 14-283; minimum, 20; maximum, 60.

   Exeter memory phone; Stock No. 16-141; minimum, 10; maximum, 50.

   Granby phone/clock radio; Stock No. 18-714; minimum, 15; maximum, 30.

5. Record the following receipts and sales on the stock cards you prepared in Exercise 4:

   Dec. 2   Received 40 ADX Answerphones, 50 ADX cordless phones, 40 Exeter memory phones, and 25 Granby phone/clock radios.
         3   Sold 2 ADX Answerphones.
         4   Sold 1 Granby phone/clock radio.
         5   Sold 3 Exeter memory phones.
         6   Sold 8 ADX Answerphones and 18 ADX cordless phones.
         7   Sold 7 ADX Answerphones, 30 ADX cordless phones, and 2 Granby phone/clock radios.
         9   Sold 2 ADX cordless phones, 8 Exeter memory phones, and 1 Granby phone/clock radio.
        11   Sold 12 ADX Answerphones.
        12   Sold 6 Exeter memory phones and 4 Granby phone/clock radios; received 58 ADX cordless phones.
        13   Sold 25 ADX cordless phones and 11 Exeter memory phones; received 40 ADX Answerphones (special price offered).

14	Sold 15 ADX Answerphones, 28 ADX cordless phones, and 6 Granby phone/clock radios.
17	Sold 6 Exeter memory phones; received 53 ADX cordless phones and 19 Granby phone/clock radios.
18	Sold 35 ADX cordless phones.
19	Sold 8 ADX Answerphones and 11 ADX cordless phones; received 44 Exeter memory phones.
20	Sold 12 Exeter memory phones.
21	Sold 8 Granby phone/clock radios.
23	Sold 14 ADX Answerphones, 21 Exeter memory phones, and 7 Granby phone/clock radios.
27	Received 3 ADX Answerphones.
28	Received 5 Exeter memory phones.
31	Received 2 Granby phone/clock radios.

6. Use the stock cards you prepared in Exercises 4 and 5 to answer the following questions:

   a. For which items and on what dates did the balance fall below the minimum? Identify both the items and the dates.

   b. For each item in **a** above, list the reorder quantity.

   c. Did the balance go above the maximum for any item? If so, which item(s)?

   d. How many of each item were received and sold? Total the Number Received and Number Sold columns of each stock card. Then check your work by subtracting the number sold from the number received for each card. The answer should be the ending balance. If it is not, check each addition and subtraction and make the correction on the stock card.

TOPIC 3 ● ORDERING AND RECEIVING STOCK

GOALS

1. To use a stock card to prepare a purchase requisition.
2. To use a purchase requisition to request price quotations.
3. To use price quotations to prepare a purchase order.
4. To prepare and use a receiving record.

KEY TERMS

A *purchase requisition* is a form used to request that an order be placed for merchandise.

A *supplier*, or *vendor*, is a business from which merchandise is ordered.

A *purchase order* is a form sent to a supplier to order goods.

PREPARING A PURCHASE REQUISITION

Stock cards can help business managers decide what merchandise to order, in what quantity, and when. Let's see how Floyd Morrow, who is responsible for stock cards for Diane's Camera Corner, uses stock cards in the ordering process.

STOCK CARD

ITEM			STOCK NO.	
Luxar 35 mm camera			2-1720	

MINIMUM			MAXIMUM	
4			8	

DATE	NUMBER RECEIVED	NUMBER SOLD	BALANCE
19— May	3	6		6
	7		1	5 ——❷
❶——	10		2	3 ——❸

Shown above is part of the stock card you studied in Topic 2. Note the following:

1. On May 10, 2 cameras were sold.
2. The previous balance was 5, which is more than the minimum of 4.
3. The new balance is 3 (5 − 2 = 3), which is below the minimum. This means that this item should be reordered on May 10.

To decide how many to reorder, Floyd subtracts the balance on hand, 3, from the maximum, 8. Floyd should order 5 items (8 − 3 = 5).

Floyd's first step in reordering merchandise is to prepare a *purchase requisition*, a request to place an order. The purchase requisition shows when the merchandise is needed, who is making the request, and what is needed. The completed purchase requisition is given to the person who normally places orders for the store.

To complete the purchase requisition shown on page 315, Floyd Morrow:

1. Estimates, based on the stock card, that the remaining three Luxar 35-mm cameras will sell within five days. Therefore, under Date Needed he writes "May 15, 19—," which is five days from the date of the request, May 10, 19—.

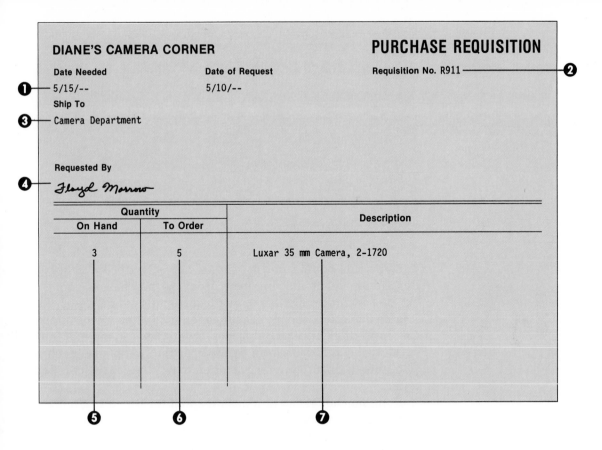

DIANE'S CAMERA CORNER

PURCHASE REQUISITION

❶ Date Needed
5/15/--

Date of Request
5/10/--

❷ Requisition No. R911

❸ Ship To
Camera Department

❹ Requested By
Floyd Morrow

Quantity		Description
On Hand	To Order	
3	5	Luxar 35 mm Camera, 2-1720

❺ ❻ ❼

2. Numbers each requisition in order with the letter "R" (for requisition) in front of the number. This is requisition R911.
3. Enters under Ship To the department of Diane's Camera Corner that is to receive the order, "Camera Department."
4. Signs his name under Requested By.
5. Enters the quantity on hand according to the stock card, 3, under On Hand.
6. Enters the quantity to be ordered, which was figured to be 5, under To Order.
7. Enters the item to be ordered and its stock number under Description.

REQUESTING PRICE QUOTATIONS

The person in charge of purchasing merchandise is usually called the *purchasing agent*. The agent keeps a list of suppliers, or vendors, and copies of their catalogs. The lists and catalogs are used to select merchandise to be ordered by the business. Part of a page from one supplier's catalog is shown on page 316.

The *purchasing agent* is the person in charge of buying merchandise from vendors and suppliers.

```
                STILL CAMERAS AND ACCESSORIES WAREHOUSE STOCK CATALOG  PAGE 54
     STOCK NO.                    DESCRIPTION                      SALE        LIST

                                                                 PRICE       PRICE

     149-1636   MAXXUM TELE SYSTEM KIT (BOD-1.7-135MM)            459.95      649.00

     149-1668   2553-600 AF 28-135MM F4/4.5 F/MAXXUM             409.95      619.00

     149-1288   MINOLTA SV TALKER (AUTOFOCUS) CAMERA             129.95      228.00

     149-1361   283-009 DISC 5 W/WRIST STRAP                      29.95       96.50

     149-1379   284-009 DISC 7 W/WRIST STRAP                      29.95      122.50

     149-1510   2557-600 MAXXUM AF 28MM F2.8 LENS                104.95      140.00

     149-1338   LUXAR 35MM CAMERA                                 77.00      150.00
```

A price quotation is the amount a supplier will charge for specific merchandise at a given time.

Some catalogs do not list prices but only stock numbers and descriptions of items. In such cases, the purchasing agent may ask two or three suppliers to quote current prices for items. To get a price quotation, the purchasing agent will often phone suppliers for up-to-date prices. For larger orders, the agent may mail a *request for quotation* form to three or four suppliers. Each supplier then is able to put its quotation in writing for the purchasing agent.

Rosa Sanchez is the purchasing agent for Diane's Camera Corner. To find out the best price for five Luxar 35-mm cameras, she phoned three suppliers and made the following notes of their prices and shipping charges:

Supplier	Price	Shipping Charges	Delivery Date
Imperial Photo Supply	$385	$ 8	May 31
West Coast Supply Co.	384	22	May 15
Maxey Cameras Inc.	385	8	May 15

Rosa looked at her notes and considered the following:

1. The cameras are needed on May 15. Rosa rejected Imperial Photo Supply because the delivery date is too late—May 31.
2. West Coast Supply has the best camera price, but when the $22 shipping charge is added, the total cost is $406 ($384 + $22 = $406).

As a result, Rosa gave the order to Maxey Cameras, because the total cost of the cameras plus the shipping charges was $393 ($385 + $8 = $393).

PREPARING A PURCHASE ORDER

The purchasing agent, Rosa Sanchez, will prepare a purchase order for the five Luxar 35-mm cameras. A *purchase order* is a form sent to a supplier to order goods.

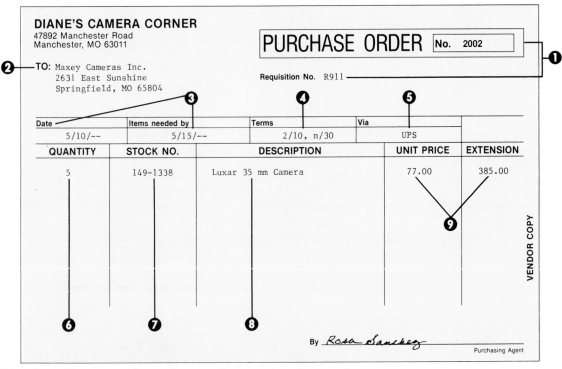

Note how Rosa completes the purchase order shown above:

1. She uses a numbered purchase order. The orders are filed by this number and can easily be located if necessary. (Purchase order numbers are often preprinted on the forms.) She also records the requisition number on the form.
2. She fills in the supplier's name and address.
3. She dates the form and tells when the order is needed.
4. She states the credit terms in the Terms block. You will learn about credit terms in Chapter 12.
5. Rosa writes the shipping terms, "UPS," which means that the cameras are to be sent by United Parcel Service.
6. She lists the number ordered in the Quantity column.
7. She writes the supplier's stock number (not Diane's Camera Corner's stock number) of the item ordered in the Stock Number column. Rosa found this number by looking in the supplier's catalog.
8. She adds a brief and clear description of the item ordered in the Description column.

9. She figures the unit price of the cameras, $77 ($385 ÷ 5 = $77). The price quoted by Maxey Cameras for five cameras is $385, not including the shipping charges. She enters both the unit price and the extension.

Rosa prepares three copies of the purchase order. She sends the original to the supplier to order the merchandise. She files the second copy in her office as a record of the order. She gives the third copy to the person who receives, opens, and checks incoming orders.

PREPARING A RECEIVING RECORD

A *receiving record* is a form that records the number and the condition of items of incoming merchandise. A copy of the purchase order may be used as the receiving record.

When a business receives a shipment of goods from a supplier, the goods must be unpacked and inspected. The person who receives merchandise must check the type and count the number of items sent as well as check to see whether any of the goods are damaged. Then the person must prepare a *receiving record*. A copy of the purchase order can be used as a receiving record. Note the following about the receiving record:

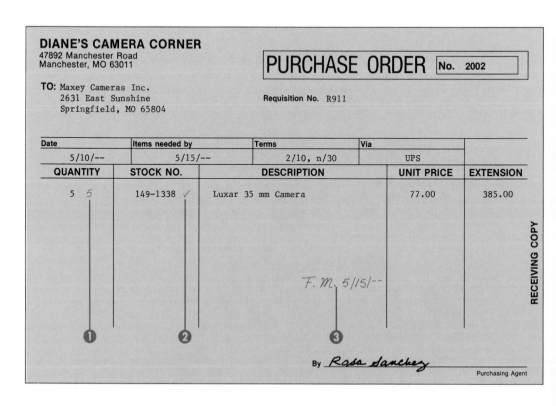

On May 15, when Floyd Morrow received the shipment from Maxey Cameras, he used a copy of the purchase order to create a receiving order. He followed these steps:

1. In the Quantity column, he wrote the number of cameras actually received beside the number ordered.
2. He placed a check mark beside the stock number to show that the correct items were received.
3. He initialed the order and dated it.

When a shipment is damaged or incorrect, Floyd notes the problem at the bottom of the receiving record.

UPDATING STOCK CARDS

Information on the receiving record is used to update the stock cards. The receiving record on page 318 was used to update the stock card for Luxar 35-mm cameras shown here.

STOCK CARD

ITEM		STOCK NO.
Luxar 35 mm camera		2-1720

MINIMUM		MAXIMUM	
4		8	

DATE		NUMBER RECEIVED	NUMBER SOLD	BALANCE
19– May	3	6		6
	7		1	5
	10		2	3
❶ 15		5		8
		❷		❸

Note the following about the May 15 entry on the stock card:

1. The date, May 15, was found on the receiving record.
2. The number received was found in the Quantity column of the receiving record.
3. The new balance, 8, was figured by adding the previous balance to the number received (3 + 5 = 8).

1. Name two inventory records that help the manager of a business make decisions about ordering merchandise.

2. What is the first step in reordering merchandise?

3. What are some things that the purchasing agent will consider in deciding which supplier should get an order?

Select one of these four records to answer each question below: stock card, receiving record, purchase order, and purchase requisition.

4. Which one has information needed to prepare a purchase requisition?

5. Which one has information needed to request price quotations?

6. Which one is used to update stock cards?

7. Which one is sent to the supplier to order merchandise?

Exercises for Topic 3

1. Use the stock card shown here to prepare Purchase Requisition R912 for the Fashion Phone Center. The date of the request is June 6, 19—, and the date needed is June 20, 19—. The order is to be shipped to the phone department. Sign your name under Requested By. The order should be for enough Exeter Memory Phones to bring the balance up to the maximum.

STOCK CARD

ITEM			STOCK NO.	
Exeter Memory Phone			*16-141*	
MINIMUM			MAXIMUM	
10			*20*	
DATE		NUMBER RECEIVED	NUMBER SOLD	BALANCE
19— *June*	*1*	*15*		*15*
	3		*4*	*11*
	6		*3*	*8*

2. Use the stock card shown here to prepare Purchase Requisition R913 for the Fashion Phone Center. The date of the request is the date the balance dropped below the minimum. The date needed is ten days after the request date. The order is to be shipped to the phone department. Sign your name under Requested By. The order should bring the balance up to the maximum.

STOCK CARD

ITEM			STOCK NO.	
ADX Answerphone			14-233	

MINIMUM			MAXIMUM	
10			40	

DATE		NUMBER RECEIVED	NUMBER SOLD	BALANCE
19— June	1	40		40
	4		18	22
	6		16	6

3. Use the price quotation information below to select a supplier for the Exeter Memory Phones requisitioned in Exercise 1. In order to be selected, the supplier must be able to deliver the merchandise on or before the date needed and at the lowest price, including shipping charges.

Supplier	Total Price	Shipping Charges	Delivery Date
National Telephone Supply	$720	$50	6/19/—
RGS Phones Inc.	734	38	6/20/—
Telecom International	720	48	6/25/—

4. Use the price quotation information below to select a supplier for the ADX Answerphones requisitioned in Exercise 2. In order to be selected, the supplier must be able to deliver the merchandise on or before the date needed and at the lowest price, including shipping charges.

Supplier	Total Price	Shipping Charges	Delivery Date
National Telephone Supply	$2,822	$125	6/14/—
RGS Phones Inc.	2,656	140	6/20/—
Eastern Communications Inc.	2,754	5% of order	6/16/—

5. Refer to the purchase requisition you prepared in Exercise 1 and the price quotation information you worked with in Exercise 3. Prepare Purchase Order 2003 to send to the supplier you selected in Exercise 3. The supplier's address is P.O. Box 10643, Duluth, MN 55809. Use the same date as the purchase requisition. Terms are 2/10, n/30. Shipping is via UPS. Remember to divide the quoted price by the number of phones to be purchased in order to find the unit price. Do not enter the shipping charges on the purchase order.

6. Refer to the purchase requisition you prepared in Exercise 2 and the price quotation information you worked with in Exercise 4. Prepare Purchase Order 2004 to send to the supplier you selected in Exercise 4. The supplier's address is P.O. Box 23127, Milwaukee, WI 53223. Use the same date as the purchase requisition. Terms are 2/10, n/30. Shipping is via UPS. Remember to divide the quoted price by the number of phones to be purchased in order to find the unit price. Do not enter the shipping charges on the purchase order.

7. On June 20, 19—, Fashion Phone Center received 12 Exeter Memory Phones, Stock No. 16-141. Using the purchase order you prepared in Exercise 5 as the receiving copy, prepare a receiving record for the incoming order. Use your own initials.

8. On June 16, 19—, Fashion Phone Center received 34 ADX Answerphones, Stock No. 14-233. Two of the phones had been damaged in shipment. Using the purchase order you prepared in Exercise 6 as the receiving copy, prepare a receiving record for the incoming order. Make a note of the damaged phones at the bottom of the form. Use your own initials.

9. Copy the stock card on page 320 or use the one in the Activity Guide. Using the information on the receiving record you prepared in Exercise 7, update the stock card.

10. Copy the stock card on page 321 or use the one in the Activity Guide. Using the information on the receiving record you prepared in Exercise 8, update the stock card. Do not include the two damaged phones in the Number Received column. They will be returned to the supplier.

TOPIC 4 ● PERIODIC INVENTORY

GOAL

1. To complete a physical inventory sheet.

KEY TERMS

A *periodic inventory* method keeps records of the items on hand on a monthly, half-yearly, or yearly basis.

A *physical inventory* is the actual counting of all items in stock.

An *inventory sheet* is a form used to list a physical inventory count.

THE PERIODIC INVENTORY METHOD

Many small retail stores, such as bookstores and novelty shops, have a large stock of many low-priced items. For such businesses, the perpetual inventory method may not be practical, because their salespersons may not have time to make a daily record of the items that are on hand after every sale and every receipt. Doing so may also be too expensive. Instead, such businesses might use the *periodic inventory* method. With the periodic inventory method, the merchandise is counted from time to time. It may be counted every month, every six months, or every year. Small stores often use this method to find the number of each item in inventory at a certain time.

TAKING A PHYSICAL INVENTORY

The actual counting of all items in stock is called a *physical inventory*. All businesses, even those using the perpetual inventory method, must take a physical inventory at least once a year. Reason: The loss of items through theft and breakage can be discovered only by taking a physical inventory. Also, the amount of inventory must be reported to the federal government for income tax purposes.

When a business takes a physical inventory, every item is counted and listed on an inventory sheet, such as the one shown on page 324.

Note the following:

1. The date the inventory is taken (December 30, 19—) and the sheet number (8) are recorded at the top.

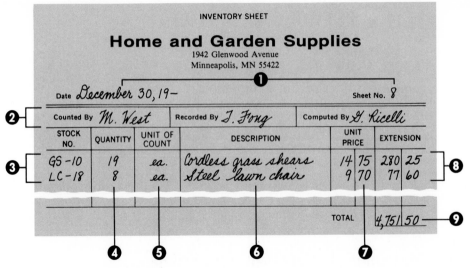

INVENTORY SHEET

Home and Garden Supplies
1942 Glenwood Avenue
Minneapolis, MN 55422

❶

Date *December 30, 19—*   Sheet No. *8*

❷ | Counted By *M. West* | Recorded By *J. Fong* | Computed By *G. Ricelli* |

❸
STOCK NO.	QUANTITY	UNIT OF COUNT	DESCRIPTION	UNIT PRICE	EXTENSION
GS-10	19	ea.	Cordless grass shears	14 75	280 25	❽
LC-18	8	ea.	Steel lawn chair	9 70	77 60
				TOTAL	4,751 50	❾

❹   ❺   ❻   ❼

2. Three different signatures are written in the spaces labeled Counted By, Recorded By, and Computed By. (A physical inventory is best taken by two people who work together as a team. One person counts the stock, and the other person records the information on the inventory sheet. Later, a third person computes the extensions.)

3. The stock number of each item is recorded in the Stock Number column.

4. The quantity of each item on hand is entered in the Quantity column.

5. The Unit of Count column shows how the item is sold—individually (*each*), by the dozen, by the pair, by the gallon.

6. The item is identified in the Description column.

7. The unit price of the item is recorded in the Unit Price column.

8. Later, the extension is computed and recorded in the Extension column.

9. The total of the extensions is recorded at the bottom of the inventory sheet.

Check Your Reading

1. What is the difference between a perpetual inventory method and a periodic inventory method?

2. Which business would most likely use a periodic inventory method: (a) a small business with many low-priced items of inventory or (b) a large wholesale supply business?

3. Why must every business that sells merchandise take a physical inventory at least once a year?

4. Why are there spaces for three different signatures on the inventory sheet illustrated on page 324?

1. Use the information below to complete Inventory Sheet 6 for Baker Brothers. The date is December 31, 19—. Compute the extensions. The inventory was counted by Phil Daly, recorded by Linda Perez, and computed by you.

Stock No.	Quantity	Unit of Count	Description	Unit Price
BB-32	18	doz.	All-Star baseballs	$48.00
SB-12	13	doz.	Solo softballs	60.00
TB-24	30	can	Court tennis balls	2.00
VB-9	15	ea.	Volli-Hi volleyballs	15.00
SKB-3	14	ea.	Rocket soccer balls	17.50

2. Use the information below to complete Inventory Sheet 4 for Modern Luggage Inc. The date is June 30, 19—. Compute the extensions. The inventory was counted by Rahmad Jammal, recorded by Juanita Soto, and computed by you.

Stock No.	Quantity	Unit of Count	Description	Unit Price
N5310	21	ea.	Carry-on	$120.00
N5627	17	ea.	Garment bag	175.00
N5831	11	ea.	Beauty case	107.50
N6120	36	ea.	Tote bag	90.00
N6342	47	ea.	Attaché	125.00
N7110	12	ea.	Weekender	45.00
N7246	51	ea.	Small duffle	33.00
N7303	60	ea.	Cargo duffle	65.00
N7900	39	ea.	Square duffle	40.00
N8172	8	set	3-piece set	300.00

Skill: Finding balances on stock cards.

Sample Problem: Check the accuracy of a completed stock card.

Number Received	Number Sold	Balance
60	—	60
—	12	48
—	7	41
—	14	27
15	—	42
—	17	25
—	13	12
20	—	32

Solution:

1. Total the Number Received and Number Sold columns.

$$
\begin{array}{cc}
60 & 12 \\
15 & 7 \\
\underline{20} & 14 \\
\text{Number received} = 95 & 17 \\
& \underline{13} \\
& \text{Number sold} = 63
\end{array}
$$

2. Subtract the total number sold from the total number received. The answer should be the ending balance.

$$
\begin{array}{r}
95 \\
-63 \\
\hline
\text{Ending balance} = \quad 32
\end{array}
$$

3. If the answer in 2 does not equal the ending balance, refigure every line on the stock card to find the error. For each line, add the number received to, or subtract the number sold from, the previous balance.

Practice: Check the accuracy of the two following stock cards. If you are using the forms in your Activity Guide, correct any errors you find in the Balance column by drawing a line through the incorrect balance and writing the correct balance above it. Do not write on the forms in your textbook.

STOCK CARD

DATE	NUMBER RECEIVED	NUMBER SOLD	BALANCE
	75		75
		12	63
		8	55
		13	42
	50		92
		39	53
		13	40
	36		76

STOCK CARD

DATE	NUMBER RECEIVED	NUMBER SOLD	BALANCE
	144		144
		37	107
		26	81
		43	48
	72		120
		18	102
		27	75
	36		111

Read each of the following statements. From the words below each statement, choose the term that best matches the statement.

1. Goods that a business has for sale.

   inventory   purchases

2. A form that lists inventory items that need to be reordered.

   low-stock report   receiving record

3. The companies from whom businesses buy goods.

   debtors   purchasers   suppliers

4. A form used to request that merchandise be ordered.

   purchase order   purchase requisition

5. The person in charge of buying goods for a business.

   purchasing agent   receiving clerk

6. A form sent to a supplier to order goods.

   purchase order   purchase requisition

7. Actual counting of all items in stock.

   perpetual inventory   physical inventory

8. A continual, day-to-day record of each item in stock.

   purchase requisition
   perpetual inventory

9. Counting merchandise from time to time.

   periodic inventory   perpetual inventory

10. The amount a supplier will charge for specific merchandise at a given time.

   credit terms   price quotation

APPLICATION
PROBLEMS

1. As an employee of Cashman's Department Store, you are to prepare stock cards for these four new inventory items:

   Takeaway steam travel iron; Stock No. 5342; minimum, 12; maximum, 30.
   Italia manicure set; Stock No. 5271; minimum, 15; maximum, 40.
   Becker shoe shiner; Stock No. 5018; minimum, 10; maximum, 25.
   Nocord rotary razor; Stock No. 5068; minimum, 18; maximum, 50.

2. Record the following receipts and sales for the week of November 2 on the stock cards you prepared in Problem 1:

Nov. 2 Received 30 Takeaway steam travel irons, 40 Italia manicure sets, 25 Becker shoe shiners, and 50 Nocord rotary razors.

3 Sold 2 Takeaway steam travel irons, 4 Italia manicure sets, 1 Becker shoe shiner, and 5 Nocord rotary razors.

4 Sold 3 Takeaway steam travel irons, 4 Italia manicure sets, 3 Becker shoe shiners, and 7 Nocord rotary razors.

5 Sold 4 Takeaway steam travel irons, 5 Italia manicure sets,

Supplier	Total Price	Shipping Charges	Delivery Date
Weyland Supply Inc.	$1,092	$48	11/14/—
Bombach Wholesalers Ltd.	1,131	none	11/14/—
Erie-Cawer Enterprises	1,053	38	11/19/—

2 Becker shoe shiners, and 8 Nocord rotary razors.

6 Sold 3 Takeaway steam travel irons, 5 Italia manicure sets, 4 Becker shoe shiners, and 10 Nocord rotary razors.

7 Sold 5 Takeaway steam travel irons, 5 Italia manicure sets, 2 Becker shoe shiners, and 9 Nocord rotary razors.

3. Use the stock cards you prepared in Problems 1 and 2 to answer the following questions:

   a. For which item(s) did the balance fall below the minimum?

   b. For each item in **a** above, list the reorder quantity.

   c. Did the balance go above the maximum for any item? If so, which item(s)?

   d. How many of each item were received and sold? Total the Number Received and Number Sold columns of each stock card. Then check your work by subtracting the number sold from the number received for each card. The answer should be the ending balance. If it is not, check each line and make the correction on the stock card.

4. In Problem 3 you should have answered that the balance fell below the minimum for one item, the Nocord rotary razor. If that was not your answer, recheck your work. Use the Nocord rotary razor stock card to prepare Purchase Requisition R7073. The date of the request is the date the balance dropped below the minimum. The date

needed is seven days from the request date. The order is to be shipped to the Travel Goods Department. Sign your name under Requested By. The order should bring the balance up to the maximum.

5. Use the price quotation information above to select a supplier for the Nocord rotary razors you requisitioned in Problem 4. In order to be selected, the supplier must be able to deliver the merchandise on or before the date needed and at the lowest price, including shipping charges.

6. Refer to the purchase requisition you prepared in Problem 4 and the price quotation information you worked with in Problem 5. Prepare Purchase Order 74630 to send to the supplier you selected in Problem 5. The supplier's address is P.O. Box 1147, Milwaukee, WI 53201. Use the same date as the purchase requisition. Terms are 2/10, n/30. Shipping is via UPS. Remember to divide the quoted price by the number of items to be purchased in order to find the unit price.

7. On November 14, 19—, Cashman's Department Store received 39 Nocord rotary razors, Stock Number 5068. Using the purchase order you prepared in Problem 6 as the receiving copy, prepare a receiving record for the incoming order. Use your own initials.

8. Using the information on the receiving record you prepared in Problem 7, update the stock card for Nocord rotary razors.

9. Use the information on page 329 to complete the first four lines of an inventory sheet

Stock No.	Quantity	Unit of Count	Description	Unit Price
5018	18	ea.	Becker shoe shiner	$49.95
5068	31	ea.	Nocord rotary razor	69.50
5271	22	ea.	Italia manicure set	45.00
5342	14	ea.	Takeaway steam travel iron	39.95

for Cashman's Department Store. The date is November 30, 19—. Compute the extensions. The inventory was counted by Anna Woolhauser, recorded by Felix Dorn, and computed by you.

CHAPTER 12

ACCOUNTS PAYABLE PROCEDURES

In Chapter 11 you learned how inventory records help the manager of a business decide which items to order, how much of each item to order, and when to place each order. The order itself is placed by sending a purchase order to the supplier.

When the supplier ships the order, the supplier also sends a bill for the merchandise. To the store receiving the order, this incoming bill is called a *purchase invoice*.

In this chapter you will learn how to process purchase invoices and how to find discounts and due dates on invoices. You will also use the invoices as accounts payable records. *Accounts payable* are the amounts a store owes to suppliers for goods that have been purchased on credit.

TOPIC 1 ● PURCHASE INVOICES

GOALS

1. To compare the invoice with the purchase order and the receiving record.
2. To check the extensions and the total on an invoice.

KEY TERMS

To the buyer or purchaser, a *purchase invoice* is an incoming bill sent by the supplier.

To the supplier, a *sales invoice* is an outgoing bill sent to a customer.

Accounts payable include all amounts owed to suppliers for goods that have been purchased on credit.

PROCESSING PURCHASE INVOICES

The supplier sends an invoice to the purchaser for the goods that have been shipped. The purchaser thinks of this invoice as a purchase invoice because it lists the goods purchased. The seller thinks of it as a sales invoice because it lists the goods sold. For example, Kelly Cosmetic Company considers the invoice shown on the following page as a purchase invoice, but Jacobs Chemical Company, the seller, considers it a sales invoice.

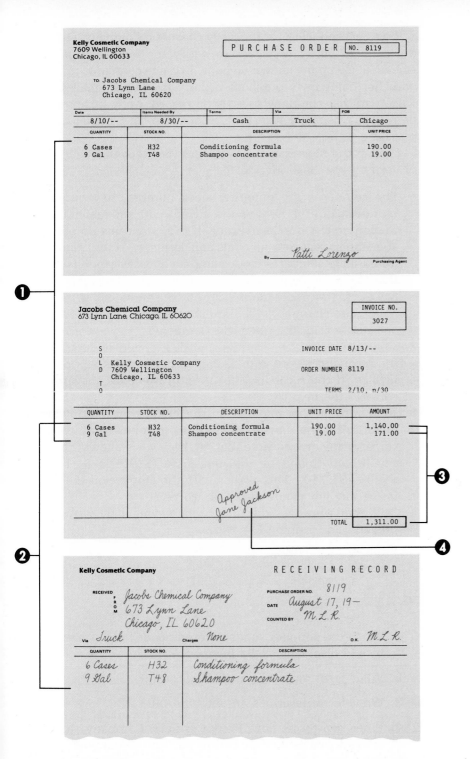

❶

Kelly Cosmetic Company
7609 Wellington
Chicago, IL 60633

PURCHASE ORDER NO. 8119

TO Jacobs Chemical Company
673 Lynn Lane
Chicago, IL 60620

Date	Items Needed By	Terms	Via	FOB
8/10/--	8/30/--	Cash	Truck	Chicago

QUANTITY	STOCK NO.	DESCRIPTION	UNIT PRICE
6 Cases	H32	Conditioning formula	190.00
9 Gal	T48	Shampoo concentrate	19.00

By _Patti Lorenzo_
Purchasing Agent

Jacobs Chemical Company
673 Lynn Lane, Chicago, IL 60620

INVOICE NO.
3027

S
O
L   Kelly Cosmetic Company
D   7609 Wellington
     Chicago, IL 60633
T
O

INVOICE DATE 8/13/--

ORDER NUMBER 8119

TERMS 2/10, n/30

QUANTITY	STOCK NO.	DESCRIPTION	UNIT PRICE	AMOUNT
6 Cases	H32	Conditioning formula	190.00	1,140.00
9 Gal	T48	Shampoo concentrate	19.00	171.00
			TOTAL	1,311.00

Approved
Jane Jackson

❸

❷

❹

Kelly Cosmetic Company

RECEIVING RECORD

RECEIVED
FROM _Jacobs Chemical Company_
      673 Lynn Lane
      Chicago, IL 60620

Via _Truck_   Charges _None_

PURCHASE ORDER NO. _8119_
DATE _August 17, 19—_
COUNTED BY _M.L.R._

O.K. _M.L.R._

QUANTITY	STOCK NO.	DESCRIPTION
6 Cases	H32	Conditioning formula
9 Gal	T48	Shampoo concentrate

Purchase invoices should always be verified before they are
paid. *Verifying* an invoice means checking that it is accurate and
complete.

Jane Jackson works at the Kelly Cosmetic Company. One of her duties is to verify invoices. To verify the invoice from Jacobs Chemical Company shown on page 331, she compares the invoice with her company's purchase order. She also compares the invoice with her company's receiving record. Kelly Cosmetic Company uses a separate form for a receiving record, not a copy of the purchase order.

Look at the illustration as you learn the steps that Jane follows to verify a purchase invoice:

1. She compares the quantity, stock number, description, and unit price of each item on the invoice with the matching information on the purchase order. If the quantities do not agree, she either reorders any missing items or returns any extra items. Jane compares stock numbers and descriptions to check that the right supplies have been shipped. She compares unit prices. If the prices do not agree, she finds out if the prices have been changed or if there is an error. If there is an error, she notifies Jacobs Chemical Company.

2. Jane compares the quantity and description of each item on the receiving record with each quantity and description on the invoice. If the receiving record and invoice do not agree, she corrects the invoice.

3. Jane verifies the amounts on the invoice by multiplying the quantity by the unit price. She also computes the total. She corrects any errors. Note that on the invoice shown, the quantity (6) multiplied by the unit price ($190) is $1,140 (6 × $190 = $1,140). This agrees with the amount on the invoice. Is the amount of the next item correct?

4. Jane then approves the invoice for payment by writing "Approved" and signing her name.

Check Your Reading

1. When the supplier sends ordered goods to a business, what else is also sent to the business?

2. What term describes an incoming bill?

3. What term describes an outgoing bill?

4. What two forms does Kelly Cosmetic Company check purchase invoices against before paying the supplier?

5. How do you show that an invoice has been approved for payment?

1. On May 15, 19—, Dalton Gift Shop sent the following purchase order to Atlanta Supply Corporation.

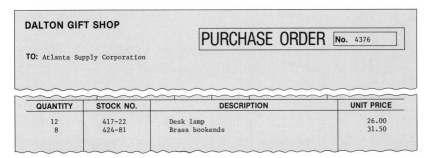

DALTON GIFT SHOP

PURCHASE ORDER   No. 4376

TO: Atlanta Supply Corporation

QUANTITY	STOCK NO.	DESCRIPTION	UNIT PRICE
12	417-22	Desk lamp	26.00
8	424-81	Brass bookends	31.50

On May 25, 19—, Dalton Gift Shop received this purchase invoice from Atlanta Supply Corporation:

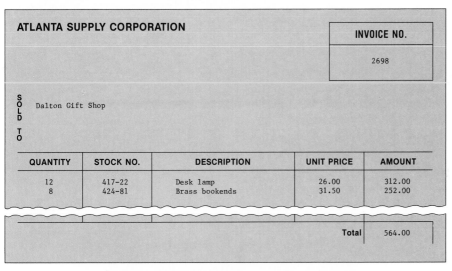

ATLANTA SUPPLY CORPORATION

INVOICE NO.

2698

SOLD TO Dalton Gift Shop

QUANTITY	STOCK NO.	DESCRIPTION	UNIT PRICE	AMOUNT
12	417-22	Desk lamp	26.00	312.00
8	424-81	Brass bookends	31.50	252.00
			Total	564.00

On May 25, 19—, Dalton Gift Shop received the following merchandise from Atlanta Supply Corporation:

Quantity	Stock No.	Description
12 ea.	417-22	Desk lamp
8 pr.	424-81	Brass bookends

a. Does the invoice agree with the purchase order?
b. Does the invoice agree with the items actually received?
c. Are the extensions and total on the invoice correct?
d. Should the invoice be approved for payment as received?

2. As an employee of Dalton Gift Shop, you are to check the extensions and totals of all purchase invoices. Check each of the following invoices. Follow the procedures listed in your Activity Guide to check each invoice. Remember: If there is an error in an extension, the total is also likely to be incorrect.

a.

Quantity	Stock No.	Description	Unit Price	Total
6 ea.	5453	Jewel chest	$71.00	$426.00

b.

Quantity	Stock No.	Description	Unit Price	Total
30 ea.	6870	Aroma disk player	$15.50	$465.00
12 ea.	6863	Vanity trio	27.75	333.00
				$798.00

c.

Quantity	Stock No.	Description	Unit Price	Total
18 ea.	5050	Wet/dry shaver	$26.70	$480.60
36 ea.	5076	Shower caddy	7.75	279.00
				$659.60

d.

Quantity	Stock No.	Description	Unit Price	Total
10 ea.	5665	Oak bookshelf	$25.00	$250.00
6 ea.	5641	Brass change dish	8.25	49.50
6 ea.	5658	Brass clock	65.25	391.50
				$691.00

e.

Quantity	Stock No.	Description	Unit Price	Total
4 ea.	4151	Wool hat	$23.65	$ 93.60
12 pr.	9255	Medium wool gloves	8.38	100.56
12 pr.	9256	Large wool gloves	8.38	100.56
				$294.72

f.

Quantity	Stock No.	Description	Unit Price	Total
5 sets	9360	Koala golf club covers	$11.73	$58.65
8 ea.	9318	Golf care kit	7.76	62.08
				$120.73

g.

Quantity	Stock No.	Description	Unit Price	Total
15 ea.	5055	Emergency CB	$54.77	$821.55
25 ea.	8653	Rechargeable flashlight	14.46	316.50
12 ea.	2018	Cordless mini vac	31.20	374.40
6 ea.	2024	Tool and knife set	55.34	332.04
				$1,844.49

h.

Quantity	Stock No.	Description	Unit Price	Total
4 ea.	3812	Nordock 450× telescope	$178.75	$715.00
2 ea.	3829	Nordock 600× telescope	276.84	553.68
1 ea.	3820	Nordock reflector tel.	443.90	443.90
				$1,722.58

i.

Quantity	Stock No.	Description	Unit Price	Total
9 ea.	6771	Gumball machine	$15.49	$139.41
12 ea.	5506	Cheese set	12.63	151.56
15 ea.	7245	Wood nutcracker	8.75	131.25
6 ea.	9755	Sleigh with candy	14.88	89.28
				$511.50

j.

Quantity	Stock No.	Description	Unit Price	Total
30 ea.	8255	Calligraphy kit	$ 6.32	$189.60
24 ea.	8823	Art activity set	8.57	203.28
10 ea.	8802	Wood art chest	12.85	128.50
16 ea.	8800	Crayon case	4.67	74.72
				$596.10

GOALS

1. To find the credit period of an invoice.
2. To find the discount period of an invoice and the net amount due.
3. To find the due date of an invoice.

KEY TERMS

On an invoice, the *terms* notation tells the purchaser when the invoice must be paid and what cash discount, if any, may be taken.

The *credit period* is the period of time allowed for the payment of the net amount of an invoice.

The *discount period* is the period of time allowed for the payment of an invoice less a discount.

FINDING THE CREDIT PERIOD

The *terms* of an invoice tell how soon the purchaser must pay the invoice. The period of time allowed for payment of an invoice is called the *credit period*. For example, the terms on an invoice dated June 1 are n/30. This means that the purchaser must pay the net, or full, amount within 30 days. The letter ''n'' stands for ''net.'' Since there are 30 days in June, the invoice must be paid by July 1.

FINDING THE DISCOUNT PERIOD AND THE AMOUNT DUE

The terms also tell the purchaser whether a cash discount may be taken. Suppose that the terms are 2/10, n/30. The code 2/10 means that the purchaser can subtract 2 percent off the total price if the invoice is paid within 10 days of the date of the invoice. The cash discount is 2 percent, and the discount period is 10 days. The code n/30 means that if the purchaser does not take the discount by paying within the 10-day discount period, then the total of the invoice must be paid within 30 days.

Suppose you receive an invoice dated March 26 for $400. The terms are 2/10, n/60. The discount period is 10 days, and the credit period is 60 days. The discount rate is 2 percent. To take advantage of the discount, you would find the due date and the amount to be paid as follows.

1. To find the last day of the discount period, count forward 10 days from March 26.

Count: 1   2   3   4   5   6   7   8   9   10
Date: 3/27 3/28 3/29 3/30 3/31 4/1 4/2 4/3 4/4 4/5

The last day of the discount period is April 5.

2. To find the amount to be paid, find the discount by multiplying the total amount of the invoice by 2 percent, or 0.02.

$$\begin{array}{r} \$400 \\ \times 0.02 \\ \hline \$8.00 \end{array}$$

Then subtract the discount from the amount of the invoice.

$$\begin{array}{r} \$400.00 \\ -8.00 \\ \hline \$392.00 \end{array}$$

If you pay the invoice by April 5, you pay $392. If you decide not to take the discount, you must pay the full amount ($400) within 60 days of March 26. In other words, the *due date*, the date payment is due, is 60 days from March 26.

FINDING THE DUE DATE

To find the due date of the invoice dated March 26, use the calendar in the margin and follow these steps:

1. Count the number of days left in March after March 26 (5).
2. Add the number of days in the next month (April) to the number of days left in March (30 + 5 = 35).
3. Subtract this amount from the number of days in the credit period (60 − 35 = 25).
4. The due date is the 25th day of the next month (May 25).

Sometimes the terms are n/EOM. *EOM* means "end of month" and *n* means "net." Thus n/EOM means that the net amount has to be paid by the end of the month of the invoice date. Some suppliers even allow a cash discount if the invoice is paid within a certain number of days after the end of the month. For example, if the terms are 3/10 EOM, n/60, a 3 percent cash discount can be taken if the invoice is paid within 10 days after the end of the month of the invoice date. If the purchaser does not pay within the discount period, the net amount of the invoice must be paid within 60 days of the invoice date.

MARCH						
S	M	T	W	T	F	S
				1	2	3
4	5	6	7	8	9	10
11	12	13	14	15	16	17
18	19	20	21	22	23	24
25	26	27	28	29	30	31

APRIL						
S	M	T	W	T	F	S
1	2	3	4	5	6	7
8	9	10	11	12	13	14
15	16	17	18	19	20	21
22	23	24	25	26	27	28
29	30					

MAY						
S	M	T	W	T	F	S
		1	2	3	4	5
6	7	8	9	10	11	12
13	14	15	16	17	18	19
20	21	22	23	24	25	26
27	28	29	30	31		

1. If the invoice terms are n/30, what is the credit period?

2. If the invoice terms are n/30, how much of the invoice amount must be paid within the credit period?

3. If the invoice terms are 2/10, n/30, what is the discount period?

4. If the invoice terms are 2/10, n/30, what percentage discount may be taken if the invoice is paid within the discount period?

5. If an invoice is dated September 10 and the terms are 3/10 EOM, n/60, what is the latest date on which the discount may be taken?

Exercises for Topic 2

1. Within how many days must the net amount of an invoice be paid if the terms are:
   a. n/30?   **c.** 2/10 EOM, n/60?
   b. 2/10, n/30?   **d.** n/EOM (invoice date is May 1)?

2. Glad Tidings Jeans Shop received 15 invoices, which are listed below. For each, find the due date of the credit period. Most of the invoices offer a cash discount. For the invoices that have discount terms, find the due date of the discount period and the amount to be paid if the discount is taken. If the discount amount has a fraction of a cent, round off the fraction to the nearest whole cent.

	Invoice Date	Invoice Amount	Terms
a.	January 5	$ 450.00	n/30
b.	January 28	265.00	4/10, n/30
c.	March 12	1,207.00	1/15, n/30
d.	April 6	336.00	2/20, n/60
e.	April 21	187.00	3/10, n/60
f.	May 8	13,423.80	3/10, n/30
g.	July 9	9,628.30	2/10, n/60
h.	August 10	693.40	2/10, n/30
i.	September 2	202.88	n/60
j.	September 12	3,561.20	2/10 EOM, n/60
k.	October 7	931.24	2/30, n/60
l.	November 5	29,328.56	n/EOM
m.	December 18	722.50	3/10, n/60

TOPIC 3 ● ACCOUNTS PAYABLE PROCEDURES

GOALS

1. To post purchase invoices to creditors' accounts.
2. To post purchase returns to creditors' accounts.
3. To post payments made to creditors to their accounts.

KEY TERMS

A *creditor's account* is a form used to record credit purchases, purchase returns, payments, and the balance owed to a supplier. A separate form is kept for each creditor. A creditor's account is an account payable.

Purchase returns are items returned to a supplier for credit.

A *credit memo* is a form sent to the purchasing business by the supplier to show that credit has been given for items returned.

In Topic 1, you learned that Kelly Cosmetic Company purchases merchandise on credit. Together, the amounts that Kelly Cosmetic Company owes its creditors for goods and services bought are its *accounts payable*. For example, if Kelly Cosmetic Company has three invoices from Jacobs Chemical Company totaling $3,985, then Jacobs Chemical Company is an account payable of $3,985.

Kelly Cosmetic Company keeps a separate account payable for each creditor. Each account shows the total amount that Kelly Cosmetic Company owes each creditor. It is similar to the customers' accounts you learned about in Chapter 10. Remember: Accounts kept for charge customers are accounts receivable because a business receives money from its customers. Accounts kept for creditors are accounts payable because a business pays out money to its creditors.

POSTING PURCHASE INVOICES

Before a creditor's invoice is filed, information from it is posted to the creditor's account. John Antonucci, an accounting clerk at Kelly Cosmetic Company, posted information from the invoice to the account payable for Jacobs Chemical Company. The invoice is called a *source document* because it is the source of information for keeping records.

Look at the invoice and the account payable on the next page.

Jacobs Chemical Company
673 Lynn Lane, Chicago, IL 60620

INVOICE NO.
3027

```
S
O
L   Kelly Cosmetic Company
D   7609 Wellington
    Chicago, IL 60633
T
O
```

INVOICE DATE 8/13/--

ORDER NUMBER 8119

TERMS n/30

QUANTITY	STOCK NO.	DESCRIPTION	UNIT PRICE	AMOUNT
6 Cases	H32	Conditioning formula	190.00	1,140.00
9 Gal	T48	Shampoo concentrate	19.00	171.00

Approved Jane Jackson

Account No. 481 **6**

	TOTAL	1,311.00

1 Name *Jacobs Chemical Company*   Account No. *481*
Address *673 Lynn Lane, Chicago, IL 60620*

	DATE	EXPLANATION	POST. REF.	DEBIT	CREDIT	BALANCE
2	Aug. 17		3027		1311 00	1311 00
			3		**4**	**5**

Note that John Antonucci:

1. Writes the name, the address, and the account number of the creditor at the top of the form.
2. Records the date that the invoice is posted (August 17, 19—) in the Date column.
3. Adds no explanation for this invoice since the invoice number (3027) is recorded in the Posting Reference column.
4. Records the invoice amount ($1,311) in the Credit column.
5. Records the account balance ($1,311) in the Balance column. In this case, the balance is the same as the amount of the invoice.
6. Writes the account number on the invoice to show that it has been posted and is ready for filing.

POSTING PURCHASE RETURNS

Every so often, Kelly Cosmetic Company receives damaged merchandise. Damaged items, which are returned to the supplier, are called *purchase returns.*

A purchase return is deducted from the amount owed to the creditor. When the creditor receives the returned items, the creditor prepares a *credit memo* and sends it to the purchaser. The credit memo for purchases is similar to the credit memo for sales that you studied in Chapter 10.

Note how John posts the credit memo to the account payable for Jacobs Chemical Company shown below the credit memo.

Jacobs Chemical Company
673 Lynn Lane, Chicago, IL 60620

CREDIT MEMORANDUM

No.   CM588

TO: Kelly Cosmetic Company
      7609 Wellington
      Chicago, IL 60633

DATE: 8/23/--

Your account has been credited as follows:

Quantity	Article	Stock No.	Unit Price	Extension
1 bag	Powder base formula	R93	86.75	86.75

account number 481 ❺

Name   *Jacobs Chemical Company*   Account No.   *481*
Address *673 Lynn Lane, Chicago, IL 60620*

	DATE	EXPLANATION	POST. REF.	DEBIT	CREDIT	BALANCE
❶	19— *Aug.* 17		3027		1 3 1 1 00	1 3 1 1 00
	26		CM588	8 6 75		1 2 2 4 25
		❷		❸		❹

To post the credit memo, John:

1. Records the date that the credit memo is posted (August 26, 19—) in the Date column.
2. Adds no explanation because the credit memo number (CM 588) is recorded in the Posting Reference column.
3. Records the amount of the credit memo ($86.75) in the Debit column, because Kelly Cosmetic Company no longer owes this amount.

4. Computes and then records the new balance of the account in the Balance column. The new balance is found by subtracting the debit from the old balance ($1,311 − $86.75 = $1,224.25).
5. Writes the account number on the credit memo to show that it has been posted and is ready for filing. John files the credit memo in the same folder as the invoice for the returned items.

POSTING PAYMENTS

Two or three days before an invoice is due, John Antonucci removes the invoice from the file and pays it. John uses the check stub or a carbon copy of the check as the source document for posting to the creditor's account. A carbon copy of a check used to pay the balance due on the Jacobs Chemical Company account is shown here. The words "Copy—Not Negotiable" mean that the check cannot be cashed.

NO. 1812   Kelly Cosmetic Company   22-1 / 960

MO.	DAY	YR.	PAY TO THE ORDER OF	Jacobs Chemical Company	AMOUNT
9	10	--		673 Lynn Lane	$1,224.25
				Chicago, IL 60620	

Twelve hundred twenty-four and 25/100---------------------------------DOLLARS

Robert Velosky
AUTHORIZED SIGNATURE

FIRST NATIONAL BANK
Chicago, IL 60612

COPY— NOT NEGOTIABLE

⑆960⑉022⑆ 437⑉9711⑈

Name **Jacobs Chemical Company**   Account No. **481**
Address **673 Lynn Lane, Chicago, IL 60620**

DATE	EXPLANATION	POST. REF.	DEBIT	CREDIT	BALANCE
Aug. 17		3027		1311 00	1311 00
26		CM588	86 75		1224 25
Sept. 10		CK1812	1224 25		— 00

❶ ❷ ❸ ❹

Note how John posts information from the check copy to the account payable of the Jacobs Chemical Company. John:

1. Records the date of the check (September 10, 19—) in the Date column.
2. Adds no explanation because the check number (Check 1812) is recorded in the Posting Reference column.
3. Records the amount of the check ($1,224.25) in the Debit column.
4. Computes and then records the new balance of the account in the Balance column. John finds the balance by subtracting the amount of the check from the old balance ($1,224.25 − $1,224.25 = 0). When the balance is zero, John writes "—00" in the Balance column.

Check Your Reading

1. Explain the difference between accounts receivable and accounts payable.

2. What form is used as the source document to post an amount owed to a creditor to the creditor's account?

3. What form is used as the source document to post a purchase return to a creditor's account?

4. What source document is used to post a payment to a creditor to the creditor's account?

5. Tell whether each of the following increases or decreases the balance of a creditor's account:
   a. A purchase on credit
   b. A purchase return
   c. A payment to the creditor

Exercises for Topic 3

1. As an employee in the accounts payable department of Greenworld Manufacturing Company, you are responsible for setting up new creditors' accounts and posting purchases, purchase returns, and payments.

   a. Set up an account for each of the following new creditors by entering each name, address, and account number at the top of a creditor's account payable form.

Name and Address	Account Number
Northeast Fabricators Inc. 1437 Cabot Avenue Boston, MA 02184	1478
Redi-Wear Paint Co. P.O. Box 2177 Anderson, IN 46011	1479
Imperial Plastics Inc. 1400 Thompson Circle Atlanta, GA 30344	1480

b. Post the following information to the correct account in your Activity Guide.

Jan. 3 Received Invoice 2419 from Northeast Fabricators Inc. for the amount of $425.

5 Received Invoice 8940 from Redi-Wear Paint Co. for the amount of $190.

7 Received Invoice 1612 from Imperial Plastics Inc. for the amount of $1,000.

15 Received Invoice 2630 from Northeast Fabricators Inc. for the amount of $638.50.

17 Received Credit Memo 418 from Redi-Wear Paint Co. for the amount of $55.

19 Received Invoice 1678 from Imperial Plastics Inc. for the amount of $650.

24 Issued Check 1711 to Northeast Fabricators Inc. for the amount of $1,063.50.

26 Received Invoice 9236 from Redi-Wear Paint Co. for the amount of $400.

28 Received Credit Memo 207 from Imperial Plastics Inc. for the amount of $150.

31 Received Invoice 2844 from Northeast Fabricators Inc. for the amount of $377.85.

31 Issued Check 1781 to Redi-Wear Paint Co. for the amount of $535.

31 Issued Check 1782 to Imperial Plastics Inc. for the amount of $1,000.

2. As an employee in the accounts payable department of Logan Lock and Key Company, you are responsible for setting up new creditors' accounts and posting purchases, purchase returns, and payments.

a. Set up an account for each of the following new creditors by entering each name, address, and account number at the top of a creditor's account form.

Name and Address	Account Number
Tidewater Steel Company Box 5121, Bayside Station Virginia Beach, VA 23455	3124
Avalon Manufacturing Company 2000 West Lebanon Street Avalon, NJ 08202	3125
Elkhart Printing Company 142 Forsyth Avenue Detroit, MI 48202	3126

b. Post the following information to the correct account in your Activity Guide.

Mar. 1 Received Invoice 3824 from Tidewater Steel Company for the amount of $2,264.73.

3 Received Invoice 72411 from Avalon Manufacturing Company for the amount of $8,044.58.

4 Received Invoice 8010 from Elkhart Printing Company for the amount of $766.02.

13 Received Invoice 4192 from Tidewater Steel Company for the amount of $1,890.20.

15 Received Credit Memo 6212 from Avalon Manufacturing Company for the amount of $267.71.

16 Received Invoice 8237 from Elkhart Printing Company for the amount of $1,861.15.

25 Issued Check 9180 to Tidewater Steel Company for the amount of $4,154.93.

27 Received Invoice 72968 from Avalon Manufacturing Company for the amount of $3,606.89.

28 Received Credit Memo 1271 from Elkhart Printing Company for the amount of $420.

29 Received Invoice 4305 from Tidewater Steel Company for the amount of $947.82.

31 Issued Check 9207 to Avalon Manufacturing Company for the amount of $11,383.76.

31 Issued Check 9208 to Elkhart Printing Company for the amount of $346.02.

MATH SKILLBUILDER

Skill: Computing discounts and payments due.

Sample Problem: Find the amount of the discount and the amount to be paid on an invoice of $200 if a 2 percent discount is taken.

Solution:

1. Change the discount rate (2 percent) to a decimal:

$$2 \text{ percent} = 0.02$$

2. Multiply the amount of the invoice ($200) by the discount rate (0.02) to find the amount of the discount:

$$\$200 \times 0.02 = \$4$$

3. Subtract the discount from the invoice amount to find the amount to be paid:

$$\$200 - \$4 = \$196$$

Practice: Find the discount and the amount to be paid on each invoice. If necessary, round your answer to the nearest cent.

	Invoice Amount	Discount Rate
a.	$ 25.00	1%
b.	100.00	1%
c.	250.00	1%
d.	181.10	2%
e.	243.43	3%
f.	1,000.00	4%
g.	1,014.18	5%
h.	3,144.89	6%
i.	7,248.03	3%
j.	1,005.68	2%

VOCABULARY SKILLBUILDER

Read each of the following statements. From the words below each statement, choose the term that best matches the statement.

1. An incoming bill.

   credit memo   purchase invoice

2. An outgoing bill.

   accounts payable   sales invoice

3. Amounts owed to suppliers for goods purchased on credit.

   accounts payable   creditor's account

4. Period of time allowed for the payment of the net amount of an invoice.

   credit memo   credit period

5. Period of time allowed for the payment of an invoice less a discount.

   credit period   discount period

6. Notation on an invoice that tells the purchaser when the invoice must be paid and what cash discount, if any, may be taken.

   sales invoice   terms

7. A form used to record credit purchases, purchase returns, payments, and the balance owed to a supplier.

   accounts payable   creditor's account

8. A form sent to the purchasing business by the supplier to show that credit has been given for items returned.

credit memo   purchase invoice

9. Items that are returned to a supplier for credit.

purchase invoice   purchase returns

APPLICATION PROBLEMS

As an employee in the accounts payable department of Dana's Clothing Store, you are responsible for setting up new creditors' accounts, checking purchase invoices, posting purchase invoices to creditors' accounts, and figuring due dates for the payment of purchase invoices.

1. Set up an account for the two new creditors on the right by entering each name, address, and account number at the top of a creditor's account form.

2. Check the extensions and total of the purchase invoices on pages 347–349. Follow the procedures listed in the Activity Guide to check each invoice. Remember: If there is an error in an extension, the total is also likely to be incorrect.

Name and Address	Account Number
Goldberg and Dell Fashions 1414 Murray Hill Station New York, NY 10016	4240
Sunshine Apparel Manufacturers 30304 Old Chelsea Station New York, NY 10011	4241

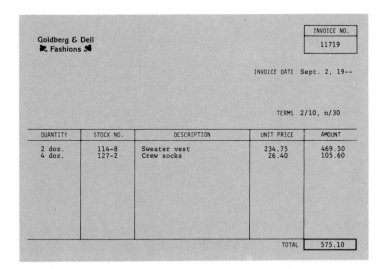

Goldberg & Dell
Fashions

INVOICE NO.
11719

INVOICE DATE Sept. 2, 19--

TERMS 2/10, n/30

QUANTITY	STOCK NO.	DESCRIPTION	UNIT PRICE	AMOUNT
2 doz.	114-8	Sweater vest	234.75	469.50
4 doz.	127-2	Crew socks	26.40	105.60
			TOTAL	575.10

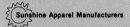

Sunshine Apparel Manufacturers

			INVOICE NO.
			793414

INVOICE DATE Sept. 7, 19--

TERMS 1/10, n/60

QUANTITY	STOCK NO.	DESCRIPTION	UNIT PRICE	AMOUNT
38	29-1441	Unlined jacket	48.75	1,852.50
45	29-1466	Silk dress	84.79	3,815.55
9	32-2002	Fur-trimmed coat	260.00	2,340.00
			TOTAL	8,008.15

Goldberg & Dell Fashions

			INVOICE NO.
			11990

INVOICE DATE Sept. 16, 19--

TERMS 2/10, n/30

QUANTITY	STOCK NO.	DESCRIPTION	UNIT PRICE	AMOUNT
124	138-02	Prewashed jeans	17.63	2,186.12
85	167-41	Wool slacks	38.27	3,252.95
60	143-81	Western shirt	28.40	1,704.00
18	147-20	Linen suit	118.45	2,133.72
			TOTAL	9,276.79

Sunshine Apparel Manufacturers

			INVOICE NO.
			793606

INVOICE DATE Sept. 21, 19--

TERMS 1/10, n/60

QUANTITY	STOCK NO.	DESCRIPTION	UNIT PRICE	AMOUNT
2 doz.	23-4118	Running suit	186.55	373.10
75	26-0615	Cotton blouse	21.12	1,584.00
24	14-1701	Corduroy jumper	48.00	1,152.00
40	32-2018	Leather jacket	83.25	3,330.00
			TOTAL	6,439.10

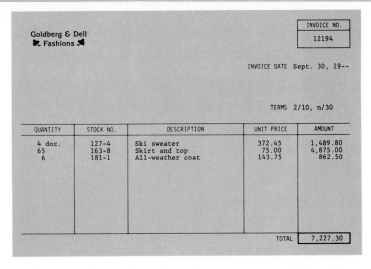

Goldberg & Dell Fashions

INVOICE NO.
12194

INVOICE DATE Sept. 30, 19--

TERMS 2/10, n/30

QUANTITY	STOCK NO.	DESCRIPTION	UNIT PRICE	AMOUNT
4 doz.	127-4	Ski sweater	372.45	1,489.80
65	163-8	Skirt and top	75.00	4,875.00
6	181-1	All-weather coat	143.75	862.50
			TOTAL	7,227.30

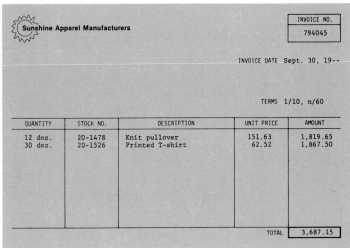

Sunshine Apparel Manufacturers

INVOICE NO.
794045

INVOICE DATE Sept. 30, 19--

TERMS 1/10, n/60

QUANTITY	STOCK NO.	DESCRIPTION	UNIT PRICE	AMOUNT
12 doz.	20-1478	Knit pullover	151.63	1,819.65
30 doz.	20-1526	Printed T-shirt	62.52	1,867.50
			TOTAL	3,687.15

3. Post each of the purchase invoices you checked in Problem 2 to the correct creditor's account that you prepared in Problem 1. Remember to post the corrected total if you found an error in the invoice. In the Activity Guide, write the creditor's account number on each invoice to show that it has been posted.

4. For each of the purchase invoices in Problem 2, find the following:

a. The due date of the credit period

b. The due date of the discount period

c. The amount to be paid if the discount is taken

CHAPTER 13

PAYROLL RECORDS

Payroll records list and summarize information about earnings. Accurate and complete payroll records are important for two reasons. First, each employee must receive the correct amount of pay when it is due. Second, the federal government requires employers to report information on the earnings of their employees. Thus every business, no matter how large or small, must have procedures for keeping accurate payroll records.

TOPIC 1 ● COMPUTING TIME AND EARNINGS

GOALS

1. To compute regular hours worked.
2. To compute overtime hours worked.
3. To compute regular earnings.
4. To compute overtime earnings.
5. To prepare a payroll earnings record.

KEY TERMS

Regular earnings are the amount earned for all hours worked during the regular workweek (usually 40 hours). This does not include overtime hours.

Overtime earnings are the amount earned for hours worked beyond the regular (40-hour) workweek.

Gross earnings include regular earnings plus overtime earnings.

A *time card* is a record of hours worked for one employee.

Ella Watson, who works for the Sovran Company, is paid an hourly rate for her work. Each morning when Ella arrives at work, she punches a *time card* on a time clock. She takes her time card from a rack and puts the card into the slot on the time clock. The clock then prints or stamps the time on the card. Ella also punches the time card when she leaves for lunch, when she gets back from lunch, and when she leaves for the day.

Ella's time card includes the following:

- The date of the last working day of the week (Week Ending)
- The employee's number, which is the social security number

Days	Regular				Overtime		Daily Totals
	In	Out	In	Out	In	Out	
Mon.	8^{00}	12^{00}	1^{00}	4^{05}			7
Tues.	7^{55}	12^{00}	1^{00}	4^{00}			7
Wed.	8^{00}	12^{10}	1^{05}	4^{10}			7
Thurs.	8^{00}	11^{55}	1^{00}	4^{00}			7
Fri.	8^{05}	11^{55}	1^{00}	4^{10}			7
Sat.							
Sun.							

Week Ending May 16, 19 --

No. 264-51-3208

Name Watson, Ella

		Hours	Rate	Earnings
	Regular			
	Overtime			
Days Worked	Total Hours		Gross Earnings	

- The employee's name
- The time the employee arrives (In) and leaves (Out) each day
- The total hours worked each day (Daily Totals)
- Space for weekly earnings at the bottom of the card

COMPUTING TIME WORKED

Dante Amani works in the payroll office at Sovran. At the end of each week, Dante gets all the time cards and computes the time worked by each employee. Dante follows certain steps to compute daily totals on a *time analysis* form, such as the one shown here.

Days	Daily Totals		Analysis
	A.M.	P.M.	
Mon.	4	3	4:05 considered as 4:00
Tues.	4	3	7:55 considered as 8:00
Wed.	4	3	12:10, 1:05, and 4:10 considered as 12:00, 1:00, 4:00
Thurs.	4	3	11:55 considered as 12:00
Fri.	4	3	8:05, 11:55, and 4:10 considered as 8:00, 12:00, 4:00

Look at Ella Watson's time card and her time analysis as you read the steps below:

1. First Dante finds the regular hours of work. At the Sovran Company, different employees work different hours. Dante finds that Ella Watson's regular hours are from 8 a.m. to 12 noon and from 1 p.m. to 4 p.m. Ella's daily total is seven hours. Her weekly total is 35 hours (5 days × 7 hours = 35 hours).

2. Dante does not count extra time beyond Ella's regular 35 hours unless the extra time is approved by Ella's supervisor. For example, Ella's time card shows that she punched out at 4:10 p.m. on Wednesday. Since the extra time was not approved by her supervisor, Ella will not be paid for the extra time.

3. Dante checks for late arrivals and early departures. The Sovran Company deducts wages only if an employee is more than five minutes late getting to work or five minutes early leaving work. Since Ella was not more than five minutes late getting to work or five minutes early leaving work, Dante counts each day as a full day. In the Daily Totals column next to each day that Ella worked, Dante writes "7." Read the Analysis column in the time analysis on page 351 to see how Dante counts late arrivals and early departures.

4. For late arrivals and early departures of more than five minutes, the Sovran Company deducts wages based on the quarter-hour time system. In this system, late arrivals and early departures of more than five minutes are computed to the nearest quarter hour. For example, arriving at 8:06, 8:07, or 8:08 is considered as arriving at 8:15, and a quarter hour's pay is deducted from the employee's wages.

RECORDING WEEKLY EARNINGS ON TIME CARDS

After Dante Amani fills in the Daily Totals column, he then completes the bottom of Ella's time card. He checks his work carefully to be sure it is accurate.

Week Ending					May 16, 19 --		
No. 264-51-3208							
Name Watson, Ella							

Days	Regular				Overtime		Daily Totals
	In	Out	In	Out	In	Out	
Mon.	8⁰⁰	12⁰⁰	1⁰⁰	4⁰⁵			7
Tues.	7⁵⁵	12⁰⁰	1⁰⁰	4⁰⁰			7
Wed.	8⁰⁰	12¹⁰	1⁰⁵	4¹⁰			7
Thurs.	8⁰⁰	11⁵⁵	1⁰⁰	4⁰⁰			7
Fri.	8⁰⁵	11⁵⁵	1⁰⁰	4¹⁰			7
Sat.							
Sun.							

❷

	Hours	Rate	Earnings
❶ Regular	35	8.00	280.00 ❸ ❹
Overtime			

| Days Worked ❺ 5 | Total Hours | 35 | Gross Earnings 280.00 |

1. Dante fills in the total regular hours for the week (35) under Hours.
2. He fills in the hourly rate of pay ($8) under Rate.
3. Dante multiplies the number of regular hours by the hourly rate (35 × $8 = $280). He enters the result, the amount earned for regular hours worked, under Earnings.
4. Since Ella Watson did not work any overtime, or extra hours, Dante leaves the Overtime spaces blank.
5. Dante then fills in Days Worked, Total Hours, and Gross Earnings. *Gross earnings* are the total amount of earnings before deductions such as taxes.

Fractions of Hours Ella Watson usually works seven full hours each day. In some weeks, however, she works more or fewer than seven full hours each day. For example, on May 19 Ella worked four hours in the morning and two and a half hours in the afternoon for a total of six and a half hours, as shown on her time card.

Week Ending				May 23, 19 --		

No. 264-51-3208

Name Watson, Ella

Days	Regular				Overtime		Daily Totals
	In	Out	In	Out	In	Out	
Mon.	8^{00}	12^{00}	1^{00}	3^{30}			*6.5*
Tues.	8^{00}	11^{55}	1^{00}	4^{05}			*7*
Wed.	8^{00}	12^{00}	1^{00}	4^{10}			*7*
Thurs.	8^{05}	11^{55}	1^{00}	4^{10}			*7*
Fri.	7^{55}	12^{10}	1^{00}	4^{30}			*7.75*
Sat.							
Sun.							

		Hours	Rate	Earnings
	Regular	*35.25*	*8.00*	*282.00*
	Overtime			
Days Worked *5*	Total Hours	*35.25*	Gross Earnings	*282.00*

In the quarter-hour time system, it is possible to have $\frac{1}{4}$-hour, $\frac{1}{2}$-hour, and $\frac{3}{4}$-hour fractions as part of a daily total. On a time card, these fractions are recorded as decimals:

$$\frac{1}{4} \text{ hour (15 minutes)} = 0.25 \text{ hour}$$

$$\frac{1}{2} \text{ hour (30 minutes)} = 0.5 \text{ hour}$$

$$\frac{3}{4} \text{ hour (45 minutes)} = 0.75 \text{ hour}$$

Thus Ella's daily total for Monday has been recorded as "6.5" (instead of "$6\frac{1}{2}$") because decimals are easier to add. For example:

Daily Totals

6.5

7

7

7

7.75

Weekly total   35.25

Time and a half refers to the hourly pay rate for overtime, which is figured by multiplying the regular hourly pay rate by $1\frac{1}{2}$ (one and a half).

Overtime People who work overtime usually are paid $1\frac{1}{2}$ times their regular hourly pay rate for any hours worked over 40 hours a week. The $1\frac{1}{2}$-times rate is commonly called *time and a half*

In one week, Arnold Lowenstein worked 40 regular hours and 8 overtime hours at the Sovran Company. His regular hourly pay rate is $10 an hour. For all hours worked over 40 hours a week, Arnold receives time and a half, or $15.

$10 (regular hourly pay rate)
+5 (half of regular hourly pay rate)
$15 (time and a half, or overtime pay rate)

Here is how his gross earnings are computed:

40 hours at $10: $400
8 hours at $15: +120
Gross earnings: $520

Week Ending _____ May 23, **19** __

No. 374-63-4772 _____

Name Lowenstein, Arnold _____

Days	Regular				Overtime		Daily Totals
	In	Out	In	Out	In	Out	
Mon.	8^{00}	12^{00}	1^{00}	5^{00}	5^{00}	7^{00}	10
Tues.	7^{55}	12^{05}	12^{55}	5^{00}			8
Wed.	7^{55}	12^{00}	1^{05}	5^{00}			8
Thurs.	8^{00}	11^{55}	1^{05}	5^{00}	5^{00}	7^{05}	10
Fri.	8^{05}	11^{55}	1^{00}	5^{05}			8
Sat.					9^{00}	1^{00}	4
Sun.							

		Hours	Rate	Earnings
	Regular	40	10.00	400.00
	Overtime	8	15.00	120.00
Days Worked 6	Total Hours	48	Gross Earnings	520.00

Unlike the Sovran Company, Sun Plastics and some other businesses pay overtime on a *daily* basis rather than a weekly basis. Any hours worked over the regular workday are treated as overtime. At Sun Plastics, Rosa Tuomisto's regular workday is eight hours. During one week she worked a total of 39 hours, as shown here:

Day:	M	T	W	T	F
Hours:	7	9	7	10	6

On Tuesday, Rosa worked nine hours—one hour more than her regular workday. On Thursday, she worked two extra hours. Thus Rosa worked three hours overtime that week. Her regular rate of pay is $10 an hour, and her overtime rate is $15 an hour. Her gross pay is computed as follows:

36 hours at $10: $360
3 hours at $15: +45
Gross earnings: $405

Rosa earned a total of $405.

PAYROLL EARNINGS RECORD

A *payroll earnings record* is used to record the hours and earnings of all employees for a payroll period. The payroll earnings record shown below is for a one-week payroll period.

SOVRAN COMPANY   **PAYROLL EARNINGS RECORD**

For the week ended _May 16,_ 19 __—__

EMPLOYEE NUMBER	NAME	REGULAR HOURS	REGULAR RATE	REGULAR EARNINGS	OVERTIME HOURS	OVERTIME RATE	OVERTIME EARNINGS	GROSS EARNINGS
218-44-3992	Sharon Tesch	38	7 30	277 40	0	— 00	— 00	277 40
264-51-3208	Ella Watson	35	8 00	280 00	0	— 00	— 00	280 00
336-26-4843	James Manuel	40	8 00	320 00	2	12 00	24 00	344 00
446-34-6215	Gloria Lopez	40	8 50	340 00	8	12 75	102 00	442 00
510-65-3618	Bess Brooks	40	8 00	320 00	8	12 00	96 00	416 00
612-06-2185	Roy Montoya	38	8 00	304 00	0	— 00	— 00	304 00
Totals				1,841 40			222 00	2,063 40

A *payroll earnings record* is a form used to record the hours and the earnings of all employees for a payroll period.

On this payroll earnings record, note the following:

1. Each employee is listed by employee number and by name. The employee number is the employee's social security number.
2. The regular hours, regular rate, and regular earnings are entered from the time card of each employee.
3. If an employee's time card lists any overtime, the time card computations are checked. The overtime hours, overtime rate, and overtime earnings are then recorded.
4. The overtime earnings, if any, are added to the regular earnings to find the gross earnings.

5. When the data for all the employees have been entered, the three earnings columns are totaled and verified.

1. List two reasons why it is important to keep accurate and complete payroll records.

2. What is the purpose of the In and Out columns on a time card?

3. What is needed before an employee can be paid for overtime hours?

4. If a time card shows that an employee of Sovran Company arrived at work at 7:55 a.m., and the employee's regular workday begins at 8 a.m., from what time will the hours worked be figured?

5. In the quarter-hour time system, if an employee punches in at 9:12 a.m., from what time will the hours worked be figured? Assume that the employee's workday begins at 9 a.m.

Exercises for Topic 1

1. Essex Medical Center employs the people listed below. Their regular hours are also listed, and their time cards are shown on pages 358 and 359. For each employee, compute the number of hours worked each day, the total hours worked during the week, and the weekly earnings. Essex Medical Center uses the quarter-hour time system. Late arrivals and early departures of five minutes or less are not counted. No overtime has been approved.

Name		Regular Hours	
a. Burks, A. R.	8:30 a.m.–12 noon	1 p.m.–4:30 p.m.	
b. Galdos, N.	8:30 a.m.–12 noon	1 p.m.–4:30 p.m.	
c. Liebert, G. H.	8:30 a.m.–12:30 p.m.	1 p.m.–4 p.m.	
d. Ponczka, E. E.	8:30 a.m.–11:30 a.m.	12 noon–4:30 p.m.	
e. Sotos, W. G.	7:30 a.m.–12 noon	1 p.m.–4:30 p.m.	
f. Yung, C.	7:30 a.m.–12 noon	1 p.m.–4:30 p.m.	

Card 1

Week Ending April 29, 19 --

No. 499-21-7645

Name Burks, A. R.

Days	Regular				Overtime		Daily Totals
	In	Out	In	Out	In	Out	
Mon.	8^{25}	12^{05}	1^{05}	4^{35}			
Tues.	8^{15}	12^{10}	1^{00}	4^{30}			
Wed.	8^{20}	12^{05}	1^{00}	4^{25}			
Thurs.	8^{10}	12^{05}	1^{05}	4^{45}			
Fri.	8^{15}	12^{05}	1^{05}	4^{45}			
Sat.							
Sun.							

	Hours	Rate	Earnings
Regular		8.30	
Overtime			

Days Worked	Total Hours		Gross Earnings

Card 2

Week Ending April 29, 19 --

No. 528-91-4924

Name Galdos, N.

Days	Regular				Overtime		Daily Totals
	In	Out	In	Out	In	Out	
Mon.	8^{00}	12^{00}	1^{00}	4^{30}			
Tues.	8^{15}	12^{00}	1^{00}	4^{30}			
Wed.	8^{30}	12^{00}	1^{45}	4^{40}			
Thurs.	8^{15}	11^{55}	1^{00}	4^{45}			
Fri.	8^{20}	12^{00}	12^{55}	4^{30}			
Sat.							
Sun.							

	Hours	Rate	Earnings
Regular		8.90	
Overtime			

Days Worked	Total Hours		Gross Earnings

Card 3

Week Ending April 29, 19 --

No. 354-12-2033

Name Liebert, G. H.

Days	Regular				Overtime		Daily Totals
	In	Out	In	Out	In	Out	
Mon.	8^{35}	12^{30}	1^{00}	4^{00}			
Tues.	8^{25}	12^{25}	1^{00}	4^{05}			
Wed.	8^{25}	12^{30}	1^{00}	4^{25}			
Thurs.	8^{30}	12^{30}	1^{05}	4^{00}			
Fri.	8^{35}	12^{35}	1^{00}	4^{15}			
Sat.							
Sun.							

	Hours	Rate	Earnings
Regular		6.70	
Overtime			

Days Worked	Total Hours		Gross Earnings

Card 4

Week Ending April 29, 19 --

No. 634-34-7066

Name Ponczka, E. E.

Days	Regular				Overtime		Daily Totals
	In	Out	In	Out	In	Out	
Mon.	8^{35}	11^{35}	12^{05}	4^{40}			
Tues.	8^{30}	11^{30}	12^{00}	4^{40}			
Wed.	8^{25}	11^{30}	12^{00}	4^{45}			
Thurs.	8^{00}	11^{30}	11^{55}	4^{30}			
Fri.	8^{30}	11^{35}	12^{00}	4^{25}			
Sat.							
Sun.							

	Hours	Rate	Earnings
Regular		9.10	
Overtime			

Days Worked	Total Hours		Gross Earnings

Week Ending _____ April 29, 19 --

No. 649-51-1101

Name Sotos, W. G.

Days	Regular				Overtime		Daily Totals
	In	Out	In	Out	In	Out	
Mon.	7^{25}	12^{05}	1^{05}	4^{05}			
Tues.	7^{45}	11^{30}	1^{00}	4^{40}			
Wed.	7^{30}	11^{50}	12^{55}	4^{20}			
Thurs.	8^{20}	12^{10}	1^{10}	4^{25}			
Fri.	7^{30}	11^{15}	12^{50}	3^{45}			
Sat.							
Sun.							

		Hours	Rate	Earnings
	Regular		10.00	
	Overtime			
Days Worked	Total Hours		Gross Earnings	

Week Ending _____ April 29, 19 --

No. 397-55-6814

Name Yung, C.

Days	Regular				Overtime		Daily Totals
	In	Out	In	Out	In	Out	
Mon.	7^{35}	12^{00}	1^{10}	4^{35}			
Tues.	7^{20}	12^{00}	12^{55}	4^{15}			
Wed.	7^{25}	11^{25}	1^{05}	4^{25}			
Thurs.	7^{35}	11^{55}	12^{50}	4^{05}			
Fri.	7^{40}	11^{30}	12^{55}	4^{25}			
Sat.							
Sun.							

		Hours	Rate	Earnings
	Regular		9.90	
	Overtime			
Days Worked	Total Hours		Gross Earnings	

2. Use the data from the table below to prepare a payroll earnings record for the DJR Company. The information is for the week ending July 27. The regular workday is eight hours, and the regular workweek is 40 hours. Overtime is paid on a weekly basis at time and a half. If you need help preparing the payroll earnings record, look at the one shown on page 356.

Employee Number	Employee Name	Hours Worked					Regular Hourly Rate
		Mon.	Tues.	Wed.	Thurs.	Fri.	
401-48-6066	Pooley, T. M.	7	6	7	8	8	$ 7.50
408-45-9066	Clarke, E.	8	7	9	10	8	10.00
414-59-6038	Harple, G. F.	8	8	8	9	8	8.00
478-19-6053	Baxani, C. M.	8	9	10	8	7	11.00
480-01-9219	Syjut, K. E.	9	8	9	8	8	9.00
489-76-3312	Imajo, T. K.	8	9	10	8	11	7.00

3. Use the data from the table below to prepare a payroll earnings record for the Lyons Company. This information is for the week ending May 12. The regular workday is eight hours, and the regular workweek is 40 hours. Overtime is paid on a weekly basis at time and a half.

Employee Number	Employee Name	Hours Worked					Regular Hourly Rate
		Mon.	Tues.	Wed.	Thurs.	Fri.	
527-32-9139	Anderson, D. L.	7	7	8	10	9	$ 9.90
528-88-7514	Truong, B. R.	8	8	9	8	9	12.30
530-26-4118	Jenks, D. N.	9	8	11	6	7	10.50
535-22-1431	Scafidi, L.	8	11	8	9	9	7.60
537-93-2401	Ozmar, B. J.	8	8	10	8	7	8.40
539-14-7821	Farmilo, E.	8	10	8	9	8	11.30

4. Use the data from the table below to prepare a payroll earnings record for the Kron Company. This information is for the week ending December 20. The regular workday is eight hours. Overtime is paid on a daily basis at time and a half.

Employee Number	Employee Name	Hours Worked					Regular Hourly Rate
		Mon.	Tues.	Wed.	Thurs.	Fri.	
497-54-3122	Shears, M. S.	9	11	9	2	7	$ 8.50
522-31-8691	Harris, D. G.	8	8	2	8	8	11.10
522-33-9856	Vickers, A. H.	8	6	6	6	6	8.80
541-48-0094	Coen, P. T.	4	9	8	8	8	10.40
566-71-3987	Swartz, L. N.	9	9	9	9	9	8.00
599-34-2033	Paasch, J. N.	10	10	10	8	4	9.00
615-78-6541	Mayo, A. E.	8	8	7	7	7	13.00
633-89-7295	Hart, C. L.	8	7	6	9	8	7.80

TOPIC 2 ● PIECEWORK

GOALS

1. To compute earnings for employees who are paid a straight piece rate.
2. To compute earnings for employees who are paid a differential piece rate.

KEY TERMS

Piecework is a plan for paying employees according to the number of items or jobs completed.

A *straight piece rate* is a piecework plan in which the employee is paid a fixed amount of money for each unit completed.

A *differential piece rate* is a piecework plan in which the employee is paid according to a pay scale. The piece rate per unit increases as the number of units completed increases.

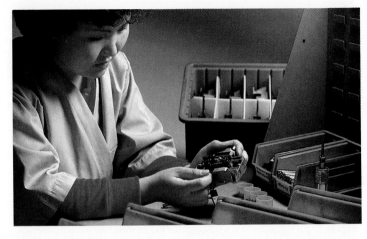

Some employees are paid for each piece or unit of work that they complete. They work on a *piecework* plan. The amount paid for each unit of work is called the *piece rate*. For example, John Vasquez assembled 40 desk lamps in one day. At a piece rate of $1.50 per lamp, John earned $60 ($1.50 × 40 = $60). John receives a *straight piece rate*, which means that John earns $1.50 for each lamp he assembles, no matter how many he assembles in one day.

When a *differential piece rate* is used, the rate of pay increases as more lamps are assembled each day. A differential piece rate pay scale looks like this:

Lamps Assembled per Day	Piece Rate
First 20	$1.50
Next 10	2.00
Over 30	2.50

Nicole Salizar assembled 28 lamps in one day. Using the differential piece rate scale, her earnings are computed as follows:

$$28 \text{ lamps} \longrightarrow \begin{cases} 20 \times \$1.50 = \$30 \\ 8 \times \$2.00 = \underline{16} \end{cases}$$
$$\text{Total earnings} = \$46$$

Beatrice Williams assembled 40 lamps in one day. Using the differential piece rate scale, her earnings are computed as follows:

$$40 \text{ lamps} \longrightarrow \begin{cases} 20 \times \$1.50 = \$30 \\ 10 \times \$2.00 = 20 \\ 10 \times \$2.50 = \underline{25} \end{cases}$$
$$\text{Total earnings} = \$75$$

1. How are earnings computed under the straight piece rate pay plan?

2. How are earnings computed under the differential piece rate plan?

Exercises for Topic 2

1. Compute the weekly earnings on a straight piece rate basis for the following employees of the Ultra Computer Corporation. The piecework rate is $1.50 per unit each day.

Name	Mon.	Tues.	Wed.	Thurs.	Fri.
a. Abdel, A. H.	41	38	34	40	39
b. Goldmann, P. H.	32	31	29	30	36
c. Lewis, R. L.	33	31	30	35	34
d. Pettus, A. G.	29	29	30	32	29
e. Trotti, B.	25	23	25	24	26
f. Wilson, D. C.	40	41	44	40	43
g. Yee, G. Y.	43	46	46	45	48
h. Zirkle, W. D.	31	34	34	36	38

2. Compute the weekly earnings on a straight piece rate basis for the following employees of the Imperial Tool and Die Company. Each employee's rate is listed below.

Name	Mon.	Tues.	Wed.	Thurs.	Fri.	Daily Piecework Rate
a. Abrams, D. L.	183	176	191	160	181	$0.28
b. Cook, A. G.	329	343	354	318	366	0.16
c. Dunn, R.	389	384	371	401	396	0.20
d. Esposito, K. J.	399	412	436	421	419	0.12
e. Farr, W. O.	1,208	1,183	1,306	1,422	1,215	0.04
f. Paulz, D. D.	218	193	240	220	310	0.24
g. Sutphin, A. L.	398	413	382	461	393	0.23
h. Terry, M. S.	512	496	483	501	491	0.15

3. Compute the weekly earnings on a differential piece rate basis for the following employees of the Magna-Max Tire Company. Use the differential piece rate scale shown here.

Units per Day	Daily Rate per Unit
First 40	$0.75
Next 20	1.00
Over 60	1.25

	Name	Mon.	Tues.	Wed.	Thurs.	Fri.
a.	Bilinski, J.	43	51	48	55	54
b.	Guthrie, R. W.	54	60	58	52	59
c.	Lyons, V. S.	67	63	63	65	64
d.	Pumo, M. A.	45	43	48	49	51
e.	Schultz, D. L.	34	39	38	36	33
f.	Syzman, T.	61	58	54	60	62

TOPIC 3 ● COMMISSION WAGES

GOALS

1. To compute earnings for employees who are paid a straight commission.
2. To compute earnings for employees who are paid a wage plus commission.

KEY TERMS

A *straight-commission* plan pays salespeople according to the total dollar amount of their sales.

A *wage-plus-commission* plan pays salespeople an hourly wage plus an amount based upon their total sales.

The earnings of many salespeople depend directly upon their sales totals. For example, Charlotte Gordon, who works part-time for J&K Shoe Store, receives a commission of 10 percent on all her sales. Her earnings depend entirely upon her sales. In other words, Charlotte works on a *straight commission*

During one week, Charlotte's sales were as follows:

Monday	Wednesday	Friday	Saturday
$210.70	$186.75	$238.12	$314.94

At the end of the day on Saturday, Charlotte's manager figured her weekly earnings by totaling her sales for the week and multiplying the total by 10 percent, or 0.10, as follows:

Monday	$210.70
Wednesday	186.75
Friday	238.12
Saturday	314.94
Total	$950.51
Commission rate	×0.10
Weekly earnings $95.0510	= $95.05

Some salespeople receive an hourly wage plus a commission for all their sales. David Selz works 40 hours a week for Danny's Sound Shop. He receives $4.50 an hour plus a commission of 5 percent on all his sales. During one week, David's sales were:

Monday	Tuesday	Thursday	Friday	Saturday
$284.51	$296.40	$248.66	$327.41	$519.62

At the end of the day on Saturday, David's manager, Brenda Holt, figured David's earnings in three steps:

1. Brenda figured the total hourly wage for the week by multiplying the hourly rate ($4.50) by the number of hours worked (40).

$$\begin{array}{r} \$4.50 \\ \times 40 \\ \hline \text{Total } \$180.00 \end{array}$$

2. She figured the commission by totaling David's sales and then multiplying the total by 5 percent, or 0.05, as follows:

Monday	$ 284.51
Tuesday	296.40
Thursday	248.66
Friday	327.41
Saturday	519.62
Total	$1,676.60
Commission rate	×0.05
Total commission	$83.8300 = $83.83

3. She added the total hourly wage to the total commission to find David's total weekly earnings.

Total hourly wage	$180.00
Total commission	+83.83
Weekly earnings	$263.83

1. Salespeople are often paid on a straight-____?____ basis.

2. How are earnings computed under the straight-commission pay plan?

3. How are earnings computed under the wage-plus-commission pay plan?

1. Using the daily sales totals below, compute the weekly earnings on a straight-commission basis for these six Thalman Department Store salespeople. The commission rate is 10 percent.

Employee	Mon.	Tues.	Wed.	Thurs.	Fri.	Sat.
a. Biddix, L.	$468.37	—	$621.89	—	$1,121.10	$ 556.80
b. Dang, C. V.	554.18	$676.21	—	$741.19	801.01	667.12
c. Harris, M.	667.44	512.21	807.32	350.00	—	834.40
d. Meli, A. P.	392.81	—	900.50	476.37	805.61	—
e. Simko, G.	530.07	392.24	676.91	—	1,107.09	—
f. Worsham, P.	—	699.80	—	963.21	1,226.81	1,463.11

2. Using the weekly sales totals below, compute the weekly earnings on a straight-commission basis for these six Star Motors salespeople. The commission rate is 3 percent.

Employee	Total Weekly Sales
a. Baldini, L. G.	$28,627.50
b. Carrico, M. A.	17,126.85
c. Haq, N.	33,662.27
d. Pappin, B. R.	8,919.60
e. Tuzzo, R. M.	14,895.05
f. Wright, J. W.	23,091.24

3. Using the daily sales totals below, compute the weekly earnings on a wage-plus-commission basis for these six Weddin Office Appliance salespeople. Each employee worked 40

hours for the week. The commission rate is 6 percent.

	Employee	Mon.	Tues.	Wed.	Thurs.	Fri.	Hourly Wage
a.	Bolstein, L. W.	$243.18	$231.12	$300.70	$256.01	$196.21	$5.25
b.	Davis, C.	219.18	246.87	224.43	272.11	242.31	6.00
c.	Huber, T. A.	304.76	220.20	218.76	212.66	344.77	5.75
d.	McMunn, A. G.	289.19	196.86	248.94	314.11	256.40	4.75
e.	Owen, A. B.	200.18	401.11	506.62	298.42	117.12	6.25
f.	Siff, W. R.	308.20	94.38	321.12	341.17	230.00	5.00

Skill: Given the starting and ending time, figuring total hours worked.

Sample Problem: Find the total hours from 9:15 a.m. to 4:30 p.m.

Solution: Depending on the time period covered, use 12 noon or 12 midnight as the base for computing. Since the time period in this problem includes 12 noon, use 12 noon as the base.

1. Count the total number of hours and minutes from 9:15 a.m. to 12 noon:
   9:15 to 10 is 45 minutes.
   10 to 12 is 2 hours.
   Total morning time: 2 hours 45 minutes

2. Count the total number of hours and minutes from 12 noon to 4:30 p.m.:

   12 noon to 4 is 4 hours.
   4 to 4:30 is 30 minutes.
   Total afternoon time: 4 hours 30 minutes

3. Add the two times together.

   $$\begin{array}{r} 2 \text{ hours } 45 \text{ minutes} \\ +4 \text{ hours } 30 \text{ minutes} \\ \hline 6 \text{ hours } 75 \text{ minutes} \end{array}$$

4. Since 60 minutes equals 1 hour, then 75 minutes equals 1 hour 15 minutes.

5. Add the 1 hour to the first column.

   $$6 + 1 = 7$$

   Answer in hours and minutes: 7 hours 15 minutes

6. Change the minutes to a decimal.

   15 minutes = 0.25 hour

7. Add the decimal to the whole hours.

   $$7 + 0.25 = 7.25$$

   Answer: 7.25 hours

Practice: Find the total hours and minutes for each of the following:

1. 8 a.m. to 12 noon
2. 9:30 a.m. to 12 noon
3. 10:15 a.m. to 12 noon
4. 11:45 a.m. to 12 noon
5. 12 noon to 2 p.m.
6. 11 a.m. to 2 p.m.
7. 8 a.m. to 4 p.m.
8. 8:30 a.m. to 3 p.m.
9. 9:45 a.m. to 4:30 p.m.
10. 8:15 a.m. to 6:45 p.m.

Skill: Computing pay at time and a half.

Sample Problem: What is the overtime pay at time and a half for an employee who works three hours overtime and makes $8 an hour?

Solution:
1. Multiply the hourly rate ($8) by time and a half (1.5) to find the overtime rate:

   $$\$8 \times 1.5 = \$12$$

2. Multiply the overtime rate by the number of overtime hours worked (3):

   $$\$12 \times 3 = \$36$$

   Answer: $36

Practice: Find the overtime pay at time and a half for each of the following. (Round to the nearest cent if necessary.)

	Overtime Hours	Hourly Rate
1.	10	$ 8.00
2.	5	9.00
3.	10	11.10
4.	8	10.30
5.	4.5	9.00
6.	2	8.40
7.	4	7.30
8.	12	8.20
9.	15	15.80
10.	3	6.83

VOCABULARY SKILLBUILDER

Read each of the following statements. From the words below each statement, choose the term that best matches the statement.

1. The amount earned for all hours worked except overtime hours.

   gross earnings   regular earnings

2. The amount earned for hours worked over 40 hours a week.

   gross earnings   overtime earnings

3. Regular earnings plus overtime earnings.

   gross earnings   payroll earnings

4. A record of hours worked for one employee.

   payroll period   time card

5. The overtime rate.

   straight piece rate   time and a half

6. A form used to record the hours and the earnings of each employee for a payroll period.

   payroll earnings record   time card

7. A piecework plan in which the employee is paid a fixed amount of money for each unit or job completed.

   differential piece rate plan
   straight piece rate plan

8. A piecework plan in which the employee is paid according to a pay scale that increases per unit as the number of units completed increases.

   differential piece rate plan
   straight piece rate plan

9. A plan for paying salespeople according to the dollar amount of their sales.

   straight-commission plan
   wage-plus-commission plan

10. A plan for paying salespeople an hourly wage plus an amount based upon their total sales.

    straight-commission plan
    wage-plus-commission plan

Week Ending				January 9, 19 --		
No. 573-12-9874						
Name Holdren, W. T.						

Days	Regular				Overtime		Daily Totals
	In	Out	In	Out	In	Out	
Mon.	8³⁰	12⁰⁰	1⁰⁰	4³⁰			
Tues.	8³⁰	12⁰⁰	1¹⁰	4⁴⁰			
Wed.	8²⁵	12⁰⁰	1⁰⁰	5⁴⁵			
Thurs.	8³⁵	12⁰⁵	1⁰⁵	4³⁰			
Fri.	8³⁰	12⁰⁵	1⁰⁰	4⁴⁰			
Sat.							
Sun.							

		Hours	Rate	Earnings
	Regular		8.40	
	Overtime			
Days Worked	Total Hours		Gross Earnings	

Week Ending				January 9, 19 --		
No. 589-33-0562						
Name Santos, G. K.						

Days	Regular				Overtime		Daily Totals
	In	Out	In	Out	In	Out	
Mon.	8³⁰	12⁰⁰	1⁰⁰	5³⁰			
Tues.	8²⁵	12⁰⁰	1⁰⁵	4⁴⁰			
Wed.	8³⁰	12⁰⁰	1⁰⁵	4⁴⁰			
Thurs.	8³⁰	12⁰⁰	1⁰⁵	4³⁵			
Fri.	8²⁰	12⁰⁰	1⁰⁰	4⁴⁵			
Sat.							
Sun.							

		Hours	Rate	Earnings
	Regular		10.15	
	Overtime			
Days Worked	Total Hours		Gross Earnings	

1. Compute the number of hours worked during the week and the weekly gross earnings for each of the employees whose time cards are shown above. Use the quarter-hour time system. Do not count late arrivals or early departures of five minutes or less. The regular hours are 8:30 a.m. to 12 noon and 1 p.m. to 4:30 p.m. The workweek is Monday to Friday. No overtime has been approved.

2. You are employed as a payroll clerk for Conway and Freeman. Your job is to do the payroll computations. Compute the total hours, regular earnings, overtime earnings, and gross earnings for the employees whose time cards are shown on the next two pages. Their regular hours are from 8 a.m. to 12 noon and from 1 p.m. to 5 p.m. from Monday to Friday, a workweek of 40 hours.

   To compute lateness or overtime, consider any part of a half hour a full half hour, but ignore amounts of 5 minutes or less. Thus if an employee is between 6 and 30 minutes late, deduct a half hour for lateness. Overtime has been approved. If an employee works 30 minutes or more beyond regular time or works on Saturday, pay the employee time and a half. This overtime is paid for all hours worked over 40 hours a week.

3. Use the time cards you worked with in Problem 2 to prepare a payroll earnings record for Conway and Freeman. The record is for the week ending July 22.

Card 1

Week Ending July 22, 19 --

No. 493-80-5297

Name Burks, A. D.

Days	Regular				Overtime		Daily Totals
	In	Out	In	Out	In	Out	
Mon.	8 00	12 02	1 00	6 00			
Tues.	7 55	12 01	12 56	7 00			
Wed.	7 50	12 00	12 58	7 30			
Thurs.	8 00	12 04	1 02	6 30			
Fri.	7 58	12 05	12 59	5 00			
Sat.	7 59	12 00					
Sun.							

		Hours	Rate	Earnings
	Regular		10.20	
	Overtime			
Days Worked	Total Hours		Gross Earnings	

Card 2

Week Ending July 22, 19 --

No. 534-66-4392

Name Cueno, A. C.

Days	Regular				Overtime		Daily Totals
	In	Out	In	Out	In	Out	
Mon.	7 50	12 02	1 00	7 30			
Tues.	8 00	12 00	12 54	6 00			
Wed.	7 52	12 02	12 58	7 00			
Thurs.	7 58	12 05	12 59	6 30			
Fri.	8 00	12 03	12 57	5 00			
Sat.	7 56	12 00					
Sun.							

		Hours	Rate	Earnings
	Regular		7.90	
	Overtime			
Days Worked	Total Hours		Gross Earnings	

Card 3

Week Ending July 22, 19 --

No. 587-20-2986

Name Happel, R. C.

Days	Regular				Overtime		Daily Totals
	In	Out	In	Out	In	Out	
Mon.	8 20	12 00	1 00	5 30			
Tues.	8 04	12 03	1 02	6 00			
Wed.	8 10	12 01	1 01	5 00			
Thurs.	8 00	12 00	1 00	6 30			
Fri.	8 02	12 03	1 02	5 00			
Sat.							
Sun.							

		Hours	Rate	Earnings
	Regular		11.00	
	Overtime			
Days Worked	Total Hours		Gross Earnings	

Card 4

Week Ending July 22, 19 --

No. 652-87-3433

Name Lau, H. H.

Days	Regular				Overtime		Daily Totals
	In	Out	In	Out	In	Out	
Mon.	9 00	12 05	1 02	6 00			
Tues.	9 10	12 02	1 00	5 00			
Wed.	7 55	12 00	12 55	4 00			
Thurs.	7 58	12 03	12 59	5 30			
Fri.	7 59	12 00	12 52	5 00			
Sat.	8 00	12 05					
Sun.							

		Hours	Rate	Earnings
	Regular		9.80	
	Overtime			
Days Worked	Total Hours		Gross Earnings	

Week Ending				July 22, 19 --		

No. 329-86-7910

Name Alonso, H.

Days	Regular				Overtime		Daily Totals
	In	Out	In	Out	In	Out	
Mon.	8^{00}	12^{05}	1^{00}	5^{04}			
Tues.	7^{57}	12^{00}	12^{58}	3^{00}			
Wed.	8^{40}	12^{03}	12^{55}	6^{00}			
Thurs.	7^{59}	12^{07}	1^{02}	7^{30}			
Fri.	8^{02}	12^{01}	12^{52}	6^{30}			
Sat.							
Sun.							

		Hours	Rate	Earnings
	Regular		9.60	
	Overtime			
Days Worked	Total Hours		Gross Earnings	

Week Ending				July 22, 19 --		

No. 358-99-0002

Name Bess, C. F.

Days	Regular				Overtime		Daily Totals
	In	Out	In	Out	In	Out	
Mon.	7^{55}	12^{00}	1^{02}	5^{00}			
Tues.	9^{00}	12^{05}	12^{53}	5^{02}			
Wed.	8^{30}	12^{03}	12^{58}	5^{04}			
Thurs.	8^{00}	12^{01}	12^{56}	7^{30}			
Fri.	7^{50}	12^{04}	12^{57}	6^{30}			
Sat.	8^{00}	12^{00}					
Sun.							

		Hours	Rate	Earnings
	Regular		8.80	
	Overtime			
Days Worked	Total Hours		Gross Earnings	

4. Use the data from the table below to prepare a payroll earnings record for the Cycle Company. This information is for the week ending August 13. The regular workday is eight hours, and the regular workweek is 40 hours. Overtime is paid on a weekly basis at time and a half.

Employee Number	Employee Name	Mon.	Tues.	Wed.	Thurs.	Fri.	Sat.	Hourly Rate
308-21-7759	Riley, S. G.	8	8	7	7	8	3	$ 7.50
329-60-5814	Lau, C. K.	7	9	7	7	7	4	8.50
348-75-8932	Mraz, J. A.	7	6	8	8	5	4	8.00
386-99-1106	Weddle, G.	8	7	7	7	6	3	9.80
394-44-2198	Bock, J. R.	8	10	8	7	4	4	7.50
410-32-7698	Bremmer, A.	2	10	9	9	8	4	7.00
437-05-0061	Zito, J. L.	10	8	9	10	7	3	10.00
459-73-8929	Smith, P. A.	7	8	8	7	7	4	8.50

5. Compute the weekly earnings on a differential piece rate basis for the following employees of the Daskun Watch Company. The differential piece rate scale is shown here:

Units per Day	Rate per Unit
First 10	$3.00
Next 5	4.00
Over 15	5.00

Employee	Mon.	Tues.	Wed.	Thurs.	Fri.
a. Arjona, J. D.	14	16	15	17	15
b. Crostic, A. C.	17	18	16	15	17
c. Hughes, J. W.	21	20	19	19	20
d. Melfi, J.	13	16	14	12	17
e. Scouras, C. M.	19	20	18	19	21
f. Yun, H. H.	22	18	19	21	18

6. Compute the weekly earnings on a wage-plus-commission basis for the following Central Furniture Mart salespeople. Each employee worked 35 hours for the week. The commission rate is 5 percent.

Employee	Weekly Sales	Hourly Wage
a. Askew, W. W.	$8,126.18	$7.50
b. Campanello, A. S.	8,728.05	6.75
c. Davis, C.	6,314.44	7.50
d. Gratz, C.	7,079.52	7.00
e. Hiltz, L. H.	6,364.59	6.75
f. Link, G. R.	8,419.06	7.50

CHAPTER 14

TAX RECORDS AND PAYROLL REPORTS

In Chapter 13 you learned how to compute *gross earnings*, the total amount an employee earns before any deductions are made. The amount of money a worker actually gets is called *net pay* or *take-home pay*. Net pay is what is left after all deductions are subtracted from the gross earnings. Some deductions, such as social security tax and income tax, are required by law. Other deductions, such as insurance and savings plans, may be required by an employer or chosen by a worker. Deductions not required by law are called *voluntary deductions*.

The federal government requires businesses to submit reports of their employees' earnings and deductions. In this chapter you will learn how to compute and report payroll deductions.

TOPIC 1 ● SOCIAL SECURITY TAX

GOALS

1. To complete an application form for a Social Security account number.
2. To use a table to find the amount of FICA tax to be withheld from employees' earnings.
3. To compute FICA taxes for self-employed people.

KEY TERMS

The federal *social security program* provides benefits to retired and disabled people.
FICA stands for the Federal Insurance Contributions Act, the federal law that established the social security program.
A *social security number* identifies one person's social security account.

Our federal government has a social security program that provides money for people who are retired or disabled. The idea of this program is simple. If you work, you pay a social security tax to the government. The business you work for pays an amount equal to what you pay. If you retire or are disabled, you receive benefits, or payments, from the federal government.

Federal law requires that you pay money into the federal social security program. The law is called the Federal Insurance Contributions Act, or FICA. This is why the social security tax is also called FICA tax.

Chapter Fourteen: TAX RECORDS AND PAYROLL REPORTS ● **373**

SOCIAL SECURITY NUMBER

Working people pay social security taxes. When you get a job, you will be asked for your social security number. Each number is used to identify one person's social security account.

If you do not have a social security number, you can get one at the Social Security Administration office nearest you. You can also get an application form at your local post office and then mail the completed form to the Social Security Administration. When you apply for a social security number, you must be able to prove (1) who you are, (2) how old you are, and (3) that you are a United States citizen. You can prove who you are with identification such as your driver's license, school identification card, or medical record. You can prove your age and your citizenship with a birth certificate, church record of birth or baptism, or hospital record of birth.

A few weeks after you apply, you will receive your social security card and number. Throughout your lifetime, the Social Security Administration will use this number to record your earnings, your tax payments, and your benefits. You will use your social security number as identification on federal income tax returns, bank records, military service records, and other important records. Many businesses use the social security number as an employee identification number. Many colleges use the social security number as a student identification number. Some states even use the social security number as identification on a driver's license.

Theresa Diaz applied for a social security number. To fill out the form shown on the following page, Theresa:

1. Printed her full name and current mailing address.
2. Checked the boxes to show her citizenship, sex, and ethnic group.
3. Wrote her birthdate, her age, and the name of the city and state where she was born.
4. Wrote her mother's and father's full names, using her mother's maiden name.
5. Checked the box to show that she had not requested a social security number before. (If she had been completing the form to correct her account information or replace a lost social security card, she would have written her social security number on line 10c.)
6. Wrote the date and her home and work telephone numbers.
7. Signed the form and marked that she was applying for the social security number for herself.

Retired persons receive social security benefits to help pay their living expenses.

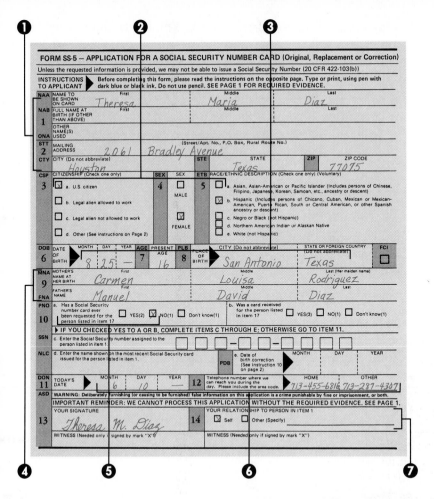

A short time later, Theresa received this social security card:

COMPUTING SOCIAL SECURITY (FICA) TAX

As you already learned, FICA requires employees to pay a social security tax. Employers, too, must pay a tax equal to what the employee pays. Even self-employed people must pay FICA taxes.

The tax is a certain percentage of each employee's taxable wages. *Taxable wages* are the amount of income subject to FICA tax deductions. This amount is set by the government and is

Taxable wages are the amount of income subject to FICA tax deductions.

changed from time to time. Tax rates, too, are changed from time to time. Note, for example, the changes in rates for the years 1988, 1989, and 1990 and after for employees, employers, and self-employed people:

Taxpayer	1988	1989	1990 and after
	TAX RATE (PERCENT)		
Employee	7.51	7.51	7.65
Employer	7.51	7.51	7.65
Self-employed person	13.02	13.02	13.30

For example, Myrna Watts is self-employed. Last week, she earned $368. Using the 13.02% rate, Myrna computed her FICA tax as follows:

$$\$368 \times 0.1302 = \$47.9136, \text{ rounded to } \$47.91$$

Note that tax amounts should always be rounded to the nearest cent.

To find tax amounts without computing, the government gives employers a social security tax table. A partial tax table is shown below.

Wages at least	But less than	Tax to be withheld
27.90	28.03	2.10
28.03	28.17	2.11
28.17	28.30	2.12
28.30	28.43	2.13
28.43	28.57	2.14
28.57	28.71	2.15

Wages at least	But less than	Tax to be withheld
99.14	99.27	7.45
99.27	99.42	7.46
99.42	99.54	7.47
99.54	99.67	7.48
99.67	99.80	7.49
99.80	99.94	7.50
99.94	100.07	7.51

Wages at least	But less than	Tax to be withheld
92.48	92.61	6.95
92.61	92.74	6.96
92.74	92.88	6.97
92.88	93.01	6.98
93.01	93.15	6.99
93.15	93.28	7.00

Wages	Taxes
100	$ 7.51
200	15.02
300	22.53
400	30.04
500	37.55
600	45.06
700	52.57
800	60.08
900	67.59
1000	75.10

The table lists tax amounts for wage ranges up to $100. Then a section at the bottom of the table gives the tax amount for even hundreds of dollars from $100 to $1,000.

Leon Roberts earned a weekly salary of $92.70 from his part-time job. His employer:

1. Used the Wages at Least and the But Less Than columns on the tax table to find the line for $92.70.
2. Located the line for wages at least $92.61 but less than $92.74, which shows that the tax to be withheld is $6.96.
3. Withheld $6.96 from Leon's paycheck as a Social Security deduction.
4. Contributed $6.96 as the employer's payment to the Social Security fund.

Rachel Steinberg's monthly earnings were $2,528.40. To figure her Social Security tax:

1. Look on the Social Security tax table for the line that includes $28.40.
2. Locate the line for wages at least $28.30 but less than $28.43. This line shows that the tax to be withheld is $2.13.
3. Look at the bottom of the table for the tax on wages of $500. You should find $37.55.
4. Look at the bottom of the table for the taxes on wages of $1,000. You should find $75.10. To get the tax on wages of $2,000, multiply $75.10 by 2 to get $150.20.
5. Add $2.13, $37.55, and $150.20 to get a total of $189.88.

Rachel and her employer would each pay $189.88 into the social security fund.

For large wage amounts such as Rachel's, you may find it easier to compute the FICA tax rather than use the table. Simply multiply the gross earnings by the FICA rate.

$2,528.40 × 0.0751 = $189.8828, rounded to $189.88

Check Your Reading

1. What term describes gross earnings minus deductions?

2. Give one example of a deduction that is required by law.

3. What federal program gives payments to retired and disabled persons?

4. Name two proofs of your identity or your age that you may use to apply for a social security number.

5. The FICA deduction from Sally Robertshaw's weekly paycheck was $18.40. What was the total amount contributed to Sally's social security account that week? Explain.

1. Fill in a social security account application form for yourself.

2. The weekly gross earnings for part-time and full-time employees at the Phillips Furniture Company are listed below. Use the social security tax table to figure the tax to be withheld from each worker's paycheck.

   a. $28.10
   b. $399.25
   c. $628.50
   d. $199.92
   e. $93.11
   f. $627.99
   g. $93
   h. $2,292.87
   i. $128
   j. $992.50
   k. $100
   l. $392.50

3. The names of five self-employed persons and their monthly gross earnings are listed below. Compute the amount of FICA tax each person must pay. Multiply each person's earnings amount by 0.1302 (13.02 percent). Round off tax amounts to the nearest cent.

   a. Doug Griffith $2,300
   b. Beth Ann Lewis $4,474
   c. Maria Costillo $3,766.50
   d. Charles Kowalski $4,257.85
   e. Hilda Jansen $3,480.72

4. You are an accountant who keeps records for eight self-employed people. Their gross earnings for last year are listed here. Figure the FICA tax for each client. Use a tax rate of 13.30 percent. (None of these clients earned more than the maximum amount subject to FICA tax.)

   a. $26,697.48
   b. $34,236.55
   c. $41,575
   d. $19,488.37
   e. $33,785.95
   f. $31,467.40
   g. $40,750
   h. $28,389.76

TOPIC 2 ● FEDERAL INCOME TAX

GOALS

1. To complete an Employee's Withholding Allowance Certificate (Form W-4).
2. To use a table to find the amount of federal income tax to be withheld from employees' earnings.

KEY TERMS

Income tax is a government charge on an individual's earnings or other sources of income.

The *tax withheld* is the amount the employer subtracts from an employee's wages for income taxes.

A *withholding allowance* frees an amount of income from taxes.

The federal government must have money to pay for national defense, health programs, education programs, foreign aid, and other needs. To pay for these programs, the federal government collects income tax. Anyone with income must pay federal income tax. Income includes any money you receive, such as wages, tips, or income from stocks and bonds. For most people, income taxes are withheld from their wages by the employer. This means that the employer deducts, or subtracts, a certain amount from your wages and pays this amount toward your income taxes.

The amount withheld is based on an estimate of your wages for the year. Each pay period, the employer deducts a portion of your estimated total tax. Then, once a year you must compute the exact amount of income tax owed and report this information.

The form you use to compute and report your federal income tax is called an *income tax return*. You must complete this form and send it to the Internal Revenue Service (IRS) by April 15 for the previous year.

Income taxes pay for many kinds of government programs. One example is aid for certain school programs.

EMPLOYEE'S WITHHOLDING ALLOWANCE CERTIFICATE (FORM W-4)

To know how much federal income tax to withhold from each worker's wages, an employer must know three things: (1) the employee's gross earnings (which you learned to compute in Chapter 13), (2) the employee's marital status, and (3) the number of *withholding allowances* the employee claims. All this information is on the Employee's Withholding Allowance Certificate, popularly called *Form W-4*. The employer keeps each employee's

Form W-4 is used by employees to claim withholding allowances and to supply other information the employer needs for income tax withholding.

A *withholding allowance* frees an amount of income from taxes.

Form W-4 on file for use in figuring the amount of income tax to be withheld.

PAYROLL DEDUCTIONS FOR FEDERAL INCOME TAX

The *Employer's Tax Guide* includes the tables used to find the amount of federal income tax to be withheld from an employee's paycheck.

Completed W-4 forms provide employers with one source of information for withholding income tax. In addition, the federal government provides the *Employer's Tax Guide* to help businesses figure payroll deductions. The *Guide* has tables that show how much to withhold based on (1) the length of the pay period, (2) the marital status, and (3) the number of allowances. Parts of two tables are shown on page 381. One is for single persons paid weekly, and the other is for married persons paid monthly. Use the two columns at the left of each table to find the range of wage amounts. The other columns list allowances from 0 through 10.

Tony Centopani receives a weekly salary of $485 from the Jamison Equipment Company. Using the information from Tony's Form W-4, his employer:

1. Notes that Tony marked that he is married but wants his taxes withheld at the higher single rate

2. Selects the Single Person—Weekly Payroll Period tax table to find Tony's taxes

3. Uses the two columns on the left to find the wage range for $485

4. On the line for wages at least $480 and but less than $490, goes across to the column for 2 allowances (which Tony claimed on his Form W-4) and finds the amount of tax: $81

5. Adds to the $81 the additional $10 deduction Tony listed on his form W-4 to get $91

The employer withholds $91 from Tony's paycheck.

STATE AND LOCAL INCOME TAXES

A number of states, counties, and cities also tax their citizens' incomes and require employers to withhold tax money. The procedure for computing the amount to be withheld is similar to the procedure you learned for federal income tax. The rates, however, are much lower.

SINGLE Persons–WEEKLY Payroll Period

And the wages are–		And the number of withholding allowances claimed is–										
At least	But less than	0	1	2	3	4	5	6	7	8	9	10
		The amount of income tax to be withheld shall be–										
$320	$330	$46	$40	$35	$29	$24	$18	$13	$7	$2	$0	$0
330	340	47	42	36	31	25	20	14	9	3	0	0
340	350	50	43	38	32	27	21	16	10	5	0	0
350	360	53	45	39	34	28	23	17	12	6	2	0
360	370	55	46	41	35	30	24	19	13	8	3	0
370	380	58	48	42	37	31	26	20	15	9	4	0
380	390	61	51	44	38	33	27	22	16	11	5	1
390	400	64	54	45	40	34	29	23	18	12	7	2
400	410	67	56	47	41	36	30	25	19	14	8	3
410	420	69	59	49	43	37	32	26	21	15	10	4
420	430	72	62	52	44	39	33	28	22	17	11	6
430	440	75	65	55	46	40	35	29	24	18	13	7
440	450	78	68	57	47	42	36	31	25	20	14	9
450	460	81	70	60	50	43	38	32	27	21	16	10
460	470	83	73	63	53	45	39	34	28	23	17	12
470	480	86	76	66	55	46	41	35	30	24	19	13
480	490	89	79	69	58	48	42	37	31	26	20	15
490	500	92	82	71	61	51	44	38	33	27	22	16
500	510	95	84	74	64	54	45	40	34	29	23	18
510	520	97	87	77	67	56	47	41	36	30	25	19
520	530	100	90	80	69	59	49	43	37	32	26	21
530	540	103	93	83	72	62	52	44	39	33	28	22
540	550	107	96	85	75	65	55	46	40	35	29	24
550	560	110	98	88	78	68	57	47	42	36	31	25
560	570	114	101	91	81	70	60	50	43	38	32	27
570	580	117	104	94	83	73	63	53	45	39	34	28
580	590	121	108	97	86	76	66	56	46	41	35	30
590	600	124	111	99	89	79	69	58	48	42	37	31
600	610	128	115	102	92	82	71	61	51	44	38	33
610	620	131	118	106	95	84	74	64	54	45	40	34
620	630	135	122	109	97	87	77	67	57	47	41	36
630	640	138	125	113	100	90	80	70	59	49	43	37
640	650	142	129	116	103	93	83	72	62	52	44	39
650	660	145	132	120	107	96	85	75	65	55	46	40
660	670	149	136	123	110	98	88	78	68	58	47	42

MARRIED Persons–MONTHLY Payroll Period

And the wages are–		And the number of withholding allowances claimed is–										
At least	But less than	0	1	2	3	4	5	6	7	8	9	10
		The amount of income tax to be withheld shall be–										
1,920	1,960	258	234	210	187	163	139	115	92	68	44	22
1,960	2,000	264	240	216	193	169	145	121	98	74	50	27
2,000	2,040	270	246	222	199	175	151	127	104	80	56	32
2,040	2,080	276	252	228	205	181	157	133	110	86	62	38
2,080	2,120	282	258	234	211	187	163	139	116	92	68	44
2,120	2,160	288	264	240	217	193	169	145	122	98	74	50
2,160	2,200	294	270	246	223	199	175	151	128	104	80	56
2,200	2,240	300	276	252	229	205	181	157	134	110	86	62
2,240	2,280	306	282	258	235	211	187	163	140	116	92	68
2,280	2,320	312	288	264	241	217	193	169	146	122	98	74
2,320	2,360	318	294	270	247	223	199	175	152	128	104	80
2,360	2,400	324	300	276	253	229	205	181	158	134	110	86
2,400	2,440	330	306	282	259	235	211	187	164	140	116	92
2,440	2,480	336	312	288	265	241	217	193	170	146	122	98
2,480	2,520	343	318	294	271	247	223	199	176	152	128	104
2,520	2,560	354	324	300	277	253	229	205	182	158	134	110
2,560	2,600	366	330	306	283	259	235	211	188	164	140	116
2,600	2,640	377	336	312	289	265	241	217	194	170	146	122
2,640	2,680	388	344	318	295	271	247	223	200	176	152	128
2,680	2,720	399	355	324	301	277	253	229	206	182	158	134
2,720	2,760	410	366	330	307	283	259	235	212	188	164	140
2,760	2,800	422	377	336	313	289	265	241	218	194	170	146
2,800	2,840	433	389	344	319	295	271	247	224	200	176	152
2,840	2,880	444	400	355	325	301	277	253	230	206	182	158
2,880	2,920	455	411	367	331	307	283	259	236	212	188	164
2,920	2,960	466	422	378	337	313	289	265	242	218	194	170
2,960	3,000	478	433	389	345	319	295	271	248	224	200	176
3,000	3,040	489	445	400	356	325	301	277	254	230	206	182
3,040	3,080	500	456	411	367	331	307	283	260	236	212	188
3,080	3,120	511	467	423	378	337	313	289	266	242	218	194

Check Your Reading

1. Name three programs paid for with federal tax money.

2. What information does Form W-4 provide an employer for withholding income tax?

3. What two facts must be known to select the correct tax table?

1. Find the amount of federal income tax to be withheld for each of the married employees listed below. Use the table on page 381.

Name	Allowances	Monthly Wages
a. Komiko, A.	2	$2,435
b. Washinsky, L.	4	2,157
c. Richardson, B.	1	2,823
d. Loesing, J.	3	2,274

2. Use the following information to select the correct tax tables on page 381. Then find the amount to be withheld for each employee.

Name	Payroll Period	Marital Status	Allowances	Additional Deductions	Wages
a. Ramirez, L.	Weekly	Single	1	$10	$ 418
b. Brown, J.	Monthly	Married	4	0	3,025
c. Stebbins, W.	Weekly	Single	2	20	642
d. Kopes, R.	Monthly	Married	1	40	1,956
e. Comley, M.	Monthly	Married	6	0	2,378
f. Herrick, C.	Weekly	Single	3	15	585

TOPIC 3 ● PAYROLL REGISTER

GOALS

1. To record voluntary payroll deductions.
2. To prepare and prove payroll registers.
3. To write payroll checks.

KEY TERMS

Voluntary payroll deductions are not required by law.
A *payroll register* is a record of earnings and deductions for all employees.

VOLUNTARY PAYROLL DEDUCTIONS

You have studied two payroll deductions that are required by law: social security tax and income tax. *Voluntary deductions* are either required by an employer or chosen by the employee. For example, some businesses require their employees to contribute to a group health insurance plan. In some industries workers who belong to labor unions have their union dues deducted from their paychecks. In addition, employees may choose to have payroll deductions for contributions to the United Fund or some other charity. Some workers belong to credit unions and have payroll deductions for savings or for loan payments. Employers must record voluntary deductions such as these to be sure that the correct payments are made.

Payroll deductions may include health insurance to help pay employees' medical, dental, and hospital expenses.

PAYROLL REGISTERS

Evelyn Wetherell is in charge of payroll reports for Davis Building Supply. One of her duties is to prepare payroll registers. A *payroll register* contains complete payroll data for all employees for one pay period.

Look at the payroll register shown on the following page to follow Evelyn as she records the payroll data for the first employee, Robert Brinkman:

1. First, Evelyn begins a new payroll register by entering the beginning and ending dates of the pay period and the date on which employees are paid.

| | | Robert Brinkman | | | | | | | | | | | | |
EMPLOYEE NUMBER	NAME	TAX TABLE	ALLOW-ANCES	HOURS	REGULAR	OVERTIME	TOTAL	FEDERAL INCOME TAX	FICA	INSUR-ANCE	OTHER	TOTAL	AMOUNT	CH. NO.
363-57-4424	Robert Brinkman	S	2	40	390 00	—00	390 00	44 00	29 29	12 00	10 00	95 29	294 71	978
536-40-7895	Jeremy King	M	1	38	475 00	—00	475 00	76 00	35 67	15 00	5 00	131 67	343 33	979
427-23-6577	Rita Lopez	S	2	43	360 00	40 50	400 50	47 00	30 08	12 00	—	89 08	311 42	980
237-53-2335	Richard Montoya	M	4	40	410 00	—00	410 00	37 00	30 79	18 00	20 00	105 79	304 21	981
344-78-9502	Evelyn Wetherell	S	1	39	395 85	—00	395 85	54 00	29 73	10 00	—00	93 73	302 12	982
					2030 85	40 50	2071 35	258 00	155 56	67 00	35 00	515 56	1555 79	

DAVIS BUILDING SUPPLY
For the Week Beginning February 5 19— and Ending February 9 19— Paid February 16 19—

PAYROLL REGISTER

EMPLOYEE DATA — EARNINGS — DEDUCTIONS — NET PAY

2. Evelyn enters Robert's employee number, which is his social security number.
3. She enters Robert's name.
4. Evelyn writes the letter "S" in the Tax Table column, so she will use the single person's tax table to figure Robert's withholding.
5. Evelyn enters the number "2" in the Allowances column because Robert claims two withholding allowances.
6. Evelyn records the hours that Robert worked (40).
7. Evelyn records Robert's regular pay ($390) in the Regular Earnings column. He did not work any overtime, so Evelyn writes "—00" in the Overtime Earnings column. Then she enters the total in the Total Earnings column. If Robert had worked overtime, the total would have been regular earnings plus overtime earnings.
8. Evelyn uses tax tables to find Robert's income tax and FICA tax and enters the amounts in the appropriate Deductions columns.
9. Evelyn records Robert's other deductions—$12 for insurance and $10 for the credit union—in the Insurance and Other Deductions columns.
10. Evelyn enters the total for all Robert's deductions in the Total Deductions column.
11. Evelyn computes Robert's net pay by subtracting his total deductions from his total earnings.
12. When Evelyn makes out Robert's payroll check, she enters the check number in the last column.

After Evelyn has entered payroll data for all employees, she proves the payroll register, as follows:

1. Evelyn draws a single line under the last entries in the Earnings, Deductions, and Net Pay sections.
2. She totals all the dollar amounts in each column.

3. Evelyn adds the totals of the Regular Earnings and Overtime Earnings columns. The result should be the same as the total of the Total Earnings column.
4. She adds the totals of the Federal Income Tax, FICA, Insurance, and Other columns. This figure should match the total of the Total Deductions column.
5. Evelyn subtracts the total of the Total Deductions column from that of the Total Earnings column. If she has done her work accurately, the result will equal the total of the Net Pay column.
6. She draws a double line under all the totals to indicate that the payroll register has been proved.

PAYROLL CHECKS

After Evelyn completes and proves the payroll register, she prepares a paycheck for each employee. Davis Building Supply uses *voucher checks* for its payroll. A voucher check has a statement attached to it showing the employee's earnings and deductions for the pay period.

A voucher check includes a statement of earnings and deductions.

Look at the voucher check below. Evelyn prepared this check for Robert Brinkman by recording the following data on the voucher:

The ending date of the pay period

The hours worked

The regular earnings

The overtime earnings, if any

The total earnings

The income tax deduction

The FICA tax deduction

The insurance deduction

The other deductions, if any

The total deductions

The net pay amount

The check number

2/9/--	40	390.00	--	390.00	44.00	29.29	12.00	10.00	95.29	294.71	978
Period Ending	Hours Worked	Regular	Overtime	Total	Income Tax	FICA	Insurance	Other	Total	Amount	Ck.No.
			Earnings				Deductions			Net Pay	

Employees Pay Statement
Detach and retain for your records.

Davis Building Supply
Providence, RI

Davis Building Supply
418 North Main
Providence, RI 02903

Payroll Check No. 978   87-21/640

Feb. 16, 19 --

Pay To The Order of _____ Robert Brinkman _____ $ 294.71

Two hundred ninety-four and 71/100------------------------------------ Dollars

FIRST BANK AND TRUST
PROVIDENCE, RI 02906

Wanda Davis

⑆0640⑈0021⑆ 324⑈0340⑈

Then, on the payroll check itself, Evelyn typed the check number, the date the check was written, Robert's full name, and the amount of the check in both figures and words. She had the check signed by Wanda Davis, the treasurer of Davis Building Supply.

When Robert receives his check, he tears off the voucher before he deposits or cashes the check. The voucher is his record of earnings and deductions for that pay period.

1. Name two examples of voluntary payroll deductions.

2. If a business pays its employees on a weekly basis, how many payroll registers would be prepared during a year?

3. What information would you find in the Tax Table column of a payroll register?

4. How do you compute an employee's net pay?

5. How do you verify the accuracy of the payroll register?

6. What is the purpose of the voucher portion of a paycheck?

Exercises for Topic 3

1. Use the data from the following table to prepare a payroll register for Fleschner Enterprises. The information is for the monthly pay period beginning April 1 and ending April 30, and the employees will be paid on May 7. None of the employees had overtime earnings. Find the federal income tax to be withheld from each employee's paycheck, from the tax table for married persons on page 381. To find the FICA tax, compute the tax at a rate of 7.51 percent of gross earnings. Assume that none of the employees has exceeded the maximum taxable wages for FICA. The employees will be paid with checks numbered 572 through 576. After listing the data for all employees, prove the payroll register.

Employee Number	Employee Name	Allow- ances	Regular Earnings	Insur- ance	Other Deductions
799-23-6751	Adams, D.	2	$2,445	$30	$10
764-45-2773	Finkel, L.	5	2,988	45	
747-38-1288	Leopold, R.	3	2,205	35	5
739-87-2359	Munilla, S.	1	2,657	25	25
782-92-3276	Stevens, J.	4	3,085	40	

2. You are employed in the payroll department of Culver Manufacturing Company. Use the information below to prepare and prove a payroll register for the week of March 8 to 12. The employees will be paid one week after the end of the pay period. Compute the regular earnings, overtime earn-

ings, and gross earnings for each employee. Consider any hours over 40 approved overtime, which is paid at time and a half. Find the federal income tax to be withheld from each employee's paycheck from the table for single persons on page 381. The amounts to be deducted for FICA can be found using the percentages on page 376. None of the employees has exceeded the maximum taxable wages for FICA.

Employee Number	Employee Name	Allow-ances	Hours Worked	Hourly Rate	Insur-ance	Other Deductions
568-77-4301	Culver, Steve	2	45	$12.75	$10	$15
579-36-0092	Havier, Marie	1	40	10.30	8	
545-28-9014	McDaniels, Joe	2	38	10.65	10	5
532-75-4144	Reubens, Pat	3	47	9.90	12	5
556-32-8773	Winkler, Terry	1	37	11.55	8	

3. Use the data from the payroll register you completed in Exercise 2 to prepare the voucher checks for all five employees. Number the checks 1285 through 1289. Sign your name on the checks. Record the check number on the payroll register after you write each check.

TOPIC 4 ● EMPLOYEE EARNINGS RECORD

GOALS

1. To prepare employee earnings records.
2. To prove employee earnings records.
3. To complete Wage and Tax Statements (Form W-2).

KEY TERMS

An *employee earnings record* shows one employee's earnings, deductions, and net pay for every pay period.

A *quarter* is one-fourth of a year. Each quarter is equal to 3 months or 13 weeks.

The *year-to-date earnings* are the running total of earnings since the beginning of the year.

A *Wage and Tax Statement (Form W-2)* shows an employee's earnings and the amounts withheld for social security and income taxes for the entire previous calendar year.

The federal government requires employers to keep records of each worker's earnings and payroll deductions. The form on which this data is recorded is called an *employee earnings record.*

At the end of each pay period, information from the payroll register is recorded on each worker's employee earnings record. At the end of each quarter, the employee earnings records are totaled and proved. A *quarter* of a year includes 13 weekly, 6 semimonthly, or 3 monthly pay periods. At the end of the year, the information from the employee earnings record is used to complete a Wage and Tax Statement (Form W-2) for the employee.

Larry Sorenson works in the payroll department of Deluxe Interiors. After completing the payroll register and writing payroll checks, his next duty is to update the employee earnings record for each worker. Shown below is Lisa Francisco's employee earnings record.

EMPLOYEE EARNINGS RECORD FOR YEAR 19 ___

Name *Lisa J. Francisco*
Address *4893 Hillside Drive*
Los Angeles, CA 90044
Telephone No. *243-6781*
Date of Birth *October 13, 19—*

Employee No. & Social Security No. *913-72-6334*
Marital Status *M; use Single table*
Withholding Allowances *1*
Position *Salesperson*
Date Employed *April 3, 19—*

PAY PERIOD ENDING	RATE PER HOUR	HOURS	EARNINGS			DEDUCTIONS					NET PAY	YEAR-TO-DATE EARNINGS
			REGULAR	OVERTIME	TOTAL	FEDERAL INCOME TAX	FICA	INSURANCE	OTHER	TOTAL		
Jan. 6	9.25	38	351 50	— 00	351 50	45 00	26 40	12 00	5 00	88 40	263 10	351 50
13	9.25	40	370 00	— 00	370 00	48 00	27 79	12 00	— 00	87 79	282 21	721 50
20	9.25	42	370 00	27 75	397 75	54 00	29 87	12 00	5 00	100 87	296 88	1119 25
27	9.25	40	370 00	— 00	370 00	48 00	27 79	12 00	— 00	87 79	282 21	1489 25

At the beginning of the year, Larry started a form for Lisa by listing her name, address, telephone number, birthdate, social security number, and marital status and the number of withholding allowances she claims, her position, and the date she was first employed by Deluxe Interiors. Each week Larry then lists at the bottom of Lisa's employee earnings record the following information:

- The date the pay period ended
- Lisa's hourly pay rate
- The number of hours she worked
- Lisa's regular, overtime, and total earnings
- The amounts of Lisa's deductions for federal income tax, FICA, and insurance, as well as any other deductions
- The total amount deducted from Lisa's paycheck

- The net pay that Lisa received
- The year-to-date earnings, the running total of how much Lisa has earned so far this year

QUARTERLY PROOF OF EMPLOYEE EARNINGS RECORDS

Larry totals and proves each employee earnings record at the end of every quarter. Lisa's employee earnings record for the first quarter of the year, January through March, is shown below.

EMPLOYEE EARNINGS RECORD FOR YEAR 19 ___

Name _Lisa J. Francisco_
Address _4893 Hillside Drive_
Los Angeles, CA 90044
Telephone No. _243-6781_
Date of Birth _October 13, 19—_

Employee No. & Social Security No. _913-72-6334_
Marital Status _M; use Single table_
Withholding Allowances _1_
Position _Salesperson_
Date Employed _April 3, 19—_

PAY PERIOD ENDING	RATE PER HOUR	HOURS	EARNINGS			DEDUCTIONS					NET PAY	YEAR-TO-DATE EARNINGS
			REGULAR	OVERTIME	TOTAL	FEDERAL INCOME TAX	FICA	INSURANCE	OTHER	TOTAL		
Jan. 6	9.25	38	351 50	— 00	351 50	45 00	26 40	12 00	5 00	88 40	263 10	351 50
13	9.25	40	370 00	— 00	370 00	48 00	27 79	12 00	— 00	87 79	282 21	721 50
20	9.25	42	370 00	27 75	397 75	54 00	29 87	12 00	5 00	100 87	296 88	1119 25
27	9.25	40	370 00	— 00	370 00	48 00	27 79	12 00	— 00	87 79	282 21	1489 25
Feb. 3	9.25	37	342 25	— 00	342 25	43 00	25 70	12 00	5 00	85 70	256 55	1831 50
10	9.25	40	370 00	— 00	370 00	48 00	27 79	12 00	— 00	87 79	282 21	2201 50
17	9.25	40	370 00	— 00	370 00	48 00	27 79	12 00	5 00	92 79	277 21	2571 50
24	9.25	44	370 00	55 50	425 50	62 00	31 96	12 00	— 00	105 96	319 54	2997 00
Mar. 3	9.50	39	370 50	— 00	370 50	48 00	27 82	12 00	5 00	92 82	277 65	3367 50
10	9.50	40	380 00	— 00	380 00	51 00	28 54	12 00	— 00	91 54	288 46	3747 50
17	9.50	38	361 00	— 00	361 00	46 00	27 11	12 00	5 00	90 11	270 89	4108 50
24	9.50	40	380 00	— 00	380 00	51 00	28 54	12 00	— 00	91 54	288 46	4488 50
31	9.50	40	380 00	— 00	380 00	51 00	28 54	12 00	5 00	96 54	283 46	4868 50
Quarterly Totals			4785 25	83 25	4868 50	643 00	365 64	156 00	35 00	1199 64	3668 83	

These are the steps Larry uses to total and prove the record:

1. Larry draws a single line under the entries for the last (thirteenth) week of the quarter.
2. Larry totals the Regular Earnings column, the Overtime Earnings column, and the Total Earnings column. To be sure his work is accurate, he adds the totals of the Regular Earnings and Overtime Earnings columns. The result should equal the total of the Total Earnings column. Larry also checks to see

that the total of the Total Earnings column is the same as the year-to-date earnings for the last week of the quarter.

3. He totals each of the columns in the Deductions section. He adds the totals of the Federal Income Tax, FICA, Insurance, and Other Deductions columns. This sum should match the total of the Total Deductions column.

4. Larry totals the Net Pay column. He proves his work by subtracting the sum of the Total Deductions column from the sum of the Total Earnings column. The result should be the same as the total of the Net Pay column.

5. Larry draws a double line under all the totals to show that the employee earnings record has been proved. Note that the Year-to-Date Earnings column is not totaled; it already gives a running total of the gross earnings.

WAGE AND TAX STATEMENT (FORM W-2)

Before January 31 of each year, employers are required to give each employee a Wage and Tax Statement (Form W-2) for the previous year. Form W-2 is a statement of the total wages paid and the amounts of income tax and social security tax that were withheld during that year. The employer sends one copy of Form W-2 directly to the IRS. The employee receives three copies of Form W-2: one to file with the federal tax return, one to file with the state or local tax return, and one for the employee's records.

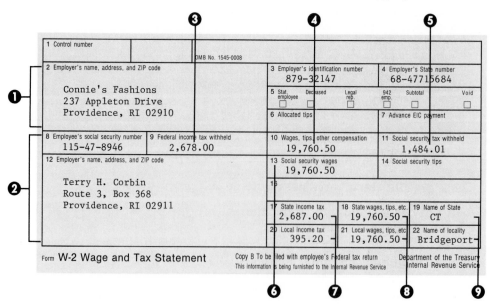

Notice that the Form W-2 shown on page 390 contains the following information:

1. Employer's name, address, and identification numbers
2. Employee's social security number, name, and address
3. Federal income tax withheld from the employee's wages
4. Total wages paid that were subject to federal income tax
5. Social security tax withheld from the employee's wages
6. Total wages paid that were subject to social security tax
7. State and local income taxes withheld from the employee's wages
8. Total wages paid that were subject to state and local income taxes
9. Name of state and locality, such as a city or a county

Check Your Reading

1. Deluxe Interiors has 15 employees. How many employee earnings records will the business need?
2. How often should employee earnings records be updated?
3. When are employee earnings records totaled and proved?
4. What does the term *year-to-date earnings* mean?
5. What form shows an employee's total earnings and taxes withheld for the previous year?

Exercises for Topic 4

1. Use the data from the table on the following page to prepare an employee earnings record for yourself. Fill in your name, address, telephone number, and date of birth. Fill in your social security number (if you do not have one, make up a number for yourself). Assume that you are single and that you claim one allowance. Your date of employment is April 1 and you are paid on a semimonthly basis. You have no overtime, so your total earnings are the same as your regular earnings. Compute the total deductions, net pay, and year-

to-date earnings for each pay period. At the end of the quarter (June 30), total and prove the employee earnings record. Check your calculations carefully.

PAY PERIOD ENDING	RATE PER HOUR	HOURS	REGULAR EARNINGS	DEDUCTIONS			
				FEDERAL INCOME TAX	FICA	INSURANCE	OTHER
April 15	7.85	80	628 00	122 00	47 16	20 00	15 00
30	7.85	96	753 60	167 00	56 60	20 00	— 00
May 15	7.85	88	690 80	146 00	51 88	20 00	15 00
31	7.85	94	737 90	160 00	55 42	20 00	— 00
June 15	8.35	80	668 00	136 00	50 17	20 00	15 00
30	8.35	79	659 65	132 00	49 54	20 00	— 00

2. Alvin Habenstein has been a dispatcher for Interstate Trucking Company since September 1, 19—. His address is 3742 Maple Street, St. Louis, MO 63177, and his telephone number is (314) 555-317number is 477-53-6891. He is married and claims three withholding allowances. Use the information from the table below to prepare an employee earnings record for Alvin. Compute the total earnings, total deductions, net pay, and year-to-date earnings for each weekly pay period. At the end of the quarter, total and prove Alvin's employee earnings record.

PAY PERIOD ENDING	RATE PER HOUR	HOURS	EARNINGS		DEDUCTIONS			
			REGULAR	OVERTIME	FEDERAL INCOME TAX	FICA	STATE INCOME TAX	LOCAL INCOME TAX
Jan. 5	10.25	40	410 00	— 00	66 00	30 79	20 50	8 20
12	10.25	39	399 75	— 00	64 00	30 02	19 99	8 00
19	10.25	42	410 00	30 75	71 00	33 10	22 04	8 82
26	10.25	40	410 00	— 00	66 00	30 79	20 50	8 20
Feb. 2	10.25	40	410 00	— 00	66 00	30 79	20 50	8 20
9	10.25	38	389 50	— 00	62 00	29 25	19 48	7 79
16	10.25	41	410 00	15 38	68 00	31 95	21 27	8 51
23	10.25	40	410 00	— 00	66 00	30 79	20 50	8 20
Mar. 2	10.75	37	397 75	— 00	64 00	29 87	19 89	7 96
9	10.75	40	430 00	— 00	69 00	32 29	21 50	8 60
16	10.75	43	430 00	48 38	77 00	35 93	21 50	9 57
23	10.75	40	430 00	— 00	69 00	32 29	21 50	8 60
30	10.75	40	430 00	— 00	66 00	32 29	21 50	8 60

3. Use the information below to prepare Wage and Tax Statements (Form W-2) for three employees of Interstate Trucking Company, 1020 Lakewood Drive, St. Louis, MO 63168. The employer's identification number is 234-93711, and the employer's state number is 78-23634479. Leave blocks 1, 5, 6, 7, 14, and 16 blank. The amount of wages will be the same for blocks 10, 13, 18, and 21. The locality is St. Louis.

Employee	Wages	Federal Income Tax	Social Security Tax	State Income Tax	Local Income Tax
a. Alvin Habenstein 3742 Maple St. St. Louis, MO 63177 477-53-6891	$23,320.75	$2,244.00	$1,751.39	$1,130.50	$466.40
b. Adriana Alvarez 417 Clark Ave. Apt. 3 St. Louis, MO 63118 489-47-2236	31,455.00	4,032.00	2,362.27	1,687.35	629.10
c. David Twenter 2370 King Road St. Louis, MO 63126 495-82-7064	27,893.50	3,240.00	2,094.80	1,393.58	557.86

Skill: Rounding to the nearest cent.

Sample Problem: Round $7.2385 and $35.3926 to the nearest cent.

Solution:

1. When working with dollars and cents, find the second digit to the right of the decimal point. This is the digit to be rounded.

$7.2385	$35.3926
↑	↑
Digit to be rounded	Digit to be rounded

2. Check the next digit to the right. Is it 5 or more, or is it less than 5?

$7.238	$35.392
↑	↑
5 or more	Less than 5

3. Because the 8 in $7.238 is more than 5, add 1 to the 3 and drop the 8: $7.24. Because the 2 in $35.392 is less than 5, simply drop the 2: $35.39.

4. Answers: $7.24 and $35.39

Practice: Round the following amounts to the nearest cent:

1. $5.876
2. $13.423
3. $27.314
4. $89.955
5. $107.672
6. $375.489
7. $642.217
8. $1,231.991
9. $2,578.396
10. $2,871.995

Skill: Computing social security tax.

Sample Problem: The social security tax rate is 7.65 percent. Compute the tax on wages of $1,893.47.

Solution:

1. Change 7.65 percent to a decimal by moving the decimal point two places to the left. The result is 0.0765.

2. Multiply 0.0765 by $1,893.47 as if the decimal points were not there:

$$\begin{array}{r} \$1893.47 \\ \times 0.0765 \\ \hline 946735 \\ 1136082 \\ 1325429 \\ \hline \$144850455 \end{array}$$

3. Count the total number of digits to the right of the decimal point in the two numbers you multiplied. In this problem there were six (4 + 2).

4. Count from right to left that number of digits (six in this case). Place the decimal point in that position:

$144.850455.

5. Answer: $144.85 (rounded to the nearest cent)

Practice: Find the social security tax for each of the following. Round each answer to the nearest cent.

1. 7.65% of $178.95
2. 7.65% of $236.44
3. 7.65% of $589.62
4. 7.65% of $675.35
5. 7.65% of $1,534.58
6. 13.30% of $1,872.31
7. 13.30% of $2,356.50
8. 13.30% of $2,749.75
9. 13.30% of $3,481.63
10. 13.30% of $3,966.42

Read each of the following statements. From the words below each statement, choose the term that best matches the statement.

1. Record of one employee's earnings, deductions, and net pay for every pay period.

employee earnings record
gross earnings

2. Government charge on the amount people receive from earnings or other sources.

dependents   gross earnings
income tax

3. Form that shows an employee's earnings and the amounts withheld for taxes during the previous year.

Employer's Tax Guide
Wage and Tax Statement (Form W-2)

4. The total amount earned before deductions are made.

gross earnings   net earnings

5. Federal program that provides benefits to retired and disabled persons.

Internal Revenue Service   social security

6. Federal agency that collects income taxes.

Internal Revenue Service
Social Security Administration

7. Includes tables used to find the amount of federal income tax to be withheld.

Employer's Tax Guide
required deductions

8. Deductions that are not required by law.

required deductions
voluntary deductions

9. Record of earnings and deductions for all employees for one pay period.

employee earning record
payroll register

10. Form used to supply information the employer needs for income tax withholding.

Employee's Withholding Allowance
    Certificate (Form W-4)
Wage and Tax Statement (Form W-2)

APPLICATION
PROBLEMS

1. As an employee in the payroll department of Kwan Lee Oriental Imports, you are responsible for preparing payroll registers. The employees are paid weekly and receive time and a half for all hours worked over 40 hours a week. The information for the week of January 9 to 13 is shown in the second table on page 396. The employees are paid on January 16 with Checks 348 to 352. Prepare a payroll register using the table on page 376 to find the FICA taxes to be deducted. Find the amount of federal income tax to be withheld from the table on page 396. After listing all five employees, total and prove the payroll register.

SINGLE Persons–WEEKLY Payroll Period

And the wages are–		And the number of withholding allowances claimed is–										
At least	But less than	0	1	2	3	4	5	6	7	8	9	10
		The amount of income tax to be withheld shall be–										
$320	$330	$46	$40	$35	$29	$24	$18	$13	$7	$2	$0	$0
330	340	47	42	36	31	25	20	14	9	3	0	0
340	350	50	43	38	32	27	21	16	10	5	0	0
350	360	53	45	39	34	28	23	17	12	6	2	0
360	370	55	46	41	35	30	24	19	13	8	3	0
370	380	58	48	42	37	31	26	20	15	9	4	0
380	390	61	51	44	38	33	27	22	16	11	5	1
390	400	64	54	45	40	34	29	23	18	12	7	2
400	410	67	56	47	41	36	30	25	19	14	8	3
410	420	69	59	49	43	37	32	26	21	15	10	4
420	430	72	62	52	44	39	33	28	22	17	11	6
430	440	75	65	55	46	40	35	29	24	18	13	7
440	450	78	68	57	47	42	36	31	25	20	14	9
450	460	81	70	60	50	43	38	32	27	21	16	10
460	470	83	73	63	53	45	39	34	28	23	17	12
470	480	86	76	66	55	46	41	35	30	24	19	13
480	490	89	79	69	58	48	42	37	31	26	20	15
490	500	92	82	71	61	51	44	38	33	27	22	16
500	510	95	84	74	64	54	45	40	34	29	23	18
510	520	97	87	77	67	56	47	41	36	30	25	19
520	530	100	90	80	69	59	49	43	37	32	26	21
530	540	103	93	83	72	62	52	44	39	33	28	22
540	550	107	96	85	75	65	55	46	40	35	29	24
550	560	110	98	88	78	68	57	47	42	36	31	25
560	570	114	101	91	81	70	60	50	43	38	32	27
570	580	117	104	94	83	73	63	53	45	39	34	28
580	590	121	108	97	86	76	66	56	46	41	35	30
590	600	124	111	99	89	79	69	58	48	42	37	31
600	610	128	115	102	92	82	71	61	51	44	38	33
610	620	131	118	106	95	84	74	64	54	45	40	34
620	630	135	122	109	97	87	77	67	57	47	41	36
630	640	138	125	113	100	90	80	70	59	49	43	37
640	650	142	129	116	103	93	83	72	62	52	44	39
650	660	145	132	120	107	96	85	75	65	55	46	40
660	670	149	136	123	110	98	88	78	68	58	47	42

Employee Number	Employee Name	Allow- ances	Hourly Rate	Hours Worked	Insur- ance	Other Deductions
837-46-8291	Seong Cho	2	$10.25	40	$12	$ 5
856-33-7384	Wen-li Fan	1	10.60	39	10	
829-17-9356	Michael Hogan	2	10.05	42	12	8
859-75-3764	Chin Ho Park	3	10.75	43	14	
872-38-4912	Carol Simmons	1	10.35	40	10	10

2. Paula Kelly has worked since June 15, 19—, as a carpenter for Wilder Construction Company, 937 Piedmont Avenue, Atlanta, GA 30303. Paula was born on February 20, 19—, and her social security number is 327-46-7591. She lives at 5172 Sentry Road, Atlanta, GA 30328, and her telephone number is (404) 555-6882. Paula is single and claims one withholding allowance. She is paid on a semimonthly basis, that is, twice a month.

PAY PERIOD ENDING	RATE PER HOUR	HOURS	EARNINGS		DEDUCTIONS			
			REGULAR	OVERTIME	FEDERAL INCOME TAX	FICA	STATE INCOME TAX	LOCAL INCOME TAX
Oct. 15	12.50	88	1100 00	— 00	187 00	82 61	121 00	22 00
31	12.50	96	1200 00	— 00	215 00	90 12	132 00	24 00
Nov. 15	12.50	90	1100 00	37 50	193 00	85 43	125 13	22 75
30	12.50	80	1000 00	— 00	159 00	75 10	110 00	20 00
Dec. 15	12.50	84	1000 00	75 00	179 00	80 73	118 25	21 50
31	12.50	96	1200 00	— 00	215 00	90 12	132 00	24 00

Use the information from the table above to prepare an employee earnings record for Paula for the fourth quarter of 19—. Paula's year-to-date earnings at the end of the third quarter were $19,837.50. Compute her total earnings, total deductions, net pay, and year-to-date earnings for each pay period in the fourth quarter. At the end of the quarter, total and prove Paula's employee earnings record.

Prepare a Wage and Tax Statement (Form W-2) for Paula. Her total deductions during the first three quarters of 19— were as follows: federal income tax, $3,393; social security tax, $1,489.80; state income tax, $2,218.13; and local income tax, $396.75. Add these amounts to her fourth-quarter totals to get Paula's total taxes withheld for the year. The employer's identification number for Wilder Construction Company is 538-956623, and the employer's state number is 98-1354672.

COMPUTER APPLICATION

Exploring Computers in Recordkeeping

In Part 2 you explored the uses of spreadsheet, graphics, and database computer programs. Other, more specialized programs are used in business to keep many of the sales, purchases, inventory, and payroll records that you studied in Part 3.

Large businesses use computers that can store millions of items of information. These large computers are called mainframes. The programs, or software, used on mainframes are usually written by a programmer who works for the company. Many medium-sized businesses have their own midsized computers, called *minicomputers.* These businesses may purchase ready-made programs from a software vendor or hire their own programmers. Smaller businesses, and departments within larger businesses, frequently use small *microcomputers* to keep records and prepare reports. The ready-made programs that are used with microcomputers are usually purchased from a software vendor or computer store. Such software is available for hundreds of recordkeeping applications. Examples of three of these are discussed here.

An *accounts receivable* program enables the business to record its credit sales and returns on a computer disk instead of on paper. The disk contains a record for each customer of the business. When a customer makes payment on account, the computer operator keys in the customer's account number, the date, and the amount of the payment. The computer figures the balance automatically. At the end of the month, the computer prints a statement for each customer.

An *inventory* program is designed to help the business order goods on time and avoid keeping too much merchandise on hand. Inventory programs are tied in with sales programs so that each sale of an item is automatically deducted from the inventory of that item. When the stock level reaches a low point, the computer prints a purchase order to restock the item. When the items that have been ordered are received, the computer operator keys in the quantity of each item. In this way the manager always knows exactly how much stock is on hand.

A *payroll* program is used to keep records of the time worked, the pay, and the deductions for each employee. When someone is hired, the computer operator keys in such information about the person as rate of pay, withholding allowances, and regular work hours. Each day as the employees check in and out, the computer records their arrival and departure by reading the magnetic strip on their identification badges. This information is used by the computer to figure each employee's weekly wages. The computer may then send instructions to other computers at the employees' banks to deposit the net pay in their checking accounts. The employees receive printed vouchers showing how much was deposited and how much was withheld.

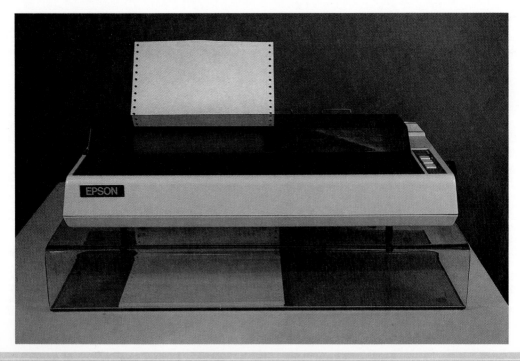

EARNINGS	HOURS	CURRENT	YEAR TO DATE	DEDUCTIONS	CURRENT	YEAR TO DATE
REGULAR PAY		2 416 67	4 833 34	FICA	181 49	362 98
TOTAL PAY		2 416 67	4 833 34	FEDERAL	282 00	564 00
				STATE	96 26	192 52
				TAX DEF SAVINGS	100 00	200 00
				COMP MED-FAM	57 25	114 50
				CREDIT UN LOAN	117 31	234 62
				NET PAY	1 582 36	3 164 72

Jones & Hamilton, Inc. and Subsidiaries

SOCIAL SECURITY NUMBER	DEPT.	CO.
104-00-5326	0069	01

PERIOD ENDING	FED. EX.	STATE EX.
02/28/-	02	02

NET PAY TRANSMITTED TO:

MARYLAND BANK & TRUST
ACCT. #91724-0

STATEMENT OF EARNINGS NOT NEGOTIABLE

JOHN SCHUSTER
201 NORTH AVE.
BALTIMORE
MD   21217

30259918

Check Your Reading

1. What are large business computers called?

2. What are midsized business computers called?

3. What are small business computers called?

4. Name three special business applications for which computer software is available.

5. Explain how one of the three applications in question 4 is used to keep business records.

Shoes for Sports is a wholesale firm that sells a limited line of athletic footwear to retail stores. As a temporary employee for the company, you will keep two weeks' records for purchases, accounts payable, inventory, sales, and accounts receivable. In addition, you will assist in preparing the payroll. The activities in this project are based upon the information in Chapters 10 through 14.

Your work is divided into three phases: setting up your records, keeping records of daily transactions, and assisting with the payroll.

Setting Up Your Records

1. The first activity in setting up your records is to establish three new creditors' accounts. You will remember that creditors, or suppliers, are businesses that sell to your firm on account. Set up an account for each of these creditors by entering each name, address, and account number at the top of a creditor's account form. You will be responsible for keeping each of these accounts up to date during your employment.

Name and Address	Account Number
National Shoe Manufacturers 1200 Pullman Avenue Portland, OR 97204	88
Cushion Tread, Inc. P.O. Box 13000 Orlando, FL 32809	89
Brandt-Zoffer Postfach 2616 8520 Erlangen West Germany	90

2. Your next assignment is to prepare stock cards for four new inventory items for which you will be responsible. Fill in the following information on four stock cards:

Cushion Tread roadrunner; stock no. 7212; minimum, 1,200; maximum, 3,000.

Brandt-Zoffer pacer; stock no. 816; minimum, 1,800; maximum, 3,600.

National wings-away; stock no. 1420; minimum, 1,500; maximum, 2,500.

National turf-wings; stock no. 1440; minimum, 3,000; maximum, 4,500.

3. Shoes for Sports has assigned you to keep records for six new retail customers. Your final activity in setting up your records is to establish an account for each of the following customers by entering each name, address, and account number at the top of a customer account form:

Name and Address	Account Number
Disco-Sportsworld 824 Burlington Drive Detroit, MI 48203	1171
JBR Sports 6200 Vista Boulevard Deer Harbor, WA 98243	1172
Jog and Play Footwear 1800 Crofts Drive Louisville, KY 40205	1173
The Pacesetter, Inc. 1140 Stephens Court Des Moines, IA 50311	1174
Red Top Sporting Goods 7612 Burns Avenue Boston, MA 02169	1175
Run & Racquet Shop 820 Main Street Xenia, OH 45383	1176

Keeping Records of Daily Transactions

You will be in charge of keeping records for four kinds of transactions: purchases on account, sales on account, payments to creditors, and receipts from customers. Follow these instructions for each:

1. *Purchases of merchandise on account.* The policy of Shoes for Sports is to record purchases on the day the merchandise is received.

Sample transaction:

June 17   Purchased on account and received from National Shoe Manufacturers, 4,500 pairs of National turf-wings at $14 a pair and 2,500 pairs of National wings-away at $12.50 a pair.

Steps to follow in recording the transaction:

Step 1.   Record the purchase in the creditor's account for National Shoe Manufacturers that you prepared when setting up your records. Enter the date, the amount of the purchase in the Credit column, and the balance. For the sample transaction above, figure the amount of the purchase as follows:

Multiply: 4,500 × $14 = $63,000
Multiply: 2,500 × $12.50 =   31,250
Add: $94,250

Step 2.   Record the receipt of the items purchased on the stock cards you prepared when setting up your records. For example, on the stock card for National wings-away, enter June 17 in the Date column, 2,500 in the Number Received column, and 2,500 in the Balance column. Remember also to record the receipt of the National turf-wings shoes on that stock card.

2. *Sales of merchandise on account.* The policy of Shoes for Sports is to record sales on the day merchandise is shipped.

Sample transaction:

June 18   Sold on account and shipped to JBR Sports, 800 pairs of Cushion Tread roadrunners at $26.30 a pair.

Steps to follow in recording the transaction:

Step 1.   Record the sale in the customer's account for JBR Sports that you prepared when setting up your records. Enter the date, the amount of the sale in the Debit column, and the balance. For the sample transaction above, figure the amount of the sale as follows:

Multiply: 800 × $26.30 = $21,040

Step 2.   Record the sale of the items on the correct stock card. For example, on the stock card for Cushion Tread roadrunners, you will already have made a June 17 entry. To record the sale, record June 18 in the Date column, 800 in the Number Sold column, and 2,200 (3,000 − 800 = 2,200) in the Balance column.

3. *Receipts of payments on account from customers.*

Sample transaction:

June 26   Received check from Red Top Sporting Goods for payment on account, $4,185.

To record this transaction, turn to the customer's account for Red Top Sporting Goods, enter the date, the amount received in the Credit column, and the new balance.

4. *Payments on account to creditors.*

Sample transaction:

June 27   Issued check to Brandt-Zoffer for payment on account, $65,700.

To record this transaction, turn to the creditor's account for Brandt-Zoffer, enter the date, the amount paid in the Debit column, and the new balance.

Daily Transactions

Record the following transactions according to the instructions on pages 401 and above.

June 17   Purchased on account and received from National Shoe Manufacturers, 4,500 pairs of National turf-wings at $14 a pair and 2,500 pairs of National wings-away at $12.50 a pair.

17   Purchased on account and received from Cushion Tread, Inc., 3,000 pairs of Cushion Tread roadrunners at $19.75 a pair.

17   Purchased on account and received from Brandt-Zoffer, 3,600 pairs of Brandt-Zoffer pacers at $18.25 a pair.

18   Sold on account and shipped to JBR Sports, 800 pairs of Cushion Tread roadrunners at $26.30 a pair.

18   Sold on account and shipped to Red Top Sporting Goods, 225 pairs of National turf-wings at $18.60 a pair.

19   Sold on account and shipped to Disco-Sportsworld, 400 pairs of Brandt-Zoffer pacers at $24.25 a pair.

20   Sold on account and shipped to Jog and Play Footwear, 275 pairs of National wings-away at $16.60 a pair.

20   Sold on account and shipped to The Pacesetter, Inc., 650 pairs of Brandt-Zoffer pacers at $24.25 a pair.

20   Sold on account and shipped to Run & Racquet Shop, 175 pairs of National turf-wings at $18.60 a pair.

21   Sold on account and shipped to Red Top Sporting Goods, 650 pairs of Cushion Tread roadrunners at $26.30 a pair and 250 pairs of Brandt-Zoffer pacers at $24.25 a pair.

21   Sold on account and shipped to JBR Sports, 350 pairs of National wings-away at $16.60 a pair and 325 pairs of National turf-wings at $18.60 a pair.

24   Sold on account and shipped to Disco-Sportsworld, 400 pairs of Cushion Tread roadrunners at $26.30 a pair.

24   Sold on account and shipped to Run & Racquet Shop, 400 pairs of National wings-away at $16.60 a pair.

25   Sold on account and shipped to Red Top Sporting Goods, 300 pairs of National turf-wings at $18.60 a pair.

25   Sold on account and shipped to Jog and Play Footwear, 300 pairs of Brandt-Zoffer pacers at $24.25 a pair.

25   Sold on account and shipped to The Pacesetter, Inc., 175 pairs of Brandt-Zoffer pacers at $24.25 a pair.

26   Purchased on account and received from Cushion Tread, Inc., 1,850 pairs of Cushion Tread roadrunners at $19.75 a pair.

26   Sold on account and shipped to Run & Racquet Shop, 250 pairs of National turf-wings at $18.60 a pair.

26   Received check from Red Top Sporting Goods for payment on account, $4,185.

27   Purchased on account and received from National Shoe Manufacturers, 1,025 pairs of National wings-away at $12.50 a pair.

27   Issued check to Brandt-Zoffer for payment on account, $65,700.

27   Received check from JBR Sports for payment on account, $21,040.

27 Received check from The Pacesetter, Inc., for payment on account, $15,762.50.

28 Sold on account and shipped to Jog and Play Footwear, 500 pairs of Cushion Tread roadrunners at $26.30 a pair.

28 Sold on account and shipped to Run & Racquet Shop, 525 pairs of National wings-away at $16.60 a pair.

28 Issued check to National Shoe Manufacturers for payment on account, $94,250.

28 Issued check to Cushion Tread, Inc., for payment on account, $59,250.

28 Received check from Disco-Sportsworld for payment on account, $20,220.

Assisting with the Payroll

Your final job as a temporary employee of Shoes for Sports is to assist with the payroll for the second week of your employment.

You have been asked to complete payroll records for four of the employees in your department. The payroll supervisor will then check your work and make it part of the full weekly payroll for the company. Follow these steps:

1. Compute time worked and earnings for each employee. Shown here are time cards for the four employees.

The regular hours of work are 8 a.m. to 12 noon and 1 p.m. to 5 p.m. The workweek is Monday to Friday. Overtime has been approved for hours worked in excess of 40 a week. The quarter-hour time system is used. Late arrivals or early departures of five minutes or less are not counted.

2. On the time cards in your Activity Guide, record regular and overtime hours, overtime rates, and regular and overtime earnings; enter number of days worked; and record total hours and gross earnings. Do not write on the time cards shown here.

Week Ending _____ June 28, 19 __

No. 176-27-9091

Name Burge, Rolf

Days	Regular				Overtime		Daily Totals
	In	Out	In	Out	In	Out	
Mon.	7^{55}	11^{05}	12^{55}	5^{00}			
Tues.	7^{55}	12^{00}	1^{00}	4^{55}			
Wed.	8^{00}	12^{00}	12^{55}	5^{00}			
Thurs.	7^{55}	11^{55}	1^{00}	4^{55}			
Fri.	8^{00}	12^{05}	1^{05}	5^{05}			
Sat.							
Sun.							

		Hours	Rate	Earnings
	Regular		8.50	
	Overtime			
Days Worked	Total Hours		Gross Earnings	

Week Ending _____ June 28, 19 __

No. 302-14-5918

Name McMinnis, Sarah

Days	Regular				Overtime		Daily Totals
	In	Out	In	Out	In	Out	
Mon.	7^{55}	12^{00}	1^{00}	5^{00}			
Tues.	8^{00}	12^{05}	12^{55}	5^{05}			
Wed.	7^{55}	11^{55}	1^{05}	5^{00}	6^{00}	9^{00}	
Thurs.	7^{55}	12^{05}	1^{00}	5^{05}	6^{05}	9^{05}	
Fri.	8^{05}	12^{00}	12^{55}	4^{55}			
Sat.							
Sun.							

		Hours	Rate	Earnings
	Regular		7.40	
	Overtime			
Days Worked	Total Hours		Gross Earnings	

Time Card — Melesco, Naomi

Week Ending June 28, 19 --

No. 414-76-6012

Name Melesco, Naomi

Days	Regular				Overtime		Daily Totals
	In	Out	In	Out	In	Out	
Mon.	7^{55}	12^{05}	12^{55}	5^{00}			
Tues.	8^{45}	12^{00}	1^{00}	5^{05}			
Wed.	8^{00}	12^{05}	1^{05}	4^{55}			
Thurs.	8^{00}	11^{55}	12^{55}	4^{55}			
Fri.	8^{00}	11^{55}	12^{55}	5^{05}			
Sat.							
Sun.							

		Hours	Rate	Earnings
	Regular		9.00	
	Overtime			
Days Worked	Total Hours		Gross Earnings	

Time Card — Sanchez, Raoul

Week Ending June 28, 19 --

No. 321-40-1799

Name Sanchez, Raoul

Days	Regular				Overtime		Daily Totals
	In	Out	In	Out	In	Out	
Mon.	8^{05}	11^{55}	1^{05}	5^{05}			
Tues.	8^{00}	12^{00}	1^{00}	5^{00}			
Wed.	8^{00}	12^{00}	12^{55}	4^{55}	6^{00}	9^{05}	
Thurs.	8^{05}	11^{55}	12^{55}	4^{05}			
Fri.	8^{05}	12^{05}	12^{55}	5^{00}			
Sat.							
Sun.							

		Hours	Rate	Earnings
	Regular		7.60	
	Overtime			
Days Worked	Total Hours		Gross Earnings	

3. Prepare a payroll register for the four employees. Time and a half is paid for all hours worked over 40 hours a week. The employees are paid on July 1 using Checks 1014, 1015, 1016, and 1017. Multiply each employee's total earnings by 0.0751 to find the FICA taxes to be withheld. Find the amount of federal income tax to be withheld by using the tax table for single persons on page 381. The employees have the following numbers of allowances: Rolf Burge, two; Sarah McMinnis, three; Naomi Melesco, one; Raoul Sanchez, two.

4. Total and prove the payroll register.

BASIC
ACCOUNTING
RECORDS

CHAPTER 15

INTRODUCTION TO ACCOUNTING

Business owners and managers need answers to questions such as these. How much money are we making (or losing)? Can we afford to give everyone a raise? Can we open a branch office? Do we have enough money to increase our advertising? Accounting records help business people answer these questions.

Accounting is based on three items called the *fundamental elements*. These are *assets*, *liabilities*, and *owner's equity*. Any event that causes a change in one or more of these fundamental elements is called a *business transaction*. Accounting, then, is the recording, summarizing, and analyzing of business transactions.

Recording A business's records are similar to personal records. By recording what happens, business managers obtain a clear financial picture. Records answer such questions as: How many sales were made October 14? What did the business purchase in July?

Summarizing Business records are used in summarizing. Reports are made by grouping information from different records. Reports answer questions such as: How much money has the business made so far this year?

Analyzing Business reports are used in analyzing. They give managers the information needed to make business decisions, such as whether to open a new store. Business reports also give bank officers, investors, and other people outside the business information to use in analyzing and in making decisions, such as whether to lend money to or invest money in the business.

In this chapter you will learn how the three fundamental elements—assets, liabilities, and owner's equity—fit together. They make up a financial statement, or report, called a *balance sheet*. A balance sheet shows the assets, liabilities, and owner's equity of a business on a certain date.

TOPIC 1 ◆ ASSETS, LIABILITIES, AND OWNER'S EQUITY

GOALS

1. To define assets, liabilities, and owner's equity.
2. To compute owner's equity, given total assets and total liabilities.
3. To complete a balance sheet, including the heading, Assets section, Liabilities section, and Owner's Equity section.

KEY TERMS

A *balance sheet* is a report that shows the assets, liabilities, and owner's equity of a business on a certain date.

Assets are things of value owned by a business.

Liabilities are debts owed by a business.

Owner's equity is the difference between a business's assets and its liabilities.

The *accounting equation* is assets = liabilities + owner's equity.

In accounting, things of value that are owned by a business are called *assets.* Assets are listed in the Assets section of the balance sheet.

Jill Owen enjoyed working in a travel agency. When she had saved enough money to open her own travel agency, she made down payments on the furniture and office machines needed. Then, on August 25, she opened the Global Travel Service.

On September 1, after operating her new business for one week, Jill had the following assets: $1,570 in cash, furniture that cost $4,600, office machines that cost $3,000, and $1,530 in accounts receivable. *Accounts receivable* are amounts that customers owe businesses for goods or services sold on credit.

Global Travel, for example, has two accounts receivable: Will Dean owes Global $700 for a vacation, and Dana Massi owes $830 for a business trip. These accounts are assets because Global Travel will receive cash for them in the future.

Accounts receivable are amounts customers owe to a business.

RECORDING ASSETS ON A BALANCE SHEET

The heading and the Assets section of Global Travel's balance sheet as of September 1 is shown below. The form is divided into a left side and a right side.

❶

❷ ❸ ❺ ❼

Global Travel Service
Balance Sheet
September 1, 19—

Assets			
Cash		1570 00	
Accounts Receivable:			
Will Dean	$ 700.00		
Dana Massi	830.00	1530 00	
Furniture		4600 00	
Office Machines		3000 00	
Total		10700 00	

❹ ❻

Note the following:

1. The three-line heading, which is centered at the top of the balance sheet, answers the questions "Who?" "What?" and

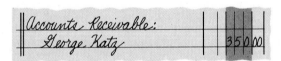 *(margin note, left column)* The *heading* of a balance sheet answers the questions "Who?" "What?" "When?"

"When?" It gives the full name of the business (Global Travel Service), the title of the statement (Balance Sheet), and the date.

2. Assets are always listed on the left side of the balance sheet. The title "Assets" is centered on the first line. Then each asset is listed at the margin under this title. The amount of each asset is recorded in the money column next to the asset.

3. Cash is always listed first. Cash includes the amount of money in the bank and the amount of money the business has on hand. Businesses use different methods for listing the assets that come after cash. In this book we will always list cash first, then accounts receivable, and then all other assets in alphabetical order.

4. No dollar signs and decimal points are used on ruled accounting paper (unless the amounts are not in the money columns).

5. The title "Accounts Receivable" is followed by a colon to indicate that account names will follow. Under the title are the names of the customers who owe money to the business (Will Dean and Dana Massi). Note that the names are indented and are listed in alphabetical order. (The term Accounts Receivable is often abbreviated Accts. Rec.)

   The individual amounts owed are listed to the left of the money column with a single rule under the last amount. Only the total is recorded in the money column.

   If there is only one account receivable, the amount is recorded in the money column, as shown here:

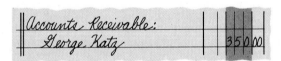

6. An amount in even dollars is written with two zeros in the cents part of the money column.

7. The assets are always totaled after the right side of the balance sheet is finished. The reason is that the totals for assets, liabilities, and owner's equity must be on the same line. The assets total is entered in this illustration, however, to show you how the Assets section would look after the balance sheet is completed.

   When the right side is totaled, the assets are then totaled. A single rule is drawn across the money column. On the next line, the word "Total" is centered in the first column, and the total amount ($10,700) is written in the money column. A double rule is drawn under the total amount to show that all assets have been listed. (Note: Lines are always drawn with a ruler.)

RECORDING LIABILITIES ON A BALANCE SHEET

In accounting, debts that are owed are called *liabilities*. The businesses or people to whom the money is owed are called *creditors*. Liabilities are recorded on the right side of the balance sheet. They are listed in the Liabilities section.

On September 1 the Global Travel Service had the following liabilities: $2,600 owed to the Decor Company and $2,000 owed to Mini Machines, Inc. These are amounts that Jill Owen owes for furniture and office machines that she bought. They are called *accounts payable*. Accounts payable are liabilities because they are debts that the business must pay at some future time.

A creditor is a business or a person to whom money is owed.

Accounts payable are amounts owed by a business for items purchased on credit.

The heading, the Assets section, and the Liabilities section of the balance sheet for the Global Travel Service on September 1 are shown below.

Global Travel Service
Balance Sheet
September 1, 19—

Assets			Liabilities			
Cash	1570 00		Accounts Payable:			❶
Accounts Receivable:			Decor Company $ 2,600.00			
Will Dean $700.00			Mini Machines, Inc. 2,000.00	4600 00		❷
Dana Massi 830.00	1530 00		Total Liabilities	4600 00		❸
Furniture	4600 00					❹
Office Machines	3000 00					
Total	10700 00					

Note the following:

1. Liabilities are listed on the right side of the balance sheet. The title "Liabilities" is centered on the first line.
2. Global's liabilities are two accounts payable. The title "Accounts Payable" (or "Accts. Pay.") is written at the margin and is followed by a colon. Under the title the names of the creditors are listed in alphabetical order. Note that the names are indented. The individual amount owed to each creditor is written outside the money column with a single rule under the last amount. The total is then recorded in the money column. If there had been only one account payable, the amount would have been recorded in the money column, as shown here.

3. When all liabilities are entered, a single rule is drawn under the last amount in the money column and the amounts are added. On the next line, the title "Total Liabilities" is indented, and the total amount ($4,600) is entered next to it in the money column.
4. A double rule is not drawn under total liabilities because the right side of the balance sheet has not yet been completed.

A *note payable* is a written promise to pay a certain amount in the future.

If there had been other types of liabilities, such as notes payable and mortgage payable, they would also have been listed. A *note payable* is a written promise to pay a certain amount in the future. A *mortgage payable* is a long-term debt, usually made to pay for a building or property. In the Liabilities section below, accounts payable are listed first, then notes payable, and then mortgage payable. They are listed in "time order"—that is, accounts payable are usually due within a short period of time, notes payable are due within a somewhat longer period of time, and a mortgage payable is usually paid over a long period of several years.

RECORDING OWNER'S EQUITY ON A BALANCE SHEET

In accounting, the difference between a business's assets and its liabilities is called *owner's equity*. It is also sometimes called *net worth*.

Assets, liabilities, and owner's equity are shown in the accounting equation as follows:

$$\text{Assets} = \text{Liabilities} + \text{Owner's Equity}$$

Global Travel's total assets are $10,700 and its total liabilities are $4,600. What is Jill Owen's owner's equity? Remember: Total assets must equal total liabilities and owner's equity.

The owner's equity can be found by subtracting the total liabilities from the total assets: $10,700 − $4,600 = $6,100. Therefore, Jill has $6,100 in owner's equity.

$$\begin{array}{ccc} \text{Assets} & = & \text{Liabilities} + \text{Owner's Equity} \\ \$10,700 = & \$4,600 & + \quad \$6,100 \end{array}$$

The balance sheet for Global Travel Service on September 1 is completed by entering the owner's equity, as shown below:

Global Travel Service					
Balance Sheet					
September 1, 19—					
Assets		**Liabilities**			
Cash	1 570 00	Accounts Payable:			
Accounts Receivable:		Decor Company $2,600.00			
Will Dean $700.00		Mini Machines, Inc. 2,000.00	4 600 00		
Dana Massi 830.00	1 530 00	Total Liabilities	4 600 00		
Furniture	4 600 00		❹		
Office Machines	3 000 00	**Owner's Equity**			❶
		Jill Owen, Capital ❷	6 100 00		❸
Total	1 0 700 00	Total	1 0 700 00		❺

❻

Note the following on the completed balance sheet:

1. Owner's equity is listed on the right side of the balance sheet, one blank line after the Liabilities section. The title "Owner's Equity" is centered in the column.

2. "Jill Owen, Capital" is written at the margin. The word "Capital" always follows the owner's name. (*Capital* means the owner's investment.)
3. The owner's equity amount ($6,100) is entered in the money column opposite "Jill Owen, Capital." This amount was found by using the accounting equation.
4. A single rule is drawn under the owner's equity amount.
5. The word "Total" is centered on the next line. Remember that a double rule was not drawn under the total liabilities amount when the Liabilities section was completed. Reason: The total liabilities amount is now added to the owner's equity amount, and the total of these two amounts is written in the money column next to the word "Total." A double rule is now drawn under the total to show that the right side of the balance sheet is complete.
6. The totals of the two sides of the balance sheet are equal. Each side totals $10,700.

The word "Total" is on the same line on both sides of the balance sheet. The double rule drawn under the total in each money column shows that all entries are complete and that the amounts are in balance.

Check Your Reading

1. What are the three fundamental elements of accounting?

2. What is the name of an event that changes one or more of the three fundamental elements of accounting?

3. What are the three main activities of accounting?

4. What financial statement shows the assets, liabilities, and owner's equity of a business on a certain date?

5. Define (a) assets, (b) liabilities, and (c) owner's equity.

6. What is the accounting equation?

7. If assets are $7,500 and liabilities are $2,500, what is the amount of owner's equity?

8. What three questions are answered by the heading of a balance sheet?

9. What is the difference between an account receivable and an account payable?

10. What two numbers are always equal on a balance sheet?

1. Complete the following accounting equations by supplying the missing amounts.

   Assets   = Liabilities + Owner's Equity
   a. $95,000 = $8,000 +   ?
   b. $23,546 = $9,346 +   ?
   c. $22,500 = $3,350 +   ?
   d. $31,250 = $8,708 +   ?
   e. $18,435 = $6,345 +   ?
   f. $9,605 = $1,205 +   ?
   g. $45,349 = $9,728 +   ?
   h. $20,090 = $5,900 +   ?

2. Prepare the heading and the Assets section of a balance sheet for Wanda Gratz, dentist. On May 31 Dr. Gratz's assets were Cash, $9,448; Accts. Rec./John Morris, $1,080; Dental Equipment, $66,720; Furniture, $10,460; Office Machines, $1,980.

3. Prepare the heading and the Assets section of a balance sheet for Swif-T Cleaners. Be sure to arrange the assets in proper order before listing them. On June 30 the business's assets were Office Machines, $2,100; Cash, $6,950; Truck, $11,200; Dry Cleaning Equipment, $89,750.

4. Prepare the heading, the Assets section, and the Liabilities section of a balance sheet for the P&L Parking Lot. On March 1 the business had the following assets: Cash, $4,800; Building, $22,000; Land, $130,000; Office Equipment, $1,850. The business also had the following liabilities: Notes Payable, $32,000; Accts. Pay./National Cement, $16,900; Accts. Pay./Sanchez, Inc., $6,800.

5. Prepare the heading, the Assets section, the Liabilities section, and the Owner's Equity section of a balance sheet for the Lakeside Theater, which is owned by Vernon Lopez. (Remember that owner's equity is found by subtracting liabilities from assets.) On November 30 the theater had the following assets and liabilities. Remember to list them in the proper order on the balance sheet. Mortgage Payable, $136,000; Accts. Rec./Marlowe Co., $6,490; Accts. Pay./Wayne-Faraday Film Co., $2,180; Building, $198,000; Cash, $11,966; Furniture, $35,700; Accts. Pay./NuVu Films, $3,550; Equipment, $64,000.

TOPIC 2 ◆ ACCOUNTS

The equipment that the Lincoln High School Band bought is recorded in the Equipment account. The money owed for the equipment is recorded in the Accts. Pay./Music World Inc. account.

A balance sheet is like a photograph. If you take a picture at a party, the picture is a record of how everyone looked at that moment. If you take another picture later, the record is never quite the same. The balance sheet is also a picture—a financial picture. It shows the financial health, or position, of a business on a certain date. The balance sheet items change as the owner buys equipment and merchandise, pays expenses, sells merchandise, or receives cash. However, the owner does not make up a new balance sheet every time something is bought or sold. Instead, the owner records changes in accounts that represent the balance sheet items.

An *account* contains financial information for one item only. The simplest form of account is a *T account*. As shown below, it is shaped like the letter "T":

ACCOUNT TITLE	
DEBIT	**CREDIT**

A T account has a title and two sides, separated by a line. The left side is called the *debit* side; the right side is called the *credit* side. A Cash account with $2,000 recorded on the debit side is shown below.

Cash
$2,000

The title of the account is written at the top. Note also that the amount ($2,000) is written with a dollar sign and a comma.

A Cash account with $2,000 recorded on the debit side and $500 recorded on the credit side is shown below.

Cash	
$2,000	$500

OPENING ACCOUNTS

When a new business opens, the owner prepares a balance sheet, as Hazel Perlman did for the Custom Cleaning Service. Her first balance sheet is shown below.

Custom Cleaning Service
Balance Sheet
February 1, 19—

Assets		Liabilities	
Cash	1500 00	Accounts Payable:	
Accounts Receivable:		Hudson, Inc.	2700 00
Willis James	130 00		
Equipment	4000 00	Owner's Equity	
Furniture	400 00	Hazel Perlman, Capital	3330 00
Total	6030 00	Total	6030 00

The balance sheet is also shaped like the letter "T." On a balance sheet, assets are listed on the left side of the "T." Liabilities and owner's equity are listed on the right side of the "T."

In other words, balance sheet information is arranged according to the accounting equation, as follows:

Assets = Liabilities + Owner's Equity
$6,030 = $2,700 + $3,330

The amounts on the left side of the balance sheet are *debit* amounts. The amounts on the right side of the balance sheet are *credit* amounts. Note that the total debits and the total credits for the Custom Cleaning Service are equal. Each totals $6,030. The total amount listed on the left side of a balance sheet must always equal the total amount listed on the right side.

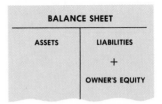

BALANCE SHEET	
ASSETS	LIABILITIES
	+
	OWNER'S EQUITY

BALANCE SHEET	
6,030	2,700
	+
	3,330
6,030	6,030

The accounting clerk opens an account for each item on the balance sheet. *Opening an account* means writing the title at the top of the account and recording the balance in the account. The balance sheet for the Custom Cleaning Service shows that it has $1,500 in cash. Thus the accounting clerk opens an account titled "Cash." Since assets are listed on the left side of the balance sheet, the amount of cash is recorded on the left side, the debit side, of the Cash account. Recording an amount on the left side of an account is known as *debiting the account*. A separate account is opened for each of the other assets on the balance sheet. The amount of each asset is debited to the proper account.

The balance sheet shows that the Custom Cleaning Service owes $2,700 to Hudson, Inc. Thus the accounting clerk opens an account for Hudson, Inc. Since liabilities are listed on the right side of the balance sheet, the amount owed to Hudson, Inc., is recorded on the right side, the credit side, of the account. Recording an amount on the right side of an account is known as *crediting the account*. An account is also opened for Hazel Perlman, Capital. This account is where Hazel Perlman's owner's equity is recorded. Since owner's equity is listed on the right side of the balance sheet, the amount is recorded on the right side, the credit side, of the Hazel Perlman, Capital account. After the accounting clerk has opened all the accounts, the accounts appear as shown here.

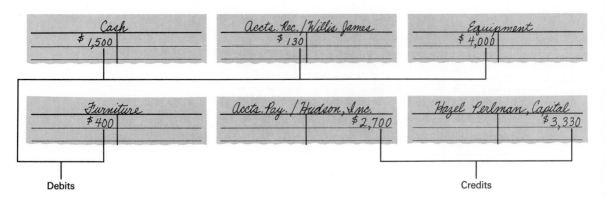

The debit amounts and the credit amounts from all the accounts of the Custom Cleaning Service are as follows:

Debits	=	Credits
$1,500		$2,700
130		3,330
4,000		
400		
$6,030	=	$6,030

Note that the totals are equal.

1. What is the left side of a T account called?

2. What is the right side of a T account called?

3. What does debiting an account mean?

4. What does crediting an account mean?

5. Draw a T account and title it "Cash."
   a. Record $72,300 on the debit side and $8,000 on the credit side of the account.
   b. How much larger is the debit side than the credit side?

6. Draw a T account and title it "Cash."
   a. Record $2,321.58 on the debit side and $630.40 on the credit side of the account.
   b. How much larger is the debit side than the credit side?

7. On what side of the balance sheet are assets listed?

8. On what side of the balance sheet are liabilities listed?

9. On what side of the balance sheet is owner's equity listed?

1. The balance sheet for Carla's Shoe Repair is shown below.
   a. Open T accounts for the asset, liability, and owner's equity items on the balance sheet.
   b. List and total the debits and the credits from the accounts. Do the total debits equal the total credits?

Carla's Shoe Repair
Balance Sheet
September 30, 19—

Assets		Liabilities	
Cash	3000 00	Accounts Payable:	
Equipment	2500 00	Furniture Mart	1500 00
Furniture	3000 00		
		Owner's Equity	
		Carla Dent, Capital	7000 00
Total	8500 00	Total	8500 00

2. The balance sheet for the Reliable Delivery Company is shown below.
   a. Open T accounts for the asset, liability, and owner's equity items on the balance sheet.
   b. List and total the debits and the credits from the accounts. Do the total debits equal the total credits?

Reliable Delivery Company
Balance Sheet
February 28, 19—

Assets		Liabilities	
Cash	6 000 00	Accounts Payable:	
Accounts Receivable:		Donnley Company	4 800 00
Drake Company	3 800 00		
Truck	9 300 00	Owner's Equity	
		S. J. Ferlito, Capital	14 300 00
Total	19 100 00	Total	19 100 00

3. The T accounts for Margo's Landscaping Service are shown below.
   a. List and total the debits and the credits from the accounts to prove that the total debits equal the total credits.
   b. Prepare a balance sheet from the T accounts. Date the balance sheet December 31, 19—.

Cash
| $2,800 | |

Accts. Rec./Lee Wong
| $600 | |

Truck
| $8,100 | |

Accts. Pay./Drummond Inc.
| | $2,100 |

Margo Walters, Capital
| | $9,400 |

GOALS

1. To record transactions involving increases and decreases in asset accounts.
2. To record transactions involving increases and decreases in liability accounts.
3. To record transactions involving increases and decreases in owner's equity.

KEY TERMS

The *debit side* is the left side of an account. The *credit side* is the right side of an account.

CHANGES IN ASSET ACCOUNTS

Changes in accounts are usually the result of business transactions. For example, there are four asset accounts on the balance sheet for the Custom Cleaning Service. These asset accounts are Cash, Accts. Rec./Willis James, Equipment, and Furniture.

Business transactions, such as receiving cash, paying cash, buying equipment, and buying furnitue, would cause changes in these accounts.

Custom Cleaning Service Balance Sheet February 1, 19—			
Assets		**Liabilities**	
Cash	1500 00	Accounts Payable:	
Accounts Receivable:		Hudson, Inc.	270 00
Willis James	130 00		
Equipment	4000 00	Owner's Equity	
Furniture	400 00	Hazel Perlman, Capital	3330 00
Total	6030 00	Total	6030 00

For example, assets are listed on the left side of the balance sheet. Thus increases in assets are recorded on the left side, the debit side, of the asset accounts. Decreases in assets are recorded on the right side, the credit side, of the asset accounts.

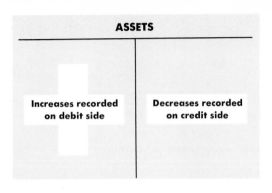

ASSETS

| Increases recorded on debit side | Decreases recorded on credit side |

Increase assets on the debit side, the left side, of an account.

The Custom Cleaning Service opened with $1,500 in cash on hand. After the amount of cash from the balance sheet is recorded, the Cash account appears as follows:

Cash
| $1,500 | |

Decrease assets on the credit side, the right side, of an account.

Now Hazel Perlman buys a $65 lamp for her office. The $65 decreases Cash. Thus the $65 is recorded on the credit side of the account. After the decrease is recorded, the Cash account appears as follows:

Cash
| $1,500 | $65 |

Hazel Perlman invests an additional $600 of her own money in her business. The $600 increases Cash. Thus the $600 is recorded on the debit side of the account. After the increase is recorded, the Cash account appears as follows:

Cash
| $1,500 | $65 |
| 600 | |

TRANSACTIONS INVOLVING TWO ASSETS

At least two accounts change with every transaction.

At least two accounts change with every business transaction. Sometimes the accounts are both asset accounts. When Hazel Perlman bought a lamp for $65 in cash, the following two changes took place: (1) The asset Furniture increased $65 and (2) the asset Cash decreased $65.

Before Hazel bought the lamp, the accounts for Cash and Furniture appeared as follows:

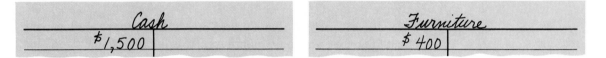

Cash		*Furniture*	
$1,500		$ 400	

After the purchase of the lamp was recorded in the accounts, the accounts appeared as follows:

Cash.		*Furniture*	
$1,500	$ 65	$ 400	
		65	

The Furniture account was debited for $65 to show an increase in that asset. The Cash account was credited for $65 to show a decrease in that asset.

CHANGES IN LIABILITY ACCOUNTS

Liabilities are listed on the right side of the balance sheet. Thus increases in liabilities are recorded on the right side, the credit side, of liability accounts. Decreases in liabilities are recorded on the left side, the debit side, of liability accounts.

Increase liabilities on the credit side, the right side, of an account.

Decrease liabilities on the debit side, the left side, of an account.

LIABILITIES

Decreases recorded on debit side	Increases recorded on credit side

The balance sheet for the Custom Cleaning Service showed one liability account—Accts. Pay./Hudson, Inc. Hazel Perlman bought cleaning equipment for $2,700 on credit from Hudson, Inc., when she started her business. After the amount owed was recorded, the Accts. Pay./Hudson, Inc. account appeared as follows:

Accts. Pay. / Hudson, Inc.

	$2,700

Shortly afterward, Hazel paid $700 of her debt to Hudson, Inc. The $700 that she paid decreases the liability to Hudson, Inc. Thus the $700 is recorded on the debit side of the liability account. After the decrease in the liability was recorded, the Accts. Pay./Hudson, Inc. account appeared as follows:

Accts. Pay. / Hudson, Inc.

$ 700	$2,700

Hazel then bought a $400 electric waxer on credit from Hudson, Inc. The $400 owed increases the liability. Thus the $400 is recorded on the credit side of the liability account. After the increase in the liability was recorded, the Accts. Pay./Hudson, Inc. account appeared as follows:

Accts. Pay. / Hudson, Inc.

$700	$2,700
	400

TRANSACTIONS INVOLVING ASSETS AND LIABILITIES

When Hazel Perlman paid Hudson, Inc., $700 toward the cleaning equipment, the following changes took place: (1) The asset Cash decreased $700 and (2) the liability Accts. Pay./Hudson, Inc. decreased $700. After this transaction was recorded, the accounts appeared as follows:

Cash

$1,500	$ 65
600	700

Accts. Pay. / Hudson, Inc.

$ 700	$2,700

When Hazel bought the $400 electric waxer on credit from Hudson, Inc., the transaction affected two accounts: Equipment and Accts. Pay./Hudson, Inc. The following changes took place:

(1) The asset Equipment increased $400 and (2) the liability Accts. Pay./Hudson, Inc. increased $400. After the transaction was recorded, the accounts appeared as follows:

Equipment		Accts. Pay./Hudson, Inc.	
$ 4,000		$ 700	$ 2,700
400			400

Remember that increases in asset accounts are recorded by debiting the accounts. This is because assets are listed on the left side of the balance sheet. Increases in liability accounts are recorded by crediting the accounts. This is because liabilities are listed on the right side of the balance sheet.

CHANGES IN OWNER'S EQUITY

Owner's equity is listed on the right side of the balance sheet. Thus increases in owner's equity are recorded on the right side, the credit side, of the owner's equity account. Decreases in owner's equity are recorded on the left side, the debit side, of the owner's equity account.

Increase owner's equity on the credit side, the right side, of an account.

Decrease owner's equity on the debit side, the left side, of an account.

OWNER'S EQUITY

Decreases recorded on debit side	Increases recorded on credit side

The title of the owner's equity account is the owner's name followed by a comma and the word "Capital"—for example, "Hazel Perlman, Capital." The owner's equity account for Hazel Perlman appeared as follows after the balance sheet amount was recorded. The $3,330 is the original amount of owner's equity.

Hazel Perlman, Capital	
	$3,330

Hazel invested an additional $600 in her business. This transaction increased the owner's equity account by $600. Since increases in owner's equity are shown as credits, the $600 is recorded on the credit side of the account. After the increase was recorded, Hazel Perlman, Capital appeared as follows:

Hazel Perlman, Capital

| | $3,330 |
| | 600 |

Later, Hazel withdrew $200 from the business for personal use. This transaction decreased the owner's equity account by $200. Since decreases in owner's equity are shown as debits, the $200 is recorded on the debit side of the account. After the decrease was recorded, Hazel Perlman, Capital appeared as follows:

Hazel Perlman, Capital

| $ 200 | $ 3,330 |
| | 600 |

TRANSACTIONS INVOLVING ASSETS AND OWNER'S EQUITY

When Hazel invested $600 cash in her business, the transaction affected two accounts: Cash and Hazel Perlman, Capital. The following changes took place: (1) The asset Cash increased $600 and (2) the owner's equity account Hazel Perlman, Capital increased $600.

Then Hazel withdrew $200 in cash from her business for personal use. The transaction affected the same two accounts: Cash and Hazel Perlman, Capital. The following changes took place: (1) The asset Cash decreased $200 and (2) the owner's equity account Hazel Perlman, Capital decreased $200.

Cash

$ 1,500	$ 65
600	700
	200

Hazel Perlman, Capital

| $ 200 | $ 3,330 |
| | 600 |

Remember that increases in asset accounts are recorded by debiting the accounts. Decreases in asset accounts are recorded by crediting the accounts. Increases in owner's equity accounts are recorded by crediting the accounts. Decreases in owner's equity accounts are recorded by debiting the accounts.

Check Your Reading

1. Write the word "debit" or "credit" for each of the following to tell on which side of an account each is recorded:
   a. Decrease in a liability
   b. Increase in owner's equity
   c. Increase in an asset
   d. Decrease in owner's equity
   e. Increase in a liability
   f. Decrease in an asset

2. At least how many accounts change with every transaction?

3. On which side of the balance sheet are assets listed? liabilities? owner's equity?

4. If equipment is bought with cash, which accounts are affected? How is each classified (asset, liability, or owner's equity)?

5. In Question 4, which account is debited and which account is credited?

Exercises for Topic 3

1. Open a T account for Cash.
   a. Write the word "debit" on the correct side. Write the word "credit" on the correct side.
   b. Write the word "increase" on the side where increases in assets are recorded. Write the word "decrease" on the side where decreases in assets are recorded.

2. Open a T account for Furniture.
   a. Record $800 in the Furniture account. This is the original cost of several pieces of furniture that the business owns.
   b. One of the original pieces of furniture cost $100. It broke and was thrown away. Record the $100 decrease in the Furniture account.
   c. The business bought more furniture for $300. Record the $300 increase in the Furniture account.

3. Open a T account for Cash.
   a. Record the amount of cash on hand, which is $4,000.
   b. Record a cash payment of $400.
   c. Record a cash payment of $160.
   d. Record a cash receipt of $500.

4. Open a T account for Cash and a T account for Furniture.
   a. Record the amount of cash on hand, which is $3,000.
   b. Record the cost of furniture on hand, which is $1,400.
   c. Record in the two accounts the purchase of a desk for $500.
   d. How much cash is on hand after the purchase? What is the total cost of the furniture on hand?

5. Open a T account for Accts. Pay./Patti Company.
   a. Record the original liability of $650 in the account.
   b. Record a decrease of $200 in the account.
   c. Record an increase of $600 in the account.

6. The balance sheet for the Gomez Company is shown below. Open T accounts for the asset and liability items on the balance sheet. Then record the following transactions in the T accounts. Remember that each transaction causes changes in two accounts.
   a. Bought a table (Furniture) for $275 in cash.
   b. Bought a cash register (Equipment) for $800 on credit from the Nolan Company.
   c. Paid $200 to the Nolan Company.
   d. Bought an adding machine (Equipment) for $315 in cash.

Gomez Company				
Balance Sheet				
June 30, 19—				
Assets		Liabilities		
Cash	4200 00	Accounts Payable:		
Equipment	900 00	Nolan Company		1100 00
Furniture	1400 00			
		Owner's Equity		
		Felipe Gomez, Capital		5400 00
Total	6500 00	Total		6500 00

7. Open a T account for Ethel Bailey, Capital.
   a. Record the original owner's equity of $8,000.
   b. Record a decrease of $775 in owner's equity.
   c. Record an increase of $2,000 in owner's equity.

8. Open T accounts for the asset, liability, and owner's equity items on the balance sheet shown below for José's Machine Shop. Then record the following transactions in the T accounts. Remember that each transaction changes two accounts. (Save your work for Exercise 4, Topic 4.)
   a. Bought new machinery for $1,200 in cash.
   b. Received $250 from Michael Wargo.
   c. Paid $400 to Teresa Mancuso.
   d. Bought machinery for $800 on credit from Teresa Mancuso.
   e. José Gomez invested $1,750 in cash in his business.

José's Machine Shop
Balance Sheet
August 31, 19–

Assets		Liabilities	
Cash	3 400 00	Accounts Payable:	
Accounts Receivable:		Teresa Mancuso	1 600 00
Michael Wargo	950 00		
Machinery	3 150 00	Owner's Equity	
		José Gomez, Capital	5 900 00
Total	7 500 00	Total	7 500 00

TOPIC 4 ◆ ACCOUNT BALANCES

GOALS

1. To pencil-foot T accounts.
2. To compute account balances.
3. To prove debit and credit balances.

KEY TERMS

The *account balance* is the difference between the debits and the credits in an account.

A *debit balance* exists when the total debits are larger than the total credits.

A *credit balance* exists when the total credits are larger than the total debits.

Pencil-footing is writing column totals in small figures at the bottom of each column.

The *account balance* is the difference between the debits and the credits in an account. To find the balance, you total the debits and the credits in the account and subtract the smaller total from the larger total. If the debits are larger, the balance is a *debit* balance. If the credits are larger, the balance is a *credit* balance.

FINDING ACCOUNT BALANCES

The Cash account for the Custom Cleaning Service has a debit balance of $1,135. To find the balance of this account:

Steps in finding an account balance:

1. Add debits and pencil-foot.
2. Add credits and pencil-foot.
3. Subtract smaller amount from larger amount.

1. Add the debits: $1,500 + $600 = $2,100. Write the total ($2,100) in small pencil figures directly under the last entry on the debit side of the account. This process is called *pencil-footing.*

2. Add the credits: $65 + $700 + $200 = $965. Pencil-foot the total ($965) under the last entry.

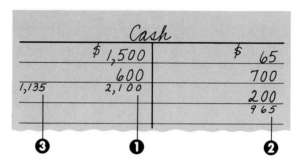

3. To find the account balance, subtract the smaller total from the larger total: $2,100 − $965 = $1,135. The balance is a debit balance because the larger total was on the debit side. Thus it is recorded on the debit side of the account. Write the difference ($1,135) in small pencil figures to the left of the pencil-footing ($2,100).

Note that the account below has a credit balance of $2,400. Since the debit side has only one entry, it is not necessary to pencil-foot this side. The credits total $3,100, as shown by the pencil-footing. To find the account balance ($2,400), subtract the debit amount from the total credits: $3,100 − $700 = $2,400. The balance is a credit balance. Thus it is recorded on the credit side of the account.

PROVING DEBIT AND CREDIT BALANCES

The accounts of the Custom Cleaning Service are pencil-footed and balanced, as shown below:

Debit Balances = Credit Balances

Debit Balances	Credit Balances
$1,135	$2,400
130	3,730
4,400	
465	
$6,130 =	$6,130

Note the result of adding the debit and the credit balances of the accounts: The total debit balances equal the total credit balances. If there are no errors in recording transactions in the accounts, the total of the debit balances will always equal the total of the credit balances.

Total debit balances must always equal total credit balances.

Cash

$ 1,500	$ 65
600	700
1,135 2,100	200
	965

Accts. Pay. / Willis James

	$ 130

Equipment

$ 4,000	
400	
4,400	

Furniture

$ 400	
65	
465	

Accts. Pay. / Hudson, Inc.

$ 700	$ 2,700
	400
2,400	3,100

Hazel Perlman, Capital

$ 200	$ 3,330
	600
3,730	3,930

Check Your Reading

1. What term describes the difference between the debits and credits in an account?

2. What term describes totaling items in accounts in small pencil figures?

3. If the left side of an account has a larger total than the right side, what kind of balance does the account have?

4. If the debit balances and the credit balances of all accounts are added, should total debits equal total credits?

Exercises for Topic 4

1. Draw the Cash account shown here. Enter the amounts that are recorded in the account.
  a. Pencil-foot each side of the account.
  b. Find the balance, and record it in small pencil figures.

Cash		
$2,400		$400
500		275
		525

2. Draw the Accts. Pay./Gem Corporation account shown here. Enter the amounts that are recorded in the account.
  a. Pencil-foot the account.
  b. Find the balance, and record it in small pencil figures.

Accts. Pay. / Gem Corporation		
$210		$400
		300
		715

3. The accounts for the McQueen Company are shown below. Copy the accounts and the entries in the accounts.
  a. Pencil-foot the accounts. Find the balances, and record them in the accounts.
  b. List and total the debit balances. List and total the credit balances. Are the total debit balances and the total credit balances equal?

Cash		
$1,200		$300
100		

Accts. Rec. / Martha Dixes		
$300		

Accts. Rec. / Larry Bauer			*Furniture*	
$200	$100		$1,200	
			500	

Equipment			*Truck*	
$100			$5,200	
350				
200				

Notes Payable			*Accts. Pay. / Wilcox Company*	
$200	$200		$200	$200
	300			350

Accts. Pay. / Ryan Furniture Company			*Irma McQueen, Capital*	
$100	$500			$8,000
100				

4. Use the accounts that you prepared in Exercise 8 of Topic 3 to do the following work:

a. Pencil-foot the accounts. Find the balances, and record them in the accounts.

b. List and total the debit balances. List and total the credit balances. Are the total debit balances and the total credit balances equal?

5. The balance sheet for the Troutdale Repair Shop shows the following asset, liability, and owner's equity items: Cash, $6,000; Equipment, $4,000; Furniture, $900; Accts. Pay./ Furniture Mart, $600; Bret Parson, Capital, $10,300.

a. Open T accounts for these asset, liability, and owner's equity items.

b. Record the following transactions in the accounts:

Bret Parson invested an additional $1,500 in cash.
Bought some work tables for $600 in cash.

Bought equipment for $1,600 in cash.
Paid $300 to the Furniture Mart.
Bought chairs for $250 on credit from the Furniture Mart.

c. Pencil-foot the accounts. Find the balances, and record them in the accounts:

d. List and total the debit balances. List and total the credit balances. Are they equal?

6. The balance sheet for the Lightning Delivery Service shows the following asset, liability, and owner's equity items: Cash, $7,500; Accts. Rec./Sylvia Epps, $300; Trucks, $9,900; Accts. Pay./Ellen's, Inc., $1,500; Laura Lasky, Capital, $16,200.

a. Open T accounts for these asset, liability, and owner's equity items.

b. Record the following transactions in the accounts:

Laura Lasky withdrew $400 in cash from the business.
Received $150 from Sylvia Epps on account.
Sold a used truck for $2,700 in cash.
Paid $800 to Ellen's, Inc.
Laura Lasky invested an additional $1,000 in cash in the business.
Bought a used truck for $6,000 on credit from Ellen's, Inc.

c. Pencil-foot the accounts. Find the balances, and record them in the accounts.

d. List and total the debit balances. List and total the credit balances. Are they equal?

MATH SKILLBUILDER

Skill: Finding account balances.

Sample Problem: Find the balance of the following account:

Cash	
$2,640.00	$600.10
776.50	58.75
2,327.94	

Solution:

1. Total the debit side of the account.

   $2,640.00 + $776.50 + $2,327.94 = $5,744.44

2. Total the credit side of the account.

   $600.10 + $58.75 = $658.85

3. Subtract the smaller total from the larger total. The difference is the balance of the account.

   $5,744.44 − $658.85 = $5,085.59

Answer: Debit balance of $5,085.59

Practice: Find the balance of the following accounts:

1.
Ella Vest, Capital	
$1,229.63	$ 4,506.73
2,472.36	8,774.27
	38,837.16

2.
Mortgage Payable	
$861.55	$94,812.27
429.73	5,624.18
	6,507.33

3.
Accounts Payable/Empire Co.	
$1,649.68	$6,221.50
141.92	898.34
	1,219.00

4.
Accounts Receivable/Cardinal Corp.	
$63,421.92	$37,410.00
8,190.09	30,006.12
17,278.61	1,198.77
34,419.88	

VOCABULARY SKILLBUILDER

Read each of the following statements. From the words below each statement, choose the term that best matches the statement.

1. Recording, summarizing, and analyzing business transactions.

   accounting   debiting   recordkeeping

2. Money on hand and in the bank.

   accounts receivable   cash   credit

3. A record that shows how the assets, liabilities, and owner's equity of a business fit together.

   balance sheet   budget
   income statement

4. The debts of a business.

   assets   liabilities   owner's equity

5. Items of value owned by a business.

   assets   credit   liabilities

6. A long-term debt usually made to pay for a building or property.

   account payable   mortgage payable

7. An amount owed to a business by a customer for goods or services bought on credit.

account receivable   note receivable

8. Assets, liabilities, and owner's equity.

fundamental elements   transactions

9. The difference between a business's assets and liabilities.

accounts receivable   owner's equity

10. A business or a person to whom money is owed.

creditor   debtor   liability

11. The minimum number of accounts that change with each transaction.

none   one   two

12. The right side of an account.

credit   debit   T account

13. When total debits are larger than total credits.

credit balance   debit balance

14. Entries recorded on the credit side of liability accounts.

decreases   increases

15. One type of account that is listed on the right side of the balance sheet.

asset   owner's equity

16. The simplest form of an account.

Cash account   T account

17. Entries recorded on the debit side of liability accounts.

decreases   increases

18. Entries recorded on the debit side of asset accounts.

decreases   increases

19. When total credits are larger than total debits.

credit balance   debit balance

20. The difference between the total debits and total credits in an account.

balance   owner's equity

21. The side on which assets are listed on the balance sheet.

left side   right side.

22. Entries recorded on the credit side of the owner's equity account.

decreases   increases

23. The side on which liabilities are listed on the balance sheet.

left side   right side

24. Entering an amount on the left side of an account.

crediting   debiting

25. A record containing financial information for one item only.

account   balance sheet

26. The left side of an account.

credit side   debit side

27. Entries recorded on the debit side of the owner's equity account.

decreases   increases

28. Recording an amount on the right side of an account.

crediting   debiting

29. Entries recorded on the credit side of asset accounts.

decreases   increases

APPLICATION PROBLEMS

1. Indicate whether each of the balance sheet items that are listed below is an asset, a liability, or an owner's equity item.

   a. Cash

   b. Accts. Pay./Diaz Company

   c. Building

   d. Office Equipment

   e. Accts. Rec./Susan Sullins

   f. Mortgage Payable

   g. Karl Miller, Capital

   h. Notes Payable

2. Complete the following accounting equations.

   Assets = Liabilities + Owner's Equity

   a. $5,900 = $2,000 + ?

   b. $25,000 = $4,600 + ?

   c. $18,650 = $3,410 + ?

3. Prepare a balance sheet for the Drake Health Club, owned by Julie Frayer. Date the balance sheet May 31. The assets and the liabilities of the business are Cash, $7,314; Building, $140,000; Equipment, $39,800; Supplies, $7,345; Accts. Pay./Ames, Inc., $5,400; Mortgage Payable, $117,000; Notes Payable, $18,000.

4. Prepare a balance sheet for the Surfway Golf Range, owned by Esther Dey. Date the balance sheet July 31. The assets and the liabilities of the business are Cash, $3,986; Building, $8,000; Equipment, $91,500; Land, $230,000; Supplies, $4,050; Tractor, $8,760; Accts. Pay./Lester Marx, $4,400; Accts. Pay./Zenith Goods, $1,743; Mortgage Payable, $200,000.

5. For each of the T accounts below, answer the following questions: Which side (debit or credit) is larger? How much larger?

   a.
Cash	
$500.00	$50.00

   b.
Accts. Rec./Bing Company	
$996.20	$445.23

   c.
Equipment	
$14,945.00	$945.80

   d.
Car	
$7,940.50	

   e.
Accts. Pay./R. M. Crandall	
$98.51	$920.43

   f.
Monique Hunt, Capital	
$4,980.50	$12,000.00

   g.
Furniture	
$4,423.00	$918.20

   h.
Accts. Pay./Joanne Nash	
$33.88	$41.73

   i.
Notes Payable	
$800.00	$4,200.00

   j.
Notes Receivable	
$900.00	$213.50

6. The balance sheet for the Fixit Shop is shown on page 436.

   a. Open T accounts for the asset, liability, and owner's equity items on the balance sheet.

The Fixit Shop
Balance Sheet
March 31, 19—

Assets			Liabilities		
Cash	4200	00	Accounts Payable:		
Accounts Receivable:			Sally Smith	700	00
Hector Lopez	400	00			
Machinery	2400	00	Owner's Equity		
			Fred Robbins, Capital	6300	00
Total	7000	00	Total	7000	00

b. List and total the debits and the credits from the accounts. Do the total debits equal the total credits?

7. The balance sheet for the Alpha Company shows the following asset, liability, and owner's equity items: Cash, $19,000; Accts. Rec./Frank Hooks, $400; Accts. Rec./Trudy Brown, $1,000; Equipment, $34,000; Supplies, $7,000; Accts. Pay./Norwood Company, $1,200; Notes Payable, $38,000; Victor Wang, Capital (amount to be determined).

a. Open T accounts for these asset, liability, and owner's equity items. Find and record the amount of the Victor Wang, Capital account.

b. Record the following transactions:

Victor Wang withdrew $200 worth of supplies for his personal use. (This decreased both Supplies and owner's equity.)
Received $600 from Trudy Brown.
Sold used equipment for $800 in cash.
Paid $300 to the Norwood Company.
Received $200 from Frank Hooks.
Victor Wang invested an additional $4,000 in cash in the business.

Paid $6,000 for a note due.
Bought new equipment for $1,800 on credit from the Norwood Company.

c. Pencil-foot the accounts. Find the balances, and record them in the accounts.

d. List and total the debit balances. List and total the credit balances. Are the total debits and credits equal?

8. The balance sheet for the NRV Company shows the following asset, liability, and owner's equity items: Cash, $5,900; Accts. Rec./Robert Bruzzi, $1,050; Equipment, $14,000; Furniture, $5,000; Trucks, $16,750; Accts. Pay./Morley Company, $4,150; Accts. Pay./Gally Furniture, $1,300; Joyce Pace, Capital (amount to be determined).

a. Open T accounts for these asset, liability, and owner's equity items. Find and record the amount of the Joyce Pace, Capital account.

b. Record the following transactions in the accounts:

Paid $200 to Gally Furniture.
Bought new furniture for $600 on credit from Gally Furniture.

Received $450 from Robert Bruzzi.
Joyce Pace withdrew $1,000 in cash from the business.
Paid $2,150 to Morley Company.
Sold used equipment for $1,900 in cash.
Paid $300 to Gally Furniture.
Sold a used truck for $3,600 in cash.

c. Pencil-foot the accounts. Find the balances, and record them in the accounts.

d. List and total the debit and credit balances. Are the total debits and credits equal?

CHAPTER 16

THE GENERAL JOURNAL AND LEDGER ACCOUNTS

In Chapter 15 you recorded changes in balance sheet items by debiting and crediting accounts. In this chapter you will learn how to record such changes, which are called *transactions*, in a journal before they are entered into accounts. A *journal* is a record of all business transactions by date. A journal is important because it provides a daily log of all business transactions.

There are several ways to keep journals. For example, a journal can be kept by a computer or by hand. A journal can be in the form of sheets of paper in a book, a collection of file folders, a computer disk, or a magnetic tape. The journals you will work with will be on sheets of paper that can be kept in a binder.

TOPIC 1 ◆ THE GENERAL JOURNAL

GOALS

1. To name the five column headings of the general journal.
2. To locate and provide information about the Date column, the money columns, and the pages of the general journal.
3. To state three reasons for recording transactions in a journal.
4. To make the opening entry in the general journal.
5. To journalize transactions in a general journal.

KEY TERMS

A *journal* is a record of all business transactions by date.
The *general journal* is the journal most often found in business.
The *opening entry* is the first journal entry to record original balance sheet items.
To *journalize* means to enter information about a transaction in a journal.

There are several kinds of journals, but the journal most often found in business is the *general journal*. The top of a journal page is shown on the following page. Note the following:

1. The title "General Journal" tells the name of the journal.
2. There is a place for the page number of each sheet in the journal. Pages are numbered as they are used.

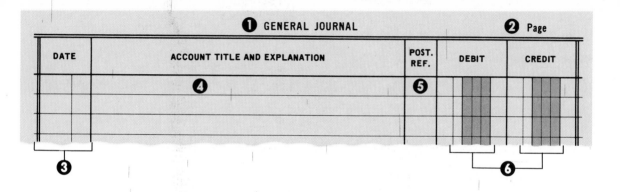

DATE	ACCOUNT TITLE AND EXPLANATION ④	POST. REF. ⑤	DEBIT	CREDIT

③   ⑥

3. The Date column is divided into two sections, one for the month and one for the day.
4. There is an Account Title and Explanation column.
5. There is a Posting Reference (Post. Ref.) column.
6. The Debit and Credit columns are the money columns. They have vertical rules to keep the numbers lined up.

JOURNALIZING PROCEDURE

Beverly Davis, owner of Bev's Craft Corner, bought a $400 type-writer on credit from the Wells Corporation. This transaction caused two changes: (1) The asset Equipment increased and (2) the liability Accts. Pay./Wells Corporation increased. (Remember: To increase an asset, you debit the account. To increase a liability, you credit the account.) Thus the Equipment account must be debited for $400, and the Accts. Pay./Wells Corporation account must be credited for $400. The debits and credits for this transaction are journalized in the general journal.

To *journalize a transaction* means to enter the information about the transaction in a journal. The information comes from a source document. *Source documents* are the original records of transactions. Examples of source documents are sales slips, invoices, receipt copies, and check stubs. The record of a transaction in a journal is called an *entry*. The entry shown on the following page was made in the general journal to record the purchase of the typewriter. The invoice shown with it is the source document of the transaction.

Note the following about the general journal entry:

Journalizing means entering the information about a transaction in a journal.

Source documents include sales slips, cash register tapes, purchase orders, check stubs, and time cards.

An *entry* is a record of a transaction in a journal.

1. The year is entered on the first line. It is written in small figures at the top of the left section of the Date column. The month and day are also entered on the first line. The month is

Wells Corporation

650 Briggs Avenue
Jacksonville, Florida 33207

SOLD TO: Bev's Craft Corner
29 West Main Street
Nashville, TN 37205

REC'D FEB 3

DATE Jan. 28, 19--
ORDER NO. 213

INVOICE NO. 1106
TERMS n/30

QUANTITY	STOCK NO.	DESCRIPTION	UNIT PRICE	AMOUNT
1	27-P12	Office Master Electronic Typewriter	400.00	400.00

GENERAL JOURNAL   Page 2

DATE	ACCOUNT TITLE AND EXPLANATION	POST. REF.	DEBIT	CREDIT
Feb. 3	Equipment ❷	❺	400 00	
	Accts. Pay./Wells Corporation ❸			400 00
	❹ Bought new typewriter.			

❶

Steps in journalizing:
1. Record the date.
2. Record the debit.
3. Record the credit.
4. Record the explanation.

abbreviated. The year is entered only once on a page—at the top of the page—unless the year changes. The month is also entered only once on a page unless the month changes. The day is recorded once for each transaction.

2. The account to be debited is always entered first. Looking at the invoice, the accounting clerk sees that a typewriter has been purchased. Typewriters are equipment, and equipment is an asset. Since Bev's Craft Corner now has more equipment, assets increase. To increase assets, debit the account. The title of the account is entered in the Account Title and Explanation column on the same line as the date. In this case, the account title is Equipment. The debit amount ($400) is entered in the Debit column.

3. The account to be credited is entered next. Again looking at the invoice, the accounting clerk sees that it is from the Wells Corporation. Bev's Craft Corner has bought the typewriter on credit from the Wells Corporation. Thus Bev's Craft Corner will owe $400 to the Wells Corporation. This transaction increases a liability, Accts. Pay./Wells Corporation. To increase a liability, credit the account. The title of the account credited is entered on the line following the debit. Note that the day is not repeated. The title of the account to be credited is indented under the title of the account debited. In this case, the title of the account to be credited is Accts. Pay./Wells Corporation. The credit amount ($400) is entered in the Credit column. Note that the debit amount and the credit amount are equal. In every transaction recorded in a journal, the total debits and the total credits must be equal.

4. An explanation of the transaction is indented on the line below the credit in the Account Title and Explanation column.

5. The Posting Reference column is not used in journalizing. It is used during the posting procedure, which will be explained in Topic 2.

There are several reasons for recording transactions in a journal:

- ◆ The journal shows you the order of transactions by date.
- ◆ The journal shows you the debit and the credit for each transaction together. (The debit and the credit for each transaction are recorded separately in the accounts.) By recording the debit and the credit together, you can easily see from the journal entry that debits and credits are equal.
- ◆ The journal entry gives you more information about a transaction than an account entry does. The explanation for each journal entry gives you extra information.

Reasons for journalizing:
1. Provides a daily record of transactions.
2. Provides both the debit and the credit for each transaction.
3. Provides an explanation of each transaction.

JOURNALIZING THE OPENING ENTRY

The first entry in a general journal is an entry to record the original balance sheet items—assets, liabilities, and owner's equity. This entry is called the *opening entry*. The balance sheet for Bev's Craft Corner on February 1 is shown below.

Bev's Craft Corner
Balance Sheet
February 1, 19—

Assets ❶		Liabilities	
Cash	1000 00	Accounts Payable:	
Accounts Receivable:		Wells Corporation ❷	100 00
Michael Gallo	50 00		
Equipment	300 00	Owner's Equity	
Furniture	800 00	Beverly Davis, Capital	2050 00
Total	2150 00	Total	2150 00

		GENERAL JOURNAL			Page
DATE		ACCOUNT TITLE AND EXPLANATION	POST. REF.	DEBIT	CREDIT
Feb.	1	Cash		1000 00	
		Accts. Rec./Michael Gallo		50 00	
❶		Equipment		300 00	
		Furniture		800 00	
❷		Accts. Pay./Wells Corporation			100 00
		Beverly Davis, Capital			2050 00
❸		To record Feb. 1, 19—, balance sheet amounts.			

Note the following about the opening entry:

1. The asset accounts shown on the balance sheet are recorded together in the journal. The amounts of all asset accounts are entered in the Debit column.
2. The liability and the owner's equity accounts shown on the balance sheet are also recorded together in the journal. The amounts of these accounts are entered in the Credit column.
3. The explanation is indented below the title of the last account credited. It gives information about the opening entry.

In the opening entry for Bev's Craft Corner, the total of the debit amounts equals the total of the credit amounts. The accounting clerk cannot tell just by looking at the entry that the total debits equal the total credits. The clerk adds the amounts on a separate sheet of paper or on a calculator.

JOURNALIZING TRANSACTIONS

The accounting clerk for Bev's Craft Corner has recorded the following transactions in the general journal during the first week of February:

	GENERAL JOURNAL				Page 2
DATE	**ACCOUNT TITLE AND EXPLANATION**	**POST. REF.**	**DEBIT**	**CREDIT**	
❶ Feb. 3	Equipment		400 00		
	Accts. Pay./Wells Corporation			400 00	
	Bought new typewriter.				
❷ 4	Furniture		200 00		
	Accts. Pay./Desk-O-Rama			200 00	
	Bought desk.				
❸ 6	Accts. Pay./Desk-O-Rama		200 00		
	Cash			200 00	
	Paid on account.				

Note the following:

1. The first entry records the purchase of a new typewriter for $400 on credit from the Wells Corporation on February 3.
2. The February 4 entry records the purchase of a $200 desk on credit from Desk-O-Rama. This transaction increased the asset Furniture and increased the liability Accts. Pay./Desk-O-Rama.

Thus the Furniture account was debited for $200, and Accts. Pay./Desk-O-Rama was credited for $200.

3. The February 6 entry records a cash payment of $200 on account to Desk-O-Rama. This transaction decreased the liability Accts. Pay./Desk-O-Rama and decreased the asset Cash. Thus Accts. Pay./Desk-O-Rama was debited for $200, and Cash was credited for $200.

Check Your Reading

1. Name the five column headings of the general journal.

2. Why does the Date column in the general journal have two sections?

3. How many spaces are there for numbers in each of e money columns of the general journal?

4. How are pages numbered in the general journal?

5. Look at the general journal entry shown on page 440.
   a. What account was debited? How do you know?
   b. Is the account that was debited an asset, a liability, or an owner's equity account?
   c. Does the debit represent an increase or a decrease in the account?
   d. What account was credited? How do you know?
   e. Is the account that was credited an asset, a liability, or an owner's equity account?
   f. Does the credit represent an increase or a decrease in the account?

6. If a company pays cash for a new desk, which asset increases and which asset decreases?

7. If the asset Furniture increases, do you debit the Furniture account?

8. If the asset Cash decreases, do you debit the Cash account?

9. If a liability decreases, do you debit the liability account?

10. Is an account payable an asset or a liability?

Exercises for Topic I

1. Journalize the following transactions in a general journal:

   Mar. 2 Bought a new typewriter for $815 on credit from Office Supplies, Inc. (Office Equipment and Accts. Pay./Office Supplies, Inc.).

3 Bought a chair for $115 on credit from the Simmons Furniture Company (Furniture and Accts. Pay./Simmons Furniture Company).

2. The balance sheet for Marty's Plumbing, Inc., is shown below. Make the opening entry in the general journal. Use the date of the balance sheet as the date of the opening entry.

Marty's Plumbing, Inc.
Balance Sheet
March 1, 19—

Assets		Liabilities	
Cash	3000 00	Accounts Payable:	
Equipment	700 00	Ace Machine Company	600 00
Furniture	1400 00		
		Owner's Equity	
		Marty Haskett, Capital	4500 00
Total	5100 00	Total	5100 00

3. The balance sheet for the Custom Cleaning Service is shown on page 415. Make the opening entry for the business in the general journal. Use the date of the balance sheet as the opening entry date.

4. The balance sheet for Copy King is shown below.

Copy King
Balance Sheet
February 1, 19 —

Assets		Liabilities	
Cash	900 00	Accounts Payable:	
Accounts Receivable:		Brown Company $1,500.00	
Marge Simeri	50 00	City Garage 30.00	1530 00
Machinery	3000 00	Total Liabilities	1530 00
Office Supplies	100 00		
Truck	1600 00	Owner's Equity	
		Bruce Fell, Capital	4120 00
Total	5650 00	Total	5650 00

a. Make the opening entry in the general journal.

b. Journalize the following in the general journal:

> Feb. 2 Bought a new $1,000 copying machine on credit from the Brown Company.
>
> 5 Paid $30 on account to City Garage.
>
> 7 Returned the new copying machine bought on February 2 to the Brown Company because machine did not work properly.

5. Journalize the following transactions for the Mesa Company in a general journal. Use these account titles: Office Equipment, Store Equipment, Accts. Pay./Austin Company, Accts. Pay./Bianco Company, and Rita Mesa, Capital.

> May 1 Bought shelves costing $300 on credit from the Austin Company. (Shelves for the store are Store Equipment.)
>
> 2 Paid $300 to the Austin Company on account.
>
> 3 Rita Mesa, the owner, took an old adding machine for her personal use. The adding machine cost $175. (This transaction decreased the asset Office Equipment and decreased the owner's equity account Rita Mesa, Capital.)
>
> 4 Bought a file cabinet for $175 on credit from the Bianco Company.
>
> 5 Rita Mesa brought a typewriter from her home to use in the business. The typewriter cost $400. (This transaction increased the asset Office Equipment and the owner's equity account Rita Mesa, Capital.)

TOPIC 2 ◆ LEDGER ACCOUNTS AND POSTING

GOALS

1. To explain the use and purpose of columns and data on a ledger account.

2. To identify a given numbered account as an asset, a liability, or an owner's equity account.

3. To post entries from the general journal to ledger accounts.

KEY TERMS

A *ledger* is a record of all transactions by account.

A *ledger account* is a record of transactions for one asset, liability, or owner's equity item that is kept in a ledger.

A *chart of accounts* is a list of the titles and numbers of a business's accounts.

Posting means transferring information from the journal to the ledger accounts.

Review the accounting practices you have learned:

Accounting equation:
Assets = Liabilities +
Owner's Equity.

- ♦ When a business is started, a balance sheet is prepared according to the accounting equation: Assets = Liabilities + Owner's Equity. Assets are listed on the left side of the balance sheet. Liabilities and owner's equity are listed on the right side of the balance sheet.
- ♦ The assets, liabilities, and owner's equity shown on the balance sheet are recorded in the general journal. This entry is called the *opening entry.*
- ♦ As business transactions occur, changes take place in assets, liabilities, and owner's equity. The transactions are entered in the general journal to record the changes.

Accounts kept
in file folders.

Binder for ledger accounts.

LEDGER ACCOUNTS

Computer disks for keeping
accounts.

There is a ledger account for every item on the balance sheet. The ledger accounts are very much like the T accounts discussed in Chapter 15. They are called *ledger accounts* because they are kept in a ledger. A *ledger* is a record of all transactions by account. Just as there are many ways to keep journals, there are many ways to keep ledgers. A ledger can be kept by hand or by computer. A ledger may be pages of accounts in a book. A ledger can also be a collection of file folders, a computer disk, or a magnetic tape. A ledger account may have two sides, like a T account, or it may have special debit and credit columns. A ledger is important because it provides information about everything that happened in any account. The ledger accounts you will work with will be pages that can be kept in a binder.

The ledger accounts you will use do not have left and right sides like T accounts. Instead, the kind of ledger account you will use has special columns for debits, credits, and balances as shown on the next page. This is called the *balance ledger* form because it always shows the balance of the account.

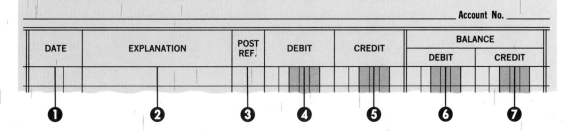

DATE	EXPLANATION	POST REF.	DEBIT	CREDIT	BALANCE	
					DEBIT	CREDIT

Account No. _____

①②③④⑤⑥⑦

Note the following about the ledger account:

1. The first column of the ledger account is the Date column.
2. The second column of the ledger account is the Explanation column. When an entry requires an explanation, the explanation is recorded in this column. For most entries, however, the Explanation column is left blank.
3. The third column of the ledger account is the Posting Reference column. This column is explained later.
4. The fourth column is the Debit column. The amount of each debit is entered in the Debit column.
5. The fifth column is the Credit column. The amount of each credit is entered in the Credit column.
6. The sixth column is the Debit Balance column. If an account has a debit balance after a transaction is posted, the balance is recorded in this column.
7. The seventh column is the Credit Balance column. If an account has a credit balance after a transaction is posted, the balance is recorded in this column.

The title of an account, such as Cash or Equipment, is centered at the top of the form when the account is opened. The number of the account is written to the right of the words "Account No."

ACCOUNT TITLES AND NUMBERS

The titles and numbers of a business's accounts are listed on a chart of accounts. The numbers are assigned according to a system. In the system used by Bev's Craft Corner and many other businesses, each account has a three-digit number. The first digit of each account number shows the type of account. The first digit of asset accounts is 1; of liability accounts, 2; of owner's equity accounts, 3. The next two digits of each account number stand for the order of the account within its group. For example, the number of the first asset account is 101. The number of the first liability account is 201. The number of the first owner's equity account is 301.

Gaps are left in the sequence of numbers. In this way, new accounts can easily be added and numbered as the business grows. For example, the next asset account after 101 may be 107. Five more accounts could then be added at a later date—102, 103, 104, 105, and 106.

POSTING

Transferring information from the journal to the ledger accounts is called *posting*. Posting may be done every day, every week, or at other times, depending on the needs of the business.

The general journal below shows the opening entry of Bev's Craft Corner. The ledger page below it shows the Cash account after the opening entry has been posted.

Look at the journal and ledger pages as you study these steps in the posting process:

1. The year, the month, and the day (Feb. 1, 19—) are entered in the Date column of the account. The year and the month are not repeated for other entries unless the month changes or a new page is started.

2. An explanation, if needed, is written in the Explanation column. In this case, the words "Opening entry" are written. This

explanation keeps the opening balance of the account separate from the amounts posted to the account later.

3. The abbreviation and the page number of the journal from which the data is posted are entered in the Posting Reference column of the account. In this case, the letter "J" and the page number "1" are entered in the Posting Reference column of the Cash account. The J stands for general journal.

4. The amount is entered in either the Debit or the Credit column. In this case, $1,000 is entered in the Debit column because the amount came from the Debit column of the journal.

5. The account balance is determined and then recorded in either the Debit Balance column or the Credit Balance column. In this case, because the account contains a single debit entry of $1,000, it has a debit balance of $1,000. This figure is written in the Debit Balance column. A new balance is calculated after each posting.

6. The number of the ledger account to which the entry was posted is entered in the Posting Reference column of the general journal. In this case, the number of the Cash account (101) is entered in the Posting Reference column.

These steps are followed in posting all debit entries from the general journal. The same steps are followed in posting credit entries from the general journal except that the credit column of the ledger account is used. The ledger account for Accts. Pay./Wells Corporation shows how a credit entry is posted.

Accts. Pay./Wells Corporation   Account No. 221

| DATE | EXPLANATION | POST REF. | DEBIT | CREDIT | BALANCE | |
					DEBIT	CREDIT
Feb 1	Opening entry	J1		100 00		100 00

As additional entries are posted, the balance of the account is refigured, as shown below.

Accts. Pay./Wells Corp.   Account No. 221

| DATE | EXPLANATION | POST REF. | DEBIT | CREDIT | BALANCE | |
					DEBIT	CREDIT
Feb 1	Opening entry	J1		100 00		100 00
2	Invoice 231	J1		400 00		500 00
3	Check 301	J1	200 00			300 00

In the example above:

1. The first balance is $100, the opening entry.

2. The next balance is $500, found by adding the second entry of $400 to the balance in line 1.
3. The next balance is $300, found by subtracting the debit entry of $200 from the balance in line 2.

Check Your Reading

1. Where is the title of a ledger account written?

2. Give an example of an account title.

3. Where is the number of a ledger account written?

4. To answer the following questions, refer to the system for numbering accounts explained in this topic.
   a. If an account is numbered 201, is it an asset, a liability, or an owner's equity account?
   b. If an account is numbered 301, is it an asset, a liability, or an owner's equity account?
   c. Which digit(s) tell you the order of the account within its group?
   d. Why are gaps left in the sequence of account numbers?

5. What term means transferring information from the journal to the ledger accounts?

Exercises for Topic 2

1. Post the opening entry from the general journal shown on page 448 to the ledger accounts listed below.

Account Title	Account Number
Cash	101
Accts. Rec./Michael Gallo	111
Equipment	141
Furniture	151
Accts. Pay./Wells Corporation	221
Beverly Davis, Capital	301

2. Post the opening entry for Quail's Delivery Service from the general journal shown on the following page to the ledger accounts. The accounts are numbered as follows:

Account Title	Account Number
Cash	101
Office Furniture	131
Office Machines	141
Truck	151
Accts. Pay./Lawford's, Inc.	211
Accts. Pay./Fernandez Company	212
Robert Quail, Capital	301

GENERAL JOURNAL   Page 1

DATE	ACCOUNT TITLE AND EXPLANATION	POST. REF.	DEBIT	CREDIT
July 1 19—	Cash		2400 00	
	Office Furniture		1100 00	
	Office Machines		1840 00	
	Truck		5200 00	
	Accts. Pay./Lawford's, Inc.			1800 00
	Accts. Pay./Fernandez Company			1240 00
	Robert Quail, Capital			7500 00
	To record July 1, 19—, balance sheet amounts.			

3. Assume that you work for the Village Service Station.
   a. Make the opening entry in the general journal to record the assets, liabilities, and owner's equity shown on the balance sheet below.

Village Service Station
Balance Sheet
January 1, 19—

Assets		Liabilities		
Cash	1960 00	Accounts Payable:		
Office Furniture	1350 00	Bidwell Motors	$1,150.00	
Office Machines	900 00	O'Brien Company	2,160.00	
Truck	4900 00	Total Liabilities		3310 00
		Owner's Equity		
		Phyllis Fowlkes, Capital		5800 00
Total	9110 00	Total		9110 00

b. Post the opening entry from the general journal to the ledger accounts. The accounts are numbered as follows:

Account Title	Account Number
Cash	101
Office Furniture	111
Office Machines	121
Truck	131
Accts. Pay./Bidwell Motors	201
Accts. Pay./O'Brien Company	211
Phyllis Fowlkes, Capital	301

c. Journalize the following transactions in the general journal, and post them to the ledger accounts:

Jan. 3 Bought a used truck on credit for $3,000 from Bidwell Motors.

4 Paid $700 to the O'Brien Company on account.

9 Paid $500 to Bidwell Motors on account.

Accts. Pay. / Darrow Corp. Account No. 222

DATE		EXPLANATION	POST REF.	DEBIT	CREDIT	BALANCE	
						DEBIT	CREDIT
Feb.	1	Opening entry	J1		700 00		700 00
	2	Invoice 579	J1		650 00		1350 00
	5	Check 101	J1	700 00			650 00
	6	Credit Memo CM-6	J1	200 00			450 00

The above shows ledger account postings and balances. Study it to see how each new posting must be added to or subtracted from the previous balance to obtain a new balance.

For the following ledger accounts, find the balance after each posting. Do not write your answers in the textbook.

1.

Accts. Pay. / Able Corp. Account No. 223

DATE		EXPLANATION	POST REF.	DEBIT	CREDIT	BALANCE	
						DEBIT	CREDIT
Mar.¹⁹⁻	1	Opening entry	J1				950 00
	2	Check 203	J1	450 00			
	3	Check 205	J1	500 00			
	5	Invoice 6221	J1		275 00		

2.

Accts. Pay. / Baker Corp. Account No. 224

DATE		EXPLANATION	POST REF.	DEBIT	CREDIT	BALANCE	
						DEBIT	CREDIT
Mar.¹⁹⁻	1	Opening entry	J1		500 00		
	2	Check 204	J1	500 00			
	3	Invoice 7101	J1		320 00		

3.

Accts. Pay. / Delta, Inc. _____ Account No. 225

DATE		EXPLANATION	POST REF.	DEBIT	CREDIT	BALANCE	
						DEBIT	CREDIT
Mar.¹⁹⁻	1	Opening entry	J1		100 00		
	2	Invoice 921	J1		1250 00		
	3	Credit memo	J1	400 00			
	5	Check 206	J1	850 00			

VOCABULARY SKILLBUILDER

Read each of the following statements. From the words below each statement, choose the term that best matches the statement.

1. The journal most frequently found in business.

   general journal   sales journal

2. Entering the information about a transaction in the journal.

   journalizing   posting

3. The amount recorded first in a journal entry.

   credit   debit   liability

4. The record of a transaction in a journal.

   credit   debit   entry

5. The entry to record the original balance sheet items.

   memorandum entry   opening entry

6. Sales slips, sales invoices, receipt copies, purchase invoices, check stubs, and time cards.

   entries   source documents

7. A record of all business transactions by date.

   balance sheet   journal

8. Accounts kept in a ledger.

   ledger accounts   T accounts

9. The first column of a ledger account.

   Date   Debit   Explanation

10. Transferring information from the journal to the ledger.

    closing   journalizing   posting

11. Titles and numbers of a business's accounts.

    chart of accounts   journal

12. A record of all transactions by account.

    account   journal   ledger

1. The balance sheet for the Grant Realty Company is shown below. Make the opening entry in the general journal.

Grant Realty Company
Balance Sheet
August 1, 19—

Assets		Liabilities	
Cash	2 160 00	Notes Payable	2 000 00
Accounts Receivable:		Accounts Payable:	
Cynthia Wong	800 00	William Clark	500 00
Office Equipment	1 500 00	Total Liabilities	2 500 00
Office Supplies	375 00		
Truck	3 000 00	Owner's Equity	
		David Grant, Capital	5 335 00
Total	7 835 00	Total	7 835 00

2. Post the opening entry that you made in Problem I to the ledger accounts. The accounts are numbered as follows:

Account Title	Account Number
Cash	101
Accts. Rec./Cynthia Wong	111
Office Equipment	131
Office Supplies	141
Truck	151
Notes Payable	201
Accts. Pay./William Clark	211
David Grant, Capital	301

3. Journalize the following transactions in the general journal of the Grant Realty Company.

Aug. 3 Received $300 on account from Cynthia Wong.
4 Paid $250 on account to William Clark.
5 The owner, David Grant, withdrew $500 in cash from the business.
6 David Grant withdrew $25 of office supplies for his personal use.
6 Gave a promissory note for $2,850 in exchange for a used truck for the business.

4. Post the entries that you made in Problem 3 from the general journal to the ledger accounts.

CHAPTER 17

SPECIAL JOURNALS: PURCHASES AND CASH PAYMENTS

In addition to the general journal discussed in Chapter 16, many businesses also use special journals. A *special journal* is used only for one type of transaction. In this chapter, you will learn how to use two kinds of special journals: the *purchases journal* and the *cash payments journal.*

The use of special journals makes journalizing and posting easier. For example, if a business uses a purchases journal, only one line is needed to enter each purchase. This is easier than recording purchases in the general journal, where at least three lines are needed for each entry. Also, the debits are not posted individually when a purchases journal is used. At the end of the month the debits are totaled, and the total is then posted to the Purchases account.

TOPIC I ◆ JOURNALIZING AND POSTING PURCHASES

GOALS

1. To journalize credit purchases in a purchases journal.
2. To post entries from a purchases journal to ledger accounts.
3. To pencil-foot, total, and rule a purchases journal.
4. To journalize purchases returns and allowances.

KEY TERMS

A *purchases journal* is a special journal used only for purchases of merchandise on credit.

The *Purchases account* is a temporary owner's equity account that is used to record all purchases of merchandise that a business makes.

A *purchase return* is merchandise returned by a business.

A *purchase allowance* is merchandise kept by a business for a lower price.

To be recorded in the purchases journal, a transaction must meet both of these tests:

1. The transaction must be a purchase on credit, not for cash.
2. The transaction must be a purchase of goods for resale.

Merchandise for resale includes all goods that a business buys to sell.

Goods that a business buys and intends to sell are called *merchandise for resale.* If a business purchases a typewriter for office

Checking invoices is an important part of the recordkeeping at Bev's Craft Corner.

use, the typewriter is not merchandise for resale. However, if the business buys 200 oil paint kits to sell to someone else, the oil paint kits are merchandise for resale.

A purchase is journalized when the invoice is received from the supplier. On September 25 Bev's Craft Corner bought needle-point kits for $500 on credit from Hobbies, Inc. On October 1 Bev's Craft Corner received an invoice for the merchandise. After Beverly Davis, the owner, checked the invoice, she gave it to the accounting clerk. The accounting clerk used the data on the invoice to journalize the purchase.

If the accounting clerk had recorded the invoice in a general journal, the entry would appear as shown below.

	GENERAL JOURNAL				Page 2
DATE	ACCOUNT TITLE AND EXPLANATION	POST. REF.	DEBIT	CREDIT	
Oct. 19— 1	Purchases		500 00		
	Accts. Pay./Hobbies, Inc.			500 00	
	Invoice B147 for merchandise				
	purchased on credit.				

Note that the date the invoice was received is the date used in journalizing the purchase. The Purchases account is debited, and the liability Accts. Pay./Hobbies, Inc. is credited.

Since Bev's Craft Corner makes a great many purchases of merchandise on credit, the business uses a purchases journal.

The invoice received from Hobbies, Inc., on October 1 was recorded in the purchases journal shown here:

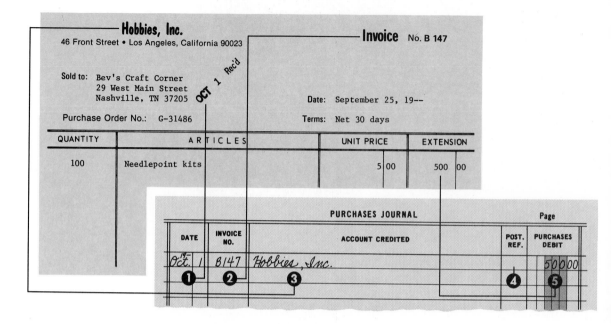

Note the following about this entry in the purchases journal:

1. The date the invoice was received is entered in the Date column.
2. The invoice number is entered in the Invoice Number column.
3. The name of the business from which the purchase was made is entered in the Account Credited column. Note that the abbreviation "Accts. Pay." is not used before the name of the creditor because every entry in the purchases journal is credited to an account payable. Thus only the name of the creditor is written.
4. The Posting Reference column is left blank. It will be used when the entry is posted.
5. The amount of the invoice is entered in the Purchases Debit column.

Each entry in the purchases journal is credited to an account payable.

Compare the entry in the general journal on page 457 with the entry in the purchases journal. Both entries are for the same invoice. But the accounting clerk wrote only one line to record the entry in the purchases journal, instead of four lines in the general journal.

Here is how other purchases of merchandise on credit are recorded in the purchases journal of Bev's Craft Corner. It is important that the date, invoice number, account, and amount to be checked are accurate.

DATE	INVOICE NO.	ACCOUNT CREDITED	POST. REF.	PURCHASES DEBIT
Oct. 1	B147	Hobbies, Inc.		500 00
8	B263	Hobbies, Inc.		160 00
28	4172	Monarch Wholesalers		112 40
31	3-84L	Rainbow Art Supplies, Inc.		31 18

POSTING FROM THE PURCHASES JOURNAL

Bev's Craft Corner purchases merchandise for resale on credit from three suppliers. They are Hobbies, Inc., Monarch Wholesalers, and Rainbow Art Supplies, Inc. A ledger account is kept for each creditor. After an invoice is recorded in the purchases journal, the entry is posted as a credit to the creditor's account in the ledger. Postings to the creditors' accounts are usually made daily so that the amount owed to each creditor is always known. At the end of the month, all the debits in the purchases journal are totaled. The total is posted as one amount to the Purchases account.

Postings to creditors' accounts are made daily. The debit to the Purchases account is posted at the end of the month.

DAILY POSTING

The accounting clerk for Bev's Craft Corner posted the October 1 entry from the purchases journal to the Accts. Pay./Hobbies, Inc. account as shown below.

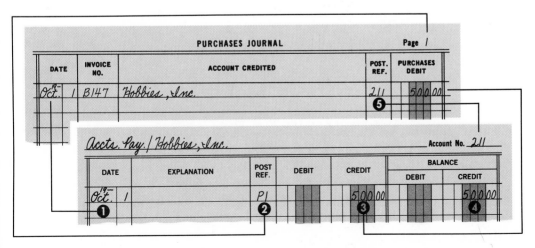

Note the following about the posting to the Accts. Pay./ Hobbies, Inc. account:

1. The date is entered in the Date column.
2. The letter "P," which stands for the purchases journal, and the page number "1" are entered in the Posting Reference column.
3. The amount of the purchase is entered in the Credit column.
4. The amount of the account balance is written in the Credit Balance column.
5. The number of the Accts. Pay./Hobbies, Inc. account (211) is entered in the Posting Reference column of the purchases journal on the line where the entry for Invoice B147 appears. This shows that the posting of the entry is finished. It is the last step in the daily posting procedure.

END-OF-MONTH POSTING

At the end of the month, the purchases journal is totaled and ruled. Then the accounting clerk posts the purchases for the month to the Purchases account. The total debit amount, rather than the individual debits, is posted at this time. If there were 20 purchases on credit during the month, only 1 posting would be made, instead of 20 postings.

A *temporary account* is used to gather information for only one period of time.

The Purchases account is a temporary owner's equity account. *Temporary accounts* are accounts that are used to gather information for only one period of time, such as a year. At the end of the period, the balance of each temporary account is reduced to zero by transferring it to another account. Then the temporary account is reopened so that it can be used to gather information for the new period.

The Purchases account is debited for merchandise purchased.

The cost of merchandise recorded in the Purchases account decreases owner's equity until the merchandise is sold. Therefore, the purchase of merchandise is debited to the Purchases account.

The purchases journal and the Purchases account of Bev's Craft Corner are shown on the following page. Look at these illustrations as you study the following steps for posting from the purchases journal to the Purchases account:

1. On the last day of the month, the purchases journal is pencil-footed and totaled. The date is entered, and "Purchases Debit" is written in the Account Credited column. A double rule is drawn under all columns of the purchases journal except the Invoice Number column and the Account Credited column.

PURCHASES JOURNAL — Page 1

DATE	INVOICE NO.	ACCOUNT CREDITED	POST. REF.	PURCHASES DEBIT
Oct. 19— 1	B147	Hobbies, Inc.	211	500 00
8	B263	Hobbies, Inc.	211	160 00
28	4172	Monarch Wholesalers	212	112 40
31	3-84L	Rainbow Art Supplies, Inc.	213	31 18
31	4893	Monarch Wholesalers	212	85 14
31	3-10R	Rainbow Art Supplies, Inc.	213	137 87
31		Purchases Debit	501	1026 59

Purchases — Account No. 501

DATE	EXPLANATION	POST REF.	DEBIT	CREDIT	BALANCE DEBIT	BALANCE CREDIT
Oct. 19— 31		P1	1026 59		1026 59	

2. The date is entered in the Date column of the Purchases account.
3. The abbreviation "P1" is entered in the Posting Reference column of the Purchases account to show that the information has been posted from page 1 of the purchases journal.
4. The total of the Purchases Debit column of the purchases journal is entered in the Debit column of the Purchases account.
5. The account balance is written in the Debit Balance column.
6. The number of the Purchases account (501) is entered in the Posting Reference column of the purchases journal. It is written on the same line as the total of the Purchases Debit column. This is the last step in the end-of-month posting procedure.

PURCHASES RETURNS AND ALLOWANCES

Sometimes merchandise arrives in a damaged condition. Sometimes merchandise is unsatisfactory for other reasons. Perhaps the merchandise is the wrong color or the wrong size. In such cases the business can (1) return the merchandise or (2) keep the merchandise and get a reduction in the price. If the business returns the merchandise, the return is called a *purchase return*. If the business keeps the merchandise for a lower price, the price reduction is called a *purchase allowance*. In either case a credit memo will be issued.

Bev's Craft Corner returned the needlepoint kits that it ordered from Hobbies, Inc. The invoice for the order is shown on page 458. Hobbies, Inc., sent a credit memo to Bev's Craft Corner. A *credit memo* shows how much credit has been given for a return or an allowance.

A *credit memo* is a record showing how much credit has been given for a return or an allowance.

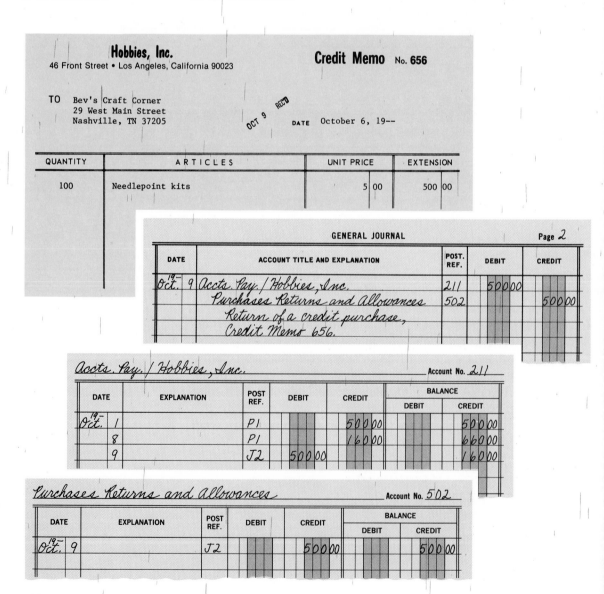

Hobbies, Inc.
46 Front Street • Los Angeles, California 90023

Credit Memo No. 656

TO Bev's Craft Corner
29 West Main Street
Nashville, TN 37205

OCT 9 REC'D

DATE October 6, 19—

QUANTITY	ARTICLES	UNIT PRICE	EXTENSION
100	Needlepoint kits	5 00	500 00

GENERAL JOURNAL Page 2

DATE	ACCOUNT TITLE AND EXPLANATION	POST. REF.	DEBIT	CREDIT
Oct. 9	Accts. Pay./ Hobbies, Inc.	211	500 00	
	Purchases Returns and Allowances	502		500 00
	Return of a credit purchase,			
	Credit Memo 656.			

Accts. Pay./ Hobbies, Inc.   Account No. 211

DATE	EXPLANATION	POST REF.	DEBIT	CREDIT	BALANCE DEBIT	BALANCE CREDIT
Oct. 1		P1		500 00		500 00
8		P1		160 00		660 00
9		J2	500 00			160 00

Purchases Returns and Allowances   Account No. 502

DATE	EXPLANATION	POST REF.	DEBIT	CREDIT	BALANCE DEBIT	BALANCE CREDIT
Oct. 9		J2		500 00		500 00

The accounting clerk for Bev's Craft Corner uses the data on the credit memo from Hobbies, Inc., to make an entry in the general journal to record the return of the merchandise. Note the following about the credit memo, the general journal entry, and the postings to the accounts shown on page 462:

- The date the credit memo was received is the date used in journalizing the return.
- The liability account, Accts. Pay./Hobbies, Inc., is decreased because Bev's Craft Corner now owes $500 less to Hobbies, Inc. Thus the account is debited for $500.
- Owner's equity is increased by the return. Thus a temporary owner's equity account called *Purchases Returns and Allowances* is credited for $500. Note that although the return results in a decrease in the amount of purchases, it is not credited to the Purchases account. Bev's Craft Corner records its purchases returns and allowances in a separate account.
- The debit from the general journal entry is posted to the Accts. Pay./Hobbies, Inc. account. The credit is posted to the Purchases Returns and Allowances account.

The *Purchases Returns and Allowances* account is a temporary owner's equity account.

The Purchases Returns and Allowances account is used to record purchase allowances as well as purchase returns. A purchase allowance is recorded in the same way as a purchase return.

Check Your Reading

1. What kinds of journals are the purchases journal and the cash payments journal?

2. Are debits posted individually from a purchases journal?

3. Are credits posted individually from a purchases journal?

4. Would a purchases journal be used to record the purchase on credit of a new desk for office use?

5. Would a purchases journal be used to record the purchase of merchandise for cash?

6. When a business returns merchandise to the seller, does the business receive a purchase allowance?

7. Would a purchases journal be used to record the purchase of merchandise on credit?

1. Journalize the following purchases of the Stokes Supply Company in a purchases journal. The date given is the date the invoice was received.

June 1 Purchased merchandise on credit for $165.90 from Howard Lumber, Invoice 4193-2.
      2 Purchased merchandise on credit for $95.32 from the Martinez Company, Invoice 32-101.
      4 Purchased merchandise on credit for $55.87 from the Keno Corporation, Invoice J2830.
      6 Purchased merchandise on credit for $232 from the Simms Corporation, Invoice 91-43E.
      9 Purchased merchandise on credit for $67.78 from the Ruiz Hardware Company, Invoice 27146.
      10 Purchased merchandise on credit for $39.29 from Hanley Wholesalers, Invoice 34-176.
      11 Purchased merchandise on credit for $98.75 from Howard Lumber, Invoice 4875-3.
      12 Purchased merchandise on credit for $175.50 from the Simms Corporation, Invoice 91-57M.
      12 Purchased merchandise on credit for $145.85 from the Sutton Company, Invoice 0017-C.
      13 Purchased merchandise on credit for $71.43 from the Ruiz Hardware Company, Invoice 27507.

2. Refer to the entries in the purchases journal that you prepared for Exercise 1.
   a. Open the following ledger accounts: Accts. Pay./Hanley Wholesalers, 201; Accts. Pay./Howard Lumber, 202; Accts. Pay/Keno Corporation, 203; Accts. Pay./Martinez Company, 204; Accts. Pay./Ruiz Hardware Company, 205; Accts. Pay./Simms Corporation, 206; Accts. Pay./Sutton Company, 207; and Purchases, 501.
   b. Post the entries from the purchases journal to the creditors' accounts.
   c. Pencil-foot, total, and rule the purchases journal.
   d. Post the total of the purchases journal to the Purchases account.

3. Journalize the following transactions of the Sally Rosen Company. Use a purchases journal for the first two transactions and a general journal for the third transaction.

June 1 Received Invoice 6291 for $658 for merchandise purchased on credit from the Tappenden Supply Company.

7   Received Invoice 6326 for $987.50 for merchandise purchased on credit from the Tappenden Supply Company.

8   Received Credit Memo 291 for $300 from the Tappenden Supply Company for returned merchandise.

4. Open the following ledger accounts: Accts. Pay./Tappenden Supply Company, 201; Purchases, 501; and Purchases Returns and Allowances, 502.

   a. Post the entries from the purchases journal and the general journal prepared in Exercise 3 to the accounts.

   b. Pencil-foot, total, and rule the purchases journal. Date the total June 30.

   c. Post the total of the purchases journal to the Purchases account.

5. Look at the purchases journal on page 461.

   a. Post the entries from the purchases journal to the following ledger accounts: Accts. Pay./Hobbies, Inc., 211; Accts. Pay./Monarch Wholesalers, 212; and Accts. Pay./Rainbow Art Supplies, Inc., 213.

   b. Post the total of the purchases journal to the Purchases account, 501.

TOPIC 2 ◆ JOURNALIZING AND POSTING CASH PAYMENTS

GOALS

1. To journalize transactions in a cash payments journal.
2. To post entries from a cash payments journal to ledger accounts.
3. To pencil-foot, total, and rule a cash payments journal.

KEY TERMS

A *cash payments journal* is a special journal used only for cash payment transactions.

Expenses are amounts paid to run a business.

Revenue is the amount that a business earns by selling goods or services.

An *expense account* is a temporary owner's equity account.

You probably pay cash for most of the goods and services you want and need—a hamburger, a sweater, a bus ride, a tape. The owner of a business does the same thing, often paying cash for supplies, salaries, rent, and merchandise. Paying out cash is one of the most common business transactions.

Advantages of cash pay-
ments journal:
1. Each entry uses only one
   line.
2. Total credits are posted
   as one amount.

To keep track of cash payments, many businesses use a cash payments journal. A *cash payments journal* is a special journal used only for recording cash payments. This special journal makes it easier to record and later post cash payments.

When a cash payments journal is used, only one line is needed to enter each cash payment. The credits to the Cash account can be added and posted as a total at the end of the month. This means that each separate credit does not have to be posted.

Check stubs are used to journalize cash payments.

Check stubs are used as source documents for cash payments in the cash payments journal. On October 10 Beverly Davis wrote a check for $160 to Hobbies, Inc. The accounting clerk used the information on the check stub to make this entry in the cash payments journal.

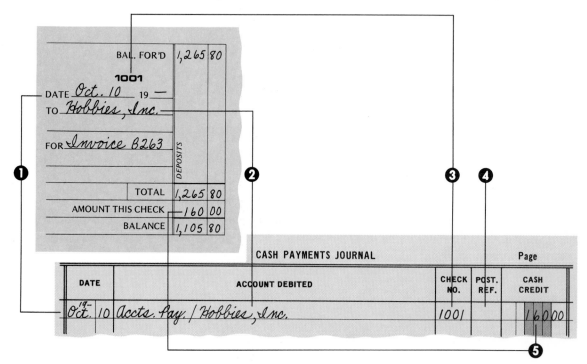

Note the following about the check stub and the entry in the cash payments journal:

1. The date that the check was written is entered in the Date column.
2. The account that must be debited is entered in the Account Debited column.
3. The check number is entered in the Check Number column.
4. The Posting Reference column is left blank. It will be used when the entry is posted.
5. The amount of the check is entered in the Cash Credit column.

EXPENSES

A business must pay out money for items that are needed to run the business. The amounts that are paid out to run a business are called *expenses*. Rent, salaries, supplies, telephone, and advertising are all examples of expenses.

The amount that a business earns by selling goods or services is called *revenue*. When the expenses of a business are less than its revenue, the business has a profit, or a *net income*. When expenses are greater than revenue, the business has a *net loss*.

Expenses cause decreases in owner's equity. Expenses are kept separate from owner's equity, however, so that the owner can see exactly how expenses affect the business's net income or net loss. An expense account is opened for each expense. An *expense account* is a temporary owner's equity account. Since expenses decrease owner's equity, the expense account is debited for each expense amount.

When a cash payment is made for an expense, the owner's equity decreases temporarily and Cash decreases. Thus a cash payment made for an expense is journalized by debiting an expense account and crediting the Cash account. Since this type of transaction involves a cash payment, the cash payment is journalized in the cash payments journal.

Part of a page from the cash payments journal of Bev's Craft Corner is shown below. There are five debits to expense accounts and two debits to liability accounts. There is also a debit to the Purchases account because a purchase of merchandise was made for cash.

CASH PAYMENTS JOURNAL

Page

DATE	ACCOUNT DEBITED	CHECK NO.	POST. REF.	CASH CREDIT
Oct. 10	Accts. Pay. / Hobbies, Inc.	1001		160 00
10	Salaries Expense	1002		50 00
11	Store Expense	1003		6 75
13	Rent Expense	1004		100 00
14	Purchases	1005		47 50
15	Office Expense	1006		22 00
17	Salaries Expense	1007		50 00
17	Accts. Pay. / Monarch Wholesalers	1008		74 30

COMMONLY USED EXPENSE ACCOUNTS

Account	Examples of Expenses Recorded in Account
Advertising Expense	Newspaper ads and ads on radio and on TV
Delivery Expense	Gas and oil, repairs, and tires for delivery equipment
Insurance Expense	Fire and liability insurance
Miscellaneous Expenses	Cleaning and window washing
Office Expense	Stationery, postage, and computer paper
Rent Expense	Rent
Salaries Expense	Employees' wages
Store Expense	Wrapping paper, window display materials, sales slip books, and cash register tapes
Tax Expense	Federal, state, and city taxes
Utilities Expense	Heat, light, water, and telephone

POSTING FROM THE CASH PAYMENTS JOURNAL

The individual debits in a cash payments journal are posted regularly during the month.

The credits in a cash payments journal are posted as a total at the end of the month.

Steps in posting cash payments:
1. Post the debits to individual accounts daily.
2. Post the credit to the Cash account at the end of the month.

The debits that are recorded in the cash payments journal are posted individually to the ledger accounts. This posting is done regularly during the month. The credits recorded in the cash payments journal are totaled at the end of the month. Then only the total is posted to the Cash account.

Part of a page from the cash payments journal of Bev's Craft Corner and four ledger accounts are shown on the following page. Look at them as you study the steps for posting from the cash payments journal to the ledger accounts.

1. The first entry in the cash payments journal is posted to the Accts. Pay./Hobbies, Inc. account. The date is entered in the Date column. (The other entries in that account for October 1, 8, and 9 were posted from the purchases journal and the general journal.)
2. The letters "CP," which stand for the cash payments journal, and the page number "1" are entered in the Posting Reference column. CP1 shows that the information came from page 1 of the cash payments journal.
3. The amount is entered in the Debit column of the account.

CASH PAYMENTS JOURNAL — Page 1

DATE	ACCOUNT DEBITED	CHECK NO.	POST. REF.	CASH CREDIT
Oct. 19— 10	Accts. Pay./Hobbies, Inc.	1001	211	160 00
10	Salaries Expense	1002	517	150 00
11	Store Expense	1003	518	6 75
31	Cash Credit		101	683 24 / 683 24

Accts. Pay./Hobbies, Inc. — Account No. 211

DATE	EXPLANATION	POST. REF.	DEBIT	CREDIT	BALANCE DEBIT	BALANCE CREDIT
Oct. 19— 1		P1		500 00		500 00
8		P1		160 00		660 00
9		J2	500 00			160 00
10		CP1	160 00			— 00

Salaries Expense — Account No. 517

DATE	EXPLANATION	POST. REF.	DEBIT	CREDIT	BALANCE DEBIT	BALANCE CREDIT
Oct. 19— 10		CP1	150 00		150 00	

Store Expense — Account No. 518

DATE	EXPLANATION	POST. REF.	DEBIT	CREDIT	BALANCE DEBIT	BALANCE CREDIT
Oct. 19— 11		CP1	6 75		6 75	

Cash — Account No. 101

DATE	EXPLANATION	POST. REF.	DEBIT	CREDIT	BALANCE DEBIT	BALANCE CREDIT
Oct. 19— 1	Balance	✓			1500 00	
31		CP1		683 24	816 76	

4. The account balance is entered in the Credit Balance column.
5. The number of the Accts. Pay./Hobbies, Inc. account (211) is entered in the Posting Reference column of the cash payments journal to show that the entry has been posted.
6. The second entry in the cash payments journal is posted to the Salaries Expense account. It is posted in the same way as the previous entry. The date is entered in the Date column. The abbreviation "CP1" is entered in the Posting Reference column. The amount is entered in the Debit column of the account. The account balance is entered in the Debit Balance column. The number of the Salaries Expense account is entered in the Posting Reference column of the cash payments journal.

7. The third entry in the cash payments journal is posted to the Store Expense account. The same posting procedure is followed.
8. At the end of the month, the cash payments journal is pencil-footed, totaled, and ruled. Note that "Cash Credit" is written in the Account Debited column on the same line as the total of the Cash Credit column.
9. The total of the cash payments journal is posted to the Cash account. First, the date is entered in the Date column of the account. Then the abbreviation "CP1" is entered in the Posting Reference column. Next, the total is entered in the Credit column. Finally the account balance is entered in the Debit Balance column.
10. The number of the Cash account is entered in the Posting Reference column of the cash payments journal. This shows that the total has been posted.

Do you see how using a special journal for cash payments makes posting easier? If there had been 20 cash payments during the month, 19 posting operations would have been saved by recording the cash payments in the cash payments journal.

Check Your Reading

1. Is a cash payments journal used for all payments of cash?

2. Would a cash purchase of merchandise be journalized in the cash payments journal?

3. Would a cash purchase of office supplies be journalized in the cash payments journal?

4. Does a business have a net loss when expenses are less than revenue?

5. Is an expense account a temporary liability account?

6. List two advantages of using a cash payments journal.

Exercises for Topic 2

1. Use a cash payments journal to journalize the following transactions of the Horning Company. Use these accounts: Cash; Accts. Pay./Edwards, Inc.; Purchases; Advertising Expense; Delivery Expense; Insurance Expense; Miscellaneous Expenses; Office Expense; Rent Expense; Salaries Expense; and Tax Expense.

Sept. 3 Issued Check 2237 for $750 for a cash purchase of merchandise.

4 Issued Check 2238 for $68.25 for gas for the truck (Delivery Expense).

5 Issued Check 2239 for $600 to Edwards, Inc., for payment on account.

6 Issued Check 2240 for $650 for rent.

7 Issued Check 2241 for $895 for salaries.

9 Issued Check 2242 for $220 for insurance.

9 Issued Check 2243 for $84 for repairs to the cash register (Miscellaneous Expenses).

10 Issued Check 2244 for $95.40 for stationery and supplies.

11 Issued Check 2245 for $145 for advertising signs.

16 Issued Check 2246 for $85 for store cleaning (Miscellaneous Expenses).

18 Issued Check 2247 for $78.95 for a new tire for the truck (Delivery Expense).

19 Issued Check 2248 for $368 for a cash purchase of merchandise.

20 Issued Check 2249 for $535 for city taxes.

25 Issued Check 2250 for $25 for a credit bureau listing (Miscellaneous Expenses).

27 Issued Check 2251 for $57 for window cleaning (Miscellaneous Expenses).

28 Issued Check 2252 for $321.60 for a cash purchase of merchandise.

2. Continue your work for the Horning Company:

a. Open the following ledger accounts: Cash, 101; Accts. Pay./Edwards, Inc., 201; Purchases, 501; Advertising Expense, 502; Delivery Expense, 503; Insurance Expense, 504; Miscellaneous Expenses, 505; Office Expense, 506; Rent Expense, 507; Salaries Expense, 508; and Tax Expense, 509. Then enter a debit balance of $6,600 in the Cash account. Enter a credit balance of $960 in the Accts. Pay./Edwards, Inc. account. Date the balances September 1. (When recording beginning balances in accounts, enter the date, write the word "Balance" in the Explanation column, enter the amount of the balance, and place a check mark in the Posting Reference column.)

b. Look at the cash payments journal that you prepared for Exercise 1. Post the entries from the cash payments journal to the accounts.

c. Pencil-foot, total, and rule the cash payments journal. Date the total September 30. (Use the illustration on page 469 as a model.)

d. Post the total of the cash payments journal to the Cash account.

3. Do the following work for the Alvarez Gift Shop:

    a. Open the following accounts, and enter the credit balances shown: Accts. Pay./Lloyd and Brent, 201, $800; Accts. Pay./Kruger Company, 202, $350; Accts. Pay./Tomar Brothers, 203, $375; and Accts. Pay./Young Corporation, 204, $400. Date the balances March 1.

    b. Journalize the following transactions in a cash payments journal.

Mar. 1	Issued Check 107 for $200 to Tomar Brothers for payment on account.
3	Issued Check 108 for $400 to Young Corporation for payment on account.
4	Issued Check 109 for $275 to Kruger Company for payment on account.
5	Issued Check 110 for $500 to Lloyd and Brent for payment on account.
5	Issued Check 111 for $175 to Tomar Brothers for payment on account.

    c. Post the entries from the cash payments journal to the accounts.

Read each of the following statements. From the words below each statement, choose the term that best matches the statement.

1. A reduction in price for damaged merchandise kept by a business.

   purchase allowance   purchase return

2. A journal used for only one type of transaction.

   general journal   special journal

3. A special journal used only for purchases of merchandise on credit.

   general journal   purchases journal

4. An account such as Purchases Returns and Allowances.

   asset account
   temporary owner's equity account

5. The time when purchases are posted to the Purchases account if a purchases journal is used.

   at the end of a day
   at the end of a month

6. A temporary owner's equity account.

   Cash   Furniture   Purchases

7. Merchandise returned by a business.

   purchase allowance   purchase return

8. A business form showing how much credit has been given for a purchase return or allowance.

   credit memo   invoice

9. Goods that a business buys and intends to sell.

   merchandise for resale
   purchases returns

10. The time when purchases are posted to creditors' accounts from the purchases journal.

    daily   monthly   weekly

11. The time to post credits recorded in the cash payments journal.

    at the end of a month   during a month

12. The amount that a business earns by selling goods or services.

    expenses   revenue

13. The number of lines that one entry uses in a cash payments journal.

    four   one   three   two

14. The result when expenses are less than revenue.

    net income   net loss

15. The time to post debits recorded in the cash payments journal.

    at the end of a month   during a month

16. Source documents used to journalize cash payments.

    check stubs   invoices

17. The result when expenses are greater than revenue.

    net income   net loss

18. The column of the Cash account to which the total of the cash payments journal is posted.

    Credit column   Debit column

19. A temporary owner's equity account.

Cash   Salaries Expense

20. Amounts paid to run a business.

expenses   revenue

APPLICATION PROBLEMS

1. Journalize the following transactions for the Jackson Brothers Company. Use a purchases journal for all purchases of merchandise on credit and a general journal for all purchases returns and allowances.

July 2   Received Invoice 1407 for $1,205 for merchandise purchased on credit from the Excello Equipment Company.

2   Received Invoice 49921 for $900 for merchandise purchased on credit from Medford Cement Products.

3   Received Invoice 424R for $535 for merchandise purchased on credit from Bayshore Laboratories.

5   Received Invoice 437R for $412 for merchandise purchased on credit from Bayshore Laboratories.

5   Received Invoice 50040 for $480 for merchandise purchased on credit from Medford Cement Products.

5   Received Invoice 1483 for $2,800 for merchandise purchased on credit from the Excello Equipment Company.

6   Received Invoice 440R for $706 for merchandise purchased on credit from Bayshore Laboratories.

6   Received Invoice 1493 for $1,150 for merchandise purchased on credit from the Excello Equipment Company.

6   Received Credit Memo 747 for $50 from Medford Cement Products for damaged merchandise.

6   Received Invoice 1512 for $920 for merchandise purchased on credit

from the Excello Equipment Company.

6   Received Credit Memo 181 for $375 from Bayshore Laboratories for returned merchandise.

2. Open the following ledger accounts for the Jackson Brothers Company: Accts. Pay./ Bayshore Laboratories, 201; Accts. Pay./ Excello Equipment Company, 202; Accts. Pay./Medford Cement Products, 203; Purchases, 501; and Purchases Returns and Allowances, 502.

a. Post the entries from the journals prepared in Problem 1 to the accounts.

b. Pencil-foot, total, and rule the purchases journal. Date the total July 31.

c. Post the total of the purchases journal to the Purchases account.

3. Do the following work for the Palace of Jeans Clothing Store.

a. Open the following ledger accounts: Cash, 101; Accts. Pay./Curle Company, 201; Purchases, 501; Advertising Expense, 502; Delivery Expense, 503; Insurance Expense, 504; Miscellaneous Expenses, 505; Office Expense, 506; Rent Expense, 507; and Salaries Expense, 508. Enter a debit balance of $9,826 in the Cash account. Enter a credit balance of $594 in the Accts. Pay./Curle Company account. Date the balances October 1.

b. Journalize the following transactions in a cash payments journal. All payments are made by check. The check numbers are in numeric order beginning with Check 101.

Oct. 1 Paid $70 for an ad in the *Daily News Reports*.
   3 Purchased merchandise for $384 in cash.
   4 Paid $700 for salaries.
   5 Paid $80 for stamps.
   7 Paid $30 for window washing.
   8 Paid $594 to Curle Company on account.
   10 Purchased merchandise for $350 in cash.
   11 Paid $24.80 for gas for the truck.
   12 Paid $142 for an insurance premium.
   17 Paid $625 for rent.
   19 Paid $53 for cleaning the store.
   20 Paid $14 for stationery.
   22 Paid $65.45 for a new tire for the truck.
   25 Paid $84.80 for repairs to lighting fixtures in the store (Miscellaneous Expenses).
   28 Paid $73 for an advertising sign.

c. Post the entries from the cash payments journal to the accounts.
d. Pencil-foot, total, and rule the journal.
e. Post the total of the cash payments journal to the Cash account.

4. Do the following work for Vicky's Variety Shop:

a. Open the following ledger accounts: Cash, 101; Accts. Pay./Amer Company, 201; Accts. Pay./Butcher Company, 202; Accts. Pay./Lahl Corporation, 203; Accts. Pay./Pierre Paper Company, 204; Accts. Pay./Rollo Company, 205; and Purchases, 501.
b. Enter a cash balance of $18,000 in the Cash account. Date the balance April 1.

5. Journalize the following transactions for Vicky's Variety Shop. Use both a purchases journal and a cash payments journal. The date given is the date the invoice was received or

the check was issued.

Apr. 1 Purchased merchandise on credit for $150 from the Pierre Paper Company, Invoice 1314.
   1 Purchased merchandise on credit for $780 from the Rollo Company, Invoice 262.
   5 Purchased merchandise on credit for $82.50 from the Amer Company, Invoice 420B.
   7 Paid $90 to the Pierre Paper Company on account, Check 428.
   7 Purchased merchandise on credit for $400 from the Butcher Company, Invoice 1124.
   15 Paid $380 to the Rollo Company on account, Check 429.
   15 Purchased merchandise on credit for $130 from the Amer Company, Invoice 478B.
   15 Paid $150 to the Butcher Company on account, Check 430.
   18 Paid $82.50 to the Amer Company on account, Check 431.
   22 Purchased merchandise on credit for $282 from the Lahl Corporation, Invoice 9201K.
   23 Purchased merchandise for $417 cash, Check 432.
   30 Paid $230 to the Lahl Corporation on account, Check 433.
   30 Paid $250 to the Butcher Company on account, Check 434.
   30 Paid $60 to the Pierre Paper Company on account, Check 435.

a. Post the entries from the purchases journal and the cash payments journal to the accounts opened in Problem 4.
b. Pencil-foot, total, and rule the purchases journal.
c. Post the total of the purchases journal to the Purchases account.
d. Pencil-foot, total, and rule the cash payments journal.
e. Post the total of the cash payments journal to the Cash account.

CHAPTER 18

SPECIAL JOURNALS: SALES AND CASH RECEIPTS

The money that a business earns is called *revenue*. Most businesses earn their revenue by selling merchandise or services. *Merchandise* includes items such as T-shirts, radios, hamburgers, sleeping bags, cars, and books. *Services* include TV repairs, guitar lessons, and movies. When you buy merchandise, you receive a product that you may keep. When you buy a service, you receive assistance or entertainment. Can you think of other examples of merchandise and services?

Sales of merchandise and services are often credit sales, rather than cash sales. The customer who bought the merchandise or service on credit will pay for it later by cash or check. In this chapter you will learn how to record credit sales in a special journal called a *sales journal*. You will also learn how to record receipts of cash in another special journal, the *cash receipts journal*.

TOPIC 1 ◆ JOURNALIZING AND POSTING SALES

GOALS

1. To journalize transactions in a sales journal.
2. To post entries from the sales journal to ledger accounts.
3. To pencil-foot, total, and rule the sales journal.
4. To journalize entries to record sales returns and allowances.

KEY TERMS

A *sales journal* is a special journal used only to record sales of merchandise or services on credit.
A *sales account* is a temporary owner's equity account that is used to record all sales of merchandise or services that a business makes.
A *sales return* is merchandise returned by a customer.
A *sales allowance* is unsatisfactory merchandise kept by customer for a lower price.

Sales entered in a sales journal must be both:
1. Sales of merchandise or services
2. Sales on credit

Many businesses record sales on credit in a special journal called a *sales journal*. Using a sales journal makes it easier to journalize and post credit sales. If a business uses a sales journal, only one line is needed to record the entry for a sale. Also, the credits to the Sales account are posted as a total at the end of the month. To be recorded in a sales journal, a transaction must be (1) a sale of merchandise or services and (2) a sale on credit.

Since Bev's Craft Corner makes many sales on credit, the business uses a sales journal. Look at the sales slip and journal page below to see how the sale made to the Crafts Club on October 1 is journalized. Note that only one line is needed for the sales journal entry.

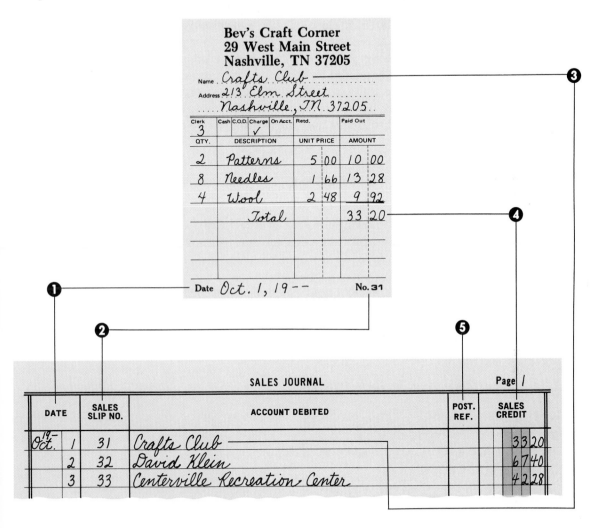

Also note that:

1. The date of the sale is entered in the Date column.
2. The sales slip number is entered in the Sales Slip Number column.
3. The name of the customer is entered in the Account Debited column. All entries in the sales journal are debited to accounts receivable. Thus it is not necessary to use the abbreviation "Accts. Rec." before the customer's name.

Each entry in a sales journal is debited to an account receivable.

4. The amount of the sale is entered in the Sales Credit column.
5. The Posting Reference column is left blank. It will be used when the entry is posted.

POSTING FROM THE SALES JOURNAL

Postings to accounts receivable are made daily.

A credit to the Sales account is made at the end of the month.

Bev's Craft Corner sells merchandise on credit to many people and associations and keeps a ledger account for each account receivable. A sale on credit is entered in the sales journal. Then the sale is posted as a debit to the ledger account. Posting is usually done daily so that Bev's Craft Corner always knows just how much each account receivable owes. At the end of the month, the credits are totaled and posted as one amount to the Sales account.

DAILY POSTING

The accounting clerk of Bev's Craft Corner posted the October 1 entry from the sales journal to the account receivable as shown below.

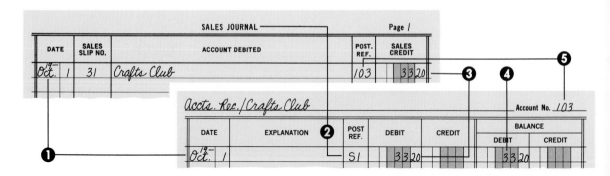

1. The date is entered in the Date column of the account.
2. The letter ''S,'' which stands for sales journal, and the page number ''1'' are entered in the Posting Reference column of the account. S1 shows that the data came from page 1 of the sales journal.
3. The amount of the sale is entered in the Debit column of the account.
4. The account balance is entered in the Debit Balance column.
5. The number of the Accts. Rec./Crafts Club account (103) is entered in the Posting Reference column of the sales journal to show that the entry was posted.

END-OF-MONTH POSTING

The accounting clerk posts the total of the sales journal as a credit to the Sales account at the end of the month. This posting is done after the sales journal has been pencil-footed, totaled, and ruled.

The amount of sales recorded in the Sales account temporarily increases the owner's equity. At some point, Bev's Craft Corner must subtract from sales the amount spent to buy the merchandise that is later sold. Because the increase to owner's equity is temporary, the Sales account is used. The Sales account is a temporary owner's equity account. Remember: To increase owner's equity, credit the account.

The sales journal and the Sales account of Bev's Craft Corner at the end of October are shown below. Look at these records as you study how to post the total from the journal to the account.

Sales temporarily increase owner's equity.

1. The sales journal is pencil-footed and totaled. The date is entered. "Sales Credit" is written in the Account Debited column on the same line as the total of the Sales Credit column. A double rule is drawn under the Date, Posting Reference, and Sales Credit columns.
2. The date is entered in the Date column of the Sales account.
3. The total of the Sales Credit column of the sales journal is entered in the Credit column of the Sales account and the account balance is entered in the Credit Balance column.
4. The abbreviation "S1" is entered in the Posting Reference column of the Sales account to show that the information has been posted from page 1 of the sales journal.
5. The number of the Sales account (401) is entered in the Post-

ing Reference column of the sales journal to show that the total has been posted.

SALES RETURNS AND ALLOWANCES

When a customer returns merchandise that was sold on credit, the seller gives the customer a credit memo. The credit memo shows that the customer's account is being credited for a *sales return*. The seller also gives a credit memo to a customer to show a *sales allowance*, which is a reduction in the price of unsatisfactory merchandise that the customer decides to keep. The seller keeps a copy of the credit memo and uses it to make an entry in the general journal.

Returns and allowances for sales are recorded in an account called *Sales Returns and Allowances*. This account, like Sales, is a temporary owner's equity account. Since sales returns and allowances decrease owner's equity, the account is debited.

Bev's Craft Corner
29 West Main Street
Nashville, TN 37205

CREDIT MEMO   No. 101

TO   Crafts Club
213 Elm Street
Nashville, TN 37205

October 6, 19--

QUANTITY	ARTICLES	UNIT PRICE	EXTENSION
2	Patterns returned because of misprintings.	5 00	10 00

	GENERAL JOURNAL			Page 2

DATE	ACCOUNT TITLE AND EXPLANATION	POST. REF.	DEBIT	CREDIT
Oct. 6	Sales Returns and Allowances	402	10 00	
	Accts. Rec./Crafts Club	103		10 00
	Return of a sale on credit, Credit Memo 101.			

The Crafts Club returned the model airplane kits that were purchased on credit from Bev's Craft Corner on October 1. Bev's Craft Corner then sent the Crafts Club a credit memo. The return of merchandise caused a decrease in owner's equity and a decrease in the asset account Accts. Rec./Crafts Club. Thus Sales

Returns and allowances decrease owner's equity.

Returns and Allowances is debited, and Accts. Rec./Crafts Club is credited. The entry that the accounting clerk for Bev's Craft Corner made in the general journal to record this transaction is shown on the preceding page. Note that the credit memo number is included in the explanation.

For a return or an allowance:
1. Debit the Sales Returns and Allowances account.
2. Credit the account receivable.

The accounting clerk for Bev's Craft Corner used the information from the general journal to post to the Sales Returns and Allowances account as shown here.

DATE	EXPLANATION	POST REF.	DEBIT	CREDIT	BALANCE	
					DEBIT	CREDIT
Oct. 6		J2	10 00		10 00	

Sales Returns and Allowances   Account No. 402

❶ ❷ ❸ ❹

1. The date is entered in the Date column of the account.
2. The abbreviation "J2" is entered in the Posting Reference column of the account to show that the information came from page 2 of the general journal.
3. The amount is entered in the Debit column of the account.
4. The account balance is entered in the Debit Balance column.

The number of the Sales Returns and Allowances account (402) is entered in the Posting Reference column of the general journal to show that the entry has been posted.

Look at the Accts. Rec./Crafts Club account below to see how the accounting clerk posted the entry for the sales return from the general journal to this account.

DATE	EXPLANATION	POST REF.	DEBIT	CREDIT	BALANCE	
					DEBIT	CREDIT
Oct. 1		S1	33 20		33 20	
6		J2		10 00	23 20	

Accts. Rec. / Crafts Club   Account No. 103

❶ ❷ ❸ ❹

1. The date is entered in the Date column of the account.
2. The abbreviation "J2" is entered in the Posting Reference column of the account to show that the information came from page 2 of the general journal.
3. The amount is entered in the Credit column of the account.
4. The account balance is entered in the Debit Balance column.

The number of the Accts. Rec./Crafts Club account (103) is entered in the Posting Reference column of the general journal to show that the entry has been posted.

Check Your Reading

1. Is a sales journal used for cash sales?

2. Would a credit sale of a service be recorded in a sales journal?

3. Would a credit sale of merchandise be recorded in a sales journal?

4. Is the Sales account a temporary owner's equity account?

5. Is each entry in a sales journal debited to an account payable?

6. Would a credit sale of an old desk that was used in the business be recorded in a sales journal?

7. Do sales decrease owner's equity?

8. Do sales returns and allowances decrease owner's equity?

Exercises for Topic 1

1. Sales on credit for the Mahlman Appliance Company follow. Journalize the sales in a sales journal. The sales slips are numbered in order, beginning with Sales Slip 60 for Jan Bartlett.

Sept. 1 Sold merchandise on credit for $36 to Jan Bartlett.
       2 Sold merchandise on credit for $90.45 to Paul Lipke.
       3 Sold merchandise on credit for $95.50 to Anna Santos.
       4 Sold merchandise on credit for $95 to Chaing Lee.
       5 Sold merchandise on credit for $145 to Sam Monroe.
       5 Sold merchandise on credit for $78.29 to Jan Bartlett.
       6 Sold merchandise on credit for $95.50 to Sam Monroe.

6 Sold merchandise on credit for $97.80 to Anna Santos.

8 Sold merchandise on credit for $85.65 to Paul Lipke.

9 Sold merchandise on credit for $91.10 to Chaing Lee.

10 Sold merchandise on credit for $176.55 to Jan Bartlett.

12 Sold merchandise on credit for $110 to Chaing Lee.

12 Sold merchandise on credit for $65.98 to Sam Monroe.

13 Sold merchandise on credit for $267.45 to Anna Santos.

2. Continue your work for the Mahlman Appliance Company.
   a. Open the following ledger accounts: Accts. Rec./Jan Bartlett, 102; Accts. Rec./Chaing Lee, 103; Accts. Rec./Paul Lipke, 104; Accts. Rec./Sam Monroe, 105; Accts. Rec./Anna Santos, 106; and Sales, 401.
   b. Look at the sales journal that you prepared for Exercise 1. Post the entries from the sales journal to the customers' accounts.
   c. Pencil-foot, total, and rule the sales journal. Date the total September 14.
   d. Post the total of the sales journal to the Sales account.

3. Do the following work for Bev's Craft Corner:
   a. Open the following ledger accounts: Accts. Rec./Centerville Recreation Center, 102; Accts. Rec./Crafts Club, 103; Accts. Rec./David Klein, 104; and Sales, 401.
   b. Post the entries from the sales journal of Bev's Craft Corner shown on page 479 to the customers' accounts.
   c. Post the total of the sales journal shown on page 479 to the Sales account.

4. Do the following work for the Paris Boutique:
   a. Open the following ledger accounts: Accts. Rec./Jackie Schultz, 102; Sales, 401; and Sales Returns and Allowances, 402.
   b. Journalize the following transactions. Use a sales journal for the first two transactions and a general journal for the last transaction.

   Oct. 1 Sold merchandise on credit for $375 to Jackie Schultz, Sales Slip 40.

   15 Sold merchandise on credit for $79.95 to Jackie Schultz, Sales Slip 61.

15 Issued Credit Memo 143 for $125 to Jackie Schultz for returned merchandise.

c. Post the entries from the sales journal to the customer's account.
d. Post the entry from the general journal to the Sales Returns and Allowances account and to the customer's account.
e. Pencil-foot, total, and rule the sales journal. Date the total October 15.
f. Post the total of the sales journal to the Sales account.

TOPIC 2 ◆ JOURNALIZING AND POSTING CASH RECEIPTS

GOALS

1. To journalize transactions in a cash receipts journal.
2. To post entries from a cash receipts journal to ledger accounts.
3. To pencil-foot, total, and rule a cash receipts journal.

KEY TERMS

A *cash receipts journal* is a special journal used only to record cash receipts.
A *memorandum entry* is an entry that is not posted.

In Chapter 17 you learned that paying cash is a very common business transaction. Receiving cash is also a very common transaction. Most *cash receipts* come from two sources:

1. Sales of merchandise or services for cash
2. Payments from customers for merchandise or services sold on credit

Many businesses have a special journal called the *cash receipts journal* for recording cash receipts. A cash receipts journal makes it easier to journalize and to post cash receipts.

JOURNALIZING CASH RECEIPTS

How to record cash receipts from cash sales and from customers paying on account:
1. Debit Cash.
2. Credit Sales or the customer's account.

Whenever cash is received, the Cash account is debited. The account to be credited depends on the transaction. For example, an amount received from a sale of merchandise for cash would be credited to the Sales account. An amount received from a customer who is making a cash payment on account would be credited to the customer's account.

Bev's Craft Corner uses a cash receipts journal. The entries are made from receipt tapes and customers' checks. Look at the cash receipts journal shown below as you study how to record entries in the cash receipts journal.

Records used in journalizing cash receipts:
1. Receipt tapes or sales slips
2. Checks from customers

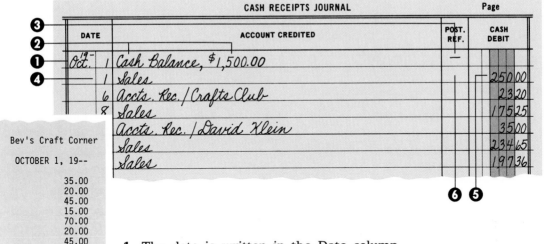

| | CASH RECEIPTS JOURNAL | | | Page | |
DATE	ACCOUNT CREDITED	POST. REF.	CASH DEBIT		
Oct. 1	Cash Balance, $1,500.00	—			
1	Sales		250 00		
6	Accts. Rec. / Crafts Club		23 20		
8	Sales		175 25		
	Accts. Rec. / David Klein		35 00		
	Sales		234 65		
	Sales		197 36		

Bev's Craft Corner

OCTOBER 1, 19--

	35.00
	20.00
	45.00
	15.00
	70.00
	20.00
	45.00
TOTAL	250.00

1. The date is written in the Date column.
2. "Cash Balance" and the amount are written in the Account Credited column at the beginning of each month.
3. A dash is placed in the Posting Reference column to show that the entry for the cash balance should not be posted. It is not posted because it does not result from a transaction. This type of entry is called a *memorandum entry*.
4. The date of the first transaction is entered in the Date column. The information comes from the receipt tape of cash sales for the past week. The title of the account to be credited (Sales) is entered in the Account Credited column.
5. The amount of cash sales is entered in the Cash Debit column. (Bev's Craft Corner records cash sales on a weekly basis. Other companies record cash sales more frequently.)
6. The Posting Reference column is left blank. It will be filled in when the entry is posted.

All remaining transactions are journalized in a similar way. Information for accounts receivable transactions is taken from the checks sent by customers to make payments on their accounts.

POSTING FROM THE CASH RECEIPTS JOURNAL

The accounting clerk for Bev's Craft Corner posts the credits recorded in the cash receipts journal to the ledger accounts every

The credits in the cash receipts journal are posted daily. day. At the end of the month, the clerk totals and rules the cash receipts journal. Then the clerk posts the total of the debits to the Cash account.

CASH RECEIPTS JOURNAL
Page 1

DATE	ACCOUNT CREDITED	POST. REF.	CASH DEBIT
Oct. 19— 1	Cash Balance, $1,500.00	—	
1	Sales	401	250 00
6	Accts. Rec. / Crafts Club	103	23 20
8	Sales	401	1 75 25
15	Accts. Rec. / David Klein	104	35 00
15	Sales	401	234 65
22	Sales	401	1 97 36
31	Cash Debit	101	1 27 6 50 / 1 27 6 50

6   **5 8**

Accts. Rec. / Crafts Club
Account No. 103

DATE	EXPLANATION	POST REF.	DEBIT	CREDIT	BALANCE DEBIT	BALANCE CREDIT
Oct. 19— 1		S1	33 20		33 20	
6		J2		10 00	23 20	
6		CR1		23 20	— 00	

❶   **❷**   **❸**   **❹**

Cash
Account No. 101

DATE	EXPLANATION	POST REF.	DEBIT	CREDIT	BALANCE DEBIT	BALANCE CREDIT
Oct. 19— 1	Balance	✓			1500 00	
31		CP1		6 83 24	8 16 76	
31		CR1	1 27 6 50		2 09 3 26	

❼

Part of the cash receipts journal of Bev's Craft Corner and two of its ledger accounts are shown on page 486. Look at these records as you read the following steps for posting entries in the cash receipts journal to the ledger accounts. The example given is for the entry dated October 6.

The total of the debits in the cash receipts journal is posted to Cash at the end of the month.

1. Every day, each individual credit is posted to the proper ledger account. The date is recorded in the Date column of the account.
2. The letters "CR" and the page number "1" are entered in the Posting Reference column of the account. CR stands for the cash receipts journal. CR1 shows that the information came from page 1 of the cash receipts journal.
3. The amount is recorded in the Credit column of the account.
4. The balance is entered in the account.
5. The number of the ledger account is written in the Posting Reference column of the journal to show that the entry has been posted.
6. At the end of the month, the cash receipts journal is pencil-footed, totaled, and ruled. "Cash Debit" is written in the Account Credited column on the same line as the total of the Cash Debit column.
7. The total is posted to the Cash account. The Date, Debit, Posting Reference, and Debit Balance columns are filled in.
8. The number of the Cash account (101) is written in the Posting Reference column of the journal.

Check Your Reading

1. Is a cash receipts journal used for credit sales?

2. Would a cash sale of merchandise be recorded in a cash receipts journal?

3. Would a cash purchase of merchandise be recorded in a cash receipts journal?

4. Are credits in the cash receipts journal posted daily?

5. Is the total of the cash receipts journal posted as a debit to the Cash account?

6. How is cash receipts journal abbreviated in the Posting Reference column of a ledger account?

Exercises for Topic 2

1. Journalize the following cash balance and transactions of the Tredway Sales Company in a cash receipts journal.

Sept. 1 Cash balance, $1,750.
2 Received $450 for rent of office space. (Credit Rental Revenue.)
3 Received $95.75 on account from Max Brewster.
4 Received $536.98 from cash sales.
6 Received $612.50 from cash sales.
8 Received $73.50 on account from Iris Van Horn.
9 Received $75.65 from cash sales.
10 Received $75 from the sale of an old office desk. (Credit Office Furniture.)
11 Received $198.75 from cash sales.
12 Received $175 on account from Kate Orzech.

2. Continue your work for the Tredway Sales Company.
   a. Open the following ledger accounts and enter the balances shown: Cash, 101, $1,750; Accts. Rec./Max Brewster, 102, $135.75; Accts. Rec./Kate Orzech, 103, $225; Accts. Rec./Iris Van Horn, 104, $178.40; Office Furniture, 105, $975; Sales, 401; and Rental Revenue, 402. Date the balances September 1.
   b. Look at the cash receipts journal that you prepared for Exercise 1. Post the entries from the cash receipts journal to the accounts.
   c. Pencil-foot, total, and rule the cash receipts journal.
   d. Post the total of the cash receipts journal to the Cash account.

3. Do the following work for the Montez Manufacturing Company:
   a. Open the following ledger accounts, and enter the balances shown: Cash, 101, $22,400; Accts. Rec./Howard Dix, 102, $350; Accts. Rec./Joan Pientka, 103, $1,834.60; Accts. Rec./Donna Timko, 104, $2,550; Office Furniture, 105, $6,000; Sales, 401; and Rental Revenue, 402. Date the balances October 1.
   b. Journalize the following cash balance and transactions in a cash receipts journal:

   Oct. 1 Cash balance, $22,400.
   2 Received $285 on account from Joan Pientka.
   6 Received $900 for parking lot rent.
   8 Received $1,477.20 from cash sales.
   9 Received $260 from the sale of used office furniture.
   10 Received $2,800.50 from cash sales.
   14 Received $3,090 from cash sales.
   17 Received $285 on account from Joan Pientka.
   19 Received $2,200 rent for building.

20	Received $750 on account from Donna Timko.
23	Received $300 from the sale of a used desk.
25	Received $175 on account from Howard Dix.
26	Received $250 on account from Donna Timko.
30	Received $285 on account from Joan Pientka.
31	Received $4,117.50 from cash sales.

   c. Post the entries from the cash receipts journal to the accounts.

   d. Pencil-foot, total, and rule the cash receipts journal.

   e. Post the total of the cash receipts journal to the Cash account.

TOPIC 3 ◆ PROVING CASH

GOALS

1. To prove cash according to the cash journals and the checkbook balance.
2. To make a memorandum entry in a cash receipts journal to record the beginning cash balance.

KEY TERM

Proving cash means comparing the ending cash balance according to the cash journals with the checkbook balance.

The accounting clerk for Bev's Craft Corner proves cash at the end of each month using the total of the cash receipts journal, the total of the cash payments journal, and the cash balance in the checkbook. To find the ending cash balance according to the data in the cash journals, the clerk uses the following formula:

$$
\begin{array}{ccccc}
\text{Beginning} & & \text{Total} & \text{Total} & \text{Ending} \\
\text{Cash} & + & \text{Cash} & - \quad \text{Cash} & = \quad \text{Cash} \\
\text{Balance} & & \text{Receipts} & \text{Payments} & \text{Balance}
\end{array}
$$

On a separate piece of paper, the clerk prepares a cash proof. The clerk follows the steps listed below.

1. Record the beginning balance from the cash receipts journal.
2. Record the total cash receipts for the month from the cash receipts journal.
3. Add the beginning balance and the total cash receipts to get the total cash available during the month.
4. Record the total cash payments made during the month from the cash payments journal.

CASH RECEIPTS JOURNAL · Page 1

DATE	ACCOUNT CREDITED	POST. REF.	CASH DEBIT	
Oct.¹⁹⁻ 1	Cash Balance $1,500.00	—		❶
31	Cash Debit	101	1,276.50	❷

CASH PAYMENTS JOURNAL · Page 1

DATE	ACCOUNT DEBITED	CHECK NO.	POST. REF.	CASH CREDIT	
Oct.¹⁹⁻ 10	Accts. Pay./Craftland Supply Corporation	1001	211	160 00	
31	Cash Credit		101	683 24	❹

Cash Proof

Beginning Cash Balance	$ 1,500.00	❶
Add Total Cash Receipts	1,276.50	❷
Total Cash Available	2,776.50	❸
Less Total Cash Payments	683.24	❹
Ending Cash Balance	2,093.26	❺

BAL. FOR'D	2,093 26	❺
1057		
DATE_____19___		
TO_____		
FOR_____	DEPOSITS	
TOTAL		
AMOUNT THIS CHECK		
BALANCE		

5. Subtract the total cash payments from the total cash available during the month. The result is the *ending cash balance*. Compare it with the checkbook balance. The amounts should be equal.

After cash has been proved for October, the accounting clerk makes a memorandum entry in the cash receipts journal. The entry records the beginning cash balance for November 1. The accounting clerk uses the ending cash balance for October 31 as the beginning cash balance for November 1.

Check Your Reading

1. What three items of information are used to prove cash?

2. What is the formula for finding the ending cash balance according to the information in the cash journals?

3. The ending cash balance on April 30 will be the beginning cash balance on what date?

1. Do the following work for the Wedgewood Shop:
   a. Open the following ledger accounts: Cash, 101; Delivery Equipment, 102; Office Equipment, 103; Store Equipment, 104; Sales, 401; Purchases, 501; Delivery Expense, 502; Miscellaneous Expenses, 503; Office Expense, 504; Rent Expense, 505; and Salaries Expense, 506. Enter a balance of $4,500 in the Cash account. Date the balance March 1.
   b. Journalize the following cash balance and transactions in a cash receipts journal and in a cash payments journal. All payments are made by check. The checks recorded in the cash payments journal should be numbered in order, starting with Check 56.

Mar.	1	Cash balance, $4,500.
	2	Paid $600 for rent for March.
	2	Paid $550 for the purchase of merchandise.
	3	Paid $2,400 for a used delivery truck.
	4	Paid $575 for counters and showcases for the store.
	5	Received $2,540 from cash sales.
	6	Paid $45 for gasoline for the truck.
	7	Paid $175 for the clerk's salary.
	9	Paid $14 for stationery and stamps.
	10	Received $1,756 from cash sales.
	11	Paid $200 for the purchase of merchandise.
	12	Paid $8.70 for the delivery of a package.
	13	Received $1,817 from cash sales.
	14	Paid $175 for the clerk's salary.
	16	Paid $210 for a used desk for the office.
	17	Paid $5.84 for postage.
	18	Received $980 from cash sales.
	19	Paid $455 for the purchase of merchandise.
	20	Received $2,119 from cash sales.
	21	Paid $175 for the clerk's salary.
	23	Paid $745 for the purchase of merchandise.
	24	Paid $115 for an electric bill. (Debit Miscellaneous Expenses.)
	24	Received $1,783 from cash sales.
	26	Paid $32 for maintenance for the truck.
	27	Received $1,400 from cash sales.
	28	Paid $175 for the clerk's salary.
	30	Paid $447 for the purchase of merchandise.
	30	Paid $85 for a telephone bill. (Debit Miscellaneous Expenses.)

c. Post the entries from the cash receipts journal and the cash payments journal to the accounts.
d. Pencil-foot, total, and rule the journals.
e. Prove cash according to the cash journals and the checkbook. The checkbook balance on March 31 is $9,707.46.
f. Post the totals of the journals to the Cash account.
g. Make a memorandum entry in the cash receipts journal to record the beginning cash balance for April 1.

TOPIC 4 ◆ MULTICOLUMN CASH JOURNALS

GOALS

1. To journalize entries in a multicolumn cash receipts journal.
2. To journalize entries in a multicolumn cash payments journal.
3. To post from multicolumn cash journals to ledger accounts.
4. To pencil-foot, total, and rule multicolumn cash journals.

KEY TERM

A *multicolumn journal* has special columns.

As you have seen, the cash receipts journal and the cash payments journal save time because individual entries do not have to be posted to the Cash account. Only the totals of the Cash columns in the journals are posted. This posting is done at the end of each month. Sometimes special columns are provided in the cash journals to save time in posting to other accounts that are used often. Journals with special columns are called *multicolumn journals*.

CASH RECEIPTS JOURNAL

Sheila Polk owns the Upbeat Music Shop. Most of the business's cash receipts come from two sources: selling musical instruments and repairing musical instruments. Revenue from sales is recorded in the Sales account, and revenue from repairs is recorded in the Repair Revenue account. Because most of Upbeat's cash receipts come from these two sources, the business uses a cash receipts journal with a Sales Credit column and a Repair Revenue

Credit column. Cash receipts from other sources are recorded in a General Ledger Credit column. The advantage of using these special columns is that posting to the Sales account and to the Repair Revenue account is then necessary only once a month.

The cash receipts journal of the Upbeat Music Shop is shown below. Look at the journal as you read about the procedures used to post from it to the ledger accounts.

1. Entries in the General Ledger Credit column are posted daily. The account numbers are written in the Posting Reference column of the journal to show that the amounts have been posted individually.
2. Entries in the Sales Credit column and the Repair Revenue Credit column are totaled and posted at the end of the month. Dashes are placed in the Posting Reference column to show that the entries are not posted individually.
3. At the end of the month, a single rule is drawn across the amount columns of the cash receipts journal and these columns are pencil-footed. The accuracy of the totals is checked by adding the totals of the three credit columns. The result should equal the total of the Net Cash Debit column.

A dash in the Posting Reference column means that the entry is not posted individually.

General Ledger		Net Cash Debit $5,567.55
Credit. $1,325.80		
Sales Credit 3,695.00		
Repair Revenue		
Credit. 546.75		
Total Credits. $5,567.55	= Total Debits $5,567.55	

4. The totals are written in ink. A double rule is drawn across all columns except the Account Credited column.
5. A check mark is placed in parentheses below the total of the General Ledger Credit column to show that the total should

A check mark means that a total is not posted.

not be posted. The entries in this column were posted individually during the month.

6. The total of the Sales Credit column is posted to the Sales account. The number of the Sales account (401) is entered in parentheses below the total of the Sales Credit column in the cash receipts journal to show that this amount has been posted.

7. The totals of the Repair Revenue Credit column and the Net Cash Debit column are posted to the proper ledger accounts— Repair Revenue and Cash. The account numbers are written in parentheses below the column totals in the cash receipts journal to show that these amounts have been posted.

8. After cash has been proved, the beginning cash balance for June 1 is written in the cash receipts journal.

CASH PAYMENTS JOURNAL

Many of the cash payments made by the Upbeat Music Shop are for purchases of merchandise and for store expenses. Thus the two accounts most frequently debited in the business's cash payments journal are Purchases and Store Expense. The Purchases account is used for all merchandise that Sheila Polk buys for resale. The Store Expense account is used for wrapping paper, twine, sales slip books, window display materials, and other small items used in the store.

To save time in journalizing and posting, Upbeat uses a cash payments journal that has three special columns: General Ledger Debit, Purchases Debit, and Store Expense Debit. The journal has a Net Cash Credit column as well.

Look at the cash payments journal below as you read about the procedures used to post from it to the ledger accounts.

	DATE	ACCOUNT DEBITED	CHECK NO.	POST. REF.	GENERAL LEDGER DEBIT	PURCHASES DEBIT	STORE EXPENSE DEBIT	NET CASH CREDIT	
	19— May 2	Store Expense	817	—			31 00	31 00	
②	3	Purchases	818	—		600 00		600 00	
①	4	Office Expense	819	506	2 25			2 25	③ ④
	31	Totals			98 60	2046 50	287 88	2432 98	
					(✓)	(501)	(508)	(101)	

⑤   ⑥

1. Entries in the General Ledger Debit column are posted daily during the month. The account numbers are placed in the Posting Reference column of the journal to show that these amounts have been posted individually.
2. Entries in the Purchases Debit and Store Expense Debit columns are not posted individually. These columns are totaled and posted at the end of the month. Dashes are placed in the Posting Reference column to show that these entries are not posted individually.
3. At the end of the month, a single rule is drawn across each amount column, and the columns are pencil-footed. The accuracy of the totals is checked by adding the totals of the three debit columns. The result should equal the total of the Net Cash Credit column.

General Ledger	Net Cash Credit..... $2,432.98
Debit ....$ 98.60	
Purchases Debit..... 2,046.50	
Store Expense Debit.. 287.88	
Total Debits ....$2,432.98 =Total Credits........ $2,432.98	

4. The totals are written in ink. A double rule is drawn across all columns except the Account Debited column and the Check Number column.
5. A check mark is placed in parentheses below the total of the General Ledger Debit column to show that this amount should not be posted. The individual amounts were posted during the month.
6. The totals of the Purchases Debit, Store Expense Debit, and Net Cash Credit columns are posted. The account numbers are written in parentheses below the column totals in the cash payments journal to show that the amounts have been posted.

The following illustrations provide a review of the procedures used to journalize and post transactions for purchases of merchandise on credit and sales of merchandise on credit.

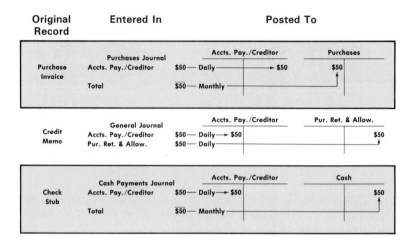

Review of transactions for purchases on credit.

Review of transactions for sales on credit.

Check Your Reading

1. Use the review of transactions for purchases on credit (shown above) to answer the following questions:
   a. In what journal is the data from the purchase invoice entered? To what accounts is the entry posted?
   b. In what journal is the data from the credit memo entered? To what accounts is the entry posted?
   c. In what journal is the data from the check stub entered? To what accounts is the entry posted?

2. Look at the review of transactions for sales on credit (see page 496) to answer the following questions:

a. In what journal is the data from the sales invoice entered? To what accounts is the entry posted?

b. In what journal is the data from the credit memo entered? To what accounts is the entry posted?

c. In what journal is the data from the customer's check entered? To what accounts is the entry posted?

Exercises for Topic 4

1. Edward Wagner owns a furniture store. He both sells and repairs furniture. The business uses multicolumn cash journals. The cash receipts journal has General Ledger Credit, Sales Credit, and Repair Revenue Credit columns, as well as a Net Cash Debit column. The cash payments journal has General Ledger Debit, Purchases Debit, and Store Expense Debit columns, as well as a Net Cash Credit column.

a. Open the following ledger accounts: Cash, 101; Accts. Pay./Dunlap Wholesale Company, 201; Sales, 401; Repair Revenue, 402; Purchases, 501; Advertising Expense, 502; Delivery Expense, 503; Insurance Expense, 504; Miscellaneous Expenses, 505; Office Expense, 506; Salaries Expense, 507; and Store Expense, 508.

Enter a balance of $3,000 in the Cash account. Enter a balance of $211.20 in the Accts. Pay./Dunlap Wholesale Company account. Date the balances January 2.

b. Journalize the following transactions in the cash receipts journal and in the cash payments journal. All payments are made by check. Checks should be numbered in order, beginning with 121.

Jan. 2 Cash balance, $3,000.

2 Paid $75 for cleaning (Miscellaneous Expenses).

3 Received $300 for furniture repair.

4 Paid $80 for an ad in the *Weekly Times.*

4 Received $978 from cash sales for the week.

5 Paid $24 for oil for the delivery truck.

5 Received $185 for furniture repair.

7 Paid $345 for the purchase of merchandise.

9 Received $73 for furniture repair.

9 Paid $184 for new glass for the store window.

9 Paid $30 for a headlight for the delivery truck.

9	Paid $248 for insurance on the store.
10	Paid $14 for stationery for the office (Office Expense).
11	Received $1,140 from cash sales for the week.
13	Paid $211.20 to Dunlap Wholesale Company on account.
14	Paid $880 in salaries.
14	Paid $6.25 for wrapping paper for use in the store (Store Expense).
16	Paid $375 for the purchase of merchandise.
16	Paid $35 for advertising.
17	Received $730 for furniture repair.
18	Received $1,576 from cash sales for the week.
19	Paid $523 for the purchase of merchandise.
20	Paid $17 for postage (Office Expense).
21	Paid $38.26 for gas and oil for the delivery truck.
23	Paid $65 for the purchase of merchandise.
25	Received $986.75 from cash sales for the week.
25	Paid $81 for the light and water bill (Miscellaneous Expenses).
26	Paid $35.35 for the telephone bill (Miscellaneous Expenses).
27	Paid $1,572 for the purchase of merchandise.
28	Paid $920 in salaries.
30	Paid $755 for the purchase of merchandise.
30	Paid $38.62 for supplies for the store (Store Expense).
31	Paid $655 for the purchase of merchandise.

c. Post the entries in the General Ledger Credit and General Ledger Debit columns to the accounts.
d. Pencil-foot, total, and rule the journals.
e. Prove cash according to the cash journals and the checkbook. The checkbook balance on January 31 is $1,761.07.
f. Post the totals of the journals to the following accounts: Cash, Sales, Repair Revenue, Purchases, and Store Expense.
g. Make a memorandum entry in the cash receipts journal to record the beginning cash balance for February 1.

Read each of the following statements. From the words below each statement, choose the term that best matches the statement.

1. The time to post the credit to the Sales account from the sales journal.

   end of day   end of month   end of year

2. Goods returned by a customer.

   sales allowance   sales return

3. The number of lines needed for one entry in a sales journal.

   four   one   three   two

4. The amount that a business earns by selling merchandise or services.

   cash   credit   revenue

5. A special journal used to record only sales on credit.

   purchases journal   sales journal

6. The time to post from the sales journal to customers' accounts.

   end of day   end of month

7. Unsatisfactory merchandise kept by a customer for a lower price.

   sales allowance   sales return

8. A record that contains information used to journalize a credit sale.

   purchase invoice   sales slip

9. Comparing the ending cash balance according to the cash journals with the checkbook balance.

   journalizing   posting   proving cash

10. Mark(s) used to show that an entry is not posted.

    check mark   dash   parentheses

11. The time to post debits from the cash receipts journal.

    end of day   end of month

12. A journal with special columns.

    general journal   multicolumn journal

13. A record that contains information used to journalize cash received on account.

    check from customer   check stub
    purchase invoice

14. A journal used to record only the receipt of cash.

    cash payments journal
    cash receipts journal

15. A record that contains information used to journalize a purchase on credit.

    check stub   purchase invoice

16. Mark(s) used to show that a total is not posted.

    check mark in parentheses   dash

17. The time to post entries from the General Ledger Credit column of the cash receipts journal.

    end of day   end of month

APPLICATION PROBLEMS

1. Do the following work for The Sound Shop, a music store.

a. Open the following ledger accounts: Accts. Rec./Mary Furtado, 102; Accts. Rec./Rick Lowe, 103; Sales, 401; and Sales Returns and Allowances, 402.

b. Journalize the following transactions. Record the transactions of August 7, 10, and 14 in a general journal. Record all the other transactions in a sales journal.

Aug. 2 Sold merchandise on credit for $500 to Rick Lowe, Sales Slip 120.

3 Sold merchandise on credit for $186 to Mary Furtado, Sales Slip 127.

4 Sold merchandise on credit for $1,602 to Rick Lowe, Sales Slip 149.

5 Sold merchandise on credit for $77 to Rick Lowe, Sales Slip 168.

6 Sold merchandise on credit for $325 to Mary Furtado, Sales Slip 182.

7 Issued Credit Memo 83 for $303 to Rick Lowe for returned merchandise.

9 Sold merchandise on credit for $650 to Mary Furtado, Sales Slip 193.

10 Issued Credit Memo 84 for $325 to Mary Furtado for returned merchandise.

12 Sold merchandise on credit for $410 to Rick Lowe, Sales Slip 206.

13 Sold merchandise on credit for $189 to Mary Furtado, Sales Slip 209.

14 Issued Credit Memo 85 for $410 to Rick Lowe for returned merchandise.

c. Post the entries from the sales journal and the general journal to the customers' accounts. Be sure to post the entries in order by date.

d. Pencil-foot, total, and rule the sales journal. Date the total August 31.

e. Post the total of the sales journal to the Sales account.

2. Do the following work for the Home Decorating Store:

a. Open the following ledger accounts, and enter the balances shown: Cash, 101, $2,850; Accts. Rec./Tina Arness, 102, $20; Accts. Rec./Jack Barton, 103; Accts. Rec./Sally Brown, 104, $18; Accts. Rec./Jeffrey Carlin, 105, $26; Accts. Rec./Ann Colt, 106; Accts. Rec./Peter Dixon, 107, $15; Accts. Rec./Julie Kent, 108; Accts. Rec./George McDonnell, 109; Accts. Rec./Lucia Perez, 110; Accts. Pay./Benson and Lox, 201; Accts. Pay./Curtis Company, 202; Accts. Pay./Robertson and Company, 203; Accts. Pay./Valdez Company, 204; Accts. Pay./Ralph Waldo, 205; Sales, 401; and Purchases, 501. Date the balances November 1.

b. Journalize the following transactions. Use a purchases journal, a cash payments journal, a sales journal, and a cash receipts journal. Record the beginning cash balance of $2,850 in the cash receipts journal.

Nov. 1 Sold merchandise on credit for $20 to Ann Colt, Sales Slip 4100.

2 Purchased merchandise on credit for $180 from Benson and Lox, Invoice A623.

3 Received $14 from Ann Colt on account.

4 Sold merchandise on credit for $14 to Tina Arness, Sales Slip 4101.

6 Purchased merchandise on credit for $150 from the Valdez Company, Invoice 9807.

8 Purchased merchandise on credit for $175 from the Curtis Company, Invoice 1142-3.

10 Sold merchandise on credit for $30 to George McDonnell, Sales Slip 4102.

12 Paid $180 to Benson and Lox on account, Check 612.

13 Purchased merchandise on credit for $210 from Ralph Waldo, Invoice 458.

16 Sold merchandise on credit for $40 to Julie Kent, Sales Slip 4103.

16 Sold merchandise on credit for $35 to Peter Dixon, Sales Slip 4104.

18 Sold merchandise on credit for $15 to Ann Colt, Sales Slip 4105.

19 Received $15 from Sally Brown on account.

20 Received $16 from Jeffrey Carlin on account.

22 Purchased merchandise on credit for $85 from Robertson and Company, Invoice 27-143.

22 Paid $175 to Curtis Company on account, Check 613.

24 Sold merchandise on credit for $38 to Lucia Perez, Sales Slip 4106.

26 Received $20 from Tina Arness on account.

27 Sold merchandise on credit for $18 to Jack Barton, Sales Slip 4107.

29 Purchased merchandise on credit for $105 from Benson and Lox, Invoice A923.

29 Purchased merchandise on credit for $72 from Ralph Waldo, Invoice 574.

c. Post the entries from the journals to the accounts.

d. Pencil-foot, total, and rule the journals.

e. Prove cash according to the cash journals and the checkbook. The checkbook balance on November 30 is $2,560.

f. Post the totals of the journals.

g. Make a memorandum entry in the cash receipts journal to record the beginning cash balance on December 1.

CHAPTER 19

THE TRIAL BALANCE AND FINANCIAL STATEMENTS

In Chapters 16, 17, and 18 you learned how to journalize and post business transactions. In posting, you recorded information about increases and decreases in asset, liability, and owner's equity accounts. The owner of a business, however, cannot get a good picture of how the business is doing by simply looking at these accounts. Every month or so, therefore, the business will summarize the information in all the accounts. This summary is called a *trial balance*. Then the business will use information in the trial balance to prepare financial statements that show how the business is doing. In this chapter you will learn how to prepare the trial balance and financial statements.

TOPIC 1 ◆ THE TRIAL BALANCE

GOALS

1. To prepare a trial balance.
2. To find errors in a trial balance that is out of balance.

KEY TERMS

A *trial balance* is a record summarizing ledger accounts and proving that total debits equal total credits.
In balance means that total debits equal total credits on the trial balance.
Out of balance means that total debits and total credits are not equal on the trial balance.

ACCOUNT BALANCES

The total debit balances and total credit balances in the ledger accounts should be equal. A trial balance proves that they are equal.

The ledger accounts for Bev's Craft Corner on December 31 are shown on pages 503 through 505.

Note the following about these accounts:

1. Each account is numbered according to the following plan:

Asset accounts, 101 to 199
Liability accounts, 201 to 299
Owner's equity accounts, 301 to 399
Revenue accounts, 401 to 499
Expense accounts, 501 to 599

2. The *Merchandise Inventory* account is an asset account. This account shows the cost of the merchandise that a business has on hand at the beginning of an accounting period. The cost of the merchandise inventory on December 1 was $825.

3. Some accounts have debit balances, and others have credit balances. For example, asset accounts normally have debit balances. Liability and owner's equity accounts normally have credit balances.

Cash   Account No. 101

DATE	EXPLANATION	POST REF.	DEBIT	CREDIT	BALANCE DEBIT	BALANCE CREDIT
Dec. 1	Balance	✓			3050 00	
31		CR1	4165 00		7215 00	
31		CP1		3123 00	4092 00	

Accts. Rec. / Centerville Recreation Center   Account No. 102

DATE	EXPLANATION	POST REF.	DEBIT	CREDIT	BALANCE DEBIT	BALANCE CREDIT
Dec. 7		S2	135 00		135 00	

Accts. Rec. / Crafts Club   Account No. 103

DATE	EXPLANATION	POST REF.	DEBIT	CREDIT	BALANCE DEBIT	BALANCE CREDIT
Dec. 1	Balance	✓			20 00	
10		S2	56 00		76 00	
11		J2		5 00	71 00	

Equipment _____ Account No. _141_

DATE		EXPLANATION	POST REF.	DEBIT	CREDIT	BALANCE	
						DEBIT	CREDIT
Dec.$^{19-}$	1	Balance	✓			300 00	
	3		J1	400 00		700 00	

Furniture _____ Account No. _151_

DATE		EXPLANATION	POST REF.	DEBIT	CREDIT	BALANCE	
						DEBIT	CREDIT
Dec.$^{19-}$	1	Balance	✓			800 00	
	4		J1	200 00		1000 00	

Merchandise Inventory _____ Account No. _161_

DATE		EXPLANATION	POST REF.	DEBIT	CREDIT	BALANCE	
						DEBIT	CREDIT
Dec.$^{19-}$	1	Balance	✓			825 00	

Notes Payable _____ Account No. _201_

DATE		EXPLANATION	POST REF.	DEBIT	CREDIT	BALANCE	
						DEBIT	CREDIT
Dec.$^{19-}$	6		J1		400 00		400 00

Accts. Pay./Craftland Supply Corporation _____ Account No. _211_

DATE		EXPLANATION	POST REF.	DEBIT	CREDIT	BALANCE	
						DEBIT	CREDIT
Dec.$^{19-}$	17		P1		205 00		205 00

Accts. Pay. / Wells Corporation — Account No. 221

DATE	EXPLANATION	POST REF.	DEBIT	CREDIT	BALANCE DEBIT	BALANCE CREDIT
Dec. 19— 1	Balance	✓				1 0 0 00
3		P1		4 0 0 00		5 0 0 00
6		J1	4 0 0 00			1 0 0 00

Beverly Davis, Capital — Account No. 301

DATE	EXPLANATION	POST REF.	DEBIT	CREDIT	BALANCE DEBIT	BALANCE CREDIT
Dec. 19— 1	Balance	✓				5 1 1 8 00
31		J1		5 0 0 00		5 6 1 8 00

Sales — Account No. 401

DATE	EXPLANATION	POST REF.	DEBIT	CREDIT	BALANCE DEBIT	BALANCE CREDIT
Dec. 19— 31		S2		1 9 5 0 00		1 9 5 0 00

Purchases — Account No. 501

DATE	EXPLANATION	POST REF.	DEBIT	CREDIT	BALANCE DEBIT	BALANCE CREDIT
Dec. 19— 31		P1	8 6 5 00		8 6 5 00	

Rent Expense — Account No. 516

DATE	EXPLANATION	POST REF.	DEBIT	CREDIT	BALANCE DEBIT	BALANCE CREDIT
Dec. 19— 3		CP1	1 8 5 00		1 8 5 00	

Salaries Expense — Account No. 517

DATE	EXPLANATION	POST REF.	DEBIT	CREDIT	BALANCE DEBIT	BALANCE CREDIT
Dec. 19— 31		CP1	4 0 0 00		4 0 0 00	

PREPARING A TRIAL BALANCE

A trial balance is a listing of the titles and the numbers of a business's accounts along with the account balances. The accounts are arranged in numeric order on the trial balance. The debit balances are entered in the left money column, and the credit balances are entered in the right money column. After all the balances are entered, the amounts in the columns are added to find the total debit balances and the total credit balances.

The trial balance prepared on December 31 by the accounting clerk for Bev's Craft Corner is shown below. Note the following:

❶

Bev's Craft Corner
Trial Balance
December 31, 19—

ACCOUNT TITLE	ACCT. NO.	DEBIT	CREDIT
Cash	101	4092 00	
Accts. Rec./Centerville Recreation Center	102	135 00	
Accts. Rec./Crafts Club	103	71 00	
Equipment	141	700 00	
Furniture	151	1000 00	
Merchandise Inventory	161	825 00	
Notes Payable	201		400 00
Accts. Pay./Craftland Supply Corporation	211		205 00
Accts. Pay./Wells Corporation	221		100 00
Beverly Davis, Capital	301		5618 00
Sales	401		1950 00
Purchases	501	865 00	
Rent Expense	516	185 00	
Salaries Expense	517	400 00	
❹		8273 00	8273 00

❷ **❸** **❺** **❻**

1. The heading of the trial balance is centered at the top of the form.
2. Only accounts that have balances are listed. The accounts are entered in numeric order. The title, the number, and the balance of each account are listed.
3. A single rule is drawn across the Debit and the Credit columns after the last balance is listed.
4. The Debit and the Credit columns are pencil-footed.

5. If the totals of the Debit and the Credit columns are equal, the totals are written on the line under the single rule.

6. A double rule is drawn under the totals of the Debit and the Credit columns.

When the total debit balances and the total credit balances are equal, the trial balance is *in balance.* When the total debit balances and the total credit balances are not equal, the trial balance is *out of balance.* If the trial balance is out of balance, the accounting clerk must find the error or errors.

FINDING ERRORS ON A TRIAL BALANCE

To find errors on a trial balance, an accounting clerk must follow the seven steps explained below. Study each step carefully.

1. Check the addition of the Debit and the Credit columns of the trial balance. Are the columns added correctly?

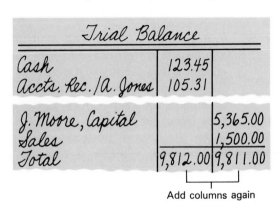

Add columns again

2. Compare the balance of each account with the balance on the trial balance. Have the account balances been copied correctly on the trial balance?

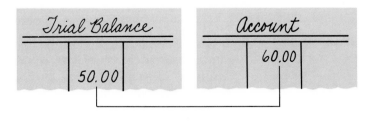

3. Check the balance of each account. Has it been computed accurately?

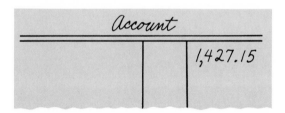

4. Find the difference between the totals of the Debit and the Credit columns of the trial balance. If the difference is $30, for example, look through the journals and ledger accounts for a $30 entry that may not have been posted or may have been posted twice.

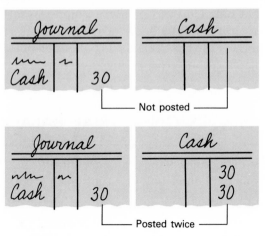

5. Divide the difference between the totals of the trial balance columns by 2. If the difference is $30, for example, look for a $15 item posted to the wrong balance column of an account. A $15 debit may have been posted as a credit, or a $15 credit may have been posted as a debit.

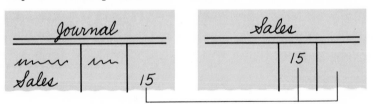

6. If the difference can be evenly divided by 9, look for a transposition, or switching, of two numbers. A $36 difference, for example, is evenly divided by 9. This error may be due to a transposition of numbers, such as 173 or 137.

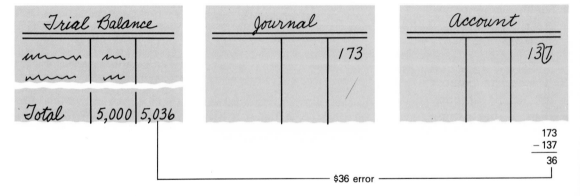

7. Check the accuracy of the postings from the journals to the ledger accounts.

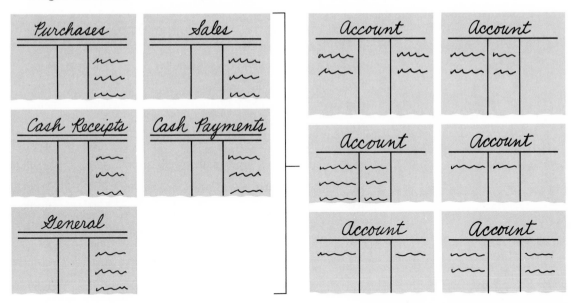

Check Your Reading

1. What is the name of the record that summarizes all the information in the ledger accounts and proves that the total debits equal the total credits?

2. What kind of balance does an account have if total credits are less than total debits?

3. What kind of balance does an account have if total debits are greater than total credits?

4. Is the Merchandise Inventory account classified as an asset, a liability, or an owner's equity account?

5. If an account has a zero balance, should it be listed on the trial balance?

6. In what order are accounts listed on a trial balance?

Exercises for Topic I

1. On April 30, the ledger accounts of Reilly's Accessory Store contained the balances listed below. Prepare a trial balance. Date it April 30 of the current year. If your trial balance is out of balance, use the first four steps shown on pages 507 to 508 to find the error.

Acct. No.	Account Title	Balance	Type of Balance
101	Cash	$2,600	Debit
102	Notes Receivable	500	Debit
103	Accts. Rec./Martin Avon	100	Debit
104	Delivery Equipment	4,000	Debit
105	Furniture	2,000	Debit
106	Merchandise Inventory	1,500	Debit
201	Notes Payable	700	Credit
202	Accts. Pay./Desmond White	600	Credit
301	Kathleen Reilly, Capital	9,750	Credit
401	Sales	2,500	Credit
501	Purchases	1,400	Debit
502	Miscellaneous Expenses	200	Debit
503	Rent Expense	500	Debit
504	Salaries Expense	750	Debit

2. On May 31, the ledger accounts of the Hymer Company contained the balances listed below. Prepare a trial balance. Date it May 31 of the current year. If your trial balance is out of balance, use the first four steps shown on pages 507 to 508 to find the error.

Acct. No.	Account Title	Balance	Type of Balance
101	Cash	$3,350	Debit
102	Notes Receivable	400	Debit
103	Accts. Rec./Felicia Webb	500	Debit
104	Delivery Equipment	4,200	Debit
105	Furniture	1,550	Debit
106	Merchandise Inventory	3,500	Debit
201	Notes Payable	950	Credit
202	Accts. Pay./Howard Katz	1,450	Credit
301	Paula Hymer, Capital	9,940	Credit
401	Sales	5,000	Credit
501	Purchases	2,000	Debit
502	Miscellaneous Expenses	375	Debit
503	Rent Expense	625	Debit
504	Salaries Expense	840	Debit

GOALS

1. To classify accounts as asset, liability, owner's equity, revenue, or expense accounts.
2. To state whether a given account normally has a debit balance or a credit balance.
3. To prepare an income statement for a service business.
4. To prepare a balance sheet for a service business.

KEY TERMS

The *financial statements* are the income statement and the balance sheet.

A *service business* is one that provides a service and does not sell merchandise.

An *income statement* is a record of revenue, expenses, and the results of a business's operations for an accounting period.

A *balance sheet* is a record of a business's financial condition on a certain date.

In Topic 1 you learned that the trial balance is used to prove that the total debits and the total credits in the ledger accounts are equal. The trial balance also provides the information needed to prepare up-to-date financial statements for a business. The *financial statements* of a business are the income statement and the balance sheet. Now you will see how the trial balance is used in preparing financial statements for a service business.

REVIEW OF ACCOUNTS AND ACCOUNT BALANCES

An accounting clerk must be familiar with all the accounts used by a business. The clerk must know the classification of each account. For example, is an account an asset account, a liability account, an owner's equity account, a revenue account, or an expense account? The accounting clerk must also know how the accounts are arranged within each classification. For instance, some accounts are arranged alphabetically within a classification.

Study the trial balance of Domino's Parcel Delivery on page 512. Since Domino's Parcel Delivery does not sell merchandise but provides a service, it is called a *service business*.

1. The first five accounts on the trial balance of Domino's Parcel Delivery are the *balance sheet accounts*. The balance sheet accounts

Domino's Parcel Delivery
Trial Balance
June 30, 19—

ACCOUNT TITLE	ACCT. NO.	DEBIT	CREDIT
Cash	101	1 250 00	
Delivery Equipment	102	2 500 00	
Office Furniture	103	900 00	
Notes Payable	201		1 300 00
Vincent Reed, Capital	301		2 700 00
Delivery Revenue	401		1 200 00
Miscellaneous Expenses	501	225 00	
Rent Expense	502	150 00	
Salaries Expense	503	175 00	
		5 200 00	5 200 00

The *balance sheet accounts* are assets, liabilities, and owner's equity.

are assets, liabilities, and owner's equity. They are shown in the table below.

Balance Sheet Accounts	Classification	Type of Balance
Cash	Asset	Debit
Delivery Equipment	Asset	Debit
Office Furniture	Asset	Debit
Notes Payable	Liability	Credit
Vincent Reed, Capital	Owner's equity	Credit

The *income statement accounts* are revenue and expenses.

2. The last four accounts on the trial balance of Domino's Parcel Delivery are the *income statement accounts*. The income statement accounts are revenue and expenses.

Income Statement Accounts	Classification	Type of Balance
Delivery Revenue	Revenue	Credit
Miscellaneous Expenses	Expense	Debit
Rent Expense	Expense	Debit
Salaries Expense	Expense	Debit

THE INCOME STATEMENT

The accounting clerk prepares an income statement from the information on the trial balance. An *income statement* is a record of revenue and expenses that shows the results of the operations of a business for an accounting period. An *accounting period* is the time covered by an income statement. The time covered may be a month, a quarter (three months), six months, or a year, depending on the business.

The income statement is prepared from the income statement accounts on the trial balance. Note the income statement accounts on the trial balance of Domino's Parcel Delivery on page 512.

Domino's Parcel Delivery has a monthly accounting period. The income statement below has been prepared for the month ended June 30. Look at it as you note the following:

An *accounting period* is the time covered by an income statement.

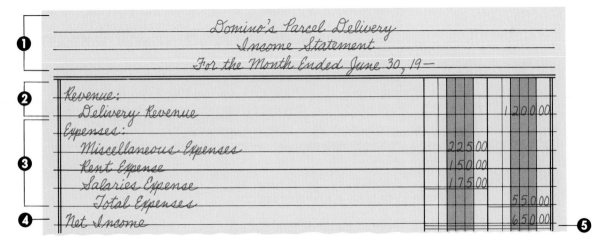

1. The heading is centered at the top of the income statement. The heading lists the name of the business, the name of the statement, and the accounting period covered by the statement.

2. The first section of the income statement is the Revenue section. The title "Revenue:" is entered next to the margin on the first line of the statement. The information for the Revenue section is taken from the trial balance. The sources of revenue are indented and listed under the title. If there is only one source of revenue, the amount from that source is entered in the right money column. If there is more than one source of revenue, the amount from each source is entered in the left money column, and a single rule is drawn under the last amount. Then the total amount is entered in the right money column.

The sections of the income statement are the Revenue, Expenses, and Net Income or Net Loss sections.

3. The second section of the income statement is the Expenses section. The title "Expenses:" is entered next to the margin on the line under the Revenue section. The information for the Expenses section is taken from the trial balance. Each expense is indented and listed under the title. Again, if there is only one expense, the amount is entered in the right money column. If there are several expenses, the amount of each expense is entered in the left money column, and a single rule is drawn under the last amount. Then the total amount is entered in the right money column opposite the words "Total Expenses." These words are indented under the last expense.

A *net income* exists when revenue is greater than expenses.

A *net loss* exists when expenses are greater than revenue.

4. The third section of the income statement is the Net Income or Net Loss section. A single rule is drawn across the second money column under the amount of total expenses. Then the amount of total expenses is subtracted from the amount of total revenue. The difference is entered on the next line.

   If revenue is greater than expenses, the difference is the *net income* for the accounting period. If expenses are greater than revenue, the difference is the *net loss* for the accounting period. The income statement for Domino's Parcel Delivery shows a net income of $650. "Net Income" is written next to the margin on the line under the Expenses section. The amount of net income is entered on the same line.

5. A double rule is drawn across the two money columns of the income statement to show that the statement is completed.

THE BALANCE SHEET

The balance sheet is prepared after the income statement is completed. The *balance sheet* is a record of the financial condition of a business on a certain date. It shows the assets, the liabilities, and the owner's equity of a business. The balance sheet is prepared after the income statement because the amount of net income or net loss shown on the income statement must be entered on the balance sheet. The net income or net loss is used to find the total owner's equity.

The balance sheet is prepared from the balance sheet accounts on the trial balance and from the Net Income or Net Loss section of the income statement. Note the balance sheet accounts on the trial balance of Domino's Parcel Delivery shown on the facing page. Look at the balance sheet as you note the following:

1. The heading is centered at the top of the balance sheet. The heading lists the name of the business, the name of the statement, and the date of the statement. Note that the date on the

Domino's Parcel Delivery
Trial Balance
June 30, 19—

ACCOUNT TITLE	ACCT. NO.	DEBIT	CREDIT
Cash	101	1250 00	
Delivery Equipment	102	2500 00	
Office Furniture	103	900 00	
Notes Payable	201		1300 00
Vincent Reed, Capital	301		2700 00

Domino's Parcel Delivery
Balance Sheet
June 30, 19—

Assets		Liabilities	
Cash	1250 00	Notes Payable	1300 00
Delivery Equipment	2500 00		
Office Furniture	900 00	Owner's Equity	
		Vincent Reed, Capital $2,700.00	
		Net Income 650.00	
		Total Owner's Equity	3350 00
Total	4650 00	Total	4650 00

balance sheet consists of a month, a day, and a year. Unlike the income statement, the balance sheet is not for a period of time. The balance sheet shows the business's condition for one day only.

2. The information for the Assets section of the balance sheet is taken from the trial balance. The title "Assets" is centered on the first line on the left side of the balance sheet. Under the title, each asset is listed at the margin. The amount of each asset is entered in the money column. Then the word "Total" and the total amount of assets are entered. However, the total is entered only after the right side of the balance sheet is completed.

3. The information for the Liabilities section of the balance sheet is taken from the trial balance. The title "Liabilities" is centered on the first line on the right side of the balance sheet. Under the title, each liability is listed at the margin. If there is more than one liability, the amounts of the liabilities are entered to the left of the money column. Then "Total Liabilities"

is written, and the total amount is entered in the money column. However, when there is only one liability, the word "Total" is not entered.

4. A line is skipped under the Liabilities section, and the title "Owner's Equity" is centered on the next line. Each owner's equity item is entered to the left of the money column. The first item in the Owner's Equity section is the capital account. This information is taken from the trial balance.

   The second item in the Owner's Equity section is the net income. This information is taken from the income statement. The amounts of the owner's equity items are added, and the words "Total Owner's Equity" are indented on the next line. The total amount is entered in the money column.

5. A single rule is drawn across the money column on the left side and across the money column on the right side. Both rules must be on the same line. The word "Total" is entered under the Assets section and also under the Liabilities and the Owner's Equity sections. The amounts on each side are added. The totals are entered in the money columns. Note that both totals are equal. Double rules are drawn under the totals in the left and the right money columns to show that the balance sheet has been completed.

The capital account plus net income (or less net loss) equals total owner's equity.

Check Your Reading

1. Classify each account as an asset, a liability, an owner's equity, a revenue, or an expense account.

a. Notes Payable	**f.** Office Furniture
b. Miscellaneous Expenses	**g.** Delivery Revenue
c. Delivery Equipment	**h.** Supplies Expense
d. Salaries Expense	**i.** Cash
e. Rosa Dunn, Capital	**j.** Rent Expense

2. For each account above, tell which type of balance, debit or credit, the account normally has.

3. Name the three classifications of balance sheet accounts.

4. Name the classifications of income statement accounts for service businesses.

5. Name an example of an asset account, a liability account, and an expense account.

6. How do the dates on an income statement and a balance sheet differ?

1. The trial balance for the Regal Cleaning Service is shown below.

Regal Cleaning Service
Trial Balance
September 30, 19 –

ACCOUNT TITLE	ACCT. NO.	DEBIT	CREDIT
Cash	101	1500 00	
Cleaning Equipment	102	1000 00	
Office Furniture	103	800 00	
Notes Payable	201		300 00
Anne McKay, Capital	301		2545 00
Cleaning Revenue	401		1000 00
Miscellaneous Expenses	501	120 00	
Rent Expense	502	200 00	
Salaries Expense	503	225 00	
		3845 00	3845 00

a. List the balance sheet accounts under these headings: "Account," "Classification," and "Type of Balance."

b. List the revenue and expense accounts under these headings: "Account," "Classification," and "Type of Balance."

2. The titles of the accounts of Rico's Repair Shop are given below. List the accounts in the order that they would appear on the trial balance. (The correct order is assets, liabilities, owner's equity, revenue, and expenses. The expense accounts should be arranged alphabetically.) Indicate the classification and the type of balance for each account. Arrange the information under these headings: "Account," "Classification" and "Type of Balance."

Rent Expense
Rico Gonzalez, Capital
Cash
Notes Receivable
Accts. Rec./
 Jim Menzies

Miscellaneous Expenses
Repair Revenue
Repair Equipment
Notes Payable
Accts. Pay./Elman
 Company

Dave's Printing Service
Trial Balance
August 31, 19—

ACCOUNT TITLE	ACCT. NO.	DEBIT	CREDIT
Cash	101	2075 00	
Accts. Rec. / Jane Redmond	102	400 00	
Printing Equipment	103	1510 00	
Truck	104	4400 00	
Accts. Pay. / Archer Print Supplies	201		650 00
Dave DiCarlo, Capital	301		7035 00
Printing Revenue	401		2350 00
Advertising Expense	501	100 00	
Miscellaneous Expenses	502	150 00	
Salaries Expense	503	1400 00	
		10035 00	10035 00

3. Do the following work for Dave's Printing Service:

   a. Prepare an income statement for the month ended August 31 of the current year. The trial balance for August 31 is shown above.

   b. Prepare a balance sheet dated August 31 of the current year.

4. Do the following work for Lynn Wolfe, attorney:

   a. Prepare an income statement for the month ended March 31 of the current year. The trial balance for March 31 is shown on the facing page.

   b. Prepare a balance sheet dated March 31 of the current year.

5. Do the following work for Specialty Cleaners:

   a. Prepare an income statement for the month ended May 31 of the current year. The trial balance for May 31 is shown on the facing page.

   b. Prepare a balance sheet dated May 31 of the current year.

Lynn Wolfe, Attorney
Trial Balance
March 31, 19—

ACCOUNT TITLE	ACCT. NO.	DEBIT	CREDIT
Cash	101	700 00	
Law Books	102	1500 00	
Office Equipment	103	600 00	
Office Furniture	104	1600 00	
Notes Payable	201		800 00
Lynn Wolfe, Capital	301		1690 00
Fee Revenue	401		3720 00
Miscellaneous Expenses	501	210 00	
Rent Expense	502	825 00	
Salaries Expense	503	775 00	
		6210 00	6210 00

Specialty Cleaners
Trial Balance
May 31, 19—

ACCOUNT TITLE	ACCT. NO.	DEBIT	CREDIT
Cash	101	1800 00	
Building	102	16000 00	
Cleaning Equipment	103	6200 00	
Store Equipment	104	1000 00	
Notes Payable	201		6500 00
Gunnar Lundgren, Capital	301		16870 00
Cleaning Revenue	401		3800 00
Advertising Expense	501	350 00	
Miscellaneous Expenses	502	250 00	
Salaries Expense	503	1570 00	
		27170 00	27170 00

TOPIC 3 ◆ FINANCIAL STATEMENTS FOR A MERCHANDISING BUSINESS

GOALS

1. To explain the difference between beginning and ending merchandise inventories.
2. To prepare an income statement for a merchandising business.
3. To prepare a balance sheet for a merchandising business.

KEY TERMS

A *merchandising* business sells goods to obtain revenue.

The *cost of goods available for sale* equals the beginning inventory plus purchases.

The *cost of goods sold* equals the cost of goods available for sale less the ending inventory.

The *gross profit on sales* equals revenue less the cost of merchandise sold.

A merchandising business prepares the same financial statements as a service business—the income statement and the balance sheet. A *merchandising* business, however, sells goods to obtain its revenue. Thus it has a *merchandise inventory.*

MERCHANDISE INVENTORY

A business's merchandise inventory is one of its assets. The *merchandise inventory* includes all items of merchandise on hand in the business. It also includes all items of merchandise in the warehouse (if the business has one). The *beginning merchandise inventory* is the cost of the merchandise inventory of a business at the beginning of an accounting period.

During an accounting period two things happen to the beginning merchandise inventory: (1) Items purchased increase the merchandise inventory. (2) Items sold decrease the merchandise inventory. The list below explains how merchandise inventory changes:

1. *September 1.* The merchandise on display on September 1 was part of the beginning merchandise inventory for Nancy's Cards and Books. On September 1, at the start of the accounting period, the total cost of this beginning merchandise inventory was $2,035.
2. *September 9.* On September 9 Nancy's Cards and Books received merchandise that had been purchased from a supplier. The merchandise was placed in stock. The receipt of these items increased the merchandise inventory.

Joe Allen is a salesperson at Nancy's Cards and Books. He is also responsible for keeping records of beginning and ending merchandise inventory.

3. *September 12.* On September 12 merchandise was sold to a customer. This sale decreased the merchandise in stock. Thus the merchandise inventory decreased.
4. *September 30.* Because of the changes that take place during an accounting period, a business's merchandise inventory at the end of the period is not the same as the merchandise inventory at the beginning of the period. The merchandise inventory of a business at the end of an accounting period is called the *ending merchandise inventory.* In order to find the ending merchandise inventory, the store must count all the items in the merchandise inventory.

The job of counting inventory is called *taking inventory.* On September 30 a salesperson at Nancy's Cards and Books took inventory. After inventory was taken, the salesperson computed the cost of the inventory. The total cost of the ending merchandise inventory at Nancy's Cards and Books on September 30 was $2,540.

THE INCOME STATEMENT

The beginning merchandise inventory of Nancy's Cards and Books was entered on the September 30 trial balance. This entry is shown below. On the trial balance, note that Merchandise Inventory is listed among the assets, after Accts. Rec./James Bell.

Nancy's Cards and Books
Trial Balance
September 30, 19—

ACCOUNT TITLE	ACCT. NO.	DEBIT	CREDIT
Cash	101	3125 00	
Accts. Rec. / James Bell	102	220 00	
Merchandise Inventory, Sept. 1, 19—	103	2035 00	
Store Equipment	104	5000 00	
Notes Payable	201		3000 00
Nancy James, Capital	301		5865 00
Sales	401		6200 00
Purchases	501	3130 00	
Miscellaneous Expenses	502	240 00	
Rent Expense	503	300 00	
Salaries Expense	504	800 00	
Store Supplies Expense	505	215 00	
		15065 00	15065 00

Ending Merchandise Inventory
September 30, 19—
$2,540

In a merchandising business an accounting clerk prepares the income statement in this way. The clerk uses the income statement accounts on the trial balance and the amounts of both the beginning and the ending merchandise inventory. The amount of the beginning merchandise inventory is already on the trial balance. Thus the only information that the accounting clerk needs to prepare the income statement is the data on the trial balance and a notation of the amount of the ending merchandise inventory.

Look at the income statement shown on the facing page and note the following:

1. The heading is centered at the top.
2. The Revenue section consists of one item—Sales. Since there is only one item, the amount is entered in the right money column.
3. The Cost of Goods Sold section follows the Revenue section. The title "Cost of Goods Sold" is aligned with the title "Revenue."
4. The amount of the beginning merchandise inventory (taken from the trial balance) is entered in the left money column.

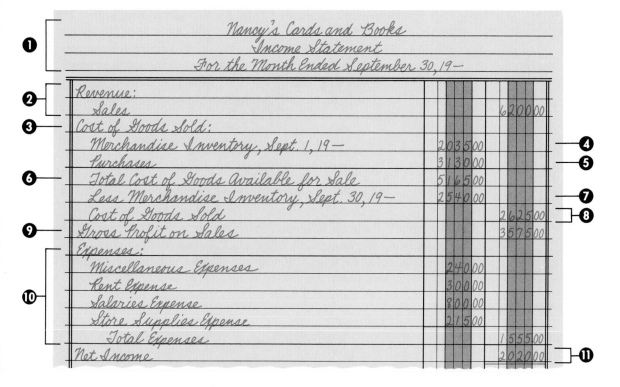

Nancy's Cards and Books
Income Statement
For the Month Ended September 30, 19—

① ② ③ ④ ⑤ ⑥ ⑦ ⑧ ⑨ ⑩ ⑪

Revenue:		
Sales		6 200 00
Cost of Goods Sold:		
Merchandise Inventory, Sept. 1, 19—	2 035 00	
Purchases	3 130 00	
Total Cost of Goods Available for Sale	5 165 00	
Less Merchandise Inventory, Sept. 30, 19—	2 540 00	
Cost of Goods Sold		2 625 00
Gross Profit on Sales		3 575 00
Expenses:		
Miscellaneous Expenses	240 00	
Rent Expense	300 00	
Salaries Expense	800 00	
Store Supplies Expense	215 00	
Total Expenses		1 555 00
Net Income		2 020 00

5. The amount of purchases (taken from the trial balance) is entered in the left money column.

6. A single rule is drawn under the purchases amount. The amount of the beginning merchandise inventory and the amount of purchases are then added. The total, which is entered in the left money column, represents the total cost of the goods available for sale during the month.

7. The amount of the ending merchandise inventory is entered in the left money column. This amount is found on the notation shown beneath the trial balance.

8. A single rule is drawn under the ending inventory amount. Then this amount is subtracted from the total cost of the goods available for sale. The difference is entered in the right money column opposite the words "Cost of Goods Sold." A single rule is drawn under the cost of goods sold amount.

9. The Gross Profit on Sales section follows the Cost of Goods Sold section. The amount of the gross profit on sales is found by subtracting the amount of the cost of goods sold from the amount of the revenue.

10. The Expenses section follows the Gross Profit on Sales section. The expenses are taken from the trial balance. The amounts of the expenses are entered in the left money column. A single rule is drawn under the last amount. The total of all expenses is then entered in the right money column

opposite the words "Total Expenses." A single rule is drawn under this amount.

11. The total of the expenses is subtracted from the gross profit on sales. The difference is entered in the right money column opposite the words "Net Income." A double rule is drawn under both money columns to show that the income statement has been completed.

THE BALANCE SHEET

The accounting clerk gets information to prepare the balance sheet of a merchandising business from several places. The necessary information comes from the balance sheet accounts on the trial balance, from the notation of the ending merchandise inventory, and from the net income on the income statement.

Nancy's Cards and Books
Trial Balance
September 30, 19—

ACCOUNT TITLE	ACCT. NO.	DEBIT	CREDIT
Cash	101	3125 00	
Accts. Rec. / James Bell	102	220 00	
Merchandise Inventory, Sept. 1, 19—	103	2035 00	
Store Equipment	104	5000 00	
Notes Payable	201		3000 00
Nancy James, Capital	301		5865 00
Sales	401		6200 00
Purchases	501	3130 00	
Miscellaneous Expenses	502	240 00	
Rent Expense	503	300 00	
Salaries Expense	504	800 00	
Store Supplies Expense	505	215 00	
		15065 00	15065 00

Ending Merchandise Inventory
September 30, 19—
$2,540

Study the procedures that the accounting clerk followed in preparing the balance sheet for Nancy's Cards and Books. Look at the trial balance, the notation of the ending merchandise inventory, income statement, and the balance sheet, shown on this and the facing pages.

Nancy's Cards and Books
Income Statement
For the Month Ended September 30, 19—

Revenue:		
Sales		6 200 00
Cost of Goods Sold:		
Merchandise Inventory, Sept. 1, 19—	2 035 00	
Purchases	3 130 00	
Total Cost of Goods Available for Sale	5 165 00	
Less Merchandise Inventory, Sept. 30, 19—	2 540 00	
Cost of Goods Sold		2 625 00
Gross Profit on Sales		3 575 00
Expenses:		
Miscellaneous Expenses	240 00	
Rent Expense	300 00	
Salaries Expense	800 00	
Store Supplies Expense	215 00	
Total Expenses		1 555 00
Net Income		2 020 00

Nancy's Cards and Books
Balance Sheet
September 30, 19—

Assets		Liabilities	
Cash	3 125 00	Notes Payable	3 000 00
Accts. Rec./James Bell	220 00		
Merchandise Inventory	2 540 00	Owner's Equity	
Store Equipment	5 000 00	Nancy James,	
		Capital $5,865.00	
		Net Income 2,020.00	
		Total Owner's Equity	7 885 00
Total	10 885 00	Total	10 885 00

Note the following:

1. The heading is centered at the top of the balance sheet.
2. The Assets section is completed from the information on the trial balance and from the notation of the ending merchandise inventory. The amount of the beginning merchandise inventory shown on the trial balance is not used because it does not represent the merchandise inventory as of September 30.

3. The Liabilities section is completed from the information on the trial balance.
4. The Owner's Equity section is completed by adding the amount of net income from the income statement to the amount of the capital account shown on the trial balance. The sum of these two amounts is the total owner's equity.
5. The Assets section is totaled. The Liabilities and Owner's Equity sections are totaled. Double rules are then drawn under the total amounts to show that the balance sheet has been completed.

Check Your Reading

1. Define merchandise inventory.

2. Define beginning merchandise inventory.

3. Define ending merchandise inventory.

4. Give two reasons for the difference between the beginning merchandise inventory and the ending merchandise inventory.

5. What is meant by ''taking inventory''?

6. What kind of account is Merchandise Inventory?

7. Does the Merchandise Inventory account have a debit balance or a credit balance?

Exercises for Topic 3

1. Do the following work for Hardy's Stationery Store:
   a. Prepare an income statement for the month ended March 31 of the current year. Use the information from the trial balance and from the notation of ending merchandise inventory shown on the following page.
   b. Prepare a balance sheet dated March 31 of the current year.

2. Do the following work for the Safari Gift Shop:
   a. Prepare an income statement for the month ended May 31 of the current year. Use the information from the trial balance and from the notation of ending merchandise inventory shown on the following page.
   b. Prepare a balance sheet dated May 31 of the current year.

Hardy's Stationery Store
Trial Balance
March 31, 19—

ACCOUNT TITLE	ACCT. NO.	DEBIT	CREDIT
Cash	101	2710 00	
Accts. Rec. / James Garland	102	320 00	
Merchandise Inventory, Mar. 1, 19—	111	1500 00	
Office Equipment	121	1470 00	
Notes Payable	201		975 00
Deena Hardy, Capital	301		4735 00
Sales	401		4950 00
Purchases	501	2940 00	
Advertising Expense	511	180 00	
Delivery Expense	512	360 00	
Miscellaneous Expenses	513	270 00	
Salaries Expense	514	910 00	
		10660 00	10660 00

Ending Merchandise Inventory
March 31, 19—
$2,250

Safari Gift Shop
Trial Balance
May 31, 19—

ACCOUNT TITLE	ACCT. NO.	DEBIT	CREDIT
Cash	101	3200 00	
Accts. Rec./ James Sommers	102	975 00	
Merchandise Inventory, May 1, 19—	111	2290 00	
Store Equipment	121	4120 00	
Notes Payable	201		1330 00
Accts. Pay./ Marsha Goodman	211		500 00
Ronald Karr, Capital	301		6795 00
Sales	401		9980 00
Purchases	501	4500 00	
Advertising Expense	511	275 00	
Insurance Expense	512	410 00	
Miscellaneous Expenses	513	430 00	
Rent Expense	514	915 00	
Salaries Expense	515	1490 00	
		18605 00	18605 00

Ending Merchandise Inventory
May 31, 19—
$1,890

Read each of the following statements. From the words below each statement, choose the term that best matches the statement.

1. The trial balance when debits equal credits.

   in balance   out of balance

2. How accounts are arranged on a trial balance.

   alphabetic order   numeric order

3. The balance that results when debits are larger than credits.

   credit balance   debit balance

4. The trial balance when debits and credits are not equal.

   in balance   out of balance

5. A record proving that the total debits equal the total credits in the ledger.

   balance sheet   trial balance

6. The balance that results when credits are larger than debits.

   credit balance   debit balance

7. An account that shows the cost of goods on hand at the beginning of an accounting period.

   Merchandise Inventory   Purchases

8. A financial statement.

   income statement   trial balance

9. Assets, liabilities, and owner's equity.

   balance sheet accounts
   income statement accounts

10. Revenue and expenses.

    balance sheet accounts
    income statement accounts

11. The time covered by an income statement.

    accounting period   one day

12. A financial statement.

    balance sheet   cash account

13. A business that provides a service and does not sell merchandise.

    merchandising business   service business

14. The result when expenses are less than revenue.

    net income   net loss   revenue

15. The result when expenses are greater than revenue.

    net income   net loss   revenue

16. A record of a business's financial condition on a certain date.

    balance sheet   income statement

17. The amount of time covered by a balance sheet.

    accounting period   one day   one year

18. Transactions that increase merchandise inventory.

    cash   purchases   sales

19. Transactions that decrease merchandise inventory.

cash   purchases   sales

20. Revenue less the cost of goods sold.

gross profit on sales   net income

21. All goods on hand and in the warehouse.

merchandise inventory   purchases

22. Counting the number of items in stock.

taking inventory   totaling

23. The gross profit on sales less expenses.

cost of goods sold   net income

24. The beginning inventory plus purchases.

cost of goods available for sale
net income

25. The cost of goods available for sale less the ending inventory.

cost of goods sold
gross profit on sales

APPLICATION PROBLEMS

1. Prepare a trial balance for the Novak Company as of June 30 of the current year. The business's accounts and balances are as follows: Cash, 101, $2,050; Notes Receivable, 102, $600; Accts. Rec./Larry Krause, 103, $1,200; Delivery Equipment, 104, $5,400; Furniture, 105, $2,400; Merchandise Inventory, 106, $2,200; Notes Payable, 201, $900; Accts. Pay./Ruth Williams, 202, $2,000; Sharla Novak, Capital, 301, $10,075; Sales, 401, $7,400; Purchases, 501, $4,250; Miscellaneous Expenses, 502, $475; Rent Expense, 503, $650; and Salaries Expense, 504, $1,150.

2. Do the following work for Dana's Auto Repair:

a. Prepare a trial balance for January 31 of the current year. The business's accounts and its balances on January 31 are listed here: Notes Payable, 201, $2,300; Truck, 103, $4,050; Salaries Expense, 503, $745.30; Repair Revenue, 401, $2,985.50;

Cash, 101, $2,755.35; Miscellaneous Expenses, 501, $465.85; Dana Torrez, Capital, 301, $21,881; Rent Expense, 502, $650; and Repair Equipment, 102, $18,500.

b. Prepare an income statement for the month ended January 31 of the current year.

c. Prepare a balance sheet dated January 31 of the current year.

3. Assume that you are an accounting clerk for the Galaxy Gift Shop. Perform the following jobs:

a. Prepare an income statement for the month ended March 31 of the current year. Use information from the trial balance and the notation of ending merchandise inventory shown on the following page.

b. Prepare a balance sheet dated March 31 of the current year.

Galaxy Gift Shop
Trial Balance
March 31, 19—

ACCOUNT TITLE	ACCT. NO.	DEBIT	CREDIT
Cash	101	3936 82	
Accts. Rec./Frank Edwards	102	470 00	
Merchandise Inventory, March 1, 19—	103	2721 05	
Store Equipment	104	7300 00	
Notes Payable	201		4000 00
Joanne Daniels, Capital	301		8501 55
Sales	401		8966 80
Purchases	501	4097 00	
Miscellaneous Expenses	502	663 45	
Rent Expense	503	725 00	
Salaries Expense	504	1175 03	
Store Supplies Expense	505	380 00	
		21468 35	21468 35

Ending Merchandise Inventory
March 31, 19—
$3,578.85

CHAPTER 20

ACCOUNTS RECEIVABLE AND ACCOUNTS PAYABLE

As you have learned, many businesses use special journals. A business may use a general journal, a sales journal, a cash receipts journal, a purchases journal, and a cash payments journal. Likewise, many businesses also use more than one ledger. A business may use a general ledger, an accounts receivable ledger, and an accounts payable ledger.

If a business with hundreds of customers and creditors had to post all its transactions to a general ledger, the ledger would have to be very large. Instead, many businesses keep all their customers' accounts in an *accounts receivable ledger* and all their creditors' accounts in an *accounts payable ledger*. All other accounts are then kept in the *general ledger*.

TOPIC 1 ◆ ACCOUNTS RECEIVABLE

GOALS

1. To post from a sales journal and a cash receipts journal to an accounts receivable ledger.
2. To prepare a schedule of accounts receivable.

KEY TERMS

An *accounts receivable ledger* is a record of all customers' accounts.
The *Accounts Receivable controlling account* is a general ledger account that summarizes the balances of all the customers' accounts in the accounts receivable ledger.
A *schedule of accounts receivable* is a list of customers and the amounts they owe.

Most of the information in the accounts receivable ledger is posted from the sales journal and the cash receipts journal.

POSTING FROM THE SALES JOURNAL

Jane Abels is an accounts receivable clerk for Confections Unlimited, which sells candy to stores and restaurants. Whenever Jane receives a sales invoice from the sales department, she enters the information from the invoice in the sales journal. Then Jane posts the entry to the customer's account in the accounts receivable ledger. Look at the illustration below as you follow Jane's procedure for journalizing and posting.

CONFECTIONS UNLIMITED
742 Wayne Avenue
Belmont, CA 94002

INVOICE NO. **607**

SOLD TO ⌈Baker's Candy Store
1005 James Street
San Jose, CA 95125⌋

SHIP TO ⌈Same⌋

INVOICE DATE 4/1/--

TERMS N/30

Cust. Order No.	Date	Shipped Via	FOB	No. of Cartons
312	3/24/--	Truck	San Jose	3

QUANTITY SHIPPED	STOCK NO.	DESCRIPTION	UNIT PRICE	AMOUNT
25 boxes	B-21	Chocolate-covered mints	1.30	32.50
40 boxes	C-35	Continental chocolates	2.90	116.00
		TOTAL		148.50

SALES JOURNAL   Page *5*

DATE	INVOICE NO.	ACCOUNT DEBITED	POST. REF.	AMOUNT
❶ apr. 1	607	Baker's Candy Store	✓ ❹	148 50

Name *Baker's Candy Store*
Address *1005 James Street, San Jose, California. 95125*

DATE	EXPLANATION	POST. REF.	DEBIT	CREDIT	BALANCE
apr. 1		S5	148 50 ❷		148 50 ❸

1. Jane uses the date of the invoice for the sales journal entry. She enters the invoice number, the account name, and the amount.
2. Jane posts the entry from the sales journal to the customer's account in the accounts receivable ledger. Since the amount is money owed to the company, the amount is posted as a debit.
3. Note that the account has a Balance column. Whenever debits are entered, Jane adds them to the amount in the Balance column. Whenever credits are entered, Jane subtracts them from the amount in the Balance column. In this way, Jane knows at all times how much is due from a customer. (Unlike the general ledger accounts, the customers' accounts in the accounts receivable ledger have only one balance column. Because all customers' accounts normally have a debit balance, it is not necessary to provide two balance columns in these accounts.)
4. Jane places a check mark in the Posting Reference column of the sales journal to show that the amount has been posted. She uses only a check mark because the accounts receivable at her firm are not numbered in the accounts receivable ledger. Instead, they are kept in alphabetic order. A larger business would probably assign numbers to the customers' accounts.

Making candy is only part of the business at Confections Unlimited. It is also necessary to keep careful financial records.

At the end of the month, Jane Abels totals and rules the sales journal. She posts the total to the general ledger as a debit to an account called Accounts Receivable and as a credit to the Sales account. If Jane posted the total only as a credit to the Sales account, the debits and credits in the general ledger would not be equal. To keep the debits and credits equal, the Accounts Receivable account has been set up in the general ledger.

The Accounts Receivable account in the general ledger is called a *controlling account* because it provides a summary of all the balances of the customers' accounts in the accounts receivable

SALES JOURNAL

Page 5

DATE	INVOICE NO.	ACCOUNT DEBITED	POST. REF.	AMOUNT
Apr. 19– 1	607	Baker's Candy Store	✓	148 50
2	608	E Street Market	✓	257 25
2	609	Larkin's Drugstore	✓	57 00
2	610	Oriole Restaurant	✓	114 75
3	611	Arlington Drugstore	✓	28 00
5	612	Harman's Sweet Shop	✓	71 50
8	613	Market Basket	✓	88 25
8	614	Turnpike Cafe	✓	35 00
9	615	Baker's Candy Store	✓	63 00
10	616	Stein's Supermarket	✓	210 00
11	617	Cole's Drugstore	✓	68 00
12	618	Arlington Drugstore	✓	73 40
15	619	Turnpike Cafe	✓	115 00
15	620	E Street Market	✓	140 50
17	621	Harman's Sweet Shop	✓	86 20
22	622	Baker's Candy Store	✓	115 00
23	623	Cole's Drugstore	✓	51 00
24	624	Stein's Supermarket	✓	115 50
25	625	Market Basket	✓	37 50
30	626	Cole's Drugstore	✓	34 50
30		Accounts Receivable Debit/Sales Credit	102/401	1 909 85 1 909 85

❶ ❸ ❺

Accounts Receivable

Account No. 102

DATE	EXPLANATION	POST REF.	DEBIT	CREDIT	BALANCE DEBIT	BALANCE CREDIT
Apr. 19– 30		S5	1 909 85		1 909 85	

❷

Sales

Account No. 401

DATE	EXPLANATION	POST REF.	DEBIT	CREDIT	BALANCE DEBIT	BALANCE CREDIT
Apr. 19– 30		S5		1 909 85		1 909 85

❹

ledger. Look at the illustration on the preceding page as you read the steps Jane follows to post the total of the sales journal to the general ledger:

1. After Jane pencil-foots the sales journal at the end of the month, she enters the date and the amount. Then she writes the words "Accounts Receivable Debit/Sales Credit."
2. Next, Jane posts the total amount of the sales journal as a debit to the Accounts Receivable account in the general ledger.
3. Jane enters the account number of the Accounts Receivable account in the Posting Reference column of the sales journal. She writes the number in small figures.
4. Jane then posts the total amount of the sales journal as a credit to the Sales account.
5. Jane writes the number of the Sales account in the Posting Reference column of the sales journal. She writes the number in small figures next to the number of the Accounts Receivable account. She separates the two numbers with a slash mark (/).

POSTING FROM THE CASH RECEIPTS JOURNAL

Confections Unlimited uses a multicolumn cash receipts journal. All cash received on account from customers is recorded in this journal. Look at the illustrations on pages 536 and 537 to see how Jane Abels makes entries in the cash receipts journal and then posts to the ledger accounts.

1. Jane uses a dash in the Posting Reference column of the journal for all entries that are not posted.
2. Each day, Jane posts the amounts in the Accounts Receivable Credit column to the customers' accounts.
3. The amounts that Jane posts to the customers' accounts are credit amounts.
4. At the end of the month, Jane pencil-foots, totals, and rules the cash receipts journal.
5. Jane posts the total of the Accounts Receivable Credit column as a credit to the Accounts Receivable controlling account in the general ledger.
6. Jane writes the account number of the Accounts Receivable account in parentheses under the total of the Accounts Receivable Credit column in the cash receipts journal to show that the amount has been posted.
7. Jane posts the total of the Sales Credit column to the Sales account. She posts the total of the Net Cash Debit column to the Cash account.

A dash in the Posting Reference column of a journal means that an entry is not posted.

DATE	ACCOUNT CREDITED	POST. REF.	GENERAL LEDGER CREDIT	ACCOUNTS RECEIVABLE CREDIT	SALES CREDIT	NET CASH DEBIT
19– Apr. 1	Cash Balance, $2,114.38	—				
1	Sales	—			374 00	374 00
2	Sales	—			205 00	205 00
4	Sales	—			350 00	350 00
5	Baker's Candy Store	✓		148 50		148 50
8	Sales	—			297 35	297 35
9	Sales	—			305 40	305 40
9	Larkin's Drugstore	✓		57 00		57 00
10	Sales	—			175 50	175 50
12	Sales	—			256 00	256 00
15	Sales	—			349 00	349 00
15	Arlington Drugstore	✓		101 40		101 40
16	E. Street Market	✓		257 25		257 25
17	Sales	—			310 00	310 00
19	Sales	—			251 00	251 00
22	Oriole Restaurant	✓		114 75		114 75
24	Baker's Candy Store	✓		63 00		63 00
25	Sales	—			375 00	375 00
26	Sales	—			206 00	206 00
26	Cole's Drugstore	✓		119 00		119 00
30	Sales	—			410 00	410 00
30	Totals			860 90	3864 25	4725 15
				860 90	3864 25	4725 15
				(102)	(401)	(101)

① ④ ⑥ ③ ⑦

Name Baker's Candy Store
Address 1005 James Street, San Jose, California 95125

DATE	EXPLANATION	POST. REF.	DEBIT	CREDIT	BALANCE
19– Apr. 1		S5	148 50		148 50
5		CR6		148 50	— 00
9		S5	63 00		63 00
22		S5	115 00		178 00
24		CR6		63 00	115 00

Accounts Receivable — Account No. *102*

DATE	EXPLANATION	POST REF.	DEBIT	CREDIT	BALANCE DEBIT	BALANCE CREDIT
Apr. 30 (19—)		S5	1 90 9 85		1 90 9 85	
30		CR6		8 60 90	1 04 8 95	

❺

SCHEDULE OF ACCOUNTS RECEIVABLE

A schedule of accounts receivable is prepared at the end of each month. This schedule is used to prove that the total of the balances of the customers' accounts in the accounts receivable ledger equals the balance of the Accounts Receivable controlling account in the general ledger.

Confections Unlimited
Schedule of Accounts Receivable
April 30, 19—

Baker's Candy Store	1 1 5 00
Cole's Drugstore	3 4 50
Total Accounts Receivable	1 04 8 95

Accounts Receivable — Account No. *102*

DATE	EXPLANATION	POST REF.	DEBIT	CREDIT	BALANCE DEBIT	BALANCE CREDIT
Apr. 30 (19—)		S5	1 90 9 85		1 90 9 85	
30		CR6		8 60 90	1 04 8 95	

A *schedule of accounts receivable* is a list of the customers of a business and the amounts that they owe. The last amount in the Balance column of each customer's account is the amount listed on the schedule.

Part of a schedule of accounts receivable prepared at Confections Unlimited is shown on page 537. If all the postings are correct, the total of the schedule of accounts receivable should be the same as the balance of the Accounts Receivable controlling account. Note that in this case the two amounts are the same.

Check Your Reading

1. What accounts are kept in an accounts receivable ledger?

2. In what order are accounts receivable kept in many small businesses?

3. Does a dash in the Posting Reference column of a journal mean that the entry has been posted?

4. Which two journals provide most of the information that is posted to the accounts receivable ledger?

5. In what ledger is the Accounts Receivable controlling account found?

Exercises for Topic I

1. Do the following work for Confections Unlimited:
   a. Open accounts for these customers:

   Arlington Drugstore
   140 Elm Street
   San Carlos, CA 94077

   Baker's Candy Store
   1005 James Street
   San Jose, CA 95125

   Cole's Drugstore
   108 Main Street
   Campbell, CA 95008

   E Street Market
   2400 E Market
   San Jose, CA 95123

   Harman's Sweet Shop
   1734 Birch Street
   Gilroy, CA 95020

   Larkin's Drugstore
   102 South Street
   Gilroy, CA 95020

   Market Basket
   3420 Lee Highway
   Campbell, CA 95008

   Oriole Restaurant
   1724 Oak Boulevard
   Saratoga, CA 95070

   Stein's Supermarket
   2500 Cox Street
   San Jose, CA 95122

   Turnpike Cafe
   45 Ridge Turnpike
   Santa Cruz, CA 95060

b. Post the entries in the sales journal on page 534 and the entries in the cash receipts journal on page 536 to the customers' accounts. Post all entries from both journals by date. In other words, do not post all the entries from the sales journal first and then post all the entries from the cash receipts journal.

2. Prepare a schedule of accounts receivable for Confections Unlimited. The total of the schedule of accounts receivable should be $1,048.95, the same as the balance of the Accounts Receivable controlling account on page 537. If your total is not correct, check the postings. Then check the balances in the customers' accounts to see that they have been computed correctly. Finally, check to see that you have correctly transferred the balances to the schedule of accounts receivable.

TOPIC 2 ◆ ACCOUNTS PAYABLE

GOALS

1. To post from a purchases journal and a cash payments journal to an accounts payable ledger.
2. To prepare a schedule of accounts payable.

KEY TERMS

An *accounts payable ledger* is a record of all creditors' accounts.

The *Accounts Payable controlling account* is a general ledger account that summarizes the balances of all the creditors' accounts in the accounts payable ledger.

A *schedule of accounts payable* is a list of creditors and the amounts owed to them.

An accounts payable ledger is similar to an accounts receivable ledger, except that it is a record of creditors' accounts rather than customers' accounts. Most of the information in the accounts payable ledger is posted from the purchases journal and the cash payments journal.

POSTING FROM THE PURCHASES JOURNAL

When Martin Kovak, an accounts payable clerk for Confections Unlimited, receives a purchase invoice from the purchasing department, he enters the information from the invoice in the purchases journal. Martin then posts each entry from the purchases journal to the creditor's account in the accounts payable ledger. The amount is posted as a credit amount. Martin places a check mark in the Posting Reference column of the purchases journal to show that the amount has been posted. In a small business like Confections Unlimited, accounts in the accounts payable ledger are kept in alphabetic order, not by account number.

Many small businesses keep their accounts payable in alphabetic order.

At the end of the month, Martin totals the purchases journal and posts its total to the general ledger. The total must be posted twice—once as a debit to Purchases and once as a credit to the controlling account. This keeps the debits and the credits equal. The *Accounts Payable controlling account* provides a summary of all the balances of the creditors' accounts in the accounts payable ledger. Look at the illustrations below and on the following page, and read the steps Martin follows as he posts the total of the purchases journal to the general ledger:

1. Martin pencil-foots, totals, and rules the purchases journal. He writes the date and the words ''Purchases Debit/Accts. Pay. Credit.''
2. Martin posts the total amount of the purchases journal as a debit to the Purchases account.
3. He writes the number of the Purchases account in the Posting Reference column of the purchases journal.

	DATE	INVOICE NO.	ACCOUNT CREDITED	POST. REF.	PURCHASES DEBIT
	Apr. 2	3648	National Candy Company	✓	426 15
	3	4290	Supreme Candies, Inc.	✓	250 00
	4	A-974	Palmer Confectionery	✓	358 50
	5	C-873	Craig Candy Company	✓	503 70
	8	399C	National Candy Company	✓	273 40
	12	8742	Old World Chocolates	✓	176 80
	15	5908	Supreme Candies, Inc.	✓	187 40
	18	E-453	Craig Candy Company	✓	263 00
	22	9264	Old World Chocolates	✓	123 00
	24	D-463	Palmer Confectionery	✓	207 00
	25	8003	Supreme Candies, Inc.	✓	93 30
	25	874F	National Candy Company	✓	217 50
	26	E-506	Palmer Confectionery	✓	32 50
	30	M-164	Craig Candy Company	✓	148 20
	30	9826	Old World Chocolates	✓	55 00
	30		Purchases Debit/Accts. Pay. Credit	501/202	3 315 45

PURCHASES JOURNAL   Page 4

Purchases

Account No. 501

DATE	EXPLANATION	POST REF.	DEBIT	CREDIT	BALANCE DEBIT	BALANCE CREDIT
19— Apr. 30		P4	331545		331545	

②

Accounts Payable

Account No. 202

DATE	EXPLANATION	POST REF.	DEBIT	CREDIT	BALANCE DEBIT	BALANCE CREDIT
19— Apr. 30		P4		331545		331545

④

4. Then Martin posts the total amount of the purchases journal as a credit to the Accounts Payable controlling account in the general ledger.
5. Finally, Martin writes the number of the Accounts Payable controlling account in the Posting Reference column of the purchases journal.

POSTING FROM THE CASH PAYMENTS JOURNAL

Confections Unlimited uses a multicolumn cash payments journal. During the month, Martin Kovak posts the amounts in the Accounts Payable Debit column to the creditors' accounts. The amounts posted are debit amounts. At the end of the month, Martin pencil-foots, totals, and rules the cash payments journal.

Look at the illustrations on page 542 as you read the steps that Martin follows to post the totals from the cash payments journal.

1. First Martin places a check mark under the total of the General Ledger Debit column. If there were any amounts in this column, they would have been posted to the general ledger during the month. Thus the total is not posted.
2. Martin posts the total of the Accounts Payable Debit column to the Accounts Payable controlling account in the general ledger.
3. Then Martin writes the number of the Accounts Payable account in parentheses under the total of the Accounts Payable Debit column in the cash payments journal.

DATE	ACCOUNT DEBITED	CHECK NO.	POST. REF.	GENERAL LEDGER DEBIT	ACCOUNTS PAYABLE DEBIT	NET CASH CREDIT
Apr. 10	National Candy Company	876	✓		426 15	426 15
15	Palmer Confectionery	882	✓		358 50	358 50
18	Craig Candy Company	910	✓		503 70	503 70
18	Supreme Candies, Inc.	911	✓		250 00	250 00
25	National Candy Company	1024	✓		273 40	273 40
30	Craig Candy Company	1108	✓		263 00	263 00
30	Old World Chocolates	1109	✓		299 80	299 80
30	Totals				2374 55	2374 55
				(✓)	(202)	(101)

❶ ❸ ❹

Accounts Payable   Account No. 202

DATE	EXPLANATION	POST REF.	DEBIT	CREDIT	BALANCE DEBIT	BALANCE CREDIT
Apr. 30		P4		3315 45		3315 45
30		CP4	2374 55			940 90

❷

4. Martin posts the total of the Net Cash Credit column to the Cash account in the general ledger.

SCHEDULE OF ACCOUNTS PAYABLE

A schedule of accounts payable is prepared at the end of each month. This schedule is used to prove that the total of the balances of the creditors' accounts in the accounts payable ledger equals the balance of the Accounts Payable controlling account in the general ledger.

A *schedule of accounts payable* is a list of the creditors of a business and the amounts that are owed to each creditor. The last amount in the Balance column of each creditor's account is the amount listed on the schedule.

Part of a schedule of accounts payable prepared at Confections Unlimited is shown on the following page. Note that the total of the schedule of accounts payable is the same as the balance of the Accounts Payable controlling account.

Confections Unlimited
Schedule of Accounts Payable
April 30, 19—

Craig Candy Company	148 20	
National Candy Company	217 50	
Total Accounts Payable		940 90

Accounts Payable _____ Account No. 202

DATE	EXPLANATION	POST REF.	DEBIT	CREDIT	BALANCE DEBIT	BALANCE CREDIT
Apr. 30 19—		P4		331 5 45		331 5 45
30		CP4	237 4 55			940 90

1. What accounts are kept in an accounts payable ledger?

2. In what order are accounts payable kept in many small businesses?

3. Is the information about accounts payable posted twice? Explain.

4. Which two journals provide most of the information that is posted to the accounts payable ledger?

5. In what ledger is the Accounts Payable controlling account found?

6. Does a schedule of accounts payable take the place of an Accounts Payable account in the general ledger?

1. Do the following work for Confections Unlimited:
   a. Open accounts for these creditors:

   Craig Candy Company   Palmer Confectionery
   8142 Michigan Avenue   1947 Park Boulevard
   Chicago, IL 60619   Atlanta, GA 30312

National Candy Company   Supreme Candies, Inc.
247 Bond Street   120 Concord Turnpike
Burlington, VT 05401   Wichita, KS 67206

Old World Chocolates
45 Bell Avenue
Stockton, CA 95201

     b. Post the entries in the purchases journal on page 540 and the entries in the cash payments journal on page 542 to the creditors' accounts. Post all entries from both journals by date. In other words, do not post all the entries from the purchases journal first and then all the entries from the cash payments journal.

   2. Prepare a schedule of accounts payable for Confections Unlimited.

VOCABULARY
SKILLBUILDER

Read each of the following statements. From the words below each statement, choose the term that best matches the statement.

1. The record in which all customers' accounts are kept.

accounts payable ledger
accounts receivable ledger

2. A list of customers and the amounts that they owe.

schedule of accounts payable
schedule of accounts receivable

3. The order in which accounts are kept in the accounts receivable and accounts payable ledgers in most small businesses.

alphabetic order   numeric order

4. General ledger accounts that summarize the balances of the customers' accounts and the creditors' accounts.

controlling accounts   purchases accounts

5. Mark(s) used to show that an entry is not posted.

check mark   dash   parentheses

6. The record in which all creditors' accounts are kept.

accounts payable ledger
accounts receivable ledger

7. The record in which all accounts except individual accounts for customers and creditors are kept.

general ledger   sales journal

8. A list of all creditors and the amounts that are owed to them.

schedule of accounts payable
schedule of accounts receivable

9. When schedules of accounts receivable and payable are prepared.

daily   end of month

APPLICATION
PROBLEMS

1. Do the following work for the Sunnyside Paint Supply Company:

a. Prepare a schedule of accounts receivable. Use the following information taken from the business's accounts receivable ledger on January 31.

Customers' Accounts and Account Balances
Ajax Hardware Center, $1,532
Bigelow Paint Store, $875.50
Farinacci's Paint Shop, $1,404
Murphy's Hardware Store, $1,585.75
Royal Paint Shop, $657.85
Wysocki's Hardware Store, $983

Accounts Receivable — Account No. 102

DATE	EXPLANATION	POST REF.	DEBIT	CREDIT	BALANCE DEBIT	BALANCE CREDIT
19— Jan. 31		S1	9993 60			
31		CR1		2955 50		

b. The Accounts Receivable controlling account is shown above. The totals of the sales journal and of the cash receipts journal have been posted. Find and record the balances of the account in your Activity Guide. Then compare the balance of the Accounts Receivable controlling account with the total of the schedule of accounts receivable. The two amounts should be the same.

2. Do the following work for the Sunnyside Paint Supply Company:

a. Prepare a schedule of accounts payable. Use the following information taken from the business's accounts payable ledger on January 31.

Creditors' Accounts and Account Balances

Armor Paint Corporation, $1,524
Emerman Paint Company, $1,125
National Paint Corporation, $975.75
Peterson Paints, Inc., $1,145.35
Swindell Paint Company, $465

b. The Accounts Payable controlling account is shown below. The totals of the purchases journal and of the cash payments journal have been posted. Find and record the balances of the account in your Activity Guide. Then compare the balance of the Accounts Payable controlling account with the total of the schedule of accounts payable. The balance of the account and the total of the schedule should be the same.

Accounts Payable — Account No. 202

DATE	EXPLANATION	POST REF.	DEBIT	CREDIT	BALANCE DEBIT	BALANCE CREDIT
19— Jan. 31		P1		8436 40		
31		CP1	3201 30			

COMPUTER APPLICATION

Exploring Computers in Accounting

In addition to the specialized computer programs that you explored at the end of Part 3, numerous software packages are available for double-entry accounting systems. Such packages are called general ledger programs, and most

```
                        RAINBOW CARD SHOP
                         TRIAL BALANCE
                        SEPTEMBER 30, 19--


ACCOUNT TITLE                        ACCT.   DEBIT        CREDIT
                                      NO.


CASH                                  101    3125.00
ACCTS. REC./JAMES BELL                102     220.00
MERCHANDISE INVENTORY, SEPT. 1, 19--  103    2035.00
STORE EQUIPMENT                       104    5000.00
NOTES PAYABLE                         201                 3000.00
NANCY JAMES, CAPITAL                  301                 5865.00
SALES                                 401                 6200.00
PURCHASES                             501    3130.00
MISCELLANEOUS EXPENSES                502     240.00
RENT EXPENSE                          503     300.00
SALARIES EXPENSE                      504     800.00
STORE SUPPLIES EXPENSE                505     215.00
                                            15065.00     15065.00
```

include subsidiary ledgers for accounts receivable and accounts payable. Many general ledger programs also include a payroll application.

When a general ledger software program is first set up, the operator keys in the number, title, and beginning balance of each account in the general ledger. In addition, information about each customer and creditor is keyed in to the related subsidiary ledger.

As day-to-day transactions take place, the computer operator uses source documents to determine which accounts are affected by each transaction, then keys in the debit and credit entries. The computer automatically posts each entry to the correct ledger account.

At the end of a fiscal period, the computer operator obtains a printed trial balance simply by selecting the trial balance choice on the accounting program menu. (A *menu* is a list of choices on a computer screen.)

The computer operator keys in any necessary corrections if the trial balance does not balance. Then the operator selects the income statement and balance sheet choices from the menu, and the computer automatically

```
                        RAINBOW CARD SHOP
                        INCOME STATEMENT
                FOR THE MONTH ENDED SEPTEMBER 30, 19--


REVENUE:
   SALES                                                    6200.00
COST OF MERCHANDISE SOLD:
   MERCHANDISE INVENTORY, SEPT. 1, 19--        2035.00
   PURCHASES                                   3130.00
   TOTAL COST OF MERCHANDISE AVAILABLE FOR SALE 5165.00
   LESS MERCHANDISE INVENTORY, SEPT. 30, 19--  2540.00
   COST OF MERCHANDISE SOLD                                 2625.00
GROSS PROFIT ON SALES                                       3575.00

EXPENSES:
   MISCELLANEOUS EXPENSES                        240.00
   RENT EXPENSE                                  300.00
   SALARIES EXPENSE                              800.00
   STORE SUPPLIES EXPENSE                        215.00
      TOTAL EXPENSES                                        1555.00

NET INCOME                                                  2020.00
```

prepares and displays each of these statements on the screen.

If the managers of a business ask for printouts of the income statement and balance sheet, they can be prepared. In addition, lists of individual accounts receivable and accounts payable can be printed. Many general ledger accounting programs also permit the computer operator to print both customer statements and checks to vendors. Thus, general ledger accounting programs enable a business to computerize a large number of its recordkeeping tasks.

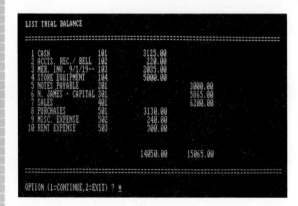

Check Your Reading

1. Double-entry accounting software programs are also called ____?____ programs.

2. Most accounting software programs include subsidiary ledgers for ____?____ and ____?____.

3. What information is keyed in when a general ledger software program is first set up?

4. What does the computer operator use to determine which accounts are affected by daily transactions?

5. How does the computer operator prepare a balance sheet using a general ledger software program?

PROJECT 4 — CASTLE JEWELERS

Castle Jewelers is a small retail jewelry store. The accounting records and procedures of this business are similar to those of many small businesses.

About the Business

Castle Jewelers is owned and managed by Martha Castle. The store sells and repairs jewelry and silverware. Martha does all the purchasing and selling. There are two employees: a technician and an accounting clerk. The technician repairs watches and other items. The accounting clerk keeps the accounting records and prepares financial statements. Don Sheehan, the technician, has been working at Castle Jewelers for five years. You have just been hired as the new accounting clerk.

Martha, the owner, shows you around the store and points out some unusual pieces of jewelry. Next, she introduces you to Don and shows you what his work involves. Finally, Martha takes you to your desk in the back office. She shows you where the accounting records are kept. She also gives you a folder that contains information about the accounting records and procedures of Castle Jewelers. Now Martha leaves you alone in your office so that you can get acquainted with the accounting system of the business.

Here is a summary of the information in the folder.

The accounting records of Castle Jewelers include five journals and three ledgers. The journals used are a purchases journal, a cash payments journal, a sales journal, a cash receipts journal, and a general journal. The ledgers used are a general ledger, an accounts receivable ledger, and an accounts payable ledger. These journals and ledgers are used for journalizing and posting.

Journalizing

The transactions of the business are journalized daily. The journalizing procedures of Castle Jewelers are as follows.

Purchases on Credit The business purchases all its merchandise on credit. The purchases of merchandise on credit are recorded in the purchases journal. The owner checks each purchase invoice received from a supplier. The approved invoice is given to the accounting clerk. The clerk uses the information on the invoice to make an entry in the purchases journal.

Cash Payments The business makes all cash payments by check. The cash payments are recorded in the cash payments journal. The owner writes the checks. The accounting clerk uses the information on the check stubs to make entries in the cash payments journal. The business's cash payments journal contains five money columns. The columns are General Ledger Debit, Accounts Payable Debit, Employee Income Taxes Payable Credit, FICA Taxes Payable Credit, and Net Cash Credit.

Sales on Credit The business makes many sales on credit. The sales on credit are recorded in the sales journal. A sales slip is prepared for each sale on credit. The sales slip consists of two copies. One copy is given to the customer, and the other copy is kept by the store. The accounting clerk uses the information on the copy of the sales slip kept by the store to make an entry in the sales journal.

Cash Receipts The business receives cash from three different sources. The sources are listed below.

1. Cash sales

2. Repair work (which must be paid for in cash)

3. Cash paid on account (by customers who have purchased merchandise on credit)

All cash receipts are recorded in the cash receipts journal. At the end of each day, after cash is proved, the detailed audit strip from the cash register is given to the accounting clerk. The information on the detailed audit strip is used by the accounting clerk to make entries in the cash receipts journal. The accounting clerk also uses the checks received from customers to make entries in the cash receipts journal. The business's cash receipts journal contains four money columns. They are Accounts Receivable Credit, Sales Credit, Repair Revenue Credit, and Net Cash Debit.

Other Transactions Transactions that cannot be recorded in the special journals are recorded in the general journal.

Posting

The individual entries in the journals are posted daily. The totals of the special journals are posted at the end of the month.

Daily Posting The daily posting procedure used by the accounting clerk at Castle Jewelers is as follows:

1. The entries in the purchases journal are posted to the creditors' accounts in the accounts payable ledger.

2. The entries in the General Ledger Debit column of the cash payments journal are posted to the general ledger.

3. The entries in the Accounts Payable Debit column of the cash payments journal are posted to the creditors' account in the accounts payable ledger.

4. The entries in the sales journal are posted to the customers' accounts in the accounts receivable ledger.

5. The entries in the Accounts Receivable Credit column of the cash receipts journal are posted to the customers' accounts in the accounts receivable ledger.

6. The entries in the general journal are posted to the general ledger.

Monthly Posting The journals are pencil-footed, totaled, and ruled at the end of the month. Then the totals of the special journals are posted. The monthly posting procedure used by the accounting clerk at Castle Jewelers is as follows:

1. The total of the purchases journal is posted to the general ledger. The Purchases account is debited, and the Accounts Payable account is credited.

2. The total of the sales journal is posted to the general ledger. The Account Receivable account is debited, and the Sales account is credited.

3. The total of the Accounts Receivable Credit, the Sales Credit, the Repair Revenue Credit, and the Net Cash Debit columns of the cash receipts journal are posted to the general ledger.

4. The totals of the Accounts Payable Debit, the Employee Income Taxes Payable Credit, the FICA Taxes Payable Credit, and the Net Cash Credit columns of the cash payments journal are posted to the general ledger.

Preparing Financial Statements

Castle Jewelers operates on the basis of a monthly accounting period. At the end of each month, the accounting clerk prepares the financial statements. A schedule of accounts receivable, a schedule of accounts payable, a trial balance, an income statement, and a balance sheet are prepared.

Your First Assignment

Before you begin the everyday task of journalizing and posting transactions, Martha

Castle, the owner, asks you to do the following:

1. Open the general ledger accounts. The accounts are in your Activity Guide. The chart of accounts for Castle Jewelers is shown below. Record the following debit balances in these accounts: Cash, $12,000; Accounts Receivable, $8,220; Furniture and Fixtures, $22,950; and Merchandise Inventory, $36,000. Record the following credit balances in these accounts: Notes Payable, $27,000; Accounts Payable, $5,700; and Martha Castle, Capital, $46,470. Use the date May 1 for all balances.

CHART OF ACCOUNTS
Castle Jewelers

Account Number	Account Title
101	Cash
102	Accounts Receivable
103	Furniture and Fixtures
104	Merchandise Inventory
201	Notes Payable
202	Accounts Payable
203	Employee Income Taxes Payable
204	FICA Taxes Payable
301	Martha Castle, Capital
401	Sales
402	Repair Revenue
501	Purchases
502	Advertising Expense
503	Miscellaneous Expenses
504	Office Supplies Expense
505	Payroll Taxes Expense
506	Rent Expense
507	Salaries Expense
508	Store Supplies Expense

2. Record the balances in the customers' accounts in the accounts receivable ledger. The accounts are in your Activity Guide. The balances are shown on the schedule of accounts receivable below. Use the date May 1 for all the balances.

CASTLE JEWELERS
Schedule of Accounts Receivable
April 30, 19—

Lucy Childs	1,050.00
Alice Fink	1,008.00
Jeff Greene	1,038.00
Charles Lopez	285.00
Linda Mull	600.00
Marv Rosner	975.00
Alex Toth	1,314.00
Roy Venero	1,053.00
Suzanne Verba	222.00
Louise Woods	675.00
Total Accounts Receivable	8,220.00

3. Record the balances in the creditors' accounts in the accounts payable ledger. The accounts are in your Activity Guide. The balances are shown on the schedule of accounts payable below. Use the date May 1 for all balances.

CASTLE JEWELERS
Schedule of Accounts Payable
April 30, 19—

Carbo Wholesale Jewelers	2,400.00
Kendall Company	1,335.00
Manila Corporation	1,005.00
Staunton Company	960.00
Total Accounts Payable	5,700.00

4. Number the journal pages in your Activity Guide. Each of your journals should begin with page 5.

5. Make a memorandum entry in the cash receipts journal to record the cash balance of $12,000 on May 1.

Daily Assignments

The transactions of Castle Jewelers for the month of May are given on page 551. You are to record each transaction in one of the journals. After you have journalized all the transactions for a day, you must post the individual entries to the ledger accounts.

May 1 Purchased merchandise on credit for $705 from Kendall Company, Invoice 567-10. Record the invoice in the purchases journal. Enter the date, the invoice number, and the name of the creditor in the proper columns. Then enter the amount of the invoice ($705) in the Purchases Debit column.

1 Issued Check 501 for $1,875 in payment of the May rent. Record this transaction in the cash payments journal. Enter the date, the title of the account to be debited (Rent Expense), and the check number in the proper columns. Then enter the amount of the transaction ($1,875) in the General Ledger Debit column and in the Net Cash Credit column.

1 Sold merchandise on credit for $75 to Charles Lopez, Sales Slip 101. Record this transaction in the sales journal. Enter the date, the sales slip number, and the name of the customer in the proper columns. Then enter the amount of the sale ($75) in the Sales Credit column.

1 Received $45 on account from Charles Lopez. Record this transaction in the cash receipts journal. Enter the date and the name of the customer in the proper columns. Then enter the amount ($45) in the Accounts Re-

ceivable Credit column and in the Net Cash Debit column.

1 Received $120 on account from Louise Woods. Record this transaction in the cash receipts journal. Follow the same procedure as you did for the previous transaction.

1 After cash is proved each day, the accounting clerk uses the information on the detailed audit tape to record the total amount of cash received from repairs and the total amount of cash received from cash sales. The total received for repairs on May 1 was $148.50. Record this amount in the cash receipts journal. Enter the date in the Date column and an explanation (Repairs) in the Account Credited column. Then enter $148.50 in the Repair Revenue Credit column and in the Net Cash Debit column. Place a dash in the Posting Reference column because this entry will not be posted individually. The total received for cash sales on May 1 was $195.75. Record this amount in the cash receipts journal. Enter the date in the Date column and an explanation (Cash Sales) in the Account Credited column. Then enter $195.75 in the Sales Credit column and in the Net Cash Debit column. Place a dash in the Posting Reference column.

Post the individual entries for May 1 from the journals to the ledgers. Follow the daily posting routine described previously on page 550.

2 Received $153 on account from Roy Venero. Journalize this transaction.

2 Issued Check 502 for $286.35 to the Northwestern Power Company in payment of an electric bill. Journalize this transaction. Debit Miscellaneous Expenses.

2 Issued Check 503 for $342 to the Allen Fuel Oil Company in payment

of a fuel oil bill. Journalize this transaction. Debit Miscellaneous Expenses.

2 Issued Check 504 for $29.25 to the Jeweler's Convention in payment of an admission fee. Journalize this transaction. Debit Miscellaneous Expenses.

2 The detailed audit strip for May 2 shows that $129.75 was received from repairs and $496.50 was received from cash sales. Journalize these cash receipts.

   Post the individual entries for May 2 from the journals to the ledgers.

3 Sold merchandise on credit for $78 to Paul Arnstein, Sales Slip 102. Journalize this transaction.

3 Received $78 on account from Jeff Greene. Journalize this transaction.

3 Received $450 on account from Lucy Childs. Journalize this transaction.

3 Issued Check 505 for $356.28 and Check 506 for $489.36 in payment of salaries. You have a weekly salary of $480, less deductions of $87 for federal income tax withholding and $36.72 for FICA tax. Don Sheehan has a weekly salary of $675, less deductions of $134 for federal income tax withholding and $51.64 for FICA tax. Record the salary payments in the cash payments journal. Your salary payment should be recorded as follows. Enter the date, the title of the account to be debited (Salaries Expense), and the check number (505) in the proper columns. Then enter the amount of the salary ($480) in the General Ledger Debit column, the amount of the income tax withholding ($87) in the Employee Income Taxes Payable Credit column, the amount of the FICA tax ($36.72) in the FICA Taxes Payable Credit column, and the amount of the

net pay ($356.28) in the Net Cash Credit column. Now record the salary payment to Don Sheehan.

3 Purchased merchandise on credit for $510 from Carbo Wholesale Jewelers, Invoice 2-652A. Journalize this transaction.

3 The detailed audit strip for May 3 shows that $270 was received for repairs and $616.35 was received for cash sales. Journalize these cash receipts.

   Post the individual entries for May 3 from the journals to the ledgers.

5 Sold merchandise on credit for $375 to Calvin Webber, Sales Slip 103.

5 Received $105 on account from Calvin Webber.

5 Received $120 on account from Alex Toth.

5 Issued Check 507 for $60 to the Flag Paper Company for wrapping paper. Debit Store Supplies Expense.

5 Issued Check 508 for $126 to the *Daily News* for an advertisement.

5 The detailed audit strip for May 5 shows that $67.50 was received for repairs and $392.25 was received for cash sales.

   Post the individual entries for May 5 from the journals to the ledgers.

6 Received $105 on account from Marv Rosner.

6 Received $150 on account from Linda Mull.

6 Issued Check 509 for $375 to the Kendall Company in payment on account.

6 The detailed audit strip for May 6 shows that $84.75 was received for repairs and $436.50 was received for cash sales.

   Post the individual entries for May 6 from the journals to the ledgers.

7 Received $72 on account from Suzanne Verba.

7 Purchased merchandise on credit for $112.50 from the Staunton Company, Invoice 8-X-64.

7 The detailed audit strip for May 7 shows that $49.50 was received for repairs and $330 was received for cash sales.

Post the individual entries for May 7 from the journals to the ledgers.

8 Received $45 on account from Charles Lopez.

8 Purchased merchandise on credit for $195 from the Manila Corporation, Invoice 26503.

8 The detailed audit strip for May 8 shows that $66 was received for repairs and $431.25 was received for cash sales.

Post the individual entries for May 8 from the journals to the ledgers.

9 Sold merchandise on credit for $756 to Robert Harrison, Sales Slip 104.

9 Received $150 on account from Robert Harrison.

9 Received $1,008 on account from Alice Fink.

9 Issued Check 510 for $73.50 for stationery. Debit Office Supplies Expense.

9 Issued Check 511 for $1,200 to Carbo Wholesale Jewelers in payment on account.

9 The detailed audit strip for May 9 shows that $97.50 was received for repairs and $227.25 was received for cash sales.

Post the individual entries for May 9 from the journals to the ledgers.

10 Sold merchandise on credit for $225 to Louise Woods, Sales Slip 105.

10 Received $78 on account from Paul Arnstein.

10 Issued Check 512 for $356.28 and Check 513 for $489.36 in payment of salaries. Refer to the payroll transaction of May 3 for the information about earnings and deductions needed for the journal entries.

10 Purchased merchandise on credit for $337.50 from the Staunton Company, Invoice 8-Y-15.

10 The detailed audit strip for May 10 shows that $126.75 was received for repairs and $406.50 was received for cash sales.

Post the individual entries for May 10 from the journals to the ledgers.

12 Sold merchandise on credit for $67.35 to Roy Venero, Sales Slip 106.

12 Issued Check 514 for $525 to the Kendall Company in payment on account.

12 The detailed audit strip for May 12 shows that $195 was received for repairs and $121.95 was received for cash sales.

Post the individual entries for May 12 from the journals to the ledgers.

13 Purchased merchandise on credit for $110.55 from the Kendall Company, Invoice 567-98.

13 The detailed audit strip for May 13 shows that $99.75 was received for repairs and $160.50 was received for cash sales.

Post the individual entries for May 13 from the journals to the ledgers.

14 Issued Check 515 for $216 to Midland Telephone Company in payment of a telephone bill. Debit Miscellaneous Expenses.

14 The detailed audit strip for May 14 shows that $67.50 was received for repairs and $83.25 was received for cash sales.

Post the individual entries for May 14 from the journals to the ledgers.

15 Received $45 on account from Charles Lopez.

15 Purchased merchandise on credit for $750 from the Staunton Company, Invoice 8-Y-78.

15 Issued Check 516 for $315 to Station KXOC for a radio advertisement.

15 The detailed audit strip for May 15 shows that $106.50 was received for repairs and $436.50 was received for cash sales.

Post the individual entries for May 15 from the journals to the ledgers.

16 Sold merchandise on credit for $85.50 to James Farnsworth, Sales Slip 107.

16 Received $156 on account from Robert Harrison.

16 Issued Check 517 for $105 to the Marx Supply Company for gift boxes. Debit Store Supplies Expense.

16 The detailed audit strip for May 16 shows that $73.50 was received for repairs and $217.50 was received for cash sales.

Post the individual entries for May 16 from the journals to the ledgers.

17 Sold merchandise on credit for $135 to Dorothy Emerson, Sales Slip 108.

17 Received $210 on account from Jeff Greene.

17 Received $180 on account from Louise Woods.

17 Issued Check 518 for $356.28 and Check 519 for $489.36 in payment of salaries. Refer to the payroll transaction of May 3 for the information about earnings and deductions needed for the journal entries.

17 Purchased merchandise on credit for $540 from the Kendall Company, Invoice 568-33.

17 The detailed audit strip for May 17 shows that $186.75 was received for repairs and $526.50 was received for cash sales.

Post the individual entries for May 17 from the journals to the ledgers.

19 Sold merchandise on credit for $60 to Suzanne Verba, Sales Slip 109.

19 Purchased merchandise on credit for $210 from Carbo Wholesale Jewelers, Invoice 2-749A.

19 Issued Check 520 for $450 to the Manila Corporation in payment on account.

19 The detailed audit strip for May 19 shows that $90.75 was received for repairs and $394.50 was received for cash sales.

Post the individual entries for May 19 from the journals to the ledgers.

20 Sold merchandise on credit for $90 to Joseph Garber, Sales Slip 110.

20 Received $30 on account from Joseph Garber.

20 Donated a necklace worth $120 to the Pioneer Club for its annual auction for charity. Record this transaction in the general journal. Debit Advertising Expense for $120, and credit Purchases for $120. Write a brief explanation of the transaction beneath the entry.

20 The detailed audit strip for May 20 shows that $105 was received for repairs and $121.50 was received for cash sales.

Post the individual entries for May 20 from the journals to the ledgers.

21 Purchased merchandise on credit for $330 from the Manila Corporation, Invoice 26805.

21 The detailed audit strip for May 21 shows that $100.50 was received for

repairs and $271.50 was received for cash sales.

Post the individual entries for May 21 from journals to the ledgers.

22 Received $45 on account from Charles Lopez.

22 Issued Check 521 for $36 to Bulldog Hi-Lites, a high school newspaper, for advertising.

22 The detailed audit strip for May 22 shows that $147 was received for repairs and $165 was received for cash sales.

Post the individual entries for May 22 from the journals to the ledgers.

23 Sold merchandise on credit for $450 to Louis Franklin, Sales Slip 111.

23 Received $75 on account from Louis Franklin.

23 Received $144 on account from Alex Toth.

23 Issued Check 522 for $75 to the Marx Supply Company for display materials. Debit Store Supplies Expense.

23 Issued Check 523 for $360 to the Staunton Company in payment on account.

23 The detailed audit strip for May 23 shows that $168 was received for repairs and $212.10 was received for cash sales.

Post the individual entries for May 23 from the journals to the ledgers.

24 Sold merchandise on credit for $192 to Jeff Greene, Sales Slip 112.

24 Received $217.35 on account from Roy Venero.

24 Issued Check 524 for $356.28 and Check 525 for $489.36 in payment of salaries. Refer to the payroll transaction of May 3 for the information about earnings and deductions needed for the journal entries.

24 Purchased merchandise on credit for $90 from the Staunton Company, Invoice 8-Z-39.

24 Issued Check 526 for $720 to Carbo Wholesale Jewelers in payment on account.

24 The detailed audit strip for May 24 shows that $160.50 was received for repairs and $660 was received for cash sales.

Post the individual entries for May 24 from the journals to the ledgers.

27 Purchased merchandise on credit for $136.50 from Carbo Wholesale Jewelers, Invoice 2-986A.

27 Issued Check 527 for $690 to the Staunton Company in payment on account.

27 The detailed audit strip for May 27 shows that $104.25 was received for repairs and $163.50 was received for cash sales.

Post the individual entries for May 27 from the journals to the ledgers.

28 Sold merchandise on credit for $150 to Robert Harrison, Sales Slip 113.

28 Issued Check 528 for $76.50 for office file folders.

28 The detailed audit strip for May 28 shows that $60 was received for repairs and $270.75 was received for cash sales.

Post the individual entries for May 28 from the journals to the ledgers.

29 Sold merchandise on credit for $120 to Calvin Webber, Sales Slip 114.

29 Received $30 on account from Calvin Webber.

29 Received $85.50 on account from James Farnsworth.

29 Purchased merchandise on credit for $121.50 from the Staunton Company, Invoice 9-A-45.

29 The detailed audit strip for May 29 shows that $30.75 was received for

repairs and $59.25 was received for cash sales.

Post the individual entries for May 29 from journals to the ledgers.

30 Sold merchandise on credit for $184.50 to Carl Cleveland, Sales Slip 115.

30 Received $124.50 on account from Carl Cleveland.

30 Received $45 on account from Charles Lopez.

30 Issued Check 529 for $51 to the Marx Supply Company for window display materials. Debit Store Supplies Expense.

30 The detailed audit strip for May 30 shows that $96 was received for repairs and $225 was received for cash sales.

Post the individual entries for May 30 from journals to the ledgers.

31 Sold merchandise on credit for $143.85 to Clifford Waxman, Sales Slip 116.

31 Received $45 on account from Clifford Waxman.

31 Received $135 on account from Dorothy Emerson.

31 Received $150 on account from Calvin Webber.

31 Received $60 on account from Joseph Garber.

31 Received $600 on account from Lucy Childs.

31 Received $117 on account from Jeff Greene.

31 Received $750 on account from Roy Venero.

31 Received $270 on account from Marv Rosner.

31 Issued Check 530 for $356.28 and Check 531 for $489.36 in payment of salaries. Refer to the payroll transaction of May 3 for the information about earnings and deductions needed for the journal entries.

31 The detailed audit strip for May 31 shows that $75.75 was received for repairs and $270 was received for cash sales.

Post the individual entries for May 31 from journals to the ledgers.

End-of-Month Assignment

Martha Castle now asks you to complete the following end-of-month work for Castle Jewelers for May:

1. Pencil-foot, total, and rule the special journals.

2. Post the totals of the special journals. Follow the monthly posting procedure described on page 550.

3. Record the employer's share of the FICA taxes in the general journal. The amount of the employer's share for May is equal to the total amount of FICA taxes withheld from the employees' salaries during the month. Enter the date (May 31) in the general journal. Then debit Payroll Taxes Expense for $441.80 and credit FICA Taxes Payable for $441.80. Write below the entry: "To record employer's share of FICA taxes for May." Post the entry.

4. Prepare a schedule of accounts receivable. Prove the schedule by comparing the total with the balance of the Accounts Receivable controlling account in the general ledger.

5. Prepare a schedule of accounts payable. Prove the schedule by comparing the total with the balance of the Accounts Payable controlling account in the general ledger.

6. Prepare a trial balance dated May 31. Make sure that the debit and credit totals are equal.

7. Prepare an income statement for the month ended May 31. The ending merchandise inventory on May 31 is $37,300.

8. Prepare a balance sheet dated May 31.

INDEX

PHOTO CREDITS